RABBLE-ROUSER
FOR PEACE

ALSO BY JOHN ALLEN

Editor, The Rainbow People of God, *by Desmond Tutu*
Editor, The Essential Desmond Tutu

RABBLE-ROUSER
FOR PEACE

The Authorized Biography of
DESMOND TUTU

JOHN ALLEN

*To Lilie & Nancy,
Very best wishes,
John Allen*

2.14.20(3

London • Sydney • Auckland • Johannesburg

3 5 7 9 10 8 6 4 2

Published in 2007 by Rider, an imprint of Ebury Publishing.
First published in the USA by The Free Press, a division of
Simon & Schuster, Inc., in 2006.

Ebury Publishing is a Random House Group company.

Copyright © John Allen 2006
Map copyright © Timothy Allen 2006

John Allen has asserted his right to be identified as the author of this Work
in accordance with the Copyright, Designs and Patents Act 1988.

The Random House Group Limited Reg. No. 954009

Addresses for companies within the Random House Group can be found
at www.randomhouse.co.uk

A CIP catalogue record for this book is available from the British Library.

The Random House Group Limited supports The Forest Stewardship
Council (FSC), the leading international forest certification organisation.
All our titles that are printed on Greenpeace approved FSC certified
paper carry the FSC logo. Our paper procurement policy can be found
at www.rbooks.co.uk/environment

Mixed Sources
Product group from well-managed
forests and other controlled sources
www.fsc.org Cert no. TT-COC-2139
© 1996 Forest Stewardship Council
FSC

Printed in the UK by CPI Cox & Wyman, Reading, RG1 8EX

ISBN 9781846040641

Copies are available at special rates for bulk orders. Contact the sales
development team on 020 7840 8487 or visit
www.booksforpromotions.co.uk for more information.

To buy books by your favourite authors and register for offers, visit
www.rbooks.co.uk

CONTENTS

God bless Africa
Guard our children
Guide our leaders
And give us peace
*—adapted from a prayer
by Trevor Huddleston,
Community of the Resurrection*

RABBLE-ROUSER
FOR PEACE

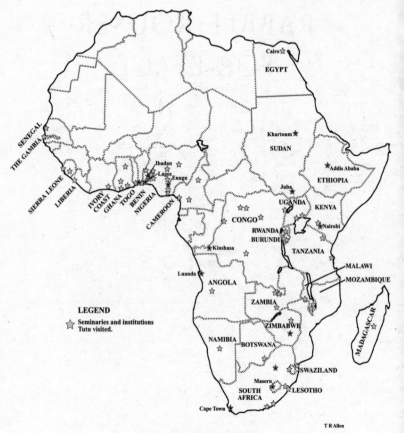

Tutu's Travels in Africa

T R Allen

LEGEND

⭐ Seminaries and institutions Tutu visited.

Cairo ⭐

EGYPT

Khartoum ⭐

SUDAN

⭐ Addis Ababa

ETHIOPIA

Juba ⭐

UGANDA   KENYA

SENEGAL

THE GAMBIA

SIERRA LEONE

LIBERIA

IVORY COAST

GHANA

TOGO

BENIN

NIGERIA

Ibadan

Lagos

Enugu

CAMEROON

CONGO

RWANDA

BURUNDI

⭐ Nairobi

⭐ Kinshasa

TANZANIA

MALAWI

MOZAMBIQUE

Luanda

ANGOLA

ZAMBIA

ZIMBABWE

MADAGASCAR

NAMIBIA   BOTSWANA

SWAZILAND

Maseru

SOUTH AFRICA

LESOTHO

Cape Town

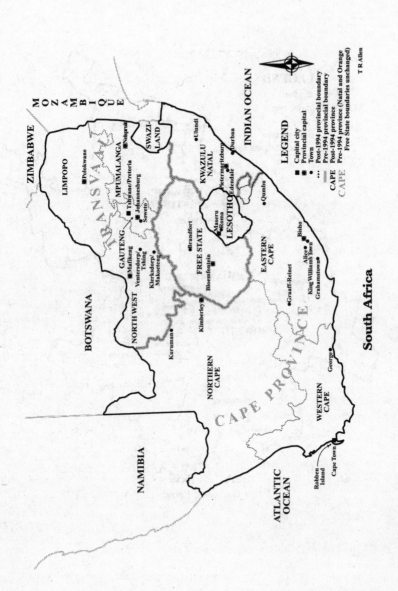

South Africa

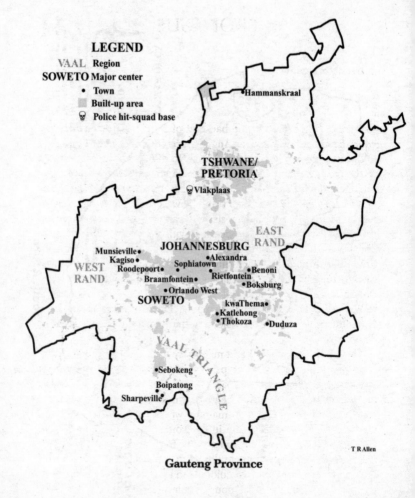

Gauteng Province

LEGEND

VAAL — Region
SOWETO — Major center
• Town
▮ Built-up area
☠ Police hit-squad base

Hammanskraal

TSHWANE/
PRETORIA

☠ Vlakplaas

EAST
RAND

JOHANNESBURG

Munsieville •
Kagiso •
Roodepoort •
Braamfontein •
• Orlando West
SOWETO

Sophiatown
• Alexandra
Rietfontein
• Benoni
• Boksburg

kwaThema •
• Katlehong
• Thokoza
• Duduza

WEST
RAND

VAAL TRIANGLE

• Sebokeng
Boipatong •
Sharpeville •

PROLOGUE

Desmond Tutu tensed in the backseat of his car as he left Bishops-court, his official residence as Anglican archbishop of Cape Town, late in the afternoon of Wednesday, March 16, 1988. A tight knot formed in the pit of his stomach. Usually this happened when he was summoned to defuse confrontations in the city's black townships, regular occurrences in which he often stood between two groups spoiling for a fight: on the one side, defiant students carrying bricks and stones; on the other, heavily armed policemen with fingers on their triggers. Today was different. As Tutu's chaplain and driver, Chris Ahrends, drove out through the imposing white gate posts, he turned north toward the city center (downtown Cape Town), where the arch-bishop had an appointment at Tuynhuys, the Cape Town office of P. W. Botha, also known as Piet Wapen ("Piet Weapon") or die Groot Krokodil ("the Great Crocodile"). Botha was the state president of South Africa.

The thirteen-kilometer (eight-mile) drive from Bishopscourt to Tuyn-huys offered an array of snapshots symbolizing past and current oppression. Bishopscourt was part of an estate owned by South Africa's first white settler in the seventeenth century. The archbishop's home—a large whitewashed two-story mansion with acres of gardens—was the oldest privately owned house in the country. The agapanthus and cannas that grew there were said to come from stock planted by Dutch colonists. Beyond the estate, to the south, were the remains of a wild almond hedge, grown by the colonists to keep out of their settlement the likes of Tutu—the indigenous people of South Africa. In 1988, Tutu's second year as archbishop, he was living in Bishopscourt ille-gally, having refused to ask for permission to live in what apartheid designated a "white area."

The route into the city ran along the eastern flank of Table Moun-tain, originally covered by fynbos (fine, or delicate, bush), the beautiful vegetation—unique to the southwestern tip of Africa—that makes up the smallest and richest of the world's floral biomes. Now the slopes were built up and occupied by the wealthiest Capetonians, whites who had displaced the fynbos with big houses and gardens in which they grew foreign, if also beautiful, plants from their countries of origin. As Tutu's car rounded Devil's Peak on the northeastern corner of the mountain, he could look out over Table Bay, the harbor that had attracted Dutch sailors as a refreshment station on their way to the east. Beyond the harbor was Robben Island, used since the earliest days of colonialism to jail any who dared resist the incursions of the settlers. Farther down the hill, just before the car dipped into the city center, an enormous scar of overgrown, rubble-strewn land came into view. This was District Six, which had been a shabby and poverty-stricken, but nevertheless a vibrant and thriving multiracial community until the 1960s, when Botha initiated a process that led to its destruction and the deportation of its people to windswept sandy wastes far out of town.

Ahrends pulled up at Botha's office a few minutes before 6 PM. This building too dated back to Dutch rule: the original structure, de Tuyn-huys (the "Garden House"), had been built by the Dutch East India Company as a guesthouse alongside the gardens which supplied passing ships. Tutu had been there before, but never at a time of such high tension between church and state. Three years earlier, in September 1984, the third major uprising against apartheid—the one that was to start its final collapse—had begun in the industrial area around the Vaal River, south of Johannesburg. Just a few weeks previously, on February 24, 1988, Botha's police minister, Adriaan Vlok, had outlawed the activities of seventeen organizations involved in the uprising, including coalitions representing two of the country's largest political forces. In response, the South African Council of Churches had convened an emergency meeting of church leaders, who resolved to pick up where the banned organizations had left off. The church leaders also decided to fly to Cape Town, seat of South Africa's parliament, to convey their decision to the government.

On Monday, February 29, 25 church leaders and about 100 other clergy and lay workers gathered at St. George's Cathedral, Cape Town, which backed onto the government complex incorporating Parliament and Tuynhuys. At a short service, the general secretary of the Council of Churches, Frank Chikane, read out a petition addressed to Botha and members of Parliament. The Anglican activist Sid Luck-ett instructed members of the congregation in the precepts of nonviolent direct action. He warned them that although the police, already swarming outside, were unlikely to use tear gas in the city center, they had used dogs, sjamboks (rawhide whips), and water cannons before.

Then, row by row, arms linked, the congregation went out of the cathedral, the church leaders wearing their robes of office, intent on delivering the petition to Parliament. In the front row were Tutu; Chikane; the Catholic archbishop of Cape Town, Stephen Naidoo; the president of the Methodist Church, Khoza Mgojo; and the president of the World Alliance of Reformed Churches, Allan Boesak. A line of blue-uniformed policemen, arms also linked, swung out across the street to block their way. An officer with a bullhorn told the protesters that their action was illegal. He warned them to disperse. They refused and knelt on the sidewalk. The police arrested the leaders, marched them away, and then opened up on the rest of the procession with a water cannon. A few of the clergy clung to parking meters, but others were sent tumbling down the street. That night, BBC Television's South African correspondent told his viewers: "The church has unmistakably taken over the front line of antiapartheid protest."

However, the church leaders' protest was not the subject of Tutu's appointment at Tuynhuys on March 16. He was there on a pastoral mission, to plead for the lives of the Sharpeville Six, five men and a woman facing execution. They were from an area best known for a massacre that took place there in 1960, and they had been convicted of killing the deputy mayor of Sharpeville on the first day of the Vaal uprising in 1984. Their case had generated an international campaign for clemency—not only had the police investigators assaulted witnesses and suspects, but most of those convicted were accused not of contributing directly to the deputy mayor's death but simply of being part of a crowd acting in common purpose with the killers. On Monday, March 14, the sheriff of the Supreme Court in Pretoria had informed the six that they were to be hanged on Friday, March 18. Wardens had measured the circumference of their necks, and their heights and weights, so that the hangman could calculate the size of the nooses and the length of the ropes. Then the prisoners had been led to a place in Pretoria's Central Prison that was called the "pot" because its occupants' emotions were said to boil over as they contemplated their death.

As Tutu waited to see Botha, the Sharpeville Six were thirty-seven hours away from execution. The next evening, Thursday, the six could expect a treat—a whole deboned chicken—for supper. Fellow prisoners would help them through the night by singing African choruses. On Friday morning, chaplains would pray with them. Wardens would pull white hoods over their heads, then lift up flaps over their faces so they could see the steps of the gallows. The gallows chamber was designed to hang seven people at a time. Each of the six could expect a warden to lead him or her to a place on a trapdoor marked by two painted feet. The hangman would then drop the flaps over their faces, put nooses over their heads, and pull a lever, and the trapdoor would fall away.

When news came of the impending executions, Tutu called the ambassadors of Botha's closest allies—Britain, the United States, and Germany—and asked to speak urgently to their heads of government. Margaret Thatcher telephoned him the same day, as did Ronald Reagan's secretary of state, George Shultz. Both assured him that they were urging clemency. The British ambassador, Robin Renwick, carried a message from Thatcher to the South African government that afternoon. Reagan made a personal appeal to Botha, and Shultz called the foreign minister, R. F. (Pik) Botha, to underline its seriousness. Helmut Kohl made a similar appeal on behalf of the twelve governments of the European Community, and Kohl's foreign policy adviser telephoned Tutu on Wednesday to brief him.

Tutu and his personal assistant, Matt Esau, went into Botha's office. It was the first time Esau had met Botha, and he was struck by the president's size; alongside Tutu, who stood only about 1.6 meters (five feet four inches) tall, Botha was, in Esau's words, a groot, fris Boer (a "big, beefy Afrikaner"). Esau was also struck by the lighting—and Robin Renwick wrote later that being received in Botha's dimly lit study conjured up images of what it must have been like to call on Hitler in his bunker. Botha was accompanied by the director general of his office and by one or two cabinet ministers.

Tutu told Botha he was not appealing for the Sharpeville Six on legal grounds. As a minister of the gospel he had come to plead for mercy, which was not to be confused with justice. He was opposed to the death penalty in principle—in 1982 he had successfully pleaded for the lives of white South African mercenaries sentenced to death for trying to overthrow the government of the Seychelles islands. Hanging the Sharpeville Six, he now warned, could spark new violence, particularly because the following Monday, March 21, was the anniversary of the 1960 Sharpeville massacre. It would be a statesmanlike act, Tutu said, to grant a reprieve. Botha replied that South Africa's courts were independent and he did not want to encroach on them. He operated within certain limits when he exercised his prerogative to grant clemency; this case did not fall within those limits. Botha provided only a glimmer of hope: the trial judge was hearing an application for a stay of execution in Pretoria, he said. If the court decided there were other circumstances that he needed to look at, he would do so.

At that point the atmosphere deteriorated. Botha said there was something else he wanted to discuss: the church leaders' petition. The original of the document had been mailed to the president the day after the abortive march, somewhat wrinkled after being drenched by the water cannon. Botha handed Tutu a four-page reply, then started to berate him. Wagging his finger in the belligerent style that was his trademark, he excoriated the archbishop for instigating an illegal march; for allegedly drawing up the petition only after the march; for supposedly marching in front of a communist flag; for advocating sanctions; for supporting the outlawed liberation movement, the African National Congress (ANC); and for having the temerity to invite Thatcher, Reagan, and Kohl to interfere in South Africa's domestic affairs.

At first Tutu restrained himself. Botha's behavior was not out of character—he was said to drive his own cabinet ministers to tears. But as Tutu tried and failed to get a word in edgewise, and Botha jumped from point to point, an anger born of decades of observing the consequences of apartheid stirred within him. Tutu thought to himself: "Our people have suffered for so long. I might never get this chance again." Shaking a finger back at Botha, he said: "Look here, I'm not a small boy. Don't think you're talking to a small boy. I'm not here as if you're my principal. . . . I thought I was talking to a civilized person and there are courtesies involved."

The meeting then became a confused melee. Tutu accused Botha of lying when he told a newspaper the marchers had no petition. Well, said Botha, why didn't you bring it to my door? Did the president think, asked Tutu, that the archbishop had so much influence that he could lead responsible church leaders into a march without the petition? Botha replied, Did you tell them it was unlawful to march? Tutu said he had never marched in front of a red flag—he had not been present at the event to which Botha referred. He did not want sanctions, but he certainly wanted a new South Africa. And time and again he had said he did not support the ANC's armed struggle, but he did support their objective of a nonracial, democratic South Africa. Botha said, no, the ANC wanted a socialist dictatorship; moreover, blacks had a higher standard of living in South Africa than anywhere else on the continent. And had Tutu seen what the white Dutch Reformed Church—of which Botha was a member—had said? "Dat jy, Aartsbiskop Tutu, is op 'n heillose pad! Dit is wat hulle sê!" ("That you, Archbishop Tutu, are on a wicked path! That's what they say!") Botha asked Tutu to cite any instance when Jesus broke a law. Tutu cited a number of instances. Those were religious laws, said Botha. But that was the law that controlled society, came the rejoinder. Tutu's declaration of patriotism had one of Botha's ministers leaping to his president's defense. "I love this country," Tutu said, "I love it more than you do. Our people"—he meant black South Africans—"fought against the Nazis. You didn't!" Tutu accused Botha of supporting the Ossewa Brandwag (Ox Wagon Sentinels), an Afrikaner nationalist group that had opposed South Africa's entry into World War II. "It's not true," the minister protested. "This president, he destroyed the Ossewa Brandwag."

As accusation mounted on accusation, Tutu repeatedly told Botha, "I take exception to what you're saying." When he decided there was no point in continuing, he said, "Thank you," and prepared to leave. Botha barked back: "You're arrogant inside and outside my office. You can take your exceptions! Good-bye!" Driving back to Bishopscourt, Tutu told his chaplain: "We didn't even shake hands." Recounting the story later, he said ruefully that both he and Botha had behaved like little boys: "I don't know whether that is how Jesus would have handled it. But at that moment I didn't actually quite mind how Jesus would have handled it. I was going to handle it my way." The following morning, Thursday, March 17, lawyers at the resumed court hearing for the Sharpeville Six in Pretoria found a judge transformed. He was accommodating and for the first time appeared sympathetic. That afternoon he granted a stay of execution. After months in the courts, the case went back to Botha later in the year, and he replaced the death sentences with long terms of imprisonment.

In the weeks following March 16, Botha conducted an acrimonious exchange of correspondence with Chikane and Tutu. Chikane laid the groundwork for a national program of civil disobedience, launched in May under the banner "Standing for the Truth." Early in June, Botha asked the police minister, Vlok, to stay behind after a meeting of his State Security Council at Tuynhuys. What, Botha asked, were the police going to do to stop the Council of Churches? Vlok went away to consider the options. At a follow-up meeting, Botha told Vlok that the council's headquarters, Khotso House ("House of Peace"), in Johannesburg, had become a "house of danger." The police must "render it unusable." How that was to be done was left up to Vlok.

Two months afterward, a police team, headed by a death squad officer who was subsequently dubbed "Prime Evil," drove late one night to the Johannesburg city center (downtown Johannesburg). They broke into Khotso House and stuffed eight backpacks, each carrying seven to ten kilograms (about fifteen to twenty-two pounds) of Soviet bloc military explosives, between the elevator shafts. They activated electronic time switches and left. By some miracle, the building's caretaker survived the ensuing blast virtually unscathed. But the occupants of a nearby apartment house were not as lucky: twenty-eight were injured, some seriously. Peter Storey, a Methodist leader who had taken part in the march on Parliament, was called out to help retirees living in apartments operated by his church across the street from Khotso House. "We were met by a scene out of hell," he said later. "Dazed old people were wandering about in their nightdresses and pajamas, some whimpering, others in shock, many bleeding from lacerations. Miraculously, none had been seriously injured." As Tutu surveyed the wrecked building a few days later, he had cause to remember a warning from Botha on March 16: "You are leading people to confrontation," Botha had said. "If you want confrontation, you're going to get confrontation. You must tell the people: they're going to get confrontation."

CHAPTER 1

CHILD OF MODERN
SOUTH AFRICA

"My father was a Xhosa and my mother a Motswana. What does that make me?"

> –Desmond Tutu, in the 1980s, ridiculing
> apartheid's obsession with ethnicity.

"A Zulu!"

> –Harry Belafonte, political activist,
> responding from the audience.

Desmond Tutu's birthplace at Makoeteng in South Africa's North West Province is easy to visit. A short walk from the busy shops and offices of Klerksdorp, a town founded by white settlers in the nineteenth century, it is a peaceful spot, flat but near a rocky koppie, or small hill, covered with bushes and trees where the children of the black township played. At the foot of the hill are the remains of a plantation of eucalyptus trees. Here, until Desmond was four, his older sister, Sylvia, collected fallen branches to make a fire at which they would warm themselves on cold winter mornings in the highveld. With the help of a resident, the visitor can trace the foundations of the house in which Desmond was born–the place where, according to African tradition, his umbilical cord was buried.

Seventy-five years after Tutu's birth, however, there was nothing else to show that a black community had once lived at Makoeteng. Klerksdorp's "location," as whites called it, was too close to town for their comfort. In the decade after the formal policy of apartheid was adopted in 1948, after the Tutus had left, its people were uprooted at gunpoint and moved six kilometers (four miles) away. In its place, the town council established a white suburb and named it Neserhof after a local family. In 2006, the area around the Tutu home was an open stretch of flat land, unused except for a strip of green grass where an entrepreneur had built a golf driving range. Large bungalows with well-cultivated gardens, on big plots of land, surrounded the empty space. Amid the trees below the hill was a golf course—golf having been long associated in South Africa with white privilege. The very name of Makoeteng, given to the area after the advent of democracy, reflected its destruction: in the language of the area, "makoeteng" describes the broken remnants of the mud-brick houses remaining after the location was razed.

Although the dispossession of black South Africans began with the arrival of the Dutch in the seventeenth century, for the Tutu family, its effects can be traced back to the British, and culminated between 1955 and 1980, when many places dear to the family—homes, schools, churches, and entire communities—were either wiped off the map or taken over by apartheid.

Desmond Mpilo Tutu was born on October 7, 1931. He was very much a child of modern South Africa, directly descended on both sides from the country's two largest language and cultural groupings. His mother, Aletta Dorothea Mavoertsek Mathlare, the strongest formative influence on his life, was a Motswana, from the Sotho-Tswana linguistic group. The chiefdoms of this group have lived in the central and northwestern interior of South Africa for at least 800 years, by one estimate since AD 350, and are renowned for having built settlements accommodating thousands of people by the seventeenth century. Grandfather Mathlare once owned cattle near Fochville, between Klerksdorp and Johannesburg. His daughter was born and grew up in Boksburg, one of the mining towns strung out across the Reef, the industrial conglomeration built over the gold-bearing reefs stretching east and west of Johannesburg. Her African name, Mavoertsek, might reflect the high infant mortality rate at the time she was born. It means "Get away!"—something one might say to a bothersome child or dog. She was letlomela, one born after the sibling before her had died. In African tradition, such a child would be named so as to diminish her importance, so the gods would not take her away also. No one ever called her by her full name; it was shortened to Matse, and her family called her Ausi ("big sister") Matse.

In Boksburg, Matse Mathlare met and married Zachariah Zelilo Tutu, who was about four years her senior. Desmond speculated that his father's second name, meaning weeping, may have been given to him because he too was letlomela. Zachariah was born in 1901 in the town of Gcuwa in the eastern Cape, and was brought up in Qumbu, about 140 kilometers (90 miles) away. He was proud to be a Xhosa-speaker, part of the Nguni group of peoples; and he was, in Desmond's words, "quite arrogant. . . . He thought that Xhosas were God's gift to the world. . . . He didn't think the Batswana* were very smart. . . . I don't know why he married my mother, because he thought that any-one who was not Xhosa was a lesser breed in many ways." Once Matse was married, she spoke her husband's mother tongue in their home. According to Desmond's sister, Sylvia Morrison, "She didn't say a word in her language, even if she was very angry. . . . According to our custom, she was married to a Xhosa, and so she had to do every-thing in the Xhosa way. This was a Xhosa home."

Zachariah was descended from a unique section of the Xhosa-speaking people known as amaMfengu. Some historians ascribe its existence as a group to the invasion of the British. The major groups that trace their ancestry to a person named Xhosa–amaGcaleka and amaRharhabe, and other Xhosa-speakers such as amaMpondo or abeThembu (the group to which Nelson Mandela belongs)–are cohe-sive sets of clans with common histories.† In contrast, amaMfengu originated as clusters of refugees of varied heritage who came together and became defined as a group only from the 1820s on. How the group was formed is part of a heated debate among South African his-torians over the tumultuous events of the southeastern seaboard and interior of South Africa during the early nineteenth century.

In the traditional version of the story, a ruthless and sadistic military innovator named Shaka led a revolution in northern Nguni society, using his hitherto minor Zulu chiefdom as the base from which to develop a powerful centralized kingdom stretching over large parts of what is now the province of kwaZulu-Natal.‡ By this account, Shaka unleashed a whirlwind, scattering defeated leaders in all directions. They in turn plundered other groups in a chain reaction, called the Mfecane, that spread mayhem across southern Africa. Among the refugees who fled south from kwaZulu into areas occupied by the Xhosa-speaking southern Nguni peoples were amaMfengu, Desmond

---

* Batswana is the plural of Motswana. The language is Setswana.
† The lowercase prefixes ama- and abe- designate the plural form of nouns in IsiXhosa; the prefix isi- modifies the noun to describe the language.
‡ The prefix kwa- designates a place: thus, the place of the Zulus.

Tutu's paternal ancestors. Their name was apparently derived from the IsiXhosa verb ukumfenguza, meaning "to wander about seeking service," and was thus a description of the group's status rather than its ethnic origin. Although amaMfengu were incorporated into Xhosa society, they were underdogs, discriminated against and exploited. In this telling of history, the British rescued the group, whom they called Fingoes, from the Xhosa overlords.

Since the 1960s, a far more nuanced picture has emerged. A number of historians now argue that black societies did not generate the Mfecane on their own but were transformed by factors ranging from drought and the overcrowding of land to the depredations of colonial forces and the colonists' need for labor. Moreover, they suggest that although some amaMfengu were from dispersed chiefdoms in the north, the group actually incorporated Xhosa-speaking refugees from chiefdoms attacked by British colonial forces as they invaded the eastern Cape from the west.

In this new narrative, amaMfengu included thousands of Gcaleka and Rharhabe women and children coerced into working on farms, others who saw no option but to seek work from the settlers to survive, groups who attached themselves to newly established Christian missions, and mercenaries employed by the British to counter Xhosa guerrilla tactics. Some historians now contend that the very concept of a "Fingo tribe" was an invention by settlers to hide from the Colonial Office in London the true identify of the Xhosa women and children they had abducted and illegally pressed into forced labor. Whatever their origins, a strong strand of opinion in Xhosa society regarded amaMfengu as collaborationists with the British, traitors to the Xhosa paramount chief to whom they owed allegiance. Phyllis Ntantala, the mother of South African cabinet minister Pallo Jordan, related that when her husband, A. C. Jordan, was being introduced to her relatives in the 1930s, they were impressed that he could claim Mpondomise citizenship, "thus showing he was no collaborating Mfengu. Such things are still important in the world we come from."

Certainly, at and beyond the frontier with white settlers, Desmond Tutu's paternal forebears lived farther from their roots than other groups, settling at mission stations, in "locations" alongside white towns, or on rural land from which the British had expelled defeated communities. They adapted themselves to the new order, converting to Christianity earlier and in greater numbers than other groups, setting up as traders and commercial farmers, and breaking with African tradition by adopting individual land ownership. They seized the opportunities for formal western education offered by missionaries, and as a result they were placed in a leading position when blacks in the Cape Colony began to organize politically and to register to vote for the legislature in the late nineteenth century. John Tengo Jabavu, an Mfengu teacher who worked closely with Cape liberals, founded South Africa's first black-owned newspaper, *Imvo ZabaNtsundu* ("Black Opinion"), in 1884. He declared that it would work for black unity and identified his audience as stretching across the subcontinent, from Table Bay (Cape Town) to Port Natal (Durban), from Pretoria (Tshwane) to Port Elizabeth.

In the twentieth century, amaMfengu gained a reputation as the educated elite of black society. When the modern South Africa was created in 1910–joining in a union two former British colonies, Natal and the Cape; and two former Afrikaner republics, Transvaal and the Orange Free State–Jabavu was in the delegation that traveled to London to try to persuade the British government not to ratify the constitution, because it denied the vote to most blacks. Fifteen years later, it was two Mfengu brothers who persuaded Nelson Mandela's father to send him to school. In his autobiography Mandela described amaMfengu as "our clergymen, policeman, teachers, clerks and interpreters."

It is this view, rather than that of amaMfengu as collaborationists, that leaders of the democratic South Africa now promote. In the early 1990s, Desmond Tutu visited Mangosuthu Buthelezi, the modern-day political leader of the Zulu nationalism to which Shaka gave birth, in the kwaZulu capital of Ulundi. As Buthelezi proudly showed Tutu a statue of Shaka, he also expressed admiration for amaMfengu as the educators of black South Africans. Mandela, in an interview with the present author, played down the characterization of amaMfengu as traitors, citing Thembu history: "When we were being attacked by the Gcalekas, the Thembus ran away. It was amaMfengu who defended Thembuland. . . . They were given an area after that, and the king said, 'Nobody should ever say that person's a Fingo. Any person who says so here will be punished.' Now even today, in Thembuland, you can't say so-and-so is an Mfengu." Mandela also emphasized that among those jailed with him for life in 1964 were leaders with Mfengu antecedents such as Raymond Mhlaba and Govan Mbeki, father of his successor as president, Thabo Mbeki.

Tutu rarely discusses his ethnic roots. In general, South Africans do not refer simultaneously to their heritage and their nationality as, for instance, Irish- or Italian-Americans do. In particular, many black South Africans spent the latter half of the twentieth century shying away from talking about, or even disclosing, their origins to outsiders. This was because apologists for apartheid used ethnicity to justify white minority rule in South Africa. There was, they said, no such person as a black South African, and thus no black majority. The country had ten black "nations," none of them much bigger than the white "nation." Each of these ten was to be allowed to rule itself in its own "homeland." In the years of Tutu's campaigning against apartheid, he described his origins only to attack the policy of forcing citizenship in these homelands on black South Africans.

Nevertheless, Tutu was brought up to regard IsiXhosa as his mother tongue. After using its "click" sounds in blessings at the end of church services, he teases western audiences by saying that it is the "language of heaven." In the Xhosa tradition, the Tutus traced their descent through the male line—not through their surname, which means "ash," but rather through isiduko, praise names given to the founders of the clans of which they are part. There is no direct analogy between the concept of a clan and an extended family in European culture; one historian has described a Xhosa clan as "a group of lineages who did not quite understand how they were related to each other, but who believed through their common clan name and clan praises that they shared a common ancestor." Nelson Mandela became widely, and affectionately, known in South Africa by his clan name, Madiba. The Tutu family's principal clan name is Tshezi, but Desmond also traced his lineage in Xhosa society through other isiduko: Tshibase, Dlaba, and Umkhontombovu ("Red Spear").

Zachariah Tutu trained as a primary school teacher at Lovedale, the preeminent educational institution established by Scottish missionaries in the eastern Cape in the nineteenth century. Lovedale's graduates spread out through South Africa, staffing the church schools that educated the overwhelming majority of black pupils. Zachariah apparently took a post in Boksburg. He was better educated than Matse; she received only a primary school education, training in domestic science at Tiger Kloof, the center for Batswana education established by the London Missionary Society in the northern Cape.

In the late 1920s, Zachariah was offered a teaching post in Klerksdorp. Before whites arrived, the site of the town was on the eastern edge of the area of influence of Tau ("Lion"), a chief of the Tswana-speaking Barolong people. By some accounts, Tau's descendants had been dislodged from the region by Nguni groups during the Mfecane, but the stability and wealth of the Barolong town at nearby Thabeng impressed pioneer missionaries in the 1820s. The first whites to appropriate the land in the area were the descendants of Dutch, Huguenot, and German settlers who left the Cape Colony in the 1830s and trekked across what they named the Vaal ("ash-colored") River. The Voortrekkers—pioneers also known as boere, or farmers, and later as Afrikaners—founded Klerksdorp on a tributary of the Vaal named Schoonspruit ("Clear Stream"). The town took its name from a magistrate named le Clercq—descended from the same Huguenot settler as South Africa's last white president, F. W. de Klerk—and it was the first white settlement in what later became the Zuid-Afrikaansche Republiek, also known as the Transvaal.

Desmond Tutu's birthplace was thus intimately associated with white rule north of the Vaal. Moreover, Tutu was born very near another site of significance for Afrikaner nationalism: a memorial to 149 adults and 968 children who died in a British concentration camp in Klerksdorp. The camp was established during the second of the Afrikaners' nineteenth-century wars of independence. In the first of these wars, the Transvaal defeated a British attempt to annex its territory in 1878. In the second, between 1899 and 1902, the Transvaal and the Orange Free State republics resisted British designs on the Transvaal's newly discovered gold fields. They lost, after a long-drawn-out war of attrition in which Boer guerrillas raided British regular troops, who in turn herded the guerrillas' families into camps to stop them from resupplying the fighters. The result was the death by disease of 6,000 Afrikaner women and 22,000 children. Black people were relegated to a marginal role in the war, serving mostly as noncombatants on both sides; but they too were swept up into camps, where 14,000 died. The deaths of black people went almost unnoticed by white public opinion—there was no memorial to black victims in Klerksdorp until 2000—but the deaths of Afrikaner civilians left a legacy of bitterness that scarred twentieth-century South Africa. In 1996, nearly a century after the second war, Tutu was to apply its lessons in the service of his postapartheid mission when he chaired the Truth and Reconciliation Commission.

Most of Klerkdorp's town histories from the apartheid era make only elliptical references to the indigenous people who lived there when the trekkers arrived, referring to "problems with the black population," "robberies" and "a threatened attack by blacks," the last of which was met by the raising of a commando to chase them off. The black residential area which later became known as Makoeteng was established in 1907, a short way downstream from the original white settlement, to house workers who served the settler community. When Tutu was born, it was known simply as the "native location." Until well into the twentieth century, whites confined their definition of a native to a black South African; many whites, even if their families had been in Africa for generations, styled themselves Europeans.

In the 1930s, Klerksdorp's black residents lived on plots that were big by the standards of townships established later. They built their own houses and kept cattle, sheep, and poultry. There was no sewerage system—sanitation workers collected buckets of night soil from outside homes and took them away in carts pulled by mules or donkeys. Only whites were enrolled as voters in elections for the seven-man town council. Issues affecting black residents were brought to the council by the Native Location Advisory Board. Black people were rarely named individually in council minutes; exceptionally, one minute of the time records that "Native L. Maloi" applied for the refund of the proceeds of the sale of his heifer by the town pound. Municipal wages for white laborers were four or five shillings a week, as against two shillings sixpence for black laborers. In 1933, when Tutu was two, a delegation from the Joint Council of Whites and Natives told the town's public health committee that the black community was suffering greatly as a result of unemployment; the delegation success-fully asked the committee to approve a plan to allocate a piece of land for 100 vegetable plots for black residents—on the condition that they would not compete with white growers by selling their produce in the town market.

The community was diverse, mostly Tswana-speaking but including Sotho- and Xhosa-speakers and a few Indian traders. Children swam in the river and played and picked berries on the slopes of the nearby koppie. There was an African Methodist Episcopal church as well as a Dutch Reformed church, but the biggest churches were the Anglican and Methodist. Zachariah Tutu was principal of the Methodist primary school. As in other black communities across the country, the term "church school" meant exactly that: classes were held in the main church sanctuary, a different class in each corner. The Tutu family lived in the schoolmaster's house, which was about 5.5 meters (eighteen feet) long and two meters (6.5 feet) wide and was built of mud bricks on a stone foundation in the yard of the Methodist mission. Later during his stay in Klerksdorp, Zachariah Tutu formed an amalgamated community school known as Itereleng, meaning "do for yourselves." In this and other communities in which he worked, he was known as ZZ Tutu, and his wife as Matichere ("wife of the teacher").

Biographical sketches of Desmond Tutu often note that he grew up in a gold-mining area. In fact, though, the large mines for which the area has become known were sunk after the Tutus had left Klerksdorp. After a short gold boom in the 1880s, mining diminished; and it did not become important again until after the development of more efficient means of extracting gold from ore and the capacity to sink some of the deepest mines in the world. In the weeks before and after Tutu's birth, the local weekly, the *Klerksdorp Record and Western Transvaal News,* reflected an agricultural community based on the farms established by the Voortrekkers, with notices announcing stock sales and "delicious purified milk" from a dairy close to town. Whites could feel in contact with the wider world: advertisements for "Rinko Talkies" feature the "First Talkie Western: Call of the West"; Charlie Chaplin "in the supreme laugh-sensation of the century, City Lights"; and the Marx brothers in "the Talking, Singing Musical Comedy Hit: The Cocoanuts." Klerksdorp had good rail connections to Johannesburg in one direction and to the diamond-mining city of Kimberley, and beyond it to Cape Town, in the other. The dirt road to Johannesburg was being improved: "A tractor-grader is at work on the Johannesburg-Potchefstroom road with good effects on the corrugated surfaces which are the bane of motorists."

However, two decades after union in 1910, contrasts between the positions of Briton and Boer were still evident in the newspaper. Christmas and New Year excursions to England on Royal Mail ships such as the *Windsor Castle, Balmoral Castle,* and *Edinburgh Castle* were advertised for those wanting to return to what many still saw as "home." The news columns reported discussion of the "Poor White" problem in the Afrikaner community by members of the Carnegie Commission (whose study was financed by the Carnegie Corporation of New York). Typically for a Transvaal town, there was a small Jewish community: "Master Maurice Boner wishes to thank all relatives and friends for good wishes and presents received on the occasion of his Barmitzvah."

Klerksdorp's black residents were referred to in the news columns only as a source of trouble, usually in court reports and often only by their first names. The union between the British and Afrikaners had been disastrous for them. The constitution denied blacks–68 percent of the population–the vote in three of its four constituent provinces: the Transvaal, the Orange Free State, and Natal. In the Cape, black and "Coloured" (mixed race) voters retained the franchise, but property and income qualifications restricted their numbers to 15 percent of the electorate. The delegation, including Jabavu, that went to London to lobby against the constitution was denied a hearing at the House of Commons. By the time the delegates met the secretary of state for the Colonies, the British government had already committed itself to ratifying the law as agreed on by the whites.

Three years after union, in the words of Sol Plaatje, South Africa's preeminent early black writer, "Awaking on Friday morning, 20 June 1913, the South African Native found himself, not actually a slave, but a pariah in the land of his birth." This was a consequence of the implementation of the Natives Land Act, which set aside less than 8 percent of the country as segregated "reserves" for blacks. The law became the first part of an interlocking system of law and practice that robbed black South Africans of their ability to remain self-sufficient and turned them into units of cheap labor: when their work was needed, the requirement that they pay poll taxes forced them into the cash economy, in the towns and down the mines; when it was not needed, a system of pass laws banished them to the reserves. The effects could be seen in a court report from the Klerksdorp Record in October 1931:

Next came a batch of natives, whose delinquency was either failure to produce tax receipts or being without passes–5 shillings or five days' for the former charge; 10 shillings or five days' for the pass offence was the punishment. . . . A young native, for deserting the service of Mr. C. J. Swart, Elandsheuvel, was ordered to receive six cuts.

Petty theft from whites drew prison sentences:

Ben Shabala–who was last week found guilty of the theft of five fowls belonging to Mr. C. A. van Wyk, of Doornplaat–was sentenced to six weeks' hard labour.

Two twenty-year-old natives named William N'Sale and George Moleti, have appeared before Mr. F. W. Ahrens, Magistrate, on a charge of theft, it being alleged that one or both broke open a penny-in-the-slot sweet machine at Mr. Dale's store and extracted sweets to the value of

7 shillings. . . . William, against whom there were previous convictions, . . . was sentenced to three months' hard labour; while George, who had one conviction for theft last year, was given six weeks' hard labour.

Altercations between blacks and whites had a predictable outcome. In one case, a "young lad named Hendrik Weyers" was assaulted by "a fifteen-year-old native named Hezekiah," who said he struck the white boy because stones were thrown at him. Hezekiah was charged, not Hendrik.

Desmond was the second boy to be born to the Tutu family. The first, Sipho ("gift"), died in infancy. Desmond was described by his family as having been sickly from birth—hence his hopeful second name, Mpilo, or "life," given to him by his paternal grandmother. He was never told why his father named him Desmond but assumed that this name must have been related to a book, or perhaps a piece of music. His older sister, Sylvia, called him Mpilo, as did Nelson Mandela much later. The rest of the family called him Boy. Although that name was not on his baptismal certificate, he used it as a third name on formal documents from his school years until the mid-1970s. Then he dropped it. However, unknown to the Tutus, at least one person outside the family continued to use it—a security policeman who was assigned to monitor his activities referred to him as Boy as a form of disparagement.

In the first years of his life, Desmond became very ill. The family did not know this, but it later became apparent that he had contracted polio. There was no vaccine against polio at the time, and in black townships it was associated with fly-borne infections from sewage buckets. Its incidence rose in summer when the buckets sat in the hot sun awaiting collection. In South Africa, the disease had a mortality rate of 10 to 25 percent. If a patient was going to die, it usually happened in the first eight days. For a family like the Tutus, there was little to be done other than to keep the patient comfortable and wait. Sylvia remembered her brother's life hanging by a thread: "We had really lost all hope. My dad had prepared . . . [for] a funeral." Although he recovered relatively well, the effects of the polio remained noticeable for the rest of his life—his right hand had atrophied, giving him a weak grip when shaking hands. He frequently rubbed it to improve the circulation and warm it; in the early 1980s the state-controlled television news service zoomed in on his hands during hearings of a government inquisition, to portray him as a miscreant wringing his hands in guilt. The polio was followed by a serious accident. As he and Sylvia warmed themselves at the fire outside their home one morning, his flannel pajamas caught fire. "He was a stubborn somebody," recalled Sylvia. "It was so cold he wanted to get close to the brazier and heat himself. . . . When I tried to stop him, he wouldn't." He was hospitalized with serious burns that scarred his thigh for life.

Tutu's earliest memories were of isolated scenes during his early childhood in Klerksdorp: he carried into adulthood images of being taken fishing on the handlebars of his father's bicycle; of waking up to find the room in which he was sleeping filled with musical instruments—drums, kettledrums, and trumpets; and, vaguely, of tinkling the keys of a piano in their house. The instruments were for a troop of Pathfinders—a group similar to Boy Scouts—which his father led.

The Tutus left Klerksdorp when Desmond was four, and went to a smaller town 70 kilometers (45 miles) farther up the Schoonspruit River. Unlike Makoeteng, the location to which they moved in 1936—named Tshing—still exists. In a region of extensive forced removals under apartheid, there is irony in this, for Tshing adjoins Ventersdorp, the farming dorp, or small town, that became synonymous in the last days of white rule with the most violently racist resistance to its abolition. Ventersdorp was the home of Eugene Terre'blanche and his Afrikaner Weerstandsbeweging ("Afrikaner Resistance Movement"), which exploited neo-Nazi imagery to put on South Africa's most telegenic—if not its most dangerous—displays of intransigence in the face of change.

Tshing is on the edge of town, where the bare red earth of the backyards and dirt streets around the old Tutu home contrast with the thorn trees and yellow grass of the undulating highveld savanna beyond. The Tutus lived in a simple rectangular building, flat-roofed at that time, in the yard of the Methodist church, which accommodated the junior classes of the school of which ZZ was principal. The house had three rooms: the parents' bedroom; a kitchen; and a living room, which doubled as a bedroom for the children at night. There was no electricity, and study at home in the evenings was by candlelight. Asked seventy years later to recollect images of himself in Tshing, Tutu described a child in shorts and a shirt, nearly always barefoot, enveloped in winter by one of his father's old overcoats, with the sleeves rolled up. Shoes were worn only for formal occasions, perhaps to church on Sundays. He recalled the time with nostalgia: "Life was actually quite full. It was fun. . . . Although we weren't affluent, we were not destitute either."

Desmond saw himself as an average, sociable township child, who joined others in making pieces of wire into toy cars with shoe polish cans for wheels, or playing soccer with a tennis ball in the strip of land, across the street from the church, that separated Tshing from the white section of Ventersdorp. Sometimes he resisted chores: "My sisters liked to say there were times when I was lazy. . . . I would cry or stamp my foot and get very upset because I was asked to go and fetch water." The effects of his early illness were apparent throughout his childhood. His younger sister, Gloria Radebe, recalled, "We would be playing with him and then you would see him going into the house and sleeping. . . . He was very delicate."

In Tshing Desmond began the eight years of kindergarten and primary schooling that were customary for those black children who could go to school. There were no desks in his first "classroom"– listening to their teachers, the children sat on the low, backless benches used by worshippers on Sundays; when they needed to write, they sat on the floor and used the benches as desks. (Sixty years afterward, during a visit to a rural school, Tutu broke down in tears at seeing children studying in the same conditions.) He was naturally right-handed but, as a result of the polio, learned to write with his left. He learned Afrikaans, which was, with Setswana, the lingua franca in Ventersdorp. Encouraged by his father, he developed a love of reading. There was little if any indigenous South African children's literature. When Tutu was bishop of Johannesburg, he wrote to a young correspondent:

I enjoyed [as a child] reading Lamb's Tales from Shakespeare and Aesop's Fables, as well as books containing well-known stories such as Red Riding Hood, Snow White and the Seven Dwarfs, Jack and the Beanstalk. You must not tell your teacher but my father, who was a school teacher, allowed me to read comics. . . . I believe I developed a great love for English in this way. Most people believe that comics encourage sloppy language.

While living in Tshing, the Tutus had a third son, Tamsanqa ("blessing"). Like Sipho, he died in infancy. Losing two of five children was not exceptional for a black South African family–infant mortality was high in black communities at the time. Desmond remembered Tamsanqa's death; his father, who he assumed must have quarreled with the local minister, conducted the funeral himself. Perhaps as a result of losing her two other sons, Desmond's mother poured out her love and affection onto him. Both Sylvia and Gloria regarded Desmond as being their mother's favorite child. "Even if he was wrong, my mother used to take his side," Gloria said. Desmond returned his mother's love and regarded her as the single greatest influence on his life:

> I resemble her in many ways. She was stumpy, and she had a big nose like mine. And I hope that I resemble her in another respect: [she] . . . was very, very gentle and compassionate and caring, always taking the side of whoever was having the worst of an argument. . . . She was also quite incredible about wanting to share. . . . She never cooked just enough for the family. She always imagined that there was going to be somebody [else] who came and for whom she must dish up. . . . Even when we didn't have a great deal she would want to share even that little bit that we had.

If Matse Tutu's compassion for the underdog goes partway toward explaining the stands her son later took as a spiritual leader and campaigner for human rights, one element of his father's behavior may explain the depth of his anger when he saw unprovoked and unmerited suffering.

Desmond Tutu was fond of his father, enjoyed Zachariah's sense of humor, and was impressed by his commitment to education and his skill as a conductor of school choirs. During South Africa's transition to democracy, he frequently quoted one of his father's aphorisms: "Don't raise your voice. Improve your argument." And the young Desmond "fumed inside," as he put it, to hear a white shop assistant, "a slip of a child," call his father "Boy." But in one respect he neither admired nor had sympathy for Zachariah:

> He drank often. I would say that it was excessive. . . . It wasn't something that happened every day, but when it happened it was awful. . . . [He] was a brilliant teacher but maybe he could have been even better had he not drunk as much as he used to. . . . Sometimes he beat up my mother. I really got very, very angry and wanted to take him on. I couldn't, I was small. . . . I don't know whether I wasn't close to hating him for how he sometimes treated my mother.

Still, ZZ's drinking did not prevent him from providing for his family: "We were poor, but we never starved," said Gloria. ZZ fished in a nearby stream to supplement the family's food and earned extra money by taking photographs at local weddings, often being paid with eggs, chickens, or piglets.

Sixty years after being taught by ZZ Tutu, Elizabeth Machocho Kgosiemang, still living in Tshing, remembered him as an outstanding teacher whose strictness was legendary: "We had to speak English during school hours, or we would be reported and receive a hiding." Sylvia Morrison recalled her father administering corporal punishment to the whole school; her own humiliation at being singled out during a school assembly for failing to do her homework, and receiving strokes across her hand, was seared into her memory.

As the principal's son, Desmond was the first child in the township to have a bicycle. Sometimes he ran errands for his parents, riding into Ventersdorp to buy meat or the *Rand Daily Mail,* the Johannesburg morning newspaper. It was there that he had his first encounters with white children:

I once rode past a group of white boys. They shouted at me: "Pik." I thought they meant a pickax with which you dig holes, so once I reached a safe distance I shouted back: "Graaf!" ("spade"). Only later did I realize they were shouting "Pikswart" ("pitch-black").

His experiences with whites were mixed; looking back as an adult, he found it remarkable that he could lay out a newspaper on the sidewalk of a street in Ventersdorp and read, undisturbed, while white pedestrians stepped around him. He also had his first experience of how South African society was ordered:

Once I saw black children scavenging in the dustbins of the white school for sandwiches which the children had thrown away after their break. [The government provided school lunches for whites.] I didn't know the political reasons for that. It just seemed strange that they could throw away perfectly good fruit and sandwiches.

I just thought life was organized in such a way that white people lived in the nice part, you lived in the township, and that was how God organized it. You knew you had to enter the post office through a separate entrance, and generally get treated like dirt. You didn't question it.

One of the uses to which ZZ put his copy of the *Mail* was keeping his pupils up-to-date on the progress of World War II. Many black

South Africans supported the war despite having lost the last of their minimal political rights three years before its outbreak. In 1936, the white parliament had voted, by a margin of 169 to eleven, to strip black voters in the Cape of their franchise. Parliament was much less certain that it wanted to fight Hitler–in 1939 the vote to declare war on Germany was carried by only eighty-one votes to fifty-nine; and Afrikaner Nationalists–among them John Vorster and P. W. Botha, future prime ministers with whom Tutu was to clash–joined the Ossewa Brandwag, whose leader admired the Nazis and collaborated with the Germans.

The black schoolchildren of Tshing supported South Africans who volunteered to fight the Italians and Germans in East Africa and North Africa. Desmond and his friends would stand at the side of the road to wave good-bye to convoys going to war. Among those who fought Rommel's Panzergruppe Afrika and Afrika Korps in North Africa were 15,000 black support troops, in roles such as drivers, cooks, clerks, laborers, stretcher-bearers, and orderlies, often armed only with ceremonial assegais. Desmond and his family were very proud that his father's younger brother, J. P. Tutu, volunteered for service: "It was actually a great honor to have someone in the army," he once told an Afrikaner journalist.

In about 1941, Matse Tutu returned to the Reef in search of work to supplement the family income, marking the beginning of a period during which the family moved from place to place as ZZ sought a position closer to her. She found a job as a cook at Ezenzeleni ("the place where you work for yourself"), an institution for the blind established by a British couple, Arthur and Florence Blaxall, in the hills west of Johannesburg. Soon she was earning enough to send clothes home, including a new winter overcoat of the proper size for Desmond. In time he went to the Reef to be closer to her. She lived at Ezenzeleni, so when he first moved he lived with his father's aunt in the nearby township of Roodepoort West. Later he and his mother came together in a house for Ezenzeleni's staff in the township. There he shared a room with one of her coworkers. The front of the house was occupied by the Blaxalls' clerk and driver, Es'kia Mphahlele, who later became a writer and academic. Mphahlele befriended the younger Tutu, taking him jogging and teaching him to box. In Roodepoort West, Tutu attended a Methodist primary school. Later he transferred to the Swedish Boarding School, known locally as SBS, a school at St. Ansgar's Mission started by Swedish missionaries.

After a few months at SBS, Desmond moved with his father to Ermelo in the eastern Transvaal, where ZZ had a temporary appointment. Six months later they returned to the Reef, and the family was reunited in a rented house in Roodepoort West. Desmond returned to SBS to complete his primary schooling. Despite these moves, he progressed quickly: after a few months in Standard Five, where classes were held in a chapel, he was among a handful promoted to Standard Six. A shock awaited him at the end of the year, however: he failed arithmetic, and thus the exam for leaving primary school. He retained a clear memory of the day decades afterward:

> Everybody believed I was going to pass, but I didn't. At least the results said I had failed. I don't believe that, I still don't believe it. But I hadn't passed. It was one of the worst nights of my life.

As an adult, Tutu remembered himself and his classmates as having been "rather docile and thoroughly unsophisticated and naive" in the face of racism. They were not so docile, though, as to respond uncritically to a primary school history written by a Methodist missionary named Whitehead:

> We found it distinctly odd that in virtually every encounter between the black Xhosas and the white settlers, Mr. Whitehead invariably described the Xhosas as those who stole the settlers' cattle, and of the white settlers he would write that the settlers captured the cattle from the Xhosas. We did not press this point at all, or hardly at all, in class discussion: but when we were outside we would mutter that it was very funny.

While living in Roodepoort West, Tutu picked up a copy of *Ebony* magazine, imported from the United States: "I didn't know that there could be literature of that kind, with such subversive qualities, because up to that point I had come to begin to believe what white people said about us." When Jackie Robinson broke into major league baseball in 1947, Tutu read about it in *Ebony:* "I didn't know baseball from Ping Pong, but here was a guy who had made it. . . . I grew inches."

And it was while visiting his mother at Ezenzeleni that Desmond had a glimpse of how South African society might be differently ordered:

This white man in a big black hat and a white flowing cassock swept past on the way to the residence of the Blaxalls. You could have knocked me down with a feather. . . . He doffed his hat to my mother. Now that seemed a perfectly normal thing I suppose for him, but for me, it was almost mind-boggling, that a white man could doff his hat to my mother, a black woman, really a nonentity in South Africa's terms.

Tutu later identified the white man as a priest named Trevor Huddleston. However, his dating of the incident attributed it to a period before Huddleston came to South Africa. If he recalled the date correctly, the priest could have been Huddleston's predecessor, Raymond Raynes, who—like Huddleston—was spare, tall, and somewhat gaunt. Whoever he was, he gave the young boy his first memory of a monk of the Community of the Resurrection, an order whose influence was to become crucial in his life.

CHAPTER 2

PRAISE POEM TO GOD

Four times a day a group of men, usually numbering between ten and twenty, gather in an austere, high-arched chapel of bare stone pillars and white-plastered walls in the north of England. For some minutes, they sit in absolute silence, with a stillness the newcomer struggles to match. Then the Angelus is rung on the chapel bell high in a tower, the clangs being transmuted into nothing more than gentle gongs as they drift into the choir stalls. A few more seconds of silence, and then the sound of plainsong chant arises. The beauty of the group's combined voices is eclipsed only by the reverberations of its echo at the deliberate pauses halfway through and at the end of each verse.

In a routine unbroken for more than a century, the monks of the Community of the Resurrection are at prayer. In the course of a day, they chant upwards of seven psalms. Before breakfast, at six-forty-five, they say Mattins, or morning prayer. After a morning of activity, they say the midday office. They are back at six-thirty for evensong, and again before bedtime for compline. In the psalms, Bible readings, and prayers, the monks proclaim, "We enter . . . into a conversation with God's word. In this rhythm of worship we are opened to His gift of prayer together and alone." At specified times of the day, including during many meals, they observe a rule of silence. Central to their day is the Mass: "The summit of our worship is the Eucharist offered with the Church on earth and in heaven, for the sake of all creation."

The chapel is part of the community's mother house, the House of Resurrection, set in a small estate of trees and lawns on a hillside in Mirfield, a town in the West Riding of Yorkshire. To the south, across a valley, is what appears at first glance to be an unspoiled hillside, the greenery occasionally interspersed with modern housing. But that appearance is deceptive. Down the street is the Mirfield Working Men's Club. A few miles to the south is the South Yorkshire Mining Museum. When the Community of the Resurrection moved to Mirfield in 1898, the town was at the center of a textile milling and coal mining area. Forty barges a day passed along a canal in the valley. The local railway station was one of the busiest in the country. Smoke from the mills led the local bishop to observe that he could not pick a flower in his diocese without blackening his fingers. By the beginning of the twenty-first century the industrial activity had subsided and the air was cleaner; but across the canal, outlines of the past were still discernible in the uneven man-made contours of grassy mounds.

The community was developed in England's industrial north because its nineteenth-century founder, Charles Gore, and his brethren were concerned by the alienation of the Church of England from the country's working class. An aristocrat, Gore was part of a movement to revive the monastic life in England, which had been destroyed by Henry VIII during the Reformation three centuries earlier. Influenced by the Christian Socialist movement, he rejected dog-eat-dog capitalism, defended trades unions, and backed radical causes domestically and internationally. In 1902 he was denounced as "pro-Boer" when he wrote to the *Times* of London that if Britain did not act to cut the death rate in South African concentration camps, "the honour of our country will contract a stain which we shall not be able to obliterate."

The community's attempt to identify with the English working class received a mixed response at best. There were limits to how well a group of privileged Englishmen, living in the former home of a mill owner and described by local newspapers as rich, cultured, "titled," and "intellectual," could expect to get to know their neighbors. One local Anglican layman wrote, "Those gentlemen . . . knew nothing about the crudities and squalor in which workers were living, almost within a stone's throw." However, when the bishop of Pretoria invited the community to minister to workers in the Transvaal gold mines at the end of the Anglo-Boer War, he initiated one of Africa's more welcome Christian missions. Among the beneficiaries of its blend of disciplined spiritual practice and social concern was Desmond Tutu.

If we consider the history of the Christian faith in the continent as a whole, European missionaries brought nothing new to Africa. Christianity was established in North Africa earlier than in much of Europe. The late Bengt Sundkler, the Swedish missionary who, with his research assistant, Christopher Steed, wrote perhaps the most comprehensive history of this religion in the continent, has pointed out that it came to Africa as an eastern religion. The Coptic Church of North Africa traces its history to the flight of Jesus and his parents to Egypt to escape Herod, and was well established in Egypt before the arrival of Islam. When officials of the Ethiopian Orthodox Church welcomed visitors such as Desmond Tutu in the 1980s, they traced their history to the baptism of their queen's chancellor by the apostle Philip, recorded in the Acts of the Apostles. This long heritage is today increasingly commemorated by Christians in the rest of the continent: the Anglican Church in southern Africa lauds Augustine of Hippo as one of the greatest of all Christian thinkers, and its highest award for lay service is named for Simon of Cyrene, the African who helped Jesus carry his cross to Calvary.

In most of sub-Saharan Africa, though, Europeans introduced Christianity in a 400-year process that Africans today view with deep ambivalence. The missionaries had an uneven political record, acting sometimes as agents of colonialism, sometimes as critics, and often showed no respect for the religious and cultural traditions of those they came to evangelize.

The missionaries came to a continent in which the spiritual was as deeply embedded as in any human community, and probably more so than in Europe during the Enlightenment. "In Africa religion was more than just religion," according to Sundkler and Steed:

> It was an all-pervasive reality which served to interpret society and give wholeness to the individual's life and the community. The village world and the Spirit world were not two distinct separate realms: there was a continuous communication between the two. Religion was a totality, a comprehensive whole.

Yet many of the missionaries who penetrated southern Africa treated its people as blank slates waiting to be written on. These missionaries recognized neither that there was an African religious tradition nor how their own western Christian practice reflected European cultural accretions rather than the fundamentals of their faith. The tragedy of a woman named Krotoa, of the Khoikhoi people of the area now called the Western Cape, was an early example of what could happen when indigenous people were forced to adopt western culture.

In 1652, thirty years after the Dutch West India Company settled New Amsterdam on the east coast of North America, Jan van Riebeeck of the Dutch East India Company established a fueling station on the southwestern tip of Africa for ships on their way to and from the east. He set up house on a piece of land that later became the site of the official residence of Anglican archbishops of Cape Town—and thus, in time, the home of Leah and Desmond Tutu. Van Riebeeck was joined by his wife, Maria, and they are recognized as South Africa's first white settler couple. Krotoa worked for Maria, and under the name Eva became the first Khoikhoi convert to her employer's religion. So enthusiastic was she that she shared her faith with other Khoikhoi people, embraced Dutch customs, and married a settler. Soon, however, there were rumors that she had run away from home and abandoned her western attire. After her husband died, her life was said to have fallen apart, and she died a drunken convict. The official diary of the Cape cruelly recorded that she had almost become Dutch, only to return "like a dog . . . to her vomit."

The first missionaries in South Africa were Moravians who arrived from eastern Germany in 1737. They established a mission among the Khoikhoi east of Cape Town which they named Genadendal, or "Vale of Grace." (In 1994, after Nelson Mandela became president, he renamed his official residence in Cape Town Genadendal.) Their work began haltingly—it was suppressed by the Dutch for fifty years—but when the British took the Cape from the Dutch at the beginning of the eighteenth century, South Africa became one of the world's busiest fields of Christian mission. Of the early groups, the best-known is the London Missionary Society (LMS). This is partly because the explorer David Livingstone was one of its missionaries, but in South Africa also because some of his predecessors defended the rights of Khoikhoi and southern Nguni peoples. The LMS missionary Johannes van der Kemp took identification with local people a step farther than his contemporaries; far more accommodating of their culture, he appropriated the Xhosa and Khoikhoi term "uThixo" for God, became accepted as a rainmaker, married a young Malagasy slave, ate Xhosa food, lived in Xhosa huts, and was willing to accept indigenous people wearing their traditional clothing. One of his contemporaries criticized his failure to "civilize" converts: "He seems to have judged it necessary, rather to imitate the savage in appearance than to induce the savage to imitate him."

Van der Kemp was unusual in his attitude toward African culture. The prevailing view was closer to that of Livingstone's father-in-law, Robert Moffat, who deplored political agitation against colonial authorities and found traditional dress "disgusting"—he once wrote that "by the slow but certain progress of Gospel principles, whole families became clothed and in their right mind." Preaching in Moffat's church in Kuruman, in the Northern Cape, on the 150th anniversary of its establishment, Desmond Tutu devoted the main thrust of his sermon to thanking missionaries. But he also enumerated their weaknesses:

> They were seen often as one arm of the imperial might of European expansionism. . . . They thought being European was synonymous with being Christian. . . . They often made our people ashamed of being African, [saying] that God would not usually hear your prayers if you were African unless you were dressed in European clothes. . . . Often they destroyed our rich cultural traditions.

Two Xhosa prophets arose in the early nineteenth century to give spiritual sustenance to a society under siege by the British, and their example inspired later generations struggling to overcome white domination. One was Nxele, also known as Makhanda. Nxele took Christian concepts and grafted them onto Xhosa tradition, providing a religious framework for resistance to colonial aggression. During the fifth of the frontier wars against the British, he led a rebellion, was captured, and became one of the earliest leaders to be jailed on Robben Island off Cape Town. If Nxele in his role as a freedom fighter can be seen as a nineteenth-century Nelson Mandela, his contemporary Ntsikana might be regarded as the forerunner of Desmond Tutu's generation of black Christian leadership. Ntsikana became more explicitly Christian than Nxele, emphasizing prayer, penance, conversion from sin, submission to God's will, and the central place of the resurrection of Christ. In contrast to the converts who went to live alongside missionaries, he remained in his own community, dressed in a leopard skin, and worshipped in Xhosa song and dance. He developed a thoroughly African faith, rooted in Xhosa symbols.

Ntsikana's most lasting achievement is his "Great Hymn," widely seen as the pinnacle of traditional Xhosa songwriting and also as the preeminent symbol of indigenous South African Christianity. Unlike African hymn writers, who used western tunes, Ntsikana set his composition to a Xhosa wedding song. It takes the form of a traditional praise poem, composed in a call-and-response style, directed not to a living person or an ancestor but to Ulo-Thixo Omkhulu ngosezulwini ("He, the Great God, who is in Heaven"). Leah and Desmond Tutu chose the hymn to open their fiftieth wedding anniversary service at Holy Cross Church in Orlando West, Soweto, in July 2005; and the choir's glorious opening cry of "Ntsikana's Bell," summoning people to worship, brought goose bumps to many in the congregation.

The importance of Ntsikana's story is highlighted by recent research showing that most Christians in Africa were converted not by European missionaries but by fellow Africans. According to this research, the role of the missionaries was political and cultural; their African converts did most of the evangelizing. By the time the Union of South Africa was formed in 1910, the missionaries and the first few generations of converts had laid the foundations for exponential growth in the twentieth century. The first union census in 1911 reported 1.5 million black Christians; in 2001 there were 32 million. The proportion of black South Africans who were Christian rose in the same period from one-third to 80 percent. In 1911, the numbers of black and white Christians were about the same; by the end of the century, black Christians outnumbered white Christians by more than eight to one.

The Anglican Church of which Desmond Tutu became a leader began as a chaplaincy to British colonial civil and military officials. It started to grow only after 1848, when the Church of England appointed the first bishop, Robert Gray, who created five dioceses and established the Church of the Province of South Africa, an autonomous institution that in time became a constituent church of the worldwide Anglican Communion. Its first bishops were British, usually graduates of Oxford or Cambridge. In their missionary work, the Anglicans generally followed the Moravian pattern of establishing mission stations that provided schools and hospitals and grew food as well as preaching the gospel. Black evangelists took charge of their congregations if white priests were not available to direct missions. In the Transvaal, Anglican fortunes were tied to those of the empire.

The Community of the Resurrection arrived in the gold fields in 1903, after the Anglo-Boer War. "From the outset," said Alban Winter in a memoir of its first sixty years there, "we realised that the chief agents in evangelisation must be the Africans themselves and their training was one of our major tasks." The monks reflected the prejudices of their time. One wrote: "The cathechists' names are Matthew, Titus, Stephen, Michael and Apolos. Their surnames I must leave to an expert. . . . I can only say they generally seem to begin with 'M.' " Another lamented that black and white Christians did not gather around the same altar, but conceded that "of course it is quite obvious that the natives just emerging from savagery cannot be treated in the same way as whites, there must be restrictions, there must be in many ways separations." Thus whites worshipped in parishes, and blacks worshipped in "mission districts" under an "archdeacon of native missions." When the diocese of Johannesburg was formed in 1922, there were nine black priests and fifteen deacons. In 1950, when the Archdeaconry of Native Missions was abolished and black churches were merged into nonracial archdeaconries, there were thirty-four black priests, two deacons, and twenty-six catechists, most of them trained by the monks they called the "CR fathers."

Desmond Tutu was not an Anglican during his early childhood; nor did he feel an early vocation to the priesthood. He nevertheless grew up immersed in church life. His paternal grandfather, Solomon Tutu, was a minister of one of the thousands of independent African churches, which were established free of white control and which now comprise the majority of South African Christians. At the age of nine months, on June 27, 1932, Desmond was baptized in the Methodist Church for which his father worked in Klerksdorp. The Methodists were a powerful missionary force in the region. As in the Anglican church, local administration was segregated. Black Methodists were organized in the Klerksdorp African circuit, which in 1932 had eleven churches, supplemented by 120 "preaching places" in outlying areas. The circuit was served by three ordained ministers and 126 lay preachers. Centrally, church government embraced all races. Nevertheless, when the minister who baptized Tutu, Molema J. Moshoela, represented his church at its regular synod, some of its deliberations were broken up into "African representative sessions" and "European representative sessions." The Klerksdorp circuit had sixteen teachers—one of them ZZ Tutu—working in four primary schools and educating 929 pupils, an average of nearly sixty a class.

When Desmond's sister Sylvia changed churches, the family followed her, first to an African Methodist Episcopal Church, a denomination that had originated in contacts with African-Americans in the nineteenth century. Then, after she was admitted to St. Peter's School, a secondary school started by the CR fathers in Rosettenville, south of Johannesburg, the family became Anglicans. Matse became a devout member of the Mothers' Union, one of the powerful prayer and support groups for women, which make up the backbone of South African society. Most of Sunday mornings were spent in church; a service could easily last three hours. At about age seven, Desmond became a server at St. Francis Anglican Church in Tshing. The priest, Zachariah Sekgapane, would become one of Tutu's models for ministry. On some Sundays, servers went to help Sekgapane in remote rural churches. The trips were memorable for two reasons: first because they traveled by car—the Tutus had no car—and second because of how the priest treated his helpers:

> Whenever we small boys had gone with him to outstations, he would never sit down to lunch at the church without first ensuring that we had been fed. I never forgot that example of caring for veritable nonentities. . . . There are a number of people you try to emulate, and he was one of them.

After the family became Anglican, Tutu and his younger sister Gloria "played church," amusing their father by trying to chant the liturgy in the Anglican style, Desmond pretending to be the priest and Gloria the congregation. This led Desmond to fleeting thoughts of becoming a priest, though these were displaced when he was a teenager. In Roodepoort West, one of Zachariah Tutu's relatives gave Desmond an introduction to an independent church. Desmond recalled in adulthood:

> He was a shoe repairer. . . . When he went around evangelizing I carried his banner. I would walk in front of him, carrying the banner, and . . . he would sing: "Simon Petrus, Ndincedise"—"Simon Peter, help me." So the children in the location would call me Simon Petrus's child.

At age twelve Desmond took the second step of Christian initiation by renewing his baptismal vows and being confirmed in his faith. He joined dozens of other children in St. Mary's Church in Roodepoort on November 28, 1943, to be confirmed by Geoffrey Clayton, bishop of Johannesburg.

While living in Roodepoort, Tutu started high school. Firmly believing that he had not failed Standard Six, he refused to go back to primary school, so his father went to see the legendary headmaster of the Johannesburg Bantu High School, Harry Percy Madibane. Like most black teachers of his era, Madibane began his career with a primary school education and a teachers' diploma. He taught at a number of church primary schools on the Reef, becoming principal of St. Cyprian's School in Sophiatown, on the western edge of Johannesburg, two years before the community took over Anglican work in the area. Madibane decided that he wanted to begin a secondary school. He studied privately for matriculation; became one of the first black graduates of the University of the Witwatersrand; and, supported by the priests of the Community of the Resurrection, opened his first class at St. Cyprian's in 1940. The following year, he moved the school to the neighboring Western Native Township, where he developed it into a powerhouse of black education in the Transvaal. There it also became known as Western High, later Madibane High.

Madibane had a reputation as a tough, fiercely determined visionary. The journalist Casey Motsisi, writing in *Drum* magazine when the school was renamed after Madibane, reported that he was nicknamed "Horse Power" by his pupils, and "the Shark" by his teachers. "If he says a mikado is a hippo," Motsisi wrote, "trying to prove him wrong would be as effective as taking a shower without turning the water on." Nonetheless, Madibane was willing to hear ZZ Tutu's entreaties and to give his son a chance to prove himself. "And prove himself he did," wrote Tutu's classmate Stanley Motjuwadi later. "In the half-yearly exams, Des came top of all 250 Form I pupils."

Tutu began his first year at high school in 1945 with a daily train journey from Roodepoort West to Westbury station, where he joined other pupils from the East and West Rand in a walk to school. One of them was Motjuwadi. When Tutu was awarded the Nobel Peace Prize, Motjuwadi, by then the editor of *Drum*, reminisced about their schooldays:

Perhaps because we shared many disadvantages, we took to each other immediately. We were scrawny, spindly-legged kids, both wore shorts and did not have shoes for our first day at high school. For the first six months, we were housed at the Full Gospel Church and had to write on our laps or kneel on the floor to use the bench as a desk. . . . After June we were moved to Form 1A which was in a room at the communal library. Here we used desks although Des, Masing Tshabadira and I had to sit in a desk meant for two.

Desmond, forced to write left-handed because of his paralyzed right hand, crouched

like a crab while doing his dyslexic scribbling—with us relegated to the extreme end of the desk. Because of this I had many fights with this selfish southpaw. We had our lunch together, played together, travelled together. But in class we fought and fought.

There was no campus—pupils were scattered in classrooms and church buildings around Western Township. Tutu visited a laboratory only once during his school career. The library was inadequate, and there were very few games or recreational facilities. As an adult he enjoyed telling what his honest answer to an exam question would have been if asked what he observed when a science experiment was performed: "Nothing—we had to imagine from what our teachers told us you observed."

What the school lacked in material resources, it made up for in the quality of its teachers. Sixty years after starting there, Tutu remembered many of them clearly. Nimrod Ndebele, father of the writer and University of Cape Town vice chancellor Njabulo Ndebele, taught him arithmetic: "He made learning so much fun. He always had objects which he used to illustrate what up to that point had been cloaked in mystery and unrelieved gloom. . . . Nobody failed his subject. . . . He hardly had to scold any of his pupils. Everybody was eating out of his hand." Geoff Mamabolo instilled in his pupils a love of English literature and set them challenging papers: "When we went to write the [public] exams we were very upset because the examiners didn't give us a chance to show off. . . . The questions they asked were nothing like the kind of questions that Geoff Mamabolo had prepared for us." The school was in a rough neighborhood, but Madibane's reputation was such that gangsters from surrounding townships would appear before him in response to a summons relayed by boys from the school. He caned gang members, even if they did not attend the school, and challenged the girls in the school for going out with them instead of with "his" boys.

Tutu joined the most junior of the school's rugby teams, his slightness dictating that he play scrum half. This was the beginning of a lifelong love of the sport: on Saturdays, carrying sandwiches made by his mother, he caught a train on his own to the original Ellis Park rugby ground in Johannesburg and, from the small pen set aside for black spectators, watched Transvaal rugby heroes such as Jan Lotz.

Soon the family found the cost of daily train fares too high, and Desmond was sent to stay with relatives who lived closer to Western Township. For a while he went to J. P. Tutu, the uncle who had served in World War II and who now sublet a backyard shack in Annandale Street, Sophiatown. Desmond shared a room with between two and five others at any one time, and the shack was only one of many occupied by subtenants in the same yard. In the mornings, winter and summer, he washed at an open-air communal cold-water tap. Later he moved closer to school, to the home of relatives in Matsimela Street, Western Township. As in primary school, Tutu felt no burning sense of injustice about the place of black South Africans in society, although there were signs that he had inherited his mother's compassion—once, while waiting for a train on a cold railway station platform, he took off one of the two sweaters he was wearing, gave it away to a boy with none, and swore his sister Gloria to silence about the incident.

As Stanley Motjuwadi told it, much of the students' life outside the classroom revolved around finding food and supplementing their allowances:

> For lunch we used to get sixpence each. . . . We had to use some ingenuity to make it stretch, so we soon discovered a place, a soda fountain run by a Chinese in Main Street, Sophiatown. Here we would buy a chunk of bread with fish crumbs for bonsella [free], a glass of flavoured water and roasted peanuts for a tickey.* The other tickey we would put aside for the afternoon break.

Tutu bought bags of oranges to split up and sell at a profit. Motjuwadi smoused—that is, hawked—candy on the train to and from school. He claimed that he and Tutu were the best cardsharps on the train:

> We would take on workers commuting with us and never lost. A deft scratching of the heart was a hint to Des to call hearts. A scooping with the open hand was spades, and three outstretched fingers meant clubs. . . . The workers we were fleecing did not seem to mind it. In fact they admired Des' prowess and nicknamed him Professor.

Tutu and Motjuwadi caddied for white golfers at the Killarney golf course in Johannesburg's northern suburbs. "My first foray," said Desmond, "was an unmitigated disaster. I infuriated my boss because I was a real liability, losing the ball a few times." Forty years later, after being entertained at a champagne breakfast at the same golf club, Stanley wrote in his *Drum* column, "De-Kaffirnated Stan," † about what he called the informal education they received there:

---

* Three pennies.

† The title of the column was a play on "Kaffir," South Africa's most derogatory epithet for black people.

We got our first chance to learn and know mlungu [white man] at close range. Mlungu, we discovered, was good and bad, generous and mean, strong and weak. In short he was human, just like us even if our fate was to carry his golf bag.

Take for instance the guy we used to call Pisspot. His vile temper could only be matched by his awful golf. . . .

I can't recall how many shiners I collected fighting over Standard Bank's bag. SB, as we called him, was the biggest tipper at Killarney. He never shouted at caddies and bought us refreshments at the 9th hole. But there was one snag. . . . SB insisted that his caddie should not wear shoes. The reason was that he wanted the caddie to work on the ball with his toes, teeing it up and taking it out of a bad lie. SB was a cheat but we caddies all loved him.

Raasbekkie ["noisy little mouth"] could talk better than he could play golf. . . .

Mahleleshushu ["the ever-hot one"] was a darling. Always drunk and lisping, he never took golf or himself seriously.

As Desmond entered his second year of high school, the Tutus moved again, this time to a township that became their permanent home. The move was occasioned by ZZ's appointment as principal of St. Paul's Anglican School in Munsieville, which is part of present-day Mogale City, 25 kilometers (15 miles) west of Johannesburg.

At the time the Tutus settled in the area, not all of its history was recorded or widely disseminated. But the twenty-first-century visitor can experience millions of years of human history down the road from the Tutus' home. Adjacent to Mogale City is a valley recently named the "cradle of humankind," a UNESCO World Heritage Site where some of the world's most important discoveries in research on human evolution have been made. In 1947 a 2.5-million-year-old skull of the species *Australopithecus africanus,* which walked upright, was found there; and in 1998 paleontologists announced the identification of an almost complete skeleton of an australopithecine who stood four feet tall and lived between 3.2 million and 3.6 million years ago.

In its more recent history, 200 years ago, the region was home to the people of the Bapo chiefdom, who were traders and miners of gold. In the late 1820s, during the Mfecane, Mzilikazi ka Mashobane, a northern Nguni leader fleeing from Shaka, invaded, killing the Po chief and taking captive his heir, Mogale wa Mogale. Mzilikazi was in turn driven out by the Voortrekkers, who carved up the land into farms for themselves. Under Boer rule, the name of one of the farms, Paardekraal, a few miles from the Tutus' home, became associated with the Afrikaner nationalist struggle—it was where 8,000 armed settlers gathered to launch the first war of liberation against the British.

Munsieville is on the northern outskirts of the town that grew up at Paardekraal after 1887, when whites began to exploit the surrounding gold-bearing reefs. The town was named Krugersdorp, after Paul Kruger, president of the Transvaal republic, and its raison d'être is still visible in the form of a white-yellow mountain of compacted sand—the by-product of the extraction of gold from ore—which rises behind the town center. Munsieville, named after the chief health inspector, James Munsie, was established to accommodate Krugersdorp's black workers. When the Tutus arrived at house number 1132—there were no street names or street numbers—the street was, in Tutu's words, "an apology for one, with rocky outcroppings." The breeze-block house, rented from the municipality, had three small rooms. The front door led directly into a central room with a coal stove, used as the kitchen but also doubling as Gloria's bedroom. Off to one side was the sitting room-cum-dining room, which also served as Desmond's bedroom; and on the other was their parents' bedroom. (Sylvia had left home.) In one corner was a small bathroom with a concrete bathtub and a toilet.

From Munsieville, Desmond first commuted to school in Western Township. He took a taxi to Krugersdorp station, took a train to Johannesburg, and then walked to school. Soon the family was again struggling to find his fares. One morning there was no money to send him to school:

> My mother went where she was doing washing and cleaning for a white madam. She would be paid two shillings a day. . . . On this occasion I went with her and she received her two shillings to give to me. I walked to the station and then caught a train. I've never forgotten it. . . . My mother was going to work that whole day and at the end she was not going to get anything because she had already got it in the morning.

So the family turned to the church for help. They went to the Community of the Resurrection, which had opened a hostel for boys at its Sophiatown mission.

CHAPTER 3

A SENSE OF WORTH

The name Sophiatown is burned into South African cultural and political history. As a community of different races in which law-abiding residents lived peacefully together, it became an exemplar of what might have been had apartheid not been inflicted on the country. As one of a few urban settlements in which blacks were permitted to own property, it held out a hope of belonging and permanence that was usually denied them in cities and towns. As an area where planning was not tightly controlled by the authorities, it gave residents freedom to build as they wanted. As the township that "spawned onto the Reef more gangs than any other location," according to *Drum* magazine's columnist "Mr. Drum," it gave birth to the Vultures, the Berliners, the Gestapo, and the Americans. And as the wellspring of a vibrant culture of jazz, dancing, singing stars, "nice time girls," traditional beer brewed in backyards, illicit "white" liquor in shebeens, and interracial mixing, it was the home of hip klevahs, ignorant rural moegoes, uptight situations, lowlife thuggish tsotsis, and more.* The generation of writers nurtured by *Drum* and associated with Sophiatown's heyday in the 1950s variously described it as South Africa's casbah, its little Chicago and its Paris.

Of the flowering of black South African writing at the time, Es'kia Mphahlele–Desmond Tutu's childhood mentor and a former writer for *Drum*–has observed:

> The literary style of the 1950s was racy, agitated and impressionistic; it quivered with a nervous energy, a caustic wit. Impressionistic, because our writers feel life at the basic levels of sheer survival, because blacks

---

* Klevahs, streetwise people; moegoes, ignorant country folk; situations, uptight people, not streetwise; tsotsis, township thugs. These terms are used in Arthur Maimane's *Hate No More* (Kwela Books, 2000).

are so close to physical pain: hunger; overcrowded public transport in which bodies chafe and push and pull; overcrowded housing, and the accompanying choking smell and taste of coal smoke; the smell of garbage, of sewage, of street litter, of wet clothes and body heat in over-crowded houses on rainy days; baton charges at political rallies; deten-tion and solitary confinement; torture in the cells; violence between black and black. The writer attempted all the time to record minute-to-minute experience—unlike his counterpart in the former British or French colonies, who has the time and physical mobility and ease that allow him philosophical contemplation, a leisurely pace of diction.

For Lewis Nkosi, of the same generation,

Ultimately, it was the cacophonous, swaggering world of Elizabethan England which gave us the closest parallel to our own mode of exis-tence; the cloak and dagger stories of Shakespeare, the marvellously gay and dangerous times of change in Great Britain, came closest to reflecting our own condition. Thus it was possible for an African musi-cian returning home at night to inspire awe in a group of thugs sur-rounding him by declaiming in an impossibly archaic English: "Unhand me, rogues!" Indeed, they did unhand him.

There were strong American influences too. Gangsters wore, as *Drum* put it, the "latest and loudest American fashions," and the tsotsis imitated the bad guys in American gangster movies. The educated middle class listened to Miles Davis, Dizzy Gillespie, Thelonious Monk and Charlie Parker, and watched films starring black actors at the upmarket Odin Theater.

Desmond Tutu's world was not that of the shebeens. But as a fourteen-year-old schoolboy—a "township urchin," he later called himself—he was exposed to much of Sophiatown's culture. He was fas-cinated by the movies, particularly those starring African-Americans. The musical *Stormy Weather,* with Lena Horne, Cab Calloway and Fats Waller, made a strong impression: "I don't know whether it was a very good film. . . . But I don't care. Because for us it was making a political statement."

The hostel in which Tutu boarded was one of a complex of Anglican institutions and ministries centered on the Church of Christ the King in Sophiatown. The biographer of Raymond Raynes, the Community of the Resurrection's first priest in charge there, recorded that when

Raynes asked for a new church in 1935, the architect said he could build only a garage with the money Raynes was offering. Raynes asked for a "huge and holy garage," and got a church seating 2,000 and standing out against the sky at the highest point of Sophiatown. Over six years, Raynes and Dorothy Maud, an aristocratic Englishwoman who worked with him, built three churches, seven schools, and three nursery schools, serving 6,000 children. They also extended a hospital; raised money for a swimming pool; and had the township's water supply, lighting, sanitation, and roads upgraded.

Institutions such as the Sophiatown mission help to explain the ambivalence with which many Africans regarded missionaries, despite the missionaries' cultural arrogance. The schools in Sophiatown, as well as Lovedale and Tiger Kloof where ZZ and Matse Tutu were educated, were all part of what one historian has called "an enormous benevolent empire" of church schools. In the 1930s, the empire employed nearly 8,000 teachers, giving classes for more than 370,000 children. In the Eastern Cape, a network of renowned schools and colleges produced an intellectual elite, many of whose descendants helped to lead South Africa's struggle for liberation and served in the first South African cabinets of the democratic era. Mandela went to Methodist schools in the Eastern Cape. His successor, Thabo Mbeki, was educated at Lovedale. The schools were often "colonialist in their attitude and practices," wrote Mandela in his autobiography, "yet . . . their benefits outweighed their disadvantages."

Desmond Tutu, preaching at the 150th anniversary of the Moffat church in 1988, singled out the missionaries' role in education for high praise:

Many, many, many of us owe the fact of us having been educated at all to the indomitable men and women who blazed the trail to provide education for the Africans when the secular authorities were less than enthusiastic and who would hardly have been able to cope with the growing needs of the black population.

In 1943 Raymond Raynes was chosen to be superior of the Community of the Resurrection. Before returning from Sophiatown to Mirfield, he appointed Trevor Huddleston, a thirty-year-old CR father, as his successor. Tutu's descriptions of Huddleston are some of the most vivid of his early years. Like many CR fathers, Huddleston had gone to a public school and then to Oxford. That was not what struck Tutu about him, though:

> He was so un-English in many ways, being very fond of hugging people, embracing them, and in the way in which he laughed. He did not laugh like many white people, only with their teeth. He laughed with his whole body, his whole being, and that endeared him very much to black people. . . . His office would one moment have several of what he called his 'creatures' playing marbles on the floor, and the next it would be his meeting place with, say, Yehudi Menuhin, who came to play in Christ the King Church.

Huddleston was so popular that the children competed for his time. Tutu once admitted during confession to another priest that he was jealous of the attention other boys received from the monk. "I will never forget it," Tutu told the author, "because the priest told me, 'When you are standing against the wall with friends basking in the sun, there is no less sun because you are sharing it.'"

Huddleston was as enchanted with the children as they were impressed by him. In his first letter home to Mirfield, he wrote: "The children everywhere . . . are simply fascinating in their friendliness and gaiety." Children, including Tutu, were allowed to sit on his lap in his office. Fifty years later this led to an angry letter from Archbishop Tutu to a prospective biographer of Huddleston. The writer was researching an episode in 1974 in which Huddleston had a nervous collapse after being accused of sexually harassing two schoolboys in London. Responding to an inquiry about whether there had been similar allegations in South Africa, Tutu repudiated the suggestion. "I have seldom felt more devastated and even soiled by the implication of what your letter suggested," Tutu said. "How ghastly to want to besmirch such a remarkable man, so holy and so good. How utterly despicable and awful."

Huddleston encouraged young Desmond to read, once lending him a manuscript copy of Alan Paton's soon to be famous book *Cry the Beloved Country* before publication. Another of the fathers–Keith Davie–tried without success to teach Tutu Greek: "When he found I was struggling, he tried Latin, I don't think with greater success. I wasn't a very apt pupil." Another protégé of the CR fathers at this time was Khotso Makhulu, later the archbishop of Central Africa. In retirement, Makhulu emphasized the fathers' enduring contribution to the lives of their charges: "They showed us that we mattered as people. . . . They instilled in you a sense of worth."

As in Ventersdorp, Tutu became a server at Christ the King. A special attraction of the job in winter was that servers were treated by the fathers to mugs of hot coffee after services. He sometimes stayed in Sophiatown on weekends and operated a bookstall after church on Sunday, selling rosaries and prayer books to parishioners. When he returned home to Munsieville, he took his work with him. "He would study when he came back from school," recalled his sister Gloria, "then relax, play a bit, and then come back. . . . He would sleep and have his candle next to him, and at night he would wake up and study."

In about May 1947–Tutu's third year of high school–the unusual experience of a white man knocking at the family's front door in Munsieville one night brought the news that he was ill. The man was one of the fathers, and he had come to tell them Desmond had been taken from the CR hostel to Coronation Hospital, near Sophiatown, with suspected pleurisy. Desmond was diagnosed with tuberculosis and taken to Rietfontein, a sanatorium near Alexandra Township on the opposite side of Johannesburg. The development of drugs to treat tuberculosis was then in its early stages; the main form of treatment was still enforced rest and good nutrition. Tutu was confined to the sanatorium for more than eighteen months before he was considered cured.

He contracted tuberculosis toward the end of a decade-long epidemic linked to South Africa's rapid industrial growth and its failure to provide proper housing for black workers. As the country's economy boomed after the Great Depression, and continued to grow when industry diversified to replace imports during World War II, thousands of black South Africans poured into the cities in search of jobs. Conditions in townships, already beset by overcrowding, malnutrition, and disease, quickly deteriorated even more. At a service marking Johannesburg's sixtieth anniversary in 1946, Trevor Huddleston gave a sermon that included imagery from Dickens and St. Luke's Gospel. Johannesburg's history was, he said, "a Tale of Two Cities in very truth." The "stinking backyards" of Sophiatown and other townships were the result of "a criminal–a sinful–lack of vision in the years that are past, whilst Lazarus has been lying at the gate unheeded and full of sores, and Dives has fared sumptuously, has built himself skyscrapers and laid out for himself pleasure gardens every day." Between 1938 and 1945, the mortality rate from tuberculosis among black South Africans nearly doubled. In Johannesburg, although the rate was lower, it grew faster: by 140 percent over the same period.

Tutu may well have owed his life to the influence of the CR in finding him a hospital bed. By the government's own estimate, there should have been 13,000 beds for blacks with tuberculosis; there were actually only 1,850. Tutu's earliest recollection of experiencing "a God-moment, almost an epiphany," was at Rietfontein. One of his doctors called Trevor Huddleston to say that the patient was going to die. Tutu became aware of the possibility through observing the rhythm of life at the sanatorium:

> Once somebody started coughing up blood you knew it was curtains. . . . I was hemorrhaging a lot one day. . . . I remember that I went to the bathroom and I was vomiting blood and I said, "God, if it means I am going to die, OK; if I am going to live, OK. . . ." Through having said that I experienced a strange sort of peace.

The experience did not, however, make him particularly religious:

> There was a priest who used to come and bring us holy communion, a wonderful old man, Father Venables. . . . And Trevor Huddleston gave me a rosary and a pocket New Testament. . . . Maybe one began to realize that there's a great deal more to life than the material things that were happening, possibly, but I can't think that I became particularly metaphysical.

Tutu and his fellow patients were discouraged from physical activity during their confinement, so they played cards or checkers much of the time. Tutu learned about cricket without ever seeing the game played– an adult patient, a Xhosa teacher, introduced him to the radio commentaries of the BBC's celebrated John Arlott. He also read a lot. When one of Huddleston's brother monks, Dominic Whitnall, brought comics to the hospital, Tutu asked for books instead. On his next visit, Whitnall brought works by Dickens and Thackeray. Tutu's regard for Huddleston was strengthened by the priest's caring for him over the long months in the hospital. He had made his first "really good" confession to Huddleston, and the monk visited him regularly in the hospital, sometimes bringing a carload of young friends from Sophiatown. One was Stanley Motjuwadi. "Even illness could not get Des down,"

Stanley wrote later. "At times I would bring my hickory shaft 8-iron and we would hit a few shots. He would also regale me with stories about patients."

The distance between Munsieville in the west and Rietfontein on the eastern outskirts of Johannesburg made it difficult for his family to get there, but his mother was a regular visitor. When the family did go, they spent hours walking and traveling in taxis, trains, and buses to get there and back. On one of the visits, Zachariah Tutu announced that Desmond now deserved to be recognized as a man.

Nelson Mandela has written that in Xhosa tradition, becoming a man is achieved through one means only—circumcision: "In my tradition, an uncircumcised male cannot be heir to his father's wealth, cannot marry or officiate in tribal rituals. An uncircumcised Xhosa man is a contradiction in terms, for he is not considered a man at all, but a boy." This was no less so for Desmond the urban township boy. From the nineteenth century on, missionaries tried to stamp out the "heathen rites" they associated with circumcision by threat of excommunication; and they succeeded to the extent that there is still no formal church liturgy recognizing it, but they failed to stop it. Traditionally, Desmond would have joined an initiation school, going into seclusion in a rural area to survive without home comforts and receive instruction in the responsibilities of adulthood. In the hospital that was not possible, and the procedure was done surgically.

When Tutu returned to school in 1949, he had missed his first public examination, the Junior Certificate. H. P. Madibane, his headmaster, nevertheless allowed him to study for matriculation. "In spite of having lost a year," according to Motjuwadi, "Des always came out top of the class when we sat down for exams." Tutu became known for his photographic memory: "He would playfully close his eyes when a classmate asked him about something. 'Your answer is on page 179 of Duggan, three lines from the top of the page,' he would tease." He joined the debating team and won the school's prize for best speaker in 1949.

He also began to think of his future. He badly wanted to become a doctor, hoping to do research on tuberculosis. At the time he wrote his Senior Certificate, or matriculation exams, pass rates were low and first-class passes were rare. Tutu was prepared for the national examinations of the Joint Matriculation Board, which was subscribed to mainly by elite white private schools and was known for its high standards. He wrote at the end of 1950 and was awarded a second-class pass, with B's in English, Zulu, History, and Zoology; C in Afrikaans; and E in Mathematics. The result was good enough to secure him admission to study medicine at the University of the Witwatersrand, but the family could not afford the fees. Forced to look elsewhere, he turned to teaching and enrolled at a government-run teacher training college on a government scholarship.

Tutu went to teachers' college in 1951, before the National Party government which introduced apartheid had fully implemented the educational system it planned for black South Africans. But W. M. M. Eiselen, who designed the details of the system, had decided by 1934 what he wanted: first, "the three R's, elementary history and geography, nature study and religion, all taught in the vernacular. Next I would provide for Bantu subjects—Bantu history, Bantu folk-lore, Bantu songs, Bantu tribal life." So when the nineteen-year-old Desmond Tutu, Stanley Motjuwadi, Casey Motsisi, and others arrived at the new Pretoria Bantu Normal College, they associated its architecture with what Afrikaner Nationalists regarded as "Bantu" culture: the dormitories were rondavels, round hutlike structures with thatched roofs. "They said we had to develop along our own lines," Tutu quipped later, "and normal rectangular buildings were probably not good for our Bantu psyche."

A fellow student was Mmutlanyane Stanley Mogoba, who was to become a political prisoner on Robben Island, a revered presiding bishop of the Methodist Church, and the leader of the Pan Africanist Congress in Parliament. Coming from a mission school with white teachers, Mogoba was surprised at the English grades of students who had been taught by black teachers at government schools: "Here we were meeting Desmond from Madibane High who got a B in English. . . . We were taught by English-speaking teachers, some of them fresh from England, and we struggled with our C's, D's and E's." Among the lecturers at Bantu Normal were white teachers from the University of South Africa and the Afrikaans-medium University of Pretoria and two black teachers of African languages. The Afrikaners were not always proficient in English, and Motjuwadi would joke that "the queen was lying prostrate" by the end of some classes because of how her language had been mangled. Mogoba and Tutu served together on the students' representative council, where Tutu was treasurer; and for two years Tutu organized the Literary and Dramatic Society and chaired the Cultural and Debating Society.

Tutu met Nelson Mandela for the first time at college, when he was a member of the debating team and Mandela adjudicated a debate with the Jan Hofmeyr School of Social Work in Johannesburg. There was no hint of their future relationship: Mandela was a prominent Johannesburg lawyer in his mid-thirties, flamboyant, tall (nearly 1.9 meters, or six feet two inches), and deeply immersed in politics; Tutu was in his early twenties, short and slender, and politically conscious but not active. In later life, Mandela had no recollection of the meeting, and the two did not see each other again until they met in the mayor's parlor at Cape Town City Hall on February 11, 1990, the day of Mandela's release from prison. During his college years, Tutu also encountered another South African political leader of note: Robert Sobukwe, who was to break away from the ANC to lead the Pan Africanist Congress. It was Sobukwe's dedication as a teacher rather than his politics which made an impression; he gave extra lessons to pupils during school holidays in the Transvaal town of Standerton, where Tutu's sister Sylvia operated a general dealer's store.

The staff could be openly racist at the college. An education inspector freely used the worst South African racial epithet in a class; seeing a spot of ink spilled on a desk, he described it as kafferwerk (the work of "kaffirs"). Students responded in a way which was new to Tutu, who had experienced the caring of white priests and doctors: "When we were in the common room and listening to the news, if you had an accident and a white person was the victim . . . guys would cheer and say, 'One oppressor less.' " The students were also dismissive of religion, prompting Tutu to resolve that they needed to meet someone he regarded as a competent and articulate exponent of Christianity. He invited Trevor Huddleston to speak at the college. Mogoba recalled students crowding around to speak to the CR father as he visited the students in their dormitories, but in Tutu's memory the visit was overshadowed by an incident involving Canon John Tsebe, the college chaplain:

> When they went to the house of the principal of the school, who was an Afrikaner, Trevor Huddleston was ushered in through the front door and went into the lounge and was given his tea there. This black priest who was our chaplain had to go in through the kitchen, and he sat there and that was where he was given his tea.

Opportunities for a full-time university education for black students were minimal in the 1950s, but the University of South Africa (Unisa) offered a generation of teachers, clergy, and civil servants the possibility of advancement through distance learning, either by correspondence or at associated institutions. It was a white-run institution—if black students visited its offices, they used separate entrances, and graduation ceremonies were segregated. But the content of the courses was the same for all races. At Bantu Normal, students had to take five Unisa courses in their first year of training. They were encouraged to continue taking courses in the ensuing two years and to complete their bachelor's degree by correspondence during their first year of teaching. Tutu and Mogoba were among about five students in their year who did this.

Tutu took his first university degree for the extra money it would earn him as a teacher, and his motivation showed both in his attitude toward his work and in his grades. He relied almost entirely on his lecturers' notes, and he did not attend Unisa's winter school. In his best subjects—biology, education, and history—he scored between 57 and 60 percent. His worst grades were in English, 49 percent; and Zulu, 47 percent. If he had majored in the subjects he enjoyed most, he would have chosen history and English. But he was not prepared to do the extensive reading required and took sociology and Zulu instead.

Returning home from college after three years with a Transvaal Bantu Teachers' Diploma, Tutu took his first teaching position at his old school in Western Township in 1954. There he taught English to five classes—senior classes of thirty to forty pupils and junior classes of up to eighty. A member of one of his junior classes, Jiyana (GG) Mbere—now a gynecologist in Johannesburg—remembered Tutu as slim and frail: "He was a 'situation,' always in a suit and tie." Some teachers used their fists to keep order, but the new teacher used persuasion: "He used to involve us in a discussion and win us over to his point of view." Tutu moved back home to Munsieville. He marked his pupils' papers on the train to and from school, and studied for his Unisa finals by candlelight at night and in the early morning. He passed Zulu with grades of 53 and 47 percent in his final two years. Robert Sobukwe, by then working in the department of African languages at the University of the Witwatersrand, helped him with "critical advice" for his finals. In sociology, Tutu graduated with final grades of 48 and 51 percent. Another member of his graduating class was Robert Gabriel Mugabe, the future president of Zimbabwe.

After a year of teaching at Madibane's school, Tutu tired of the train travel. Since his school days, a new government secondary school for black children had been started across the street from his parents' home. It was called Krugersdorp High School and was headed by his old English teacher, Geoff Mamabolo. Tutu transferred there in 1955 to teach English and history.

A girl he had known for some years by the time he began teaching was Gloria's friend Nomalizo Leah Shenxane. She had been born in Krugersdorp; spent time in the rural town of Brits, where her father, James, was a successful small farmer; and moved back to Munsieville when her mother, Johanna, became a domestic worker for a white family in Geduld, east of Johannesburg. Leah lived with her older brother, William, in a rented room in the backyard of a landlord's house and attended St. Paul's Primary School, where she was one of ZZ Tutu's star pupils.

"The very first time I saw Desmond, he'd come from his school," she recalled after forty years of marriage. "He was a very good-looking, slim young man, and I thought: Gosh, he's quite a guy. But he never noticed me. I was at primary school. . . . It was a young girl's crush on an older boy. He just saw me as one of many girls visiting his sister." Desmond first took notice of Leah when she emerged from her final primary school exam, and he asked her how it had gone. "My naughty-girlish inclination was to turn around to hit my dress [with my hand], which was a fashionable way of saying, Go to the moon!"

Leah left Munsieville for a rural Catholic high school near Polokwane in the north of South Africa, where she studied for her Junior Certificate. Like most prospective primary school teachers at the time, she went directly on to college; and it was while she was at St. Thomas's Teacher Training College in Village Main, Johannesburg, that she and Desmond began dating. When they could meet in Munsieville, they spent afternoons walking around the township's open spaces; otherwise, they exchanged notes. "It became quite serious and hot by the time I went back to college to finish my last year," Leah remembered. "We were already talking about engagements and marriages. . . . He was quite keen to send negotiators [in] the traditional Xhosa way . . . as soon as I had finished writing exams. I pushed him back a bit and said, 'Wait a minute, let's have the results first because you know what my parents will say if I don't pass? They will say, how could you pass when you were already thinking of marriage?'"

Legally, Leah and Desmond were married at the end of June 1955, but this is not a date they ever recognized. Black clergy were not permitted to be state marriage officers, so, in Tutu's words, "you were unceremoniously processed during working hours on a weekday at the Krugersdorp Native Commissioner's Court." They did not regard themselves as actually married until a priest completed the religious ceremony in church. Leah having been raised a Catholic, they were married on July 2, 1955, in the Church of Mary Queen of Apostles, Munsieville, by Jean Verot, a missionary priest of the Oblates of Mary Immaculate. Verot made an entry in the Latin marriage register indicating that Desmond was Protestant, Leah was Catholic, and theirs was thus a marriage of "mixed religion." Like most black Christians, Desmond also observed the important custom of ukulobola—the payment of "lobola" to Leah's family upon their marriage. Like circumcision, lobola was frowned upon by early missionaries, but the CR fathers were accepting enough of the practice to help Desmond pay, not in the traditional way with cattle but with cash. By 1995, at the end of Tutu's term as archbishop, Anglican theologians had given the custom their imprimatur, recognizing it as a mechanism by which two families or clans marked their union, one moreover which actually conferred dignity upon the bride. However, another African custom which the Tutus took into their marriage—that of slaughtering a beast and spilling a little of its blood on the ground as a libation for their ancestors—continued to cause controversy in the church into the twenty-first century, despite Tutu's view that the African veneration of ancestors differs little from the Christian recognition of saints.

Desmond and Leah put down roots in the local community. To begin with, they lived in the single room used as a dining room, sitting room, and bedroom in Desmond's parents' house at 1132 Munsieville. Leah taught at a primary school in Roodepoort, to which she commuted by taxi and train. Desmond became a volunteer soccer administrator, convening the fixtures and selection committee of the Krugersdorp Bantu Football Association. After six months, they found their own home to rent. By the end of each month they had run out of money and had to buy groceries on credit from the local shop. There was only a cold-water shower, and Desmond went to his parents' home once a week for a hot bath. Despite this, according to Leah, they felt rich:

> We were quite comfortable. We had a three-room house; other people had one-room houses. We had an electrified house. Most people had unelectrified houses. The fashion at that time was to buy twin beds. . . . So we bought twin beds and used one bed. . . . The first thing you did

in the morning was to get up and make sure your stoep was shining; then you went in and made the tea or coffee and breakfast. . . . My mother-in-law liked cooking. She cooked as if she was cooking for ten . . . and she was always carrying about little dishes . . . either to my house or Gloria's house, which was not far either.

The proudest day of Desmond's life came when their first child was born in Paardekraal Hospital–renamed Yusuf Dadoo Hospital in the democratic era–in April 1956. He learned of the birth from a nurse whom he phoned to check on Leah's progress: "She said, 'She's got a boy.' I threw down the phone and ran all the way, about a mile, to my parents' house, and arrived breathless to announce that I had become a father." They named their son Trevor Armstrong Tamsanqa, after Trevor Huddleston, Louis Armstrong, and one of the brothers Desmond had lost. Sixteen months later, on the Feast of the Assumption, their first daughter was born at home in Munsieville. They called her Thandeka–meaning "lovable"–Theresa Ursula; the latter two names, her father said, were given because "we had to touch our forelocks to her mother's Roman Catholic background."

The Tutus worshipped in St. Paul's Church, a mission founded by the Community of the Resurrection. Typically for a black congregation, St. Paul's struggled financially. Correspondence with the diocesan office in Johannesburg portrayed a church constantly in debt, first over its mission bicycles, later over its car; and always behind in paying its assessments to the diocese. In November 1953, its priest in charge, Canon Peter Moñala, sent ninety-six pounds to the bishop and wrote: "If you only knew how hard I'm pulling. My people are very hard in paying their church dues. I hate to be in arrears." Tutu served the congregation in several capacities–as Sunday school teacher, assistant choirmaster, church councilor, lay preacher, and subdeacon–but felt no calling to the priesthood. It was primarily through his response to national political developments–and the ensuing confrontation between church and state, in which the Community of the Resurrection and the Anglican Church featured prominently–that he was to find his vocation.

CHAPTER 4

OBVIOUS GIFTS OF LEADERSHIP

When you talk to South Africans of Desmond Tutu's generation, especially those who lived where he grew up, they speak of the election of the Afrikaner Nationalist government of 1948 as if it portended the arrival of a plague. No matter what suffering they endured before apartheid, when they compare it with what followed they tend toward nostalgia. For the new generation of political activists who had recently founded the African National Congress Youth League, the violent suppression of a miners' strike two years earlier, in 1946, marked the moment they lost any illusion that South Africa might allow democracy at home after fighting for it abroad during World War II. But even for them, the election of 1948 was a shock. Nelson Mandela records that on election night he and Oliver Tambo, a future law partner and ANC leader in exile, were at an all-night meeting: "We barely discussed the question of a Nationalist government because we did not expect one." Emerging to see that the National Party had won, "I was stunned and dismayed."

William Beinart, professor of race relations at Oxford University, has observed that until 1948, although segregationist attitudes might have been more stringent in South Africa than in the United States or Britain's colonies, they were not much different. The newly elected government set about changing that. Beginning with laws that classified every South African by racial origin and extended bans on interracial sex and marriage, it made race the fundamental building block of society. It imposed rigid segregation between four distinct groups—white, Indian, Coloured (of mixed heritage), and black. Whites, constituting 21 percent of the population, took complete and undiluted control of national policy. They stripped Coloureds of the franchise, packing Parliament and then the courts in a five-year struggle to overcome legislative and legal defeats. Perverting the post–World War II language of decolonization and self-determination, Hendrik Verwoerd, the government's chief ideologue, repudiated the very idea of a black South African. Blacks, 68 percent of the population, were divided into ethnically based "nations" that would exercise "self rule" in "homelands" constituting about 13 percent of the land. Blacks were described in apartheid nomenclature as Bantu, a term derived from the Nguni word for "people," and the homelands became Bantustans. In Mandela's words: "The often haphazard segregation of the past three hundred years was to be consolidated into a monolithic system that was diabolical in its detail, inescapable in its reach and overwhelming in its power."

It might be added that a section of the Christian church was in large measure responsible for the policy: the Reverend David Botha, a leader of the segregated Dutch Reformed church for people classified as Coloured, created a stir at a conference of the South African Council of Churches in 1980 with an analysis of how, as he put it, the white Dutch Reformed church "conceived and gave birth to the secular gospel of apartheid." Not only did it provide a model for apartheid, with four segregated churches for people of different races; in 1935 it produced a document that formed the cornerstone of the policy.

Bringing such a plan to fruition required large-scale social engineering in which ideologues who paid no regard to human suffering forcibly uprooted whole communities of people and pushed them around South Africa like checkers on a board. A study by the Methodist Church in the Transvaal reported that in the first decade of these removals, it had to build between sixty and seventy new churches to replace those destroyed by apartheid, and it expected to have to build forty-six more. In Klerksdorp, Tutu's birthplace—including the church in which he had been baptized—was bulldozed in the late 1950s. Roodepoort West and with it Ezenzeleni, a neighboring eye hospital, the homes in which the Tutus lived, and the schools and churches they attended were all swept away, to be replaced by white suburbs. East of Johannesburg, the township of Stirtonville, near Boksburg, where Matse Tutu's family lived, was destroyed. In the Eastern Cape, the institutions that had educated ZZ and Matse Tutu were taken over: Lovedale's white staff was replaced, its high school was abolished, and its library was dispersed. Tiger Kloof—which also educated the first two presidents of neighboring Botswana and almost the whole of the country's first postindependence cabinet—was seized, declared a "black spot" in a "white area," and closed down. Most of Munsieville survived, but both Leah and William's first home in the township and St. Mary's Church, where the Tutus had been married, were destroyed.

Saint Thomas's college in Village Main, Johannesburg, where Leah had trained as a teacher, was closed. But of the removals carried out in places associated with Desmond Tutu, that in Sophiatown attracted the most publicity.

The end of Sophiatown was documented by journalists including the gangster turned poet Don Mattera, Douglas Brown of the *Daily Telegraph,* and Leonard Ingalls of the *New York Times*. What Sophiatown represented was in almost every respect anathema to the new rulers. The local white authorities had long wanted to evict its people; a white suburb, Westdene, abutted Sophiatown to the east, and others had grown up to the west. Only when the National Party came to power, however, was there the political will to develop a comprehensive strategy to implement these wishes; one that included building new houses for its black residents in a township named Meadowlands, eighteen kilometers (11 miles) out of the city, tearing people from their homes, and forcibly relocating them in ethnically segregated housing.

The first removals were scheduled for February 12, 1955. "Excitement ran high as meetings were held on township squares, street corners and in churches," Mattera wrote later. "Bands of young people marched through the streets. . . . Foreign newsmen and local journalists virtually lived in Sophiatown. They wanted to see it all; see the revolution in its initial stages. It was coming for sure, so we all believed." The government preempted resistance by acting three days early. Ingalls and Brown accompanied Huddleston as he left Christ the King to find out what was happening. In a front-page report in the *New York Times,* datelined Johannesburg, February 9, Ingalls wrote:

> The forced removal of natives from their homes in Johannesburg began today. The transfer of the first 130 Negro families from their slum dwellings to a new Government housing development beyond the city limits was carried out under close surveillance of 2,000 heavily armed policeman. . . . At 4 A.M. detachments of white and native police assembled in the pre-dawn darkness at Sophiatown and Meadowlands and on the route between them to enforce the removal plan. White officers were armed with pistols, rifles, submachine and machine guns. Native policemen carried steel-pointed spears, known as assegais, and clubs.

Noni Jabavu, J. Tengo Jabavu's granddaughter, recorded that her brother wrote to her:

Sisi [big sister], you should have been here. The Boers' pale blue eyes were glinting steelier than ever that day. Their fingers tickled the triggers of revolvers and the hands clenched and unclenched the handles of those sjambok whips until the knuckles were white.

Brown, in his report on page one of the *Telegraph,* said that the operation was "the greatest display of police strength seen in Johannesburg for many years. . . . By nightfall the homes of nearly 100 families had been destroyed—in a city that is short of 50,000 native houses. . . . All was done in the manner and on the scale of a big military operation. . . . The police used no violence and very little roughness today. Yet this unusually correct behaviour seemed only to add to the cold horror of the scene."

The community's resistance broken, the removals continued until Sophiatown was cleared. Those responsible trumpeted their achievement in the new name they gave to the suburb for Afrikaner working people which they created in place of Sophiatown: Triomf. The street names they left the same, "as if to rub salt in our wounds," said Tutu in later life, perhaps explaining why fifty years later these names were still so prominent in residents' reminiscences. The Church of Christ the King on Ray Street was sold some years later, becoming in turn a whites-only Dutch Reformed church, an Afrikaans Pentecostal church, and a boxing club. After the end of apartheid the church was reclaimed, and Trevor Huddleston's ashes were interred there; but of the hostel in which Tutu stayed, and the priory in which he ate his meals, there remained no trace.

The removal from Sophiatown was not universally unpopular. Many tenants from Sophiatown told Ingalls, after being moved to Meadowlands, that they were glad to be in new homes for which they were charged less rent. But that did not legitimize the government's behavior, as both Huddleston and the *New York Times* pointed out. In his book *Naught for Your Comfort,* Huddleston wrote: "Sophiatown WAS a slum. Those of us who have lived there would never wish to deny that. . . . But slum conditions can be removed without the expropriation of a whole area." The *New York Times* said in editorial comment on February 10 that its news report "reads uncomfortably like an account from a police state."

If the apartheid government's destruction of Sophiatown epitomized its readiness to resort to armed force to dictate where people could live, its seizure of the education system in which ZZ and

Desmond Tutu taught showed the lengths to which it would go to try to control children's minds. Historically, white authorities had little enthusiasm for educating black South Africans. In his memoir of the early days of the Community of the Resurrection in Johannesburg, Alban Winter wrote:

> Again and again I have heard Europeans say they would rather have a raw African to labour for them rather than one who had been to school. The latter, they declared, was dishonest. He knew enough to make him a clever thief or a forger of passes but not how to do an honest day's work or obey orders. . . . There was also the dislike which arises from the white man's sense of racial superiority. It irked such [people] very much to see black children with school books and slates going to school just like their own children.

In 1950 there were places at school for only a third to half of black children of school age. Government subsidies for the education of blacks were circumscribed by a formula linking them to revenue from black taxpayers, who earned the lowest wages. A tiny minority of black pupils went to secondary school–3 percent of the total school enrolment in 1950. When Tutu went to Western High in 1945, it was one of only three black high schools on the Reef. Such education as existed was nearly all provided by the churches. The church school system was grossly inadequate—one researcher has suggested that by the 1950s it was near collapse, too poor and too small to cope with the demand for education. However, as in Sophiatown, Verwoerd's solution was not to build on what had been achieved but rather to smash the system and replace it with one molded to suit his ideological predilections. In a notorious speech to Parliament, he said that the churches' "European" model of education was giving black pupils unrealistic expectations:

> The Bantu must be guided to serve his own community in all respects. There is no place for him in the European community above the level of certain forms of labour. . . . Until now he has been subjected to a school system which drew him away from his own community and misled him by showing him the green pastures of European society in which he was not allowed to graze.

Verwoerd abolished state subsidies for independent schools, forcing the churches to hand control of the schools to the government, close the schools down, or raise their own funds—something only a small fraction were able to do. In place of the church school system, he and his chief civil servant, W. M. M. Eiselen, established "Bantu education." Although Eiselen planned to double the number of pupils at school over ten years, this goal was to be achieved in part by cutting school hours from 4½ hours a day to three and introducing double sessions for teachers. And his focus was on education at its most basic level—in 1949, three in four pupils stayed in school for only four years, and he envisaged no change in this proportion.

Black leaders and church leaders alike were appalled. "This is the most evil act of all," Tambo said. "I fear for the future of our children, and for the generations of children to come." Geoffrey Clayton, the bishop who had confirmed Tutu and who now headed the Anglican Church in South Africa as archbishop of Cape Town, said the government was making black education an instrument for forwarding the National Party's ideals: "That is the recognized pattern of a totalitarian state. It is the sort of thing most of us objected to in the Nazi regime of Germany." However, the churches were in what Trevor Huddleston described as a "cruel dilemma": should they lease their school buildings to the government, facilitating implementation of an evil system, or should they turn the children out and close down the schools? Clayton and most of his bishops opted for the former: "Even a rotten system of education is better than that which young children pick up in the streets," Clayton said. Huddleston and Ambrose Reeves, Clayton's successor as bishop of Johannesburg, disagreed. Reeves told the archbishops of Canterbury and York in England: "It is my conviction that if a proposed system of education is morally indefensible, the Church has no right to assist the authorities in carrying out their plans however remotely or indirectly." On April 1, 1955, the day the schools were to be taken over, Reeves closed the forty-seven black schools of the Johannesburg diocese, leaving the parents of 13,000 children with, again in Huddleston's phrase, "the same hideous dilemma: 'Bantu Education' or the street."

Desmond and Leah Tutu, who were then in their early twenties and beginning their teaching careers, followed the debate from Munsieville. They were already teaching in government schools, and Desmond was enjoying his work: "I was probably something of a disciplinarian but I tried to discipline through the syllabus, making the students enjoy what they were doing, and saying to them: it's good to have pride." However, Verwoerd's vision for the future did not accord with theirs. "The Bantu teacher," Verwoerd had told Parliament, "must be integrated as an active agent in the ... development of the Bantu community. He must learn not to feel above his community, with a consequent desire to become integrated into the life of the European community." Verwoerd proposed to save money by replacing male junior primary teachers with women earning less, and he unashamedly promoted discriminatory pay scales: "The salaries which European teachers enjoy are in no way a fit or permissible criterion for the salaries of Bantu teachers." After discussions with Leah, Desmond decided: "I just felt I couldn't be part of this. . . . I said to myself, sorry, I'm not going to be a collaborator in this nefarious scheme. So I said, 'What can I do?' "

Desmond and Leah finalized their decision during the summer holidays at the end of the 1955 school year. Trevor Huddleston wrote a recommendation for Desmond in a letter to Redvers Rouse, the archdeacon of Johannesburg, on January 21, 1956:

> *My dear Redvers,*
>   *This is to introduce Desmond Tutu from Krugersdorp.*
>   *I have known him now for just on ten years & I have known him well. I think he is a first rate person: intelligent (he is a graduate), deeply conscientious and sincere. He now believes he has a vocation to the priesthood though he desires to go forward with further degrees first—which in his case is, I think right.*
>   *Anyhow I believe he would prove an immensely valuable priest.*
>   *Yrs affectionately*
>   *Trevor C.R.*

In later life Tutu was quite frank about how he discerned his vocation: "It wasn't for very highfalutin ideals that I became a priest. It was almost by default. . . . I couldn't go to medical school. . . . The easiest option was going to theological college." His father was unhappy about the decision—ZZ had been told by the education department's supervisor for the area that Desmond was in line for a principalship.

Later in January, Tutu asked to join the Ordinands' Guild, in which prospective priests were evaluated for training. Some months afterward he was able to speak directly to Ambrose Reeves about his ambition, when he was admitted to serve as a subdeacon in his home parish. He followed up the conversation with a letter that gives an idea of how relations between Anglican priests and their bishops were ordered at the time. In the tradition of the Church of England—an established church with Queen Elizabeth II its temporal head and its bishops formally part of state protocol lists—Anglican bishops in South Africa were addressed as if they were British peers. "My Lord," wrote Tutu, "I was advised by Father Shand [John Shand, Tutu's spiritual director] to write this letter. He says he told Your Lordship that I intended entering Theological College, God willing, in 1958. . . . Father Shand deemed it wise for me to ask Your Lordship to arrange a day when I could be interviewed by Your Lordship."

At this point differences arose between Tutu and the diocese. He decided he wanted to enter college earlier, hoping to be accepted for 1957. Diocesan officials left no written record explaining why they turned him down, but Rouse's record of an interview with Tutu on September 1, 1956, shows that he owed money on hire purchase contracts. Married for little more than a year, he still had to pay off debts of 140 pounds for furniture—perhaps including the twin beds—as well as twenty pounds for books and forty pounds for clothing. His income was forty-two pounds a month. Rouse's note indicates that Tutu could not discharge the debt until December 1957. Responding to a letter from the diocese, Tutu told Reeves on September 12 that he was "deeply disappointed at my Lord's decision." He was nevertheless undaunted, and asked Reeves to stay his hand. He had, he revealed, a very promising indication that South Africa's richest man would help financially.

Even before his meeting with Rouse, Tutu had written to Harry Oppenheimer, heir to the family fortune behind De Beers Consolidated Mines and the Anglo American Corporation. Oppenheimer was about to succeed his father as head of the empire that controlled 80 percent of the world's diamonds and 40 percent of South Africa's gold. His wealth was built on a migrant labor system in which workers were housed in single-sex hostels and separated from their families for most of the year, and in a meeting with the president-general of the ANC, Albert Luthuli, he described the ANC's demand for universal adult suffrage as excessive. But he helped finance liberal opposition parties and contributed to lawyers' costs in the major political trial of the era. He had also been brought up an Anglican. He replied to Tutu that he was "very willing to consider this matter in a sympathetic spirit." He asked for testimonials and for further information about Tutu's career and intentions.

Tutu responded, and on September 14 Oppenheimer sent a check for 200 pounds. "I wish you all success," he told Tutu, "and hope that you will be able to contribute to the building up of a spirit of greater tolerance and understanding in South Africa." Reeves's reaction to Tutu's initiative is not recorded, although given the relationship between bishops and ordination candidates it is reasonable to speculate that he would have seen it as impertinent. He was certainly not swayed by Tutu's success in settling his debt. In November he summoned Tutu to an interview at Bishop's House. Tutu later could not recall what happened at the meeting, but the day afterward he wrote to Oppenheimer offering to return the money. Oppenheimer did not want it back: "I am sorry to hear of the difficulties that have arisen," he told Tutu. "I think that the best arrangement would be that any question of your repaying the 200 pounds I gave you should stand over for a year until you know whether you will be admitted to the Theological College in 1958."

Whatever Reeves felt about Tutu's approach to Oppenheimer, the effects were temporary. On April 23, 1957, Tutu wrote:

My Lord,
*   Please accept my heartfelt thanks for your Lordship's having resolved our differences and graciously allowing me to start college next year. I was very anxious when I attended our last meeting of the Postulants' Guild as I was apprehensive of your Lordship's attitude towards me. When I told Father Huddleston about our last interview, he was more optimistic and he seems to have been borne out.*
*   Again, I thank you very much, my Lord.*
*   Yours very respectfully,*
*   DMB Tutu*

While Tutu was waiting to go to college, Dale White, a young curate in the parish of St. Peter's, Krugersdorp, offered him Greek lessons. He accepted, but the rector refused to allow White to bring him into the church buildings. The Greek lessons had to be given in a room at the top of the church tower.

In September Reeves wrote confirming that Tutu would be sent to college. Reeves asked St. Peter's College in Rosettenville, Johannesburg, to admit Tutu and in a letter to the principal requested him to watch Tutu's spending:

I was somewhat disturbed by the number of debts this man has incurred, although it is true that both he and his wife were earning a considerable sum monthly as teachers and he would no doubt have been able easily to meet these if he had continued in the teaching profession. . . . Still . . . as a priest he is never going to have the kind of income that he has been used to in these last years.

Reeves's letter, with its implication that Tutu was a spendthrift, was to give him a reputation which dogged him throughout his ministry.

The Tutus' decision to repudiate Bantu education was made at a cost to their family life as well as to their earnings. Saint Peter's was a residential college, training only men; and married students could not live there with their wives. Leah resolved to leave teaching and train as a nurse. She could find a place only hundreds of miles away, at Jane Furse Hospital in a remote part of Sekhukhuneland, far to the north of Johannesburg. When she left to become a probationer nurse in April 1958, Trevor and Thandi had to stay behind in Munsieville with Desmond's parents.

The College of the Resurrection and St. Peter was the only institution training black Anglican priests in the northern provinces of South Africa. It was run by the Community of the Resurrection, which had originally established it in wood and iron buildings in Doornfontein, near the center of Johannesburg. In 1911 the community moved to Rosettenville, at that time a sparsely populated area. Over the years, the community built up a small campus, which included the elite St. Peter's secondary school, attended by—among others—Oliver Tambo; Sylvia Tutu; and a later Bantustan leader, Lucas Mangope. But by the 1950s, white suburbs had enveloped the campus. When Tutu's class arrived in 1958, the college was living, said Alban Winter, with a "sword of Damocles suspended over our heads." Saint Peter's School had already been closed down by Bantu education; and the nonracial island, like Tiger Kloof in the Northern Cape, was what the government called a "black spot" in a white area.

St. Peter's College accommodated thirty-six students, providing training over three years. Daily college life was centered on a quadrangle bounding a chapel, kitchen, refectory, hall, lecture rooms, and shared living rooms. The students came with diverse qualifications and abilities, from ten dioceses. The biggest group, of twelve, was from Johannesburg. Five CR fathers taught them the Old and New Testament, doctrine, church history, Christian ethics, and worship. The best-educated students prepared for external exams, in Tutu's case the church's licentiate in theology (L. Th.), and learned additional subjects such as elementary Greek.

Tutu's arrival coincided with that of a new principal, Godfrey Pawson. The previous principal had thought the college's function was primarily to teach its students to pray. Pawson, one of the community's best theologians, believed educated black South Africans were leaving the church partly because the clergy were inadequately educated. Barely one candidate a year attained the L.Th. before leaving college. Pawson wanted to improve academic standards, and he singled out Tutu, the only university graduate in his class, for individual tuition. "Godfrey spotted the fact that Desmond was exceptional," according to Timothy Stanton, the vice principal. "He didn't think he was an original thinker . . . [but] he said he had a photographic memory."

Tutu threw himself wholeheartedly into the college experience. He was a precisionist in preparing the chapel's altar for communion, says Sipho Masemola, a fellow student: "Desmond would want to do it exactly correctly. He would say, 'I came for this, I must know it.' " As part of their pastoral training, senior students such as Khotso Makhulu took Desmond and others out in their long, flowing cassocks for practical training in pastoral work. Sometimes they visited local domestic servants working in white homes. On Sunday afternoons, they bicycled across southern Johannesburg to visit the youths at Diepkloof Reformatory, the institution once headed by the author Alan Paton; and patients at Baragwanath Hospital, the largest hospital in the southern hemisphere. The college was run on a shoestring, and the students did everything but cook; they washed dishes, cleaned the premises, lit the fires, and did manual labor in the garden or on the sports field two afternoons a week. Tutu was less enthusiastic about cleaning the toilets than preparing the chapel, but he did his share. He was impressed by Stanton: "I was amazed that he, the vice principal and a white man to boot, would join the black students in doing some of the menial tasks." The students gave Stanton the African name Mzalwane, which describes his spirituality and gentle friendliness.

While Desmond was at St. Peter's, the Tutus struck up one of their earliest friendships with a white family. Val and Norman Leslie were fellow members of the Fraternity of the Resurrection, a group of lay Anglican supporters of the CR. They were not part of Johannesburg's white elite, protected by wealth from black advancement. Neither were they politically active, to Tutu's knowledge, and he objects to the use of the word "liberal" in describing them: "Liberal is a swear word. They were just human . . . more really committed Christians. If anything, they should have been verkramp* [but] they used to have blacks come to their house in Orange Grove for tea. We called my father Khulu (Granddad), and they called him Khulu too. They were just remarkable people."

After forty-five years as a priest, Tutu remained unable to identify a particular moment when his pragmatic decision to seek ordination as the best available option turned into a conviction that he was doing what God had called him to do. However, once at college, "I don't think I ever did question that this was in fact right." Mainly, this was because at college he became powerfully attracted to the spiritual life, in particular as it was modeled by the monks of the CR.

In Tutu's worldview, spirituality for an African is as much a part of existence as breathing. It was one of his aphorisms that "African communist" was a contradiction in terms, if communism was defined as atheistic and materialistic. Accordingly, one might say that the students at St. Peter's did not need to be "taught" spirituality. Pawson gave weekly instruction on the spiritual life, but for Tutu the CR fathers' best lessons were taught "by example rather than precept." The college followed the rigid discipline of monastic prayer observed at Mirfield: Mattins at six-thirty in the morning, holy Eucharist at seven, silent meditation on a text at seven-thirty, a recitation of the Angelus during lectures at noon, the service of sext at one in the afternoon, evensong at six, and compline at nine, followed by strict silence until after meditation the next morning. Apart from that, Tutu would frequently come across elderly monks praying on their knees, bent over in their stalls, when he was cleaning their priory chapel. Timothy Stanton arrived in the college chapel for personal prayer at five o'clock in the morning; and Masemola and David Nkwe, a fellow student from Krugersdorp who later became bishop of Matlosane, based in Klerksdorp, observed Tutu following his example.

It is in Desmond Tutu's spirituality that the legacy of St. Peter's and the Community of the Resurrection can principally be seen. The regimen of spiritual practice that the CR fathers modeled became central to his daily life. He rarely discussed it—following the biblical injunction in Matthew 6:1 not to "parade your religion before others"—but he occasionally revealed that if his daily schedule of personal and formal prayers was disrupted, he experienced "almost a physical sen-

---

* Narrow-minded, the opposite of *verlig*, "enlightened," in the Afrikaans political vocabulary.

sation like maybe not brushing my teeth." He asked Stanton to be his confessor at college and also asked two religious orders to allocate prayer companions to help him, through prayer, to become a good priest. One was the former Dorothy Maud, Raymond Raynes's coworker, who had become Sister Dorothy Raphael of the Community of St. Mary the Virgin, at Irene north of Johannesburg. The other was Sister Mary Julian, a member of the Society of the Precious Blood, in Masite in the neighboring country of Lesotho. He kept in contact with her, and she kept him in her daily prayers, until she died in 1999.

At the end of 1958, Pawson wrote in a first-year report to Reeves that Tutu had "more than fulfilled our high expectations." He continued:

> He has exceptional knowledge and intelligence and is very industrious. At the same time he shows no arrogance, mixes in well and is popular. . . . He has obvious gifts of leadership.

Outside St. Peter's, the change of career was causing difficulties. Tutu returned home for the summer holidays to find his father on half pay and bedridden, with a heart complaint and asthma. He wrote to Pawson: "I have myself been hopelessly improvident and have no funds to fall back on and I am apprehensive about what the Bishop will say since, I believe, I have created a bad impression with his Lordship about my ability to order my finances satisfactorily." Pawson approached Reeves, saying that Tutu's conduct had been "excellent" and that other dioceses paid higher family allowances, "especially in the case of a man like Tutu who has the ability and the qualifications for earning a high salary and has been used to a high standard of living." He added, "On the other hand you seem to have knowledge which I do not share of Tutu's irresponsibility in financial matters in the past." Reeves replied that although he had "some difficulty with Tutu in the past," this did not mean that he would not deal sympathetically with him now. After the diocese drew up a report on the family's finances, Tutu was given a five-pound increase in his allowance. Thanking Reeves, he apologized for being "such an awful nuisance so often."

The church had less sympathy for Leah. At that time bishops presumed to dictate not only the lives of ordinands but those of their wives (there were no woman priests). From the outset, despite his own opposition to collaborating with Bantu education, Reeves was annoyed that Leah had given up teaching. His reason, according to Pawson, was that the diocese had to find extra money to support the family. When, after a year of nursing training, Leah was struggling with the separation from her children, Pawson wrote to a brother monk at the hospital that he hoped Leah would stay there. He acknowledged "her babes from whom she is so unnaturally separated" but said he had defended Leah "rather hotly before the Bishop" for leaving teaching and did not want to be proved wrong. At the end of Desmond's second year, Reeves suggested that Leah stop nursing because it would be impractical for her to practice after his ordination. She was given a leave of absence to return to Johannesburg to discuss the issue with Desmond, but she insisted on remaining at the hospital. In a letter to Reeves, Pawson said he hoped the bishop would agree that Desmond was right in allowing her to do what was best for her. In discussions of the tensions of family life, the feelings of the celibate monks of the CR were usually with the man; in his second-year report on Desmond, Pawson commented: "With his wife he is a model of forbearance and affectionate understanding." As it happened, Leah had to give up nursing when she became pregnant again. In August 1960 she gave birth to a girl at 1132 Munsieville. She and Desmond named their new daughter Naomi Cecilia Nontombi: Naomi after Naomi Pucher, a friend who ran a discount book club to which Desmond belonged; Cecilia after ZZ Tutu's sister; and Nontombi–"mother of girls"–because Leah had produced another girl.

Tutu's rejection of Bantu education and his sojourn in the all-consuming world of the seminary in Rosettenville took place during intensifying political ferment in the country. In the decade since the National Party had come to power, the ANC had transformed itself. Leaders of its Youth League–among them Nelson Mandela; his mentor, Walter Sisulu; Oliver Tambo; and Robert Sobukwe–had persuaded the movement to adopt a "program of action" in 1949 that replaced petitions and delegations with mass action, strikes, boycotts, and civil disobedience. The government had banned the Communist Party. In 1952 the ANC cooperated with the South African Indian Congress in a Defiance Campaign against apartheid laws, timed to coincide with white celebrations of the 300th anniversary of Van Riebeeck's arrival. Three years later, the ANC, the Indian Congress, the Coloured People's Congress, the white Congress of Democrats (which included former Communist Party members), and the South African Congress of Trade Unions convened what became the "Congress of the People." The gathering endorsed the Freedom Charter, a political manifesto which became the rallying cry of the ANC and its allies for half a century. In 1956, 20,000 women marched on the Union Buildings, the seat of government in Pretoria, in protest against the extension of the pass laws to women. There was an upsurge of rural resistance in the late 1950s. In 1957 apartheid's first political show trial began when 156 leaders of the congress were charged with treason. Soon afterward, Sobukwe and other "Africanists" suspicious of the role of communists of other races in the congress alliance broke away from the ANC and formed the rival Pan-Africanist Congress (PAC).

Faced with systematic apartheid in every sphere of life, the multiracial churches founded by missionaries—among them Anglicans, Catholics, Congregationalists, Methodists, and Presbyterians—passed resolutions condemning the policy. In general, however, they failed to translate their words into concrete action. The Anglican hierarchy acted only when the church faced direct threats to its own worship and institutions. The protest for which Clayton was best known was telling the government that bishops would refuse to obey a law imposing apartheid on services of worship and church meetings. Also, the internal life of the church reflected apartheid values. The Johannesburg diocese spent far less on black ordinands at St. Peter's College than on their white counterparts at St. Paul's College, Grahamstown, in the Eastern Cape. In the late 1950s the basic personal allowance for black students was eighteen pounds a year, compared with forty pounds for whites. Sipho Masemola recalled one student at St. Peter's, on receiving his thirty-shilling allowance at the end of the month, chanting: "Pay day! Pay day! Thirty pieces of silver!" Family allowances narrowed the gap for married black students with big families, but in 1959 Desmond Tutu's allowance of 50 pounds in total—including a family allowance of twenty-seven pounds and a book allowance of five pounds—was still ten pounds lower than that of most of his contemporaries at St. Paul's.

The events of 1960, Tutu's final year at college, were a watershed in the history of the country, and as a result in the life of the diocese of Johannesburg. On Monday, March 21, the first day of a PAC protest against the pass laws, police in the township of Sharpeville, south of Johannesburg, opened fire on a crowd of demonstrators with .38 pistols, .303 rifles, and handheld light machine guns (Sten guns). With no warning, they fired more than a 1,000 rounds of ammunition in less than a minute. The only reporter there, Humphrey Tyler of *Drum*, observed: "One policeman was standing on the top of a Saracen (armoured police vehicle) and it looked as if he was firing his Sten gun into the fleeing crowd. He was moving slowly from side to side. It looked as if he was panning a movie camera—from the hip." Sixty-nine people were declared to have died in the Sharpeville Massacre, and an estimated 185 to 190 people were injured, 70 percent of them shot in the back as they ran from the police.

At St. Peter's, the news was received as in the rest of the country. "We were in a state of shock," said Tutu, "and I think a kind of disbelief. It couldn't have happened. There was also a kind of anger at God. After the shooting, there was blood in the street. Soon after, it rained and washed away the blood. . . . It seemed God was siding with these people, even removing the evidence of what had happened." But the students did not think of joining the protests against the pass laws: "We were in some ways a very apolitical bunch."

Ambrose Reeves responded quickly. His political instincts were by this time well honed: apart from his stand against Bantu education, he had opposed the removals from Sophiatown, prompting an attack on him in Parliament by Verwoerd. He chaired the board of trustees of a defense fund for leaders on trial for treason and had brought together fourteen liberal and left-wing groups, often at odds with one another, into a consultative antiapartheid front. Told of the massacre by the CR father Keith Davie, who was then chaplain at Baragwanath Hospital, Reeves visited the injured, appointed lawyers to take statements from them, and fought off attempts by the police to block access to them. He caused an outcry among whites when he hinted that explosive dumdum bullets had been used, asking why the police had a type of bullet which "causes a small wound when it enters but a large wound where it emerges from the body." Forty years afterward, his suspicions were vindicated when Philip Frankel of the University of the Witwatersrand published new research on the massacre. It showed that the death toll was far in excess of the reported sixty-nine and included about two dozen victims of dumdum bullets whose horrendously injured bodies had been disposed of secretly the night after the massacre.

The ensuing crisis unfolded with bewildering speed. On the same day as the massacre, three people were killed in a PAC protest in Cape Town. Workers in Cape Town began to stay away from their jobs. Luthuli, Mandela, Sisulu, and other leaders of the ANC burned their passes publicly—they had previously announced their own campaign against passes but had been preempted by the PAC. The ANC called for a day of mourning on Monday, March 28, which turned into the biggest strike in the country's history, and the government introduced legislation in Parliament to outlaw the ANC and PAC.

The country seemed on the brink of revolution. The British journalist Anthony Sampson, a former editor of *Drum* magazine, on a visit to Soweto, was struck by people's confidence: "It was certainly one of those brief interims in a nation's history when it seemed that anything could happen." Sixteen African colonies were on the verge of receiving independence from European powers; six weeks before Sharpeville, the British prime minister, Harold Macmillan, had warned the South African Parliament that "the wind of change is blowing through this continent, and, whether we like it or not, this growth of national consciousness is a political fact." In the face of widespread defiance across South Africa, the police suspended arrests for violations of the pass laws. On March 30 the government declared a state of emergency, giving itself the power to ban gatherings, impose curfews, and detain people without trial. Albert Luthuli was arrested in Pretoria; arriving at the police station, he was horrified to find that Timothy Stanton's sister, Hannah, was among those being held. Tambo left the country on the orders of the ANC leadership to head the movement in exile. Economically, international confidence in South Africa collapsed; 48 million pounds was withdrawn from the country, and share prices plunged. In Cape Town, 30,000 people marched on Parliament on March 30 in what the *New York Times*'s reporter Joseph Lelyveld later described as "the most impressive assertion of disciplined black political will the white regime has had to live through in this century." The protest was defused, and a massacre was averted, when a police colonel disobeyed orders to use force to suppress it. It was, wrote Lelyveld, "an hour in which the Bastille might have been stormed in South Africa but wasn't." On the night of April 1 Reeves was tipped off that he was about to be arrested. Within three hours he fled Bishop's House in Johannesburg, and he slipped across the border to Swaziland early the next morning. On April 8, the ANC and PAC were banned. On April 9, a mentally disturbed white farmer shot and injured Verwoerd in an attempted assassination.

The government soon reasserted control. It mobilized the army reserves and forced workers back to their jobs. By early May it had arrested 18,000 people, and it began to enforce the pass laws again. Sobukwe was sentenced to three years' imprisonment for incitement. Local and foreign investors took advantage of the crisis by buying shares at the bottom of the market, British multinationals continued to support the country, and Chase Manhattan Bank, chaired by David Rockefeller, lent South Africa ten million dollars in one of a number of key interventions in the country's history. In 1961, the Afrikaner Nationalists pulled out of the British Commonwealth and declared South Africa a republic, realizing an ambition that went back to the defeat of their republics by Britain in 1902.

Sharpeville precipitated South Africa into a different era, in which the principal political movements reflecting black aspirations were forced underground. "Even then," reflected Desmond Tutu later, "I can't say that I was madly political and angry." He accepted the status quo in the church: "I didn't think that I necessarily ought to go and work in a white parish." He and his peers were nevertheless thrilled when the Anglican Church elected its first black bishop, the former St. Peter's student Alphaeus Zulu, in 1960. Students clustered around Zulu when he visited the college, calling him "My Lord" and kneeling to kiss his episcopal ring. "I think he was a little uneasy about all the titles and obsequiousness," recalled Tutu. "But we said we couldn't possibly not do it for you when we were doing it for these other people"–by which he meant white bishops. Another event that excited the students was a visit from two men who had been tried for treason: Albert Luthuli and Professor Z. K. Matthews; the latter was one of the country's most distinguished black scholars and the initiator of the Congress of the People. Luthuli and Matthews stayed with the CR fathers, and Tutu excitedly went "just to shake hands with the great men."

Tutu continued to excel in his final year at college. He competed against white students at St. Paul's and black students at other colleges for the archbishop's annual essay prize and won it with a paper on Christianity and Islam. During the year, Pawson was replaced as principal by Aelred Stubbs, a member of the CR who had been educated at Eton and Oxford. Stubbs identified Tutu as being "head and shoulders" above the other students. He thought Tutu's fellow student Lawrence Zulu, later to become bishop of Zululand and a much discussed prospect as archbishop of Cape Town, was a more original thinker: "He had the vision. I think he had the better mind. He was more thoughtful. But he didn't have the incisiveness or ambition of Desmond." Tutu also had "an extraordinary power of assimilation" and was a good judge of people: "Desmond had real feeling for people and their goodness or otherwise."

Tutu's final college report was dated July 4, 1960. It is not clear from the copy in the church's archives whether it was written by Pawson or Stubbs. It read:

> He continues to be a diligent and intelligent reader and a most receptive pupil. As Senior Student he is efficient and dependable, if sometimes a little lacking in tact and in soundness of judgement. His health causes me some anxiety; he has had no serious illness, but very easily catches cold and is of poor physique (with quite considerable skill and energy on the football field in spite of this). One or two who knew him before he came to College have spoken to me about him in vaguely disparaging terms; the only definite suggestion I have heard against him was that he was irresponsible in financial matters. That failing I am sure he has now remedied. In striving to learn theology, in seeking to develop his devotional life, in performing tasks entrusted to him, and in every other way that I can think of, he has shown himself an exceptionally conscientious person. Not long ago he seemed to be suffering from a touch of "Roman fever"; * perhaps his bishop might do well to question him about that before ordination. Though anxious to please, he has little natural charm, and will never, with his superiors at any rate, be overpopular; but his outstanding intellectual gifts, combined with well-tried moral integrity, mark him out as a man likely to be of almost unique value to the Church of the future in South Africa.

A medical report compiled ahead of Tutu's ordination said that there was little likelihood of a recurrence of his tuberculosis: "Recent X-ray shows evidence of old disease," wrote P. Gordon Smith of Baragwanath Hospital, "but no suggestion of activity. Pleural adhesions are present, which would account for his chest pain. He should be re-examined if any symptoms of reactivity appear (weight loss, cough, night sweats, etc.) and should in any case be re-examined by X-ray at yearly intervals."

Ambrose Reeves was not in Johannesburg at the end of 1960 to ordain St. Peter's newly graduated students for their customary year of service as deacons. His decision to leave South Africa in April had been contentious. His white senior advisers in the diocese had urged him to leave; and Tutu recalled that this impaired his credibility among black Anglicans. Once he was gone, the white leadership wrote accus-

---

* A suggestion that he was too close to beliefs or practices of the Roman Catholic Church.

ing him of giving too much time to "extraecclesiastical affairs" and asked him to resign. Reeves refused and insisted on returning in September. He stayed at St. Benedict's House, a retreat house run by Anglican nuns across the street from St. Peter's. Tutu and other students were amused at the police car that followed his every move. Two days after his return, the head of the security police in Johannesburg served him with a deportation order and forced him onto an aircraft leaving the country. Reeves asked the retired archbishop of Central Africa, Edward Paget, to act as vicar-general of the diocese in his place, and Paget ordained Tutu and three other deacons in St. Mary's Cathedral, Johannesburg, on December 18, 1960. Tutu, on the basis of his examination results, was chosen to read the gospel at the ordination service.

Tutu was appointed as an assistant curate in St. Alban's parish in the "Old Location" at Benoni, east of Johannesburg, where he reported to the rector, Canon Nathaniel Mokoatle. Under the pass laws, he needed permission to live and work on the East Rand, and Mokoatle had to take him to the Bantu commissioner's office to be "influxed in," as the expression went.

The Tutu family, reunited permanently for the first time in three years, had to live in a converted garage. Desmond, Leah, and their three children used the garage space as a bedroom and living room. A second room served as a kitchen. Stubbs considered the conditions "absolutely terrible." Adding to the unpleasantness, a neighbor allowed friends to use his room for their sexual liaisons. "It was almost like a brothel," remembered Tutu. They considered moving, to a parish in Soweto, but Mokoatle refused to release Tutu from an agreement committing him to St. Alban's. Tutu wrote to Stubbs in July 1961: "I cannot get to Orlando. Has its advantages as I shall not move house in the middle of the year. We are all right, don't fret."

Leah wrote to the diocese about the family's living conditions. A report compiled the following January by Archdeacon Dick Yates of Germiston recorded:

> Fr. Tutu's house has double garage doors at the front, which fit fairly well. The roof is iron and is about 8 foot high. It is unsealed. It has a small kitchen, 10 foot by 10 foot. His bedroom, which is the garage, is 15 foot by 10 foot. There is a small stove in the bedroom but there are holes where the chimney goes through the roof. There is only one latrine (bucket system) for two families with children and one other per-

son. There is no place suitable for the interviewing of parishioners in their house. The bedroom has one window, 4 foot by 3 foot, half of which opens, and one small fanlight about two foot by one foot, on the opposite side. The kitchen has one four foot by three foot window on one side only. In my opinion the accommodation is not suitable or sufficient for a married priest.

Apart from the poor living conditions, as a black clergyman in the diocese of Johannesburg Tutu earned less than his white counterparts. Although marriage allowances were equal, the basic stipend for whites was half as much again as that for blacks, and child allowances for whites were double those for blacks. Tutu earned sixty-seven rand a month in stipend and allowances as a deacon, compared with a white deacon's ninety-seven rand. As a priest he earned 72.50 rand a month, compared with 110 rand.*

After Ambrose Reeves was deported, he resigned as bishop of Johannesburg. The diocese chose in his place Leslie Stradling, an English bishop serving in Tanzania. Stradling distanced himself from Reeves's approach and told his first synod that he would follow a "middle of the road" course: "I dislike apartheid very much and I know that many of you do also, but we are not sufficiently important for our likes and dislikes to matter much."

Tutu's ordination as a priest coincided with a historic change of strategy in the struggle against apartheid. On Saturday, December 16, 1961, he and two fellow ordinands had their final interviews with their bishop. They accompanied Stradling to Christ the King, Sophiatown, where he confirmed 150 young people, and then went to what Stradling said in his diary was a "tiresome" rehearsal for the ordination the next day. "Too much is being done at the altar, away from the people," he wrote. The same day, six days after Albert Luthuli had accepted the Nobel Peace Prize in Oslo for his nonviolent opposition to apartheid, the newly formed military wing of the ANC and the South African Communist Party, uMkhonto we Sizwe ("Spear of the Nation") set off bombs at government offices and an electrical installation. Nelson Mandela and his comrades had decided that after fifty years of peaceful campaigning, the ANC, now forced underground,

* South Africa changed its currency after declaring itself a republic, replacing the pound with the rand. The exchange rate at the time was two rand to the pound, and a U.S. dollar was roughly equal to one rand.

had no choice but to resort to force. The next day, Tutu was ordained with three others at St. Mary's Cathedral.

In 1962, Tutu was transferred a short distance from Benoni to St. Philip's Church, Thokoza, an outstation of the main parish church of Natalspruit. The family moved into a municipal house across the street from the church, which was small but a vast improvement on the garage. Leah went out to teach again. Desmond's rector, Mlonyeni Voyi, put him in charge of St. Philip's, giving him the opportunity to run his own congregation. Tutu later recalled that Voyi gave him a valuable lesson in ministry: "When you tried things and they didn't work, he would say, 'My son, people are not taps (faucets). You can't just turn them on and off.' " Many parishioners were laborers or domestic workers in white suburbs. Standing at the church door after services, Tutu greeted them in the formal African way as Baba or Ntate ("Father," "Sir") and Mama or Mme ("Mother," "Ma'am"). "The priest," he said, "was regarded as somebody very important in the community. If the priest could treat them as who they really were, with reverence, perhaps they could be . . . won over." He took communion to the sick and visited the housebound in different areas on alternate weeks. He found fulfillment in giving a man communion a few hours before his death, but was haunted by his failure to minister to an elderly woman because he was not due to be in her area that week: "I could have gone to see her. I said, 'Well, no, I'll go next week.' She died before her priest came to see her." He regularly had a quiet day of prayer and meditation in Rosettenville, often traveling there on the back of Sipho Masemola's scooter.

In Benoni and Thokoza, Desmond Tutu came to know what he subsequently described as the "incredible privilege" of ministry:

> You visit people who are sick on their deathbed, and they tell you things that they probably have not shared with any other person. You are privileged to bring the holy sacrament to people at a time when they are at their lowest. But you also have the privilege of meeting up with people at their moments of great joy, when they are getting married or when they have a child baptized. And you are given the privilege of connecting people with the transcendent, connecting people with their God.

The experience gave him a passion for pastoral ministry that continued for the rest of his life. It was, however, to be one of only two short periods during which he was able to minister full time in a local congregation. Soon after he arrived in Benoni, Aelred Stubbs began to make other plans for him, and henceforth pastoral work had to be combined with, or built into, study, lecturing, or leading institutions.

When Godfrey Pawson arrived at St. Peter's College, he wrote that "whether or not the policy of apartheid prevails, the African people will, in the next 20 years, have to start providing their own leaders in ecclesiastical, as well as other spheres. I long for the day when African theological students will sit under African theological lecturers, responsible to an African principal. When that day comes . . . it will be a prelude to yet greater things."

To this end, Aelred Stubbs approached Ambrose Reeves after Tutu graduated from St. Peter's to propose that he should be trained as a theology teacher. Early in April 1961, Reeves wrote to Stubbs from the United Kingdom that he no longer had jurisdiction in the diocese, but he heartily endorsed Stubbs's idea: "Please go ahead with it. It is excellent!"

In June, Stubbs wrote to Sydney Evans, dean of King's College, London, asking him to take Tutu. Stubbs said that because there was no bishop at the time, he had only the unofficial approval of an archdeacon, "but the need of an African member of staff who can hold his own academically is so urgent, and Desmond the only suitable man known to us, so that I hope and believe that Bishop Stradling . . . will give his blessing." Evans quickly agreed: "I want this College to be used as much as possible by students from overseas." Supporting an application for admission to King's, Timothy Stanton said that Tutu had been the college's best student in his time there. He added: "I was his confessor, and so can add that he has been a regular penitent, with considerable self-knowledge." In lengthy correspondence between Stubbs, Evans, and Tutu, mostly dealing with funding, arrangements were made for him to travel to London to read for the degree of bachelor of divinity in the academic year beginning in the northern autumn of 1962. However, he still had to get a passport from the South African government.

CHAPTER 5

A BREATH OF FRESH AIR

While Nelson Mandela and most of South Africa's black political leaders were in prison, in exile, or under restriction within the country, Desmond Tutu's outspokenness as a church leader in the 1980s made him, in Mandela's words, "public enemy number one to the powers-that-be," one of those on whom extensive files were kept. However, when researchers for the Truth and Reconciliation Commission began early in the democratic era to dig into the country's past, hardly any files were to be found. The outgoing government had purged its records—the National Intelligence Service alone destroyed forty-four tons of documents and microfilm in the blast furnaces of the quasi-state iron and steel company over an eight-month period in 1993. One of the few surviving government files on Tutu was that kept by the Department of Bantu Administration and Development (BAD) on his passport applications from the 1960s. It gives an illuminating insight into how far the apartheid government went in controlling the lives of black South Africans.

The possession of a passport was, in the view of the government, "not a right but a privilege" and the applications of black South Africans to travel outside the country were carefully examined. On receiving Desmond and Leah Tutu's request for passports in March 1962, the Department of the Interior asked both the police and BAD for reports. The commanding officer of the Security Branch on the East Rand was asked to investigate the purpose of the trip, whether the Tutus were in a financial position to travel, and "whether the applicant is suspected of tendencies calculated prejudicially to affect the security of the state." Police headquarters responded that the church would pay the family's costs and that "nothing of an adverse nature concerning the applicants has come to the notice of the Police."

The BAD head office asked the Bantu Affairs Commissioner in Germiston on the East Rand for a report on 17 prescribed questions on the "abovementioned Bantu," including what their political beliefs were and whether they were considered "fit and proper persons to visit countries where there is no racial segregation." After six weeks, in mid-May the commissioner sent a three-page reply reporting that the "applicants' political tendencies are not known" and that he was unable to answer the second question. He reported that Tutu had said in one interview that Leah was a qualified nurse and intended to work in a hospital in England, but later said she was a teacher: "When these contradictory statements were pointed out to him, he shrugged his shoulders." The commissioner added that Tutu had wrongly stated during an interview that there were no facilities for "a Bantu" to study for the bachelor of divinity degree. In fact the University of South Africa offered the degree. However, the commissioner recognized that the financial aid Tutu was being offered was specifically for full-time study at King's College, and he recommended a passport. At the end of May, his boss, the chief Bantu Affairs commissioner of the Witwatersrand in Johannesburg, concurred.

The application was referred to the BAD head office in Pretoria, where in mid-July a senior official recommended that the department should not oppose a passport. Refusing it could be contentious, he said, and it was not clear on what grounds a refusal could be defended. Despite his view, the first draft of a memorandum to the minister of Bantu Administration and Development, M. D. C. de Wet Nel, drawn up by another senior official, proposed that BAD recommend against a passport. As justification, the draft cited Tutu's "contradictory statements," the option of a degree at Unisa, and a completely new consideration: that Tutu was "selected on the personal recommendation of the Rev. Joost de Blank."

The Most Reverend Joost de Blank, archbishop of Cape Town, was the flamboyant and controversial successor to Geoffrey Clayton. Although born in the Netherlands, de Blank was, like Clayton, an import from England. He has been described as a "prince archbishop" who made the archbishop's official residence at Bishopscourt a "place of minor pageantry" and behaved as if the Anglican Church were, like the Church of England, the established church in South Africa. He threw overboard the polite language in which bishops had previously criticized apartheid. Within a few months of arriving, he was under verbal assault in Parliament for describing white domination as "inhuman and unchristian." When Verwoerd, who by now had become prime minister, threatened to act against him, de Blank noted that Ver-

woerd too was Dutch-born and offered to resign and leave the country
if Verwoerd would do the same. From a pulpit in New York, he
accused the white Dutch Reformed Church of having a "warped and
inaccurate Calvinistic outlook," and after Sharpeville he tried to have
it expelled from the World Council of Churches (WCC). By the time
the Tutus applied for their passports in 1962, de Blank had softened his
views on the Dutch Reformed leaders–they had by then repudiated
some of the central tenets of apartheid at a consultation of South
African member churches of the WCC, and had in turn been slapped
down, first by Verwoerd and then by their own synods. De Blank's
relations with the government, however, remained as tense as ever;
when he was recovering from a thrombosis in England in 1962, the
minister of transport said he hoped the archbishop would stay there:
"We are tired of these political bishops in our country."

Finally, on July 27, four months after the Tutus applied for passports,
the permanent secretary to the Bantu Administration department
wrote to the minister: "The applicant's contradictory statements in
respect of his wife cast doubt on his bona fides but on the other hand
he has been awarded a bursary. It is also true that should he enrol with
the University of South Africa, he would have to maintain himself."
The next day, de Wet Nel approved the application.

While the Tutus were waiting for passports, Aelred Stubbs was
exchanging letters about money with church officials in New York.
Leslie Stradling had agreed that the diocese of Johannesburg would
pay Tutu's stipend while he was studying, and the CR was prepared to
underwrite the cost of his degree with funds originally raised for
St. Peter's School. However, Stubbs clearly wanted to conserve the
CR's resources, and he wrote to the Theological Education Fund
(TEF) of the International Missionary Council asking for help. The
TEF–established with a gift of 2 million dollars from John D. Rocke-
feller, Jr., the father of David Rockefeller; and a matching grant by nine
American Protestant churches–was an important sponsor of theologi-
cal education in Africa, Asia, and Latin America. On July 30, 1962,
James F. Hopewell of the TEF told Stubbs that a grant had been
approved: "We are pleased," he said, "to share in your desire to
increase the African representation on the . . . staff." Stubbs replied:
"This scholarship for Desmond Tutu is immensely exciting and encouraging, and I wish you could have seen his face when I told him." There
was some sensitivity about the TEF in South Africa. Tutu told Sydney
Evans at King's that on the certificate saying he had a scholarship

"no mention of the TEF should be made, since it has associations with the World Council of Churches—hardly acceptable to our government."

Desmond set off alone on his first flight, and his first journey outside South Africa, on the budget airline Trek. Norman Leslie, who had served in the South African air force in World War II, joked that its airplanes were "stuck together with chewing gum and string." The journey to London—now a direct overnight flight—took two days, with stops in Zimbabwe, Uganda, Sudan and Greece on the way.

The first leg up to Salisbury [now Harare] was rather bumpy with some low cloud. But all this was mitigated by the charming friendliness of the crew and air hostesses. Two seats away from me across the aisle was a Dr. Grobbelaar, Head of the Department of Afrikaans-Nederlands, University of Natal, who became my chum on the journey. We shared cigarettes (his!!) and beer (mine); plus our Afrikaans which served as the bond of our friendship. How true that outside the Republic white South Africans do become human again. We dined at Entebbe which was quite pleasant and it is here that the first white person addressed me as "Sir." (How snobbish can we become?)

Our next stop was Wadi Halfa. The sand in the moonlight looked like snow. I slept through much of the next leg which was not to Malta but quite excitingly to Athens.... We were put up in splendid hotels, single rooms, telephone, private bath and what-have-you. We went to the Acropolis and later in the evening to see Greek folk dances. I went with another South African to a boulevard café and had a most delicious chilled beer. I looked a proper American tourist with an open-neck shirt and camera slung over my shoulder.

Tutu spent his first weekend in England being "quite spoiled" by the writer Nicholas Mosley—biographer of Raymond Raynes—before going to stay at the London priory of the Community of the Resurrection in Holland Park. Writing to Stubbs a few days later, he said England was beautiful, the weather was glorious, he had watched the Last Night at the Proms (a concert) on television and had seen an air show: "You can tell Bro. Roger that I think I want to agree with him that until one has seen England one does not know what green is.... May I again say 'thank you' to you and the CR for this grand opportunity? I shall try very hard to be more circumspect financially, so don't fret and worry yourself on that score."

The Britain in which he arrived was a country in transition. The journalist Anthony Sampson, who was making a name for himself as a writer after returning from Johannesburg, remarked in the second of a series of books on the "anatomy of Britain" that in politics, business, law, and the universities, "the familiar chorus of 'Old Freddies'—of peers, soldiers or courtiers—has begun to troop off-stage. . . . Reverence and stuffiness are out of fashion, and nearly everyone . . . likes to think of himself as being 'anti-Establishment.' " It was the era of the rise of the Beatles and of the irreverent satirical late-night television show, *That Was the Week That Was,* hosted by David Frost. It was also a time when theology became front-page news; Bishop John Robinson shocked much of his church by advocating, in his book *Honest to God,* an end to the "crudely physical" thinking that God existed "out there" beyond outer space, and argued instead for an image of God as "the Ground of our very being." Robinson quoted approvingly a sermon by the theologian Paul Tillich saying that if the word "God" meant little to his listeners, they should perhaps forget the word and "speak of the depths of your life, of the source of your being, of your ultimate concern, of what you take seriously without any reservation."

King's College, London, was founded as an explicitly Christian institution in 1829, supported by King George IV. But by the 1960s, King's had changed radically. Religious tests and compulsory attendance at chapel had been abolished. With University College, it had become part of the University of London. The college's heritage was, however, still reflected in a theological department that operated separately from the university and in a unique autonomy exercised by the dean.

Most foreign theology students found King's hard going, and many failed. The expectations of Tutu's tutor, Joseph Robinson, can be inferred from his first-term report on his new African student. Tutu had settled down quite well, Robinson said, and produced some good work "written in admirable English." Settling down was, however, complicated by early difficulties in getting the Tutu family established in England.

Aelred Stubbs initially planned that once Desmond had found accommodation Leah would join him in London. There she hoped to complete her nursing training. Trevor, Thandi, and Naomi were to remain with Desmond's parents in Munsieville; the TEF did not have the funds to cover their travel costs. Leah, facing the prospect of a second long-term separation from her children, rebelled and wrote to Stubbs: "I really would not for anything leave my children here [for] three years."

Consulted by Stubbs, Desmond said that whether Leah remained with the children or came to London alone to worry constantly about them, he would find it equally unsettling. He acknowledged that fares would be a difficulty, and that Leah would be unable to earn money in London if the children came. "But perhaps it will be more prudent to come and I do miss them very much. The whole thing bristles with difficulties and thank you very, very much indeed for caring so much." Stubbs relented, and Leah, Trevor, and Thandi left in November on a mail ship, the *Pretoria Castle,* for Southampton, where they were met by Desmond and taken to London on the boat train. The CR, in the face of the TEF's unwillingness to cover the costs of the family, subsequently gave him an allowance to help cover their costs for the remainder of their time in Britain. Two-year-old Naomi joined them six months later after their friend Val Leslie appealed to the CR to allow her to go too.

In London, after a two-month search for accommodations, Desmond had been offered the curate's flat behind the Church of St. Alban the Martyr in Golders Green. It was small, and the floors were thin. The church's verger, living downstairs, pointedly ignored the Tutus when the children had been noisy the night before. For Leah, however, it was "beautiful"–the best home they had lived in. Less than thirty minutes' traveling time north of central London on the Underground, it was easily accessible to King's. It comprised a living room, a small kitchen, two bedrooms, and a study, so that Trevor could have a room of his own. It was given to them rent-free in exchange for Desmond's helping out with Sunday services. Trevor and Thandi were admitted to a good infants' school, thus escaping Bantu education. Trevor joined a Cub Scouts pack. "We were overwhelmed with all this generosity," Desmond wrote to Aelred Stubbs in December 1962, "especially when we arrived to find the flat almost fully furnished, even with blankets and kitchen utensils. Say a special 'thank you' to God for all this love and goodness, utterly undeserved."

In his letter to Stubbs, Tutu also reported on his first term. Sydney Evans had told him King's was pleased with his work and that he need not be anxious about his ability to complete the course. He was awarded an A in Greek and a B- for Plato. His philosophy paper was judged "good." But he was not satisfied: "I was told I should work steadily and not panic, but you know how I get worked up by exams. . . . I am feeling inadequate and am suffering from quite a huge slice of inferiority. I am too eager to do well and be impressive and so I tie myself up in knots. And my memory has been playing tricks. But thanks for your prayers. I suppose I should be pleased that staff are pleased." This privately expressed lack of confidence persisted; the next term he again received an A in Greek, was complimented by his tutor on how he had settled in his new environment, but nevertheless told Stubbs that he had "still not got on top of my work."

Tutu made an immediate impression on his classmates. At thirty, he was older than most of them; he was one of very few who were already ordained; and, said Richard Carr, "the face of a black student on C corridor in the early 1960s was bound to stand out!" Carr remembered him as "a quiet, shy, retiring man," but Mervyn Terrett, who had a locker adjacent to Tutu's in the same corridor, had a somewhat different early experience: "It was our first week. . . . He was struggling with his outdoor coat . . . and I held it for him to put his arms in. . . . He turned round and said, 'Do you know, Mervyn, you're the first white man ever to hold my coat for me!' and then burst into that typical laugh."

Learning New Testament Greek was "a great bonding struggle" for students, according to John Gillis. As members of the class settled in together, many were struck by the "giggling" relationship that Brian Oosthuysen and Tutu developed. Oosthuysen was a white South African, partly of Afrikaner descent, who had left school at age fifteen to work in the railways, developed an interest in ministry, and traveled to England to pursue it. He completed his schooling at night, arrived at King's feeling like "a country boy," and was attracted to a fellow South African who looked as out of place as Oosthuysen felt. They argued over Robinson's *Honest to God,* according to Oosthuysen: "I was saying the saviour of the church has come. . . . Desmond was saying . . . you've got to step back and be more critical, any new theory that comes along you just take up and accept." Tutu disrupted a class with an outburst of laughter when a teacher described a problem as "the nigger in the woodpile" and Oosthuysen leaned over and said: "They're talking about you, Desmond." In another class, Desmond went off into a daydream and had to ask Oosthuysen what the lecturer had been saying. "I wrote, 'Sex is here to stay,' to him. He picked it up, looked at it and . . . the cackle just ripped across the room." At Speakers' Corner in Hyde Park, Tutu and Oosthuysen shared a sense of foreboding when a man told his audience that Harold Macmillan was a knave and a fool. "We thought there was going to be trouble," says Oosthuysen. "He was going to be arrested. You can't say this about the

Prime Minister. I looked at Desmond and Desmond looked at me. We thought, God if we said this in South Africa, Special Branch would be coming. Let's move away."

Tutu told King's later that his experiences with Oosthuysen had profound consequences for him. "Brian and I would not have been in the same tertiary institutions in South Africa. . . . That mundane everyday occurrence of students sitting side by side was in fact of monumental significance. It was saying as eloquently as a massive tome that you were in fact human too." Tutu grew in other ways too; after the males-only world of St. Peter's, "being beaten by these precocious girls" at King's was a humbling experience.

He was thrilled to be taught by people who were household names in theology. Dennis Nineham's lectures on the Synoptic Gospels were "brilliant," he told Stubbs in an early letter. Writing about the work of biblical historians who suggest that the gospels of Matthew and Luke are based not only on that of Mark but on a second source, a "lost gospel" called Q, Tutu added: "It is fantastic the number of variations and the theories about Q." The intricacies of theological scholarship excited him.

Tutu described Christopher Evans in subsequent tributes as having "bowled us over with his tour de force of reading directly from the Greek unhaltingly in beautiful English, a meticulous New Testament scholar." Sydney Evans was "debonair with every hair in place . . . as eloquent as he was impeccable sartorially." Eric Mascall was "a brilliant mathematician turned into an equally brilliant theologian." Geoffrey Parrinder, a prolific author, was "one of the most eminent exponents of the comparative study of religions," who had a "warm generosity of spirit, helping his students to have a broad ecumenism that welcomed the insights of those of faiths other than their own." In time, Tutu became critical of his teachers' unconscious assumption that western theology was the only theology, but he retained an abiding respect for the analytical skills they taught him. Addressing the commemoration of King's 175th anniversary in 2004, he said that after the claustrophobia of apartheid South Africa, King's was "like a breath of fresh air." In South Africa, the purpose of education was "to regurgitate the right answers nearly always learned by rote . . . where you did and believed things because someone in authority said so. You were supposed . . . to toe the party line, to kowtow, to be obsequious." In contrast, at King's "there frequently did not seem to be one right answer. We were encouraged to examine the facts for ourselves and to arrive at the conclusion which seemed best to make sense of the available evidence." He admired his lecturers' allergy to dogma, his favourite illustration being the Old Testament scholar Peter Ackroyd's pet phrase: "It is not unreasonable to suppose . . ."

In Golders Green, a largely white middle-class suburb with a substantial Jewish community, Tutu helped the vicar, John Halsey. It was the first time Tutu had ministered to a white congregation: "I don't know what I was expecting, but it turned out that they were human beings, with the ordinary strengths and foibles, resentments and triumphs, as well as the sins of ordinary human beings." A church youth group and the Mothers' Union met regularly, and there was a formal church choir. Between his studies, Tutu preached regularly and visited parishioners. The family of Joy Alexander, who lived around the corner, became friends. Her son, Malcolm, was impressed with Desmond's calls: "My grandfather, who was quite crusty and wouldn't normally have bothered to go to church or have been visited by the church, was very pleased to see this priest who bothered to go upstairs and maybe have a glass of whisky with him." Saint Alban's was unlike the churches in which Tutu had been brought up. Black parishes in Johannesburg, many of them established by the CR, were in Anglican parlance "high church" or Anglo Catholic. The main Sunday service was a Eucharist, often called Mass as in the Catholic Church, celebrated in clouds of incense by priests wearing rich vestments. At the other end of the Anglican spectrum were "low church" evangelicals who eschewed ornamentation and made the service of Morning Prayer their central act of Sunday worship. At St. Alban's, Tutu told Aelred Stubbs, "the Churchmanship is middle; they have vestments, facilities for reservation (but no reserved sacrament*), Mattins the main service on Sunday, but they are good people, fully awake to their missionary commitment."

Leah and Desmond reveled in a country without apartheid and the pass laws. Between classes at King's, Desmond was able to go into a pub for a lunch of pork pie and cider. "There is racism in England," he said, "but we were not exposed to it. Maybe we were protected by the fact that we belonged in a church community." One of his most frequently told stories was about a bank teller in Golders Green:

---

* Consecrated bread and wine kept near the altar between services, mainly for later distribution to the sick. Devout "high church" Anglicans genuflect as they pass the reserved sacrament.

The Midlands Bank was near the tube station and I went in and stood in the queue. I was next to be served, but someone rushed in, in a desperate hurry, and wanted to jump the queue. The lady behind the counter, very gently but firmly told this guy, "Sorry it's his turn first." I grew inches. . . . I had already given way, because this was standard practice at home. I went back subsequently to the bank to tell her, "You might not know what you did for me. . . . Now you've become my pin-up."

Another story was about his experiences with London's bobbies:

Leah and I would go, perhaps to Trafalgar Square, late at night. . . . We found it almost intoxicating that a police officer . . . didn't come across to ask for your pass. You were free to walk wherever and we would often go and ask for directions, even when we knew where we were going, just so that we could hear a white police officer saying, "No sir, yes ma'am."

Apart from parishioners whom the Tutus befriended in London, they had a circle of English church friends who had served in South Africa. Desmond reestablished contact with Trevor Huddleston after seven years. Ambrose Reeves, who had offices near St. Alban's, invited them to social gatherings and paid for the family to have a ten-day holiday in Swanwick, Derbyshire, while Desmond attended a Student Christian Movement conference there. When the Tutus' last child was born in the flat in Golders Green, the older children went to stay with Margaret and Mary Comber, the sisters of Tom Comber, a former university chaplain in Johannesburg. The baby was a girl. They called her Mpho ("Gift") Andrea. She was given the name Andrea because she was born on St. Andrew's Day, in 1963.

The church also gave the Tutus entrée to a network of deeply committed Anglicans—some of them supporters of the Community of the Resurrection—from the kind of families whose names were listed in directories of England's nobility and landed gentry. Through a friend of Aelred Stubbs, they met Martin Kenyon, the Eton- and Oxford-educated son of an army officer who ran an educational charity, financed by British oil companies, that helped students from overseas in the United Kingdom. Kenyon was a gregarious and loquacious enthusiast who felt more at home among African students than among his peers, and who knew where blacks were, and were not, welcome in

London. He took Desmond for lunch at the Travellers Club in Pall Mall. There Tutu learned to spit out shotgun pellets while eating grouse during England's hunting season. Kenyon became Mpho's godfather. Leah and Desmond refused to allow the children to address him by his first name, and he resisted being called "Uncle Martin" in the South African style, so they called him "Brother Martin." Thanks to Kenyon, the interest in cricket which Tutu developed as a teenager in the hospital became a lifelong passion. Kenyon took him to watch the West Indies play England at the Lord's cricket ground in London in the summer of 1963, the year in which the British were exposed for the first time to the exuberance of Caribbean fans. Tutu saw the West Indian bowler Wes Hall fracture the arm of England batsman Colin Cowdrey with a fast ball, and England fast bowler Freddie Trueman was on top of his form, helping to take the last five West Indian second innings wickets for fifteen runs in twenty-five minutes. Tutu supported the West Indians, but when they returned in 1966 he changed his allegiance and supported England—it was the year in which Basil D'Oliveira, the black player who left South Africa to escape apartheid, made his debut as an all-rounder for England.

The Tutus did not return to South Africa during the years when Desmond was studying in England, but they did manage to go on summer vacations, thanks to the diocese of London's "Poor Clergy Holiday Fund" and the generosity of church members who opened their homes. For their first two summers, they stayed at "Burnett," the home of a Miss Hardy in the Surrey village of Cranleigh. "It was paradise," said Desmond, "a double-story house in a big yard." Black people were a curiosity in the English countryside; Trevor was asked by a new friend: "How does your mother know you are dirty?" Martin Kenyon came to visit and once took them to the coast for Trevor to swim and the girls to ride on a miniature train. On a subsequent summer holiday, Desmond and Leah used a gift of money from his parish to tour England and Scotland in a borrowed car, staying at convents and monasteries where they could.

In his second year at King's, Tutu faced a new challenge. Writing to Stubbs at the end of his first year, he bemoaned "this awful Plato [which] still remains at the first level of B-." However, he passed his New Testament exam with 84 percent and Old Testament with a B+. King's decided he could cope with a more demanding course. Tutu had a keen intelligence, Sydney Evans told Stubbs. "His results . . . are really excellent and there is no doubt he will do really well." Tutu's

teachers resolved that he should change to an honors course. This
would involve learning Hebrew, Evans told the TEF, but King's was
confident he would succeed. "You can hardly imagine how encouraging it is to receive such news!" Stubbs replied to Evans. "I perhaps pin
too much faith on a man like Desmond, because the future of the
Church in this country so largely depends on him and the few like him.
So thank you for all the care you spend on him."

Stubbs went on in the same letter to discuss finances for the ensuing
two years. He did not want Tutu to have to worry about money, he
said; neither did he want the family to become a burden on King's or
St. Alban's parish. He continued:

> I am quite ready to accept the fact that the cost of living in Golders
> Green is higher than we budgetted for, but he has not been good in the
> past about money—as no doubt you know it is the besetting fault of
> Africans, and not only Africans!—and if he is to play the part in the
> Church for which his gifts would seem to fit him he must overcome this
> fault. I'm afraid this sounds a bit pompous and schoolmasterish, which
> is probably the result of three years as Principal here!

Stubbs's comment invites certain questions: Was Tutu irresponsible
with money? Or was Stubbs racist? Or, as a single monk whose community met his basic needs, was Stubbs perhaps simply insensitive to
the everyday needs of a person maintaining a family of five? And, in
London at least, were the Tutus in any different position from that of
thousands of other Africans studying in Britain?

Forty-years later, Desmond Tutu's response to these questions was
simply to acknowledge that his handling of money was not what it
might have been. We have already seen that the hire-purchase obligations he entered into as a teacher worried Ambrose Reeves. At
St. Peter's, the CR fathers frowned on students' asking the staff for
loans; Desmond once asked Timothy Stanton for an advance on his
allowance, but was refused. The diocesan secretary, Colonel H. C. Juta,
was irritated by the complexity of Tutu's family finances; he told
Stubbs that apart from "the bother" of getting monthly foreign bank
drafts for Desmond's stipend, the diocese was paying monthly install-
ments to three shops and to Desmond's father. "It appears that of his
impositions there is no end!" he complained. Tutu's acknowledgement of his improvidence in correspondence with Pawson in 1958 was
repeated in letters to Stubbs and to Leslie Stradling during his first year

at King's. However, the improvidence to which he confessed related to his family obligations rather than his own spending habits—he had to support his parents in Munsieville as well as a family in London. Thanking Stradling for helping ZZ Tutu early in 1963, Tutu wrote:

> Of course I feel quite awful that our finances are such a shambles. He [Desmond's father] could still be earning if the school board at Krugersdorp had not refused to grant him the normal five-year extension of his services after reaching the superannuation age. . . . It is quite humiliating, but as it is in great measure our fault we must accept it with good grace. I ought to try to use all this (and perhaps having created unfavourable impressions) as a means of growing in humility.

To Stubbs he added: "It is so embarrassing to seem to be cadging, going about with a hat in your hand."

When Tutu arrived in London, Sydney Evans warned Stubbs that the TEF grant was not going to be enough to support him. Eight months later, Tutu told Stubbs, "In fact we have never been able to make ends meet at all." The parish council had paid their winter electricity bill, he had hardly been able to buy a book, and travel was almost out of the question. Thirty years later, Leah told an interviewer that once when the milkman came for his weekly payment of about a pound, Desmond made out a check, gave it to her to hand over, and hid in the bedroom. "Desmond was so ashamed to show his face. . . . I went down to give the cheque to the milkman, and he looked at me and said, 'Oh well, I'll take it next week then.' It was a waste of a cheque form." After Tutu's successful first year, the TEF made a supplementary grant and King's awarded him a scholarship of a 100 pounds a year, as well as seventy pounds to cover his tuition fees. The issue of his spending largely disappeared from the correspondence.

Changing to an honors course was "a considerable test of a man's ability," Christopher Evans said later, and he recalled no other African student who had done it. Tutu found his second year demanding and struggled with Hebrew: "The work is all over me, and the Hebrew takes up so much time." He was awarded an A in Hebrew at the end of the first term; but his tutor, Geoffrey Parrinder, felt he was neglecting other subjects. In the second term, he had a better grasp of most subjects, reported Parrinder; and by the end of the third term there was a great improvement in his essays. Ahead of his final exams, he was working until twelve-thirty AM and getting up again at three-thirty

AM. His results were mixed, but he found them quite gratifying, he told Stubbs. "I just scraped through the Hebrew with a 49 percent. But it was quite adequate for purposes of qualifying for the honours course. I just could not get the paradigm into my head, try as much as I could." But "to take the bad taste away," he said, he had earned a B+ for New Testament studies, an A- for Old Testament, and an A for Philosophy.

As Tutu entered his final undergraduate year, he began to explore staying at King's to study for a master's degree. The professorial board of King's approved the idea on the condition that Tutu would earn at least an upper second-class honors degree. Implementing the plan depended on raising more money, on securing extensions to the family's passports, and on Aelred Stubbs's willingness to wait for Desmond to join the staff of St. Peter's College. After asking Stubbs what he thought, Tutu said, "I shall probably accept your decision whatever it is." If he thought Stubbs would try to veto the plan, he was wrong. Stubbs believed the wait was worthwhile. In correspondence with the TEF about another scholarship, he quoted Z. K. Matthews, now working for the World Council of Churches in Geneva. Matthews, he said, had told the seminary during a recent visit that the greatest lack in the church was of African theologians. "While he had found a few in West Africa he had hardly come across one in Central, East, or Southern Africa." With a master's degree, Tutu would be "the best qualified non–Roman Catholic theologian in southern Africa."

The TEF gave Tutu a new grant, King's extended his scholarship, and Tutu went on to his master's degree. The diocese of Johannesburg stopped paying his stipend, believing it had played its part; but the CR stepped in and replaced the stipend from its own resources. Leah and Desmond applied at South Africa House in Trafalgar Square for extensions to their passports. The Tutus had a long wait to hear "what our overlords have decided," but the passports were extended for three years—entitling the family for the first time to travel to most western European countries and the United States. Scandinavian countries, viewed by the government as too sympathetic to South Africa's liberation movements, remained off limits.

During the summer, King's introduced a one-year master's degree in theology. This enabled Tutu to enroll for a course beginning in October 1965 and ending in September 1966, facilitating his return to teach in South Africa in January 1967. Stubbs had initially wanted him to specialize in Old Testament studies, but Evans said he had not studied enough Hebrew for that and recommended the New Testament instead. Christopher Evans suggested that Tutu should study Islam, and he did, under the supervision of Geoffrey Parrinder. He had already won the prize at St. Peter's in Johannesburg with an essay on Islam, and Sydney Evans explained to Aelred Stubbs: "As I understand his mind he wants to understand Islam better in order that he may teach Christian theology with true understanding of Islam in mind."

Awaiting the outcome of deliberations over the master's degree, the Tutus and St. Alban's parish in Golders Green began to discuss a move. St. Alban's had been "generous and kind and we have enjoyed being here," but Tutu now wanted a parish "in a less well-to-do part of London." He was not to get it. After a summer of uncertainty, and a month's holiday with Martin Kenyon's family at their country home in Lydbury North, Shropshire, Kenyon helped to arrange an appointment as an assistant curate in St. Mary's Parish in the village of Bletchingley, near Redhill in Surrey.

Bletchingley was "deep in CR country," as Tutu described it to Aelred Stubbs. The "moving spirit" behind his appointment was Uvedale Lambert, a devout Anglican, a leader of the diocese of Southwark, and a member of the church assembly of the Church of England. The Lamberts of Blechingley were an old established family in the district, who spelled the village's name without a "t," arguing that it was "a later addition, introduced by foreigners and perpetuated by civil servants." Lambert had served as high sheriff of the county. He was master of the Old Surrey and Burstow Foxhounds and hunted twice a week in the winter; one of the fondest memories which his daughter, Sarah Goad, had of him was "serving the Mass dressed up in his stock and breeches and an old tweed coat—his coat and top boots were, of course, donned at the last moment."

Tutu came to a parish that encompassed huge differences. It was in the most rural part of Southwark diocese, and tracts of farmland surrounded the village. Apart from the landed gentry, the area was home to two peers of the realm; to agricultural workers, shopkeepers, and artisans; to residents of a housing development; and to stockbrokers and Lloyd's underwriters who commuted to London from nearby Redhill station. Everyone in this multifaceted community was white, but everyone enthusiastically welcomed Desmond, Leah, and their four children, now aged from ten years to twenty-one months. Ronald Brownrigg, the rector of St. Mary's, announced their arrival the Sunday morning before they came. By lunchtime, parishioners had donated all the furnishings, linen, bedding, crockery, and cutlery needed for a family of six. After a short stay in the gardener's cottage on the estate of the Baroness Gian de Cabrol in nearby South Godstone, the family moved into the the "Clerk's House," overlooking a large stone cross in the heart of the village that commemorated "the men of Blechingley who gave their lives for King and Country in the Great War." A two-story home with a garden at the back, "it was like a palace for us," Desmond recalled. St. Mary's was fifty yards away, down a narrow lane bordered by a row of fourteenth-century cottages. Its Norman tower dated to about 1090 and the appointment of its first rector could be traced to 1293. In exchange for the house and an annual stipend of 200 pounds, Tutu did Sunday duty and two days' work, mainly visiting parishioners. He also did Sunday duties for the neighboring St. Nicholas Church, Godstone.

After three years at Golders Green, the Tutus spent little more than a year in Bletchingley. Yet to listen to them and the people of Bletchingley, one might imagine it was the other way around. "By the way people speak, you would think they spent much of their lives here," a recently arrived parishioner told the author. Forty years later, villagers remembered Leah taking part in the activities of the Women's Institute and walking to the shops around her home. They described Desmond fetching fish and chips on Friday nights on his scooter. Uvedale Lambert had given him the scooter so he could ride to London to consult Geoffrey Parrinder at King's, and residents still joked about his driving skills and how his large crash helmet almost obscured his face. He once took Leah to London with him, but she declined further offers after he drove between two converging trucks and they were nearly crushed. Trevor was remembered as the only black pupil at The Hawthorns, a private preparatory school; and Mpho was remembered as a toddler attending an infants' school with Cassandra Goad, Uvedale Lambert's granddaughter. But Desmond hated English winters, according to the organist John Ewington. "He said he couldn't pray when he was cold. So he would come to the church with his cloak on to say his prayers."

An ingredient in Tutu's popularity was his sense of humor. "He could giggle at almost anything," said Ewington, "even at the most solemn time—it was like pricking a balloon." As at King's, Tutu dealt with the issue of race by pulling it into the open, making jokes about it, and poking fun at racism. In later years he enjoyed telling of a woman who, during a visit to Shropshire, arrived for an appointment out of breath and flurried, to announce: "I'm sorry I'm late, we were working like ni . . . like Trojans." (He told such jokes only in South Africa and the United Kingdom; in the United States he usually found racial sensitivity so highly developed that most Americans did not find them funny.)

Tutu's effervescent personality became and remained one of his most striking characteristics, and his infectious laughter one of his principal gifts—which he used later in situations ranging from meeting kings and queens to defusing violent street clashes at home. At the end of his time in England, this attribute—already evident to his contemporaries at college in South Africa in the 1950s—marked him out as someone unique. Christopher Evans, invited by Tutu to preach in Bletchingley, wrote later:

> Along with his academic qualifications he has a striking personality. He has an irrepressible sense of humour, and is the life and soul of the party. . . . It was clear [in Bletchingley] that his combination of skill, forthrightness, wit and modesty had quite captivated the people—as had also his wife, who is also a striking person. In a parish of this particular kind . . . this was a remarkable achievement.

At the end of his year in Bletchingley, Tutu took exams for his M.Th. and turned in a 10,000-word essay on Islam in West Africa, which impressed both his examiners. He had learned rudimentary Arabic and became interested enough in Islam to enrol at Unisa for a Ph.D. after leaving King's. Regarding his ambition to do a thesis on "Moses in the Quran," he wrote: "Islam is a potent force in Africa. To carry on a dialogue with Muslims, we must know their faith well." But the ambition was not to be fulfilled.

Tutu was disappointed not to get a master's degree "with distinction." Evans thought that had he allowed himself eighteen months for the course instead of a year, he would have achieved this. Still, Tutu was pleased to have passed and wrote to Aelred Stubbs:

> Hurrah! Thank you all for your sustaining prayers, for there were days when I felt very much in the dumps (as I suppose I usually do about exams) and the prayers tided me over a great deal. Of course it does not mean I am any wiser than I was when I left South Africa, but I suppose it means something. You will say a private Te Deum for the success of your bold venture in sending us overseas. Thank you for all your

faith in me. I am somewhat relieved (no I am greatly relieved) that I have a tiny bit to show for the large sums of money that you have spent on us. Sometimes when I thought things were not going well academically, I used to get up in a cold sweat when I thought of all the money tied up in me. I worried too that it would queer the pitch for other chaps in the future.

A year after Tutu left King's, his former teachers were asked for a detailed assessment of his ability to take on doctoral studies. Sydney Evans, the dean, rated his social concern and his ability to think independently as average, and his ability to lead others and cooperate with colleagues and his sensitivity to the needs of others as good. Evans added that Tutu was "a delightful personality based on a strong Christian faith and discipline." Geoffrey Parrinder declared Tutu "excellent" in every attribute. "He was well above most of the students of his year," wrote Parrinder. "Mr. Tutu is a hard-working and intelligent man and deserving of the highest encouragement." The most detailed and effusive report was by Christopher Evans, who judged him an outstanding scholar: "perceptive, enthusiastic, and well balanced." Evans remained an admirer of Tutu's, even when he took a more distanced view. In 1969 he summed up Tutu's achievements at King's in a recommendation for a university teaching post:

> He was very modest—too modest in fact, as it took him some time with his particular African background to realise that he really could be a person who mattered in the eyes of his teachers. He had the instincts of a scholar, and his work was detailed and thorough. He worked very hard and read widely, and was concerned to go to the roots of a subject. He was not academic in a very narrow sense of the word, since he mixed his scholarship with a warm humanity, and as a result his contributions to a class were very much worth having.

Tutu's English friends did not perceive him as politically active during his sojourn in London. He actively promoted cross-cultural friendships, said Khotso Makhulu, who—like Tutu—was a protégé of the CR; but neither in Golders Green nor in Bletchingley did anyone recall that his sermons ever dealt with South African or overtly political issues. "First and foremost he was a pastor; there was absolutely no question," said Sarah Goad. He was, however, drawn into church committees on South Africa soon after he arrived. He once asked

Malcolm Alexander to accompany him to a church hall in a working-class area in north London, where he addressed a meeting on conditions in South Africa. At Ambrose Reeves's home, he met South African exiles in London, including a fellow resident of Krugersdorp, Yusuf Dadoo, a leader in the South African Indian Congress and the South African Communist Party. And his correspondence gives a hint of his political thinking. In a letter to Sydney Evans about a meeting addressed by a former British ambassador to South Africa, he gave early notice of the views which were to make him "public enemy number one" at home twenty years later:

> I have just come away from hearing Sir John Maud argue very persuasively and eloquently against the imposition of sanctions against South Africa. I heartily disagree with him and wish I could share his optimism. What I found heartening was the tremendous keenness and desire to grapple with what is a baffling problem, that the large audience showed.

He also kept in touch with church politics. On his way between King's and Golders Green he regularly stopped at South Africa House in Trafalgar Square to read the Johannesburg newspapers. There he saw the sensational coverage given to the first synod over which Leslie Stradling presided as the new bishop of Johannesburg. In a nine column headline on page three, the *Sunday Times* reported: "STRADLING CAUSES AN UPROAR." The bishop's statement that he was obliged to "accept" apartheid and intended to play a less active role in politics than Ambrose Reeves had caused an outcry, the report said: "Many white laymen and women were frankly enthusiastic at the idea of a 'non-political' Bishop, while others condemned the Bishop's stand and said his views had 'come like a slap in the face to the African members of the Anglican community.' " Stradling told the *Sunday Times:* "I thought it would be understood that I am opposed to apartheid. I accept it only in the sense that it is inevitable for me to do so. It is the law of the country and I have to accept it, even if I do not support it." Two days later the synod reaffirmed its stand on apartheid by passing a resolution that stated, "The policy of racial separation is contrary to the Scriptures and its practical implementation is morally wrong." In an editorial, the *Rand Daily Mail* said Stradling's resigned attitude "is exactly the state of mind which this Government has been trying to produce in the public for years. . . . Bishop Stradling may well feel

repelled by the thought of being asked to take sides in a political con-
test, but the truth is that South African politics today pose a major
moral issue and people are entitled to look to their religious leaders for
guidance."

In a decision which received less prominence, the synod accepted in
principle that the stipends paid to the black and white clergy should be
equal. However, the principle took years to implement, giving rise to
constant conflict over the interim compromises offered by the diocese's
financiers. A particularly sore point was the stipends of clergy classified
under apartheid as Coloured, who were paid less than whites but
more than blacks. A year before returning home, Tutu challenged
Stubbs on the issue in a way not seen in previous letters. Some of the
differences between stipends for blacks and Coloureds were staggering,
he said, and they reflected white society's attempts "to attach the
Coloured more firmly to the white man's cause." He also wrote:

> You may have been disturbed at the uncharitable way the Africans
> might have put over their case. But I am afraid I can't agree with you at
> all over the basic principle of it. . . . We and our friends have not
> realised how deeply the evil of race has wounded our relations, so that
> it is quite impossible or nearly so for people not to seem to have a chip
> on their shoulder. . . .
>
> No I am not bitter. It is only that one thinks of the occasions when,
> as a theological student you were not permitted to use white churches
> for African domestic servants' services even [if] the church was not
> being used by our white fellow Christians. Once the money is in the
> coffers of the Church, it is now church money and should be equitably
> distributed, and we should stop deluding ourselves about ourselves. If
> we base our decisions on race we should not be surprised that people
> should react violently.

In England, the Tutus had a "wild, wild dream"–to return to South
Africa by car through Europe, the Middle East, and Africa. It was not
realized, but with the help of St. Mary's parish, Desmond was able to
take Leah, Naomi, and Mpho with him on a pilgrimage to Jerusalem
before flying home. While Trevor and Thandi completed their school
term in Surrey, the rest of the family toured Paris and Rome briefly,
thanks to a parishioner in Bletchingley who worked for the Thomas
Cook travel agency. They went on to east Jersualem, which was still in
Jordan at the time. There Desmond studied Arabic and Greek at St.

George's College, and read philosophy to prepare himself to lecture in doctrine the following year. Being in the Holy Land, he reported home, "lights up the scriptures for you in a wonderful way and helps to disabuse one of several misconceptions." He added: "The 'gentle Jesus' just can't fit into a terrain as harsh as this." The family visited Bethlehem, Jericho, and the Dead Sea. In Jerusalem they visited Gethsemane and followed processions led by Franciscan monks to the stations of the cross: "The crowds jostle and are indifferent quite as much as on the first Good Friday."

At the end of their visit, they had what Tutu described to Martin Kenyon as an awful journey to Johannesburg. In Cairo, they were refused permission to board their onward flight. "Ethiopian Airlines would have no truck with South Africans, even black ones," Tutu wrote. "I admired their sticking to principle even at the loss of four fares." The family was confined to Cairo airport for a weekend; Leah and Naomi became badly ill with upset stomachs; and they were unable to send a message to tell their families not to meet them. They arrived home two days' late, early in December, filled with apprehension at the prospect of living under apartheid again. "You can't really prepare yourself for it," Tutu told Kenyon. "Do pray for us that we may not succumb to the temptation to hate and become bitter."

CHAPTER 6

CAMPUS PARENTS

After spending Christmas 1966 with their families on the Reef, the Tutus traveled by train to the village of Alice in the Eastern Cape for the beginning of the 1967 academic year at St. Peter's College, which had moved from Johannesburg, to be incorporated into the newly-established Federal Theological Seminary. The differences between the life they had known for the past four years and what now faced them could hardly have been greater. Leah Tutu had told Uvedale Lambert that she dreaded the difficulties of bringing the children home. In England, they went to school around the corner. In South Africa, to avoid Bantu education, Trevor (then aged ten), Thandi (nine), and Naomi (six), had to be sent to boarding schools in Swaziland, a 2,600-kilometer (1,600-mile) round trip that took three days at the beginning and end of each term. In Golders Green and Bletchingley, only lack of money kept the family from shopping and eating wherever they wished. On the way to and from Swaziland, they were not allowed inside many roadside stores but had to buy their food through windows reserved for black customers.

"I don't want to sound melodramatic," Desmond wrote to Martin Kenyon, "but it is extremely difficult being back here, having to ask permission from various white officials to visit my parents! Having to carry my heavy pass and look out for the entrances and exits meant especially for us. . . . It is as well that our Lord expected us not [to] like but [to] love our enemies and neighbours. It will be extremely difficult to love the white man as it is." After arriving in Alice, Desmond took the family to the nearby city of East London to buy secondhand furniture. At lunchtime, there was no restaurant they could use: "We had to buy fish and chips. . . . Just a few weeks ago we had been in some of the poshest places in Paris." The city's beaches were segregated, the rockiest reserved for blacks. The youngest Tutu, born in England, had no experience of segregation, her father recalled:

To get there we passed a children's playground. Mpho said she wanted to go on the swings, and I said, "No, sweetheart, you can't," and she said, "But there are other children there." You got quite sick having to say, "Yes, there are other children there, but they are not quite children like you."

The Federal Seminary, known to the staff and students as Fedsem, lay in a valley regarded by residents in the nineteenth century as the most beautiful in the Eastern Cape. During the dry winters, the landscape is enlivened by the rich orange and red shades of the local aloe plants. Noni Jabavu wrote of the "girl-like beauty" of the green countryside in summer: "As far as the eye could see, the landscape was a typically South African one, a wide expanse of rolling shallow bare hills and in the distance a jagged blue frieze of mountainous edge; and there were the dark forested apronlike folds, kloofs we called them colloquially in Afrikaans, of the . . . Amatole." However, the valley was also at the heart of the frontier over which Britons and amaXhosa wrestled in a succession of wars lasting for most of the century.

On the property occupied by Fedsem, the missionaries had built up Lovedale, the institution at which Desmond's father, Zachariah Tutu, had been trained. Lovedale not only trained teachers—at its height it included a primary school, high schools for boys and girls, a trades school, a Bible school, and a printing press that published much early literature in IsiXhosa. And adjoining its campus was the reason Fedsem was situated at Alice—the University of Fort Hare.

Many of those whose names have appeared in these pages "spent formative years at Fort Hare," as the university's postapartheid prospectus described it (the reason being that the rebelliousness of many led to their expulsion before graduation). Nelson Mandela, Mangosuthu Buthelezi, Govan Mbeki, Oliver Tambo, Robert Sobukwe, Robert Mugabe, Z. K. Matthews, Phyllis Ntantala, A. C. Jordan, Can Themba, and Alphaeus Zulu all studied at Fort Hare. Once known to local people as I-Koleji ka Jabavu, "the college of J. Tengu Jabavu," in recognition of Jabavu's role in helping to found it, Fort Hare was one of a few institutions on the continent that introduced university education for Africans. Although it operated in a segregated environment and its education was Eurocentric, for decades it represented the principal hope of full-time study for aspiring black students in southern Africa. It enrolled black, Coloured, and Indian students of all language groups, both men and women. Its staff included black professors, among them Z. K. Matthews, one of Africa's most distinguished scholars.

But like the church-run schools, such an institution had no place in the master plan of apartheid. In what the journalist Nat Nakasa of *Drum* called "The Murder of Fort Hare," the university was transferred in 1959 to the control of the Bantu Education ministry and shrunk into a tribal college for Xhosa-speakers. Outspoken staff members were fired, and a more compliant administration was installed. Most important for the churches, the government seized the university hostels in which Methodist and Presbyterian ministers were trained. Charles Ranson, an official of the Theological Education Fund in New York, visited South Africa at the time to find the churches reeling at the government's attack. At Fort Hare, the churches were unwilling to do anything that might signal acquiescence in the government's plans. One school of thought refused even to consider alternatives until the government had forced them out. In Johannesburg, St. Peter's College preferred to "wait and see" whether it would be expelled from its site in Johannesburg's southern suburbs. Ranson was therefore pleasantly surprised when, at a consultation called to discuss the future, the churches accepted the most radical of the options with which he presented them: they should amalgamate their training institutions under a single federal structure.

Simon Gqubule, Fedsem's first black lecturer and then its president, was later to remark that by bringing churches of different denominations together, "apartheid forced the church to be the church." When the Tutus arrived there, Fedsem had been operating for nearly four years and was already on its way to becoming one of South Africa's most successful ecumenical ventures. At the top of the campus was a central teaching, office, and library block, where students from all the participating churches–Anglican, Congregational, Methodist, and Presbyterian–gathered for lectures in the mornings. In the afternoons they dispersed to four denominational colleges spread out on the hillside below, where they lived, worshipped, and learned their own traditions. A staff of sixteen–said by a visiting TEF official to include more talent than any similar institution in Africa–taught the Old and New Testaments, church history, English, social ethics, logic and philosophy, liturgy, and doctrine. Courses were offered at three levels: a certificate for those who had completed only a Junior Certificate at secondary school; a diploma for those with a Senior Certificate, the normal qualification on leaving school; and a degree-level course for the minority eligible to enter a university.

Tutu taught doctrine, Old Testament, and Greek, and shared tasks such as instructing students in church administration and supervising pastoral work and fieldwork. He came well prepared to his first teaching post, according to Merwyn Castle, one of his students, who later became a bishop. "He talked from handwritten notes. He would ramble a little bit . . . but his lectures were quite amusing. He peppered them with stories and jokes and personal experiences." The students regarded Tutu as a strict grader.

Most of the staff were European or American expatriates. Very few of the prescribed textbooks were written in or about Africa. The texts included a church history by the Anglican Peter Hinchliff; an English translation of *L'enfant noir* by the Guinean novelist Camara Laye; and Paton's *Cry the Beloved Country*—the book that did so much to draw the attention of Americans to racism in South Africa. A German expatriate staff member noted that students were constantly asking questions about independent African churches, but Fedsem could give them no answers on what was clearly a burning issue. Seminary archives show that Tutu was at the heart of discussions about a new course variously called "African Studies," "The Church and its Environment in Southern Africa," and "Church and Society"; but his own recollection, particularly of his lectures on doctrine, was that he conformed to the prevailing academic milieu: "I was teaching as if I was teaching people in Europe, really. . . . I wasn't as abrasive as I should have been, considering what was happening just across the road in Fort Hare, and what was happening in the country. I'm amazed now at how innocent in some ways I was."

As in Johannesburg, St. Peter's College was staffed mostly by monks of the Community of the Resurrection. The monks, including the greatly loved Timothy Stanton, lived in a priory. They built a house specially for the Tutus with the help of a bequest left to the CR by Gian de Cabrol in Surrey. And as when Tutu was a student, St. Peter's was a tight-knit community with an all-encompassing schedule organized around worship, study, and chores. Students welcomed Tutu's arrival, partly because the atmosphere created by English monks was foreign to them. In the refectory, "You had to eat in a particular way," said Ezra Tisani, who went to college after serving a jail term as a political prisoner. "You had to not shout, keep your voices low, talk to the person next to you, which was far from being African." On Saturdays students could go into the village of Alice, or visit nurses at the nearby hospital. Liquor was banned from the campus so Anglicans might go to a local pub for a glass of sherry. After evensong, they could go across to Fort Hare to see a movie.

Tutu was the first black lecturer to be appointed to St. Peter's staff. The college council, which numbered Mangosuthu Buthelezi and Alan Paton among its members, resolved that his salary should be "on the scale of a European priest in the Diocese of Grahamstown" (under which Alice fell). With marriage and family allowances, this came to 1,760 rand a year, to which were added subsidies for water, lights, and telephone, as well as a yearly allowance of 200 rand to replace the Easter offerings that parishes gave their priests. To finance Tutu's package, the college fees paid by dioceses were raised from 250 to 325 rand a year per student. Aelred Stubbs discussed the possibility of applying for government permission to have the Tutus' children admitted to white Anglican schools in Grahamstown, 100 kilometers (60 miles) away; but before he made any progress, Trevor was admitted to a new nonracial secondary school in Swaziland, Waterford/Kamhlaba. English friends—Martin Kenyon, Uvedale Lambert, and the Comber sisters—helped to pay the fees, and their help was supplemented later by a Swedish grant through the International University Exchange Fund. Thandi and Naomi were sent to St. Michael's, a church-run primary school in Swaziland. This strained the family budget—Tutu complained about the fees in what the school told Stubbs was "a rather dismal letter . . . not quite in keeping with the image of the delightful Desmond known heretofore!" Toward the end of the Tutus' first year at Fedsem, Leah was appointed as an assistant in its library, so that she could earn a little money as well.

Fedsem was unique in South Africa in having a blanket permit from the government allowing people of all races to live on the campus. Its colleges, like the institutions that preceded them, could not admit white students; but teachers of all races and black, Coloured, and Indian students lived together, creating what Tutu once described as "an oasis of sanity and love in an otherwise arid country." Simon Gqubule's daughters called their white neighbor's mother-in-law "Granny" and played on her verandah. Mpho Tutu joined a playgroup of campus children of her own age, in which she became muddled about her race. At age four, she told somebody that she was "a nonwhite European." "I really don't know where she picked up such awful language," her father told Martin Kenyon. "She is very sensitive to racial things, wants to know why African houses are not as nice as those for so-called whites." Merwyn Castle, a Capetonian classified by apartheid as Coloured, experienced culture shock when he entered the seminary:

> In Cape Town, life was fairly segregated. We all lived in our own little pockets. . . . The only black people we saw were those who used to work at the docks. Going to St. Peter's, you were exposed to all these black guys, all speaking different languages. Every Sunday the Eucharist would be in a different language, and we'd do all the musical settings in those languages as well.

The oasis, remote as it was from urban areas, was not cut off from contemporary life. A constant stream of visitors, among them high-profile church leaders and South African liberals, addressed the students. Desmond and Leah stayed away when the former British prime minister Alec Douglas-Home came: "Although the Homes are themselves probably attractive people," Desmond told Martin Kenyon, "we thought the Conservatives had behaved abominably over issues which touched our hearts most nearly. Of course, Labour don't have such a lovely record." Staff and students were also engaged in the surrounding community, helping with feeding schemes, giving blood, and supporting child welfare clinics. "There is acute unemployment," Tutu told Kenyon, "and we have a young woman in daily to clean and help with the washing."

Fedsem's unity was hard-won; it came only from struggling together through divisive issues, both theological and political. The Anglicans were a source of many theological difficulties. The Community of the Resurrection, situated as it was at the Anglo-Catholic end of the spectrum of Anglican thought, had a history of opposition to schemes of union with Protestant churches, and it joined the seminary only after Aelred Stubbs had persuaded his brethren to override the superior's objections. Once it had joined, said Timothy Stanton, the CR fathers insisted that "we must teach our own people in our own way." "We saw ourselves as a cut above the rest," according to Merwyn Castle. "We were run like a monastery, we got up at five o'clock in the morning. We had our own fully equipped basilica of a chapel where Catholic services were performed. There was no ecumenical worship, except on a Sunday afternoon when we would all go up to the hall in the seminary buildings." In deference to Anglican sensitivities, the other three colleges waited for five years before celebrating communion together. After the Lambeth Conference of Anglican bishops in 1968 opened the way to sharing communion with other churches, the seminary resolved on joint services.

Political difficulties among the participating churches arose over whether to train degree candidates at Fort Hare. The Methodists and Presbyterians, who had trained their ministers at the "old" Fort Hare, were open to returning if a deal could be worked out respecting Fedsem's autonomy. Fort Hare negotiated concessions with the government to try to accommodate the churches, but the Congregationalists and the Anglicans were implacably opposed. The Congregational Church had relinquished a previous campus rather than compromise with Bantu education. The Anglicans were influenced by the CR's historically uncompromising rejection of Bantu education; in response to an early Methodist proposal for cooperation with Fort Hare, Aelred Stubbs wrote: "This would undoubtedly be regarded by many, in this country and outside it, as a betrayal of all that we have stood for in South Africa." When the Methodists persisted—with Gqubule dissenting—Stubbs sharpened his argument: "In dealing with Fort Hare we are not negotiating with an ordinary university, as that word is understood in the Western world. We are dealing with an institution controlled by the Bantu Education Department, which in turn is motivated by an ideology fundamentally and totally opposed to our own." Additionally, he said, "The Fort Hare degree is now of very dubious value in the academic world." With the constituent colleges of the seminary deadlocked among themselves, resentment built up in Fort Hare's administration. Shortly before Tutu joined the staff, the principal of the Methodist Church's John Wesley College wrote that Fort Hare was accusing the churches of a breach of faith, and that influential figures in the government were contemplating action against the seminary. Soon after Tutu's arrival, the chief civil servant responsible for Bantu education told Fedsem it was failing to comply with government concessions allowing it to operate: it had introduced its own degree without government permission; it was blocking its students from going to Fort Hare; and it was adopting an uncooperative, even hostile, tone toward the university.

Fedsem's internal disagreements were not confined to the debate over Fort Hare. When St. Peter's played soccer and tennis matches against the white theological students of St. Paul's College, Grahamstown, the Methodist president of the seminary told Stubbs that friends had warned him they would be playing with fire if they allowed multiracial sports events. Stubbs replied: "I must state that in my view your friends, and by implication you yourself, are capitulating to the policy of 'separate development' in precisely the way which the government wants us to do—namely by voluntarily refraining from doing things which are contrary to its policy, even though there is no law against such actions." The internal squabbling receded into the background, however, when the seminary became caught up in conflict between Fort Hare's administration and its students.

Despite the difficult relationship between Fedsem and the university administration, there was considerable interaction with Fort Hare's students. The churches used seminary lecturers as university chaplains: "I'm also Anglican chaplain to the travesty next door," was how Tutu announced his appointment to Martin Kenyon. Students new to Fort Hare—such as Thami Lokwe (later Thami Tisani), who came from Qumbu—found a "third home" at the seminary. In contrast to the teachers at Fort Hare, where Lokwe's history professor ridiculed the ability of blacks to study the subject at the postgraduate level, Desmond and Leah were seen as sympathetic parental figures. Leah provided a model for young women who, as first-generation graduates in their families, were uncertain of what was demanded of them socially and culturally. She told them to be themselves and to behave in the way they had been taught at home, implicitly reassuring them that there was nothing inferior about African manners and customs. Student couples found Desmond easier to relate to than the celibates of the CR—if Ezra and Thami danced together for too long at a Fedsem party, one of the monks would separate them, whereas Desmond celebrated students' relationships. Thami Tisani remembered Tutu teasing the students:

> One day we were coming out of a service, and he stood at the door, kissing all the girls, saying, "Guys, if you want this, you must marry." The girls were grinning, sort of confused, but tickled pink. There was no way in which it could have been misinterpreted, we were very comfortable with it. I don't know what the monks said about it but he would say, "You know what, I'm looking for wives for my students."

Unusually for the time, Tutu also invited woman students to play a formal role as servers at the Eucharist.

While the Tutus were in England, the government had driven resistance to apartheid underground or into exile. Nelson Mandela, Walter

Sisulu, and other leaders of the high command of uMkhonto we Sizwe were jailed for life and sent to Robben Island, where Nxele had been imprisoned more than a century earlier. When Robert Sobukwe of the rival PAC completed the prison term imposed on him after the Sharpeville massacre, the government passed a special law to keep him detained on Robben Island. John Vorster, the Afrikaner Nationalist politician who had been interned because of his anti-British sympathies during World War II, became the police minister and began to deploy the apparatus of a police state. In 1966 he became prime minister after Verwoerd was assassinated in Parliament by a messenger. Students at Fort Hare were afraid to discuss politics openly, according to Thami Tisani: "You had to pick up and make sense of this ANC that was now spoken about in whispers. I didn't even know what the difference was between the ANC and the PAC." The Special Branch of the police had free access to the university registrar's files and planted spies as students. In protest against the lack of academic freedom, the students refused to form a Students' Representative Council.

Students from Fort Hare looking for an environment conducive to open discussion found that they could breathe a little more easily at Fedsem. The Tutus held coffee evenings on Sundays, and N. Barney Pityana, a Fort Hare law student, was one of those who went: "They really opened their home to us [for] student evenings of really good solid, intellectual discussion and debate. That atmosphere was completely non-existent at Fort Hare." Tutu learned from his students; he was particularly impressed by the lack of bitterness of Ezra Tisani, who was studying theology but had formerly been a prisoner at Robben Island—where he was once buried to the neck and urinated on by two infamous guards. Tutu also accompanied delegations of Anglican students to meetings of the Anglican Students' Federation and the University Christian Movement (UCM). It was at these meetings, attended by students of all races, that leaders such as Pityana and Steve Biko, a medical student at the University of Natal, concluded that if blacks wanted to challenge whites on an equal footing, they needed first to organize themselves independently, and thus launched what became known as the black consciousness movement.

Tutu was later remembered for supporting black students at an important meeting during the early stages of the development of black consciousness. In 1968, at the annual conference of the UCM, in Stutterheim in the Eastern Cape, black delegates resolved to defy the pass laws, which circumscribed their participation in the conference. They made their decision after withdrawing from the conference and con-

vening a separate blacks-only meeting. At a time when the concept of
a "black caucus" was new and controversial, Tutu joined it and backed
his students in the heated debate that followed in the conference as a
whole. "His support was important," said Pityana, "because he was one
of the chaplains, and there were some universities who were very
opposed to this."

A few months later in 1968, the student protests that had swept western Europe in the northern spring had a counterpart in a three-week
confrontation at Fort Hare. For student supporters of the UCM, the
saga began with a university mission on campus, planned by a joint
council of Christian societies with the help of the chaplains. At the end
of the mission week, the students passed resolutions on issues such as
discrimination against black university staff members, and petitioned
the administration. In the same period, Anglican students were denied
permission to hold a "Hunger Week" to raise money for food-
distribution schemes. They were told that they were at Fort Hare to
study and could help their people later. On Friday, August 16, 1968,
the government minister responsible for Bantu education visited the
campus for the inauguration of a new rector, J. M. de Wet, who had
come from a conservative Afrikaans university. Most students boycotted the ceremony. The next morning, slogans such as "Vorster Is
Identical to Hitler" were found painted on walls at the university. De
Wet called in seventeen students, including Pityana, and told them they
would be held responsible for any further disturbances. A few days
later, security police took away four of them for questioning. On
August 25, Tutu preached at a regular Sunday evening service for
Fort Hare's students. The previous Tuesday night, Warsaw Pact troops
had moved into Czechoslovakia to crush the reforms of the "Prague
spring." Tutu excited the students by preaching a sermon condemning
oppression, drawing an analogy between South Africa and eastern
Europe.

The students were given permission to hold a mass meeting on
August 27 to discuss plans for their annual spring ball, but they used it
to protest against the treatment of the seventeen. They asked the rector to meet the student body. On being told that he was away, they
held a sit-in for the last two days of the term. A week later, back for the
next term, they took up where they had left off. The students used Tutu
and the other chaplains as sounding boards to talk through their
options. Thami Tisani recalled: "I remember him specifically saying,
'For how long are you going to be yielding to them—how long are you

going to be giving in against what you believe in?' I wouldn't say that he was an instigator. I don't want to say that he told us what to do, but I do remember that he was an ear, that he listened to us." Gqubule, Tutu, and the other chaplains tried unsuccessfully to broker a meeting between the administration and the students at the beginning of the new term. On Friday, September 6, about 300 students including Thami Lokwe and Barney Pityana were informed that they had been suspended and had to disperse by three o'clock that afternoon.

Pityana, in the years that followed, became an independent-minded Anglican priest who clashed vehemently with Tutu on a number of occasions. But he never forgot how Tutu waded into the fray when the police arrived with dogs and tear gas at 3:05 PM. If this was what a priest did, Pityana thought, he wanted to be one:

> We had been surrounded by police, with dogs snarling at us. We were petrified, for nearly two hours. Some people were crying . . . The staff of the university, the white people—some of them armed—these profes-sors were watching and nobody said a word, nobody . . . Desmond [came] almost from nowhere, in a cassock . . . broke the police cordon and came to be among us. I recall moving scenes of young women kneeling to pray with Desmond for blessings. Even today when I recall that I get very emotional. For me that was the greatest example I could think of, of what to be a priest was about.

The episode was a defining moment for Tutu's ministry. It sug-gested not only that he had inherited his mother's compassion but, for the first time, that he was capable in a crisis of transforming the burn-ing sense of injustice he felt into creative ministry to victims of vio-lence. In this, his intervention foreshadowed his later ministry. More than thirty years later, he could easily conjure up the scene at Fort Hare that day:

> I can actually see police coming, and these kids sitting on the lawn, and the incredible dignity that they had. The dogs came viciously, and the natural reaction should have been that they [the students] ought to have run away, because these things came snarling at them. They didn't, it was unbelievable. They all just got up and sang Nkosi Sikelele,* and then they were taken one by one to their residences to pack up.

* An abbreviated reference to "Nkosi Sikelel' iAfrika" (God bless Africa), the hymn that is now part of South Africa's national anthem.

Some of the students had to be treated for dog bites by Miriam Gqubule and other wives of Fedsem's lecturers. Then the students were forced onto buses and taken to nearby railway stations. Students at Alice station had nothing to eat, so the chaplains bought them loaves of bread. Others were taken to remote railway junctions, where volunteers bringing food were denied access as the students waited for trains home.

Tutu had experienced discrimination throughout his life. His teaching career had been cut short by apartheid. Community after community, institution after institution, in which he lived and studied had been destroyed. But until that day in 1968 he had never witnessed firsthand the use of state power to suppress dissent. That night, he hardly slept, thinking of the students and their plight: "It made me angry with God," he remembered. In the morning Merwyn Castle saw the experience overwhelm him in the college chapel: "He broke down during prayers and wailed and wailed and cried his eyes out. . . . He wept like a baby."

In the next weeks, suspended students were told they could re-apply for admission if they brought their parents to countersign an agreement that they would obey Fort Hare's rules. But as the students had feared, those the university branded as ringleaders—twenty-one students—were denied readmission. Relations between Fedsem and Fort Hare were strained. The rector of the university claimed that leaders of the National Union of South African Students, banned from the campus, were using Fedsem as a conduit to reach Fort Hare's students. The president of Fedsem replied, deadpan: "It has always been our belief that our students should not be protected from encounter with ideas." In 1969, the rector threatened Fedsem after accusations that its students had incited a boycott of a visiting drama group: "We can . . . assure you that the matter will be taken further."

The denouement came a year after the Tutus had left Fedsem. In 1971, Fort Hare made an "offer to purchase" the seminary campus, claiming that it needed the space. Writing in the *Times* of London, Bernard Levin drew an analogy with the erection of the Berlin Wall. The South African authorities, he suggested, wanted to insulate the students at Fort Hare from the "contagion of freedom," just as the Russians sought to insulate the East Berliners. The churches refused to sell. In 1974, the government expropriated the land and buildings and gave the seminary thirty days to leave. It was the eleventh institution intimately connected with the Tutu family to be forcibly removed or closed down by apartheid.

When the government finally acted, Desmond had taken a teaching post at the University of Botswana, Lesotho, and Swaziland (UBLS) in Roma, Lesotho. His decision was a shock to the college; he had been about to become vice principal and was being groomed as the first black principal. Aelred Stubbs was upset and angry. "I don't think Desmond going off was part of the plan," said Timothy Stanton. At least one of the monks felt that Tutu was guilty of two sins: ambition and wanting to make more money. In a letter written some months after Tutu left in 1970, Theodore Simpson of the CR opposed a proposal that he should be brought back to the seminary as its first full-time president. If Tutu accepted such an offer, Simpson wrote, it would be "a tacit admission that he left us simply in order to secure a more prestigious and better paid post." Returning would show he was "someone who was primarily interested in the advancement of his own career. Most of us are here at the expense of such personal success." Moreover, he added, some doubted whether Tutu would have been a good principal, and by extension a good seminary president: "I have observed myself that he tends to live above his income, and that his handling of his personal finances is not always very wise."

Simpson's memorandum took no account of Tutu's family situation—perhaps understandably for a monk living in a community that took care of its members' basic material needs. Whether or not Tutu was a spendthrift, the attraction of the post at UBLS to a couple with four children is not difficult to see. Three of the children were living 1,300 kilometers (800 miles) from Alice, attending expensive schools. If the family had stayed in Alice, the only child still at home—Mpho, age six—would soon have had to join her siblings in Swaziland. As it was, Leah told Martin Kenyon before there was any prospect of moving: "I miss the children very much sometimes and on these occasions sink into bouts of depression. . . . I keeping hoping that we should one day settle in Swaziland or Lesotho." Moving to Lesotho enabled the Tutus to bring Naomi back from boarding school and to send her and Mpho to a school on the university campus. It cut in half the journey to ferry the older children to and from Swaziland. And the job paid education allowances for the older children and doubled Desmond's salary, to 3,570 rand a year. Aelred Stubbs, later suggested that ambition and money were part of Tutu's motives, but also linked his decision to go to

Lesotho to his family: "They were insisting that their children should not be trained under Bantu education. Desmond's educational ambitions for his children were very high indeed, and dogged he was in pursuit of them."

Notified of his new job offer, Tutu sent an emotional letter to his mentor. "My dear Aelred," he wrote. "How should I begin this missive—because I want to say things that lie too deep for words—that does sound like melodramatic histrionics. (I really am going to town in the Queen's language!) But in fact it is true." After telling Stubbs about the details of the appointment, he continued:

> You started all this racket when you got me to go to your country to study. I have been incredibly lucky don't you think? You brought me on wonderfully with your solicitude and concern and prayers. We had, as you know, a most wonderful time and made an incredible number of splendid friends and all this really through your good offices. What can one say for all these good things but an inadequate "thank you." I shall miss you. I am sentimental. You have helped us in all kinds of ways—financially, spiritually and all the other "allys" that you can think of. We are obviously excited, but there are going to be several difficulties—I shan't have my Monday off, or the days off to fetch the children. I shall have no one to tease me. . . . But from all of us accept our warmest thanks for having been the agent of so many good things that have come our way. . . . We must sing next Friday at Mass "From glory to glory advancing we praise thee O Lord" because for some odd reason I associate it especially with you—as perhaps the first hymn you taught us at Rosettenville [in Johannesburg] and I am nostalgic for some things that are difficult to recapture, but linger faintly in the depths. This [letter] is unrevised and it does not want an answer or discussion.

In an unusually intimate gesture, he signed the letter with his family nickname: "Yours affectionately, Boy."

Like Fort Hare, the University of Botswana, Lesotho, and Swaziland grew from an institution established by missionaries—in the case of UBLS, from the Pius XII Catholic University College. It was established in 1964 while the three countries that it served were preparing for independence from Britain. Also like Fort Hare, it was isolated in a rural area, in the valley where the first Catholic missionaries settled in Lesotho. Unlike Fort Hare in 1970, UBLS was nonracial and inclusive. It admitted students from all southern African countries, and it allowed free political debate. For Njabulo and Mpho Ndebele, South Africans who met and married while studying there, Roma was "a haven . . . a jewel," in Mpho's words, a "little island of peace." Students could discuss liberation politics openly, whether these involved the ANC's armed struggle or the fast-spreading black consciousness philosophy being developed by Biko, Pityana, and others. Politically aware students read the work of African revolutionaries such as Amilcar Cabral and Eduardo Mondlane, as well as Marx, Engels, Lenin, and Castro. The government of Lesotho publicly attacked left-wing student leaders such as Jama Mbeki, younger brother of Thabo Mbeki, but at that stage still respected the university's academic freedom.

The Tutus had relinquished their passports on their return from England three years earlier and now had to apply for "travel documents" to work in Lesotho. Approving the documents, the secretary for Bantu Affairs and Development told a local Eastern Cape official: "Bantu travel documents may be issued to abovementioned Bantus for the purpose of working in Lesotho provided the police report is favourable." The family moved to a house on the UBLS campus in January 1970, accompanied by their furniture, forty boxes, twelve cases, five trunks, and 900 books. In time, Desmond was appointed Anglican chaplain; and in his second year he was made warden of two student residences—Chancellor Hall and Mswati Hall—which came with free housing and honoraria totaling 600 rand a year.

As at Fedsem, most of the staff were white, many of them British and American expatriates. Also as at Fedsem, Desmond and Leah were like parents on campus, particularly to Anglican students. Desmond's pastoral style, as Nelson and Winnie Mandela were to discover many years later when their marriage was in trouble, was interventionist—he did not wait to be asked for advice. While a student was walking on campus, he or she could expect to be called over by Desmond. "There was no way you could look the other way," said Mpho Ndebele. "You tended also to open up to him; he would really confront you with issues." Leah was appointed to the office of the dean of student affairs, where she took responsibility for the welfare of students. She organized Saturday night movies, including *The Taming of the Shrew* and *The Amorous Adventures of Moll Flanders*. The latter she announced in the campus newsletter as being "the rollicking story of a ribald century that should have been ashamed of itself." One of Desmond's passions was preserving African traditions of courtesy. Njabulo Ndebele, the son of Tutu's high school arithmetic teacher, first heard Tutu when he was lecturing to a packed classroom in Oppenheimer Hall: "He bemoaned the fact that people were losing their sense of community by not recognising one another when they met on campus. He said at Roma people no longer greeted each other as they passed one another [and] that was not a good sign."

In the theology department, Tutu was in charge of teaching the Old Testament to degree students. Most were teachers being prepared to give instruction in religious knowledge, but there were some Catholic seminarians as well. One was Buti Tlhagale, later archbishop of Bloemfontein and bishop of Johannesburg. Tutu stood out from the other teachers at Roma, said Tlhagale: "He was already a very forceful personality with a presence. He taught us the Old Testament prophets. He was very strong on the role of Amos, on the role of justice, but that was all academic. We never associated it with real life. I never thought that he would actually play out that role later on." Students were interested in the new concepts of African theology and black theology, but there were no courses dealing with them. It was only some years later, when Tlhagale was studying in Rome, that he began to read articles by Tutu on black theology. Ndebele found a sympathetic hearing when he approached his chaplain about a crisis of belief. He told Tutu that he was uninspired by the church's rituals and felt he was not drawing sustenance from his faith. As Ndebele recalled, Tutu did not attempt to prescribe a solution, but there was "extreme concern that the church appeared not to be getting through to young people, to potential leaders. . . . He was really worried about that."

Off the campus, Tutu's reputation was growing in the church. At St. Peter's, he had begun to publish articles in academic journals and journals of current affairs. In Lesotho, he was on the executive board of the Lesotho Ecumenical Association, and he represented the local diocese to the rest of the Anglican church. He became an external examiner for both Fedsem and Rhodes University in Grahamstown. He traveled frequently to conferences and meetings. Even before he left St. Peter's, the demands that flowed from his being one of the church's best-qualified black theologians began to stretch him. When Joost de Blank's successor as archbishop of Cape Town, Robert Selby Taylor, asked him to be a delegate to the official Anglican-Catholic conversations in southern Africa, Tutu pointed out that he was already on the body promoting union with Protestant churches, the Church Unity Commission (CUC). Selby Taylor asked him to try to do both, and he agreed: "I hope you will not have thought I was playing hard to get. It is a great privilege to serve the church." Appointed to the council of St. Paul's College in Grahamstown, he asked Selby Taylor in 1971 to be allowed to fly to meetings. He had already lost two weeks of teaching at UBLS to Anglican-Catholic and CUC meetings, he said, and he was anxious that it should not be said of black representatives that they wanted appointments to church bodies but did not honor their commitments. Tutu also had difficulties with the attitudes of white church administrators who handled his travel claims—an experience he shared with the black clergy in general. In a complaint to Selby Taylor, he protested against the tone of a letter from a church official: "He writes as if he were a headmaster hauling a schoolboy over the coals. . . . He should please refrain from imputing that we seek to milk the church."

In February 1971, while Tutu was in Johannesburg for meetings, his father, ZZ Tutu, died peacefully in his sleep. The family had seen him the Sunday before he died; on their way to Swaziland for the beginning of the school year, they stopped in Munsieville and celebrated Eucharist around the kitchen table. Under the pass laws Desmond's mother faced deportation to a Bantustan. "Mercifully the local authorities allowed her to remain as my younger sister's ward!" he told friends.

During this period Tutu also began to play a small role in deliberations on the most important issues of church and state in South Africa. In decisions dating back to a conference of the World Council of Churches (WCC) in Geneva in 1966, the WCC moved toward recognizing the legitimacy of the armed struggle that the ANC and PAC had launched after having been banned in 1960. When, in 1970, the WCC approved a proposal from its Program to Combat Racism to give humanitarian grants to liberation movements, there was an uproar in South Africa, not least among white members of the multiracial churches that belonged to the WCC. Many black Anglicans supported the grants, although this was not publicly apparent in the climate created by Vorster's Terrorism Act of 1967, a law that allowed the police to detain people indefinitely without trial, denied detainees access to the courts, and prescribed a minimum jail sentence of five years for anyone whose actions could be presumed to give even a vestige of support for the violent overthrow of the government. Tutu was appointed as one of three Anglican members of a delegation that tried to arrange a follow-up meeting with the WCC on the issue. Within South Africa, the WCC conference of 1966 set in motion a process that led to the publication in 1968 of a theological declaration, "A Message to the People of South Africa," which went well beyond saying apartheid was simply mistaken or unjust. The message declared that by elevating race to the most important human attribute, apartheid denied the central statements of the Christian gospel: "This doctrine of separation is a false faith, a novel gospel." Vorster responded with a threat: "There are clergy in South Africa who are toying with the sort of thing that Martin Luther King did in America—I want to tell them: Cut it out! Cut it out! The cloth you wear will not protect you if you do it in South Africa." The church leaders, led by Beyers Naude, an Afrikaner who had been forced out of the Dutch Reformed Church, persisted by setting up a series of commissions under the umbrella of the Study Project on Christianity in Apartheid Society (Spro-Cas) to work out the implications of the message. Tutu took part in consultations for the Spro-Cas church commission.

Although life in Lesotho offered protection from the everyday details of oppression in South Africa, the Tutus dreaded their encounters with South African officials at the border. They were often made to wait while immigration officers pulled files on them from a revolving file stand. Once Trevor, then about fifteen years old, became angry and told an officer: "What a silly fool you are!" Furious officials seized him and tried to take him away, but his parents—ignoring threats of arrest for trespassing—insisted on accompanying him and defused the confrontation. Oppression was not confined to South Africa. Lesotho held its first postindependence election just after the Tutus arrived there in January 1970. The ruling Basutoland National Party fully expected to win; but as results began to come in, it was running neck and neck with its main opponent, the Basutoland Congress Party. A blackout was imposed on the results. Arriving back from a meeting in Johannesburg, Tutu was told at the border post that the election had been suspended. The prime minister, Leabua Jonathan, declared a state of emergency and jailed opposition leaders. He also imposed a night curfew on many roads, which had the effect of prohibiting UBLS staff members and students from traveling between ten PM and six AM without a special permit from police headquarters in the capital, Maseru. The curfew was lifted just as the Tutus were leaving Lesotho, but constitutional government would not be restored until twenty-three years later.

In 1971, Denis Fahy, head of the theology department at UBLS, proposed to the university that Tutu be sent to teach theology at a satellite campus in Swaziland. Six months later, Tutu was still waiting to hear what would happen when he unexpectedly received another offer, this one from London: would he like to apply to become the Africa director of the Theological Education Fund? The TEF, the body that had helped to establish Fedsem and had paid for much of Tutu's education at King's College, was a major force in theological education in developing countries, and the post was an important one. Tutu wrote to Robert Selby Taylor: "With the uncertainty about my present job, and the challenge of this . . . [prospective] job, I have agreed to [apply] with mixed feelings."

During the recruitment process, the TEF asked Sydney Evans at King's to give a reference for Tutu. Evans had no hesitation about strongly recommending Tutu for the job, but questioned his motives:

> I find myself wondering, however, just what is moving Desmond to make this further move; whether there is here some kind of element of social advancement. I believe his time in England led him to want his own children to have the best possible kind of education, and he financially, I think, rather over-reached himself to enable them to go to the Waterford School. So summing it all up I think you would have a very fine worker in this field, if you were to appoint Desmond Tutu; though I would myself want to talk with him to know what it was that was making him want to do this rather than remain a lecturer.

A bigger obstacle than Evans's qualified reference stood in the way, however: securing a passport so that Tutu could travel to London for an interview. He applied at the South African government office nearest to Lesotho: the magistrate's court in the border town of Ladybrand. The magistrate who interviewed him gave a positive recommendation. Tutu was "a highly developed person with high moral principles," he wrote to the chief Bantu Affairs commissioner for the region. Answering the standard question of whether Tutu was a "fit and proper person to visit countries where there is no racial segregation," the magistrate said: "He is a highly educated man and should fit into any multiracial society. It does not seem as if his previous contact with a multiracial society has affected him detrimentally." On July 30, 1971, the head office of BAD asked for a police report. On August 5, a handwritten note in Tutu's file said that a passport should not be recommended, "since the report is unfavourable." The passport application was also referred to the country's principal intelligence agency, the

Bureau for State Security, generally known as BOSS. On August 6, BOSS also advised against it. Neither the police reports nor the BOSS reports were filed, but it seems clear that Tutu's activism at Alice counted against him.

Tutu's passport application was refused with no explanation. (He remained unaware of the internal discussions about him in the civil service until the writing of this book.) Without much hope of having the decision reversed, Tutu asked Robert Selby Taylor to write to the South African interior minister, Theo Gerdener, and tell Gerdener that he, Tutu, was not a politician and did not belong to a political party– and that although the TEF was a subsidiary of the WCC it was confined entirely to theological work. Concealing his true feelings about the WCC grants to liberation movements, Tutu proposed that Selby Taylor refer to the Anglican church's disagreement with the grants, and to the fact that Tutu had been chosen "to present the case of our church against the WCC." In his letter to Gerdener, Selby Taylor followed the general tenor of Tutu's advice, but refrained from any reference to the Anglicans' or Tutu's supposed opposition to the grants. He said the work Tutu was interested in was of a theological nature, that Tutu was a person in whom he had confidence, and that a refusal to allow contacts with theologians outside the country created a bad impression overseas.

Selby Taylor's appeal was sent in August 1971. Gerdener later had qualms about apartheid and broke with his party, but at that time Selby Taylor was not optimistic about Tutu's prospects. He wrote: "My fear is that this may be all I shall hear on the subject." It was all he did hear. As months passed without any further response, the Tutu family found itself in a "terrible quandary," as Desmond described it to friends in a letter that Christmas. Despite not being able to get to London for an interview, he was offered the job at the TEF. Meanwhile, UBLS continued to hope he would stay in southern Africa. Fahy recommended that the university give Tutu a promotion, based on his academic excellence, his exceptional teaching skills, and his significant contributions to the region's cultural and religious life. He also cited Tutu's "vigorous powers of argument, and his insistence that justice should be done to the African point of view."

In December, Tutu wrote in desperation directly to prime minister Vorster asking for a passport. His appeal was referred to BOSS, which reiterated its opposition. Vorster's national security adviser told the Department of the Interior: "Tutu wants to give the impression in his letter to the Honourable Prime Minister that he can be an asset to South Africa if he is allowed to take up the TEF post. Given his political attitude to the South African system so far, I very much doubt he will employ his energy in favour of the Republic of South Africa." However, it would appear that summer holiday fever came to Tutu's rescue. The letter from BOSS was written four days before Christmas. It arrived at Interior between Christmas and the New Year. By the time it received attention, Gerdener had already approved a passport. In January, the Interior Department informed Tutu of the decision, again without any explanation. He was now hopeful that he would be able to accept the post at the TEF, but he refused to take it for granted. The government had been known to confiscate a passport just after issuing it, and Leah did not have her passport yet. Tutu told the vice chancellor of UBLS: "We won't breathe freely until we are in the plane."

CHAPTER 7

TRANSFORMATION

In March 1972 the Tutus flew to Britain for Desmond to take up his post at the Theological Education Fund (TEF). Unknown to them, an attempt had been made to block the issue of a passport to Leah, but it had been overruled. The magistrate at Ladybrand had no objection; sending her application to the Bantu Affairs commissioner, he wrote: "Mrs. Tutu and her family naturally and rightly wish to accompany her husband to London where her children will continue their education." But the commissioner opposed the application, telling his head office it appeared that Leah wanted to settle permanently. The head office asked for a police report on Leah. In a decision unexplained by the contents of the file, her passport was issued late in January.

Tutu became Africa director of the TEF about a decade into the postindependence era. To most South Africans, liberated Africa was a closed book for the first half century of its existence. Black South Africans rejoiced as former Belgian, British, French, Italian, Portuguese, and Spanish colonies freed themselves from European control, but they themselves were isolated from day-to-day developments; only exiles had direct experience of most of the continent. Most whites knew and cared little about Africa's politics and looked to Europe and North America for culture.

Tutu's job was to assess and make recommendations for TEF grants to theological training institutions and students across sub-Saharan Africa. To do this, he had to travel, paying forty-eight visits to twenty-five countries over three years. (See map at front.) Plunged into the national and church politics of a region numbering about 300 million people, he learned firsthand of the challenges, successes, and failures implicit in the enormous enterprise of creating national identities, developing economies, and uniting disparate peoples arbitrarily thrown together within national boundaries imposed by European powers. One of his duties was to share reports of his trips with his fellow regional directors for Asia, the Middle East, Latin America, and the Pacific. These he wrote as he traveled, scrawling commentary day by day into a series of wire-bound reporters' notebooks.

The notebooks and the corresponding typed reports, transcribed by his personal assistant, Betty Ward, are now in the basement archives of the World Council of Churches in Geneva. They constitute a treasure trove: among notes on the minutiae of theological education across Africa is a rich, vivid account of the variety and complexity of newly independent Africa in the early 1970s. It is an account, moreover, in which can be traced the origins of the concerns Tutu was to voice during Africa's "second liberation," in the late 1980s and early 1990s, and of a profound shift in his theological thinking.

Tutu's most frequent and longest visits were to large countries with extensive theological education facilities, such as Zaire (now the Democratic Republic of Congo) and Nigeria, but he also spent considerable time in other countries in West Africa, such as Cameroon, Ghana, and Sierra Leone; in East Africa, where he visited Kenya and Uganda most often; and on his home ground in southern Africa.

His first visit was to Zaire. Its transition to liberation in 1960 was about as different from South Africa's thirty years later as one could imagine. In South Africa negotiations took four years. Its leaders haggled over every detail of the transition. Centrifugal forces threatened to tear the nation apart, and it stood constantly on the brink of an all-out civil war. The result was that by the time Nelson Mandela was inaugurated president in 1994, enough common ground had been created for the major forces in the country to identify themselves with the new order. Patrice Lumumba, the Congolese leader whose aspirations to a broad nationalism most approximated those of Mandela, was less fortunate. Independence was declared within six months after the Belgian rulers first sat down to meet Congolese leaders. On independence day in June 1960, King Baudouin of Belgium delivered a paternalistic lecture praising the brutal rule of his great-uncle, Léopold II, who had colonized the area as a personal fiefdom. Lumumba, now prime minister, countered with an unscripted, angry denunciation of the "humiliating slavery" of Belgian colonialism. The Belgians held up the official lunch while they discussed boycotting it. Within days the army rebelled against its Belgian officers. Whites were attacked, the Belgians sent in soldiers, and the United Nations intervened with a force of 19,000. Most Congolese leaders pursued regional agendas. Secessionists broke away in the southern Katanga region, supported by Belgian mining companies. Lumumba, suspicious that the UN was promoting Belgium with its continuing economic interests, asked for help from the Soviet Union, embroiling himself in global cold war politics. Congolese leaders financed by the CIA deposed him, then delivered him to Katanga, where local gendarmes led by Belgians murdered him. Recent research has shown that when a scandal began to break regarding the assassination, the Katangese and the Belgians who worked for them concocted a story about Lumumba's disappearance, exhumed his body, cut it up with knives and a hacksaw, and dissolved it in sulfuric acid.

When Tutu went to Zaire in 1972, it was ruled by one of the Congolese army officers who replaced the Belgians after the army rebellion of 1960. Colonel Joseph-Désiré Mobutu had taken over the country for some months after Lumumba was deposed, and seized control permanently in 1965. With the support of the west, he set up a one-party state, promoted indigenous African culture and practices in a process he called "authenticité," changed the name of the country to Zaire, and himself assumed the name Mobutu Sese Seko. On his first day in the capital, Kinshasa, Tutu wrote that politics was a potent force in Zaire:

> Politically [the] country [is a] military dictatorship and [the] national assembly [a] rubber stamp, but most people think it infinitely better than [the] chaotic situation which existed for five years after independence. Much corruption and bribery. Very little one can get done without "dash." The rich are feathering their nest and the poor get poorer. 27% unemployment especially among teenagers and young adults who can't get into senior high schools. The city attracts many who should remain in the country so that urbanisation brings in its train [the] usual socio-economic problems–too many chasing too few jobs, overcrowding, immorality, prostitution, drunkenness, etc.

Mobutu was determined to control any source of influence in society independent of the government. "The President," wrote Tutu, "has already united all trade unions and would like to see the church help nationalism à la Constantine." Mobutu had forced more than eighty Protestant churches and missions to merge. He conferred official recognition on a few Christian churches: on the product of the merger, the Église du Christ au Zaïre (ECZ); on the Catholic Church; and on the "Church of Jesus Christ on Earth through the Prophet Simon Kimbangu," an indigenous church inspired by a healer who was jailed by the Belgians for thirty years.

The Catholic Church, formerly closely associated with Belgian rule, shared Mobutu's desire for an authentic indigenous identity, and its cardinal promoted the Africanization of liturgy and religious leadership. However, a decree that junior branches of the governing party be established in all institutions was a "bone of contention with the RCs," Tutu noted: "Cardinal Malula jibbed at this. Is now in exile in Rome. Mobutu practising RC but won't have him back. Some seminaries consequently closed; then RC bishops conference changed its mind and acceded to government wishes."

Tutu's reports were not confined to religion and politics. In 1974 he arrived days before an event announced by the American boxing promoter Don King as the "Rumble in the Jungle": "The country is all agog with excitement at the Ali-Foreman fight. . . . Dance troupes welcome visitors at the new international airport as they arrive to attend the fight and there are signboards welcoming [Muhammad] Ali and [George] Foreman to the land of their forefathers." A staggering number of impressive buildings had gone up in Kinshasa; the city looked prosperous; and "there is the spring of a growing confidence in the jaunty walk of most Zaireans clad in the trendy African suits which political leaders such as President Mobutu, President Kaunda [of Zambia] and President Nyerere [of Tanzania] sport." Coming back to politics, Tutu said that wealth and power were being concentrated in the hands of the few and indigenization was sliding into something else: "The country was set on the road to discover and develop a genuine African lifestyle under the auspices of what was called authenticité and this was largely admirable. Now one is not quite so sure of the new cult called Le Mobutuisme."

Three years after Tutu's first visit, his concerns had crystallized:

Zaïre is passing through a very difficult time what with inflation, increasing unemployment and a host of other problems. President Mobutu must still be commended for holding together the diverse elements that make up this huge country. But he is in trouble. Someone remarked to me that if he survives the present unhappy state of affairs and is not toppled, then he is likely to go on for a very long time to come.*

Some feel that the feud between the government and the church (read Roman Catholic church, because the Protestants are largely

* Mobutu was overthrown in 1997.

docile and quiescent) is merely a diversionary tactic to draw the attention of the people away from the crisis the country finds itself in. The most disturbing feature of this whole business is the passivity of the Protestant church which appears to have lost all sense of its prophetic vocation. Now it is obviously easy from outside to advise that people should be critical of an oppressive system . . . [and] it is quite unfair to ask others to risk imprisonment, harassment and worse, all from the safety of the touchlines. But I am nevertheless deeply disturbed at this fairly widespread phenomenon in the African church. But one of the paradoxes, of course, is that nearly all of the political leaders of independent Africa have been mainly Christian. . . .

There is little freedom in Zaïre today. It is a military regime and all this is extremely galling to a black from South Africa. God be praised for the courage of some of the Roman Catholic leaders and others in the ECZ. I believe fervently that the church is going to be the salvation of Africa. If the church fails, then I am frightened for the future.

Tutu's concern that the church needed to retain its "prophetic vocation" was to emerge when he became president of the All Africa Conference of Churches in 1987, and again in postapartheid South Africa.

The second country Tutu visited while working for the TEF was Africa's giant—Nigeria. With more than twice South Africa's population, a well-run civil service, and a strong economy, it had been seen at independence in 1960 as Africa's major hope for postcolonial progress. But it too had been torn by regional tensions, leading to a series of military coups in 1966 and conflict between the predominantly Muslim north and the Christian east. The east seceded in 1967 to form the Republic of Biafra, precipitating a bitter civil war with the rest of the Nigerian federation. During the war Biafra presented itself as the victim of Muslim oppression—although half the federal army was Christian—giving the struggle religious undertones and splitting the country's church leadership.

When Tutu first went to Nigeria, the war had been over for two years and the country was ruled by General Yakubu Gowon, a Christian (as it happened an Anglican) from the north. Nigerian church leaders and academics shared with Tutu their mixed feelings about military rule: they wanted democracy but not the instability it seemed to generate. On his second visit, Tutu's informants were crediting Gowon with steadying the country: "Everybody trusts him and believes what he says. Despite [his] being a Christian, Muslim northerners have confidence in him too. The target date for return to civilian rule is 1976, but nobody looks forward to this with much enthusiasm. The people are browned off still with the machinations and machiavellianism of most politicians and they appear to be quite content under military rule." Opinions diverged far more sharply over the aftermath of the Biafran war. The wounds of the war were being healed wonderfully quickly, Tutu was told in Lagos in 1973. But in Enugu, formerly the capital of Biafra, he found "a deep hurt in the hearts" of the Igbo people.

At the TEF, Tutu had direct experience for the first time of the interaction between Christianity and Islam, which takes place on an axis running across Africa from its west coast through the nations of West Africa to the Horn of Africa in the east. He saw the Islam in Africa Project in Ibadan, a mixed Christian-Muslim city in the west of Nigeria, where he wrote that interfaith dialogue had replaced a polemical approach with what he called a "more eirenical approach." He praised the imaginative programs of the Study Center for Islam and Christianity in Ibadan, which encouraged Christians to take Muslims seriously. One plan was to help teachers in religiously mixed schools conduct multifaith worship. Traveling around the continent, Tutu also became acquainted with the University of Fort Hare's pioneering counterparts elsewhere: the University of Ibadan in Nigeria, which particularly impressed him; Makerere University in Uganda; and Fourah Bay College in Sierra Leone.

On Tutu's last extensive trip for the TEF in Nigeria in 1974, his conclusions were as varied as his first impressions had been. The "rankling Igbo resentment and sense of injustice . . . make the outlook for the future somewhat sombre. Of course Nigeria is really several nations and is but one very glowing example of the rape of Africa by the colonisers who forced their dismemberment of Africa through their voracious greed." There was still a military regime "but it is quite amazing what freedom the Press enjoys to express very sharp criticism of the powers that be." Nigeria was booming, domestic gasoline prices had been cut, and the country was enjoying its membership in the Organization of Petroleum Exporting Countries (OPEC), which had just triggered an energy crisis in developed countries by quadrupling prices. But housing and sanitation were nearly chaotic, the roads were inadequate, and too many cars were not roadworthy.

Tutu visited Kenya on his first tour of East Africa in 1972. It was richly endowed in many ways, he noted, and the capital, Nairobi, was impressive:

The city looks prosperous with much building going on. I know there are many problems, acute housing shortage, slums, the rich getting richer and the poor becoming more so, unemployment, prostitution and frustrated school leavers with nothing to do. But the first impression is of progress and development. It warms one's heart to see this when one comes from a country which constantly denigrates the black man. It is good for my own personal ego.

A coup in Kenya was unthinkable, he reported. President Jomo Kenyatta was "firmly in the saddle," the country was politically stable, and there was freedom of speech: "There is much self criticism in the ruling party KANU [Kenyan African National Union]—though the President is held generally to be beyond reproach. He is a magnificent symbol of unity and nationhood. He is greatly respected even by those who disagree with him." However, there were tribal tensions, which were mirrored in the churches: "The Luos and the Kikuyus had often been played against each other, but after independence there was a genuine desire on the part of all to work for a unified Kenya. The assassination of Tom Mboya [a cabinet minister of Luo birth] in 1969 has put paid to that. Kikuyus it is felt are entrenching themselves in all positions of authority." In 1973, Tutu visited Nairobi and Limuru a few days before celebrations of the anniversary of the country's independence. "The flags are out," he wrote. "Understandably there is much self-congratulation but one is impressed that an editorial in one of the papers says the celebrations must be tempered with a large dose of self-criticism. Perhaps it is a measure of the maturity and security here (particularly obvious after Uganda) that there is this freedom to criticise. . . . It is not clear who will succeed Kenyatta but at present Kenya is riding on the crest of a wave of glowing success and achievement."

Social conditions gave rise to reflection over whether the education of the clergy was meeting Africa's needs. After visiting a center for Masai nomadic cattle herders on the border with Tanzania, he questioned whether the church was giving appropriate training for the clergy working in rural areas. In Nairobi, after touring one of the worst slums he had ever seen, he asked:

> How do you speak about a God who loves you, a redeemer, a saviour, when you live like an animal? . . . Is the training given in the often sheltered ivory towers at all geared to speak relevantly to this and similar situations? . . . It is a whole philosophy and lifestyle in theological education that must be revolutionised so that it is fundamentally more

problem-orientated and people-centred, rather than curriculum and syllabus orientated. . . . The third world must develop its own style geared
to its own needs and maybe we could still teach others a thing or two.

During Tutu's first visit to Kenya, a church leader shared his worry
that too much of the Kenyan economy was in the hands of Asian
businessmen; in the interests of the Asians themselves, he suggested,
the economy needed more participation by blacks. Within days,
Uganda's way of dealing with the same complaint formed Tutu's first
impression of that country in the 1970s. "Arrived Entebbe 17.45," he
wrote. "Pathetic sight of Asians being packed off. This airport is
unlikely to cope with avalanche when airlift begins in earnest." The
Asian community was being expelled en masse. Away from the airport, he noted: "Uganda is beautiful with a lot of greenery because of
the abundant rains. Economically it does not give the same impression
of development and progress that one gets coming into Nairobi. Politically this is a military dictatorship with little room for dissent. The
newspapers and the radio are echoes of the Master's voice."

The "Master" was Idi Amin Dada, who had seized power eighteen
months earlier. During his rule, terminated only by an invasion from
Tanzania in 1979, he was responsible for the deaths of an estimated
300,000 people, including the country's chief justice, numerous cabinet
ministers, and an Anglican archbishop, Janani Luwum. Tutu traveled
in Uganda before the full brutality of the regime unfolded, but the pattern was clear by December 1973:

> This is a sad country. There is an overpowering sense of insecurity. Peo-
> ple just keep disappearing and nobody knows if they will be next on the
> list. There is no apparent rhyme or reason—at one moment it is some-
> one high in the echelons of Government and at the next it will be some-
> one unknown. It is government by the whim of the President. . . .
> Travelling in a car with my university host, we were discussing the sit-
> uation in the country when he said somewhat agitatedly that we should
> keep off that subject. Why? Because we were being followed by an
> army van. You just don't go discussing this sort of thing anywhere
> these days, you never know to whom you are talking. The army has
> been pampered and spoiled, and the general (Amin) has confessed to
> some that he can't control the soldiers. . . . The Americans have closed
> their Embassy because the general took umbrage at the presence
> of armed uniformed Marines after he had threatened to arrest the
> Ambassador.

At the end of his stay, Tutu had his own encounter with Amin's security agents. At Entebbe airport, they held back his aircraft while they searched his luggage. They went through his papers, but missed the report from an earlier trip describing the media as echoes of "the Master's voice" and the country as a military dictatorship: "I don't know what would have happened had they found it."

Touring the white-ruled countries of southern Africa, Tutu also had a run-in with Rhodesia's security police. When he arrived in the capital, then Salisbury, in 1973, detectives of the Special Branch were called after he asked an immigration officer not to put a Rhodesian stamp in his passport for fear of repercussions in other African countries. Two days later they searched his luggage on his way out and found essays on black theology. They told him, "This is not theology, this is politics!" He was able to hide notes he had made on South Africa and Mozambique—"I would have been truly in the soup then"—but their suspicions were again aroused when they found a letter from Betty Ward, his personal assistant, signed "Octopus." The explanation—readily understood by anyone who ever worked for Tutu, but not by the Rhodesians—was that he had given her this nickname after she said he wanted her to do so many things at once that he needed not a secretary but an octopus.

On his journeys, Tutu wrote running commentaries touching briefly on many other contemporary African issues: the last vestiges of colonial rule; the dilemmas of the independent neighbors of white-ruled countries; internal conflicts, sometimes of genocidal proportions; the colonial heritage; and neocolonial control, now more subtly exercised in church and secular society.

Mozambique was "extremely depressing," he wrote in 1973, before the Portuguese military coup that led to its independence; he preferred the clarity of apartheid's unremitting harshness. In Mozambique, he said:

the rough edges of oppression are disguised by the façade of non-discrimination, so that people should not find it too chafing and unbearable (yet mercifully they have). Any blacks who may rise despite these obstacles and who could be leaders of their people are seduced into acceptance of the status quo by being assimilated. I found I much preferred the situation at home in South Africa where you knew clearly where you stood. Assimilation says you don't count as a black but will count only as a sham white. Value and personhood lies in whiteness. What blasphemy.

In Swaziland, lying between Mozambique and South Africa, Tutu found "realms of confusion and contradiction," as King Sobhuza II dissolved parliament at the request of the majority royalist party and South Africa armed a royal force against the more liberal police and civil service. He admired Botswana, which was being punished economically by neighboring South Africa for supporting its liberation movements: "It is a wonder they still adopt such independent and critical attitudes to South Africa." Zambia had derived self-respect and pride from a costly decision to close its borders with Rhodesia, Tutu was told by church representatives. The achievements of President Kenneth Kaunda were considerable; he had done a splendid job of welding the country together; and, church leaders claimed, people in detention had only themselves to blame. But rural development had failed badly. Malawi maintained good relations with both its neighbor Zambia, and more distant South Africa, but there was no personal freedom. Under the absolutist life president, Kamuzu Banda, "too many people are whisked away and just disappear. It is a veritable one-man show."

In West Africa, Tutu returned repeatedly in his reports to military coups, to the instability generated by illogical national boundaries imposed by colonial powers, to colonial exploitation, and to Africans' continuing lack of access to economic opportunities. He arrived in Ghana, the first sub-Saharan country to get independence, the day after eight men were sentenced to face a firing squad for an attempted coup against Lieutenant-Colonel Ignatius Kutu Acheampong. People were still disgruntled with the civilian government, Tutu said, so they were prepared to tolerate army rule. Dahomey (now Benin) had experienced seven coups since independence twelve years earlier, he noted in 1972. The instability had frightened away investors, whereas next-door Togo, the site of Africa's first coup in 1963, had a stable albeit repressive government and German and French assistance. After traveling in Nigeria and Cameroon—whose common border divides fourteen ethnic groupings—he commented on how colonisers "did their job only too well to divide us up according to their whims. . . . The colonial powers have often kept together what should have been separated and separated what should have been kept united—with continuing repercussions in today's Africa."

Driving along the coast from Aného in Togo to Cotonou in Dahomey, "I was reflecting on how little all the colonial countries have done for their colonies. . . . They really exploited them and fed back very little of the wealth they bled from these countries. Poverty stares you in the face. . . . It is utterly unrealistic to expect the newly independent countries with a host of problems to tackle all of them equally effectively." He observed popular feeling against Lebanese traders; in Dahomey, he wrote that they were generating the same resentment as Asians did in East Africa. In Sierra Leone, a theologian suggested to him that "they need an Amin for the Lebanese."

Of West Africa generally, he wrote in 1972:

> There is a mood of self-reliance about but of course they are still very dependent on resources from abroad. But there is more pride in being themselves and there is movement, there is life. They will make mistakes but at least they are alive. The colonialists have done something but hardly as much as they could or should have, considering what they got out of their former colonies.

African nations that had long ruled themselves were also a subject of critical comment in Tutu's reports. In Liberia, he found tension between the descendants of freed slaves who had settled the country from the United States in the nineteenth century and the local people they had found there: "There is still this sense of two nations. The Government is actively engaged in a campaign of unification but this will be a slow process and the effects of a two nation 'policy' are only too evident in the relatively undeveloped state of the interior." He was unimpressed by American influence on the country: "I still think it rather pathetic that they should be a pale copy of the U.S. in many of their institutions—U.S. currency, similar flag, speak of Parliament buildings as Capitol, etc. Maybe they will really come into their own one day." In Ethiopia, the capital, Addis Ababa, was

> a mosaic of poverty and affluence, cheek by jowl with each other. . . . The major question is who will succeed the Emperor who is still sprightly at 80 plus—I saw him inspect the guard of honour at Nairobi airport when he and other heads of state were visiting Kenya to celebrate ten years of Uhuru. He has ruled firmly and autocratically and given the country stability. Whether the younger educated ones will contend that there are other things more precious than political stability and be prepared to do something about it, remains to be seen.

In Sudan, Burundi, and Rwanda, Tutu saw the seeds of future strife. In Sudan, conflict between the north and the south which had begun in the 1950s was brought to an end–temporarily, it later turned out–by a peace agreement in 1972. In 1975, he visited Juba in the south, where he found that the emphasis was on unity, reconciliation, and reconstruction. "Some say the rapprochement between the South (largely Christian) and the North (largely Muslim) is very tenuous and fragile and that things are often near breaking point. . . . It is difficult to make a fair assessment. But clearly official attempts and policy are to forge real links between the North and the South."

He was less sanguine about Rwanda and Burundi, where German and Belgian colonizers had highlighted group identity and treated the Tutsi minority as a ruling class. Rwanda was now ruled by the majority Hutu people, Tutu noted in 1973, but well-educated Tutsis held many important positions and students had recently protested against their influence: "They [the students] said positions in government, places in schools and university should reflect ethnic composition of nation, that is Batutsi should be cut down to size. Batutsi are being ousted from influential positions. . . . Some Tutsi have been killed, some expelled from schools." Neighboring Burundi, on the other hand, was ruled by the Tutsi minority:

Eighty-five percent of the population are made up of Bahutu who form the base of the socio-political pyramid with the Batutsi at the summit. . . . When they could not stand being the underdog any longer, the Bahutu attempted the coup of 1972. . . . The Government set up a systematic and ruthless campaign of reprisal against the Bahutu. All actual and potential leadership was exterminated. There are mass graves where schoolboys, teachers, doctors, nurses etc. are buried. The Anglicans lost about a quarter of their pastors, the Baptists 50 percent. The Anglican bishop lost a son and son-in-law while his driver lost a father and four brothers. Estimates vary as to the number killed. Some say 60,000, others say up to 200,000. There is a staggering number of widows and fatherless children. It was a ruthless attempt at genocide. The government is in full control but an illiterate Mohutu is reported as saying that they would never forget what happened. Their children would never forget and their children would merely bide their time waiting for the opportunity to wreak revenge.

The metaphor of the underdog biding his time before taking revenge lodged itself in Tutu's mind, to reemerge more than twenty years later as a theme running through his addresses during a high-profile mission to Rwanda after the genocide of 1994.

Touring seminaries and universities, Tutu dealt extensively with the expatriate western theological teachers whose replacement the grants he was dispensing were meant to facilitate. He welcomed the sensitivity of expatriates who showed an awareness of the need for indigenous teachers, and railed against those who lived in privilege. A Protestant seminary in Ethiopia evidently reminded him of the favored treatment enjoyed by white professors at Fort Hare: "Why do the expatriates live in so much better homes, segregated by a green belt from the village where the national staff live? Because the mission boards pay the rents for the missionaries and the nationals can't afford the rents. Well, damn the mission boards."

Tutu's theology was fundamentally transformed in the early 1970s in response to a range of influences: his brush with police brutality at Fort Hare, his exposure to the nascent philosophy of black consciousness, his firsthand observation of Africa's successes and failures, his debates with African theologians, and his contact with the exponents of new theologies—in particular, with the TEF's associate director for Latin America, Aharon Sapsezian, who introduced him to liberation theology.

Although Tutu was deeply grateful to King's in London for his education, his respect for his teachers' academic rigor was not necessarily matched by an admiration of their worldview. He has told of how, exploring further study, he raised with Geoffrey Parrinder the possibility of writing a doctoral thesis on black theology:

He [Parrinder] replied, quite seriously, "What is black theology?" He asked the question in a tone of voice that made it clear he had no doubt at all that it was obvious there could be no such entity. He had the unconscious arrogance of one who expected everyone to know that there really was only one kind of theology and that was theology as practised by himself and those like him, Caucasian and overwhelmingly male.

In conference papers and articles, Tutu came to reject as a fallacy the view that any theology, western or other, could be universally applicable. He argued that theology had to be "contextual"—it had to take into account the context in which believers lived. Western theologians, Tutu said, were looking for answers to questions that Africans were not asking. In England in the 1960s, his fellow students were wrestling with how to minister in a society that, under the influence of scientific progress and of interpretations which denied the transcendent, was losing its belief in God. In the west, people were embarrassed to talk about God. Some spoke of the "death of God." In his book *Honest to God,* John Robinson was trying to redefine God in ways that would make sense to westerners. Linguistic philosophy was in vogue; students examined the grammar of religious language, asking what it meant to say, "God exists." This was a legitimate exercise for western Christians, Tutu said, but it was irrelevant for Africans: "Our people did not doubt that God existed and they knew perfectly well what God meant. Nor did they need to be convinced that God was good and omnipotent."

For Tutu, there were two all-consuming questions for African Christians: first, how to replace an alien, imported way of expressing their faith with one that was authentically African; and second, how to liberate people from bondage. In South Africa, blacks were not concerned with the standard theological question of why God allowed evil and suffering in the world: "No, what they wanted to know was–why did this exquisite and excruciating suffering seem to isolate and concentrate so particularly on them?" To answer these questions, he became an advocate of two closely related but distinct schools of theology at the time: African and black. African theology, largely developed for countries that had already achieved political liberation, focused on freeing Christians from colonial cultural influences extraneous to faith. Black theology was initiated by African-American theologians in response to racism in the United States and addressed situations in which blacks were still politically oppressed.

Drawing on the exponents of African theology, Tutu said that African Christians were suffering from a kind of schizophrenia. Missionaries had expected them to become westerners before they could become Christians: "They had to deny their African-ness to become genuine Christians. . . . Virtually all things African were condemned as pagan and to be destroyed root and branch. They even had to adopt so-called Christian names at baptism because their beautiful African names were considered heathen." Most African Christians accepted this cerebrally, he said, but their psyche had been damaged by it: "African Christians . . . were shuttling back and forth between two worlds, during the day being respectable western-type Christians and at night consulting traditional doctors and slaughtering to the ancestors under the euphemisms of a 'party.' " To counter the missionaries' thinking, Tutu noted similarities between African and Old Testament concepts of God. The biblical worldview was much more congenial to Africans than to westerners, he said. Africans and Israelites shared the same thought world in their respect for their ancestors: "The African would understand perfectly well what the Old Testament meant when it said 'man belongs to the bundle of life,' that he is not a solitary individual. He is linked backwards to the ancestors whom he reveres and forward with all the generations yet unborn."

African theology had done a good job in addressing the "split in the African soul," Tutu said. "African theology has given the lie to the belief that worthwhile religion in Africa had to await the advent of the white man." But it had not gone far enough: "I fear that African theology has failed to produce a sufficiently sharp cutting edge. . . . Very little has been offered that is pertinent, say, about the theology of power in the face of the epidemic of coups and military rule, about development, about poverty." His solution was to graft black theology onto African theology. Black theology resonated strongly with black South Africans, but not always with proponents of African theology from liberated Africa. John Mbiti, an East African theologian, attacked it as a foreign import from the United States, of no direct relevance to Africa. He said it was "full of sorrow, bitterness, anger and hatred. . . . It speaks of a black God, Black Church, Black Liberation, Black this and Black that." Color was not a theological concept in the scriptures, said Mbiti. Black theology arose from the color-consciousness of American society, and it was a judgment on American Christianity. It deserved a hearing only in South Africa, where racial oppression was similar to that in the United States.

Tutu, whose first visit to the United States was for a conference on African and black theology at Union Theological Seminary in New York in 1973, did not agree with Mbiti. His most powerful defense of black theology, a paper never previously published, was written a few months after the conference in New York. It is worth quoting in some detail, not least because of the insight it gives into how within a few years he became simultaneously a defiantly outspoken advocate for black South Africans and an emotional exponent of reconciliation with whites.

Opening the paper, Tutu asked rhetorically: Why so much emphasis on black? He answered himself in a passage that might just as easily have come from the pen of Steve Biko:

It does not need much intelligence to realise that most reactions to blackness are negative ones. This is borne out to a great degree by language. When one is in a rotten mood, then one is in a black mood; the bad exception is the black sheep. In most Christian religious art, the good angels are white, the devil and his angels are black. Black is generally associated with death, white with purity and life. . . . The trouble with all these cultural reactions and customs is how easily they help to condition humans. It starts off as an innocent enough human characteristic, but soon it develops, as it has most certainly done in this instance, to a general denigration of things black and of black persons. When this happens for long enough it is not long before you, a black person, wonder whether you are not as they depict you. You begin, deep down, to have doubts about your own humanity. It sounds melodramatic. I wish it were. . . . We blacks have been defined too often in the white man's terms—we are non-white, non-European—negatives.

In a reaction against this, he continued:

The term "black" has been quite deliberately adopted so that we can describe ourselves positively. It is an assertion of our personhood, our identity in its own right, not [against] . . . anyone else. We are declaring to ourselves or to anybody else who cares to listen, that we are fundamentally subjects, not objects, persons, not things. Each one of us is an "I" not an "it." We have to say this over and over again . . . until we believe it and can act as if we really did believe in our own dignity and humanity. . . . The white man has, up to now, perhaps unconsciously yet certainly, sought to determine our existence. . . . So we use black as an epithet here because we are black; because we are each somebody. We matter, we are alive and kicking and black *is* beautiful.

Black theology repudiated western arrogance, wrote Tutu. It made no claim to be universal or final, since any theology was a product of its time.

Black theology is an engaged not an academic, detached theology. It is a gut level theology, relating to the real concerns, the life and death issues of the black man. If the white man is so made that he finds it genuinely difficult to understand the meaning of apparently straightforward sentences . . . such as "God loves you," then perhaps the white theologian is justified in being concerned with Wittgenstein, with verification principle et al. . . . Black theology seeks to make sense of the life experience of the black man, which is largely black suffering at the hands of rampant white racism, and to understand this in the light of what God has said about himself, about man, and about the world in his very definitive Word. . . . Black theology has to do with whether it is possible to be black and continue to be Christian; it is to ask on whose side is God; it is to be concerned about the humanisation of man, because those who ravage our humanity dehumanise themselves in the process; [it says] that the liberation of the black man is the other side of the coin of the liberation of the white man—so it is concerned with human liberation. It is a clarion call for man to align himself with the God who is the God of the Exodus, God the liberator, who leads his people, all his people, out of all kinds of bondage—political, economic, cultural, the bondage of sin and disease, into the glorious liberty of the sons of God.

Black might be beautiful, he continued, but it was not automatically morally superior:

Black theology is not so naïve as to think that white oppression is the only bondage from which the blacks need to be liberated. Sin and evil are as dehumanising as white racism (a peculiar manifestation of sin and evil) and . . . white racism does not exhaust all sin and evil. When the white oppressor is removed, far too often he is succeeded by his black counterpart.

In a statement presaging the outspokenness that led him into trouble from the time he returned to Johannesburg, Tutu said his paper was not a plea for acceptance or a demonstration of the academic respectability of black theology:

No, it is just a straightforward, perhaps shrill, statement about an existent. Black theology is. No permission is being requested for it to come into being. . . . Frankly the time has passed when we will wait for the white man to give us permission to do our thing. Whether or not he accepts the intellectual respectability of our activity is largely irrelevant. We will proceed regardless.

That Tutu would not wait for whites to give him permission to act became apparent soon after he was recalled to South Africa to become the first black dean of Johannesburg in 1975.

CHAPTER 8

BLOODY CONFRONTATION

A month after the Sharpeville massacre in 1960, an American official of the World Council of Churches (WCC) visited South Africa to consult with the council's member churches there. At the time, the WCC still included the white Dutch Reformed church synods, which provided a theological justification for apartheid, as well as the multiracial churches of British origin that opposed it. Reporting on the latter to his colleagues, the official wrote: "The English-speaking churches are maintaining positions of courage on the apartheid issue, but are the victims of much phariseeism because they do not back up their statements with anything like commensurate action. This is a spiritual problem for them of deep proportions." Not only did the churches fail to act on their statements; they elected very few black leaders. In the Anglican church, three-quarters of whose members were black, Alphaeus Zulu was in 1974 still the only black diocesan bishop. His diocese, Zululand, was largely rural. Control of the dioceses in South Africa's wealthiest metropolitan areas was firmly in white hands. It came as a surprise, therefore, when Desmond Tutu emerged as a top candidate to replace Leslie Stradling as bishop of Johannesburg.

Choosing a bishop for the Anglican church in southern Africa is an event surrounded by lobbying, drama, and even intrigue. Unlike the Church of England, for which bishops are selected by the government after consultation with the church, the church in South Africa elects its leaders. Representatives from every parish meet in an elective assembly to debate the strengths—and sometimes the weaknesses—of the candidates. In the Episcopal Church in the United States, bishops contend publicly for office; but in South Africa the election is secret. Adding to the sense of occasion, members of an assembly know that if they make a mistake, they cannot vote their choice out of office; unless elected by another diocese, a bishop serves until retirement, often for fifteen or twenty years. To be elected, a candidate needs two-thirds of

the votes of the clergy and two-thirds of the votes of lay members of
the assembly, representing ordinary church members. This requirement, while ensuring there is consensus on a new bishop, leads easily
to deadlocks. In a country as divided as South Africa was in the 1970s
and 1980s, it could turn elections–in the words of Peter Lee, the historian of the Johannesburg diocese–into "racial battlegrounds."

Tutu–still based in London–was the only black candidate as Johannesburg's elective assembly convened on a public holiday, Settlers'
Day, in September 1974. The assembly was chaired by Bill Burnett,
who had recently replaced Selby Taylor as archbishop of Cape Town.
Tutu was nominated by Leo Rakale, a member of the Community of
the Resurrection; and seconded by Aelred Stubbs, his old mentor. "I
was sure he would make a good bishop," Stubbs has said. "It wasn't
just a racial gimmick." In a biographical sketch compiled for the election, the assembly's advisory committee said Tutu was a priest with a
strong personality, had outstanding academic qualifications and was an
impressive speaker. "Being an extrovert, he is an easy mixer," it added.
"He has pastoral gifts, especially towards students, and is an experienced ecumenist. Widely travelled, he has a knowledge of people,
administration and current thinking in other parts of the world." Of the
other seven candidates nominated, four were already bishops elsewhere and three were leaders in their dioceses. A newspaper in Johannesburg said that "whether [Tutu] commands much backing is
questionable." Yet when voting began after three hours of debate,
Tutu drew the second highest number of votes among clergy and lay
representatives. The records of the assembly, filed in the church's
archives, show that Mark Wood, a bishop from what was then Rhodesia, drew one vote more than Tutu among the clergy; and John Carter,
the suffragan (assistant) bishop of Johannesburg, drew twenty votes
more among the laity. In the two succeeding ballots, Tutu's support did
not increase; in fact it dropped slightly among the laity. Wood and
Carter, however, picked up the votes of the candidates who were
eliminated. Then Stubbs intervened to propose that debate be
reopened. Against opposition, he prevailed. Participants in the assembly do not recall what he or other speakers said, but Tutu surged into
first place in the next round of voting. By the fifth ballot, he had double the number of votes of either of his opponents. He was, however,
well short of a two-thirds majority. The assembly adjourned for supper.

What happened during the supper break is still a matter of controversy. Black members suspected that whites lobbied to stop Tutu.

What is certain is that when the assembly reconvened, two white members nominated Timothy Bavin, who as dean of Johannesburg was the diocese's most senior priest. Bavin, an expatriate from England, had been dean for less than two years. He had earlier refused to stand; but the rules said that a nominee need not signify acceptance, and his supporters successfully proposed that the proceedings should continue without his being asked whether he would accept. The assembly debated the candidates anew, and voting resumed. In the sixth ballot, Bavin won massive support from the clergy. Tutu was the main loser among both clergy and laity. In successive ballots late into the night, Bavin's support grew steadily. After the eighth ballot, in which Bavin overtook Tutu for the first time, Burnett sought to invoke the Holy Spirit by asking the assembly to sing the hymn "Veni Creator" ("Come Holy Ghost"). Bavin won a two-thirds majority among the laity on the ninth ballot and among the clergy on the tenth. Asked by Burnett whether he accepted the election, Bavin consented.

Thirty years later some of the black clergy in the diocese of Johannesburg, believing that Bavin had blocked Tutu's election, had still not forgiven him. In fact, a comparison of voting figures with the racial composition of the assembly suggests that when Bavin was nominated, the assembly was headed not for Tutu's election but for a deadlock, created by the refusal of white lay Anglicans to accept him. Hearing the news in London, Tutu wrote to his college friend Stanley Mogoba: "Johannesburg rejected me. But I am glad mainly because they had to consider a black candidate as a very serious contender." Many years later, after serving as Bavin's successor, Tutu suggested that God had been wise: "Had I been elected at that point [1974], I am sure the shock to the system would have been a great deal more traumatic than it turned out to be in 1984, and that was quite something. The Diocese could so easily then have disintegrated."

One of Timothy Bavin's first tasks as bishop was to nominate his successor as dean and rector of St. Mary's Cathedral. He wanted to propose a black candidate to the cathedral council for two reasons: the congregation had been integrated for some years, and he felt that the way had been prepared by his own predecessor as dean, Gonville ffrench-Beytagh. He did not know Tutu but, probably influenced by the support Tutu had received in the election, decided to nominate him.

Since Desmond had started working at the head office of the Theological Education Fund (TEF) in Bromley, Kent, the Tutu family had put down roots in the area. They had taken the first steps toward buying the home in which they lived, a semidetached house in a middle-class part of nearby southeast London. Between trips for the TEF, Desmond acted as an honorary curate at St. Augustine's Church, Grove Park, around the corner from their home. The family was popular in the congregation; Naomi and Mpho were "a real pair of comics, lively, mischievous and very popular with other children," in the recollection of one parishioner; and Trevor was remembered for publicly praying for the impeachment of Richard Nixon. Desmond was known for calling worshippers after church to "roll up, roll up, get your holy handshakes" and for what the vicar of St. Augustine's, Charles Cartwright, described as his "infectious sense of gaiety and joy." Leah enrolled in adult education classes, taking yoga and psychology courses and learning automobile maintenance to help her cope during Desmond's frequent absences. She made friends through the children. Trevor was at a university close to home: Imperial College, London. Thandi, Naomi, and Mpho were at good schools, living at home. Leah was later to describe the time as one of the happiest of her life.

Against this backdrop, Bavin's invitation to Tutu precipitated a family crisis. Faced with the prospect of returning to apartheid and separation from her children again, Leah literally cried on the shoulder of Desmond's personal assistant, Betty Ward. "I had soaking wet shoulders," Ward recalled. "I remember very distinctly her saying, 'Over here I can do what I like. In South Africa I have to walk off the pavement if a white person is coming towards me.' " Leah and Desmond agonized over the decision for weeks. One evening, Leah walked out of the house on what she called a "private protest march." Asking Bill Burnett for advice, Desmond said that apart from the issue of the children's education he faced a substantial drop in income. Burnett replied that he understood the reservations and that the job would not be an easy one: "I think your coming would, however, be a clear personal witness to the Lordship of Jesus in your own life and also a proclamation by the Church that He is Lord." In Desmond's recollection, the response of the children was decisive: "We said this must be a family decision. The children said, 'Daddy, you must go back.' " Desmond told Timothy Bavin his name could go forward to the cathedral council. Leah continued to be strongly opposed: "Leah was very, very upset: It strained our marriage very much."

Tutu was elected as dean by the council of St. Mary's Cathedral on a Friday evening in March 1975. By Saturday, a day ahead of the scheduled announcement at Sunday services, the news had leaked out, and the election of the first black dean of a South African cathedral was making headlines in the South African press. A few days later Tutu told a London correspondent of a South African newspaper group that he would refuse to apply for government permission to live in the dean's official residence in the white suburb of Houghton. He categorically rejected being treated as an "honorary white," he said: "I do not want to apologise for my blackness." It was not apparent at the time, but he had begun one of the most extensive, high-pressure, prominent public ministries of any church leader of his generation.

At this point in Tutu's life, as he stepped onto the public stage, it is possible to identify the attributes that were to sustain and drive his work from then on. He assumed leadership as a South African of mixed ethnic heritage, raised in the country's most cosmopolitan metropolis, fluent in six of the country's languages, and thus—because of their similarities—able to communicate with the speakers of nine. He had personal experience of the destructive consequences of apartheid. He had the compassion of his mother, becoming an emotional, caring pastor who intuitively felt the plight of the weak and burned with outrage at abuses of power by the strong. He inherited African spirituality, which he expressed through an ordered, deliberately paced structure of praise and prayer learned from western monastic tradition. A well-educated twentieth-century theologian, acquainted with New Testament Greek and Hebrew—and a little Arabic and French—he accepted modern biblical scholarship, rejected simple fundamentalism, but never questioned his belief in God and was comfortable with traditional "God talk." He was a cross-cultural communicator with an ebullient personality, as much at ease in western as in African settings. He had experienced the issues of working in an institution that tried at the same time both to repudiate apartheid and to survive in a police state. An exponent of black self-assertiveness and black leadership, he was nevertheless committed to cooperation with whites, in church and national life. As an African, he was thrilled at the liberation of the continent from colonial control but had firsthand experience of its challenges and failures which was shared by very few South Africans.

Tutu was installed as dean by Timothy Bavin in St. Mary's Cathedral on August 31, 1975. The cathedral was filled to capacity. Archbishop Karekin Sarkissian of the Armenian Orthodox Church, the chairman of the TEF, traveled to Johannesburg for the service. The service was glorious and the music superb, Tutu wrote afterward. A senior priest in Johannesburg declared it a magnificent service and act of worship, at the end of which "I wanted to shout aloud."

Trevor and Thandi had remained in London, Trevor at his university and Thandi to complete her schooling. Desmond, Leah, and the younger girls—when they were not at school in Swaziland—went to live eighteen kilometers (11 miles) out of town in Soweto, a vast collection of twenty-eight townships southwest of the city. Whether compared with the mansions of Houghton which the Tutus had forgone, or with the smaller homes of white middle- and working-class suburbs south of Johannesburg, Soweto was poor. Nobody knew exactly how many people lived there, but estimates were around 1.5 million. Nearly half the workers of Africa's richest city lived below the poverty line. They lived in what they called "matchbox" houses, most with no ceilings or bathrooms. Many had running water only from a tap outside in the yard. Most had no electricity and thus no hot running water. Lighting in houses was by candles or paraffin lamps, but the streets were lit by powerful lights at the top of huge masts dotted throughout the townships. Cooking was done on coal fires. In winter, smoke hung over the streets until mid-morning, so that taxis and cars going to work had to keep their lights on hours after the sun was up. In August, the strong winds of early spring dusted the townships with the fine yellow sand of nearby mine dumps. Crime was far higher than in heavily policed white Johannesburg, with fifteen to twenty people murdered every weekend.

The Tutus moved into a house owned by the cathedral, but not before it was enlarged. "The diocese was very bad with its accommodation for black priests," said Tutu. "They were preparing jerry-built places for clergy." The renovated house, situated in a cluster of modest middle-class homes on the side of a hill in the township of Orlando West, was comparatively luxurious: other Sowetans called the area "Beverly Hills." Around the corner from the Tutus was the matchbox home of Nelson Mandela, in which Winnie Madikizela Mandela had lived since her husband had been jailed.

Saint Mary's was in the Johannesburg city center, near the main railway station. The congregation had been established while the city was still a gold mining camp, and the cathedral was built after Johannesburg became a separate diocese in the 1920s. When Tutu arrived, a twenty-two-story building of shops, offices, and apartments adjoining the church, planned by ffrench-Beytagh and completed under Bavin, was filling up with tenants. The congregation, numbering 1,500, was well regarded in the diocese for its social concern, its liveliness in keeping its clergy accountable, and the strength of its traditional forms of worship—although it was seen as weak in pastoral visiting, in youth work, and in evangelism. It had become multiracial in the 1960s after a nearby black church closed down and the congregations merged. Tutu came to find it still largely white, particularly on Sunday mornings. Nevertheless, as the mother church of the diocese, it was the central venue where black and white Anglicans met in Johannesburg. Services in nearly all the diocese's other churches were segregated in practice if not by policy—residents of black townships went to churches near their homes, as did whites in their suburbs; and domestic workers in the suburbs usually attended separate Sunday afternoon services conducted in indigenous languages.

Announcing Tutu's appointment, St. Mary's parish magazine said that to a committed Christian, it should make no difference whether he was "black, white or pink." The only concern should be whether he could lead effectively, and he had a seven-year term in which to prove himself. In his first letter to the parish, Tutu said he was committed to reconciliation:

> But I am certainly not committed to a cheap reconciliation. Real reconciliation cost God the death of his Son and if we are to be instruments of his peace then we must know what we are about, that we must be ready to be marked with the Cross of reconciliation, that we have to identify as Our Lord identified, with the down and out, the drug addict, the homosexual, the prostitute, the poor and downtrodden.

He followed up by suggesting that on Fridays there should be services of penitence for the sins of racism and injustice: "All our efforts in this direction," he emphasized, "must be based on the Word of God and be informed and inspired by God the Holy Spirit himself."

Denunciations of injustice were not new at St. Mary's. Ffrench-Beytagh had been outspoken against apartheid. In 1970, after he made news by arguing against a synod resolution condemning grants by the World Council of Churches to liberation movements, the government decided to demonstrate Vorster's point that antiapartheid clergy would not be protected by their status. Police planted ANC and Communist Party pamphlets in his home, then arrested him and charged him

under the Terrorism Act with furthering the aims of the ANC. The trial
court sentenced him to five years in prison for inciting people to violence and for helping the families of political prisoners. The appellate
division of the Supreme Court overturned the convictions, saying that
ffrench-Beytagh had warned of violence, not advocated it, and that in
helping prisoners' families he had not acted, as charged, with "intent to
endanger the maintenance of law and order."

The congregation was politically divided, especially over the pronouncements of the clergy. One parishioner, Noël Whitman, set off a
months-long controversy in the pages of the parish magazine with a
complaint about a sermon by Norman Montjane, the priest who had
taken Naomi Tutu to London in 1963. Whitman wrote:

> Firstly I would very much like to know where the fact that Johannes-
> burg "was built on the blood of the black man" was unearthed. . . . I
> find it most unfitting that the Cathedral pulpit be used as a political
> shouting ground. Surely one goes to the Cathedral, or any church for
> that matter, for the purpose of getting something of a spiritual nature
> from the services and not to be made to feel guilty of the colour one
> was born.

Taking issue with a statement by Tutu that white South Africans were
part of a prosperous minority in the world, Whitman asked: "Do we
really need all this jargon about the 2nd and 3rd worlds? Besides
which, it is the so-called pampered minority which keeps the developing nations off the starvation line because of their own bad management."

Despite such views, Tutu experienced no hostility from the congregation: "They were as accepting as they could be," he reflected later.
They were worried at first that he would not be allowed to perform
marriages for whites, but he was granted a government licence to do
so. In an absurd quirk of apartheid law, he could marry a white couple
or a couple classified as Coloured, but he needed a special government
exemption to marry a black couple. Conducting marriages across the
color line would have been a contravention of the Prohibition of
Mixed Marriages Act. As soon as outsiders came into the cathedral for
special services, or Tutu moved outside the precincts, he encountered
intensified racism. At a service organized for a national day of prayer
and repentance, a white woman asked, in a reference to Tutu: "What

is that boy doing there?" On visits to parishioners in their apartments near the cathedral, he was shown the tradesmen's entrances.

The cathedral had a racially mixed staff. Tutu appointed as his subdean a man eighteen years his senior, a priest widely loved and respected in the diocese. Leo Rakale, who came from a well-known clerical family, had been the first black monk to join the Community of the Resurrection, and had been a spiritual adviser to Winnie Mandela through the years of loneliness and police harassment that followed the jailing of her husband. He was also the priest upon whom Alan Paton modeled the character in *Cry the Beloved Country* who spoke the novel's best-known lines: "I have one great fear in my heart, that one day when they [whites] are turned to loving, they will find we [blacks] are turned to hating."*

Tutu's principal overt struggle with his congregation concerned not politics but updating the services. Prescribed forms of worship, published in a Book of Common Prayer originating in the sixteenth century, are central to Anglican tradition; and the cathedral was proud of its high standards in liturgy and in formal western church music. The South African church had just supplemented its South African Prayer Book of 1954 with an experimental update of important services under the title Liturgy 75. At a superficial level, this involved changes such as addressing God using "you" and "your" instead of "Thou," "Thee," and "Thy." The cathedral had adopted Liturgy 75 for smaller services but continued to use the old prayer book for high mass on Sundays. Tutu acknowledged that the new liturgy sometimes used inelegant language, but he argued that it introduced "symphony-like movement" into the service, drew worshippers in as participants, and made better use of the scriptures and of collective silence. "Please let's not bicker too much about essentially domestic matters because the world will pass us by as utterly irrelevant," he pleaded. The congregation was not persuaded: four months after his appeal, more than 80 percent of the parishioners voted against Liturgy 75. Tutu decided he had more important priorities than wasting his energy fighting them over it.

Six months into his seven-year term as dean, Tutu was asked to stand for election as bishop of Lesotho. John Maund, an expatriate who had served for twenty-five years, was retiring. While teaching at

---

* In an interview for an obituary on Rakale, Paton suggested to the present writer that although Rakale never used the phrase attributed to the character Theophilus Msimangu, it was the sort of observation he might have made.

the university in Roma, Tutu had been a member of Lesotho's diocesan synod, and lay Anglicans who were part of the country's political and social elite had been impressed. Once, during heated debate on a proposal to sanction the use of contraceptives, Desmond warned the synod against losing touch with society. In the recollection of Philip Mokuku, one of the clergy, Tutu spoke "so lovingly, so gently" that he brought the meeting around to his view. Desmond believed that Leah's reputation for hospitality while they were living at Roma had as much to do with his nomination as anything; she enjoyed entertaining visitors attending meetings at the university in their campus home.

For the Tutus, returning to Lesotho was almost unthinkable. Leah had taken on work for the Domestic Workers' and Employers' Project of the Institute of Race Relations, defending the interests of domestic workers in Johannesburg. Desmond was immersed in everyday cathedral life, beating the traffic into the city by driving in for the six-thirty or seven AM Eucharist. He loved the continued coming and going of visitors who rested in the gray stone church, stopping to pray for a few minutes on the way to or from work, or just setting down heavy shopping bags on their way to catch trains to the townships. Seeing children of all races "playing, praying, and learning and even fighting together, almost uniquely in South Africa," brought a lump to his throat. As he sat in his dean's stall watching a multiracial crowd listening to a racially mixed choir, then receiving communion from a mixed group of ministers, "tears sometimes streamed down my cheeks, tears of joy that it could be that indeed Jesus Christ had broken down the wall of partition."* He had thought he was coming back to South Africa mainly to reassure blacks that God loved them and they should assert themselves; he found that "in many ways it was whites who needed to hear this message about self-assurance and self-acceptance, that oppression dehumanized the oppressor as much as, if not more than, the oppressed."

Passionate about reconciliation, he had also slipped quickly into a public role in Johannesburg. In his first weeks as dean, he shared a platform with Winnie Mandela, where he set out theological reasons why Christians should oppose the Terrorism Act. Soon afterward he organized at the cathedral a twenty-four-hour prayer vigil for racial harmony, at which special prayers were said for people detained without

---

* A biblical reference to the wall that separated Jew from Gentile in the Temple in Jerusalem, Ephesians 2:14.

trial under the Terrorism Act. He established a symbiotic relationship with the press, one that he was to maintain and strengthen, at least with the antiapartheid media, throughout his public life. On his side, he felt that Johannesburg's English-language press was actively willing him to succeed; for their part, the journalists found him open, accessible, and articulate.

Tutu turned down the nomination for Lesotho, and appeared in a headline in the Johannesburg press as "THE DEAN WHO DOESN'T WANT TO LEAVE." Anglicans refused to take no for an answer. B. M. Khaketla, a political leader who was a former privy councilor to King Moshoeshoe II, led a delegation to Soweto to press him to stand. Khaketla told him he would not be in Maseru long—the diocese of Lesotho would be a stepping-stone to his election as archbishop of Cape Town. Leah did not want to move, but she and some family friends felt that Desmond would appear arrogant if he refused even to be considered. So he said simultaneously both that he would not decline the nomination and that he did not want to be elected. In the elective assembly in Maseru in March 1976, he was the candidate favored by lay voters from the beginning, almost reaching the requisite two-thirds majority in the first round of voting. The votes of the clergy were more evenly spread. After five ballots, most of the clergy were divided between Tutu and another candidate. Tutu's candidacy steadily gained support in successive votes, and he was elected on the eleventh ballot in the middle of the second day. The assembly adjourned to await his response.

Tutu was at a meeting in Pietermaritzburg in Natal when the telephone call he was dreading came. A little over a year after wrestling over whether to become dean, he was again faced with an agonizing choice. He said later: "There have been very few occasions when I have had such a feeling of being torn apart. Which way should I go? What is God's will for me?"

This time he had to decide overnight. He returned to Johannesburg, and he and Leah went to see Timothy Bavin the following morning. "I was crying, I think he was saying, 'Well, the Lord has spoken and you have to go.' I was looking for somebody who was going to say, 'We think you shouldn't.'" The assembly in Maseru reconvened in the afternoon to hear that he had consented. That night, he flew to London, en route to a meeting of the Anglican Consultative Council, an international consultative body, in Trinidad and Tobago. As he flew north, he wept again.

In a message Tutu left to be read in the cathedral on Sunday, he told his congregation he was "deeply desolated. . . . It has been one long agony. I hope you will all understand my decision, even if you do not agree with it." Supporting him, Bavin alluded to the fact that the congregation would have to adjust to its third new dean in four years. The Tutus did not want to go any more than the congregation wanted them to leave, he wrote. The fact that the assembly had elected Tutu knowing he would probably refuse made it seem that the hand of God was in what had happened. In a later farewell, Bavin said: "One man has—by God's grace—done more for the cause of justice, peace and reconciliation in this Diocese and City than many of us have achieved in many years . . . and that in less than a year."

In the four months between Tutu's election and his consecration as bishop, his unhappiness at having to leave the country grew rather than abated. As he read the mood of the black community, South Africa was on the verge of an explosion. His fear was based on intuition rather than analysis, but scholars and journalists have since enumerated the conditions that made a violent eruption likely in 1976. In Soweto, apart from poor living conditions, there were housing shortages. Rigid civil servants from the central government exacerbated tensions after they took administrative control of the townships away from municipal authorities. Throughout the country, black South Africans had been excluded from the decade of economic growth that followed the suppression of resistance in 1964. In the 1970s, prices rose, unemployment grew, and the quadrupling of international oil prices brought on a recession. At the same time, there was a resurgence of black political and labor mobilization. Activists of the black consciousness movement began to organize. A spontaneous outbreak of strikes at factories beginning in Durban in 1973, marked the first mass expression of dissent in nearly a decade. Academics now argue over the relative importance of these developments, but all agree on the significance to South African contemporary history of a military coup in Portugal in 1974.

Until 1975, a buffer of white-ruled countries to the north lay between South Africa and the independent African countries that became hosts of the liberation movements. Joe Slovo, the Communist Party leader and a member of the ANC's Revolutionary Council, has said that although by the mid-1970s the ANC had sent between 800 and 1,000 members for military training, "there wasn't a shot fired in anger in South Africa." In a study based on extensive interviews with the

ANC's military leaders, the journalist and former ANC activist Howard Barrell judged that by 1974 the ANC was "a near irrelevance inside South Africa." The dynamics changed when the Portuguese armed forces, drained by long wars against liberation movements in African colonies, overthrew their country's dictatorship and gave independence to Angola and Mozambique. Black South Africans were jubilant. State repression and the ANC's focus on armed struggle had left the movement without significant clandestine political networks, but black-consciousness leaders organized rallies to celebrate Mozambique's freedom. Vorster gave the appearance of shifting ground. He pursued détente with Zambia and encouraged whites in Rhodesia to negotiate with liberation movements. The alternative to a peaceful settlement was, he said, "too ghastly to contemplate."

Vorster's maneuvering to placate independent African states was accompanied by a characteristically blunt declaration that within South Africa there would be no negotiation: "In white South Africa, the whites will rule, and let there be no mistake about that." He continued with plans to make the Transkei region of the Eastern Cape the first "independent" Bantustan in 1976, stripping Xhosa-speakers of their South African citizenship and forcing "citizenship" in the Transkei on them. A liberal newspaper in Johannesburg, the *Rand Daily Mail,* which published its editorials on the front page on Saturdays, took the unusual step of giving the space to Tutu on May 1, 1976. He addressed himself to whites:

> I speak with words I hope I have chosen carefully–the issue of Transkeian citizenship is highly explosive. Blacks are being provoked beyond human endurance. . . . Do you want to make us really desperate? I have warned before and I reiterate this warning with all seriousness that desperate people will be compelled to use desperate means. . . . We don't want a bloody confrontation. I mean this with all my heart. Please do not provoke us into despair and hopelessness. Please for God's sake.

The following Monday, Tutu joined other members of the clergy from the diocese of Johannesburg in a five-day silent retreat in the church's exclusive boys' school, St. John's College, Houghton. He entered the retreat in a welter of emotions, engendered both by his impending move to Lesotho and by his sense of foreboding for the country. In a schoolboy's cell-like room, he felt called by God to write a personal plea to John Vorster. Tutu was sensitive to the implications of claiming to be inspired by God: "What do you say to justify that it is from God? The Old Testament is full of strictures against false prophets. . . . How are you able to distinguish between what is genuinely from God and what is merely personal predilection?" Yet whether or not others judged his actions as divinely inspired, he had no doubt that God acts in history. At St. John's, he was meant to be meditating and praying, not writing letters, but "I felt this pressure, I had to do this and just sat at my desk. It more or less wrote itself."

In the 2,600-word letter, he addressed the authoritarian Afrikaner leader as a family man—"I am writing to you, Sir, because I know you to be a loving and caring father and husband, a doting grandfather"—and as a fellow Christian and a victim of British imperialism: "Your people, more than any other section of the community, must surely know that in the very core of their beings . . . that absolutely nothing will stop a people from attaining their freedom." Blacks, he said, could not understand why white South Africans from many different European countries were treated as one nation, yet blacks were deemed under apartheid to form several. Black South Africans were grateful for what had been done for them, but were now claiming an inalienable right to do things for themselves. "Freedom, Sir, is indivisible," Tutu wrote, "the whites of this land will not be free until all sections of our community are genuinely free." Blacks had tried to assure whites that they would not be driven into the sea: "How long can they go on giving these assurances and have them thrown back in their faces with contempt? They say even the worm will turn." Then came the words that were to earn for Tutu the reputation of predicting the Soweto uprising six weeks later:

> I am writing to you, Sir, because I have a growing nightmarish fear that unless something drastic is done very soon then bloodshed and violence are going to happen in South Africa almost inevitably. A people can take only so much and no more. . . . I am frightened, dreadfully frightened, that we may soon reach a point of no return, when events will generate a momentum of their own, when nothing will stop their reaching bloody denouement which is "too ghastly to contemplate," to quote your words, Sir.

Tutu said he recognized that politics was the art of the possible and that Vorster could not move too far ahead of his constituency.

So blacks were ready to accept "some meaningful signs," which would demonstrate a commitment to peaceful change. Tutu cited three: accept blacks as South Africans with the right to live in urban areas, instead of as units of labor who could be arbitrarily shipped back to Bantustans; repeal the pass laws; and call a national convention of leaders recognized by their communities "to work out an orderly evolution of South Africa into a nonracial, open and just society." This included leaders in jail, Tutu said later: "Most of our people have always recognised men like Nelson Mandela and Robert Sobukwe as our true leaders."

In the weeks after sending the letter, Tutu took every opportunity to warn and cajole. He publicly supported an economic boycott to put pressure on the government: "You hear people say the blacks will be the first to be hit. Rubbish! What do you think is happening right now—they are suffering and for no purpose. At least an economic boycott would provide a purpose." At a synod of the diocese of Johannesburg, he and a white delegate proposed a resolution praising Vorster for promoting a settlement in Zimbabwe but saying that external détente had to be matched with internal détente. The resolution condemned the proposal to force Transkeian citizenship on people and adopted the three proposals Tutu had made to Vorster.

When Tutu disclosed to a journalist friend, Lambert Pringle, that he had written to the prime minister, Pringle asked to see the letter. Tutu naively gave it to him, not intending its publication, at least not yet. Pringle splashed it in full across the editorial page of Durban's newspaper the *Sunday Tribune.* Vorster refused to allow Tutu to release his reply, but Tutu let it be known that the prime minister had dismissed his initiative as political propaganda inspired by the white opposition in Párliament. The author Alan Paton, in an unsigned editorial written for the *Tribune,* said it was beyond comprehension that Vorster should regard Tutu's moderate proposals as propaganda: "Does the Prime Minister think that he can settle for less? Then he does not understand the nature of the crisis that faces the country over which he rules." Barney Pityana, who had been in and out of detention since his expulsion from Fort Hare in 1968, wrote to Tutu—his former chaplain—expressing appreciation for his stand. But, he said, Tutu was wasting his time trying to get through to Vorster as a grandfather: "You can't appeal to these people [expecting] they are going to be different from what they are. We can't reason with them. Writing letters is a useless gesture."

Tutu may have been prescient in predicting an explosion; but when it came, a few blocks up the hill from his home in Soweto, its nature took him—and the rest of Soweto's parents—by surprise. Government policy was that black secondary school children in urban areas should learn in the country's two official languages: Afrikaans and English. In Soweto there were not enough teachers qualified to teach in Afrikaans, so English dominated—until the Bantu education department decided to enforce the policy anyway. It ordered that mathematics and social studies be taught in Afrikaans. At the same time, the department abolished the final year of primary school, reducing schooling for blacks from thirteen to twelve years, in line with schooling for whites. The result was that in 1976, classes of senior primary and junior secondary school pupils in Soweto were merged, in grossly overcrowded classrooms, to be taught in a language in which not even the teachers were fluent. Parents, school boards, teachers' organizations, and principals protested, to no effect.

The rebellion started in the Phefeni Junior Secondary School around the corner from the Tutus' house. In a memoir of events at the school, Sifiso Mxolisi Ndlovu, who was fourteen at the time, has described how he and his fellow pupils, with no prompting from political groups, parents, or even older high school students, triggered a revolution. In March, they began a slowdown. On May 17, pupils in Form I and Form II went on strike and dumped their Afrikaans mathematics, geography, and biology textbooks at their principal's door. Then they forced Form III to abandon midyear exams. In the weeks that followed, they defied their parents' appeals to return to class. At least six other schools joined the boycott, for varying periods. On Sunday, June 13, high school political activists, associated with a students' organization inspired by the black consciousness movement, decided to rally behind their younger brothers and sisters. They resolved on a protest march the following Wednesday and organized it in secret, concealing their plans as far as possible from their parents and teachers.

On June 16, columns of schoolchildren converged from all over Soweto on the Orlando West school where the strike had begun, intent on marching across the valley below and up a hill on the other side to the Orlando Stadium. Numbering between 10,000 and 20,000, they carried posters with slogans such as "Down with Afrikaans," "To Hell with Bantu Education," and "If We Must Do Afrikaans, Vorster Must Do Zulu." As the singing students in the vanguard arrived, Sophie Tema of the Johannesburg newspaper *The World* saw about thirty policemen emerge from ten vans. Some students began taunting them and waving placards. So far the demonstration had been peaceful.

According to Bongani Mnguni, a photographer, the trouble started with a dog. His story was later considered a myth, but at hearings held by the Truth and Reconciliation Commission twenty years later, one of the organizers of the march, Murphy Morobe, corroborated it:

> It was not mythology. . . . It was a real dog that bit some of the students. That really raised the anger of the students. We were not doing anything we thought warranted the kind of reaction from them [the police]. . . . That dog was then killed by students who sought to protect themselves from it. The police then started opening fire.

As Sophie Tema saw it from her vantage point, the confrontation was set off by a policeman lobbing tear gas into the crowd. In return, children stoned the police. First one policeman, then others, pulled out their revolvers and began shooting at the children. Pandemonium broke out as students tried to run from the bullets and tear gas. The police gave no warnings to disperse before opening fire, nor did they make any other efforts to communicate with the marchers.

Desmond Tutu had not been involved in the buildup to the protest. He and Leah had once allowed students to use their house for a meeting; and he was later told that something was being planned, but he did not know it was a march. On the morning of the march he was in his office in the Johannesburg city center. Timothy Bavin was on vacation in Britain, and Tutu was in charge of the diocese. Told by his receptionist of reports coming from Soweto, he telephoned the most senior officer he could find at the police headquarters, John Vorster. "I said, 'What is happening?' He said, 'Oh, everything is under control.' And I said, 'Well, I hear that some children have been shot.' And he said he's not going to be cross-examined by anybody. So I said to him, 'I'm not anybody, I am the dean of this cathedral and I am the vicar-general of the Diocese of Johannesburg.' He slammed the phone on me." Tutu and Leo Rakale drove to Orlando West: "It was eerily still, as if nothing had happened. We drove around and actually saw nothing. It had been cleared, no children, there might have been some on the streets but not too many. It was extraordinarily quiet." They returned to the city, where Tutu broke down in tears as he asked fellow clergymen, "What do I say to black people about this?"

Going home that afternoon, Soweto's parents found their children rioting. Youths stood alongside roads coming from the city, ready to stone or hijack vehicles belonging to white-owned businesses. Tutu had to identify himself to get through. That night, and during the succeeding days and months, the rebellion spread first to all twenty-eight of Soweto's townships, then to others on the Witwatersrand, and then across the country. On June 17, Tutu called for twenty-four hours of prayer and fasting for the "miracle of a change of heart" by the government. On Friday, June 18, he told an emergency meeting of church leaders that the police were a law unto themselves: "If they had meant to quell a riot, they could have used fire hoses, rubber bullets but the things that were rioting were black things. . . . All the while they are relying on and using violence, the power of the bullet. Very soon we who are regarded as radical are going to be rejected by our people." He left the meeting early to return to Soweto: youths were burning down government administration buildings, post offices, beer halls, and liquor stores—the last two because students blamed drinking for their parents' failure to stand up against oppression. Vorster told the police to "maintain order at all costs." Riot police moved through the townships in armored personnel carriers known as "hippos," shooting arsonists, protestors, and students who dared to brandish their clenched fists in a salute and shout "Power." Later, men wearing camouflage outfits roamed in unmarked cars, killing children indiscriminately, sometimes as they stood in their parents' yards. In the ten months following June 16, at least 660 people were killed. Most of them were under 24.

Tutu was upset by the lack of outrage in the white community at the shooting of children. He was shocked when Bill Burnett called him on another matter and made no reference to events in Soweto. On Sunday, June 20, Tutu told his congregation at St. Mary's that their silence was "deafening" and asked them how they would have reacted had white schoolchildren been shot. In the parish newsletter, in his final remarks before going to Lesotho, he told his parishioners to take a message to their fellow whites:

> Tell them that peace and order which are found at the end of a gun barrel will be brittle, superficial and temporary: that such a peace and order will need more guns to maintain. Tell them that there can be no lasting security there. Tell them that unless radical changes are effected in the ordering of society, then South Africa cannot survive. Nobody will win. Tell them, please, before we run out of time.

Had the Soweto uprising preceded the election for bishop of Lesotho, it is likely that Tutu would have refused to stand. As it was, after June 16, leaders including Winnie Mandela pressed him to stay in Johannesburg. When he entered a two-day silent retreat at the end of June, he had not finally accepted that he would go. He wrote to Trevor Huddleston that he was in retreat "to prepare for the consecration [as bishop] or to hear what God wants me to do. I have never felt less like becoming a bishop than now." He and Leah were inclined to heed the appeals of those who wanted him to stay, but others thought this would be unfair to Lesotho: "Tim Bavin thinks my credibility would go for a loop given the fact that at the start there was this yes-no business. He thinks too that I have made a reasonable contribution here and the Government have not acted against me because they know I'm going away." On July 11, Bill Burnett consecrated Tutu a bishop during a service in St. Mary's Cathedral. "What a magnificent occasion it was," wrote a parishioner, Belinda Crisp:

> The ancient traditions–the words of the consecration ceremony, the mitred bishops, the music and movements of the High Mass, met with the power of the modern liturgy, the children gathered at the chancel steps, the TV cameras, the medley of distinguished visitors and simple folk in the congregation, the singing of much-loved hymns, the semi-formal speeches at the end of the service. Incongruous? Not a bit of it. The consecration of our dean took place in a service where pomp and fellowship were beautifully blended into a splendid whole.

Three weeks later, a crowd of thousands gathered in Maseru at the Cathedral of St. Mary and St. James to see Tutu enthroned. Those who could not get into the cathedral–a squat, cross-shaped church made of the light sandstone characteristic of the Lesotho lowlands–listened to the service on loudspeakers outside. Guests inside included King Moshoeshoe II; Queen 'Mamohato; Prime Minister Leabua Jonathan, the man who had seized power when Tutu was teaching at Roma in 1970; and members of the legislative assembly.

The Tutus moved into a different world when they went to Lesotho. The country's population was 1.2 million, compared with South Africa's 25 million. Maseru was a small town by South African standards. Only 10 percent of the country's people, the Basotho, lived in urban areas, compared with nearly half of South Africans. Two-thirds of Lesotho is covered by the Maloti Mountains, the highest in southern Africa, and Desmond had to learn to ride a horse to reach many of his mountain parishes. The country was poor, with a per capita gross domestic product only one-seventeenth of South Africa's. It had a population density twice South Africa's and only about a tenth of its land was arable. Surrounded by South Africa, it was economically dependent on its neighbor, particularly on remittances from Basotho migrant mine workers. But preaching at his enthronement, Tutu refused to see the diocese as poor: "Yes we may be in certain physical and material resources. . . . We are wonderfully rich in human and spiritual resources." Most of the twenty-three parishes of the diocese had only one priest serving the main parish church and up to twenty outstations, so he recommended that self-supporting priests should be ordained for their communities. He asked Anglicans to triple their contributions to the church. At his official residence, he upgraded the servants' accommodations, which he regarded as unworthy of a church that condemned racial discrimination.

An Anglican bishop is described as a "father in God." Tutu made it clear that he took this description seriously. "I want to be your father, please," he said at this enthronement. "I would prefer to be called 'Father' or 'Bishop' rather than 'My Lord.' Please regard Bishop's House as your home, especially those of you who don't live in Maseru. Come in when you are thirsty or tired. . . . Never use the back door or my wife and I will drive you away. Use the front door." Leah sought work in Lesotho but was denied a job because she was not a Basotho national. As a result she continued to lobby for domestic workers in South Africa, spending a week of every month in Johannesburg.

Tutu appointed as the diocese's first dean Philip Mokuku, a younger priest whom he identified as a future leader. He sent Mokuku on a tour of cathedrals in Jerusalem, Zambia, Italy, the United Kingdom, the United States, and Trinidad and Tobago. Mokuku, who went on to replace Tutu as bishop, said of him: "It was obvious to all of us that with his advent the entire diocese was going to shake. We held our breaths and it did shake." Tutu made the further education of the clergy a priority. He and Leah began conferences for the wives of clergymen (the priests were all men). He took his senior staff on retreat to assess needs and shortcomings. "It really gave us a sense of worth," said Mokuku. "His style was to come alongside people, not to turn them upside down. He was able to identify talents and gifts whose owners were not aware of them. He was a real pastor. People felt individually loved and everybody felt we now had a beloved father."

A large part of a bishop's work was to travel around his diocese, visiting people in parishes and institutions. In Lesotho, this often meant trips into the mountains. One of Tutu's journeys was described in a diary kept by David Bruno, a national church official who visited him two months after he began work:

> We leave Bishop's House in a blue Toyota truck, plus canopy, at 8.15. A fabulous day. It was Tuesday, the 9th of November. Super skies, fresh clear air and wonderful, clear views. We leave the tar after only a short way and thereafter are on dirt, mountainous roads. Over Blue Mountain Pass, which is 8,900 ft, and on over range after range, getting more and more remote. Little thatched rondavels, people ploughing on precarious slopes and a few blanketed folk. But otherwise almost deserted country. Green mountain slopes, small rushing streams, and much rock strewn across the bumpy road. So tossed about do we become, that finally the canopy sails off the back and lands on its base, quite undamaged. But it's far too heavy to lift and we leave it there. Finally after four-and-a-half hours and 130 km we arrive, battered, dusty, warm, in spite of the cold mountain air, but in one piece, at St James' Hospital, Mantsonyane.

When Tutu visited parishes in the mountains, he would travel up on a Thursday so that he could conduct services in outstations—usually in schools or other community buildings—on Friday and Saturday before the main parish service on Sunday. He and the local priest often rode for hours on horseback to get to the outstations, and this gave him a chance to get to know his clergy. In Maseru, he tried to celebrate Eucharist in a different church each weekday when he was in town. He took Mondays off and once a month went for a quiet day of prayer, often at the convent of the Society of the Precious Blood, where his prayer companion, Sister Mary Julian, was based.

Tutu developed a deep affection for Lesotho, its language, Sesotho, and its people, so much so that he continued afterward to regard it as a second home. He described Sesotho, with its gentle consonants, as "the French of Africa." He experienced the "grave and respectful politeness" toward outsiders that an early missionary traveler had identified as a national characteristic of the Basotho. Tutu was impressed because they addressed a young boy with the same respectful term—ntate, "father"—they used for an adult. He also fought hard for his diocese. When its theological students urgently needed accommodation, he appealed to his fellow bishops for help. He was traveling during the meeting at which the plea was discussed and turned down. "I have seldom felt more sick at heart and more deflated," he wrote to the bishops when he returned, "than when I read the Episcopal Synod minute regarding theological education in Lesotho. . . . What has shattered me is the complete lack of sympathy and caring. . . . I pray that Lesotho should not be treated as a mere appendage of the Republic of South Africa. We have our integrity and autonomy, as well as the peculiarities of our specific context, which should please be respected."

Tutu also admired the Basotho nation, which had been forged out of disparate groups during the Mfecane (called the Lifaqane in Sesotho) by King Moshoeshoe's ancestor, Moshoeshoe I, widely regarded as the leading southern African statesman of his time. The Tutus were friends of the royal family, dating back to when they took care of Moshoeshoe II's son during vacations while the boy was at school in England. (The son, now King Letsie III, retained warm memories of the Tutu family thirty years later and traveled to Johannesburg to attend Desmond and Leah's fiftieth wedding anniversary celebration.) Tutu's admiration, however, extended neither to Lesotho's political system nor to the interaction between politics and religion. Apart from Prime Minister Jonathan's seizure of power in 1970, there was constant skirmishing between politicians and the king; both Jonathan and his successors clashed with Moshoeshoe II, twice sending him into exile. The major religious forces were the Catholic Church and the Lesotho Evangelical Church, both founded by French missionaries. The feud between Catholics and Protestants, which the missionaries imported from Europe, was intensified by the coup of 1970, after the Catholic Church—inspired by anticommunist zeal—backed Jonathan's dictatorship against what it perceived as a left-wing opposition. As Jonathan cracked down on the opposition, driving its leaders into exile, the Evangelical Church effectively took its place. Lesotho, said Tutu, became like Northern Ireland: religious differences mirrored political divisions. Away from the country of his citizenship, Tutu did not take a conspicuous stance on local political issues, but his disapproval of Jonathan's government was well enough known for the government to complain about it to his successor, Philip Mokuku, after he left.

While Tutu was in Lesotho, South Africa's problems constantly tugged at his time and emotions. He did not think an armed struggle against apartheid had "a snowball's chance in hell" of succeeding, he said in an address in 1977. He nevertheless vigorously defended liberation movements that differed with him, in a speech in the United States in the same year:

> It is because blacks in Zimbabwe, in South Africa and in Namibia have, they believe, tried every peaceful means that they have been compelled reluctantly to resort to violence to oppose a system that has used and uses legalised and institutional violence to oppress them. . . . They have as they see it no other option. . . . And they have been flabbergasted at how most of the Western world turned pacifist all of a sudden. The same Western world lauded to the skies the underground resistance movements during the last world war.

In a circular letter to friends, he reiterated his support for sanctions. In the same letter, he recorded that Leah was "in fine fettle" despite having recently been thoroughly searched by South African officials at the border with Lesotho. She had managed to flush "incriminating material"–political literature–down a toilet before the search.

In September 1977, he was summoned home at short notice to replace Bishop Alphaeus Zulu as a speaker at the funeral of Steve Biko in the Eastern Cape. Shock had swept the country when Biko was killed in police custody. In the years since Tutu had met him, Biko had gained a reputation as the foremost advocate of black consciousness. The police had detained him under the Terrorism Act in the middle of August. They kept him in solitary confinement for nearly three weeks. Within half an hour of beginning to interrogate him on September 6, they had inflicted extensive brain injuries. They shackled him hand and foot to a grille and kept him chained for a day before calling a doctor, falsifying records to hide the delay. For five days, his condition deteriorated. When state doctors decided he should be hospitalized, the police took him in the back of a police van, without medical attention or his medical records, to a prison hospital in Pretoria, 1,200 kilometers (750 miles) away. On September 12, in the words of his lawyer, "He died a miserable and lonely death on a mat on a stone floor in a prison cell." Vorster's police minister, Jimmy Kruger, told a party congress that Biko's death "leaves me cold"–a comment Tutu was to use time and again as an example of how apartheid dehumanized the oppressor as well as the oppressed. Twenty years later four of Biko's interrogators applied to the postapartheid Truth and Reconciliation Commission (TRC) for amnesty. They confessed for the first time that they had injured him a full day earlier than they previously admitted, but maintained that they had done it accidentally in a scuffle. A committee of the TRC denied amnesty, saying it was probable that the four had attacked Biko because "they did not take kindly to his arrogant, recalcitrant and non-cooperative attitude."

Leah was in Johannesburg when Desmond was asked to preach at the funeral. Instead of returning to Lesotho to travel with him, she decided to take one of the chartered buses taking mourners to the Eastern Cape. As her bus was about to leave, the police boarded it, whipped her and others with a sjambok,* and pushed her off. She fell, spraining her ankle. When she did not get up quickly enough, another policeman called her a bitch and threatened her with a firearm.

In all, the police stopped about 1,200 mourners from going to Biko's hometown, King William's Town, but 15,000 others—and diplomats from twelve western countries—did reach the funeral. In the town's sports stadium, Tutu rallied Biko's supporters: God had called Biko to be the founding father of black consciousness, he said, "a movement by which God, through Steve, sought to awaken in the black person a sense of his intrinsic value and worth as a child of God." Biko realized that blacks could not be reconciled with whites until they asserted their humanity, since reconciliation could happen only between persons who asserted their own personhood and respected that of others. "Paradoxically," Tutu said, "we give thanks for Steve and for his life and his death. . . . Steve started something that is quite unstoppable. The powers of injustice, of oppression, of exploitation, have done their worst and they have lost. They have lost because they are immoral and wrong and our God, the God of the Exodus, the liberator God, is a God of justice and liberation and goodness. Our cause, the cause of justice and liberation, must triumph because it is moral and just and right."

The first attempt to pull Tutu back to South Africa from Lesotho was made only two months after he arrived there. John Rees, the general secretary of the South African Council of Churches (SACC), the ecumenical body representing most of the country's largest churches, had resigned. Tutu and his college friend Stanley Mogoba, now a Methodist minister, were among four candidates discussed. Tutu was nominated early in October 1976. The invitation, coming so soon after he had left, reinforced his unease at leaving South Africa at a time of crisis. He was inclined to accept, but he could not resign without the

* A rawhide whip.

approval of other Anglican bishops. He flew to Cape Town to consult with the archbishop, Bill Burnett.

In Cape Town, Tutu told Burnett that he felt he had left his people in Johannesburg in the lurch by going to Lesotho. Burnett thought there was one argument in favor of Tutu's returning to Johannesburg—the SACC needed strong leadership to prevent it from falling into the hands of secular political groups. However, on other counts Burnett was opposed: God often placed people where they did not think they should be; the credibility of the electoral process would be undermined if Tutu left so soon; and as an ecumenical agency the SACC had an ephemeral constituency. Burnett was also suspicious of liberation theology—in time he would liken it to the theology that justified apartheid. According to a note of his meeting with Tutu, he asked: "Is liberation what the Churches can and should do, for in the final analysis it will be political pressures and/or guns that decide the issue, unless the whites change. Will a black SACC change whites?" At the end of their discussion, Tutu agreed to leave the decision in the hands of the next meeting of the church's synod of bishops. The bishops advised him to turn down the invitation. Tutu told John Rees he was deeply distressed. He and Leah felt like renegades, he said, but it would have been intolerable to try to do the job without the backing of his own church.

Within a year, Tutu was back in the same position. Rees's replacement, John Thorne, a former president of the SACC, decided after three months that he would never fit into the job and resigned. The SACC executive committee decided to make a fresh approach to Tutu. The previous year its invitation had been publicized before the Anglican bishops met. This time, anxious not to put the bishops or Tutu under public pressure, they kept their plans secret. Tutu wrote to Burnett saying he was not sure he was drawn to the post; it was awful to be on the sidelines of the struggle and it was unusual to be asked to do the same job twice in a year, but he was concerned for his diocese, and King Moshoeshoe had told him he should be mindful of the confusion his departure might cause. He consulted his bishop's senate, which reluctantly said he should accept. He approached the synod of bishops with an open mind: "I think some of them maybe didn't believe me when I said, 'Look, I really do not know what is God's will for me. What you tell me I will do. If you say stay, I will stay." This time the synod unanimously agreed that Tutu should go. Burnett followed up with a pastoral letter to the Anglicans of Lesotho, telling them that the bishops had sought only to be obedient to God.

Despite the backing from Tutu's fellow bishops, his unusually short stay in Lesotho led to controversy. Trevor Huddleston supported him: "It is always so much better when things come unsought," he wrote. "I only hope the government won't get its hands on the organisation before you take it over!" But the South African Church Union, an Anglo-Catholic lobby, said that Tutu had acted for his own personal advancement, deserted his flock, and caused a scandal in the church. The sharpest words came from his most vocal critic in the diocese of Johannesburg. Roy Snyman, the rector of St. Boniface Church, Germiston, wrote in "The Axeman," his appropriately named parish newsletter:

> One wonders why the Bishop of Lesotho accepted that See in the first place if he could be tempted to abandon his responsibility so speedily for an office job of a churchy nature.... The Church needs godly, prayerful, Gospel-centred, prophetic, disciplined, seasoned, catholic-minded, sacrificial, ministers ("servants of God"), not clever-dick, worldly, socio-political manipulators.

CHAPTER 9

THE JAZZ CONDUCTOR

Desmond Tutu became executive head of the South African Council of Churches (SACC) in March 1978. Although the government had by then suppressed the uprisings that began in 1976, it would never regain the measure of control it had imposed after Sharpeville. About 4,000 young people went into exile in the eighteen months after June 16. Most of the 3,000 who joined the ANC–the largest number of recruits it had ever received–went for military training. In the weeks following June 16, a group of ANC activists recently released from Robben Island prison began, clandestinely, to advise some of the student leaders. In October 1976 a unit of the ANC's army, uMkhonto we Sizwe (MK), infiltrated South Africa through Mozambique, now liberated, and Swaziland. A young MK commander named Mosima "Tokyo" Sexwale inflicted the first injuries on government forces when he threw a hand grenade at police during an attempt to enter South Africa from Swaziland in November 1976.

As recruits returned from training in 1977, MK stepped up its attacks. In an attempt to suppress dissent after Biko's killing, the government proscribed newspapers, restricted or jailed journalists, and banned eighteen organizations, most of them proponents of black consciousness. This precipitated a resolution by the United Nations Security Council instituting a mandatory arms embargo. Commending the work of American diplomats in Africa in helping to bring about a compromise resolution, the Carter administration's secretary of state, Cyrus Vance, told them it was the first time in history that the council had invoked Chapter VII sanctions against a member state. "This action by us and other Western members," he said in a cable, "represented [a] major step taken in coordination with African states."

In retrospect, historians may consider that the tide had turned against apartheid by the late 1970s, but this was by no means clear at the time. The erosion of white power proceeded in fits and starts.

The issues Tutu and the churches had been raising—the legitimacy of a resort to arms, the use of sanctions to end apartheid, and the need for a negotiated settlement with jailed and exiled leaders—were almost absent from public debate inside the country. Before Tutu's return from Lesotho, the bête noire of whites was Andrew Young, a former aide of Martin Luther King, Jr., who was Jimmy Carter's ambassador to the United Nations. Nelson Mandela, out of sight, was also out of white people's minds. Tutu's former student in Lesotho, Buti Tlhagale, who provided young activists in Soweto with their principal venue for rallies at Regina Mundi Catholic Church in Rockville, found that they knew virtually nothing about the ANC. Overt political activity by blacks was confined to the constantly harassed leaders of the black consciousness movement and to those who worked from platforms provided by the government—notably Mangosuthu Buthelezi of kwaZulu, who used his platform to oppose "Bantustan independence" and call for the release of Mandela.

In this atmosphere, the public synods and assemblies of South Africa's largest multiracial churches—the Anglicans, Congregationalists, Methodists, and Presbyterians—provided the only high-profile representative forums in South Africa where blacks and whites could debate the country's future. When the present writer was appointed religion correspondent for a newspaper in Johannesburg in 1976, it quickly became apparent that this was a better vantage point than the whites-only Parliament from which to cover South African national affairs. Yet the number of whites in denominational ruling bodies was much higher than their numbers in the churches warranted. Only in the SACC, which attracted the most socially active, did black leadership approach representative levels. The SACC contended that it was more representative than Parliament, because in a country of 25 million, the SACC's member churches had between 12 million and 15 million adherents whereas Parliament represented only 4 million whites. "In the SACC," said Peter Storey, the vice president of the SACC who nominated Tutu as general secretary, "whites learn what it is like to be a minority and in this sense the SACC is a prototype of the future South Africa."

The SACC, like many of its ecumenical counterparts internationally, originated in missionary conferences convened in the early twentieth century to coordinate the activities of mission societies from different denominations. Its immediate predecessor, the Christian Council of South Africa, initially included the Dutch Reformed

Church, but that church withdrew at the beginning of World War II. Under Bill Burnett, the Christian Council became the South African Council of Churches in 1968. Two years later Burnett was succeeded by John Rees, a dynamic young Methodist layman. Rees transformed the SACC beyond recognition, from a body employing six people into one employing seventy and making the promotion of black leaders a priority. After he left in 1977, an Anglican member of the SACC executive committee described him as a "kind of whiz kid" who needed to be replaced by a "superhuman administrator." Rees's successor, John Thorne, was not superhuman. He was unable to bring the council under his control, and it began to run out of money.

While waiting for Tutu to take Thorne's place, the SACC executive committee temporarily brought Rees back. He went abroad to visit donors and returned with promises of money. At home, he drew up a 250-page operating manual for the council, and the executive committee decided to appoint a deputy general secretary under Tutu to handle finance and administration. Handing over to Tutu, Rees wrote a six-page memorandum giving thumbnail descriptions of twenty-seven trust funds and twenty-two divisional accounts for which he would be responsible. He also gave Tutu 14,000 rand ($12,000, or £8,400 in 1978) to help him buy the house in Orlando West where he and Leah had lived while he was dean. The money, Rees said, came from a foreign donor who wanted to remain anonymous but had earmarked it specifically for this purpose. Tutu, inheriting an organization with an annual operating budget of 3 million rand ($2.6 million, or £1.8 million in 1978), said of Rees, "I tried on his shoes and found them several sizes too large. So I decided I could not emulate John. All I could do was to be what I know how best to be—myself."

Tutu made his mark when he arrived at the SACC by introducing compulsory daily staff prayers; regular Bible study; monthly Eucharist; and, to the discomfort of many who were not Anglican, silent retreats. Activists in the international ecumenical movement were accused by conservatives of being more concerned with social structures than with their relationship with God; Tutu set out to demonstrate that the SACC was not a secular body:

> The church exists first and foremost to praise and glorify God and it cannot be otherwise for a council of churches. That is our first priority. . . . So for us prayer, meditations, Bible reading are not peripheral to our operations. These things are at the centre of our lives. We are

not embarrassed that we put God first. . . . Our pattern and example is
our Lord and Saviour Jesus Christ who could be the man for others
only because he was first and foremost a man of God, a man of prayer.

The staff at the SACC quickly concluded the opposite of Tutu's critics:
that he was a prayerful, Gospel-centered, prophetic, disciplined, and
catholic-minded servant of God.

Leah and Desmond Tutu moved back into the home in Orlando
West at a time of family transition. The house emptied, and soon they
had four children in four countries. Trevor qualified as a teacher at
King's College, London, after graduating from Imperial College with
a Bachelor of Science degree, and took a teaching post in north London. Thandi went to study at the University of Botswana in Gaborone.
Naomi enrolled at an American school, Berea College in Kentucky.
Mpho was at Waterford in Swaziland. Leah returned to the Domestic
Workers' and Employers' Project and became an assistant director of
the Institute of Race Relations. Desmond resumed his routine of leaving Soweto early to join a seven AM Eucharist at St. Mary's Cathedral
in town. From there he went to his office for personal meditation.
Through the day, meetings and interviews in his office began with
prayer. At noon, he stopped whatever he was doing to recite the
Angelus, the Catholic devotion including the Hail Mary. In his early
years at the SACC, its offices were in Koinonia, a building in the
Braamfontein office district. Later the SACC bought a larger building
in the city center, near the cathedral. It named its new headquarters
Khotso House, "House of Peace," and opened it to trade unions and
secular antiapartheid groups.

The council was the largest organization in which Tutu had worked.
He set about creating a family atmosphere, with himself as a loving but
strict father. Asserting his Anglican priesthood, he announced, to the
discomfort of some, that he preferred to be known as Father, and the
staff responded by calling him Baba ("father" or "sir" in Zulu). Morning services were used for announcements, reports on trips, and reflections on national and local events. Birthdays, anniversaries, and family
successes were celebrated, and bereavements were marked. He hugged
men and kissed women. The staff knew he was in the office by the
noise of jokes and laughter as he moved around around the building.
He insisted on punctuality—he had no patience with meetings that
started late on the "African time" observed in rural areas, where transportation was difficult or uncertain. He also disliked gossip: the staff

learned not to say anything to him about a third party unless they were willing to have their comments relayed to the person. He prohibited the staff from speculating on whether others were government informers—someone so accused was hardly likely to confess, he said, and a denial was even less likely to be believed.

At the SACC, he developed a style of leadership that he followed for the rest of his ministry: appoint a senior staff capable of taking the initiative; delegate the detailed work to it, except for writing sermons, speeches, and the most important correspondence; and keep in touch through meetings, memorandums, and copies of the outgoing correspondence of his colleagues. "He wasn't the grand planner or strategist," said Dan Vaughan, a Baptist from a conservative background who rose to a senior position under Tutu. "He followed his intuition. In that he was brilliant." One of those who went to work for him was Wetshotsile Joseph (Joe) Seremane, a former pupil from Krugersdorp. When Seremane first reestablished contact, he was disappointed in Tutu's response to the news that he had been in jail for the PanAfricanist Congress: "I could see his face closing down. And I knew that, ah, he's more sympathetic to the ANC." Still, Seremane came to admire Tutu's leadership:

> He would say, "Do it. I'm not here to spoon-feed you." Ordinary guys blossomed. Tutu made everybody feel like somebody. Then he would give meaning to what you did and elevate it to a higher level. In that free-flowing style, he was like a jazz conductor. . . . He said "You improvise." If you do it well, he'll be happy and boast about it. If you go beyond his bounds, you spoil the whole thing. If you anger him, his wrath would bring you into line.

Tutu did not often get angry in personal contacts; if he did, it was usually because he felt that his integrity was being challenged. Once he ordered out of his office an editor and reporter from the Methodist Church's newspaper who had criticized, in what he described as a scurrilous editorial, the retrenchment of the communications staff. Tutu was uncompromising in exercising what he regarded as his executive prerogatives. He once wrote to staff members who complained that he undermined them by giving discretionary grants to individuals they had already turned down: "It is quite intolerable to have one's staff reading one the Riot Act, not once but on a number of occasions. . . . I am distressed at how you are sensitive about your areas and so singularly lacking in sensitivity about the parameters of my operation and authority."

Within weeks of returning to Johannesburg, Tutu was called on to declare his position concerning perhaps the single most controversial question facing the churches: the legitimacy of the liberation movements' armed struggle. The police had captured the MK unit of which Tokyo Sexwale was part. He and his comrades were on trial for their lives in the biggest case of its kind since Mandela was jailed. The group fell squarely into the government's definition of terrorists—trained in East Germany and the Soviet Union, they carried Chinese, Czech, and Soviet weapons. The trial was important enough for the American embassy to send an observer, who reported to Washington that "police . . . maintained [a] strong show of force with machine pistols, dogs and extra policemen at the ready. Men were frisked and women had handbags searched upon entering the gallery." After six men were convicted, the prosecutor called for the death penalty. The accused decided to ask Tutu to give evidence for mitigation of the sentence. "We said, let's go back to our roots," explained Sexwale, "let's get a church person to explain how we found ourselves in the dock."

Sexwale was taken aback when Tutu arrived at court: "In walks this diminutive gnome. The pictures had not shown his height." In the witness box, Tutu told the court he was committed to change by nonviolent means: "But as attempts to bring the conditions of blacks to the notice of authorities have seemed to fall on deaf ears, there have been those who have said, 'We are not violent people but we have . . . tried everything that is nonviolent and have failed.' So some of them out of desperation, out of deep frustration, have resorted to saying that the only way that this can happen is by violent means." While he did not condone this, he told the judge, "I can understand when . . . people feel they have exhausted all nonviolent avenues." Sexwale, who later became a prominent political and business leader, was never to forget Tutu's evidence—not because the judge spared the lives of the accused but because Tutu had identified with the young at "the most dangerous period of our struggle. . . . I was not begging. We didn't want somebody who was going to be apologetic and plead for us. We needed somebody who could tell . . . why I would go to the gallows with dignity."

Tutu's attitude toward violence was in line with the SACC's policy, which combined an understanding of the reasons for taking up arms with a blanket condemnation of all violence, from whatever side it came, and an appeal to young white men facing military conscription to consider becoming conscientious objectors. At the first meeting of the SACC executive committee in March 1978, Tutu reported that the churches were now being pressed to go farther. Baldwin Sjollema, head of the WCC program that gave humanitarian grants to liberation movements, had responded to the banning of black consciousness organizations in October 1977 by accusing the WCC of fence-sitting. He said it should formally recognize the liberation movements' armed struggle as a "just rebellion." The South African church leaders disliked Sjollema, who they believed took domineering and doctrinaire positions. Tutu told the meeting he had challenged Sjollema: "How can you put that paper out without consulting us? You are doing us a disservice in putting all whites and all blacks into particular molds." Sjollema's paper was merely noted by the executive committee but the points it raised were integrated into work already being done by Wolfram Kistner, the council's director of justice and reconciliation.

Kistner, a quiet, soft-spoken, self-effacing man from a conservative German Lutheran background, was the council's theological éminence grise. He was extraordinarily prolific, year after year producing document after document exploring possibilities and recommending options for dealing with the most sensitive and controversial issues facing the churches. Radical in the original sense of penetrating to the roots of an issue, he was named by a government commission of inquiry as one of the two most influential personalities in the council (the other being Tutu). At Tutu's first national conference in 1978 Kistner presented a document on violence that attracted a flurry of public attention. Lawyers advising one South African newspaper group, fearing prosecution for inciting violence, recommended against publication. Johannesburg's largest daily newspaper published a report only after the editor in chief had signed a copy ordering that it be run in full, to ensure that the nuances enunciated by Kistner were retained.

In his paper, Kistner said the churches agreed that apartheid was fundamentally unjust, but it was meaningless to talk of a just revolution: "Violent revolutions very often result in chaos and anarchy, seldom truly benefit the poor, and are usually morally indefensible. . . . The circumstances and means of such a revolution can hardly prove wholly acceptable to God." He nevertheless questioned the consistency of the SACC's member churches—which, apart from the Quakers, had never been pacifist churches—in claiming that they rejected all violence. In place of just revolution, Kistner advocated that the churches should adopt the concept of "justifiable resistance." Drawing on the criteria for a just war developed by theologians beginning with Augustine of Hippo, he said Christians who opted for violent means of change should ask themselves questions such as these: whether all peaceful means had been exhausted; whether violence had a realistic prospect of achieving its objectives; whether the ends sought had been clearly defined; and whether the suffering caused might not vitiate the ends sought. The SACC should, he said, "encourage Christians to consider that circumstances can arise in which the right to resist evil laws becomes apparent and that a theology of resistance is both a valid and vital concept in such consideration."

The document was referred to member churches for discussion. A suggestion that churches should consider declaring that the rejection of apartheid was an obligation implicit in the profession of the Christian faith fed into a debate, which gained currency in the 1980s, particularly in the Reformed churches. But Kistner's principal recommendation went nowhere. Tutu won the support of the ten-yearly meeting of the world's Anglican bishops, the Lambeth Conference, in July 1978, after he told them that those who opted for violence were still their brothers and sisters: "Our cry is: 'Do not abandon us even when, perhaps particularly when, [the] struggle for various reasons becomes violent.'" At home, the initial Anglican response was to dodge a decision. After some debate, the church's next synod swept the issue off the table by approving a procedural measure to move to the next item of business without taking a vote. An outcry forced the issue back onto the agenda, and the synod edged toward giving legitimacy to the struggle for liberation but balked at doing more than expressing respect for everyone: pacifists, those serving in the armed forces under apartheid, and those who fought apartheid. Tutu was excluded from the synod; a church lawyer had ruled that since he was working for the SACC, his status was that of a "clergyman in retirement," and Bill Burnett had refused to invite him to join the deliberations.

It was not only racial divisions that inhibited the Anglicans—and other multiracial churches—from coming out in clear support of those who took up arms against apartheid. The imperatives of institutional survival militated against organizations with members and buildings in every community in the country defying the government to the extent of formally passing resolutions supporting its violent overthrow. Moreover, if church leaders could agree on nothing else, they agreed at least that one crucial criterion for a just war had not been met: peaceful means of working for an end to apartheid had not yet been exhausted.

So individuals who wanted to fight went into exile and joined the liberation movements. Church leaders such as Desmond Tutu remained to explore alternative means.

Tutu's instrument of choice in the peaceful struggle against apartheid became economic pressure, in the form of disinvestment and sanctions. South Africa, as Africa's mining and industrial powerhouse, depended on international investment and trade. In 1978, 26.3 billion U.S. dollars' worth of foreign capital was invested in the country: 40 percent of it British, 20 percent American, 10 percent West German, 5 percent French, and 5 percent Swiss. Debate over using the country's international ties as an instrument of pressure to end apartheid went back twenty years; after the ANC was banned and Albert Luthuli was awarded the Nobel Peace Prize, he said that economic ostracism represented the only chance of a relatively peaceful transition. In 1976, the SACC commissioned a study of foreign investment from its justice and reconciliation division, under Wolfram Kistner. At the time Tutu joined the council, this issue was the most controversial on the agenda of his first national conference. The SACC executive committee instructed Kistner to convene a consultation to prepare a draft resolution for the conference. The participants were mostly church representatives, but they also included both a left-wing academic and a businessman. The businessman was a Methodist layman, Bobby Godsell, who worked for Harry Oppenheimer's Anglo American Corporation and later became a leader of the South African gold mining industry. The two-day meeting produced a draft that refrained from calling explicitly for disinvestment but questioned whether future investment would bring about a redistribution of power. It also called on foreign countries and companies "for the sake of justice to revise radically their investment policies and employment practices." The compromise satisfied competing camps: those wanting disinvestment could argue that radical revision of policies which buttressed the status quo necessarily implied withdrawal; those rejecting it could use the wording to lobby for better employment practices.

Even this draft fell afoul of the law. A section of the Terrorism Act brought into its ambit activities that "cripple or prejudice any industry or undertaking or industries or undertakings generally or the production or distribution of commodities or foodstuffs." The SACC's lawyer pointed out that another section made it a crime to encourage any social or economic change in South Africa with the assistance of any foreign government or institution. He accordingly recommended the deletion of a clause urging foreign countries to reduce their dependence on South Africa by increasing investment in neighboring countries. The conference excluded the press from its debate on the resolution—so that the proponents of disinvestment could state their views freely—and called in the lawyer. It accepted his advice and passed the resolution without the contentious clause.

This resolution was the basis for a formula that Tutu adopted during the remainder of his time at the SACC: appeal at home and abroad for "political, diplomatic and especially economic pressure on South Africa"; point out that the Terrorism Act prescribed a minimum jail sentence of five years for economic sabotage; and invite his audiences to draw their own conclusions. Speaking to Quakers in Philadelphia in the United States in 1979, he said of the resolution: "That was the closest we could sail to the wind. We hope we have reasonably intelligent friends overseas and they ought to know what we are saying." There were, however, times when he threw caution to the winds. The first time this happened was in 1979, and his action was set off by his anger over forced removals.

The month Tutu moved to the SACC, a former member of his congregation at St. Mary's Cathedral gave South Africa a graphic portrayal of the consequences of this element of government policy. Barbara Waite was a member of the Black Sash, an organization of white women opposed to apartheid. (The name was derived from their practice of picketing cabinet ministers' public appearances; when the women began picketing in the 1950s, they wore black sashes to mourn the abolition of the Coloured franchise.) The Black Sash knew where apartheid hurt the most as a result of operating advice offices that tried to help black South Africans negotiate their way around the myriad laws and regulations controlling their lives. In a three-year project that began on her dining room table, Waite comprehensively plotted forced population removals. She used the information to draw a map of South Africa, covered with clusters of arrows and detailed annotations, that provided the first consolidated picture of the effects of governmental social engineering. Other members of the Black Sash compiled estimates showing that 2.1 million people had already been removed, and 1.7 million still faced removal. High as these figures were, they did not even include people continually being deported from urban areas under the pass laws, numbering hundreds of thousands every year.

In a visit to the Ciskei Bantustan in the Eastern Cape at the end of

June 1979, Tutu toured one of the places to which people had been removed. A conversation that lasted a few seconds was burned into his mind, and he was to repeat it in almost exactly the same words for years afterward:

> In Zweledinga I met this little girl who lives with her widowed mother and sister. I asked whether her mother received a pension or any other grant and she said, "No."
> "Then how do you live?" I asked.
> "We borrow food," she said.
> "Have you ever returned the food you have borrowed?"
> "No."
> "What happens if you can't borrow food?"
> "We drink water to fill our stomachs."

Back in Johannesburg, Tutu decided to write to the new prime minister, Pieter Willem Botha, who was always known by his initials, P. W. Botha had been defense minister for twelve years before succeeding Vorster the previous year. Faced with arms embargoes, Botha had presided over the development of a South African armaments industry—hence his nickname, Piet Wapen ("Piet Weapon"). He had come to power proclaiming reform. In the aftermath of the Soweto uprising, he told whites that apartheid was a recipe for conflict and that they needed to "adapt or die." He appointed a member of the verligte, or "enlightened," wing of his party, Piet Koornhof, to take over the old Bantu Administration and Development department. For a short while it had been referred to as the "Department of Plural Relations," and it was now renamed the Department of Cooperation and Development. Tutu's letter to Botha was to be the first in a series of impassioned private appeals—revealed in this biography for the first time—in the style of his letter of 1976 to Vorster. Tutu opened by addressing himself to Botha as a fellow Christian. He continued:

> I believe that you are unaware of the conditions that shattered me during my visit to the Eastern Cape. I am convinced that if you knew what the consequences of the massive population resettlement schemes have been on your fellow human beings and your fellow South Africans, then you and your colleagues in the Nationalist Party would long ago have called a halt to something with such distressing results. . . .
> I must be careful not to use emotive language but, Mr. Prime Minis-

ter, I cannot avoid speaking about the *dumping* of people as if they were things with little prior consultation about how they felt. . . . I cannot see how such treatment is consistent with the Gospel of Jesus Christ who said, 'Inasmuch as you did not do it to the least of these my brethren you did it not unto me.'* I am trying to be as restrained as possible because I want to confess to you that at this moment as I write I am deeply agitated and angered by what I have seen. . . .

I do not think you know that women sweep the streets of Sada for R6 [$5, or £3] a month . . . that an old man in Glenmore could earn R2.50 a day near his old home and now must pay R6.50 for the return journey to the same place. . . . I do not think you know of the little girl in Zweledinga who said she and her mother and sister lived on borrowed food and if they could not borrow food they drank water to fill their stomachs, this in a country that exports food. . . .

I will always be haunted by that little girl and I pledge myself to do all I can to see an end to what I believe to be utterly diabolical and unacceptable to the Christian conscience. . . . The Afrikaner has found it difficult to forget the concentration camps in which some of his forebears were incarcerated by the British. Black memories of the resettlement camps and villages may be equally indelible.

Botha's mother had been confined in a British concentration camp in the Anglo-Boer War, but Botha was unmoved by Tutu's plea. It was not government policy to "dump" people, he replied. He outlined the legal process involved in removals, and added: "Although it is conceded that the removal of people from established places of abode may cause inconvenience in some cases, the ultimate advantages far outweigh the initial disadvantages." Tutu's anger boiled over even before he saw Botha's reply. Visiting European donor agencies, he told a Danish television interviewer that it was "rather disgraceful" that Denmark was buying South African coal. Told that black workers would lose their jobs if coal exports were ended, Tutu said the suffering would be temporary: "It would be suffering with a purpose. We would not be doing what is happening now, where blacks are suffering, and it seems to be a suffering that is going to go on and on and on."

There was uproar at home. Botha's interior minister, Alwyn Schlebusch, said he was "disgusted." The president of the Methodist Church said that Tutu was speaking without a mandate. Right-wing Anglicans

* Matthew 25:40.

called on their leaders to distance themselves from Tutu. Bill Burnett privately disagreed with Tutu but said nothing in public. Timothy Bavin disagreed publicly but said that many people agreed with Tutu and rejected appeals to discipline him: "He is a man of deep prayer and living faith and spends more time on his knees than most of those who call for action to be taken by the Church against him." American diplomats reported to Washington that Tutu's views were widely shared by urban black leaders but were rarely aired: "Tutu is risking prosecution or banning under South Africa's security laws by advocating international boycott action. His remarks are more likely however to result in a campaign of police and press harassment of the SACC."

The prediction proved accurate. Schlebusch, who was responsible for issuing passports, summoned Tutu to a meeting in Pretoria. In what Tutu later came to suspect was part of a "good cop, bad cop" routine, Botha's cabinet decided that Koornhof should join the meeting. Koornhof had in preceding months reprieved a number of communities facing forced removal and had tried—without success—to persuade Tutu to join a government committee discussing policy toward black people living in urban areas. He had followed up with confidential talks—once at his home—with Tutu; the SACC's president, Sam Buti; and other black leaders. During an eighty-minute meeting between Tutu and the two ministers early in October 1979, Schlebusch produced a transcript of Tutu's interview with the Danish reporter. He said that Tutu was guilty of economic sabotage and pressed him to retract or apologize. Tutu responded that economic pressure was necessary to bring about fundamental change. Koornhof kept interrupting, accusing Tutu of being inconsistent by both pursuing dialogue and urging sanctions. At the end, Tutu said he wanted to talk to his family and the SACC's leaders before giving a final response. Two days later the government widened its assault. The police minister, Louis le Grange, warned the SACC to desist from irresponsible actions. Leftist spiritual leaders, he said, were conditioning blacks to believe that the existing order was unchristian and immoral, that their human rights were being denied, that they were being oppressed and exploited, and their human dignity was being infringed on.

Church leaders and the SACC executive committee met the following week in an atmosphere of crisis. They were at one in rejecting le Grange's accusations. On sanctions, they were divided. Defending his unmandated statement, Tutu said that he was committed to work for reasonably peaceful change—"reasonably" because there had already been so much violence. If fundamental change did not happen soon, however, there would be a bloodbath. He applauded Botha's reforms, such as recognition of black trade unions. But they would allow privileges only for black workers who qualified under the pass laws to live in urban areas. The overwhelming majority of black South Africans would lose their citizenship and be liable to dumping in the Bantustans. It was essential, he said, to search for nonviolent strategies to force fundamental change, including political and economic pressure from the international community. He asked his opponents to suggest alternatives that would be effective.

After some debate, Peter Storey, who chaired the meeting in the absence of Sam Buti, developed a consensus position that was adopted by the meeting: in the tradition of the Old Testament prophets, Tutu had a right to express his views as a matter of personal conscience, notwithstanding differences of opinion in the churches. The real issue, Storey said, was the need for fundamental change. The church leaders agreed unanimously to tell Schlebusch that in spite of their differences, "having heard Bishop Tutu's reasons for his statement, we share his belief that any retraction of or apology for his statement in this instance would constitute a denial of his prophetic calling. . . . We will not allow any single member of the Body of Christ to be isolated for attack."

Tutu's family also supported him. Responding to a suggestion by le Grange that Tutu talked too much, Leah told him to keep talking: "I would much rather you were happy on Robben Island than unhappy outside," she said. Trevor, now working in England, phoned to give his support; and Mpho, at school at Waterford, said she was proud of her father's reply to le Grange. Desmond wrote to Schlebusch that he had consulted the church leaders and his family: "I have also prayed about it and find I am unable to retract or apologise because I am concerned for peaceful change in this country and believe that we need the international community to persuade us to sit down and discuss the issues of fundamental change in our country."

For some months there was no overt response from the government. Tutu continued a correspondence with Koornhof, appealing on behalf of communities facing forced removal. In November he wrote another long plea to Botha, alluding to his letter of 1976 to Vorster: "I have written this letter, as I wrote one to your predecessor, in fact after much prayer and the thought of writing to you came whilst I was on my knees. . . . I have this deep commitment to try and work for peaceful change. But I am equally committed to fundamental change. . . . It will not do to try and coöpt especially urban blacks into the free enterprise system by attempting to create a so-called middle class or a core of highly-privileged blacks." He called again for a national convention and asked to meet Botha.

Covertly, government security agencies focused more closely on the churches. The police had kept Tutu under surveillance since his return from Lesotho. One of the policemen who did so was Paul Erasmus, a member of the Security Branch in Johannesburg. Disillusioned and angry, he left the police in the early 1990s, surreptitiously taking his casebooks with him. Hence, although Tutu's main police files were destroyed, it is possible to trace occasions on which Erasmus intercepted his letters, inspected his bank accounts, and spied on meetings he addressed. If an intercept warranted a report, Erasmus lodged it in Tutu's local Security Branch file: number WA/VP 4/6233. If it was important enough, it was sent to police headquarters in Pretoria for his national file: number S4/V/1171. (Apartheid was observed even in police files—the category S4 showed that Tutu was a black suspect; if he had been white, Indian, or Coloured, the prefix would have been, respectively, S1, S2, or S3.) In 1979, the Department of Justice opened the first of two files on Tutu, which it used in deciding whether to impose restriction orders on him. One of the only government files on Tutu that escaped the purges of the 1990s—the others being his passport files—it is filled mostly with press clippings.

Faced with the growing challenge from the churches in 1979, the security police enlarged their "church desk" at headquarters in Pretoria. Tutu's advocacy of sanctions posed a particular problem, according to the police brigadier who headed the desk, Willie Wentzel: "He did not hesitate to say what he felt, and he got away with it. We investigated whether he could be charged with economic sabotage after the statement over a coal boycott. . . . It was referred to the director of security legislation and eventually they decided that despite the possibility of loading the [court] bench, we would never get a conviction."

The government's response to Tutu's refusal to back down over his statement to the Danish reporter came one afternoon early in March 1980, when two officials from Schlebusch's department arrived at his office to confiscate his passport. Church leaders, including Bavin, Burnett, and Storey, condemned the government. Winnie Mandela wrote from Brandfort, the small rural town to which she was banished: "What a blunder, they need you so much yet they do this to you."

Internationally, the government gave Tutu an audience the like of which he had never enjoyed before. Robert Runcie, about to be enthroned as archbishop of Canterbury, sent Botha a confidential letter asking for reasons for taking away the passport: "I have no wish to begin my archiepiscopate by stirring up hostility to any country," he said, "but you will recognise the strength of feeling which the treatment of Bishop Tutu has already evoked." He and the twenty-four Anglican "primates" from around the world who went to his enthronement followed up with public condemnation. Paul E. Tsongas of Massachusetts, who had met Tutu in Johannesburg two months earlier, told the United States Senate that Botha's action was counterproductive and senseless. He described Tutu as a black moderate and contrasted him with revolutionaries and radicals. He and nineteen other members of Congress asked Jimmy Carter to protest. The U.S. State Department issued a formal denunciation describing Tutu as "a man of great moral stature." The previous spring, Harvard University–amid debate over its refusal to sell its stock in firms doing business in South Africa–had awarded Tutu an honorary degree. Now the university's president, Derek C. Bok, wrote a cautious protest to Botha. He was unable to ascertain all the facts, he said, but if Tutu's passport had been revoked because he spoke out for black South Africans, "the action of your government strikes a blow against basic individual freedoms, and I would like to express my strong disapproval."

Within a week, Tutu joined a newspaper editor in opening a new front. On March 4, the day Tutu's passport was seized, it was announced in Zimbabwe that Robert Mugabe, regarded as a terrorist by whites, had won the country's preindependence election. The next weekend, Percy Qoboza, editor of Johannesburg's black newspapers the *Post* and the *Sunday Post,* launched a petition for the release of South Africa's "terrorist," Nelson Mandela. At the time Mandela was a figure of remote legend, by no means the icon he later became. To the young in Soweto, Tutu and the local medical practitioner Nthato Motlana, chairman of a body called the Committee of Ten, were better known. Following up the story, a competing newspaper approached Tutu for comment on Qoboza's initiative. Tutu said he would ask the churches to support the petition. The newspaper described him as having launched a "free Mandela" campaign. Soon Tutu was telling the BBC's southern African correspondent, John Humphrys, that Mandela would be prime minister within five to ten years. A sceptical Humphrys suggested that Tutu was hopelessly optimistic. "Brother," Tutu replied, "the

Christian faith is hopelessly optimistic because it's based on the faith of a guy who died on a Friday and everybody said it was utterly and completely hopeless—ignominious defeat. And Sunday He rose."

From Robben Island, Mandela—responding to a birthday telegram from Tutu in July 1980—wrote to thank and encourage Tutu: "The will to continue fighting and the hope of victory remain one of the most splendid spiritual weapons in the hands of the oppressed people inside and outside prison, and men like you are making an invaluable contribution in feeding that fighting spirit and hope of victory." But in exile, some of Mandela's comrades were not as enthusiastic about Tutu as he was. The ANC, headed by its leader in exile, Oliver Tambo, had recently completed a thorough review of its strategies following the Soweto uprising. Influenced by a visit to Vietnam in 1978, it decided to give more attention to organizing politically within South Africa, in particular by promoting a broad-based national front with a common program. Tambo's record of discussions shortly before the "free Mandela" campaign reveals that at least some of ANC's leaders had reservations about the roles of Tutu, Motlana, and Qoboza. In notes of reports to a meeting of the ANC, Tutu was described as holding himself aloof from former close friends. Moreover, the churches operated in a pyramid structure, they started projects to obtain money instead of working according to a program of priorities, and they were under pressure regarding their use of funds. In a general comment on the reports, Tambo argued for an inclusive approach:

> We must not try to force the pace in a way which makes it an issue whether some accept the ANC line or not. We do not expect people like DT, NM and PQ to behave like revolutionaries. To castigate them because they are not measuring up to revolutionary standards would be wrong. They are people of some influence. It is this attribute we must exploit—put their influence behind and in support of our struggle, even if not in support of the ANC as such. We must not turn them into enemies. If they are enemies, we can surely neutralise them. They and the ANC have plenty in common.

Tutu and church leaders inside the country remained unaware of the exiles' discussions until long after liberation. Driven by day-to-day events affecting their members, they were about to enter both a new level of confrontation and an unprecedented dialogue with the government.

The ground for the confrontation had been laid at the previous year's national conference of the SACC. The conference, inspired partly by the moving rhetoric of Allan Boesak, the young rising star of the black Dutch Reformed churches, approved a series of proposals encouraging campaigns of civil disobedience against racial laws. Tutu was personally ambivalent about civil disobedience. Unlike Mahatma Gandhi and Martin Luther King, Jr., he did not on principle reject the use of force under all circumstances. Moreover, if disobedience involved street protests, its success depended on a government's having enough respect for human life to hesitate to massacre large numbers of demonstrators. Tutu doubted that was the case in South Africa. However, the proposals before the conference did not go as far as calling for action on the streets. They were aimed more at defying laws that forbade interracial fellowship, and Tutu strongly supported the idea that the churches should obey the "law of Jesus Christ" instead of the "law of Caesar."

At the national conference in 1980, the senior SACC staff, frustrated by the timidity of church leaders, urged them to abandon their agenda and drive to Pretoria to hold an illegal public protest. At first the staff wanted to nail the Freedom Charter of 1955 to the doors of prominent churches in the city center, imitating Martin Luther's action at the beginning of the Reformation in 1517. But the charter was closely associated with the ANC and its allies, so Tutu tried to widen support for the protest by suggesting instead a service of witness, in Pretoria's Church Square, against forced removals. If the police came to arrest them, he said, they should remain on their knees and refuse to move until they finished the service. His compromise was defeated by one vote. Militant members of the conference went away more frustrated than they had been when they arrived. Two weeks later the police in Johannesburg gave them the opportunity to act.

Early in 1980 pupils at schools began a new series of protests. These spread to Johannesburg in April, when pupils in the segregated Coloured and Indian school systems, with the support of the clergy in their areas, began boycotting classes. Among the clergy was John Thorne, the former president of the SACC who had briefly served as general secretary before Tutu. Thorne—a mild-mannered, pipe-smoking Congregationalist minister—was hardly a militant, so when the police detained him on Saturday, May 24, and took him to police headquarters in John Vorster Square, the city's religious leaders were shocked. The interrogation rooms of the security police, on the tenth floor at John Vorster Square, were notorious, a place from which detainees had been known to "fall" to their deaths. Joe Wing, general secretary of the Congregational Church and a pioneer of the ecumenical movement in South Africa, spent the weekend anxiously trying to ascertain Thorne's fate, visiting John Vorster Square, calling the head office of the security police in Pretoria, and then calling the minister of justice in Cape Town. Thorne's colleagues met and agreed that if he was not released, they would gather at the church's head office on Monday morning; hold a prayer service for him; and, in defiance of a law prohibiting public protest, walk to John Vorster Square to hand in a petition for his release. They invited leaders and ministers of other churches to join them. Among these was Timothy Bavin, who was called by Wing late on Sunday night. Bavin lived within a five-minute drive of where the protest was to begin, but he did not want to go. "All my instincts were against it," he told Bill Burnett later. "A sleepless night was followed by prayer and the Eucharist in my chapel and still I was not clear as to the leading of the Lord. . . . However, at about 8.15 I knew I had to go and, apart from moments of loss of nerve, have never doubted that this was what God was asking of us."

The fifty-member group that gathered at the Congregational Center in Braamfontein on Monday morning, dressed in clerical robes and carrying Bibles, was an unlikely amalgam of militants, liberals, and conservatives. Many members had little contact with the activists of the SACC. Some were from congregations in Johannesburg's black, Coloured, and Indian townships; others were from the wealthy white northern suburbs. Even the rector of Harry Oppenheimer's church was there. There were Protestants and Catholics, monks of the Community of the Resurrection, a visiting Canadian priest–and Leah Tutu. In accordance with the precepts of nonviolent direct action, they telephoned the police to announce what they were doing. After a short prayer service, they began their unlawful march, led by Tutu and Joe Wing, down toward Queen Elizabeth Bridge, which crosses the railway line separating the offices of Braamfontein from the Johannesburg city center. The small column, walking against the traffic but only two abreast, hardly blocking one lane, moved quietly over the bridge. If they had been allowed to walk through the western edge of the city center and on to John Vorster Square, the episode would have been short and insignificant. Instead, a posse from the police riot squad arrived, dressed in camouflage uniforms as if ready for a battle against guerillas in the bush. At their head, with a bullhorn and wearing a floppy khaki hat, was Theuns Swanepoel, who in the 1960s had been a feared interrogator of detainees such as Winnie Mandela and was notorious for his brutal suppression of the Soweto uprising.

Swanepoel stopped the march on a street corner outside the offices of Johannesburg's afternoon daily, *The Star*. It was few minutes before one of the newspaper's deadlines. Photographers raced down the stairs to capture images of riot policemen with automatic rifles, pistols, and gas masks surrounding the clergy. As the present author, then a newspaperman, who had run ahead of the marchers to file the story, dictated it to a copy typist, other reporters hung from the windows and relayed developments. "They're singing 'Onward Christian soldiers,' " called one excited journalist. "Now they're being loaded into trucks." The clergymen were transported to John Vorster Square. The riot police, unmindful of the journalists, dispersed onlookers by beating them with batons.

Just before four o'clock that afternoon, John Thorne was released. The marchers were kept overnight in communal cells segregated by race as well as gender. In the black women's cell, Leah Tutu organized a collection to help a prisoner, not connected to the protest, pay her fine. In their cells, the men prayed, sang hymns, and told stories and jokes. Tutu complained that the black men's cell was dirty, so the police had it cleaned. Then he pointed out the blankets were filthy. Clean ones were supplied. Finally, before going to sleep, he said that the group would not be able to sleep with the lights on all night. The police obliged by turning off the lights. The next morning, the marchers were reunited in the basement cells under the Johannesburg magistrates' courts. During a prayer service before the hearing, Joe Wing wept: in his time in the ecumenical movement, he had never seen denominational differences evaporate as they did then. The court appearance generated local and international headlines for a second day. With the sound of hymns from the cells resonating through the building, the police cleared the small courtroom to accommodate the fifty-three accused. They were charged, and later fined, under the Riotous Assemblies Act.

P. W. Botha was furious. In a speech three days later, he said that acts of civil disobedience furthered the aims of the ANC, and he accused the SACC of channeling millions of rand to promote unrest. Tutu sent him a telegram, asking for a meeting. An emergency gathering of church leaders endorsed the request. That weekend, Tutu, Peter Storey, and the SACC's vice-president Sally Motlana met Koornhof for discussions at his home. Churches and the government haggled for some weeks over the terms of a meeting. Botha set what Tutu called preposterous preconditions: that the SACC should declare that it rejected communism, violence, and the ANC; and that it accepted conscription for white males. In the interests of dialogue, the SACC, in Tutu's words "interpreted those conditions suitably." It said that it had never supported communism or any other ideology; that it rejected violence, including institutionalized violence perpetrated by the state; that it had never identified itself with any political movement; and that it accepted national service as long as it included nonmilitary options for conscientious objectors. For his part, Tutu made suggestions to Botha on the composition of the government delegation.

Twenty church leaders met Botha and seven of his ministers at Union Buildings, the seat of executive government in Pretoria, on August 7. The church delegation was headed by Sam Buti and included Tutu, Storey, and Burnett. The only woman at the meeting was Sally Motlana—perhaps the most militant member of the executive, she had repeatedly been detained without trial and had her passport revoked. (She was also the daughter of the CR fathers' cook who had provided meals for Tutu when he lived in their hostel in Sophiatown as a boy.) Botha, who was concentrating power in the hands of the military, brought to the meeting members of his State Security Council. He also included the ministers Tutu had asked for. For thirty years the apartheid government had either ignored or publicly assailed the multiracial churches. On the rare occasions when an interview was granted, it had lectured them. Botha gave the church leaders seventy-five minutes to put their case, and his cabinet ministers forty-five minutes to reply. The church leaders warned that the country was heading for disaster. Tutu said that hatred, bitterness, and anger were growing, and he stated four demands for government action: allow common citizenship for all in an undivided South Africa; abolish the pass laws; stop the "totally evil" population removals; and set up a single, uniform education system. Burnett confessed that he had in the past hated the government, and said it would heal both church and state if both met regularly at least during times of stress. Storey crossed swords with Botha when he warned the president that blacks did not trust the good faith of the government. Replying at the end of the meeting, Botha said he believed in Christ:

But the Christ I believe in is not a weakling. The Christ I believe in is not a jellyfish. . . . I am proud of being an Afrikaner and I am not going to ask anybody to excuse me for being one. My people fought colonialism before any other people in Africa fought it. . . . If apartheid means what our enemies make of it, I reject it. . . . I am prepared to lead my people to create new dispensations, but I am not prepared to lead them on the road of a government of one man, one vote.

Sam Buti replied that the church wanted warring parties, including exiles and prisoners, to be brought around a conference table to seek a solution which would secure the interests of both blacks and whites.

The church leaders came out of the meeting to declare that although the delegations were speaking different languages, or were on different wavelengths, at least they were talking in the same room. "I can't say the meeting is in quite the same league as that between President [Menachem] Begin and President [Anwar] Sadat," said Tutu, "but it is of the same order." Their feelings were not universally shared. Buti Tlhagale said Botha was speaking about "a different Lord from the one proclaimed by black people. . . . Is it possible for the Church to have dialogue with a government that is clearly beyond redemption?" Allan Boesak and many of his colleagues who ministered in the segregated churches set up by the white Dutch Reformed Church took a similar view. They saw those who led the traditionally English-speaking churches as tea-drinking liberals, naive in their dealings with Afrikaner nationalists. Tutu was unapologetic: "Moses went to Pharaoh repeatedly to secure the release of the Israelites. The prophets spoke repeatedly to the kings and to the people to get them to change and learn to obey God. We too as churches will go on speaking to the government until the very last moment."

Events over the following months showed that Botha was not interested in real dialogue. Although he had suggested follow-up talks, he also wanted church leaders to visit troops fighting Namibia's liberation movement, Swapo, on its border with Angola. It took four months to determine that Botha was not making the visit a precondition for further talks. While this correspondence was continuing, Tutu felt moved while on a retreat to write a separate letter to Botha. He told Botha "that you have it in you to go down in history as a truly great man who by a total dismantling of apartheid was able to usher in a period of justice, peace and reconciliation and coexistence not only in South Africa but in the entire continent." He received an acknowledgement, but no reply is on record.

After South Africa's summer holidays, in February 1981 Tutu proposed a possible agenda for a meeting. But at the same time, he told his executive committee that he was losing enthusiasm for talks. Botha was becoming more totalitarian, taking the country back to the "dark ages" of Verwoerd. The government had banned the *Post* and the *Sunday Post*. Koornhof's much-trumpeted new deal for blacks was a "horrible lie." On forced removals, he said the government was devising what the Nazis had called the final solution:

> It is not gas chambers we are talking about. But if you remove people from where they had reasonably adequate accommodation and were reasonably near places of work . . . and you dump them in the middle of nowhere . . . are you not as guilty as if you had pulled a trigger? I will be attacked for saying this. They will say I am guilty of gross exaggeration. I wish I did not have to say it. I want to be popular, I want to be loved–but not at the expense of the truth, not at the expense of our people.

The talks finally died in the aftermath of a raid by government troops on the headquarters of MK's special operations unit in Matola, Mozambique. Tutu spoke at a memorial service in Regina Mundi Church, where he said that the ANC's dead, whom many whites called terrorists, were "our sons, our fathers, our brothers." Citing the tenor of this and Tutu's other recent statements, Botha said there was no point in further discussions: "You appear to have opted for confrontation with the Government."

Perhaps the only concrete gain from the meeting of August 1980 was the return of Tutu's passport in January 1981. If its withdrawal had helped to give him an international profile, its restoration enabled the SACC a year later to capitalize on that profile. In March 1981, Tutu made a five-week visit to ten countries in Europe and North America. Storey, who was acting as the SACC's president, said that since they did not know how long he would have a passport, he should aim high. Across Europe Tutu consulted with churches and lobbied government officials and cabinet ministers, among them the German foreign minister Hans-Dietrich Genscher. In Washington, D.C., where the incoming Reagan administration was developing its policy on South Africa, he met senators including Paul Tsongas and Republican Nancy Kassebaum of Kansas, soon to play a central part in the debate over sanctions. In New York he spent an hour with the UN Secretary-General Kurt Waldheim. Addressing the UN Special Committee against Apartheid, Tutu made his customary appeal for political, diplomatic, and above all economic pressure. He saw Jeane Kirkpatrick, the new U.S. ambassador to the UN. She told him there were two poles to the administration's foreign policy: concern for Soviet expansionism, which was widely publicized; and total abhorrence of policies based on race, which was not. There was no chance of a rapprochement between the United States and South Africa as long as apartheid existed, she said, sending a signal that differed from the signal coming from the White House.

Tutu's visit upset P. W. Botha, not only because of his calls for economic pressure but most likely because the reception Kirkpatrick gave Tutu humiliated the South African government. Ten days earlier she had secretly met Botha's military intelligence chief, P. W. van der Westhuizen, at the offices of a right-wing lobby group. This army general had been granted a visa despite the State Department's ban on visits by the South African military. News of the meeting leaked out, and African diplomats at the UN protested. Kirkpatrick took the opportunity of meeting Tutu to tell him that she had rebuked van der Westhuizen, and Tutu relayed this to the press. An angry Botha told an election meeting that he was going to withdraw Tutu's passport again.

Tutu had intended to end his trip in London, where he saw officials at the Foreign Office and joined politicians and church leaders at a meeting in the House of Commons to endorse the "free Mandela" campaign. However, Storey suggested that he delay his homecoming until the dust had settled. Two senior staff members from the SACC flew to London to consult with him on whether he should come back at all. He brushed aside the idea of not returning. In the first of many displays of support, Robert Runcie appeared with him at a photo opportunity at Lambeth Palace and arranged for him to have a brief audience with the pope on the way home. Desmond and Leah flew to Rome to attend a general audience in St. Peter's Square. Afterward, John Paul II came down from the dais to spend a few minutes with them and reassured them that the church was always opposed to racism. As Tutu traveled home, the Vatican issued a public expression of the pope's dismay at the prospect of government action.

Among those observing the Tutus' arrival at the airport in Johannesburg were Paul Erasmus and about ten other security policemen. While waiting, they discussed stabbing Tutu with a sharpened bicycle spoke: "It was a pretty good opportunity," said Erasmus. "We knew there was a good chance there would be a huge crowd and he'd have to walk through the main concourse. If you looked at the state's intelligence review, which was a little weekly publication at that time, the government was frothing at the mouth. . . . I think if there had been a senior person there, the right senior person, he would have said 'Boys, don't talk kak [shit], let's do it.' Or, 'Who's prepared to do it?' The feelings were very strong at that time." The following week, as Tutu prepared for a Good Friday service, security policemen arrived at the house in Orlando West with an order for Tutu to hand over his passport. He responded to journalists that Botha was "just a pathetic little bully." A few days later, the office of the Department of Justice responsible for drawing up restriction orders opened its second file on him.

Tutu had come home to another emergency meeting, this time for church leaders and the SACC executive committee to discuss the threat to him. That evening, after the meeting had adjourned, a small group stayed behind for another, strictly confidential meeting. Tutu, Peter Storey, and Sally Motlana were joined in Tutu's office by his deputy in charge of finances, Matt Stevenson; and by the council's lawyer, Oliver Barrett. There they heard news that over the next three years was to rock the council to its core, setting its leaders at odds, threatening its racial unity, and giving the government its best chance yet to destroy the council's work. Stevenson told the group that the police had discovered SACC money invested in dozens of personal bank accounts operated by its former general secretary, John Rees.

Money, in particular its sources and its administration, had long been the SACC's Achilles' heel. Members of the multiracial churches were relatively poor financially, and the SACC depended on churches abroad for 98 percent of its income. The Evangelical Church in Germany–financed by the church tax levied on taxpayers unless they opted out–covered half the budget. The other major donors were, in order, the World Council of Churches and the Dutch, Swiss, Danish, American, Swedish, and British churches. By the standards of South African charitable organizations, the council administered large amounts of money: 17.5 million rand (in 1981, $23.5 million or £10 million) over the seven years from 1975 to 1981. But the development of financial controls had not kept pace with the council's expansion under Rees. A year before Tutu's arrival, no one was able to tell the exact state of the SACC's finances at any one time. Money was spent before it was received and at the end of 1976 the council was technically insolvent. The executive committee approved the establishment of an independent accounting service and also decided to appoint a deputy to control the finances. However, it took nearly two years to appoint the deputy—no qualified candidates applied, and approaches to laymen such as Bobby Godsell of Anglo American were unsuccessful. In the meantime, a divisional director of the SACC was discovered to have stolen money from an institution associated with the council. It took three months and considerable wrestling over racial sensitivities before charges were brought. (The director was black.) Then auditors found that the accounting service was not keeping proper accounts, so it was dismantled and an outside auditor was appointed to investigate. This auditor found that the head accountant had also been stealing money, so charges were brought against him too.

Although Tutu was largely the victim of a situation that had arisen before he took office, Storey felt he bore a measure of responsibility for the council's struggle to get on top of the problems. In 1979, Tutu was on a six-week visit to the United States—including Harvard's commencement ceremonies—when one of the first crises over finances blew up. He returned to receive a handwritten letter from Storey suggesting that he had been too slow to respond to the first reports of misdemeanors, that the SACC's divisions needed closer supervision, and that Godsell had been lost to the SACC through carelessness. Storey also criticized the length and purpose of Tutu's trips: "This past trip . . . has been referred to in my presence in scathing terms as an 'ego trip.' Questions have been asked as to whether you were paid while overseas. . . . I see this as very damaging and I beg you to look at it again."

The first indications that the government was exploiting the SACC's financial problems for its own ends came during the trials of the former employees on charges of fraud and theft. Information on the council's finances was leaked to journalists known for their close contacts with the police. Defense lawyers appeared to be receiving similar information. Both men were acquitted by magistrates who criticized the SACC's record-keeping. One of the accused, who was acquitted despite having given Tutu a written confession, then linked up with a right-wing Christian group funded by the government. He claimed to represent 4 million members, lobbied the government to retain the ban on interracial marriage, campaigned against Tutu abroad, and was ultimately awarded state honors by P. W. Botha.

Successive police ministers, and Botha himself, harried the SACC over the purposes for which it used its money. Its smaller divisions and projects were uncontroversial—theological education, mission and evangelism, a women's desk, and a choir project. A bursary fund, accounting for 11 percent of the SACC's budget, was alleged to favor the children of radicals. The council's development arm, which used 15 percent of its budget, was accused of exploiting unemployment for political ends. But the government's main targets were the Dependants' Conference and the Asingeni Relief Fund, each of which accounted for a quarter of the budget. The Dependants' Conference, allocated 4.2 million rand over seven years, gave maintenance grants, money for schooling, and other help to hundreds of political prisoners, typically men banished to rural areas after serving long prison sentences for their activities in the ANC. While prisoners were still in jail, the conference helped their dependents, usually women who had children and were unemployed or had low-paying jobs. It also sponsored family visits to prisoners on Robben Island, covering train fares to Cape Town, accommodating family members in a hostel near the railway station, and taking them to board the prison ferry to the island.

The Asingeni Fund was started by John Rees on June 16, 1976, to provide relief grants to the residents of Soweto after the uprising. Its name, meaning "we will not go in," reflected the SACC's identification with pupils boycotting classes. Most of its money–4.4 million rand in its first six years–went to lawyers defending residents on charges such as public violence. Rees paid out the rest in hundreds of cash grants for funeral costs, food, clothing, schooling, and transport. He operated the fund on the same basis as the clergy ran poor funds–payments were made entirely at his discretion, and the recipients' names were kept confidential. In a local church, this was done to maintain the confidentiality of the pastoral relationship; in the SACC, it protected recipients from victimization by the government. Tutu, more confident that the black community did not feel it needed the protection, abolished the cash grants and issued checks to named recipients. He also operated with a subcommittee, although Asingeni remained a discretionary fund without a budget. Over time, the fund broadened its scope, making relief payments for striking workers, paying for buses to Steve Biko's funeral, helping Robert Sobukwe's widow with funeral costs, covering administration costs for the "free Mandela" campaign, and covering the legal costs of a major Pan-Africanist Congress trial and the inquest into the killing of Biko.

The small, confidential meeting that was held on Tutu's return from Rome in April 1981 was the first of a series in which he, Storey, Motlana, Stevenson, and Barrett wrestled with the news about Rees. They heard that between 1976 and early May 1978–two months after Tutu assumed office–Rees had deposited 296,000 rand of the SACC's money in fifty-one bank accounts under his control. The police said they had found evidence of the payments when investigating one of the other fraud cases. They asked the SACC to press charges. Tutu's initial instinct at the first meeting was to express unease about Rees: outside the hearing of the police, he said that while the council had confidence in Rees's integrity, it was theoretically possible a crime had been committed. There were also racial overtones: the council had brought charges against a suspect who was black, but hesitated when a suspect was white. At the back of his mind, undisclosed to the meeting, was an incident that had occurred three weeks after he arrived at the SACC: Rees had requisitioned a check for 60,000 rand; Tutu had asked him what it was for; and Rees had told him it was for grants from the Asingeni Fund. Tutu had not been happy with the explanation, but he did not pursue it. Similarly, he did not dissent when, in April 1981, the SACC officers told the police they would not charge Rees. They said he had been given absolute discretion to use funds as he saw fit, and he could not be judged to have behaved improperly at the first whiff of suspicion. They did not say it, but the depth of their trust in Rees was matched only by the depth of their suspicion of the police's motives. Before the meeting adjourned, Storey, who was Rees's pastor, said he would almost certainly have to resign from the SACC if it brought charges against Rees.

The meeting sent Barrett to ask Rees about the money. Rees said some of it was from the Asingeni Fund and had been channeled to victims of political unrest through his accounts to safeguard their identities. But he had also been operating another discretionary fund, named Actipax, completely independent of the SACC. While waiting for money to come from abroad for Asingeni, he had sometimes borrowed money from Actipax. Most of the SACC checks made out to his personal accounts were repayments of these loans. After some months of investigation and discussion, the SACC officers accepted his explanation but said that his withdrawals of Asingeni's money after Tutu's arrival–totaling 90,000 rand–were irregular. They asked him to certify for auditing purposes that they were reimbursements to Actipax.

The SACC's response proved inadequate. First, during one of the fraud trials the police publicly revealed the payments to Rees. Newspapers that usually supported the SACC turned on the council. Worse for Tutu, a defense lawyer suggested that Rees had bought Tutu's silence with the 14,000-rand donation toward the house in Orlando West when he took office. Tutu felt sickened by the accusation and by the possibility Rees had used the SACC's money to help him pay for his house—as he drove home on the evening of the disclosure, he shrank at the prospect that his neighbors in Soweto might think that he was pursuing only material gain. He asked Rees to provide evidence of the source of the 14,000 rand: "I am very anxious and cannot go on living under this cloud of suspicion and innuendo," he wrote. Rees certified that the money did not belong to the SACC and named a German donor as the source of the gift. But the donor denied making it, so Tutu took out a loan to repay the money. A few days after the newspapers' criticism, at the end of October 1981, the executive committee resolved to appoint a senior independent lawyer to convene a commission of inquiry into its administration. P. W. Botha seized the opening: within days he announced the appointment of a government commission. Its terms of reference covered far more than finances: the whole operation of the SACC was to be investigated.

Tutu and the SACC were forced into the defensive for much of the time during his final years there. The police arrested John Rees during the council's national conference in 1982 and put him on trial. The judge, Richard Goldstone, was no stooge of apartheid—he subsequently became a member of South Africa's postapartheid Constitutional Court and the first chief prosecutor of the war crimes tribunal for Yugoslavia. He found the story about Actipax highly improbable and convicted Rees of fraud. But he said that the SACC had been irresponsible to give Rees so much discretion, accepted that he had not acted out of greed, and imposed an unusually light sentence—a fine and a suspended prison term.

Goldstone also said that Rees had developed an inflated sense of his own mission and had shown uncharacteristic arrogance in failing to transfer control of the funds to Tutu. Wolfram Kistner observed that Tutu was deeply hurt by the unwillingness of a white officer of the council to entrust control of funds to a black successor. This hurt was publicly displayed at the SACC's national conference after the trial ended. Delivering his annual report, Tutu made a stinging attack on Rees, on Rees's defenders, and on liberals in "fashionable white suburbs" who had suggested that the SACC had deserted Rees at his time of need:

I resent such treatment and conduct. For goodness sake, I did not defraud the SACC of its money. I did not betray the trust placed in me. . . . I did not lie. These wrongs were committed by John Rees. . . .

Those who want Mr. Rees to be a martyr must look for another cause. The case was a straightforward criminal prosecution. . . . Mr. Rees does not know perhaps know what his actions have cost this council. We have lost an outstanding President. . . . My staff are divided with the blacks on one side and some whites on the other. He has succeeded where the Government had failed. His crime is grist to the Government's mill.

Debate on the report at the conference took up nearly five hours of valuable time. It ended with an endorsement of the executive committee's judgment that Rees had deceived the council and Tutu had acted with integrity.

Tutu's reference to losing a president concerned the resignation of Peter Storey. Tutu had grown close to Storey, who had nominated him as general secretary. As vice president, Storey had chaired many of the council's meetings at crises during the frequent absences of Sam Buti, and he formally became president in 1982. He was an articulate, hands-on leader, the epitome of tough love and a forceful teller of what he believed to be the truth—whether addressing Tutu privately on his absences abroad or publicly defending Tutu's right to speak his mind. He and Tutu had been to prison together and seen the prime minister together. They had also, they learned later, once nearly died together. Trying to visit detainees in the most blatantly corrupt of the "independent" Bantustans, Venda, in South Africa's far north, they were themselves detained for some hours, declared "prohibited immigrants," and ordered out of the territory. On the way out, their escort of about a dozen armed men in two vehicles forced their car into the bush, stopped at a clearing, searched their trunk, and roughed them up. The men's leader told them, "We can kill you here and nobody will find you," but eventually he let them go. In the late 1990s, a white former military officer seconded to Venda told Storey and Tutu that he had ordered them killed and still did not know why his orders had not been carried out.

However, Storey's declaration of trust in John Rees before the trial began had made it impossible for him to continue as president. After Rees's conviction, he and Tutu had what he called a "flaming row" over Tutu's precipitate public comments to the press over the implications of the case. They quickly restored their relationship with mutual written apologies, but Storey had already decided that his continued presidency would imperil the SACC's unity.

While the SACC threatened to tear itself apart over the Rees affair, the government commission investigating it took up so much staff time, energy, and money that the independent commission mandated by the executive committee never sat. The government commission, headed by a senior judge, C. F. Eloff, appointed to head its investigation Klaus von Lieres und Wilkau, a state lawyer who had been a member of a press commission that devoted nearly as many pages in its report condemning the SACC as it did the press. The SACC retained one of South Africa's foremost lawyers, Sydney Kentridge, who had appeared for the Biko family at the inquest into Steve Biko's death. The commission contracted chartered accountants to examine the SACC's finances and itself studied 21,000 documents. At public hearings, the main threat to the SACC was presented by the police. They argued that the council represented the views of its foreign funders, not its member churches, and accused it of building the credibility of the ANC: among Tutu's sins was that he had publicly described Tambo as "a person of Christian conviction and sincerity in his desire for peace and justice." The police asked the commission to recommend that the council be declared an "affected organization" under South African law; such a declaration would have barred it from receiving foreign funding.

At the request of the Eloff Commission, Johan Heyns–later a leader of the white Dutch Reformed Church–analyzed Tutu's evidence. Heyns opened the way for government action against the SACC by pointing out that it was technically not a church, only a coordinating body. Tutu's proposition that the Bible was a revolutionary document was understandable, he said, but dangerous in South Africa's circumstances. Black theology was also dangerous. Heyns's solution was that theology and church life should be depoliticized, and that whites, in their historical role as initiators in South Africa, had to set the example. However, another Afrikaner theologian, David Bosch of the University of South Africa, drew an analogy between the role of the SACC and that of Afrikaans churches when Afrikaners were poor and powerless. A wise government ought to welcome a critical voice, even if it sounded radical, he told Eloff.

Tutu's evidence to the Eloff Commission rooted the SACC's work in its faith. Allister Sparks, the *Observer*'s correspondent in South Africa, described it as an extraordinary three-hour performance, perhaps the greatest sermon of Tutu's life: "It made for a curious scene, the little black bishop delivering his profound theological lecture strewn with biblical quotations and ecclesiastical allusions to a stony-faced white audience." Tutu said God had created the universe to be a cosmos in which harmony and unity would reign. But sin had disturbed the divine intention, creating a chaos of disharmony and separation:

> In the face of this, God then sent his Son to restore that primordial harmony to effect reconciliation. By becoming a real human being through Jesus Christ, God showed that he took the whole of human history and the whole of human life seriously. He demonstrated that he was Lord of all life, spiritual and secular, sacred and profane, material and spiritual. We will show that scripture and the mainstream of Christian tradition and teaching know nothing of the dichotomies so popular in our day which demand the separation of religion from politics. These I will demonstrate are deeply theological matters which affect the nature, work and attitudes of the SACC. Our God cares that children starve in resettlement camps, the somewhat respectable name for apartheid's dumping grounds for the pathetic casualties of this vicious and evil system. The God we worship does care that people die mysteriously in detention. . . . I might add that if God did not care about these and similar matters, I would not worship him for he would be a totally useless God. Mercifully, he is not such a God.
>
> I will show that the central work of Jesus was to effect reconciliation between God and us and also between man and man. Consequently, from a theological and scriptural base, I will demonstrate that apartheid, separate development or whatever it is called is evil, totally and without remainder, that it is unchristian and unbiblical. . . . If anyone were to show me that apartheid is biblical or Christian, I have said before and I reiterate now, that I would burn my Bible and cease to be a Christian.

Storey delivered a powerful and emotional eighty-four-page rebuttal of the police submission. Leaders of the SACC's member churches declared their support. After the police said that the SACC was being manipulated by South Africa's enemies abroad, church leaders from Europe and the United States came to testify that the council set the agenda for the activities they financed. Robert Runcie sent an international Anglican delegation. It included his secretary for Anglican Communion affairs, Terry Waite, who towered over Tutu, leading friends who saw a newspaper photograph of the two together to ask

Tutu, "Why were you kneeling?" In the view of Dan Vaughan, the deputy general secretary of the SACC, Tutu's handling of the Eloff inquiry turned the situation around. Tutu took important strategic decisions, he gave the inquiry his full attention and, above all, he rallied staff morale: "He often said afterwards that this was our finest hour in what were potentially the council's darkest days."

Eloff's 450-page report, taken up in Parliament early in 1984, revealed little that was not already in the public arena. It found that the SACC had failed to disclose having received money from governments—namely the Danish, Dutch, Swedish, and Finnish governments—as well as from churches. It had also tried to hide the fact that it used the World Council of Churches to launder money from a United Nations trust fund for victims of persecution under apartheid laws. The commission's central conclusions were in defense of government policy: the SACC aimed "to obstruct the government in its declared endeavour to effect change by a process of evolutionary development, in which the emphasis is to be on the rights of minorities." Civil disobedience, the covert discouragement of disinvestment, and the support of draft resisters were not in the national interest, Eloff said. He recommended that economic sabotage be made a crime and that the law controlling welfare organizations be amended to include the SACC. But Eloff accepted that the SACC set its own agenda and rejected the principal police proposal: "In no way was I going to recommend that it become an affected organization," he told the present writer. "It would have sounded the death knell for the SACC, and it would have been perceived as an attack on the Church."

When the report was first published, the extent to which it threatened the SACC was not clear, and Tutu launched an attack against it. He wrote a letter of complaint to Eloff and publicly questioned the commission's facts, judgments, and conclusions: "The commission did not boast a single professional theologian in its membership," he said, "so how could it be expected to pass fair judgement on an organisation whose very reason for existence is theological? It really was like asking, speaking respectfully, a group of blind men to judge the Chelsea Flower Show." On the day the report was released, a member of the SACC's staff appealed to a visiting Norwegian television journalist, Einar Lunde, for the support and protection the Nobel Peace Prize would offer. Lunde replied he was confident that the Norwegian Nobel Committee, which awards the prize, was watching developments in South Africa. His confidence was not misplaced.

CHAPTER 10

A FIRE BURNING IN MY BREAST

Desmond Tutu's growing prominence in the late 1970s and early 1980s produced a sharply polarized reaction. Black journalists wrote adulatory features on him, accompanied by inspirational quotations. His outspokenness made an impact on Nelson Mandela and Mandela's comrades on Robben Island. Black South Africans in townships named their children after him. Buti Tlhagale's predecessor as Catholic bishop of Johannesburg joked about how when he asked young Catholics who their bishop was, many would reply, "Tutu!" But whites' anger against him was first expressed in obscene phone calls and death threats from the far right. In 1978, incited by the security police, eight extremists wearing crash helmets stormed past the SACC's security desk and into Tutu's office, where they screamed abuse and threw "thirty pieces of silver"—five-cent pieces—at his feet. A group calling itself the Wit Kommando ("White Commando") threatened him repeatedly, once with a letter telling him, "Kaffir—lay off whites or die." Tutu first drew up his wishes for his funeral when another extremist group, the Wit Wolwe ("White Wolves"), threatened to kill him on a particular day. Their threat had an unexpected result: as a gesture of reassurance, three members of the staff came together to sing the Twenty-Third Psalm for him at the SACC's morning prayer service. He was enchanted, and the group, as the Khotso House Trio, became a permanent fixture of the SACC's worship at times of commiseration and celebration.

Anonymously produced propaganda against Tutu began to circulate in response to his campaigns for economic pressure and against forced removals. After his visit to the United States and Europe in 1981, pamphlets attempting to discredit him were distributed in the names of the "United Trade Union Council" and the "Young Christian Workers—Group Nine." No one in the union movement or the churches knew of the existence of such bodies. After Tutu led a week of prayer and fasting against forced removals, a leaflet from a supposed "Commission for

Reconciliation and Peace" defended removals, arguing that people were being rescued from slums. A security agency's report drawn up in the same period, marked "top secret," and placed in one of Tutu's files at the Department of Justice said that the churches were embarrassing the government internationally by exploiting forced removals. "The resettlement of blacks," the report said, "is at present one of the most important themes of the church assault on the present order." The government's campaign against Tutu was taken to a new level in September 1981, when the police minister Louis le Grange gave Parliament what turned out to be a preview of the government's case to the Eloff Commission. In a wide-ranging speech, le Grange charged Tutu with promoting disinvestment, the evasion of military service, civil disobedience, labor unrest, and the aims and objects of the ANC. Le Grange concluded his address with an appeal to church members to repudiate Tutu.

Le Grange's plea fell on well-prepared ground among white Christians. Most members of the SACC's churches did not read the pro-apartheid Afrikaans press, but the state-controlled South African Broadcasting Corporation (SABC) could regularly be relied on to devote its early morning commentary to agitation against Tutu. *The Citizen,* a newspaper founded with government money secretly given to an agricultural fertilizer magnate, regularly lambasted Tutu under headlines such as "Tu-Tu Much!" and "Shut Up!" As polarization persisted, so did hostility from many other English-language newspapers. By 1984, Tutu was the black leader white South Africans most loved to hate. This was to be expected among unrepentant racists. What was more threatening to Tutu's base in the SACC was that white liberals began to turn against him.

Tutu's extraordinary gift for communication across racial lines, his potential as a reconciler, and the reason it went unfulfilled as the struggle against apartheid reached its apogee, were all captured by the journalist Lin Menge of Johannesburg in a feature in the *Rand Daily Mail* in 1981. She wrote:

> One minute he seems to be whipping up a riot. The next minute he has stopped it, cold. And then he has his audience laughing. That is the push-pull emotional buffeting Bishop Tutu's critics would have suffered if they had gone along to the South African Council of Churches' public meeting this week. One minute whites were being swept along, submerged, in a black political tirade; the next minute, they were

being set down, safe and sound, on the sunny banks of racial amity. And after each dunking, whitey came a little closer to seeing the big black bishop, not as the monster who threw him in and held him down, but the nice uncle who pulled him out. But of course the detractors of the SACC did not turn up to see the wicked Bishop Tutu for themselves.

Helen Suzman, a liberal member of Parliament for more than twenty years, was a white South African who had regular contact with Tutu; she took up individual hardship cases with the government for him and joined the Tutu's family celebrations. Her views on sanctions were diametrically opposed to his; nevertheless they had a warm personal relationship. In correspondence, Tutu addressed Suzman—fourteen years his senior and a tough fighter who had taken personal abuse from P. W. Botha—as "My dear Child." (Entering into the spirit of his correspondence, she once signed a letter "The dear Child.") The writer Alan Paton, on the other hand, had little contact with Tutu. Although he had ghosted a newspaper editorial supportive of Tutu's letter to Vorster in 1976, six years later he was more ambivalent. He told his longtime friend and correspondent Trevor Huddleston in a letter in 1982 that he had just seen a documentary film featuring Tutu:

He is a great character, make no mistake about that, but I was more attracted to him after seeing the film than I had been before. Since then however he has made some speeches which seem to me deliberately provocative. Just as Andre Brink's* provocativeness has damaged his art, so I am afraid that Tutu's provocativeness will damage his religion. One week he makes a speech of Christian love and the next week he makes a speech which sends shivers down the spines of white Christians.

Although Paton did not identify the offending speeches, Tutu's orations at the time had taken on a note of angry defiance. The apartheid government, he would say—and continued to say, in more or less the same words, until Mandela was released in 1990—was trying to defend a lie, a totally evil and bankrupt system. Nothing it could do to him or the SACC, he said, would stop him from speaking out:

* South African novelist.

You [the government] are mere mortals. You are not gods. Many like yourselves tried to take on the church in the past when they too thought they were unassailable. Nero thought so, Hitler thought so, Mussolini thought so, so did Idi Amin and Bokassa. Where are they today? They bit the dust quite comprehensively. You, like they if you don't repent and mend your ways, will end up as the flotsam and jetsam of history . . . but the Church of God will continue.

Bill Burnett was another who voiced his unease at Tutu's no-holds-barred approach. Asked to join the week of prayer and fasting against forced removals, Burnett agreed but invoked the warning in Matthew's Gospel against performing such activities for the purpose of being seen by others. He admonished Tutu: "I am increasingly disturbed by the way calls to prayer, and sometimes fasting, are used to be directed at men rather than offered to God. . . . I know only too well that it is not difficult to misuse even God as we become involved in the power struggles of our time." (By the time Tutu became archbishop, he had conceded Burnett's point. Although he issued calls for prayer and fasting, he would not allow publicity to be given to the details of his own usually strict fasts.) On the eve of his retirement, Burnett became more outspoken in his private correspondence. He dismissed as rhetoric a proposal by Tutu, made during the campaign against forced removals, that the churches should excommunicate those who perpetrated apartheid. Burnett told a fellow bishop that the rhetoric would continue because "Desmond is Desmond and has not only an image to maintain, but a necessity to seem to retain the initiative," but that it would cease to have any power when nothing resulted.

As confrontation with the government grew, Burnett and some of the leaders of other churches went to see P. W. Botha in ecumenical delegations that excluded the SACC. The tension between the Anglican archbishop's office in Cape Town and Tutu in Johannesburg eased considerably, however, when Burnett retired and Philip Russell, who was the bishop of Natal and a long-serving member of the SACC executive committee, was chosen in Burnett's place. Church leaders still sometimes met the government without the SACC present, and Russell was not uncritical of Tutu; he once contested Tutu's use of the phrase "God has taken sides on behalf of the poor," saying he preferred the formulation that God had a particular concern for the poor. However, soon after Russell assumed office the church's synod of bishops rallied in Tutu's defense against the government, quoting St. Paul: "The whole body suffers when one of its members is hurt."

The indignation of most white English-speaking South Africans at criticism by black leaders such as Tutu was bolstered by their assertion that apartheid was being reformed in a steady process of evolution. Had apartheid in sports not been abolished? Had Harry Oppenheimer not persuaded fellow business leaders to form a foundation to improve conditions in Soweto? Had P. W. Botha not legalized black trade unions in response to the needs of the business community? And had Botha not risked his power base and split his party by reforming the constitution to include people of color in Parliament? White lay Anglicans, feeling that an Afrikaner Nationalist government was taking account of their business interests for the first time, were as anxious as any in the white community for Botha to prevail.

Ironically, it was Botha's tinkering on the edges of the apartheid system that led to the final train of events culminating in its downfall. In 1983, white voters approved in a referendum a new constitution, which created separate chambers of Parliament for Coloured and Indian South Africans. The "reforms," far from sharing power, entrenched it in white hands. They installed Botha in an executive presidency. They assigned Coloured and Indian legislators permanent minority status, leaving these legislators unable even to form alliances with the opposition in the white chamber. The majority of black South Africans—those of purely African descent—continued to be excluded from Parliament altogether; they were to have the right to vote only for local authorities and in Bantustan governments. The conferences, assemblies, and synods of the SACC's member churches rejected the new constitution outright. In a resolution that pulled their views together at the next national conference, the SACC said the constitution "perpetuates division on racial lines . . . and does not move in any way towards the achievement of a common society and common citizenship." Tutu described the constitution as failing even to acknowledge the existence of black South Africans. But the church leader who took the most important initiative in organising opposition was Allan Boesak.

By 1983, Boesak was becoming one of the most prominent anti-apartheid voices of the South African church, particularly internationally. The previous year he had been elected president of the World Alliance of Reformed Churches at a meeting that isolated the white Dutch Reformed Church by declaring apartheid a heresy. He had narrowly missed election as moderator of the synod of his own Dutch Reformed Mission Church, the largest single church in the Coloured community. He was a powerful preacher; some people likened him, as an orator, to Martin Luther King, Jr. In January 1983, Boesak was invited to address a meeting to revive the Transvaal Indian Congress, a partner of the ANC in the Congress Alliance of the 1950s. There Boesak called for the formation of a united front of churches, civic associations, trade unions, student organizations, and sports bodies to oppose the government's constitutional proposals. His appeal resonated with activists from the congress tradition; and seven months later, in August 1983, the United Democratic Front (UDF), encompassing 575 affiliates, was launched in Cape Town. The founding conference of the UDF elected as its leaders three presidents, all veterans of the ANC, among them Albertina Sisulu, the wife of Walter Sisulu. It also named a list of famous "patrons" including religious leaders. Tutu, who did not attend the launch, was one of them.

The contrasting roles of Tutu and Boesak in the biggest show of support for the ideals of the ANC since its banning highlighted significant differences in their styles. Boesak, with a fine, sharply-honed political mind, worked in the world of organizational strategy and politics. Tutu kept his distance from the political process, choosing rather to follow his intuition. Late-night meetings in smoke-filled rooms were not for him; he once told the present writer: "I'm not a thinker, I can't analyze things. I'm a feeling person; maybe I get inspirations." In the 1970s, Buti Tlhagale at Regina Mundi Church regarded Tutu and Nthato Motlana as two key figures in Soweto, without whose presence the annual commemoration on June 16 would dissolve into chaos. Tutu, however, saw Motlana, not himself, as the political leader; Tutu might preach liberation, but his constituency was the church and his mandate the Christian gospel. The three best examples of why religious leaders should keep out of party politics, he would say, were Abel Muzorewa in Zimbabwe, Archbishop Makarios in Cyprus, and the Ayatollah Khomeini in Iran.

Tutu also tried to keep himself politically nonaligned. In accordance with the positions taken by many of the SACC's member churches, he rejected the role that apartheid allocated to the homelands and their leaders. Beyond that, he attempted to keep his distance from party activity. When an activist of the Pan Africanist Congress (PAC) complained to him about his support of the "free Mandela" campaign, he replied that he did not support any one group but Mandela was the most effective symbol around which to lobby for the release of all leaders. He countersigned a plea by his daughter Naomi that antiapartheid activists in the United States support the PAC as well as the ANC. And he deplored rifts that opened up regarding the commemorations of June 16, between rival supporters of black consciousness and the Freedom Charter. Two months before the launch of the UDF, he helped to inaugurate a "National Forum"—which became closely associated with the black consciousness movement—to bring the two sides together. "Why are we so often at one another's throats?" he asked the meeting. "Why are we so keen to denigrate one another and impute the worst motives to one another and actually sabotage the liberation struggle . . . whilst the enemy rolls about in uncontrollable mirth?"

The UDF's first high-profile activity was a successful campaign against elections for the Coloured and Indian houses of Parliament set up under the new constitution. In August 1984, only 18 percent of those eligible to vote in Coloured elections turned out. On September 2, 24 percent of Indian voters went to the polls. The next day events in black townships grabbed the country's attention. Activists affiliated to the UDF in the townships of the industrialised Vaal triangle, south of Johannesburg, called a strike in protest against a 56 percent rent increase imposed by the local council, which had been elected by only 15 percent of eligible voters. They unwittingly set off a low-intensity civil war in the country's black townships, which, although it ebbed and flowed, was not to end finally until liberation ten years later.

Patrick Noonan, an Irish Franciscan who served in the Vaal townships, has written a compelling account of the uprising, which began on the day he called "black Monday," September 3, 1984—two days before P. W. Botha was elected executive president under the new constitution. Snippets from Noonan's diary for black Monday suggest the atmosphere in which countless clergy and lay church workers ministered during the last years of apartheid:

> Petrus Mokoena hurriedly buys koki pens and cardboard boxes to help with the making of placards. . . . The Security Police are cruising around in their dark-windowed cars. . . . Bus commuters, attempting to go to work in defiance of the "declared" one-day anti-rent-rise stay-away, were being stoned. . . . At 11 AM an enormous crowd appeared on the horizon. . . . The police withdrew from the church to the lower part of the section that would later be known as "Beirut" in Moshoeshoe Street, obviously unprepared for such a massive throng of people. And then it happened. A camouflaged military helicopter, like a giant steel crab, roared up from behind the marchers at rooftop

level, spraying teargas into the crowd. "O Nkosi yami! Safa saphela! Kwenzenjani kwelilizwe lethu?" (Oh my God! We're all going to be killed. What is going on in our land?), Lucas shouted. Panic, screaming, chaos, people trampled underfoot, running in all directions, anger . . . Our phones ring all day for more information on the breaking news. The Vaal Triangle is burning. Black smoke curling skywards dots the townships' landscape.

Fourteen residents of the township died and thirty-two were injured, at least eight of them policemen, on the first day of the protests. Tutu, who had sent one of the SACC's most experienced fieldworkers, Thom Manthata, to the Vaal in the buildup to the rent boycott, telegraphed Louis le Grange on September 4 and asked him to meet church leaders. "This is the time for statesmen," Tutu said. On September 6, as Tutu and the SACC's leaders held an emergency meeting on the situation, a government delegation toured the township. At one point the group—which included le Grange; the defense minister, Magnus Malan, an army general turned politician who headed P. W. Botha's security apparatus; and the local member of Parliament, F. W. de Klerk—was forced to make a detour when angry residents blocking the way refused to disperse. By the end of the month, ninety people were dead, among them five councilors targetted as collaborationists. (One was deputy mayor Kuzwayo Jacob Dlamini, whose death led to the trial of Sharpeville Six.) In October the government augmented the police by ordering the army into the townships for the first time. "As far as we're concerned," said le Grange, "it is war, plain and simple."

In the following weeks and months, Noonan observed later, the townships "boiled and simmered and boiled over again. . . . It was a time of terror, mass arrests, burning tires, arson, political funerals, the destruction of state property, and of meetings. Emergency meetings, urgent meetings and ad hoc meetings between the state, the people and the churches." As community leaders were arrested or went into hiding, the clergy had no option but to step into their places: "In this knife-edge atmosphere, there was no way back to the presbytery or friary except through the gauntlet of a people demanding your assistance." Tutu had to delay the beginning of long-overdue sabbatical leave in the United States to respond to the crisis. On a pastoral visit to the East Rand, he prayed with an elderly woman whose six-year-old grandson had been shot dead by police as he played in her yard. There could hardly have been a more appropriate moment for the world to recognize peacemaking in South Africa, and Tutu would soon be telling the story of the grandmother in Oslo.

Questions of peace and violence in South Africa were not new to the Norwegian Nobel Committee, the body elected by the Norwegian Storting (parliament) to award the Peace Prize under the will of Alfred Nobel. In 1961, when the committee awarded the 1960 prize to Albert Luthuli, it expressed surprise that the struggle of black South Africans had remained peaceful. "Their patience is remarkable; their moral strength in the struggle boundless," the committee chairman, Gunnar Jahn, remarked in his presentation speech. In fact, the ANC's patience ran out six days after Luthuli received the award; its military wing, uMkhonto we Sizwe (MK), set off its first bombs on December 16, 1961. The Norwegians appear to have learned after the prize was announced but before it was conferred that violence had become likely: Luthuli told at least one Norwegian in Oslo that notwithstanding his own feelings on the issue, he had felt bound at a meeting with the ANC's leaders some months earlier to accept a decision to embark on sabotage. The Norwegians did not know when sabotage would begin and, given the operational autonomy of MK, it is unlikely that even Luthuli knew. However, knowledge of a decision in principle to resort to violence may have influenced the closing words of Jahn's speech, in which he said that if the struggle "degenerates into bloody slaughter . . . let us remember him [Luthuli] then and never forget that his way was unwavering and clear. He would not have had it so."

The award to Luthuli created what the secretary of the Norwegian Nobel Committee, Geir Lundestad, has identified as a new category of peace prize, which in the half century that followed became the largest single category, recognizing those who strove to establish respect for human rights. As international attention focused on South Africa in the aftermath of the Soweto uprising, increasing numbers of South Africans were nominated for the prize, usually by their admirers overseas. In 1981, three South Africans were nominated: Helen Suzman (for the second time), Tutu, and Mangosuthu Buthelezi. The prize was awarded to an organization, the Office of the UN High Commissioner for Refugees. Suzman and Tutu were both nominated again in 1982, when the prize went to two recipients who fell within the most traditional application of the award criteria—the disarmament campaigners Alva Myrdal of Sweden and Alfonso Garcia Robles of Mexico. In 1983, discussion of South Africa intensified when Nelson Mandela was nominated for the first time. His nomination, from a large group of west European parliamentarians, posed a challenge to the Nobel Committee because he had been jailed for planning armed rebellion and his current thinking was unknown. Tutu was not initially nominated that year, so, in an apparent attempt to widen the number of South Africans to be considered, his name was added to the list from within the committee by its chairman, Egil Aarvik. The prize was awarded to Lech Walesa, leader of Solidarity in Poland.

There is evidence that at least some members of the Nobel Committee saw South Africa as providing an alternative candidate in 1983 if the situation in Poland deteriorated and became unstable before the prize was announced. In 1984, with South Africa already in the minds of committee members, several influences came to bear on the committee. In February, the Eloff Commission's report was published in Cape Town while the Norwegian television journalist Einar Lunde happened to be in the country. As well as visiting the SACC, Lunde went to Sebokeng in the Vaal triangle, where he interviewed an elderly woman who had witnessed police killing children. When Lunde edited the footage back in Norway, tears began to flow down his cheeks. He had gone to school with the sons of Egil Aarvik. He spontaneously picked up the phone and called Aarvik. "You've got to give the prize to South Africa this year," he blurted out. "This year is more important than ever before." He described his visit to South Africa and said he had documentation to support his case. Aarvik asked him to send it to the committee, and he did, accompanied by a covering letter that strongly backed the SACC for the prize. Over the same period, Aarvik was hearing about Tutu in particular from a close friend, Gunnar Lislerud, a Norwegian bishop who had been a missionary in South Africa. Lislerud was one of the foreign church leaders who gave evidence to the Eloff Commission in support of the SACC, and he sent the committee a ten-page recommendation backing Tutu. South Africa was on the verge of civil war, Lislerud wrote; the SACC was one of very few organizations fighting apartheid that the government had not banned; and a Peace Prize would make it difficult for the government to act against Tutu and the SACC. Lunde and Lislerud found Aarvik receptive—he was himself a former church official, and as a Christian Democrat parliamentarian in 1961 he had denounced the Sharpeville massacre in strong language during a speech to the Storting.

Six South African names were among those before the Nobel Committee in 1984: Tutu, Suzman, Buthelezi, and Mandela, who had all been proposed previously; and Oliver Tambo and the SACC (in its institutional capacity), now nominated for the first time. Mandela, Suzman, and the SACC were nominated from outside; but the names of Tutu, Buthelezi, and Tambo were added by the committee, apparently to ensure that its list was comprehensive. No records of the committee's deliberations are kept, but the available evidence suggests that it was by no means certain until the final stages that the award would go to South Africa, partly because Luthuli had already received the prize for the same struggle there. Nor was Tutu the inevitable choice: he was held by some to represent specifically Christian opposition to apartheid when in reality the opposition was far wider. Ultimately, however, the committee appears to have seen Tutu as less controversial than Mandela or Buthelezi. It selected him, as Aarvik said in his presentation speech, as "a unifying leader figure in the campaign to solve South Africa's apartheid problem by peaceful means."

Tutu was on sabbatical at the General Theological Seminary of the Episcopal Church when the Nobel Committee made its decision. On the afternoon of Monday, October 15, a member of the staff of the Norwegian mission to the United Nations called the dean of the seminary, James C. Fenhagen, and made an appointment for Norway's ambassador to the United Nations to visit the campus in New York's Chelsea neighborhood the next morning. At evensong, Fenhagen told the seminary only that an announcement was due the next day. If Tutu had won the prize, the chapel bells would ring. That night Leah found the tension almost unbearable; perhaps the ambassador was coming to say that the award was going to someone else. Desmond slept badly: "It was almost like waiting for exam results. It had happened twice before that people said I was a strong candidate, and the letdown then was very hard." At nine o'clock in the morning, when the ambassador, Tom Eric Vraalsen, was shown up to the Tutus' apartment, he was carrying a bouquet of flowers for Leah. "It was a giveaway," she said. "I had a big lump in my throat and I thought my heart had stopped." As the bells began to ring, classes stopped, the students and staff crowded into the chapel, and the Tutus entered to tears and a standing ovation. Desmond took a moment of silence to read Psalm 139 to himself:

O Lord you have searched me out and known me:
    You know when I sit or when I stand

you comprehend my thoughts long before.
You discern my path and the places where I rest:
you are acquainted with all my ways.
For there is not a word on my tongue:
But you Lord know it altogether.
You have encompassed me behind and before:
and have laid your hand upon me.

The congregation prayed and sang hymns of thanksgiving. Tutu
thanked them in turn: "This is our award. It says something about the
Christian church. . . . This is wonderful that you share in it." He then
went out and stood on the grass in the seminary's enclosed courtyard
for a news conference. He could hardly have chosen a better place
than New York to focus international attention on South Africa. As
telegrams piled up alongside birthday cards from the week before, he
did a stream of interviews through the day, warning of a bloodbath if
the international community did not exert pressure to force the South
African government to negotiate an end to apartheid. Peter Jennings of
ABC asked what Tutu meant when he said he was a man of peace, but
not a pacifist:

   Tutu: "Well, it means I would understand when people pick up
   arms and I would not condemn them. . . . Gandhi said that his methods
   would probably not have applied in Nazi Germany."
   Jennings: "Are you comparing South Africa to Nazi Germany in this
   instance?"
   Tutu: "Oh, I do, yes. . . . I would say, the gas chambers were probably more efficient and more clean . . . [but] if you put children in places
   where, that you know that they will starve, you are as guilty as those
   who stoke up gas chambers."

Tutu also compared the struggle against apartheid to that against
communism. Referring to the previous year's award to Lech Walesa,
he told the *MacNeil/Lehrer NewsHour* that his award "is saying that
those who oppose apartheid are in many ways like those who oppose
communism."
   The next day, Desmond and Leah went home to celebrate. They
brought with them Naomi and Mpho, who were both studying at
American universities. They flew first on the Concorde to London,
where Robert Runcie and Terry Waite, a battery of cameras and lights

behind them, met them at Heathrow Airport. Desmond addressed a
news conference, and the family took an overnight flight to Johannesburg. On Thursday, jubilant supporters, led by Allan Boesak, met the
family at the airport there, cheering, dancing, and singing in a raptur-
ous welcome. They carried placards reading "Apartheid: Good-Bye to
You" and "Welcome, Baba." Ignoring dozens of uniformed and plainclothes police—and instructions that singing was not allowed in the
arrivals hall—they welcomed the Tutus with the national anthem recognized by black South Africans: "Nkosi Sikelel' iAfrika" ("God Bless
Africa"). At Khotso House, Beyers Naude, South Africa's most prominent Afrikaner Christian dissident, fought back tears as he voiced the
hope that one day his people would come to understand Tutu's message. Tutu replied that he accepted the award especially on behalf of
"those who are called the little people—the ones whose noses are
rubbed in the dust every day."

> This award is for mothers, who sit at railway stations to try to eke out an
> existence, selling potatoes, selling mealies [maize, or corn], selling pro-
> duce. This award is for you, fathers, sitting in a single-sex hostel, sepa-
> rated from your children for 11 months a year. This award is for you.
> This award is for you, mothers in the KTC squatter camp [Cape Town],
> whose shelters are destroyed callously every day, and who sit on soak-
> ing mattresses in the winter rain, holding whimpering babies. . . . This
> award is for you, the 3.5 million of our people who have been uprooted
> and dumped as if you were rubbish. This award is for you.

Congratulatory messages poured in from around the world—from
heads of state and from Tutu's sister Gloria: "Congrat. Bro. Well Done,
Your sister, Gugu." From exile in Zamiba, ANC's leader Oliver Tambo
telegraphed that Tutu was a worthy successor to Luthuli. From Stanger
in Natal came greetings from Luthuli's widow, Nokukhanya. Nelson
Mandela, transferred from Robben Island to a mainland prison in
Cape Town, wrote a letter of congratulation, but the prison authorities
refused to send it.

Beyers Naude's emotional welcome was an allusion to white South
Africa's hostile reception of the news. Both P. W. Botha and his foreign
minister, R. F. (Pik) Botha responded with "no comment." In Johannesburg the Afrikaans daily, *Beeld,* said that the award was one of the
strangest yet: "Tutu stands for anything but peace." The first SABC
radio news bulletin with the news carried it as the last item. Television

news aimed at whites first carried a ten-second report as its sixth item, then moved it up to second place, but with no reports of celebrations, congratulations, or implications. A political commentary on the radio presumed to tell the Nobel Committee that it had misinterpreted Alfred Nobel's will; and an attack on television showed footage of Tutu delivering an impassioned speech, allowing his voice to emerge only for an isolated phrase, with no context, featuring the word "violence." *The Citizen* said that if South Africa had truly been like Nazi Germany, "Bishop Tutu would not have been around to carry on his campaign."

Alan Paton wrote a newspaper article in the form of an open letter to Tutu, which congratulated him but then continued on an unexpectedly sour note: "I have never won a prize like that. I am afraid that my skin is not the right colour." Tutu was the first black man since Luthuli to assume a position of national responsibility, Paton said. This would require a measure of wisdom and courage that had never been required "and certainly has never been shown before." He ended the piece by questioning Tutu's political morality: "I do not understand how your Christian conscience allows you to advocate disinvestment. . . . It would go against my own deepest principles to advocate anything that would put a man—and especially a black man—out of a job." At the other end of the political spectrum, the exiled South African Communist Party was delighted by the award but upset that Tutu had put communism in the same category as apartheid and Nazism:

> The SACP throughout the seven decades of its history has stood uncompromisingly by the principle of equal rights for all South Africans irrespective of race, creed or colour. . . . There are no deprived or oppressed peoples in the Soviet Union today—no ghettoes, no slums, no colour bars. . . . The glib equation of apartheid with "Nazism and Communism" is an affront to history and reason, an insult to the liberation movement in general, a desecration of the memory of some of our foremost martyrs and freedom fighters.

During his four-day trip home, Tutu visited his mother, now eighty, who was living with his sister Sylvia. It was to be the last time he saw her; she died at the end of November. On Sunday he spent the day celebrating at his home parish, St. Augustine's, Orlando West, in traditional Soweto Anglican style: with a three-hour Eucharist using five languages—English, IsiXhosa, IsiZulu, Sesotho, and Setswana—and featuring incense, bells, western hymns, and African choruses. The only musical instruments were the voices of the congregation, accompanied by hand clapping and foot stamping. He also discussed what to do with the prize money of 192,000 dollars. (He shared some with his family and the staff of the SACC and gave the rest to a scholarship fund for South African students in exile.)

Tutu's relationship with St. Augustine's was born of a longing for pastoral ministry. He had first asked Timothy Bavin for a part-time appointment to a local parish when he arrived at the SACC, and Bavin agreed to institute him as rector of St. Augustine's some years later. His desire to be a pastor was not confined to a local level; after a year at the SACC, he told a friend that he wanted at some stage to return to the Anglican Church as a diocesan bishop. The prospect was first raised by the election to replace Bill Burnett when he retired as archbishop of Cape Town in 1981. As in Johannesburg in 1974, Tutu did not appear to be a strong candidate. Cape Town was the mother diocese of the Anglican Church in southern Africa; and the archbishop was its most senior bishop and head of the church, chosen only after years of service in another large diocese. Tutu had nineteen months of episcopal experience, in one of the church's smaller dioceses. The strongest candidate, Michael Nuttall, was one of the church's finest intellects and had been bishop of Pretoria for five years. Yet Tutu's nomination deadlocked the assembly. On the third day, the synod of bishops chose Philip Russell, who was the most senior bishop under Burnett and was within a few years of retirement. This gave Tutu's supporters time to rally support for him before the next election.

After the deadlock in 1981, Anglicans promoting Tutu as a future archbishop of Cape Town resolved that if they were to succeed, they needed first to get him elected as bishop of a major South African diocese. How they did this is a remarkable story of domestic and international intrigue involving–albeit unwittingly in some cases–Timothy Bavin, Philip Russell, Njongonkulu Ndungane (a senior Anglican church official), Terry Waite, Robert Runcie, Margaret Thatcher, Queen Elizabeth II of the United Kingdom, an elective assembly of the diocese of Johannesburg, the synod of bishops, and the South African security police.

Bavin had proved a unifying figure since his election in Johannesburg, admired by Tutu among many others. For activist clergymen such as Dale White–the priest who had taught Tutu Greek in the 1950s–he was, however, much too conservative. In the early 1980s, White began to lobby local and English church officials, including

Terry Waite, to have Bavin offered a diocese in England. At the same time, Waite, after visits to South Africa, suggested to Robert Runcie that Tutu was in an exposed position in the SACC and that his position would be strengthened if he was brought back fully into the Anglican Church. "We wanted to get him to be first of all a bishop of a diocese," Waite told the present writer. "We [also] felt . . . that he was the man who could be one of the first black Africans in a position of real prominence in South Africa, which clearly meant Cape Town." Runcie, who had once taught Bavin, made preliminary overtures to him about returning to England, to which Bavin gave noncommittal answers.

In 1983, Runcie pursued the idea at an assembly of the World Council of Churches in Vancouver. Tutu had made an impact on the assembly: the government had refused him a travel document, then changed its mind, so he arrived only toward the end of proceedings, to be greeted by a standing ovation when he made a dramatic entrance at a midnight peace vigil. Runcie asked one of the South Africans present—whom he did not identify—whether, if the Church of England could engineer a vacancy for Bavin, Tutu's supporters could get him elected bishop of Johannesburg: "He said he thought they could," Runcie told a biographer. "And I said, 'And if you manage that, do you think that when Philip Russell . . . retires in two years' time, you could get Desmond translated* there?' And he thought they could." Separately, Runcie urged Tutu to consider returning from the SACC to a diocese, but did not disclose any further plans.

Eight months later, in May 1984, the British prime minister, Margaret Thatcher, wrote to Bavin asking whether she could submit his name to the queen as a candidate for the diocese of Portsmouth in England. The letter came as a complete surprise. Runcie wrote and telephoned to urge him to accept. Bavin, by now thoroughly committed to South Africa and to the diocese, took more than a month to decide. He told his fellow bishops that it was only during Mass at the end of a retreat that he was confirmed in his belief that God was calling him to return to England: "Not without a struggle, [I] offered my obedience to Him. . . . I hope that never again do I find myself so torn between my personal preferences and what I believe to be God's will." Twenty years later, Bavin told this writer that he had no idea of Runcie's motive in offering him Portsmouth: "It would have made the decision that much harder, since I was anxious to do what I believed God was

* Technical term for moving a bishop already serving in one diocese to a new see.

calling me to do. But then, God can act through the schemes of archbishops as well as through elective assemblies." Tutu told the author
that he did not recall when he learned about what Runcie and Waite
called their "good diplomacy." The SACC's files show that in August
1984, he said in the course of a letter to Waite: "I note that you for your
part have fulfilled your side of the bargain. It is now up to us here
though I think we do not have a snowball's chance in hell–never
mind. We will have a go and hope that the Holy Spirit will do His bit."

No one, of course, could have known that by the time Johannesburg's elective assembly convened, Tutu would be a Nobel laureate.
This, added to his episcopal experience in Lesotho and his vast local
and international exposure, might have given his supporters the hope
that he was a far stronger candidate than he had been ten years earlier.
Trevor Huddleston, lobbying against another candidate, told his
brother monks that the diocese would not be able to ignore Tutu, and
"if they do it will be a very sad day for Johannesburg." But Huddleston,
who had been away from South Africa for nearly thirty years, had not
reckoned with the obduracy of white Anglican opinion.

The elective assembly convened at St. Barnabas College, a nonracial
church school in the western suburbs of Johannesburg, on Tuesday,
October 23–the day after Tutu arrived back in New York from his brief
visit home. Five candidates were nominated. Tutu, proposed by
Michael Corke, the principal of St. Barnabas; and seconded by David
Nkwe, an old college friend and one of Soweto's best-known clergymen, was the only black candidate. Most of the first day was taken up
debating the nominees. From the first round of voting, soon after five
PM, the front-runners were Tutu and Peter Lee, a socially active evangelical from Johannesburg's northern suburbs. Tutu drew most of the
clergy's votes, and he and Lee had about the same number of lay
votes. But as other candidates were eliminated, Tutu's vote remained
the same while Lee's grew by leaps and bounds. By the third ballot,
Lee had more clergy votes than Tutu and the requisite two-thirds
majority of lay votes. Tutu continued to lose support. By the sixth
round Lee was within five votes of a two-thirds majority among the
clergy, and thus of election as bishop.

Then the assembly reopened debate. Participants were unclear,
twenty years later, about what had changed the minds of the electors.
The assembly minutes indicate that it was an impassioned session. A
black layman's speech had a white layman walking out in protest.
One participant believed that a speaker who warned the largely Anglo-

Catholic diocese that it was about to elect an evangelical bishop played a particularly persuasive role. What is clear is that when voting resumed later that night, the clergy's support swung dramatically in favor of Tutu. He overtook Lee in clergy votes and doubled his lay support. The assembly then adjourned overnight. But through another four rounds of voting on the second day, the number of lay votes cast for Tutu remained almost the same, never exceeding the number of black parishes in the diocese. As this became apparent, first Lee and then Tutu began to lose votes. As the deadlock continued, Lee asked for, but was refused, permission to withdraw from the election. More and more voters opted out altogether. By the eleventh ballot, one-third of the assembly refused to vote for either candidate. Exhausted, the meeting delegated the decision to the synod of bishops. As in 1974, Tutu could not draw the support of white parishioners. "Blocking was the order of the day," one senior white priest told Philip Russell, who chaired the assembly. The eyes of the Anglican world might have been on the diocese of Johannesburg, but the white laity was having none of Tutu—Nobel laureate or not.

On the eve of the bishops' synod, the government took a hand. Under an eight-column headline on the front page of the newspaper with the largest circulation in the country, the *Sunday Times,* a journalist best-known for publishing material fed to him clandestinely by the security police reported that the church stood on the brink of its most serious crisis in years. "A revolt by moderate bishops" seemed set to block Tutu's election, he wrote. The list of bishops named as supporting Tutu was probably accurate; but the list of those named as being against Tutu was largely fanciful. The report in the *Sunday Times* suggested that the synod promised all the tension and intrigue of a papal election and could drag on all week.

The bishops were infuriated by the obvious attempt to dictate the church's decision. They arrived at Modderpoort for their synod during the course of Monday. Philip Russell took part in pushing for a quick decision. By Tuesday they had chosen Tutu.

Black Anglicans celebrated. Many whites fumed, becoming angrier and angrier with Tutu as he toured the United States and Europe during his sabbatical. In London, at St. Paul's Cathedral, he said that most black South Africans thought anything would be better than apartheid: "If the Russians were to come to South Africa today then most blacks who reject communism as atheistic and materialistic would welcome them as saviours." On *This Week with David Brinkley,* he warned that everybody in South Africa would suffer if there was widespread violence, "and it may be that a white skin would be a horrible disadvantage." Visiting Robert Runcie at Canterbury Cathedral the day before receiving the peace prize, he struck a lighter note: "Leah says so many things are happening to us lately, with the Nobel Prize and the see of Johannesburg, that at the rate we're going she's worried she might wake up one morning and find she's sleeping with the pope!"

Philip Russell became a secondary focus of white people's outrage. A woman from Natal asked him how someone with a white skin could be expected to support a church harboring a "disciple of doom." Another correspondent sent Russell a newspaper clipping accusing Tutu of insulting the pope by telling Leah's joke. The churchwardens of Christ Church, Mayfair, in Johannesburg, wrote: "We pray that once Bishop Tutu takes up his post, he will concentrate on his pastoral duties to the exclusion of 'bloodbath' politics."

Desmond, Leah, their four children, a delegation of the SACC's staff and members of the executive committee went to Oslo for the presentation of the peace prize on December 10 and for the events surrounding it—a torchlight parade of 2,000 past the laureate's balcony at the Grand Hotel, a banquet with reindeer on the menu, Tutu's Nobel lecture, and celebrations with unions and the church. They were joined by friends from abroad, among them Martin Kenyon, Terry Waite, and James and Eulalie Fenhagen. Trevor Huddleston was hurt not to receive a formal invitation. When he was told informally that he was expected, he wrote, five days before the ceremony, that if he had received a month's notice he would have been able to rearrange his schedule and come. As Egil Aarvik completed his presentation speech in the hall at Oslo University, the Aula, a Norwegian official approached an aide to King Olav V and told him there had been a bomb threat. The king waved him away; but the proceedings were stopped by police, the king left under protest, and the hall was cleared for eighty minutes—an act unprecedented in the history of the prize—while bomb-sniffing dogs were brought in. The threat, later found to have been made by a Norwegian neo-Nazi, was a hoax. By the time the ceremony reconvened, the orchestra had disappeared. In an impromptu gesture that made a lasting impression on the assembly, Tutu summoned the South Africans present to the stage to sing "Nkosi Sikelel' iAfrika." For Waite, "it absolutely made the day." "It changed the whole mood," recalled James and Eulalie Fenhagen. "They just took over, and it was so joyful."

Tutu returned to South Africa after visits to Sweden, Denmark,

Canada, Tanzania, and Zambia. At a news conference in Johannesburg, he issued an ultimatum on sanctions, linked to three conditions that he had been advocating for most of the previous year. He would call for economic sanctions, he said, if within eighteen to twenty-four months the government did not abolish the pass laws, allow the families of migrant workers to live with them, and increase investment in the education of blacks. When a black journalist said that some people would feel Tutu's Nobel Prize would inhibit the struggle for liberation, he acknowledged this possibility: "I am surprised that radical blacks are still willing to say we are their leaders. What have we got to show for all our talk of peaceful change? Nothing."

On Sunday, February 3, Desmond Tutu returned to St. Mary's Cathedral. There, in the church in which he had been ordained deacon and priest, served as dean, and been consecrated as a bishop, he was enthroned as the sixth bishop of Johannesburg. The three-hour service reflected the cultural and linguistic heritage of both Tutu and his diocese. As members of the congregation waited for the service to begin, they listened to Bach's Fantasia in G. The opening procession was to a hymn in English, "Guide Me, O Thou Great Redeemer." Standing down the street from the railway station he had used as a boy, clad in a cope and miter of cream and red, Tutu hammered his staff on the closed west door three times. The door was opened, Philip Russell led him into the cathedral, and the choir sang an anthem set to music by Bruckner. The Gloria ("Glory to God in the Highest") and the Nicene Creed were sung in IsiXhosa. Sally Motlana read from the Old Testament lesson in Sesotho; and Beyers Naude read from the New Testament in Afrikaans. Simeon Nkoane—who was one of two bishops suffragan in the diocese and a monk of the Community of the Resurrection—chanted the Gospel; and Sigisbert Ndwandwe, the other bishop suffragan, led the prayers. Tutu preached for an hour—"too long," said Russell in a letter to Timothy Bavin. The dean, Tutu's former student Merwyn Castle, presented him to the congregation. Soweto choirs, including the choir from St. Augustine's, joined the cathedral choir. The Khotso House Trio and a visiting choir, Imilonji ka Ntu, contributed items, and the congregation sang traditional African choruses. The cathedral was packed. There were few whites from the northern suburbs, noted the former bishop, Leslie Stradling; he attributed this to the time of the service, two o'clock on a Sunday afternoon.

One of the white Anglicans attending was Harry Oppenheimer,

who heard Tutu amend his ultimatum on sanctions. To the conditions previously enumerated, Tutu added two more: the government should declare an end to forced removals and to stripping blacks of their South African nationality. He gave notice, he said in his sermon, that if the dismantling of apartheid had not started within eighteen to twenty-four months, he would call for punitive economic sanctions, whatever the legal consequences. Recognizing that many whites felt he had been foisted on them, he tried to reassure them he was not the "horrid ogre" he was made out to be, emphasizing his belief in the centrality of the spiritual life and noting that his positions were based on the Bible and that he was committed to dialogue and reconciliation. But he said that, like the Old Testament prophet Jeremiah, he had no choice but to speak his mind. If Jeremiah tried to suppress God's word, it became imprisoned within him like "a fire burning in his breast."[*] When God's children hurt, said Tutu, he too could not keep quiet.

He also announced that he hoped to be bishop of Johannesburg until he retired, "unless it becomes abundantly clear that God wills me to do otherwise." In a quiet moment the day before the enthronement, Philip Russell, mindful of Tutu's short service in Lesotho, had given him a lecture: "I said to Desmond, 'If you do Johannesburg, you have to stick at it.' I felt like his grandmother." Tutu took no umbrage—his response, written some days later and invoking the name of Russell's wife, was typical of the teasing interaction he had developed with the archbishop:

> Just a short inadequate note to thank you most fervently for your part in my enthronement. Thank you for the words of counsel on the Saturday. I appreciate your concern. I must say it pains me to have to say all these nice things to you. I am an incorrigible masochist and I tolerate you only for Eirene's sake. Lucky dog, you!"

Moving from an ecumenical agency back into a diocese, Tutu decided that a bishop's calling to be a focus of unity required that he should attempt anew to distance himself from any appearance of partisan political alignment. While he continued to say locally and abroad that he identified with the ANC's objective of a nonracial, just, and democratic South Africa, he resigned as a patron of the UDF. Within the diocese, he spent much of his time wooing white Anglicans. Much

[*] Jeremiah 20:7–9.

of his first pastoral letter was aimed at dealing with white parishoners' concerns. At St. Martin's-in-the-Veld, in the wealthy northern suburbs, 500 parishioners packed the church hall to ask him his views on issues ranging from sanctions to the virgin birth. He was a great success in most of the parishes he visited, the monks of the Community of the Resurrection reported to their brethren in Mirfield.

Instead of living permanently in Soweto, as he had done when he was dean, he and Leah made themselves more accessible to whites by splitting their time between their own home in Orlando West and the official bishop's residence in the northern suburbs. When three senior white lay officers offered to resign so that Tutu could make his own appointments, he decided their attitude demonstrated that he should retain them. He appointed Peter Lee–the principal alternative candidate for bishop–as "canon missioner" of the diocese, and one of the diocese's most senior white priests as his executive assistant; the priest was later to tell a colleague in Cape Town that Tutu was the most caring and vital person he had ever met. Tutu had to counter rumors that a trip to attend Naomi's graduation in Kentucky was paid for by the diocese–in fact, he reported to the diocesan council, the trip had generated donations of 80,000 rand, of which one-fourth would go to the SACC and the rest to mission and outreach in the diocese. He also moved to secure his base among the clergy by rejecting an austerity budget that froze stipends for the clergy. At the end of his first year in office, he went on a tour to the United States, where he raised 500,000 dollars for the diocese and the SACC. He called for daily Eucharist, fasting, and prayer and for teaching to change attitudes and overcome racial divisions.

As Tutu established his leadership more securely, he invited the clergy, lay officers, and outside experts to bring to diocesan meetings different perspectives on the insurrection in black townships. While these reports helped diocesan leaders to identify with the challenges faced by the clergy in the townships, and with Tutu's need to support them, some could not help noticing that his "crisis ministry" disrupted diocesan business. Peter Lee later wrote that Tutu and the diocese were subject to what he described as "intolerable pressures" and "unbelievable strain." No one experienced these more than priests and bishops who were, in different ways, harassed by the police. Merwyn Castle, who was gay, was ensnared in a police trap and charged for activity that would later be protected by South Africa's bill of rights. The trap was a way of getting at Tutu: the police told Castle they would hush up the case and withdraw the charge if he agreed to become an informer. Rather than spy on Tutu, Castle chose what he privately called the "excruciating" pain of a public trial. Tutu instructed him to resign. About 1,000 people signed a petition asking Tutu and the cathedral council to reject the resignation, but it was accepted—a decision that haunted Tutu for years. When Tutu came to the diocese, the rector of the Sharpeville parish, Geoff Moselane, who had hosted community meetings before the uprising in the Vaal triangle, was being detained. After Moselane had been in prison for six months without charges, Tutu and his suffragan bishops, carrying their pastoral staffs, led twenty-seven other members of the clergy on a march from St. Mary's Cathedral to John Vorster Square to petition for his release. Recalling the outcome of the march in 1980, the diocesan secretary, Sid Colam, followed the clergy at a safe distance with thousands of rand stuffed into his pockets, for bail. The money was not needed—the protest ended with Tutu having tea with the divisional commissioner of police in his office. (Moselane, Thom Manthata of the SACC, and twenty other national and community leaders, one of them former black consciousness leader Mosiuoa Lekota, were subsequently tried on charges of treason arising from the Vaal uprising.)

An episcopal office provided no protection from victimization. The police gasoline-bombed the home of Sigisbert Ndwandwe, the suffragan bishop responsible for the western part of the diocese, which included Klerksdorp and Ventersdorp. Then they arrested him on charges of public violence, released him, rearrested him, strip-searched him in public, and held him in "preventive detention" for ninety-nine days on the basis of a claim that he had conspired to murder policemen. On the East Rand, Simeon Nkoane's eighty-two-year-old mother was awoken at one o'clock in the morning by the sound of bricks and gasoline bombs crashing through the windows of their home. The perpetrators were not identified, but other residents of the community whose homes were bombed that night saw a group of black and white men, suspected of being the police, leaving the scene. Five days afterward, a series of events began to unfold that would be fully explained only a decade later, during hearings of the postapartheid Truth and Reconciliation Commission.

According to the version of events put out by police at the time, seven young activists died at midnight on June 25, 1985, when they blew themselves up while trying to attack the homes of black policemen in three East Rand townships. An eighth activist died in a limpet mine explosion when he tried to sabotage an electrical substation. Two reporters for *The Star*, briefed by unnamed "military experts," said that "an incredible twist of irony and ignorance" may have been responsible for "one of the strangest terrorism episodes in the history of southern African insurgency." The seven had used Soviet hand grenades specially manufactured without time-delay devices for use in booby traps. Six had their right hands blown off. The death of the man killed by the limpet mine was "a mystery." On the same night, Simeon Nkoane's home was again gasoline-bombed. When he went to a window to peer outside, three shots were fired in his direction. Confusion and anger reigned in the three townships.

Two weeks later, Desmond Tutu withdrew from the three-yearly meeting of the Anglican Church's highest ruling body, its provincial synod, and went to Duduza township, near the white town of Nigel, to help Nkoane and other members of the local clergy bury four of the dead. In the days leading up to the service, ten people had been shot dead by police in the area. As was the custom of the time, crowds gathered in a soccer stadium, the only space big enough for the funeral. Four thousand or 5,000 residents gathered; their number was swelled by pupils boycotting school. Kingston Erson, CR, wrote to his brother monks in Mirfield that evening:

> Many hundreds of youths were on the grandstand and some on the roof, singing and dancing. In front of them in about the middle of the field were three iron tables, with a loudspeaker system, and in front of the tables were four coffins on chairs. The wind was reasonably fresh and the dust was soon swept up and covered clothes and hair. . . . There were speeches and songs by the young leaders and teachers of the schools in Duduza. The families of the bereaved sat in front and listened patiently to many short speeches. The mood was pretty electric and [the young people] danced and sang and surrounded the coffins, guarding them as it were, many with clenched fists. . . . Simeon introduced the day with prayers and Desmond made a short but well-received speech. . . . Once during the funeral service the police/army appeared at a distance and the mood of the crowd soon became angry.

At the end of the service, the clergy accompanied the families of the dead to the local cemetery. Leaving the graveside after the committal of the bodies, Tutu and Nkoane came across a frenzied crowd of young mourners beating, kicking, and whipping a man they suspected of being an impimpi, a police informer. The youths had overturned the man's car, set it on fire, and pummeled him to the ground. Shouting, "Impimpi, impimpi, burn him!" they doused him with gasoline. They had lifted him up, ready to throw him onto his flaming car, when Tutu and Nkoane waded into the maelstrom. Shorter than many of the youths, the priests in their long purple cassocks were barely visible to spectators as the crowd jostled and pushed them. As Tutu reached the center, the victim–bleeding from the head–clung to Tutu's legs. Pleading with the youths and nearly in tears, Tutu helped Nkoane to pull the man away and put him into a car.

As Nkoane drove the injured man away to a hospital, youths beat their fists on the roof the the car. They then turned to Tutu. "Why don't you allow us to deal with these dogs in the same way they treat us?" shouted a youngster brandishing a sjambok. If you saved an impimpi, he implied, you must be a collaborationist. "Don't you believe when I say ours is a noble and righteous struggle?" retorted Tutu. "Why must we use the very same methods as the 'system'? . . . Why don't we use methods of which we will be proud in years to come?" Joined by dozens more youths, the youngster said that the "system" had killed four of their comrades, and that informers were going to sell others out. Tutu said he understood their anger but he would not allow them to kill people. "Do you recognize us as your leaders?" he asked. Grudgingly, the youths did. "Then . . . why don't you do as we tell you? . . . What is the point in claiming to recognize our leadership when in fact you don't?"

One of those who attended the funeral at Duduza was a local activist, Maki Skhosana. In the weeks after the killings with the hand grenades, rumors began to circulate about her. She was, it was said, the girlfriend of the man who had supplied the doctored grenades. Skhosana's sister warned her to flee, but she refused, proclaiming her innocence. At a subsequent funeral in Duduza, on July 20, the "comrades," her fellow activists, caught up with her. The first her sister knew about it was when three young woman passed her house on the way from the funeral, shouting slogans and saying that they had "burned Maki." Rushing to the scene, she identified Skhosana's body by the feet. A large rock covered the head and chest. Maki's head had been gashed open, her teeth had been smashed, and her body was scorched. Broken glass had been pushed up between her open legs. As her family prepared to bury her, they were shunned. Comrades threatened to burn down the premises of the local undertaker, and the family had to contract a white undertaker from the nearby town to arrange the funeral, almost clandestinely. Maki Skhosana's killing was not the first of its kind: youths had inaugurated the "necklace"–a burning tire placed around a victim's neck–some months earlier. But this killing played into P. W. Botha's hands. Television footage was broadcast internationally, and Botha cited its brutality as justification for declaring the first state of emergency since the Sharpeville massacre of 1960.

Tutu, who had not been at the funeral where Skhosana was killed, returned to the East Rand for yet another funeral the following week. This funeral was for fourteen people killed in unrest in the township of KwaThema. It was the first large gathering under the state of emergency. Thirty thousand people welcomed Tutu to the local sports stadium with an ovation that lasted twelve minutes. He spoke standing on a table in the middle of the stadium, serried rows of young comrades moving rhythmically up and down in the war dance called the toyi-toyi in the stands behind him. He told the crowd that many people around the world supported the struggle for freedom. But scenes such as the killing of Skhosana had led these people to question whether blacks were ready for freedom. South Africans had a cause that was noble, he added:

> We have a cause that is just. We have a cause that is going to prevail. For goodness' sake, let us not spoil it by the kind of methods that we use. And if we do this again, I must tell you that I am going to find it difficult to be able to speak up for our liberation. I will find it difficult–it is already difficult in this country to talk the truth, but if we use methods such as the one that we saw in Duduza, then, my friends, I am going to collect my family and leave a country that I love very deeply, a country that I love passionately.

Some in the crowd booed. For the most part his words were received in silence. Soon afterward, he was supposed to speak at a funeral rally in the Eastern Cape. His hosts did not arrive at the airport to fetch him, and he could find no alternative transportation. A local priest told him that the community was very annoyed with him.

The full truth behind the events of June and July 1985 in the East Rand emerged only after the cause had prevailed. The ANC, in one of its contributions to feeding the flames of revolt, had dispatched several hundred MK soldiers into the country as shock troops, each equipped with a Kalashnikov rifle, a few thousand rand, and perhaps a dozen grenades. Their task was to give township "grenade squads" rudimentary training to attack government targets. When two men known simply as "Mike" and "James" approached the activists in the East Rand and offered them training amid deserted gold mine dumps, the activists believed their instructors were from the ANC. Maki Skhosana became Mike's girlfriend and probably introduced him to some of the activists. Unknown to her or the others, Mike and James were askaris, ANC guerrillas who had been recruited by the police, and who were putting into effect a plan developed and approved at the highest levels of government.

Johannes Velde van der Merwe, the national police commissioner in F. W. de Klerk's administration, applied to the Truth and Reconciliation Commission in 1996 for amnesty for murdering the eight activists in the East Rand, and for attempting to murder seven others who survived the explosions. Van der Merwe told the amnesty committee that he was deputy head of the security police when he conceived the plan. Its purpose was to protect black policemen and councilors, to eliminate anyone prepared to join the armed struggle, and to discredit MK. It had been approved by Louis le Grange, the police minister. Police technicians had disabled the time-delay mechanisms of the Russian-made grenades. The limpet mine was similarly modified, to kill the only activist who could identify "Mike." The plan was carried out by Unit C1 of the security branch, which ran death squads out of a farm called Vlakplaas southeast of Pretoria. The Truth Commission granted amnesty to thirteen policemen for the crime, including commanding officers, members of the death squad, technicians, and explosives experts who "investigated" the blasts.

Botha's emergency regulations of July 1985 gave security forces extraordinary powers of arrest, detention, censorship, and control of public assembly in thirty-six magisterial districts around Johannesburg and in the Eastern Cape. Tutu warned that the "iron fist" would not end the unrest; if the emergency did manage to restore a level of calm, it would be "illusory, sullen, and superficial." He renewed an offer he had made when he was enthroned in February, to broker talks between the government and authentic black leaders. He asked Botha for an urgent meeting, at which he planned to urge the release of Nelson Mandela. For five days newspaper headlines speculated on the possibility of talks. Then, in a calculated snub, Botha said he would be prepared to meet church leaders who repudiated civil disobedience.

He then agreed to meet a delegation headed by Philip Russell, but not until three weeks later.

In the meantime, Tutu was being called on to speak at funeral after funeral. As the only opportunities for black South Africans to give voice to their political aspirations, the funerals attracted thousands of young people. Activists sang revolutionary songs and performed the toyi-toyi around coffins, taunting the police and troops in armored personnel carriers. The funerals were followed by unequal clashes between heavily armed security forces and youngsters wielding stones. In a self-perpetuating cycle, the clashes produced more killings, which led to more funerals, which produced new clashes and new killings. The police tried to quell protests by imposing restrictions on the funerals, forbidding the burial of more than one person at a time, outlawing marches to cemeteries, and prohibiting political speeches. Addressing 10,000 mourners at the funeral of three teenage boys shot dead in a small Free State town, Tutu said he would ignore the restrictions: "I will not listen to people who tell me what to preach. . . . I will preach the Gospel of Jesus Christ. . . . If they pass laws which are quite unjust, quite intolerable, then I will break the law."

Five days later, at the funeral in the East Rand of a sixteen-year-old girl shot by the police after an earlier funeral, Tutu defied the restrictions for the first time, then interposed himself between the police and the crowd to defuse a confrontation. He condemned the emergency regulations and pleaded with the government to lift them: "Please allow us to bury our dead with dignity. Please do not rub our noses in the dust. We are already hurt; we are already down. Don't trample on us. We are human beings; we are not animals. And when we have a death, we cry like you cry." The police had ordered the family to bury their daughter before noon and had prescribed the routes to the cemetery. When noon came, dozens of armored vehicles and hundreds of policemen and soldiers surrounded an angry crowd of about 1,500. The police ordered the young people to disperse. In twenty minutes of negotiations, Tutu persuaded a police colonel to supply buses to the cemetery. Then he persuaded the youngsters to use the buses. Tutu thanked the colonel: "In trying to maintain unreasonable laws, you were reasonable and well-behaved." To journalists, he said that the children scared him: "They have an incredible recklessness. They all think they are going to die. They . . . think that if this is the way they are going to get their freedom, then so be it."

In February 1986, after defusing another explosive situation in

Alexandra township, Johannesburg, Tutu came as close as he ever felt to having a crowd turn against him. Because Alexandra was near white residential areas northeast of the city, security forces had, since the uprising of June 1976, suppressed resistance there with a brutality exceptional even by their standards. A confrontation at a funeral on February 15 set off three days of violence during which nineteen people were killed. Residents stayed at home from work, and students boycotted school. The township was on a knife-edge. Residents wanted the security forces to withdraw. A delegation from the SACC argued with the police for more than an hour before being allowed past roadblocks sealing off the township. Tutu pleaded with a crowd of 30,000 in a football stadium to disperse and not to confront the security forces. He would, he said, take up their demands with the government. Tutu and five church and community leaders flew to Cape Town, where P. W. Botha refused to see them and referred them to a deputy minister. They returned to Alexandra empty-handed. Tutu told a crowd, this time of 40,000, that he had brought no concessions. He begged youths not to make themselves cannon fodder. He was booed and shouted at from the stands: "It's not enough. The death of our people must be avenged. Down with Botha!" On his way out, a gang of youths blocked the way to his car. Once he had left, they said, the police would attack them. They were not going to tolerate it: "As soon as you leave here we will deal with the police in our own way." Said Peter Storey, who had been on the dais with Tutu: "I wish every white South African could have been at the stadium to see the anger of the people . . . to see what apartheid has done to the generations of this country."

The uprising that originated in the Vaal triangle was like a whirlwind, which nobody could ignore. It both sucked into its vortex and strengthened other forces ranged against apartheid. Responding to events at the Vaal, Thabo Mbeki, the ANC's director of information and publicity, broadcast an appeal from exile to make the country "ungovernable." The ANC managed to establish sporadic "insurrectionary zones" in some townships. Later Oliver Tambo called on supporters to "take the struggle into the white areas of South Africa." However, as the struggle against apartheid entered its final stages, the most important effect of the uprising was to unleash financial sanctions against apartheid.

From abroad, South Africa in 1985 seemed to be going up in flames. Night after night, television news bulletins carried footage of burning cars, property, and sometimes people. On July 31, two days after P. W.

Botha refused to meet Tutu, the French government announced a ban–largely symbolic–on investment in South Africa. On the same day, Chase Manhattan Bank, which had come to the government's rescue after Sharpeville in 1960, decided to call in its loans to South Africa and freeze unused lines of credit. It was a business decision; the loans constituted less than half a percent of the bank's assets, and the political agitation to which they gave rise outweighed their usefulness. The value of the rand began to slide. South African businessmen dubbed Willard Butcher, David Rockefeller's successor as chairman of Chase, the "Butcher of the rand." Other American banks followed suit. One slashed South Africa's credit rating. Some Swiss and German banks increased loans at interest rates as much as 4 percent above normal.

As the crisis developed, South African businessmen and foreign creditors looked to P. W. Botha to restore confidence. He was scheduled to address a party congress on August 15. Rumors spread that he would announce substantial reforms. Speculation raced through the diplomatic corps, and CNN scheduled a live transmission of his speech. But what he had to say had been oversold. He reacted belligerently to being put under pressure, and the world saw his typically aggressive, finger-wagging style. The rand fell by 20 percent overnight. On August 27 it reached a record low. The government suspended trading on the Johannesburg Stock Exchange and in foreign exchange for four days, then declared a moratorium on debt repayments while new terms were negotiated.

The debt crisis demonstrated that financial sanctions had an unexpectedly strong potential to force change. In September the government made proposals to end the pass laws and restore citizenship in South Africa to blacks. It was too little, too late, said Tutu and the UDF: "Things that . . . would have had a tremendous impact a few months ago are now damp squibs." When creditor banks began negotiations on repayment terms, Tutu and Beyers Naude, who had succeeded him as the SACC's general secretary, signed a letter–written by Allan Boesak and a dissident banker in Cape Town, Terry Crawford-Browne–appealing to them to make the rescheduling of repayments conditional on the resignation of the government and its replacement by one responsive to the needs of all South Africans. The bankers, deeply uncomfortable at having morality or democracy dragged into their business, made no such demands; but their negotiators privately told Pretoria that it had to send out some signals indicating a readiness to make political reforms. Before the negotiations in March and April

1986, Botha temporarily lifted the state of emergency and opened Parliament with a speech in which he raised the prospect of releasing Mandela.

By early 1986 Tutu had already indicated that he would change the position on sanctions he had outlined when he became bishop of Johannesburg. Then, he had given the government eighteen to twenty-four months to make reforms. In October 1985, he shortened that time: addressing the political committee of the UN General Assembly in New York, he said that the situation had developed "desperately badly" and now the world should apply sanctions if apartheid had not been dismantled within six months. The timing of his formal declaration was dictated by developments in the Anglican Church. Philip Russell was retiring, and Tutu was again a candidate for archbishop of Cape Town. The election was set for April 14, and Tutu wanted the elective assembly in no doubt as to where he stood.

He spent Easter praying over his final decision. On April 2, he held a news conference at St. Alban's Church in Johannesburg, where his office was based. In a long statement, he said that South Africa was on the edge of a catastrophe worse than Vietnam. He spelled out his efforts to bring about peaceful change over the previous ten years: his letter to Vorster; the abortive meeting with Botha in 1980; his interventions to defuse confrontation; his dialogue with the government and Afrikaners in the face of criticism from within the black community. He said that although Botha had acted with courage on coming to power, the president had since shown, to turn an English expression around, that he did not have "the convictions of his courage." Nothing Botha had said indicated that he was serious about dismantling apartheid—in fact, he had just given the foreign minister, Pik Botha, a dressing-down for suggesting that one day South Africa would have a black president. Those who opposed sanctions by arguing that they would hurt the people they were meant to help were hypocritical. Blacks were killed, mainly by the security forces, almost as if they were flies: more than 1,200 since August 1984. He had heard hardly a squeak of protest from whites who claimed to be concerned about blacks' suffering. Botha had refused to meet him and whites pilloried him. Recent polls showed that more than 70 percent of black South Africans supported sanctions of some sort. Very little in South Africa had changed without international pressure. He concluded:

I have no hope of real change from this government unless they are forced. We face a catastrophe in this land and only the action of the international community by applying pressure can save us. Our children are dying. Our land is bleeding and burning and so I call the international community to apply punitive sanctions against this government to help us establish a new South Africa–non-racial, democratic, participatory and just. This is a non-violent strategy to help us do so. There is a great deal of goodwill still in our country between the races. Let us not be so wanton in destroying it. We can live together as one people, one family, black and white together.

Tutu's announcement elicited a reaction unprecedented in its division along racial lines. Black political organizations–with the exception of homeland leaders–supported him. From whites–conservatives and liberals alike, and businessmen in particular–there was an outcry. Helen Suzman said she was opposed to sanctions, although if they were imposed, Botha and not Tutu should be blamed. Some newspapers made their attacks personal. The *Sunday Times* turned against Tutu his reconciliatory gesture of using the official bishop's residence in Johannesburg's white suburbs: it reported that while he advocated that other blacks should suffer, he had a choice of two houses. Moreover, he flew abroad frequently, often first-class; he had a chauffer-driven car; and his children had been educated at private schools. The security file kept on him by the Department of Justice reflects intense scrutiny of his call and the controversy it created.

There were, however, no threats of action from the government. Legal steps against Tutu were unlikely, the government press reported. Underlying much of the heat of white people's reaction was the uneasy, if unacknowledged, recognition that the future was slipping out of their control. Until whites were prepared to abandon apartheid completely, what they thought was of little importance. What now mattered was what the international community thought, particularly western countries with the closest economic ties to South Africa.

CHAPTER 11

OUR BROTHERS AND SISTERS

One strength of South Africa's struggle for democracy was that it was multifaceted, conducted by many leaders, in many arenas and in many countries. In the churches, Desmond Tutu had distinctive qualities, which gave him a high public profile; but he was just one of dozens of similarly-minded campaigners. Church pulpits and assemblies provided an unrivaled array of platforms at a time when few others were available in the black community; but as the independent trade unions grew in the late 1970s and 1980s, they became a more powerful institutional force for liberation than church denominational structures. And outside the country, the cause was furthered by South Africans—Oliver Tambo and Thabo Mbeki preeminent among them—within and outside the diplomatic offices of the ANC and PAC, supported by a network of sympathizers the size of which was second to none in the history of Africa's twentieth-century liberation. Nonetheless, Desmond Tutu made a powerful and unique contribution to publicizing the antiapartheid struggle abroad, nowhere more so than in the United States.

Links between South Africa and the United States go back to the eighteenth century, when American whalers and traders did business in Cape Town. American mining engineers were reported by Mark Twain to have had a good reputation in the Reef gold fields. During the nineteenth century, the two countries also became marginally involved in each other's wars. Capetonians witnessed one of the battles in the American Civil War when the *Alabama,* a Confederate raider, fired on and then captured a Union ship in Table Bay in 1862, inspiring a folk song, "Daar Kom die Alabama" ("There Comes the Alabama"). Later, an Irish-American brigade joined the Transvaal Republic's fight against the British. America's most important early influence on modern South Africa, however, was through education.

In the nineteenth century, the American Board of Commissioners for Foreign Missions sent a party to South Africa with the ambitious aim of converting the whole Zulu nation in one generation. It may have overreached itself in that respect, but it exerted an influence out of proportion to its numbers. The mission it established—Groutville, named for Aldin Grout, one of the first missionaries—was home to Albert Luthuli, and he received his first schooling there. John Langal-ibalele Dube, the grandson of an early convert, went for his further education to Oberlin College, in Ohio. One of his cousins, Pixley ka Isaka Seme, graduated from Columbia University. Seme went home to become the founding father of the African National Congress, and Dube was its first president. Another president of the ANC, the physi-cian A. B. Xuma of Sophiatown, was educated at Tuskegee Institute in Alabama and received his medical training at Marquette University, the Jesuit school in Wisconsin. A woman described by Xuma as "the mother of African freedom in this country," Charlotte Maxeke, first president of the ANC Women's League, studied at the African Meth-odist Episcopal (AME) Church's Wilberforce University in Cleve-land, and was instrumental in introducing the AME Church to South Africa.

The African-American community first welcomed Tutu to the United States. He had originally hoped to visit there in the summer of 1965, when King's College recommended him for a forty-five-day travel scholarship from the U.S. State Department. He wanted to study what a professor at King's had told him was exhilarating theol-ogy, and he also regarded a visit as "an opportunity to see integration at work." But after an interview at the American embassy in London, he was turned down; and did not travel to the United States until 1973, when he met exponents of black and African theology. Working for the Theological Education Fund and based in London, he also met Robert Powell, head of the Africa desk of the National Council of Churches of Christ in the United States. Powell and Tutu quickly became friends: they were both Anglican (Episcopalian) priests; they enjoyed each other's sense of humor; and Tutu impressed Powell as an articulate speaker with a deep-rooted faith. Powell began to seek out pulpits from which Tutu could boost Africa's cause in American churches. His wife, Bernice Powell, a deacon at Riverside Church—an institution that benefited from John D. Rockefeller Jr.'s philanthropy—initially had some difficulty persuading the church's minister, William Sloane Coffin, Jr., to invite Tutu to preach: "I almost had to sign with blood, because nobody had heard of Desmond Tutu. I remember Bill Coffin saying, 'Are you sure?' I said believe me, this is important, this is good. He's a good preacher, he has a message that folks need to hear." Reaction to Tutu's sermon was positive, and another door opened to him.

In Harlem, the Powells introduced Tutu to Frederick Boyd Williams at the Church of the Intercession, an Episcopal Church at West 155 Street. Williams and Wyatt Tee Walker, once chief assistant to Martin Luther King, Jr., were the founders of a coalition of black churches against apartheid; and the first time Tutu preached at Intercession, there were signs on the front lawn reading: "U.S. Out of South Africa– End Apartheid Now!" Williams saw in Tutu "a child-like quality . . . a mischievousness that I loved," but he was more impressed with Leah. He was particularly taken with her accounts of organizing domestic workers. A southerner, he had been raised by his godmother, his great-grandmother, and his mother, and he identified in Leah a person of like mind: "Black women have been our backbone. I saw it in Leah, a quiet strong current. You don't mess with strong black women."

Tutu's first close contact with white Episcopalians was with members of the prosperous 2,400 member congregation of St. James's Church on Madison Avenue in New York. He had met the church's rector, Hays Rockwell, in 1976, at the church meeting in Trinidad and Tobago to which he had flown the day he accepted election as bishop of Lesotho. They were both theological consultants, and their friendship began as they compiled daily reports together, then adjourned to a nearby bar. When Rockwell became rector soon afterward and invited Tutu to preach, the members of the congregation were charmed. They gave his diocese in Lesotho the proceeds of their next spring fund-raising drive to buy him a four-wheel-drive vehicle for the mountains and to build the accommodation for his theological students that he had sought unsuccessfully from the South African bishops. It was the beginning of a relationship as profound, in its own way, as that with the black church community. Tutu widened his circle when he met American bishops in South Africa and in 1978 at the Lambeth Conference of Anglican bishops from around the world–the trip that got him into trouble with Peter Storey at the SACC in 1979 was one to the diocese of Jack Spong, the bishop in Newark, New Jersey. Later, John Walker, the respected bishop of Washington, became a close friend and invited him to preach from the pulpit of the National Cathedral in Washington D.C. Tutu was also introduced to Manhattan's oldest Episcopal church, Trinity Church at the top of Wall Street, in 1979, when he addressed for the first time the annual conference of the Trinity Institute. This too was the beginning of a long relationship, during which he spoke repeatedly at Trinity's conferences. The parish of Trinity, financed by its extensive real estate holdings in the Hudson Square district of Manhattan, gave substantial support to his ministry.

Complementing his work with the churches, Tutu was introduced to a wider spectrum of people in politics, the media, and society by a friend he made in Lesotho, Frank Ferrari of the African-American Institute (subsequently renamed the Africa-American Institute). Ferrari was the consummate American lobbyist, with friends and contacts across independent Africa, at the United Nations in New York, and in Washington, D.C. He was a devout Catholic and an admirer of the Catholic movement, the Young Christian Workers; and he was attracted to Tutu as a revolutionary whose actions were consistent with what the liberation movements were doing and what his faith dictated. He introduced Tutu to members of Congress from the late 1970s. As Tutu became better known, Ferrari worked with church officials to arrange his schedules in New York and Washington, D.C. At the same time, journalistic coverage of Tutu was raising his profile. In 1980 the *New York Times*'s correspondent John F. Burns visited him at home in Orlando West and identified him as one of the most influential black critics of the government. The next year, the columnist Anthony Lewis named him as perhaps the most articulate spokesman for black people; and the *Washington Post* published an opinion piece from him on its op-ed page. After the government appointed the Eloff Commission, the *Times*'s bureau chief in Johannesburg, Joseph Lelyveld, wrote a 6,000-word article on Tutu for the Sunday magazine. Leyleveld painted an appealing picture of a bishop he described as unusually pious and prayerful but at the same time irrepressible, "a quicksilver spirit that can be somber and joyful at once," expressing himself alternately in a sonorous voice and in "high-pitched yelps of delight and giggles."

One reason Tutu liked traveling was to get away from the stifling, often menacing, atmosphere at home. In London he and Leah stayed with Livingstone and Nzimazana Mqotsi, South African exiles they had befriended while living there. They used the Mqotsis's home in southeast London as a base from which to do business, visit other old friends, and stroll to the local pub. In New York the Tutus stayed with Bob and Bernice Powell or Hays and Linda Rockwell. At the Rockwells' apartment, the Tutus took over the bedroom of their daughter, Martha. Desmond delighted in doing what would be unthinkable in Johannesburg–taking the blond eight-year-old girl by the hand to buy rum-raisin ice cream at a local store. After he lost his passport the first time, the children of St. James's sent him drawings that they called "passports of love." He pasted these on the wall of his office and replied with an emotional letter, which was testimony to how he missed being unable to escape the oppression of apartheid:

> How does one start a letter from a full heart as I have? I thought I knew that you loved us but in recent days the evidence of the warmth of your caring and compassion and love have been quite overwhelming. . . . As I dictate this letter I have closed my eyes and I can see your apartment. I see us sitting at table by candlelight and you, Hays, trying to impress us by holding forth on one topic or another and Linda, as gracious as ever, a beautiful, charming hostess, and Martha and Sarah; or we are in your lounge listening to Miriam Makeba or dancing away; or we are in St. James and I am about to hold forth; or it is in the morning and I am jogging; and these are vignettes that I will always carry with me.

In 1982, Tutu's lack of a passport became an irritant in relations between the apartheid government and the Reagan administration. Columbia University followed General Seminary, Harvard, and Kent University in England in resolving to confer an honorary degree on Tutu. At the request of the Democratic congressman Charles B. Rangel of New York, the State Department made a special appeal that Tutu be allowed to travel. South Africa rejected the plea, prompting an expression of disappointment from the assistant secretary responsible for Africa. Pretoria's rebuff backfired when Columbia left an empty chair for Tutu at its commencement ceremonies and announced that for only the third time in its history, it would seek to award the degree off campus. (The first time had been in 1861, when Abraham Lincoln could not leave Washington during the Civil War, and the second in 1979, when a stroke left Supreme Court Justice William O. Douglas unable to travel.) If South Africa denied entry to Columbia, the university threatened, it would keep an empty chair for Tutu at every ceremony until he received his degree. (In an irony of which Columbia was probably unaware, it awarded the degree later that year at the University of the Witwatersrand, the institution to which Tutu had been admitted to study medicine but which he could not afford to attend. He had dozens of honorary degrees from foreign universities before this or any other white South African university recognized him. The South Africans waited until the 1990s, when there was no longer any risk of a white backlash.)

Tutu's passport became a test of the administration's policy toward Pretoria for Democrats and moderate Republicans alike. Nancy Kassebaum, the Republican chairman of the Senate subcommittee on Africa, said that South Africa's refusal to heed American representations called into question the premise that being friendly to Botha's government would achieve more results than being unfriendly. The Episcopal Church added pressure when it invited Tutu to address its national convention in New Orleans in September 1982. Another speaker at the convention was the church's most prominent layman, George H. W. Bush. The church told South African diplomats that their government would embarrass Reagan's vice president if it refused Tutu a passport. On September 1, while Tutu was giving evidence to the Eloff Commission in Pretoria, a junior official disrupted the proceedings by shouting from the doorway that he was needed. The commission adjourned, and Tutu went out to be told by an official from the interior ministry that the minister, F. W. de Klerk, had granted him a "temporary and limited travel document." Since the government could apparently not decide to which ethnic Bantustan Tutu belonged, the document said his nationality was "undeterminable at present."

In the United States, Tutu had—in the words of Daniel P. Matthews, rector of Trinity Church, Wall Street—"a genius for intuitively sensing his audience." Tutu was in peak oratorical form when he spoke in New Orleans. In the recollection of Edmond Browning, later the Episcopal Church's presiding bishop, he overwhelmed the convention. He began with a self-depreciating story that he usually told when he was introduced in fulsome terms, about a woman who turned to her son after the tribute at her husband's funeral and said: "I think we're at the wrong funeral." He joked about his last name: when he had to give his name and room number at a conference—"Tutu, four-five-three"—he said he sounded like an escaped convict. To repeated laughter and applause, he went on to ridicule and attack apartheid. The government had for a short period renamed its department of Bantu Affairs the Department of Plural Relations, he said: "Presumably now we [blacks] were plurals, one of whom would be that very odd thing, a singular plural—and perhaps one coming from the countryside would be a rural plural." By appointing the Eloff Commission, the government had put not the

SACC but Christianity on trial, as if South Africa were behind the iron curtain. The SACC believed in negotiation and discussion: "It is our government who want and who will cause bloody confrontation and violent revolution." Adopting the words of the Anglican Eucharist, he included Episcopalians as participants in the South African churches' struggle against apartheid. The South African government, he said, did not understand what the SACC was when it began the Eloff inquiry:

> We are not a fly-by-night, tu'penny, ha'penny, merely human organization. No, we are part of the church of God! What a tremendous thing that you are our brothers and sisters. Hey! Thank you. Thank you. Thank you for bringing to life what it means to us to be the church of God. Maybe you don't know. I will tell you just what it means to experience as almost a physical thing to be borne up, to be upheld by the love and the prayers and the concern and the laughter and the joy of so many around the world. I told the Commission that anybody was being really foolhardy to take on the Church of God. (Extended laughter and applause.)
>
> I said, hey, I belong to this divine, this supernatural organism, which includes the living in what we call the church militant, which includes the dead in what we call the church quiescent, which includes the saints in glory in what is called the church triumphant. So that although it is a nonsense for the world, we can say in the central act of our worship, hey, we join with the angels and the archangels and the whole company of heaven—we down here are up there, and we glorify God and say, "Holy, Holy, Lord God of Hosts, heaven and earth are full of your glory. . . ." God, you are good, you are good! They can remove a Desmond Tutu, they can remove the SACC, but the Church of God goes on.

The convention's standing ovation lasted several minutes. During the convention, Tutu also preached at Grace Episcopal Church, New Orleans, where he addressed white people's fears. White South Africans, he said, were not inhuman. They weren't "sprouting horns or tails. They're just ordinary people like you and me . . . people who are scared. Wouldn't you be if you were outnumbered five to one?"

To the American church, Tutu brought an exceptional combination of Anglo-Catholic spirituality, biblical evangelical zeal, and rigorous theology. For Hays Rockwell, he rose above traditional divides:

Just when you think you're going to characterize him as this, that or the other, ideologically or in terms of churchmanship, he escapes such categories. He's a deeply Catholic man in the sense that he's inclusive, encompassing of the faith. He's Anglo-Catholic, there's no question, but he never would make that his primary way of addressing the church. He is able to proclaim the gospel with such energy because he believes in the evangelical mandate–not as an ideological thing but because that's what his faith requires of him. He reaches into individual lives in a way that's transformative. The range of his voice represents the range of his faith and of his intellect. Very few evangelical preachers are as profoundly intellectual as he is, though he would scorn that word. His faith is beautifully informed by his learning, his knowledge.

In the judgment of Fred Williams, Allan Boesak had Martin Luther King's power to rouse a crowd; he had the cadences, repetition, and harmony that are part of an American preacher's repertoire. Tutu did not, but he brought something else, Williams said:

He's a crossover artist. Black preaching of an evangelical style scares the bejesus out of most white mainline Protestants. They don't think they're supposed to experience emotion. Desmond appeals to that emotional level without scaring them to death, because his humanity comes across in a wave and they hear the emotion. It's sort of like making love without screaming. They know they are loved, but they don't have to give a "Whoop!" He becomes transfigured and it becomes transparently real when he's in the pulpit. There is something of the otherworldly that shines through his eyes and in his smile and in his voice and in the way he closes his eyes and holds up his hands and lifts up his head that just lifts you into the upper realms.

Adding to the effectiveness of his message in the United States, Tutu's faith was communicated as part of his public image. In South Africa, Britain, and Australia, where even correspondents reporting on religion rationed their use of the "G-word," his words were usually shorn of their context. In most American cities, when he rooted his views in biblical texts and spoke about God, journalists reported him as doing so.

As the campaign to boycott apartheid intensified, Tutu's church sponsors took him to speak to other organizations lobbying against American companies that did business with South Africa–college groups, unions, and municipalities. Hays Rockwell used contacts made through his wealthy parish to set up meetings with businessmen. The meetings were virtually clandestine at first: "These heads of banks . . . didn't want to be associated with a communist agitator. I don't think they really believed he was a communist, they just thought he was stirring things up. [But] within a very short time after a meeting began, they were charmed by Desmond into wanting at least to extend the conversation. In some cases, over time, they altered their poses on investment and trade."

F. W. de Klerk based the issuance of a travel document to Tutu for New Orleans on the "theological nature" of the conference. Tutu interpreted this widely–"Everything I do is theological"–and Frank Ferrari worked with the churches to set up meetings for him in New York and Washington that were typical of the array of organizations and leaders he could gain access to: philanthropic foundations including the Carnegie Corporation and the Ford Foundation; UN Secretary-General Javier Perez de Cuellar; Protestant and Catholic church leaders; the Congressional Black Caucus; Congressman William H. Gray III; senators Nancy Kassebaum and Edward Kennedy; leaders of the House and Senate subcommittees on Africa. On this and other visits, the Rockwells and the movie magnate Arthur Krim–who was also part of the delegation from Columbia University that flew to Johannesburg to award the degree–held dinner parties where Tutu mixed with entertainers, activists, journalists, and businesspeople. In Ferrari's experience, Tutu moved effortlessly from group to group, person to person, with transparent authenticity and consistency:

> There was never a conflict between the man and the politician–he was first and foremost the priest against social injustice and oppression. . . . When he walked into a room, it was not the Nobel laureate, not the bishop . . . not the articulate spokesperson, but the humility and commitment and dedication of this person that struck everyone [and] his irrepressible personality with his magnificent sense of humor.

Tutu had as little hesitation now in asking people for money as he had when he wanted to go to theological college. Leah often joked that he was a professional beggar. After Robert Powell's early death, Bernice Powell* helped Tutu begin a scholarship fund for young South

---

* She later remarried, becoming Bernice Powell Jackson.

Africans who went into exile after the Soweto uprising. Tutu made a contribution to the fund from his Nobel Prize, but most of the money had to be found in the United States. Tutu asked Bernice Powell to raise it: "He taught me that if you believe in what you're doing you should have no problem at all in asking people to give you money." Neither was Tutu greatly concerned with controversy over its sources; he told Powell to accept donations from Coca-Cola at a time when its role in South Africa was being questioned. "He was very clear: take the money, we need it to get these kids to school, nobody else is giving money, take the money." Tutu also did not hesitate to ask for more than he was offered. Hays Rockwell recalled that his church offered to sponsor one black priest for one year at a New York seminary: "So he [Tutu] said 'Right,' and sent us a priest, with his wife and three sons, for three years. He said, 'You don't want to separate that man from his family, do you?' And, 'One year doesn't do it. He needs to get the degree doesn't he?'"

The breadth of Tutu's support base created tension within it. African-Americans, who in Washington were most comfortable with working with the Congressional Black Caucus, were suspicious of Ferrari's range of contacts. (In time, Tutu would come to joke publicly that Ferrari was "my contact with the FBI.") The issue that needed most managing, however, was between blacks and whites in the American church. To many African-Americans, their white compatriots had gutted Martin Luther King Jr.'s message of its power—in Bernice Powell's words, in the fifteen years since King's murder they had "pasteurized and homogenized" him. Now they were venerating Tutu and deploring apartheid, while downplaying racism in their own backyard. Powell was unhappy with Tutu's attitude toward whites, and in the early years of their relationship he irritated her: "He's too nice to white people. He takes too much from them and he's too nice to them. . . . As I got to know more [black] South Africans, I [realized] he wasn't by himself. They're all too nice to them." Once, Fred Williams and Bernice Powell took Tutu, in Williams's words, "to the woodshed" and told him that he was spending too much time with "white folks on the East Side" and too little with black leaders.

When Powell ran Tutu's Refugee Scholarship Fund, she took charge of his American schedule, balancing the demands made on him by different groups and trying to ensure that he was not exploited simply as a celebrity. For his part, Tutu remarked privately that he found African-Americans to be angrier than black South Africans, a judgment not on them but on the failure of white Americans to appreciate the depth of the pain left by slavery and racism. Under apartheid, Tutu said, black South Africans knew where they stood with whites. African-Americans, although guaranteed equality under the Constitution, found that they kept hitting glass ceilings. (After he chaired South Africa's Truth and Reconciliation Commission, Tutu made one of the themes of his speeches as he traveled in the United States an appeal for Americans to undertake a similar exercise.)

P. W. Botha's domestic attempt to win legitimacy by introducing a new constitution in 1984 was accompanied by regional and international diplomacy. Pretoria reached an agreement on the way forward in interminable negotiations over the future of Namibia, a former German colony that South Africa claimed to rule under a UN mandate. Using its regional power, it forced neighboring Mozambique and Swaziland to sign security accords. Botha's diplomacy had little impact in parts of Europe—on a visit in March 1984 Tutu was reassured by the Danish and Dutch foreign ministers that their governments maintained a strongly antiapartheid line; and in Oslo the Norwegian foreign minister supported a hearing on Pretoria's aggression against its neighbors which he and Thabo Mbeki of the ANC addressed. Elsewhere, particularly among South Africa's main trading partners, governments were inclined to reward Botha. In June 1984 Botha pulled off what Tutu called a "splendid diplomatic coup"—a seven-nation European tour in which he was received by leaders including the British prime minister and the West German chancellor.

Tutu approved of the cool reception Botha was given in most countries. But it was small comfort. Trevor Huddleston tried but failed to persuade Margaret Thatcher not to receive Botha. Tutu wrote to Thatcher and Helmut Kohl in Bonn asking whether they would have collaborated with Hitler and Stalin. "It seemed," he reported to the SACC's foreign partners, "they were saying to blacks that we were expendable, that we should not really trust whites when it came to the crunch because they would club together against us because blood was thicker than water." More upsetting, Pope John Paul II agreed to receive Botha. In March the pope had given Tutu a private audience in a gesture interpreted as support of the SACC after the Eloff Commission's report. Now, said Tutu, the pope had given the victims of apartheid "a slap in the face."

Officials of the Reagan administration were delighted by Botha's European tour: it was a way of giving him western recognition without having to face the diplomatic and domestic fallout of consorting too closely with him themselves. The principal architect of the administration's South Africa policy was Chester Crocker, the assistant secretary of state for Africa. Before his appointment in 1981, he was on record as recognizing that Botha's reforms could well be what he called an "elaborate smokescreen for a limited co-optation strategy aimed at wooing urban black and rural homeland elites into collaboration with the whites." But as an academic expert on Pretoria's military machine, he believed that coercive power was firmly in white hands, and he identified Afrikaner leaders such as Botha and Piet Koornhof as "pragmatic, flexible, determined . . . modernizers." So he propagated a policy that he called "constructive engagement in the region as a whole," with three objectives: combating Soviet influence in southern Africa, encouraging "white-led change in the direction of real power-sharing," and strengthening the capacity of blacks to take part in changing the system.

Tutu met Crocker a number of times during Reagan's first term and found him a powerful advocate and "a good and very intelligent man." However, Tutu saw him and the administration as being obsessed with communism—their diplomacy was dominated by the complex negotiations linking a withdrawal of Cuban troops from Angola to independence for Namibia. Crocker argued, to the present writer, that this strategy cleared the way for negotiations in South Africa: "What we did to P. W. in a sense is what Gorbachev did to us [the United States]. We took away his enemy and we took away his excuse [for not negotiating]." Whatever the merits of his case for the long-term outcome of his strategy, the administration's policy failed within South Africa on two levels.

First, Crocker went into office suggesting that Americans' empathy for the suffering of black people should be balanced by empathy for what he sympathetically described as "the awesome political dilemma in which Afrikaners and other whites find themselves." As conflict intensified in the early 1980s, this approach alienated the administration from broad swaths of black South African opinion. Crocker's phrase "constructive engagement" became a dirty word. Second, as the administration lost touch with black people's thinking, it lost its capacity to interpret what was actually happening in South Africa. The CIA accurately predicted in 1981 that the pace of reform would not be adequate to satisfy black people's demands over the next two to three years, and that racial tension would rise. "But," Crocker admitted to this writer, "I wouldn't claim that we foresaw any of what actually happened in terms of the UDF . . . and the urban areas catching fire the way they did. Or that we knew quite how that would play out." The Americans' failure to appreciate the anger in the townships, combined with internal divisions in the Republican Party, was to bring about the worst foreign policy defeat of Reagan's presidency, one in which Desmond Tutu played a considerable part.

The Nobel Peace Prize, Tutu often observed, transformed the way he was perceived: "One day no one was listening. The next, I was an oracle." There are a few documented cases in which governments attributed to him a direct and immediate role in changing their policies on apartheid. In December 1984, after receiving the prize, he visited Canada, where he was given a standing ovation in Parliament and met Brian Mulroney, the new Conservative prime minister. Mulroney was profoundly influenced by Tutu, according to Edward Lee, the Canadian ambassador to South Africa. "After their meeting I was recalled to Ottawa for consultations. At a full Cabinet meeting at Meech Lake, I observed Mulroney and [the foreign minister Joe] Clark convince the Cabinet that Canada should invoke political and economic sanctions, and take the lead in the Commonwealth and at the UN on this issue, despite the total opposition of Thatcher and Reagan." In May 1985, the French Socialist government invited Tutu, Mother Teresa, and other Nobel laureates to Paris for an international conference on human rights. During the visit, Prime Minister Laurent Fabius, who opposed sanctions, took a stroll with Tutu from his residence to the National Assembly. Tutu said nothing about sanctions, Fabius recounted to a television interviewer, but he made a lasting impression when he commented: "A white minister walking with a black bishop without police protection—that's freedom." The remark inspired the sanctions, which were declared on the day Chase Manhattan refused to roll over its loans.

In the United States, Tutu's role was not as direct, nor were the results as quick. The announcement of the peace prize prompted formal congratulations from President Reagan, in which he recognized Tutu's nonviolent work to bring about a form of government based on the consent of the governed. Within a week—on the day Tutu was invited to address the UN Security Council in New York—a White House aide was briefing presidential counselor—and later U.S. Attorney General—Edwin Meese III with a representative sample of Tutu's attacks on the administration. "Tutu's criticism," the aide reported to

Meese, "is that constructive engagement has not appreciably helped South African blacks; rather, it has hurt them by appearing to support the apartheid system." At the Security Council meeting, the United States abstained from voting on a resolution calling for the immediate eradication of apartheid; the U.S. ambassador, Jeane Kirkpatrick, said it contained excessive language when it referred to massacres. The South African ambassador, Kurt von Schirnding, walked out of the council meeting which Tutu addressed, after announcing to the council that if the UN continued on the course it was following, "South Africa will be forced to withdraw from its path of peace. Frankly, we have had enough."

In the closing weeks of the presidential campaign of 1984, Tutu assailed Reagan's policies as a disaster for black South Africans. It was Americans' prerogative whom to elect as president, he said, but the South African government would not be crying if they chose Reagan. In Reagan's view, Tutu merited one brief response—the United States could turn its back on South Africa, or it could try to help change the situation: "Perhaps he (Tutu) isn't aware of all that we are doing." On November 6, Reagan was reelected in a landslide. African-Americans, who during the primaries had promoted Jesse Jackson as the country's first serious black presidential candidate, felt thoroughly defeated. Randall Robinson, executive director of the lobby group TransAfrica, said: "We were down so far we had to do something—you can't fall off the ground." With the help of Walter Fauntroy, congressional representative for the District of Columbia, Robinson initiated the Free South Africa Movement, a national campaign of public protest against racism the like of which had not been seen since the 1960s. On the day before Thanksgiving—a date selected, according to Fauntroy, because "there's nothing to report but turkeys"—Robinson, Fauntroy, and Mary Frances Berry, a member of the Civil Rights Commission, went to the South African embassy, demanded the release of detained leaders of the UDF, and refused to move until the demand had been met. The ambassador called the police. Fauntroy waived his congressional immunity, and the three were arrested and jailed overnight. In the ensuing weeks, reported Mary McGrory in the *Washington Post*, the daily protests that took place 500 feet from the embassy "may be the most stylized in the history of the art." Every afternoon, fifty to seventy people gathered, chanting and carrying homemade signs. Every afternoon, Robinson held a news conference at which he read "the latest outrages from Johannesburg," then named the Americans who would break the law by protesting too close to the embassy building and "provide the celebrity arrests that are the special feature of the demonstrations." Among the hundreds who joined the protest in succeeding months were members of the King family, the Kennedy family, the Congressional Black Caucus, the American Jewish Congress, Harry Belafonte, the tennis star Arthur Ashe, the comedian Dick Gregory, and the civil rights legend Rosa Parks.

By the beginning of December, a week before Tutu traveled to Oslo to receive the peace prize, conditions were such that apartheid could move to the national stage in Washington, D.C. On Sunday, December 2, Tutu preached in the National Cathedral at an interfaith service honoring the award. President Reagan returned from a weekend at Camp David to be briefed on South Africa by Chester Crocker on Monday. In a rare move, Reagan sent Crocker out to defend the administration's record to the press. Constructive engagement had been "misdescribed" and maligned, Crocker said. It was "rubbish" to say that Reagan was too soft on the South African government. The following morning, December 4, the *Washington Post* carried a sympathetic 800-word feature on the bishop with a "puckish wit and gentle manner" who had been become "a powerful voice for the anti-apartheid movement." Describing his recent appearance at the African-American Institute, it began:

> Heads turned and a murmur of appreciation spread through the celebrity-studded crowd full of tuxedos and sequined gowns. Through a side door, a diminutive black man clothed in the fuchsia robes of the Anglican Church had slipped into the ballroom of the Waldorf-Astoria. As he walked to the ballroom's platform, hundreds of guests rose in a standing ovation. Jacqueline Onassis, Sen. Edward M. Kennedy (D-Mass.) and Atlanta Mayor Andrew Young joined chief executive officers of major U.S. corporations and Wall Street lawyers in applauding Desmond Tutu.

By congressional standards, Tutu was given as effusive a welcome when he appeared on the morning the article was published at a hearing of the House Subcommittee on Africa in the Rayburn House Office Building. The Democratic chairman, Howard Wolpe of Michigan, said that the committee was deeply honored to have him. The ranking minority member, Gerald Solomon of New York, noted that it was unusual to have so many members at a meeting on Africa. Tutu said it was ironical that he was not able to address a comparable body in his own country: "Here I am, a bishop in the church of God, fifty-three years of age, who some might even be ready to risk calling reasonably responsible, and yet I cannot vote in my motherland; whereas, a child of eighteen years of age, because she is white, and only very recently Coloured and Indian, can vote." He told of how he had to postpone his sabbatical in New York because of the outbreak of violence in the Vaal triangle, of P. W. Botha's refusal to meet church leaders, of the woman in the East Rand whose grandson was shot by the police. He also told them of the killing of black South Africans during a general strike that had brought South Africa's industrial heartland to a standstill the previous month:

> Twenty-four blacks were killed during that two-day strike in November. Six thousand were sacked from their jobs. There was not a squeak of protest from the government of this country. When a priest in Poland went missing, and then his body was found, there was an outrage . . . and the media quite rightly gave it extensive coverage.* . . . I believe we are being told that this administration is not being soft on apartheid. Heaven help us when they do decide to be soft. Would the reaction and the silence have been so deafening if the casualties had been white . . . if the casualties had for instance been Jewish?
>
> Constructive engagement has worsened our situation under apartheid. . . . It is giving democracy a bad name, just as apartheid has given free enterprise a bad name. Mr Chairman, we are talking about a moral issue. You are either for or against apartheid, and not by rhetoric. You are either in favor of evil or you are in favor of good. You are either on the side of the oppressed or on the side of the oppressor. You cannot be neutral. . . . Apartheid is an evil as immoral and unchristian in my view as Nazism, and in my view, the Reagan administration's support and collaboration with it is equally immoral, evil, and totally unchristian, without remainder.

Tutu's presentation brought the members of Congress and the spectators to a standing ovation, a highly unusual gesture that violated the committee's rules. Across town in Embassy Row on Massachusetts Avenue, the police arrested three American labor leaders. Demonstra-

---

* A reference to the murder of Father Jerzy Popieluszko by Polish secret police in October.

tors also marched to South African consulates in New York, for the second successive day; and in Boston, Chicago, Los Angeles, Houston, and Seattle, all for the first time. Cracks began to appear in the Republican Party; thirty-five conservative congressmen anxious not to be seen as soft on racism–Newt Gingrich of Georgia, Tom Ridge of Pennsylvania, Robert Walker of Pennsylvania, Connie Mack of Florida, and Richard Armey of Texas were among them–sent a letter to the South African ambassador demanding an immediate end to violence in South Africa and "a demonstrated sense of urgency about ending apartheid." If this was not forthcoming, they said, they would recommend international diplomatic and economic sanctions. A letter to Reagan from Nancy Kassebaum and Richard G. Lugar, incoming chairman of the Senate foreign relations committee, criticizing the State Department's failure to speak out against apartheid, was leaked. The two senators met the South African ambassador to express concern at the arrest of leaders of the November strike. On the other side of the Republican divide, three high-ranking black members of the administration criticized the focus on South Africa. "All of us who have lived under segregation, a mild form of apartheid, are concerned," said Clarence Thomas, chairman of the Equal Employment Opportunity Commission (and later a Supreme Court justice). "But in terms of the immediate, in terms of priorities, I think we should focus more on what is happening here."

In his address to the House subcommittee on December 4, Tutu announced that he would no longer meet members of the administration, but that he might meet the president or secretary of State if invited. The next day the White House announced a meeting on Friday, December 7–Reagan's first with an antiapartheid leader. In Johannesburg the announcement was described as the second setback for Pretoria in "a day of dramatic developments"–the first being the Republican congressmen's rebellion. The meeting on Friday was scheduled to last fifteen minutes. In the event, Desmond and Leah Tutu and a senior staffer from the SACC, Dan Vaughan, spent thirty minutes in the Oval Office with Reagan, who was accompanied by Vice President George Bush, Secretary of State George Schultz, Meese, Crocker, Chief of Staff James Baker, and the national security adviser, Robert McFarlane. When Reagan ran out of time, Tutu continued discussions for another hour with Bush and Crocker.

Tutu and Reagan agreed that apartheid was repugnant. They agreed that it should be dismantled as far as possible by peaceful means.

They agreed on very little else. Tutu said that he spoke as a victim and he hoped his views would not be dismissed as "rubbish"—an allusion to Crocker's earlier statement. He told Reagan that the situation had worsened. Reagan told the press afterward that it had not. Tutu said that constructive engagement was not effective. Reagan disagreed. Tutu repeated a number of the points he had made to the House subcommittee, and added that the administration's policy on South Africa was inconsistent with its policy on Poland and Latin America. He told Reagan that his travel document described his nationality as "undeterminable at present." He mentioned six demands: (1) that violence and the use of the South African Army in townships should be ended; (2) that all detainees—not just the labor union leaders held since the November strike—should be charged or released; (3) that workers fired in the strike should be reinstated; (4) that all restriction and banishment orders, especially those imposed on Winnie Mandela, should be lifted; (5) that all population removals should be stopped; and (6) that political prisoners should be released ahead of negotiations between all authentic leaders. Reagan said that the State Department would look at some of the points.

After the meeting, Reagan told reporters in the White House briefing room that he thought Tutu had been surprised at some of what the administration was doing. There had been "a surge of violence here and there [in South Africa], and that has resulted in violence from the other side"; but quiet diplomacy had made solid progress. He went on to worsen his poor image in South Africa by referring to support for American investment as coming from "black tribal leaders there." Invoking a stereotype of a tribal Africa was nothing new in the United States; but to people whose rulers were stripping them of their South African nationality and trying to foist on them citizenship in impoverished "tribal" homelands, his phrase was offensive. Later in the day, anxious to demonstrate the results of quiet diplomacy, Reagan stopped briefly on his way to Camp David for the weekend to tell the press he had just heard that Pretoria had released eleven of the union leaders. Asked if this might not be a result of the protests at the embassy, he said he had no evidence of that.

Tutu emerged from his meetings with Reagan and Bush to tell reporters in the driveway: "It is quite clear we are no nearer to each other than before I entered the White House." Crocker felt that Tutu had "written and scripted it before he even went in to see the president. They weren't listening to each other. He [Tutu] very dogmatically rejected everything to do with the administration's approach." Crocker recalled that Reagan was asked later in the day how the meeting had gone: "I remember he said, 'Tutu? So-so.'* They just did not hit it off. . . . People would say to me, 'Chet, why on earth did you recommend that the president of the United States waste his goddamned time talking to that guy?' " In Pollsmoor Prison at Cape Town, Nelson Mandela and some of his fellow prisoners were unhappy for other reasons. Mandela told the present writer they heard that Tutu had offered to call off the campaign to boycott South Africa if Reagan met his demands, "as if he had introduced it [the boycott]. . . . He made a statement which was regarded as arrogant by many of us. . . . Some of us understood, but others did not."

After the meeting in the Oval Office, an official from the State Department told reporters that the administration might speak out more often against whites' mistreatment of black South Africans. On December 10, Human Rights Day, after Tutu had received the prize in Oslo, Reagan escalated the rhetoric. There were times, he said, when quiet diplomacy was not enough. Racism was repugnant, and the United States had to emphasize its concern and grief over the human and spiritual costs of apartheid. He called for an end to forced removals, to detention without trial, and to the imprisonment of black leaders. Peaceful change, he added, could come only through dialogue sustained by a belief in governments based on the consent of the governed. His speech failed to change perceptions of his policy. He went on to denounce Nicaragua and the Soviet Union in much harsher words.

Early in 1985, Senator Edward Kennedy visited South Africa, thus helping to keep Americans focused on apartheid. In 1966, Robert F. Kennedy had made a huge impact during a four-day visit. He spoke to 30,000 people on four university campuses; flew by helicopter to see Albert Luthuli, who was restricted in Groutville; had lunch with Afrikaner students; and met Alan Paton and Mangosuthu Buthelezi in Durban. Robert and Ethel Kennedy were mobbed in Soweto. The visit was described in the *Rand Daily Mail* as a gust of fresh air sweeping into a stuffy room. In October 1984, Tutu proposed at a lunch on Capitol Hill that the Kennedy family should return. The invitation was backed by Allan Boesak, but in the rush to set up the trip insufficient

* George H. W. Bush was to raise a laugh with this anecdote at Reagan's funeral in the National Cathedral in 2004.

attention was given to the Azanian People's Organisation (Azapo), a black consciousness group that was strongly anti-American and anti-capitalist.

The contrasts in the reception Edward Kennedy received on the day he arrived set the pattern for the days that followed. At the airport, forty activists from Azapo shouted "Kennedy Go Home", in Soweto, 500 people carrying candles gathered to welcome him to the Tutus' home, which had been renovated so that he could spend his first night in a township. In the best African tradition, the arrival of the visitor was accompanied by rain, and Tutu named Kennedy Motlalepula, "bringer of rain." Kennedy and a party from his extended family toured South Africa for a week, visiting Winnie Mandela and Mangosuthu Buthelezi, addressing American businessmen, and going to a camp where the victims of forced removals had been dumped. He was refused permission to see Nelson Mandela. On his last day in the country, 2,500 people crowded into Regina Mundi in Soweto to hear him. About 120 members of Azapo disrupted the proceedings, marching toward the altar carrying placards describing him as an imperialist and chanting "No more Kennedy!" Tutu polled the meeting on whether Kennedy should speak. The majority vociferously agreed, and part of the crowd threatened to overwhelm the protestors. Close to tears, Tutu called off the speech, saying that he did not want to give the heavily armed police outside a pretext to move in. The incident permanently damaged his relations with Azapo—he was appalled at its willingness to incur the unprecedented, gloating coverage its protests attracted from the pro-apartheid media.

Two months after Kennedy's visit, apartheid was again on television screens in the United States. Ted Koppel brought ABC's *Nightline* to South Africa for five nights of discussion between South Africans who had never debated one another before. The series began with an opening skirmish between Tutu and the foreign minister, Pik Botha. "How," Koppel asked Botha, "do you respond to this man who has just said to you he is a bishop, he is a respected world figure, and he has never been able to vote in his own land?" Botha blustered that Tutu could vote in a Bantustan but that the government was prepared to consult with black leaders to see to what extent it could resolve the problem. Would they be prepared to negotiate with Tutu? Koppel asked. If Tutu rejected violence, replied Botha. His answer was a mistake, according to a review of the show in the *New York Times*. "The last 25 years of television have taught us that images carry their own truth.

It was impossible to associate Bishop Tutu with violence, active or implied. . . . Mr. Botha, one thought, lost that debate." Twenty years later, in an interview, Botha agreed.

Back in Washington, Kennedy joined other senators–including Gary Hart of Colorado, the newly elected John Kerry of Massachusetts, and the Republican Lowell Weicker of Connecticut–in introducing legislation to impose sanctions. Tutu's was from the beginning the South African name most often cited in debates in both in the Senate and the House of Representatives. Both Democrats and Republicans batted his opinions back and forth in support of their positions. None had spoken more eloquently about South Africa's "tragic and moving situation" than Tutu, said Kerry in July 1985. Tutu could not have been more explicit in assessing "what I would call trickle-down human rights." Paul Simon of Illinois described Tutu as "a reasonable man of good judgment." In the House, William H. Gray of Philadelphia quoted Tutu's reply to critics who opposed sanctions because they threatened people's jobs: "Moral humbug." Walter Fauntroy mentioned the "Tutu Principles"–the demands that Tutu had put forward, when he was enthroned as bishop of Johannesburg, as conditions for avoiding sanctions. In the early debates Republicans were reluctant to take Tutu on, preferring to bolster their case by referring to his reluctance to call explicitly for sanctions. This was particularly so after he and Simeon Nkoane had saved the life of the suspected informer in Duduza in July 1985–that event was covered widely and elicited widespread admiration for his courage.

A key reason for Tutu's prominence was America's visceral anticommunism. Because the ANC was allied with the South African Communist Party, quoting the ANC's leaders could sink a speaker in a mire of accusations and counteraccusations. The moderate Republican Nancy Kassebaum was among those who regarded Tutu as distinct from the ANC "but still an activist voice." According to Mark Helmke, the longtime senior adviser to Richard Lugar, Tutu rose above squabbles concerning communism: "He didn't look like a communist, he didn't sound like a communist. He didn't come across as a firebrand, he didn't come across as a bomb-thrower."

During Reagan's first term as president, Africa retained its position as what Chester Crocker called the stepchild of American foreign policy. He and his colleagues at the State Department had a free hand to pursue regional diplomacy as if on a chessboard, seeking to checkmate their Soviet opponents. In Reagan's second term, developments off the board—Tutu's Nobel Prize, American domestic politics, and the township uprising—intersected to threaten their game. In Crocker's cast of characters, there were spoilers on all sides. On the left, he wrote in his memoir, "Desmond Tutu and Randall Robinson complemented each other well: the courageous . . . prelate with a sharp tongue and a well-developed taste for liberation theology, and the American activist who knew how to simplify South Africa's trauma into a series of emotive, civil rights sound bites." In South Africa, Crocker wrote, the two had "the perfect allies in their campaign to change American policy: Pretoria's ministers of brutality, perversity, stupidity, and bad timing—a collection of characters who behaved like walk-ons in a Hollywood script." Backing them up in Washington were "the out-of-power Georgetown liberals, running their dinner parties, [to whom] the arrival in Washington of Bishop Tutu, or of any visiting South African, was like the arrival of a new line of designer jeans at the local haberdasher—this is a cause, everyone's got to get with The Cause."

On the right, as apartheid became a domestic issue as well as a matter of foreign policy, the fissure between the administration and congressional Republicans—already evident in late 1984—widened. Moreover, the administration itself split. By mid-1985, in Crocker's assessment, George Bush, George Shultz, Robert McFarlane, and James Baker were all in a camp that believed the administration had to make concessions, agree to modest sanctions, and put the issue behind it. Opposing them were Republicans caricatured by Crocker as conservatives who "viewed Africa as elephant country—a place to hunt for anti-Communist trophies to hang on the wall and to demonstrate doctrinal manhood in support of [right-wing] freedom fighters." Their ranks included William J. Casey, director of the CIA, who was seeking captured Soviet weaponry from South African military intelligence to feed to the Nicaraguan contras; Reagan's new chief of staff, Donald Regan; and the White House communications director, Pat Buchanan.

The Republicans were saved from a showdown in 1985 by P. W. Botha's disastrous speech of August 15. The flamboyant Pik Botha met McFarlane and Crocker before the speech, and in a performance described by Crocker as Pik at "his thespian best," told them major reforms were in the offing. McFarlane subsequently recoiled as he watched P.W. on television. He decided that P.W. was "a mean-spirited son of a bitch" and he, Schultz, and Richard Lugar worked out a deal in which Reagan preempted Congress by proclaiming a small package of sanctions by executive order. The order banned bank loans to

South Africa, the export of computers and nuclear technology, and imports of the South African gold coin, the Krugerrand.

These limited sanctions did not impress Tutu. For weeks he had been conducting tense funerals for people shot by the police. Two weeks earlier, Reagan had told a radio station in Atlanta that South Africa had "eliminated the segregation that we once had in our own country." In pure apartheid-speak, he added: "You know we must recognize that the black majority in South Africa is a combination of minorities. There are at least ten tribal divisions there." Reagan was speaking the day after armed police and soldiers in Soweto had rounded up 800 children for boycotting school, loaded them into armored vehicles, and taken them to a police station. When ninety-four of them were brought to court three days later, an eight-year-old was among them. Trevor Tutu—who was in the courtroom with Leah—said loudly: "This is a joke! These people are clowns." In the altercation that followed, the police accused him of swearing at them; they then detained him without trial for fourteen days under emergency regulations. Against this backdrop, when Desmond Tutu was asked for his response to Reagan's sanctions, he said they were "not even a flea bite." Reagan had no real interest in the welfare of blacks: "He has really been saying blacks are expendable. He sits around in equanimity because the fatalities are black fatalities. I said [last week] he was a crypto-racist. I think I should say now he is a racist pure and simple."

In late 1985 and the first half of 1986, the British Commonwealth became the center of antiapartheid efforts and Tutu's attention in the English-speaking world. Tutu did not play as prominent a role in Britain as in the United States. First Ambrose Reeves and then Trevor Huddleston took the lead as president of the Anti-Apartheid Movement, a coalition well established by the time Tutu became a public figure. Huddleston pursued an active correspondence with Margaret Thatcher. Her views on South Africa were similar, although not identical, to those of her ideological soul mate, Ronald Reagan. She was also influenced by her friend Laurens van der Post, the South African–born storyteller. Van der Post was a friend of Piet Koornhof, an admirer of Zulu nationalism and Mangosuthu Buthelezi—whom he called "the leader of the biggest nation in South Africa"—and a scathing critic of Nelson Mandela, "a god with clay feet." Thatcher developed respect for Mandela after his release, but when van der Post visited her, according to one of her officials, "she would listen with delight, her jaw agape" to stories about the Zulus. As late as 2000 she told van der Post's biographer, "I'm on the side of the Zulus."

Robert Runcie set up an appointment with Thatcher for Tutu in London in October 1985, during a planning meeting for the Lambeth Conference of 1988. Tutu stayed with Martin Kenyon. When Tutu arrived, Trevor Huddleston was away, putting the case for sanctions to American businessmen at Trinity Church, Wall Street. But he left a letter with Kenyon urging Tutu to address Thatcher with "great directness." He continued: "I know you will—but certainly my experience with the lady was that she *will* listen to what she doesn't agree with and it *will* have an effect if one is absolutely unshaken by the 'economic' arguments. . . . We really have the best possible chances [of] getting the Commonwealth to isolate Britain on the sanctions issue."

Tutu, accompanied by Terry Waite, met Thatcher in a small upstairs study at 10 Downing Street. He told her—as he had told Reagan—that apartheid was as evil and unchristian as Nazism. She had used sanctions against Argentina at the time of the Falklands war, he said. Why could she not use them now? She replied that they would threaten jobs in both Britain and South Africa. Tutu came away after an hour of discussions "slightly more hopeful" than when he went in. He thought she seemed anxious to avoid being isolated and branded as P. W. Botha's defender. Terry Waite's impression differed: "She listened, she was coldly polite. But she gave nothing away, absolutely nothing."

The next evening, the secretary-general of the Commonwealth, Sonny Ramphal, gave a dinner for Tutu and Oliver Tambo at its headquarters at Marlborough House in London. Commonwealth diplomats, businessmen, and clergymen—Trevor Huddleston was back from New York—attended, but no one from the British government. Thatcher had banned contact with the ANC: "As far as she was concerned," said her private secretary, Charles Powell, "people who were engaged in letting off bombs and killing people were terrorists and that was that. She wasn't going to deal with them." Standing up to speak beneath frescoes of the duke of Marlborough's eighteenth-century victories, Tambo amused Tutu by introducing himself "As a well-known terrorist . . ." After dinner, the two arranged to talk at breakfast the next morning in Kenyon's home in London. One of Kenyon's clearest recollections of the occasion was of Tambo and Thabo Mbeki arriving in a minibus to be told by Tutu that Eucharist had to come before breakfast.

The Commonwealth heads of government held their regular two-yearly meeting at Nassau in the Bahamas two weeks after Tutu saw Thatcher. As Huddleston predicted, Britain was isolated. Thatcher tore into her fellow prime ministers—she described them in her memoirs as "a gang of bullies." Brian Mulroney of Canada and the Indian prime minister, Rajiv Gandhi, tried to get her to compromise. The meeting bent over backward to accommodate her. She eventually conceded a ban on the import of Krugerrands and the withdrawal of support for trade promotion with South Africa. She triumphantly described her concession to the press as only "a tiny little bit." In doing so, as her own foreign secretary, Geoffrey Howe, wrote later, she "humiliated three dozen other heads of government, devalued the policy which they just agreed, and demeaned herself."

As Tutu became disillusioned at the prospects for a change in Thatcher's policy, his anger at the British government grew. At the end of October he said that Thatcher, Reagan, and Helmut Kohl were protecting a racist government that was killing children: "Support of this racist policy is racist." He cut off contact with British officials below the rank of foreign secretary, as he had done with the Americans. In 1986 he refused to see even Howe, although he later made an exception, at Robert Runcie's request, for Britain's ambassador to South Africa, Robin Renwick. According to Charles Powell, Thatcher recognised Tutu as "a brave man, a man who was taking great risks in what he was saying and what he was doing." But Lynda Chalker, a minister at the foreign office from 1986 on, told this writer that Thatcher, brought up in a devout, churchgoing Methodist family, was offended at Tutu's suggestion that she was unchristian: "She couldn't stand Desmond Tutu. Part of that was the result of his animosity . . . [his belief] that there was no good in her." Anthony Sampson was once shocked when Tutu snubbed Chalker at a diplomatic reception: "He cut her dead." Chalker recalled that Tutu upset Queen Elizabeth, although she attributed the incident to a different period: "I was escorting Her Majesty the Queen around and [remember] him coming up with a very sharp remark. . . . She heard it and said to me afterwards: 'Why does he have to be unpleasant?' I said, 'He's just angry.' "

The most positive outcome of the Commonwealth conference in Nassau was the establishment of an "Eminent Persons Group" to promote negotiations in South Africa. Cochaired by two former heads of government—Olusegun Obasanjo of Nigeria and Malcolm Fraser of Australia—the group held extensive consultations with scores of leaders in the first half of 1986. They met Tutu early in their work—six weeks before his appeal on April 2 for punitive sanctions. They drew up a promising "possible negotiating concept" in consultation with all parties. On May 19, P. W. Botha smashed the initiative by ordering the bombing of three Commonwealth capitals–Gaborone in Botswana, Harare in Zimbabwe, and Lusaka in Zambia. On June 12 the group announced the collapse of its mission. On the same day, Botha reimposed the state of emergency.

The following afternoon, Nancy Kassebaum telephoned Chester Crocker to warn him that the previous year's consensus between the administration and the Republican-controlled Senate was breaking down. Reagan had to "get out front" on the issue fast, she told him. Introducing new legislation some weeks earlier, Edward Kennedy had quoted from Tutu's call of April 2 for sanctions and declared: "The Anti-Apartheid Act of 1986 responds to Bishop Tutu's call by seeking a broad range of specific new American economic sanctions against South Africa." In the House–controlled by the Democrats–Congressman Ronald V. Dellums of California introduced into a debate over sanctions on June 18 a bill requiring a comprehensive trade and investment embargo of South Africa. This was far more radical than the proposal under discussion, and even he was shocked when it was approved on a voice vote. The administration responded by planning a package of new initiatives, an important part of which was a major presidential speech on South Africa.

As political heat over South Africa was building up in Washington, Ronald and Nancy Reagan spent the July 4 celebrations in New York, where the president joined a ceremony in which the Statue of Liberty, newly renovated for its centennial, was unveiled and relit. During the weekend, they went up the Hudson River to stay at Kykuit, the Rockefeller estate overlooking the river at Pocantico Hills. There, Reagan was handed a fervent plea on apartheid from one of the Rockefeller "cousins," the grandchildren of John D. Rockefeller, Jr. In a handwritten letter, Mary R. Morgan, daughter of a former Republican vice president, Nelson A. Rockefeller, told Reagan that black South Africans were discriminated against, detained, manipulated, and "now violated and killed" by their government. Like Reagan, she said, she believed America should be faithful to the ideals and pursuit of freedom for oppressed peoples: "As you said last night in a moving ceremony: 'We are the keepers of the flame of Liberty.'" She continued: "In that spirit, let us take an active stand for the oppressed people of South Africa, *before* all vestiges of their moderate democratic ideals are wiped away by demands for survival and revenge." The lessons of Nazi Germany needed to be reread: "We should not wait until it's too late; wait until there is a bloodbath we can only stand and watch and regret. I beg you to take another courageous, historically sensitive position and action like you are taking for free trade."

The value of Reagan's reply, filed in the Reagan presidential library in Simi Valley, California, is that—unlike letters to congressional leaders and others, which were usually composed by the National Security Council or the State Department—it was drafted personally. Before it was sent, the president's director of correspondence noted to a colleague that Reagan had written and signed it himself, and the handwritten draft was filed. Reagan wrote:

I know an effort is being made to portray our position as one of callous disregard for the plight of the Blacks in that country. I realize, of course, that some of this is political partisanship but, at the same time, that many sincerely concerned people are unaware of what we are doing. To tell the truth, that is understandable because we have to be rather quiet if we are to be helpful.

Some of the measures that are being suggested, such as the resolution approved in the House . . . would hurt the very people we seek to help. They would also leave us completely estranged and with no possible chance of influencing the South African government. As you know, we have employed some sanctions against South Africa, but only those which would not impose economic hardships on the mainly Black workers.

We also feel that closing down American-owned businesses there would only result in the unemployment of some 80,000 Blacks. As it is, those American firms have used a policy conceived by a Black clergyman in our country, Reverend Sullivan,* with regard to employee relations. It is based on our nondiscriminatory practices here at home.

We continue to press the South African government to move toward elimination of apartheid and to enter into discussions and negotiations with responsible Black leaders. We have not hesitated in citing the immorality of present practices.

* Leon H. Sullivan of Philadelphia drew up an employers' code of conduct for U.S. companies in South Africa. He abandoned it and called for disinvestment in June 1987.

In the ten days leading up to Reagan's speech on July 22, there was a tug-of-war over its contents between the State Department and the White House. The diplomats stood by constructive engagement but proposed in their first draft that Reagan express outrage at recent events in South Africa and reach out to black leaders across the spectrum, including the ANC. At the White House, Pat Buchanan responded with language that could have come directly from Pretoria's information department. Crocker was livid: "Permitting communications director Buchanan to mess with the basics of American foreign policy was to me almost obscene." The final version of the speech–delivered in the East Room of the White House–was a mishmash of contradictory signals, which, for example, both adopted Pretoria's language justifying its refusal to negotiate with the ANC and called for Mandela to be released to take part in the political process. In the most retrograde sections of the speech, Reagan defended Botha's reforms, said Pretoria had realized that apartheid had to go, and spoke of "violent attacks by blacks against blacks" and "calculated terror" by elements of the ANC.

Tutu read the highlights of Reagan's address the day after frustrating and unproductive talks with P. W. Botha. After reimposing the state of emergency on June 12, Botha had agreed to meet Tutu for the first time since the church leaders' meeting six years earlier. Tutu spent ninety minutes with Botha on June 13, and nearly two hours on July 21. They "did not mince words," Tutu said. He told Botha that the situation in the townships was deteriorating, and tried to persuade him that trying to crush dissent was like "an aspirin or a toothpick" for toothache–it might give temporary relief, but it could not provide a solution. He also raised the issue of harassment of church leaders and the crisis in black schools. Botha said he would refer Tutu's concerns on church leaders and education to the appropriate cabinet ministers, but was otherwise unyielding. He attacked Tutu's advocacy of sanctions and said he expected Tutu to stand up against foreign intervention in South Africa's domestic affairs. After the second meeting, Botha publicly discounted Tutu's constituency–Tutu represented only a segment of only one of the country's churches, Botha said.

Tutu decided he would not mince words with Reagan either. "Your president is the pits as far as blacks are concerned," he told an American journalist. "I found the speech nauseating. . . . He sits there like the great big white chief of old [who] can tell us black people that we don't know what is good for us, the white man knows." With the South

Zachariah Zelilo Tutu,
Desmond Tutu's father.

Aletta Dorothea "Matse" Tutu, née Mathlare, Tutu's mother, with Eudy Zamille
Morrison, son of Tutu's sister Sylvia.
Tutu's mother was a powerful influence
on his life.

Desmond Mpilo Tutu
and Nomalizo Leah
Shenxane at their
wedding in 1955.

Desmond and Leah in London with,
from left, Trevor, Thandi, Nontombi, and Mpho.

Desmond and Leah in retirement in their garden at Milnerton,
Cape Town. (Photo: Benny Gool.)

Tutu at theological college with the principal, Godfrey Pawson, CR; a visiting priest, Namo Ranthite; and, on Tutu's left, his fellow student Ernest Sobukwe, brother of the political leader Robert Sobukwe.

Aelred Stubbs, CR, identified Tutu's potential as a theology teacher and sent Tutu to be trained in Britain.

Bill Burnett, a predecessor as archbishop, had a difficult relationship with Tutu.

N. Barney Pityana was inspired by Tutu's caring but later argued with him over the involvement of priests in politics.

Of the many forced removals associated with the lives of Desmond and Leah Tutu, that in Sophiatown in 1955 attracted the most publicity.

African National Congress leader Oliver Tambo was a close friend of Trevor Huddleston, who recommended both him and Tutu for the priesthood.

The spire of Christ the King, Sophiatown, remained standing above homes destroyed by apartheid. (Photo: Paul Singleton.)

Tutu could reach many of his parishes in the Lesotho mountains only on horseback. (Photo: David Bruno.)

Desmond Tutu was among about fifty protesters (including Leah Tutu) arrested on the streets of Johannesburg in 1980 for an illegal march. (Photo: *The Star*.)

Tutu and Peter Storey worked together in the South African Council of Churches during some of its stormiest years. They learned later that they had narrowly escaped being killed together.

Moments from death, a suspected
police informer clings to Tutu's legs.
In a flurry of action, Tutu and his
colleague Simeon Nkoane, CR, waded
into the crowd to save the man's life.
(Photo: Peter Magubane.)

Anxious mothers in Soweto, right, listen as Tutu negotiates the release
of their children. (Photo: Louise Gubb.)

The clergy of Cape Town declare their allegiance to Tutu in his throne–part of a choir screen from Westminster Abbey–in St. George's Cathedral.

The police teargas community leaders in Gugulethu, Cape Town, in 1989. Tutu, in cassock, is partly obscuring the educationist Jakes Gerwel, later chief of staff to President Mandela. (Photo: Rashid Lombard.)

From left, Sheikh Nazeem Mohamed, Tutu, Mayor Gordon Oliver, the church
leaders Allan Boesak and Frank Chikane (behind Boesak's shoulder), and
the United Democratic Front's leader Zoli Malindi in 1989 at a march of 30,000
people which helped open the way to Nelson Mandela's release. (Photo: Benny Gool.)

Tutu showing Nelson and Winnie Mandela through
the terraced gardens of Bishopscourt, Cape Town, the morning
after Mandela's release from prison. (Photo: Louise Gubb.)

Tutu preaching peace to angry crowds wielding makeshift weapons in Kagiso on the West Rand during the violence of the transition to democracy. (Photo: Louise Gubb.)

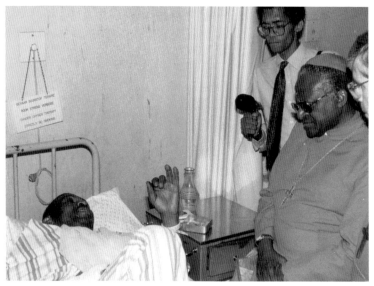

Patients at Sebokeng Hospital in the Vaal Triangle told Tutu that whites were among their attackers in the violence of 1990. Their accounts sowed the seeds of Tutu's disillusionment with F. W. de Klerk.

Tutu visiting Mangosuthu
Buthelezi at kwaZulu's capital,
Ulundi. The statue in the
background is of Shaka,
the legendary leader who
forged the Zulu nation.

Nelson Mandela–flanked by Tutu and "number two to Tutu," Michael Nuttall–
greets southern Africa's Anglican bishops a week after his release.

Tutu, his old college classmate Stanley Mogoba (left), and Michael Nuttall (not in photograph) brokered a summit between Nelson Mandela and Mangosuthu Buthelezi in 1993.

Tutu, sixty-two years old and a Nobel Peace laureate, votes for the first time. (Photo: Benny Gool.)

"This is the day for which we have waited for over 300 years." Tutu presents Mandela to crowds in Cape Town on the day of his election as president. (Photo: Benny Gool.)

Tutu traveled to the home of the former president P. W. Botha's daughter to try to persuade Botha to appear before the Truth and Reconciliation Commission. (Photo: Benny Gool.)

Former president F. W. de Klerk appeared before the TRC but upset Tutu by refusing to acknowledge that governments in which he had served had presided over systematic, state-sanctioned violence. (Photo: Benny Gool.)

Al Gore, with whom Tutu served on the board of overseers of Harvard University, joined Bill Clinton to welcome Tutu as the first South African in the Oval Office during Clinton's presidency. (White House photo, Clinton Presidential Library.)

Visiting the church at Ntarama, Rwanda. The post-genocide government took visitors to this church to show them the consequences of the international community's failure to act in 1994.

Tutu thanks Queen Elizabeth II after she presented him with the Wilberforce Medal in 1999 in recognition of his work for human rights and democracy. The medal is named after the British antislavery campaigner, William Wilberforce.

Tutu accepted an invitation to meet the Sinn Fein leader Gerry Adams at Connolly House, the party's headquarters in west Belfast, in 1998.

The tiny chapel in the backyard of Desmond and Leah Tutu's home at Orlando West. (Photo: Benny Gool.)

African government killing four-year-olds, it was nonsense to describe freedom fighters, who had used peaceful means to oppose racism for fifty years before taking up arms, as terrorists. Reagan, Thatcher, and Kohl were saying to blacks that they were dispensable: "I am quite angry. I think the west, for my part, can go to hell."

The only recorded response from any of the leaders was from Thatcher. "Bishop Tutu is entitled to say just exactly what he wishes," she told a press conference in Oslo. "So am I. I shall be more circumspect than Bishop Tutu."

The day of Reagan's address, according to Chester Crocker, was the day the administration lost the debate over sanctions. "He didn't know how to speak to race," Crocker told the present writer. "No question about it. The president had a tin ear on issues of race." On August 15, the Senate approved a bill initiated by Richard Lugar stopping flights between South Africa and the United States; banning imports of iron, steel, uranium, coal, textiles, and agricultural products; and prohibiting American companies from making new investments in South Africa. Edward Kennedy lobbied House members of the Congressional Black Caucus, urging them to accept the limited Senate bill rather than pursue the House's proposal for comprehensive sanctions. This removed the White House's last hope—that the legislation would become bogged down in a Senate-House conference. As the White House made preparations for Reagan to veto the bill, it scrambled for Senate votes to sustain the veto. White House records show that a vigorous lobbying campaign was run out of Buchanan's office from July on, using the names of Helen Suzman, Alan Paton, Mangosuthu Gatsha Buthelezi (described in one draft memo as "Gotcha Bathelesi"), members of Botha's black local authorities, and black clergymen who opposed sanctions—one of whom was the former divisional director of the SACC, who admitted to Tutu that he had forged the SACC's checks. After the Senate's vote for sanctions, the campaign focused on Republicans: Buchanan's aides scathingly called State Department personnel the "Boer bashers at State," and Buchanan proposed a newspaper op-ed article criticizing Richard Lugar.

On September 26, Reagan vetoed Lugar's bill, now known as the Comprehensive Anti-Apartheid Act. Three days later, the House of Representatives voted by a huge majority (313 to 83) to override his veto. The bill moved to the Senate for the final act on October 1 and 2. In response to Reagan's warning of lost jobs, Kennedy again quoted Tutu: "Blacks are suffering already. To end that suffering, we will support sanctions, even if we have to take on additional suffering. To whom is the international community willing to listen? To the victims and their spokesmen or to the perpetrators of apartheid and those who benefit from it?" Faced with a string of invocations of Tutu's comments from Democratic senators, the allies of the White House tackled Tutu head-on for the first time. Jesse Helms of North Carolina said Tutu represented only a minority, "and the minority he represents happens to be the violent minority." Orrin Hatch of Utah had visited South Africa in the summer recess to find, he declared, that Tutu spoke only for himself and not for his church: "Senator Kennedy's friend Bishop Tutu is not what Senator Kennedy claims him to be." Jeremiah Denton of Alabama described Tutu as "a creature of the media . . . luxuriating in his prominence."

On the day the Senate voted, Reagan placed personal calls to a number of senators in a final bid to get their votes. He was preparing for a summit with the Soviet leader, Mikhail Gorbachev, in Reykjavik; and he argued that he would appear weak and ineffective if he was defeated. His appeal was to no avail. The Senate overrode his veto, 78 to 21. It was the first and only time a veto by Reagan concerning foreign policy was not sustained, and the first override of a presidential veto on a major foreign policy question since 1972. Tutu's singular contribution to the outcome of the debate, in the view of both Democrats and Republicans in Washington, was his moral stature. "He was the perfect communicator for the moral high ground in American political life," Lugar's aide Mark Helmke told this writer. For Kennedy's senior aide Gregory Craig, "The reason he was important was that whenever we saw him, he was acting courageously and consistently with his nonviolent position and his spiritual leadership position. He was the closest thing to a Dr. King the antiapartheid movement had."

CHAPTER 12

THE HEADMASTER

Early in February 1986 a group of black Anglicans from Cape Town met at a church in Mitchell's Plain, one of the areas on the sandy Cape Flats outside the city to which apartheid had relegated the people it designated as Coloured. The group was holding a regular meeting of the diocese's Black Solidarity Group, and Desmond Tutu was on the agenda. Two months hence, the diocese would elect a replacement for Philip Russell as archbishop, and white South Africa was in one of its frenzies over Tutu's doings and sayings abroad. In Atlanta to receive the Martin Luther King Jr. Peace Prize, he had called for recognition of the ANC by the west. Vice President George Bush, a fellow guest at the first celebration of King's birthday as a federal holiday in the United States, had reportedly questioned Tutu's commitment to nonviolence. At other stops on a three-week tour, Tutu had raised the prospect of attacks on white South African schoolchildren and of black servants poisoning their employers' morning coffee. On his return home he was forced to issue a pastoral letter to Anglicans pointing out that he had been trying to show the horrors of full-scale civil war: "I was issuing a warning," he patiently explained. "I don't want to see any of this happen."

None of the controversy fazed the Black Solidarity Group. According to a record of its meeting, it decided that although Tutu had refused nomination as a candidate for archbishop, he ought at least to be considered: "The meeting was in favour of the Bishop as a nominee, and felt strongly that it was the prerogative of the Assembly to elect him despite his refusal." Five years earlier, black Anglicans had tried to delay the election to replace Bill Burnett because they felt they were underrepresented in the assembly. They had failed but had instead deadlocked the assembly. Now their representation had been improved, and the Solidarity Group resolved to lobby other clergy and lay voters before the election. They were ready for a long-drawn-out struggle; there was to be no question of rushing the election "because of a desire to get it over and done with so that we get home quicker."

On Monday, April 14, clergy and lay representatives from every parish in the diocese convened the elective assembly in the chapel of Diocesan College, the elite Anglican private school in Cape Town's southern suburbs. Since they were electing a diocesan bishop for Cape Town, they were the principal electors. But because their choice would also be metropolitan or spiritual head of the church in southern Africa, representatives from across the subcontinent, including all the bishops, also joined the assembly. The leading candidates all professed their reluctance to be nominated. Khotso Makhulu was now bishop of Botswana and archbishop of Central Africa. Michael Nuttall, the alternative to Tutu in the deadlocked election of 1981, had no pressing desire to be archbishop: he had been elected bishop in his home province of Natal only four years previously. Tutu, as we have seen, had told Johannesburg that he hoped he would be there until retirement, unless it became "abundantly clear" that God had other ideas. More important, Leah was settled in Johannesburg, deeply rooted in the Soweto community, and very unhappy at the prospect of moving.

Still, Tutu and Nuttall were both persuaded to allow their names to go forward. When Makhulu's opposition to his nomination was announced to the assembly, Tutu urged that he should remain a contender. As assembly members debated the candidates, Tutu and Nuttall sat together out of earshot in the school library, "sometimes talking together, mostly keeping silent," Nuttall wrote afterward. Nuttall prayed for "a holy indifference" to the result. He also found it unsettling to be seen foiling the prospect of South Africa's first black Anglican archbishop. He need not have worried. Late in the afternoon of the first day, on the third ballot, Tutu's nomination secured the necessary two-thirds majority among both clergy and laity. The synod of bishops voted unanimously to ratify the election. Tutu entered the school chapel with his brother bishops to a standing ovation. Accepting election, he gave a short address. He was like a lightbulb, he said: he could shine only if he was plugged into a source of power. Only if the church, its people, and their faith provided an electric current could he succeed. At seven-fifteen that evening, the doors of the chapel swung open and the news was announced to the people waiting outside. Tutu emerged to shake the hands of assembly members as they filed out. "I'm speechless," he said, "and I guess there are some who would prefer me to remain that way!" More seriously, he sought to reassure whites: "I suppose there will be some people who are not exactly enamoured of my election. They must remember that the church does not belong to Desmond Tutu." He pledged that he would not be "a one-man band about to explode on the scene. . . . The Archbishop is a focus and spokesperson for the synod of bishops usually." In Soweto, Leah wept.

The speed and unanimity of the election convinced Nuttall that God had indeed spoken, in Tutu's phrase, abundantly clearly. Other whites in the leadership were similarly persuaded. Leslie Stradling, the bishop of Johannesburg who had ordained Tutu as a priest twenty-five years earlier, confided to his diary that night that he would have preferred Nuttall, "but we have been praying a lot about it and the assembly sounds as if it was directed by a spirit of love and understanding so this is something to be accepted gladly."

As when Tutu was chosen for Johannesburg, there was shock as well as anger and disappointment among white Anglicans, some of whom left the church or withdrew financial support. Alan Paton told Mangosuthu Buthelezi in a letter that Tutu had been described as "a kind of holy man" by the new bishop of Johannesburg, Duncan Buchanan. "I am afraid that I do not get this impression of him," Paton wrote. "There is something in his personality that I do not like. Perhaps it is I who am at fault." To which Buthelezi replied: "There is something radically wrong with the personality of His Grace [Tutu], if one strings together his various statements." From within the Anglican hierarchy, the only vocal support the opposition received was from Burnett. Soon after Tutu was enthroned, Burnett wrote a long commentary in which he did not use Tutu's name but left readers in no doubt as to whom he was referring. Quoting the Letter of Jude in the New Testament, Burnett said that admission to the church had been gained by some "who pervert the grace of our God . . . and deny our only master and Lord Jesus Christ." Liberation theology, just like the theology underlying apartheid, led people to place their hope of salvation in a political manifesto instead of in the redeeming work of Jesus. Burnett attacked Tutu for "the consigning to hell of Margaret Thatcher and Ronald Reagan," whom he described as Christians in good standing. He concluded: "It would seem that we have one of the offspring of the Cuckoo of Liberation theology being inserted into the ecclesiastical nest. It is important that we recognise cuckoo chicks when we see them. By them the faith once delivered to the saints is being eroded." A counterpoint to the negative response to Tutu's election from South

Africa's minority was provided by two large services of celebration and thanksgiving in Cape Town on Sunday, September 7. In the first, more than 1,300 people crammed into the Cathedral of St. George the Martyr, mother church of the diocese, for the formal two-hour enthronement service. The diocese hired eighteen plainclothes security officers for the occasion. The cathedral was searched for bombs on Saturday night and again on Sunday morning. Monitors were set up in a hall for guests who could not be accommodated in the main church. As excitement grew before the service, hundreds of supporters without seats gathered at the northwest door, where Tutu would make his formal entrance. The service began with a procession of choirs and clergy including archbishops and bishops, clad in colourful copes and miters, from across Africa and the world. Tutu arrived, knocked on the closed northwest door three times, and was admitted and welcomed by the dean, Ted King. After proceeding to the altar, Tutu made a declaration on the gospels that he would protect the rights and liberties of the cathedral and preserve the customs of the church. The church's most senior bishop, Kenneth Oram of Grahamstown, enthroned him in the archiepiscopal chair and presented him with the primatial cross, the symbol of his authority. Philip Russell hung around his neck the diamond-encrusted Kimberley cross. The dean gave him his pastoral staff and, to a trumpet fanfare, presented him to the congregation. Most of the hymns and anthems were by western church composers—Hubert Parry, Elgar, Handel, and Bach ("Jesu, Joy of Man's Desiring")—but the Soweto choir, Imilonji ka Ntu, sang one of Tutu's favorite Sesotho hymns and a praise poem dedicated to him, "Hail, Stick of Redemption!" (Imilonji's rendering of this was "very noisy," thought Stradling.)

Tutu structured his hour-long "charge" to the diocese around three themes: the centrality of the spiritual, the church as family, and—one of his best-loved biblical themes—the principle of transfiguration. He called for daily Eucharist, fasting on Fridays, and "a whole army" of spiritual directors. But this did not imply that believers could "luxuriate" in the spirit, which was given to an individual "to goad him or her into action." Building on his belief that separating the sacred from the secular was a result of the "baneful influence" of "Hellenistic dualism" on western thought, he advocated the African worldview: God was the God of all life, whether religious or political. Families disagreed, said Tutu, and Anglicans were not expected to agree with their archbishop on every issue. As in a biological family, members of the church could not choose their sisters and brothers: "Whether I like it or not, whether he likes it or not . . . P.W. Botha is my brother and I must desire and pray for the best for him." Transfiguration, he said, was at work when an instrument of execution for criminals in the Middle East was transformed for Christians into a symbol of life—"the life-giving cross which Christians wear with pride." No individual, no situation was "untransfigurable." His address was interrupted by applause, cheering, and whistles, and at the end he received a standing ovation.

The new archbishop ended the service by proceeding out of the cathedral and blessing the diocese and city, to cheers and cries of "Viva Tutu" from the crowd outside. The only jarring notes were created by a few right-wing demonstrators, who tried to lay a wreath to mourn his coming; and by diocesan officials, who offended journalists by trying to charge international television crews exorbitant fees for footage of the service.

From the cathedral, the celebrations moved to an open-air Eucharist for 10,000 at the Cape Showgrounds, Goodwood, outside the city. Here, the real South Africa asserted itself more vigorously. The service opened with Ntsikana's Great Hymn, led by Imilonji ka Ntu, and the Soweto choir played a bigger role than in the cathedral, also leading traditional African choruses. Important parts of the liturgy were sung in IsiXhosa, and a Xhosa translation of the sermon was provided. This, observed Leslie Stradling in his diary, was new for Cape Town, where "African parishes are few and small and generally receive only crumbs." He added: "The lesson was in Afrikaans but otherwise there was no recognition that Coloureds were present." The sermon was preached by Robert Runcie, who had come from London to enjoy the fruit of his and Terry Waite's "good diplomacy" two years earlier. Exuberant youngsters chanted slogans and raised their fists in the black power salute. When Winnie Mandela arrived, bringing congratulations from her husband in nearby Pollsmoor Prison, she was mobbed. Allan Boesak was greeted with the two-syllable chant of his name customary in the Western Cape's townships: "Boes-sak! Boes-sak! Boes-sak!" When a few hundred young activists began to jog around the stadium and call for speeches by political leaders, Tutu asked Boesak and Albertina Sisulu, a president of the UDF, to speak, to the dismay of those Anglicans who felt that the sanctity of their worship was being breached. "Two unpleasantly rabble-rousing speeches . . . spoiled the atmosphere," complained Stradling.

To round off the day, Cape Town's mayor, Leon Markowitz, gave a party for the Tutus and their foreign guests, among them Coretta Scott King, widow of Martin Luther King, Jr. The event was an example of civic farsightedness—as when the mayor of Atlanta, Georgia, in 1964, persuaded its white establishment to swallow their hostility to King and attend a banquet celebrating his Nobel Peace Prize. At the dinner in Cape Town, the wife of one alderman told Canada's archbishop, Michael Peers, that the image of Tutu as vicious was so pervasive among whites that she was frightened when he approached their table. Johannesburg's civic and business leaders had not been able to find it within themselves to recognize Tutu's peace prize in 1984, and he never forgot the contrast of Cape Town's welcome.

The impact of Tutu's election and enthronement was not a result of the size of his denomination—the Catholic and the Methodist churches were larger. Nor was it because he was the first black leader of a major multiracial church—the Methodists had elected their first black national leader two decades earlier. It was rather because the Anglican Church, as in so many other former British-ruled territories, was still viewed— whether accurately or not—as the church of the English establishment. The pronouncements of Anglican archbishops automatically received more press coverage than those of other church leaders. Saint George's Cathedral, built from local sandstone in Gothic Revival style, was designed by the British architect Herbert Baker, who went on to collaborate with the architect of imperial New Delhi, Edwin Lutyens. The cathedral was in the heart of Cape Town, separated from Parliament and the president's offices at Tuynhuys only by the pedestrian precinct of Government Avenue. It was one block from the Groote Kerk ("Great Church"), mother church of first the Dutch and then the Afrikaner establishment. For the jubilant young people at Goodwood stadium, Tutu's accession to high office provided a foretaste of liberation: if a black person could take over at St. George's, and live in Bishopscourt, the big white mansion in Cape Town's most expensive suburb, could political liberation be far behind?

Tutu set about exercising authority over his new domain vigorously, appropriating old symbols and creating new ones. He began with his home and office at Bishopscourt. He and Leah had come a long way from the garage to which they were consigned when he was first ordained deacon in 1960. Bishopscourt, the seat of bishops of Cape Town since 1851, had at least eight bedrooms and three bathrooms upstairs. Downstairs were huge drawing room and dining room, a large library and kitchen, a chapel, and the archbishop's office. Some of the original walls dated back to the seventeenth century; dampness was an ongoing problem; and the house was costly to maintain. For years the diocese had spent a bare minimum on upkeep, mindful of the relative poverty of the church's black majority and feeling overwhelmed by priorities such as the cost of replacing churches for communities displaced by apartheid. Tutu, unencumbered by white liberal guilt, was confident that black Anglicans wanted the headquarters of their church under its first black archbishop to reflect an institution that was world-class. "Bishopscourt is a charming house," he wrote to the diocesan official responsible for its upkeep before he moved in, "but it is dingy and quite unattractive and inhospitable as presently ordered. It is a disgrace to the Diocese and the Province"—that is, the church across southern Africa.

The purpose of his letter was to complain that the diocesan trustees were hesitant to spend the 80,000 rand needed to renovate the house. Tutu threatened to refuse to live there if they did not back down. "I have far more important work to do than to be engaged in unedifying wrangles over this relatively unimportant issue," he said. "I cannot afford to invest precious time, emotional and nervous energy in that sort of thing when I am battling . . . on several fronts. . . . My wife does not want to come to Cape Town. If I were to tell her your recent decision my work would be cut out persuading her to come." The trustees approved the conversion of most of the upstairs rooms into two living units: a three-bedroom apartment for the Tutu family, and a one-bedroom apartment for guests. Downstairs, wall-to-wall carpeting was put down on many of the old wooden floors, to the barely disguised horror of some members of the diocese's white establishment. Tutu insisted on upgrading the accommodation provided for workers in the home and garden; for the third time he had moved into a bishop's house in which he believed the servants' quarters reflected badly on the church. Once the work was complete, he was a stickler for maintenance. He would not tolerate the deterioration in buildings and infrastructure that he sometimes encountered while traveling in Africa, and a staff member instructed to replace a lightbulb in the morning could expect to be asked that afternoon why the job had not yet been done.

Later the chapel was also renovated. A rural community development project supplied new pews. Tutu commissioned a sculptor in Cape Town to model a crucifix on Salvador Dalí's *Christ of St. John of the Cross,* in which the body of Christ leans forward off the cross in agony. Outside, the forecourt was bricked over, an outbuilding was converted into a retreat center, and office accommodation was extended. The archbishop, however, overreached himself with a feature that the present writer, working as his press secretary, privately dubbed "Tutu's folly." In a protracted episode, Tutu pressed Stephen Oliver, the archdeacon responsible for the upkeep of Bishopscourt, to build a fountain in the forecourt. Months of discussion and wrangling ensued, reflecting on the one hand the archbishop's desire for an impressive water feature of the sort he enjoyed seeing on foreign visits, and on the other the reluctance of a blunt and determinedly parsimonious Yorkshireman to spend money. The outcome was a small fountain in an oversize circular pond, which looked like a low-walled concrete farm reservoir, lacking only a creaking corrugated iron wind pump and cattle lapping at the water. The debate then turned to the plumbing. This produced results no more impressive—when the water jets were turned on low, their height did not give the feature the proportions it needed; when they were turned on high, the slightest breeze sent sheets of water streaming across the driveway. Then the fountain had to be turned off at night when a nun living in the retreat house complained that the running water was disturbing her. Tutu's successor had the pond demolished and the fountain moved to a more appropriate place in the garden.

The house was surrounded by seven hectares (seventeen acres) of land, through which the headwaters of Cape Town's Liesbeeck River flowed. From the terraced and cultivated front garden, framed by pergolas, there was a stunning view of the eastern slopes and, in winter, the waterfalls, of Table Mountain, the 1,085-meter (3,500-foot) mountain dominating the city skyline. The property was maintained by a staff of two or three presided over by a dignified head gardener, Livingstone Nakani, whose clan name, Tshawe, indicated his descent from the original Xhosa royal house. As Tutu got to know Nakani's qualities, he developed great respect for him and gave him more authority over the property. Behind a hedge flanking the garden was a swimming pool, and beyond that a piece of undeveloped land. The Tutus had playground equipment installed there and opened the pool to the diocese. White Anglicans with their own gardens and pools did not use the facility much, but parishes in black areas hired buses to bring their congregations to Bishopscourt for summer picnics. Living in Bishopscourt, Tutu told visitors, he found it easy to understand the blindness of most white South Africans, who had never visited a black township, to the suffering in their country.

Leah Tutu never came fully to terms with Bishopscourt. At a time of frequent threats on Desmond's life, Soweto was safer than Bishopscourt. Their house in Orlando West was closely hemmed in by others; they were surrounded by supportive neighbors within shouting distance; and a short, high wall separated them from the street outside. In Cape Town, the long fence around the overgrown perimeter of the estate was impossible to secure, and the burglar alarm in the house would not have prevented a serious attempt by assassins. Tutu was matter-of-fact about his security: "If I'm doing God's work," he said, "he should jolly well look after me." But Leah could never be that sanguine. Strange cars parked in the driveway overnight, though they usually belonged to friends of other residents, were a constant source of worry. Apart from the question of security, life in a suburb where properties were so big that people rarely saw their neighbors was lonely compared with life in bustling Soweto. In Cape Town, the only space Leah could count on as her own was their upstairs apartment; in Soweto, she was in complete control of their home. She loved gardening and liked to do much of the work herself; this was feasible in their small garden in Orlando West but impractical at Bishopscourt. (Sometimes on his days off in Soweto, Desmond would watch her mow the lawn.) White liberals in Leah's position did good works in Cape Town's black townships, but as a township resident herself she found that prospect awkward. As a result, when Desmond traveled outside Cape Town without her, she often took the opportunity to spend the time in Soweto, where she could join fully in community life and run her own house and garden.

Leah nevertheless played a pivotal role in her husband's work as archbishop. She prided herself on being able to read his moods and thoughts. Although feisty and independent-minded, she expressed her views discreetly, acting as a private sounding board, at times shaping his decisions by her opposition rather than her support.

Occasionally Leah's assertiveness became news—for example, when foreign visitors, perched high on their seats in tourist buses, took photographs of her over the wall of the home in Orlando West as if she were an animal in a zoo. She once called this writer in Bishopscourt from Johannesburg to say: "John, I've stoned another bus." A more detailed explanation revealed that she had been on her hands and knees in her garden when she was disturbed by tourists' flashbulbs, and she had lobbed clods of earth at the bus. A statement was issued appealing to tour operators to respect her privacy.

The pressures on Desmond's time in South Africa were such that often the best "quality time" he and Leah enjoyed as a couple was traveling abroad together. He both startled and charmed fellow airline passengers at the beginning of flights by going down on his hands and knees in first-class cabins to replace Leah's shoes with airline socks. He acknowledged as a weakness his enjoyment of the limelight, and she took pleasure in ribbing him publicly about it. At the U.S. Military Academy at West Point, New York, officer cadets once gave him an academy cap that did not fit. Someone else, he quipped, would have said they gave him a cap that was too small, but Leah said, "Your head is too big." To hosts asking about his tastes in food and drink, she said: "Think of a five-year-old."

In Cape Town, Leah was also separated from her family. Although some of the children stayed abroad after graduating, at least one or two were always to be found in Johannesburg. Mpho studied electrical engineering at Howard University in Washington, D.C.; tried without success to get work in South Africa; and returned to the United States. There she took over from Bernice Powell the scholarship fund sponsoring the studies of exiled South Africans at American universities. In 1993, she married a sportswriter for the *Boston Globe*, Joe Burris. Naomi completed a master's degree in Kentucky and pursued an academic career, studying and teaching at universities in the United States, Britain, and South Africa and carrying out research on woman-headed households in a rural area of South Africa. She married twice—first an American, then a South African—and started a fund that financed projects for South African refugees in other African countries. Thandi married and lived in Soweto until halfway through her parents' time at Bishopscourt, leading efforts to raise funds for conjoined twins who were separated in a high-profile operation in Baragwanath Hospital. She then moved with her husband, Mthunzi Gxashe, and son, Xabiso, to Atlanta, Georgia, to study health sciences and work at Emory University's School of Public Health.

Trevor returned to South Africa from Britain while his father was still at the SACC, and developed a colorful reputation from his clashes with the law. These began a year after his return, when traffic officers in Johannesburg stopped him for speeding and driving under the influence of alcohol. He had come from a society in which policemen called him "sir," and his first problem in South Africa in the 1980s was to be a black man encountering white traffic policemen. His second problem was that as a relatively well-paid employee of a multinational corporation, he drove the kind of car that traffic officers probably did not believe a black man could, or should, own. His third problem was that he knew his rights, and insisted on them. It perhaps did not help that he spoke English like a Briton. Finally, the fat really hit the fire when he told the police his name. He was kept in police cells for three days even after tests showed he was not under the influence. The state later paid him damages for wrongful detention. A year later, a soccer team for which he was playing walked off the field over a referee's treatment of him. "We believe the referee was justified in sending Trevor off for swearing at him," his captain said afterward, "but we objected when the referee referred to him as a kaffir."

Desmond and Leah had been thrilled when Trevor announced his desire to come home, albeit anxious about how he would readjust to apartheid. By 1984 they were privately concerned enough about his welfare for Desmond to write to Trevor Huddleston: "Your godson [Trevor] . . . needs your prayers desperately urgently. He worries us." Thereafter, Trevor developed a taste for confrontation with authority that reflected his father's outspokenness but not his father's judgment. In a publicity stunt for an advertising agency he was launching, he attempted to breach security measures at Johannesburg's airport. On another occasion, on leaving an aircraft in transit and being denied permission to reboard, he suggested that his calculator could detonate an explosion. He was charged and convicted under antihijacking legislation and was given a jail sentence of 3½ years. He was closer to Leah than to Desmond, but both were distraught, not least at the prospect of how white prison guards would treat a Tutu.

In 1992, his father intervened to help him. In a letter to the foreign minister, Pik Botha, Tutu wrote: "I write to you as a father with a heavy heart. My son, Trevor, has been very foolish. As you may know, he lost his appeal and will now have to serve time in prison." Tutu pointed to an instance in which the government had granted "a certain leeway" to whites facing prison. He asked Botha: "I am making a personal plea to you to ask if through your good offices something can be done to help him." Botha did not reply but made informal representations within the government on the basis that Trevor's behavior would never have been taken seriously had he been an ordinary South African's son. For more than three years, the police ignored Trevor. The press mocked their apparent inability to the find the man it now called Tutu's "maverick son."

When the Truth and Reconciliation Commission (TRC) was established under a democratic government, Trevor applied for amnesty, arguing that he had committed his offenses with political motives. In August 1997, in the midst of a dispute between the TRC–which Tutu was now chairing–and the former rulers, the police suddenly appeared at the house in Orlando West without prior notice or explanation. Accompanied by a photographer from the Afrikaans newspaper most bitterly opposed to the commission, they announced that they had come to find Trevor. His parents advised him to give himself up and serve the sentence. Four months into it, the TRC's amnesty committee freed him. Trevor's assertion of political motives had raised eyebrows, but Alex Boraine, Tutu's deputy in the commission, told critics of the amnesty decision that Tutu had been "scrupulously correct" in keeping out of his son's case. The most likely explanation for the decision is that it was taken by a panel of the amnesty committee chaired by the commission's most right-wing member, who believed in granting amnesty on the most generous terms possible. Whatever Tutu felt or said privately, he loyally defended his son in public. He repeatedly voiced his pride in the protest against the mass arrests of schoolchildren for which Trevor had been jailed for two weeks in 1985. He acknowledged that Trevor had been "naughty"–a severe judgment in Tutu's lexicon–but lashed out at the government for trying to get at him through his family. Some of the Tutus' British friends who watched Trevor growing up believed Desmond had been too much the disciplinarian, tougher on Trevor than on his sisters. In 1994 Tutu agreed, at least partly. "Part of the problem is that I have been too strict," he told a British newsmagazine. "I see myself in Trevor. Some of the weaker me, when it has surfaced in him, has made me more angry with him because I was angry with myself." He later said that the pain and anguish the family had gone through taught him "something of the impotence God feels as he watches his children making the wrong choices."

Arriving at Bishopscourt in 1986, Tutu adopted with slight changes the daily schedule he had followed in Johannesburg. Members of the household observed that his alarm was set so that he could begin personal prayers at four AM on weekdays. These he said either on his knees or crouched alongside his bed, curled up like a fetus. At five AM he took a fast thirty-minute walk on the streets outside Bishopscourt, accompanied by a staff member. In Soweto he had jogged, but he had to stop jogging after a suspected thrombosis was found in one leg. At five-thirty, he showered. He was downstairs in his study at six AM for devotional reading and work at his desk. At seven-thirty he went to the chapel to recite formal Morning Prayer with the clergy who worked at Bishopscourt. The lay staff joined them for daily Eucharist at eight. As at the SACC, Tutu was strict about punctuality: staff members who were late could expect to be asked at the exchanging of the peace: "Do you need a new watch?" Chaplains who arrived even two or three minutes late to take him out for parish visits would find he had left without them. At eight-thirty he went upstairs for breakfast with Leah—in his case a glass of orange juice. Soon after nine he was back in his office, ready to begin a series of thirty-minute appointments from ten o'clock on through the day. At eleven AM and three-thirty PM, the staff left their desks for a tea break in the library. These breaks were used as an opportunity to greet local and foreign guests, often people who could not otherwise be fitted into his schedule. He returned to the chapel for thirty minutes of personal prayer at one PM, then went upstairs for lunch and an hour-long nap. Appointments began again at three o'clock. At the end of the afternoon he was back in the chapel for evening prayer with the clergy, followed by personal prayer. He went upstairs at seven PM for a drink—usually a rum and Coke—and supper with Leah, and to watch the evening television news. If he had no outside appointments, he was usually in bed by nine or ten and asleep by eleven PM after saying the prayers known as compline.

In addition to his daily prayers, Tutu fasted until supper on Fridays and observed a "quiet day" every month and a seven-day silent retreat once a year. During the six-week Lenten fast leading up to Easter, he ate only in the evenings—typically a thick soup with meat in it. It soon became apparent to the staff at Bishopscourt that Tutu the ebullient extrovert and Tutu the meditative priest who needed six or seven hours a day in silence were two sides of the same coin. One could not exist without the other: in particular, his extraordinary capacity to communicate with warmth, compassion, and humor depended on the regeneration of personal resources, which in turn depended on the iron self-discipline of his prayers.

Tutu's jovial demeanor was not to be confused with tolerance of people he regarded as overfamiliar, particularly if he discerned racism behind their attitude. He preferred to be called "Father" rather than "Your Grace"—the form of address reflecting an archbishop's rank as a duke in British protocol—but nevertheless insisted on respect for the dignity of his office. Ted King, ten years his senior, never felt able to call Tutu by his first name: "I think this is because I feel I am in the presence of someone who never forgets his priestly character or indeed his episcopal status, who carries it with an inner dignity, quietly and firmly."

As part of his focus on the spiritual life, Tutu invited Francis Cull, an English lecturer and priest from Johannesburg, to establish an Institute of Christian Spirituality at Bishopscourt. Cull was a particular admirer of Tutu's; he directed Tutu's annual retreats, observed his prayer life growing more contemplative as time passed, and—as the person to whom Tutu made regular formal confession—credited the archbishop with considerable capacity for self-criticism. (Cull also liked to point out to visitors that when he took up residence in an outbuilding at Bishopscourt, he reversed the historical pattern: the black man now lived in the big house, he said, and the white man in the eighteenth-century slave quarters.) The church approved funds for the institute only after a long debate, which reflected tension between two conflicting desires that Tutu experienced throughout his decade at Bishopscourt: while he wanted to pursue the priorities he set for himself and the church, he did not want to look like an empire-builder.

In spite of Tutu's best intentions, the work his ministry generated took up an increasing proportion of the national church budget. The church's comptrollers found that the excitement of having as archbishop a Nobel laureate who was an icon of racial justice came at a price. The cost was eased, however, by help from foreign donors. Tutu's international renown attracted a stream of donations from sympathizers abroad, boosting the value of his "archbishop's discretionary fund" to levels hitherto unimagined. The spirituality institute was founded partly with money allocated to the national church by the United Society for the Propagation of the Gospel in Britain. Trinity Church, Wall Street—which had divested itself of 10 million dollars' worth of stock in companies doing business in South Africa—financed communications initiatives, as did the Carnegie Corporation of New York. St. James's Church on Madison Avenue—Hays Rockwell's parish—paid for a new bishop's house.

Tutu carried his attitude toward money into his new role, remaining bold in asking for it and pragmatic about from whom he accepted it. The costs of extra security and four new offices in a prefabricated building were covered by a donation from a foundation linked to Coca-Cola. (In a demonstration of the sophistication underlying the company's dominance of the world's soft drink market, when Coca-Cola worked out how to disinvest from South Africa it gave recognition to antiapartheid leaders unprecedented for a multinational company. It donated 10 million dollars to establish a foundation, run by antiapartheid leaders, to create new business, housing, and educational opportunities for black South Africans. It disposed of its shareholding in South African bottlers and moved a syrup plant out of South Africa to neighboring Swaziland. But it continued to sell its products in South Africa.)

Early in his term Tutu introduced the church's provincial secretary, Sid Colam–previously his diocesan secretary in Johannesburg–by saying: "I know how to raise money, I certainly know how to spend it, but I can't administer it. This is the man who does that." Colam performed a juggling act to ensure that Tutu's largesse did not outstrip income, issuing checks for the school fees of priests' children, paying florists' bills for never-ending bouquets and fruit baskets, recovering travel expenses from foreign hosts, and raising the alarm when he thought Tutu was running out of money. To those in the church who criticized Tutu's spending, Colam replied that Tutu was not using the tithes of parishioners or spending the money on himself. The competing demands of the traditional tasks of an archbishop and Tutu's extraordinary national and international ministry were another source of tension. In a typical twelve-month period in 1989–1990, he was out of the country for a quarter of the year on visits to churches in the rest of Africa, the Holy Land, the United States, and Canada; and on visits to universities–where he received six honorary degrees–and a military academy. For the remainder of the year, he spent a little less than half his time out of the diocese and elsewhere in southern Africa, either at church meetings or ministering in areas of conflict. Part of Tutu's problem predated his ministry. The diocese was large, stretching 150 kilometers (100 miles) east of Cape Town and more than 600 kilometers (400 miles) north to the Namibian border. Since the 1960s, archbishops had struggled to balance the dual role of bishop of a local diocese and metropolitan of a church incorporating five southern African countries (and the islands of St. Helena and Ascension in the south Atlantic). Theologians argued that the correct solution was to divide Cape Town into more manageable dioceses, each with its own bishop. The diocese resisted this and instead elected suffragan or assistant bishops to help its archbishops.

Tutu inherited two suffragans but brought to the job external demands that his predecessors had not faced. He set as a principal objective of his term the division of the diocese–and failed. This was partly because Cape Town's Anglicans wanted to be associated with the archbishop and partly because they doubted the financial viability of smaller dioceses, but another important reason advanced by black lay representatives was political: "The government has balkanized us," they argued, "and we don't want to balkanize the church." Thus Tutu had to make do with the election of a third suffragan bishop, a division of the diocese into three regions, and the allocation of a suffragan to take pastoral responsibility for each. He himself retained formal responsibility for the whole.

Tutu's national and international ministry cut into his time in the diocese—he often joked that he was the "archbishop from Cape Town"—and some of his clergy, especially younger priests, felt that he did not devote enough time to them. By most of his clergy, however, both in Johannesburg and in Cape Town, he was remembered principally as a pastor. The pew in which he prayed in the chapel at Bishopscourt held files containing photos and personal details of priests and their families. He sent them flowers on birthdays and anniversaries and when they moved into new homes. A stream of handwritten postcards flowed from his pen, written at his desk or on airplanes. He developed a ministry of prayer on the telephone (which was extended to heads of state such as Nelson Mandela, and later to Bill Clinton in the White House during his impeachment hearings). Never forgetting his failure to minister to a parishioner on the point of death twenty-five years earlier, he often made visits to hospitals to see seriously ill clergymen when he was on the way to or from Cape Town's airport.

In the Province—the church in southern Africa as a whole—Tutu coped with his workload both by delegating work to his executive officer, Njongonkulu Ndungane, and through a remarkable collaboration with Michael Nuttall, the man who a decade earlier would certainly have been elected as archbishop in preference to him. In 1989, Nuttall was elected dean of the Province, or deputy to the archbishop, by the synod of bishops. Until then the role had involved few responsibilities. Tutu set about changing that. First he invited Nuttall to accompany him on a pilgrimage to Bethlehem and Jerusalem at Christmas 1989. What developed could not easily have been predicted. Nuttall was strongly opposed to apartheid, a former member of the Liberal Party, which Alan Paton once led, but was far more cautious and restrained than Tutu. When Paton's newspaper commentary on Tutu's Nobel Prize had been published five years earlier, Nuttall wrote privately to Paton expressing gratitude for "the frank combination . . . of congratulation and criticism" in the article: "It says the sort of wise and courageous things about him [Tutu] which are very difficult for someone like myself to say." By 1989 Nuttall's views had already begun to shift—he came to support targeted sanctions—but the pilgrimage to the Holy Land signified a new approach. There, he wrote later, he found himself "in a political situation uncannily similar to our own." Speaking to religious leaders, he was asked to explain what "dean of the Province" meant. On the spur of the moment, he said that the easiest way of thinking of him was as "number two to Tutu." Tutu responded by offering the partnership as a symbol: if black and white could come together in South Africa, then Palestinians and Israelis could come together in the Middle East.

Back in South Africa, the two developed a close relationship in which Tutu consulted Nuttall on his key decisions and Nuttall joined Ndungane in taking on some of Tutu's administrative work. This eased Tutu's load, although what Nuttall treasured most was the opportunity for joint ministry in the country's political crisis. Nuttall has written a moving memoir of their relationship, *Number Two to Tutu*. For readers of church biography and South African history, it stands on its own as a valuable account of the times; but it is also worth quoting briefly Nuttall's experience of how Tutu worked with his colleagues:

> We bishops were encouraged to discover . . . the truth about ourselves behind the purple we wore, the child within, the more feminine traits, the authentic person. Out of this there emerged a leadership more free to acknowledge human frailty, to laugh or to cry, not to take ourselves too seriously. . . . Unconsciously and spontaneously he brought a new and wholesome liberty into the lives of the other bishops around him. . . . Yet it was a paradoxical liberty, for it brought with it a deeper dependence on the grace of God and on one another rather than on our own strength or status.

In church meetings, Tutu practiced a consensus-building style of leadership drawn from African tradition. He avoided divisive votes at church meetings whenever possible, instead sending the leaders of opposing camps away overnight to come up with a compromise. Bishops had a great deal of autonomy in their dioceses, so Tutu, faced with threats of splits and whites' leaving the church, laid special emphasis on building unity at the synod of bishops. A single bishop's dissent was allowed to hold up a decision until the decision was reformulated in such a way that everyone could live with it. In this forum, which met behind closed doors twice a year for a week at a time, Tutu built into a team a disparate group that varied widely in theology, culture, politics, and race. Together, they prayed, argued, laughed, took early-morning walks or runs, and kept times of silence. After evening prayer, they enjoyed "jabula"–a code for predinner drinks, drawn from the Nguni word for celebration. Tutu led from the front. Others found this over-powering at times, but he had a gift for discerning dissent and drawing it into the open. Nuttall has described in his memoir how Tutu's brother bishops–they were all male–called him "the headmaster":

> He gained that nickname because of his practice, in the free times during our regular meetings, of calling us to his room, one by one, so that he could find out how we were–"in your heart," he would often say. How were our times of quiet, our retreat, our reading and days off, our holidays? Were we safeguarding these times? Were we look-ing after ourselves, and allowing God to do so? . . . Were we looking after . . . our families? Then: "Let us have a little prayer together," and afterwards we would leave heartened or chastened, always deep in thought, a little embarrassed perhaps by our short session with "the headmaster."

Although Tutu failed to persuade the Cape Town diocese to divide, he did achieve his other main objective for the church while in office: securing approval for the ordination of women as priests. It was a cause he had long promoted. In southern Africa, the first realistic hope of ordaining women was raised in 1989, when the church's provincial synod failed by only thirteen votes to reach the two-thirds majority needed to approve this step. Tutu likened the exclusion of women to apartheid: it discriminated against people because of something they could not change–in this case, their gender. Over the next three years, bishops promoted a thorough debate on the issue. Tutu opened the provincial synod of 1992 by saying that the church was "grossly impov-erished" by the absence of women. This time the measure passed, but he restrained the synod from celebrating. Recognizing the pain of his opponents, and anxious to preserve unity, he and Nuttall proposed a resolution reassuring them "that there is a cherished place for them in (our Lord's) church, which would be impoverished without them."

Two women were soon ordained in Cape Town, and in time Tutu appointed one of them–Wilma Jakobsen–as his chaplain. In a similar gesture, he also invited Merwyn Castle–the gay priest whose resignation he had forced as dean of Johannesburg–to serve in the same position for a period. Castle's appointment was in line with the church's policy, which allowed celibate gays and lesbians to be priests. Tutu defended the policy publicly but privately acknowledged that it was not logically sustainable. Enforcing celibacy on clergy of homosexual but not heterosexual orientation, he said, was also discrimination based on an attribute people could not change. Shortly before his retirement, he asked his fellow bishops to review the policy, but he made no progress before he stepped down. The church was still wrestling with the issue a decade later in a debate to which he was to make unofficial but widely publicized contributions.

Tutu's life was based firmly in the institution of the church. He took his job as archbishop seriously. He was, however, above all else a pastor whose passion was the people to whom he was ordained to minister. His ministry was therefore outward-looking, focused on their welfare. In South Africa during the 1980s, this meant that his primary objective as archbishop, overriding all others, was the fight against apartheid. After settling in and getting to know his new diocese, he declared that for as long as he was archbishop, liberation would be the major priority on the church's agenda–"liberation from sin in all its manifestations, liberation to be all that God wants his children to be." This was reflected in the quirky political graffiti for which Cape Town was renowned. Along a highway near Bishopscourt, an anti-Tutu wit spray-painted these lines:

> I was Anglican
> Till I put Tu and tu
> Together.

To which a supporter of Tutu's added:

> Yes, but $2 + 2$
> $= 3$dom.

CHAPTER 13

INTERIM LEADER

The most farsighted members of P. W. Botha's military, police, and intelligence bureaucracy realized within a year of the spread of the Vaal uprising to other parts of the country that negotiations with the African National Congress (ANC) were inevitable. In October 1985, the Coordinating Intelligence Committee of the State Security Council convened a special meeting of generals and intelligence personnel to discuss whether it was possible to avoid talks. The consensus, noting the ANC's enormous domestic and foreign support, was that it was not–but that negotiations should be delayed until the government had the upper hand. In the words of one general quoted by the Truth and Reconciliation Commission in its summary of the committee's meeting: "This is the stage [after the government shifted the balance of power] when one can negotiate from a position of strength and can afford to accommodate the other party, given that it has largely been eliminated as a threat." A two-track strategy ensued: on one track, government emissaries secretly opened up lines of communication with Nelson Mandela in prison and the ANC in exile; on the other, the security forces refined their tactics of counterrevolutionary warfare with a view to forcing the ANC into a position of subservient partner in negotiations.

Desmond Tutu was not affected by the first track. He became aware that there was some interaction between Mandela and his jailers, but correspondence between him and Mandela had been banned by prison authorities since 1983, when they stopped Mandela from sending an innocuous letter wishing Tutu well after an ear operation.*

---

* Mandela wrote: "I sincerely hope . . . that your hearing has been completely restored, but not to the extent that you can now hear things not meant for you." Tutu first saw the letter twenty-three years after it was written, when it was retrieved from prison records in research for this book.

Later, Tutu was denied permission to visit Mandela in prison, even after Mandela was allowed to consult extensively with the UDF, with colleagues in the ANC, and with other church leaders. Tutu held consultations with the ANC's leaders in exile–they called him "Comrade Archbishop"–and urged them to suspend their armed struggle if the government agreed to talk; but he was not involved in any secret talks. In his role as archbishop, he found his ministry overwhelmed by the consequences of the second track of the government's strategy–the violent suppression of opposition.

His first intervention against violence in Cape Town was made even before he was enthroned. One of the government's tactics was "contra-mobilization"–selecting groups within black communities who were prepared to cooperate with it, pumping resources into developing their areas, and sponsoring vigilante attacks by the groups on supporters of the ANC. In June 1986, thousands of vigilante "fathers" repeatedly attacked "comrades" in a shack settlement outside Cape Town, killing about twenty people, burning and looting homes, and driving some 30,000 people from the area. Tutu flew from Johannesburg to negotiate an interim cease-fire between the groups. The police arrested not a single vigilante; local security chiefs sent the State Security Council in Pretoria a signal asking for money to pay for "a victory feast in the form of a cattle slaughter."

Once established in Cape Town, Tutu became part of a group of church leaders often called on to mediate in conflicts on the streets. Its most prominent members included Allan Boesak, who as leader of the Dutch Reformed Mission Church led twice as many Coloured congregants as Tutu; and Stephen Naidoo, the son of Hindu converts to Catholicism, who had been appointed the city's Catholic archbishop two years earlier. The three formed a strong team: Boesak brought to the group an incisive political mind, Naidoo the precise approach of a careful negotiator and Tutu a blend of rhetoric that first roused and unified crowds, then channeled their anger into creative, peaceful action. In one of their early experiences of working together, they tried to avert a confrontation at the funeral of Ashley Kriel, a guerrilla of the ANC killed by the security police in July 1987. Kriel had been an articulate, popular youth leader, described by the Cape Town activist and journalist Zubeida Jaffer as "the Che Guevara of the Cape Flats." The police imposed restrictions on his funeral, prompting Allan Boesak to telex Adriaan Vlok, the successor to Louis le Grange as police minister, warning that they were impractical and provocative. As Boesak spent the day before the funeral arguing with national police chiefs, Tutu and Naidoo appealed to the local police commissioner to keep his men away.

The police refused to lift the restrictions. Early on the morning of the funeral they summoned the church leaders to their headquarters in Cape Town. There, in front of a prominently displayed bulletin board listing police firepower, the two groups held two hours of negotiations, even as the funeral got under way. The talks ended inconclusively, with no clear agreements on the compromises that had been discussed. The police had said they would not allow ANC flags or slogans, but they would allow mourners to travel to the cemetery in buses. The church leaders arrived in the Cape Flats township of Bonteheuwel to find mourners surrounded by policemen in Casspirs, their yellow-painted armored personnel carriers, with snipers deployed on rooftops and a helicopter hovering overhead. Mourners had been tear-gassed as they left the funeral service in the Kriel family's church, and the coffin had been taken to a nearby Anglican church while they regrouped. Abandoning plans for a rally in a nearby field, the organizers of the funeral made the second church the place of their protest. "The church service becomes a mass rally and the mass rally becomes a church service," wrote Jaffer in a memoir. "Out comes the ANC flag to be draped over the coffin. Hymns merge into freedom songs and freedom songs into hymns. Tears become laughter and laughter becomes tears. Both Tutu and Boesak poke fun at the police, creating a levity essential to lowering the mood of anger." As the coffin emerged, the police tried to confiscate the flag, setting off a tussle in which a police major grappled with Allan Boesak and Moulana Faried Essack, a Muslim cleric. For Tutu, the funeral ended with a fruitless attempt to persuade a police commander on the ground to honor the agreement not to restrict the number of people traveling to the cemetery.

Tutu's attempts to mediate on the streets were made at a time of renewed tension with the government over his attitude toward armed struggle. In June 1987, he and Leah had been invited to visit Mozambique by Dinis Sengulane, the bishop of Lebombo, whose diocese covered the southern part of the country. South Africa had bludgeoned Mozambique into signing a peace accord three years earlier, forcing the closure of the ANC's military bases; but South Africa still saw Mozambique as enemy territory, ruled by marxists. The Mozambican Resistance Movement, RENAMO, sponsored by South Africa, was fighting a brutal war against the government. On the first day of Tutu's visit, a journalist asked him at a news conference in the capital, Maputo, whether he still stood by his opposition to armed struggle. "Oh, absolutely, yes," Tutu replied. "I would say that I will tell you the day I believe we must tell the world that now we have reached a point where we must use violence to overthrow an unjust system. I do not believe we are there yet." There was nothing new in Tutu's remarks; they went unreported by most journalists; and he began a tour of remote rural parishes.

A week later Tutu's party returned to Maputo to find that there was a furor at home. The Associated Press had featured Tutu's remarks in its report of the news conference. In Johannesburg, the pro-apartheid newspaper *The Citizen* headlined the AP report: "Tutu Promises to Give Signal for Violence in SA." A Mozambican newspaper misreported him as saying the time for violence had now come. The police had seized television news tapes of the statement. When a news agency sued for the return of the tapes, the police told the court that they were investigating high treason or terrorism. Tutu challenged the police: "I learn that some people have said that I'm going to stand up and say to the black people, 'You go ahead.' Who am I to take on such a presumptuous position? If that is treasonable . . . I will be only too ready to face charges."

The evening before he returned to Johannesburg, his spirits were low. Leah had left for Johannesburg early, and his public defiance was replaced by a subdued conversation with his staff. He told Matt Esau, his personal assistant, that if anything happened to him, his will and funeral instructions could be found in the bottom drawer of his desk. One of his wishes was that his family should not follow the custom of reversing photographs to hide his image during the period of mourning. Esau called ahead to Johannesburg and asked colleagues to arrange private security guards for the airport. The next day, June 29, the church commemorated the feast of St. Peter and St. Paul. In his final service in Maputo, Tutu said that Christians were meant to be witnesses to the love of God:

> We expect them to reflect the character of Jesus Christ. We expect Christians to be gentle, not always quarrelling and scratching. We expect Christians to be humble as Jesus was humble. . . . We expect Christians to be peace-loving and people who work for peace. We expect Christians to be loving. . . . We expect Christians to be people who forgive as Jesus forgave even those who were nailing him to the

Cross. But we expect Christians also to be those who stand up for the truth, we expect Christians to be those who stand up for justice, we expect Christians to be those who stand on the side of the poor and the hungry and the homeless and the naked, and when that happens then Christians will be trustworthy, believable witnesses.

The word "witness" in Greek was the word from which the English word "martyr" was derived, Tutu continued. So a martyr was a Christian who witnessed to the faith, even unto death as Peter and Paul had done. He concluded:

> And it may happen that you and I and all of us, that we may be called to witness for Jesus Christ, witness at great cost, witness even when we are made to suffer because we are Christians and perhaps even to die for the faith. Because martyrs keep happening in the church, even today. And we pray that God will strengthen us, that when the time of trial comes we can be faithful witnesses to our Lord and that God will give us his blessing so that we can be true witnesses to our Lord and Saviour Jesus Christ.

At Maputo airport, Mozambicans gave him a colorful, noisy farewell, singing choruses on the apron. He and his staff were the last passengers to board the flight. The tension was palpable as Tutu entered the South African Airways plane: it was filled with white South African officials and businessman who stared at him in total silence. An hour later, at Johannesburg's airport, he was mobbed by journalists, with cameras flashing and microphones pushed in front of his face. Two security guards escorted him through the crush and took him to a nearby hotel. Esau was to fetch him there in a rented car and drive him to meet Leah at their home in Orlando West. As another staff member was about to set off for the hotel in the car, a bystander saw that the right front tire had no tread. The rubber was worn down to the lining, and pieces of wire from the steel belt were protruding where the tread should have been. Another car was provided. A senior executive of the car rental company later preferred to blame his staff for overlooking the deterioration of the tire during months of maintenance checks rather than face up to the possibility of sabotage.

Tutu never did reach the point of deciding that violence was the only way of defeating apartheid. Instead, he joined other church leaders in exploring strategies of sanctions and civil disobedience. In doing so, he tried to live up to his declaration that as archbishop he would not be a "one-man band" but would try to speak for the bishops as a whole. Both on the use of violence and on the best means of avoiding it, he thus emphasized narrowing the gap between his positions and official church policy. The first important shift in policy that he and the church made together came five months after the controversy at Maputo.

In 1985, following the township uprisings that had begun the previous year, more than 150 South African theologians published a groundbreaking working paper, "Challenge to the Church." They said that a "kairos" moment—in Greek, a moment of truth or divine turning point—had arrived. They characterized the apartheid state as a tyranny, and accused leaders of the multiracial churches of advocating a concept of reconciliation that sought to reconcile good with evil and God with the devil. These leaders, the theologians suggested, equated the violence of state oppression with the violence of the oppressed. Was it legitimate, they asked, to condemn "the ruthless and repressive activities of the State" and "the desperate attempts of the people to defend themselves" in the same language? "Would it be legitimate to describe both the physical force used by a rapist and the physical force used by a woman trying to resist the rapist as violence?"

The "Kairos Document" was soon seen as one of the most important theological declarations of its time. Tutu did not sign it; he thought it too abrasive and too easily dismissive of the white leadership of the multiracial churches. But he supported its thrust. Moreover, thirty of its original signers—a fifth of the total—were Anglican, among them Tutu's friend from college David Nkwe and his suffragan bishops in Cape Town, Edward Mackenzie and Geoff Quinlan. Although the document did not explicitly support the armed struggle of the liberation movements, it gave such a struggle unprecedented legitimacy. In May 1987, a consultation in Lusaka, Zambia, convened by the World Council of Churches' Program to Combat Racism, took the next step and declared that the nature of apartheid "compelled" liberation movements to take up arms. This statement went before the annual meeting of the Anglican Church's provincial standing committee in November 1987. In a short debate, the bishops of Johannesburg and Pretoria, Duncan Buchanan and Richard Kraft, reported on talks they and Tutu had recently held with the ANC. Without opposition, the meeting adopted a resolution stating that it "accepted" the statement of May from Lusaka and implored church members to follow Jesus' "third way": vigorous nonviolent action for change.

The committee's decision brought down a storm of criticism, this time not just on Tutu but also on his brother bishops. A right-wing Anglican lobby, Anglicans Concerned for Truth and Spirituality, tackled Buchanan and said that the church had questioned the legitimacy of Botha's government "despite its effort at peaceful reform." White lay Anglicans wrote to report anger and confusion among them. The newsmagazine *Financial Mail* made snide comments about the "third way." The Dutch Reformed Church said that Anglicans no longer saw the church as an instrument of peace. Paul Erasmus, the security policeman who had long monitored and harassed church leaders, clandestinely produced a poster telling Anglicans that by accepting the Lusaka statement they were committing themselves to the "horrendous deeds" of the ANC and the Communist Party: murder, execution, intimidation, and "the maiming of innocent people, especially our children—both black and white." Erasmus sketched a bizarre line drawing to illustrate the poster, depicting a Ku Klux Klan figure with a skull-like face, wearing a hammer-and-sickle emblem and using a sword marked "Lusaka Statement" to slice one arm off a Christian cross.

The second major change in policy that the Anglican Church made after Tutu became archbishop had to do with sanctions. Of all the issues facing the multiracial churches in the 1980s, this was by far the most divisive. It led to deep splits not only in churches but in other antiapartheid bodies that operated legally and had support among whites. South African business, the newspapers businessmen owned, and the white opposition in Parliament were all strongly opposed to sanctions. Public debate was thus overwhelmingly weighted against them. Pro- and anti-sanctions lobbies quoted the conflicting results of opinion polls to one another, each side suggesting that black South Africans supported its view and not that of the other side. (The extent of black workers' support for sanctions tended to depend on whether pollsters' questions suggested that sanctions would lead to job losses or liberation.)

Anglican bishops were at first as divided on the matter as the leaders of any other church. The diocese of Zululand, in which Mangosuthu Buthelezi was the leading layman, had taken a formal synod resolution repudiating sanctions. Michael Nuttall supported boycotts of sports but, like Alan Paton, felt he could not be party to anything that put other people's jobs at risk. On taking office, Tutu joined his fellow bishops in a three-year process of consultation that first produced agreement not on the comprehensive sanctions he advocated but on "carefully selected and specifically targeted forms of pressure, including economic and diplomatic pressure." The agreement was taken to Anglican parishes. Almost without exception, blacks supported the call and whites rejected it. It went first back to the bishops and then to the provincial synod, the church's highest ruling body, which voted by a large majority to call for financial sanctions and an end to international air travel to and from South Africa. Nuttall credited Tutu with refraining from "bulldozing" the bishops.

By the end of 1987, the coercive powers that the government had assumed under P.W. Botha's declaration of a state of emergency had enabled it to crush any potential for a nationwide insurrection leading to the collapse of the government. Yet, as Tutu had warned Botha the day after he declared the emergency, it gave only temporary relief. On February 24, 1988, Botha gave Adriaan Vlok the power under emergency regulations to issue decrees preventing organizations or individuals from carrying out "any activities or acts whatsoever." On the same day, Vlok used the power to ban the operations of seventeen organizations associated both with the United Democratic Front and with the black consciousness movement. He also prohibited trade unions from political activity and restricted eighteen individuals, including the UDF's president, Albertina Sisulu; and Tutu's former colleague at Fedsem, Simon Gqubule.

The church leaders responded by moving to center stage with a protest march on February 29, and then Tutu had his famous finger-wagging confrontation with Botha, described at the beginning of this book. A week after the march was broken up, Cape Town's church leaders joined educationists, sports administrators, and women's leaders to form an ad hoc Committee for the Defense of Democracy. Vlok banned the committee. Its leaders called for a protest rally. The police banned that. So Tutu, Allan Boesak, and Stephen Naidoo organized a service in St. George's Cathedral to replace the rally. An American evangelical preacher, Jim Wallis, who had arrived on a visit to South Africa the previous day, has described the scene:

> Police roadblocks had been set up to keep the young people from the black townships from getting to the church service . . . but many made it anyway, surging into the sanctuary like a powerful river of energy, determination, and militant hope. There was no more room to sit or stand in the whole church. People were everywhere—in the aisles, the choir lofts, and spaces behind and in front of the pulpit.

In fiery sermons, Boesak and Tutu defiantly told the government it was headed for defeat. Boesak likened the government to the biblical rulers of Israel, Ahab and Jezebel, who followed the false god Baal.* He urged the crowd to follow the example of the prophet Elijah: "We will have to go to this Jezebel who sits in Pretoria; you and I will have to go to P. W. Ahab, and we will have to say to him . . . 'Your days are over!' " Tutu had a message for unjust rulers: "You have already lost! Let us say to you nicely: You have already lost! We are inviting you to come and join the winning side! Your cause is unjust. You are defending what is fundamentally indefensible, because it is evil. It is evil without question. It is immoral. It is immoral without question. It is unchristian. Therefore, you will bite the dust! And you will bite the dust comprehensively."

Two days later the white Dutch Reformed Church (DRC) came out on the side of the government. Its general synodical commission assailed Boesak and Tutu publicly, stating that they were on a "wicked path." They had stepped over the boundary between church and state and thus could not claim that any government action against them was an attack on the church. A delegation of Anglican bishops promptly canceled talks they had scheduled with the DRC and charged it with trying to isolate Tutu and Boesak as a prelude to state action. This delegation called an emergency meeting of all the bishops, to which Robert Runcie sent an emissary. The meeting declared to Botha: "Archbishop Desmond is our father in God, who belongs to us as we belong to him. When you touch our father in God, you touch the children of God. We shall not allow the government to isolate him."

In the meantime, Botha had replied to the petition that the church leaders carried in their attempt to march to Parliament. Addressing his reply to Tutu, he suggested that Tutu had joined a revolutionary campaign led by the ANC and the South African Communist Party to establish an atheistic, Marxist dictatorship. Botha drew an analogy between the language of the petition and that of the ANC's propaganda, highlighting words such as "justice," "peace," "democratic," "people's" and "liberation." The time for "bluffing and games" was past, he wrote:

The question must be posed whether you are acting on behalf of the kingdom of God, or the kingdom promised by the ANC and the

* 1 Kings, 18 and 19.

SACP? If it is the latter, say so, but do not then hide behind the structures and the cloth of the Christian church, because Christianity and marxism are irreconcilable opposites.

Tutu's eight-page rejoinder to Botha was the South African equivalent of Martin Luther King Jr.'s "Letter from a Birmingham Jail," achieving as much publicity as his warning to Vorster in 1976, before the Soweto uprising. He wrote that his position derived from the Bible and the teachings of the church: "The Bible and the Church predate Marxism and the ANC by several centuries. . . . Our marching orders come from Christ himself and not from any human being." He went on to lay out a detailed theological critique of apartheid and a defense of the church's duty to oppose injustice. He crammed his arguments with biblical references drawn from books ranging from Genesis to the Revelation of John. He relied repeatedly on the prophecy of Isaiah:

> Is not this what I require of you as a fast;
> to loose the fetters of injustice,
> to untie the knots of the yoke,
> to snap every yoke
> and set free those who have been crushed?*

Tutu told Botha he could not have been serious in suggesting on the basis of the church leaders' language that there was a sinister connection between them and the ANC: "If a communist were to say, 'Water makes you wet,' would you say, 'No, water does not make you wet,' for fear that people would accuse you of being a communist?" As a Christian leader, he rejected communism and Marxism as atheistic and materialistic. "I work for God's Kingdom," he concluded. "For whose Kingdom with your apartheid policy do you work? I pray for you, as I do for your ministerial colleagues, every day by name. God bless you."

The willingness of a wide cross section of South Africa's church leadership to take part in an illegal march on February 29 rallied new support for civil disobedience, bringing together the "kairos" theologians, who had promoted defiance of a tyrannical government, and pacifists who had long been urging the church to follow the nonviolent strate-

* Isaiah 58:6.

gies of Gandhi in India, King in the United States, and the campaigners who had brought down the government of Ferdinand Marcos in the Philippines. Frank Chikane, general secretary of the Council of Churches, convened a convocation of churches at the end of May that launched a national "Standing for the Truth Campaign," with the initial objective of releasing political prisoners. Tutu supported the campaign, notwithstanding his concern that the South African government would not hesitate to massacre black demonstrators. He told the SACC's leading proponent of pacifism: "I would hope we can enlist the support of more whites for direct nonviolent action since the authorities are less likely to shoot in that case." Church leaders followed up with a campaign against municipal elections, which the government was hoping would give legitimacy to local authorities it had set up in black areas. Tutu appealed for a boycott of the election–in contravention of emergency regulations–from the pulpit of St. George's Cathedral at a special service for the installation of a new dean, Colin Jones, on September 4. Two days later the police arrived at Bishopscourt with a search warrant for the audiotape of Tutu's sermon. They seized the tape, but no charges ever materialized–the main efforts by the police to undermine Tutu's influence were taking other forms.

Within weeks after Tutu sent his letter of April 8 to P. W. Botha, the state launched a covert campaign against him. Beginning in May 1988, on his return from a five-week visit to Europe and North America, protesters from police-sponsored front organizations demonstrated against him at airports. The protesters knew his unpublished flight schedules, and the airport police allowed them to violate the ban on public protests. Black demonstrators openly told journalists that they had been hired from lines at unemployment agencies. These tactics ended when Tutu's supporters began to organize counterdemonstrations, presenting foreign tourists arriving in South Africa with the spectacle of rival groups of chanting, dancing demonstrators taunting each other. In Cape Town, 400 unemployed workers arrived at Bishopscourt in buses, saying that they had been told Tutu would give them jobs. Tutu was away, but the new dean, Colin Jones, asked the staff to provide them with food and drink and invited their leaders in for talks. After an hour, the leaders emerged, stressing that the fundamental cause of black people's suffering was apartheid, which had begun long before anyone asked for sanctions. Jones contrasted the church's treatment of protesters with that meted out by the police: "We don't dish out tear gas and bullets," he said; "instead we give tea and biscuits and then we talk to the people."

In the midst of the controversy, traffic police in Johannesburg arrested Leah Tutu when she arrived late to renew her motor vehicle licence. They handcuffed her and took her to John Vorster Square, where they locked her up temporarily in a cell. When she protested, they swore at her and threatened to kick her teeth in. One night the occupants of a minibus of a type used by the police spent twenty minutes honking the horn and flashing lights on the Tutus' bedroom window in Orlando West, at a time when only a few people knew they were in Soweto. The police also printed and distributed an array of anti-Tutu pamphlets and bumper stickers. During the night before he preached at the 150th anniversary of Robert Moffat's church at Kuruman in the Northern Cape, there was an explosion nearby. The next morning churchgoers found stickers on traffic signs and gates portraying Tutu as the devil. Other stickers read "Ag (Oh) Shame Tutu! Sanctions Are Out!" and "Do not play the Tutu game of self-destruction." Early in 1989, a man claiming to be a former policeman who had served a prison sentence telephoned Bishopscourt and told a member of the staff he had been offered—and had refused to accept—a contract for 20,000 rand ($8,300, or £4,700, at that time) to kill Tutu and Frank Chikane. An attempt to set up a meeting with this man failed, and he was not heard from again.

Much of the covert harassment of antiapartheid leaders was run by a subcommittee of the State Security Council, Tak Strategiese Kommunikasie ("Strategic Communications Branch"), generally known within the security forces as Stratkom. On the committee were represented the security branch of the police, military intelligence, and the National Intelligence Service. Stratkom's operatives—such as Paul Erasmus, formerly a security policeman at John Vorster Square—told the Truth and Reconciliation Commission that its activities were of two kinds: "soft" and "hard." Propaganda and disinformation were the "soft" side of Stratkom. The "hard" side included the bombing of Khotso House, described at the beginning of this book, an arson attack on Khanya House, the headquarters of the Catholic Bishops' Conference in Pretoria; and Erasmus's firebombing of St. Mary's Cathedral in Johannesburg with what he described to the present writer as "home-made napalm"—car tires sliced up into small pieces and soaked for a few days in a twenty-liter (four-gallon) drum of gasoline in the garage of his home.

Stratkom's personnel applied to the Truth Commission for amnesty for activities that included slashing tires and loosening wheel nuts. No one, however, confessed to sabotaging Tutu's car on his return from Mozambique. Security policemen interviewed by this writer—including one who had confessed to multiple killings—were adamant that Tutu's assassination would never have been countenanced. The repercussions of killing someone with his international profile, they suggested, would have been "awesome." This explains neither the possible sabotage of his car nor the story of a 20,000-rand contract, but it does suggest that he had the Norwegian Nobel Committee to thank for being spared more serious attempts on his life.

Tutu's status as a church leader would not by itself have protected him: both Smangaliso Mkhatshwa, secretary general of the Catholic Bishops' Conference; and Frank Chikane narrowly escaped assassination. In the same year as Tutu's car was apparently sabotaged, a sniper from the security police had Mkhatshwa in his sights at Durban's airport, but his shot was obstructed by other airline passengers. Chikane suffered a series of mysterious collapses early in 1989, coming close to death each time. Specialists at the University of Wisconsin, where Chikane's wife was studying, eventually solved the mystery—toxins had been applied to his clothing. An affidavit provided later for a government inquiry into death squads alleged that the Civil Cooperation Bureau (CCB) of the South African Defence Force was responsible for putting out the contract on Chikane and Tutu, but this was never corroborated. Evidence given to the Truth and Reconciliation Commission on Chikane's poisoning was stronger; it suggested that the police broke into Chikane's suitcase at Johannesburg airport and that the CCB's agents smeared an organophosphate on a set of clothes.

The CCB was the most sinister unit of the Special Forces arm of the military. Its task was to wage war against the ANC by unconventional means, and it ran death squads using international and local criminals. Its operatives also hatched the most bizarre of all the attempts to harass Tutu—and perhaps to get at him by killing his son. The operation was called Project Apie ("Project Little Monkey"). During 1989, Eddie Webb, the major general who commanded the CCB, gave orders under which, first, a scientist in a military research laboratory performed a cesarean section on a pregnant baboon. The scientist recovered two fetuses, each of which was put in a jam jar. One was placed outside the front door of Bishop's House, Johannesburg, three years after Tutu had ceased to live there. The other fetus was flown to Cape Town, where two CCB agents climbed over the fence surrounding

Bishopscourt. One, a former detective in Johannesburg's murder and robbery unit, hung the jam jar from the branch of a tree. The other, a former policeman who had been jailed for murder and then released on parole, hammered into the earth on either side of the driveway four nails smeared with a potion supplied by what the operatives called a "witch doctor."

The men from the CCB later claimed to the Truth Commission that the plan had been put together by an anthropologist who knew about tribal superstitions. Some thought that Tutu would believe a spell had been cast over him and withdraw from public life. Others suggested that his employees would resign their jobs in fear. If this was indeed the intention, the plan was a failure. The head gardener, Livingstone Nakani, was baffled but not frightened when he found the jar. He cut it down and had it buried without even bothering to tell Tutu. But George Bizos, the human rights lawyer who cross-examined Webb at his amnesty hearing, did not believe that a unit which operated death squads would have deigned to become involved in such an absurd activity. He told Webb that the murderer who carried the nails had offered another version: there was a bigger plot, in which the next steps would be to hang the carcass of a hyena in the garden, then to poison Trevor and blame his death on tribal traditionalists who were upset at Tutu's advocacy of sanctions. Bizos put it to Webb that this, and not the scaring of Tutu or his staff, was a more likely task for the CCB to have been given. Webb denied it.

Whatever the objectives of Project Apie, the depth to which the dirty-tricks department of Africa's most powerful military force was prepared to sink might be seen as an indication that the defenders of apartheid were losing their grip on reality. That was what crossed Desmond Tutu's mind when two United States senators visited him at Bishopscourt in December 1988, soon after meeting P. W. Botha.

Sam Nunn of Georgia and David Boren of Oklahoma had traveled to South Africa to see the situation for themselves. They were Democrats, but conservative Democrats seen by the South African government as "safe" enough to be allowed in. They were also powerful, the kind of foreign leaders Botha could not afford to alienate. Nunn was chairman of the Senate's Armed Services Committee. Boren chaired the Select Committee on Intelligence, and he was traveling with his staff director, George J. Tenet, later the director of Central Intelligence. They had been to see Botha at Tuynhuys to raise questions about the detention of Smangaliso Mkhatshwa and Zwelakhe Sisulu, son of Walter and Albertina Sisulu; to ask to visit Mandela in prison; and to discuss wider issues such as the need to release political prisoners and begin negotiations. Botha was not interested in a dialogue. "Before we could even make our points," said Boren in an interview, "he went into a tirade, shaking his finger at me, almost touching my nose. He was saying things to me like, 'You Americans have no place to talk, you persecuted blacks, you killed the American Indians!' He used the word 'nigger' several times, I think trying to intimidate Ambassador Perkins [Ed Perkins, the American ambassador to South Africa] very disrespectfully. And then . . . he began to rise in his chair like he was ending the audience." Perkins, an African-American, watched, startled, as Boren reacted: "I couldn't believe what happened. Boren stuck his finger back in Botha's face and said, 'Now you listen to me! I came down here to learn something, you've been doing all the talking, now you listen to me!' Botha was stunned into silence. . . . Boren went on to make all of his points."

Nunn announced at the end of the visit that he was prepared to support tougher sanctions. Boren said that if Botha reflected the government's view, intensified sanctions were likely. Back in Washington, D.C., Boren went to see George H. W. Bush, who was an old family friend and a fellow member of Yale University's best-known secret society, Skull and Bones. Bush was about to become president, having been elected the previous month to succeed Ronald Reagan. Before Boren's trip, Bush had asked him to share his thoughts on his return. With Perkins's input, Boren drew up a list of proposals for signals that the new president could send to indicate a willingness to intensify pressure against apartheid. He took the list to Bush and spent two hours sharing his experiences. He told Bush of people who had been detained, of people who had disappeared, of his fiery meeting with Botha, and—in total contrast—of one of the most moving conversations he had ever had in his life. This had been with Albertina Sisulu, copresident of the UDF, at her home in Orlando West, just up the hill from the Tutus' house. "Ma Sisulu," as she was known in Soweto, told Boren about her efforts to create educational opportunities for young people and what needed to be done to bring blacks and whites together. Boren advised Bush that one of his signals should be to invite Sisulu to the White House.

Boren's recommendation was adopted as part of a new emphasis of the Bush administration: pressing for negotiations in South Africa.

Reagan's contact with black South Africans, apart from the one unhappy meeting with Tutu, had been limited to Mangosuthu Buthelezi. Three months after Bush's inauguration, his secretary of state, James A. Baker III, wrote to the president that early contact with "credible leaders" was vital. He made a formal proposal that Bush invite Albertina Sisulu to the White House. She was, Baker said, "the matriarch of one of black South Africa's leading political families," the wife of Walter Sisulu and the mother of Zwelakhe. "Her militant, but non-violent, leadership of the UDF, the premier anti-apartheid movement in the country, has marked Albertina as a major force in black politics." The administration's stress on negotiations came at a time when it believed Moscow had come to share its view. A secret intelligence memo, later filed in a National Security Council staff member's folder on the ANC, said in March 1989 that the ANC's information director, Thabo Mbeki—the "clear favorite" to succeed Oliver Tambo as party leader—was in Washington wanting to pursue a dialogue begun in 1986 between Tambo and George Shultz. The background to Mbeki's visit was that the Soviet Union was putting pressure on the ANC to negotiate. "Whatever Moscow's broader political motives for counseling talking rather than fighting," U.S. intelligence suggested, "the Soviets believe the ANC's military wing is ill-disciplined, badly led and heavily penetrated by South Africa. . . . Moscow will continue to give the ANC military aid, but the ANC recognizes there are new limits and conditions. Without Soviet military support, the ANC loses its major lever on Pretoria."

Before Bush had acted on Baker's memorandum, Desmond Tutu popped up to complicate matters for the White House. A week after Baker wrote to Bush, in May 1989, the administration received notice that Tutu was coming to Washington and wanted to meet the president. Tutu, Allan Boesak, Beyers Naude, and Frank Chikane had been invited by Randall Robinson—mastermind of the protests at the South African embassy in 1985—to press Bush into taking a stronger line on South Africa. Chikane had to be hospitalized in Madison, Wisconsin, after collapsing as a result of his poisoning, but the other three took part in a forum on Capitol Hill organized by liberal Democrats. The administration's internal correspondence reveals that the request for a meeting in the Oval Office for the visiting South Africans put the White House in a quandary; officials felt that Bush could not say no to Tutu, but they did not like his views on sanctions and would have preferred to deal only with Sisulu. A solution to the problem was proposed by David Passage, director for African affairs in the National Security Council, who wrote to Brent Scowcroft, Bush's national security adviser:

> Tutu is—without question—an important person. The President needs to meet with him and be attentive to his views—even while using the occasion to distance the U.S. from policies (such as "sanctions") Tutu advocates. Not to meet with him would be distorted by the President's opponents, who would portray him and his Administration as unsympathetic to the black opposition to apartheid. We need to quickly announce that the President will be meeting with Tutu.
>
> At the same time, however, we need to lay the groundwork for a broadened outreach to the black South African opposition to apartheid. There are no other significant black South African leaders presently in Washington, and it is not desirable to have the President look like he is trying to upstage Tutu while the latter is here. However, Ed Perkins . . . will be returning to Pretoria next week; I strongly recommend that he carry back with him a Presidential letter to Albertina Sisulu.

On May 18, Tutu, Boesak, and Naude became the first South Africans to meet Bush during his presidency. Bush told them he wanted to be a force for change. Tutu came away hopeful: "We do not want to be overoptimistic but there is clearly an openness to beginning new initiatives." The White House concentrated its public relations on the meeting with Sisulu and a delegation from the UDF six weeks later. Bush said in a statement welcoming her that she personified the struggle for human rights: "Mrs. Sisulu has lived a life of sacrifice for the betterment of all South Africans. At age seventy, she continues to be active in the service of others." He said apartheid was wrong and he wanted negotiations for a nonracial, democratic South Africa. From Washington, Sisulu and her delegation went to London, where Margaret Thatcher agreed to meet them. At home, Tutu was excited at the recognition of Sisulu and pleased that the United States and Britain were widening their contacts among antiapartheid leaders.

As the international community opened new doors to leaders of the liberation movements in 1989, it began to increase pressure on the government. In January, P. W. Botha suffered a stroke; stepped down as party leader, though not as president; and was replaced by his education minister, F. W. de Klerk. Preparing himself to take over the presidency from Botha later in the year, de Klerk extended his foreign contacts. James Baker heard that de Klerk wanted to visit Washington. Baker told Bush they might issue a "quiet invitation" to him as a way of ensuring that Albertina Sisulu was permitted to leave South Africa for her appointment at the White House. But there was to be no question of de Klerk's following in her or the church leaders' footsteps—Baker told Bush it would be "inappropriate" for him to receive de Klerk. In the event, de Klerk did not go to Washington, but he did visit London. There, Margaret Thatcher pressed him "pretty hard" to release Mandela, according to Charles Powell, her private secretary:

> She said to de Klerk, "Look I've held the line against sanctions, I will continue to hold the line against sanctions, I believe they are morally repugnant, but I do so on the basis that you are really going to change South Africa. I don't think sanctions are the way to do it, but there has to be change. Apartheid's simply got to go and you've got to do it. I will hold the line against sanctions to enable you to do that, and to enable you to carry people with you in doing that, but you know it is on that understanding alone."

Complementing the threat of further sanctions from white South Africa's last allies, hundreds of internal antiapartheid leaders took action in January 1989 that was to prove decisive in opening the way to the release of Mandela, the unbanning of political parties, and negotiations to end apartheid.

One of the extraordinary powers that the government gave to the police was preventive detention. Unlike other forms of detention without trial, it did not even pretend to hold out the prospect of a trial in court; it was aimed at neutralizing political opponents by simply locking them up. By the beginning of 1989, hundreds had been jailed indefinitely, some for up to thirty months. They went through "mental agony," according to Richard Goldstone, one of the few judges who visited them (he was also the judge who had tried John Rees of the SACC). Pressure from outside had failed to achieve their release, and many thought they would never be set free. About 300 detainees took matters into their own hands: they began a hunger strike. Allan Boesak announced that he would fast in solidarity with them. Tutu declined to make any announcement—he was beginning his annual Lenten fast, the details of which he never disclosed publicly. He sent appeals for pressure to James Baker, Robert Runcie, Margaret Thatcher, and the West German chancellor Helmut Kohl. He also called the police minister, Adriaan Vlok, who agreed to meet church leaders. When a delegation including Tutu, Boesak, Naidoo, Frank Chikane, and Stanley Mogoba—by then head of the Methodist Church—sat down with Vlok in Cape Town on February 16, Tutu could hardly believe what he heard. Vlok said he was very worried about the repercussions of the crisis. To the evident discomfort of the chief of his security police—the man allegedly responsible for the order to assassinate Smangaliso Mkhatshwa—the minister agreed with the delegation that the death of a hunger striker would have consequences, in Vorster's phrase of the 1970s, "too ghastly to contemplate." Church leaders had likened the hunger strikers to the Irish prisoner Bobby Sands. No, said Vlok, their situation was worse; Sands had been convicted in a court, whereas the South Africans had never been charged. He told the church leaders he would review the detentions and begin to release detainees. Vlok's cooperative attitude was not reflected in the behavior of police on the streets outside—they tried to break up a "report back" meeting in Cape Town's Metropolitan Methodist Church and brought up a water cannon as Tutu tried in vain to persuade them to allow people to gather. Neither was the crisis immediately resolved; there were disagreements over the pace and number of releases and over restriction orders imposed on newly released detainees. But by putting their lives on the line, hundreds of the country's most talented and effective political activists put themselves back in circulation.

The newly released activists joined labor union and other leaders in a coalition organized so loosely that it was difficult for the police to ban. Operating informally as the Mass Democratic Movement, they organized a national campaign of civil disobedience to protest against a general election called by the government on September 6. National church leaders said that the campaign was compatible with their own initiative, Standing for the Truth. In Cape Town, Tutu, Boesak, and Jakes Gerwel—the vice chancellor of the University of the Western Cape, a center of academic opposition to apartheid—asserted the right of local activists living under restriction orders to defy the orders and engage in peaceful political activity. Twenty activists launched what became known as the Defiance Campaign on August 6: they ignored their restriction orders and appeared before 2,000 people at a service in an African Methodist Episcopal Church in Hazendal, Cape Town. Tutu pledged that if the government acted against the restrictees, he would march in their support. He also told the crowd of an exchange with the police minister during their negotiations in February:

> I told Mr. Vlok, "You know you have lost." I said it nice and quietly, I didn't shout like now. I said: "You know you have lost, you know it from your own history. You believed you were being oppressed by the British, you fought against the British and in the end you became free. The lesson you must learn from your own history is that when people decide to be free, nothing, just nothing, absolutely nothing can stop them."

Over the next six weeks, thousands of Capetonians set about demonstrating Tutu's point in activities, planned either by the Mass Democratic Movement or by Standing for the Truth, which defied the government's ban on public protest. The church first took the campaign into the city center of Cape Town when it organized a service in support of those defying their restrictions, followed by an illegal placard demonstration outside St. George's Cathedral. It followed up with the march Tutu had promised when the police arrested and charged those breaking their restrictions.

After an "Ecumenical Defiance Service" at the cathedral on August 17, Tutu; the dean, Colin Jones; and Charles Villa-Vicencio, a professor of religious studies at the University of Cape Town led 150 marchers toward the Cape Town offices of the security police. They were thrown off balance when the police, in an exceptionally creative public relations maneuver, sent a squad of policewomen to stop them. With shaking hands and in a trembling voice, a Coloured policewoman ordered them to disperse. The marchers refused and knelt on the pavement. For a few moments it appeared that the police might have had a sinister motive. As truckloads of policemen waited out of sight, a police commander was seen nearby unloading from smaller police vans young men who looked suspiciously like members of a "jump street squad"—agents provocateur used to foment incidents in the townships. Church staff members, concerned that one of the thugs would assault a policewoman to discredit the clergy, called the attention of the media to their presence. At the head of the column, Tutu and Jones negotiated a compromise, which allowed the marchers to return to the cathedral.

Defiance intensified as the election approached. Some years earlier the Cape Town municipality had desegregated beaches within the city; but smaller, more conservative white communities farther along the coast retained apartheid on their beaches. On Saturday, August 19, hundreds of protesters flocked to the Strand, east of Cape Town. The police, backed by army troops, erected roadblocks and turned back buses of young people from black and Coloured townships, but a few hundred protesters driving their own cars got through. Tutu passed through three roadblocks before reaching the main beach at the Strand. There he found that the police, with whips and dogs, had already chased some demonstrators off the beach. Signs reading "Beach and Sea. Whites Only" had been covered by temporary placards reading "DANGER—NO ENTRY—SAP DOG TRAINING" (SAP stood for South African Police). At one point, barbed wire sealed off the beach; elsewhere a line of policemen protected the surf against the incursion. Tutu led a second demonstration up and down the beach. The police warned the protesters to disperse. If they did not, an officer carrying a megaphone announced, his men would use force, including live ammunition, against them. As people left, the police arrested photographers and television cameramen and confiscated their film. Once Tutu had gone, the police set upon the remaining protesters with whips and dogs. One priest was bitten and another, an American visiting from New York, was arrested and held for most of the day for photographing the police action.

Leaving the Strand, Tutu was summoned to Bloubergstrand, north of Cape Town. There he found a much larger group of protesters, young people from the buses that had been turned away from the Strand. Catching residents and the police by surprise, they had streamed onto the beach. A handful of policemen had driven them off with whips. One of Tutu's senior priests had been badly beaten. As Tutu arrived, an ugly confrontation was developing between about 1,000 protesters and a small police contingent, while angry white residents hurled insults at the intruders. Tutu told a police lieutenant that if they were to avoid bloodshed, the policeman needed to lend him a megaphone. Reluctantly, the policeman agreed.

Tutu proceeded to channel the emotions of the protesters, applying the style which he had developed on the East Rand, and which frequently led Albertina Sisulu to tease him by calling him a "rabble-rouser." First he would inspire the crowd with rhetoric that seemed, to the police, provocative and inflammatory. Then he would spring a question on the young activists: do you truly believe you will be free?

Caught unawares, they would respond slowly, giving him an opening to taunt them and imply that they were not nearly as radical as they claimed. Repeating the question over and over, encouraging them to shout their replies in unison, he would forge the young people into a chanting crowd with a single purpose. Finally, he would wrap up by suggesting that people who were confident that they were going to be free did not have to prove themselves by picking suicidal fights with the police. At Bloubergstrand, Tutu gave his rallying speech with the police megaphone from the back of a truck, led the youngsters in the anthem, "Nkosi Sikelel' iAfrika," and asked them to return to the buses: "You have made your point. You have broken the law. Perhaps it is time for a strategic retreat." As the buses pulled off, Tutu returned the megaphone to the lieutenant. "You see," he said, "I told you we could avoid violence." The policeman acknowledged the point grudgingly. "We won't say how," he replied.

The next day, on a Sunday afternoon, an exuberant congregation of 4,000 people of all races gathered in St. George's Cathedral. Police had banned a "people's rally" organized for the University of the Western Cape to commemorate the sixth anniversary of the founding of the UDF. Tutu had called for a "service of witness" instead. The police set up roadblocks and stopped busloads of people on their way to the service. Colin Jones won a court order against them. Groups of young people, singing, rhythmically dancing the toyi-toyi, and shouting "Viva UDF" and "Viva ANC," squeezed into every available space. The service began with the Lord's Prayer, a scripture reading, and an address in which Tutu mocked the government for its show of force the previous day: "They say apartheid is dead. Apartheid is dead? It is one of the most extraordinary corpses around! They had police, they had dogs, they had tear gas. To do what? To stop people from walking on God's beaches. . . . Dogs can walk on God's beaches! Black people can't walk on God's beaches!"

When Tutu's sermon was completed, the UDF's activists took over. One of them was Trevor Manuel, who went on after liberation to become South Africa's most successful finance minister. In 1989, he was thirty-three-years old, a hunger striker recently released from detention, and a man living under restriction. He was prohibited from addressing more than ten people, from being at any gathering where the government was criticized, and from taking part in any activity of the UDF. That Sunday, reported Ray Bonner in the *New Yorker*, Manuel was defying all this:

He approached the microphones, thrust his right arm upward, clenched his fist, opened his mouth wide, and let loose with the battle cry of the liberation movement: "A-MAN-DLA"–"Power." The cathedral erupted as the congregation roared "AWETHU"–"To the people"–in response. This was repeated several times. The congregation sang, chanted, and danced. Then Manuel said, "Comrades, there's an old Kikuyu proverb: No matter how long the night, the day is sure to come. We are gathered here today to unban our organizations." That began a procession across the church in front of the altar . . . banned organization following banned organization, each unfurling its colors and declaring itself unbanned. Finally . . . a spokesman declared, "The UDF is unbanned!"

The police kept a low profile, and the rally ended peacefully. Under Colin Jones, the cathedral took the militancy in stride, proudly calling itself the "people's cathedral" and playing a role similar to that of Leipzig's St. Nicholas Church, where the protesters who would bring down the German Democratic Republic two months later gathered regularly.

Three days after the rally, Tutu, Jones, Gerwel, and Franklin Sonn, another leading educator in Cape Town, rushed to Gugulethu on the Cape Flats to avert a clash between the police and school pupils. Black smoke was rising from burning barricades on streets across the Cape Flats as the group arrived in Gugulethu. The pupils and their teachers were determined to march on the local police station to demand the release of detainees. Tutu, fearing violence by the police, undertook to carry the pupils' grievances directly to Vlok. He persuaded them not to march. Trying to bring the protest to a peaceful conclusion, he told pupils in St. Mary's Church, Gugulethu, that they were involved in a noble struggle:

We are involved in a moral struggle. We are involved in a struggle that will succeed. We have no doubt that we are going to be free. Because we know that we are going to be free, we can afford to be disciplined, we can afford to be dignified and we need to underline the fact of this struggle being a nonviolent struggle. Therefore I ask you, when we finish here, I ask you to disperse peacefully, quietly, in a disciplined way.

The students listened. But as Tutu, Jones, and the educators left the church, the police fired tear gas at them. Coughing and wheezing, the tear gas burning their skin, their noses, and their throats, the group remonstrated with the police captain in charge. Chris Ahrends, Tutu's chaplain, lost his temper: "Who do you think you are?" he shouted. "Do you not realize who this is?"

A week later, Leah Tutu was one of 170 women arrested for trying to march from the Metropolitan Methodist Church, two blocks from the cathedral, to the British embassy, where they wanted to deliver a letter to Margaret Thatcher. Leah was held for twelve hours, then released after being arraigned in a special night session of the Cape Town magistrate's courts. The women's families turned the court appearances into an impromptu rally, singing freedom songs and giving each group of women a tumultuous welcome as they were brought to be charged. The next day Leah was again jailed for a few hours, this time with Desmond. Demonstrators from Standing for the Truth holding placards protesting against the rearrest of Trevor Manuel had been brutally beaten outside the headquarters of the security police; and the Tutus were among about thirty leading figures who were arrested as they sought to continue the protest.

As the "Defiance Campaign" reached its climax in the week before the election, Tutu became uneasy about the disparities in how he and his followers were dealt with by the police. Typically, the police treated him with kid gloves, arresting him and removing him from the scene, and then attacked ordinary protesters. Hence, when campaign leaders planned simultaneous marches on Parliament from three different points in Cape Town on Saturday, September 2, Tutu declined to take part, choosing instead to remain on standby at Bishopscourt. Watched by shoppers and tourists, the police broke up the marches with a degree of violence—shooting excepted—that they normally kept hidden from the eyes of white voters. At the cathedral they arrested the leaders, then bunched their followers together and beat them with whips and batons (night sticks). Across the street, bystanders including tourists were among a group whom they whipped and beat. At the Metropolitan Methodist Church, they brought up a water cannon mounted on a truck, stopped about twenty meters (60 feet) from the front row of marchers, and opened up on marchers with a jet of purple-dyed water. In a brief, extraordinary interlude, a protester clambered onto the truck, seized the nozzle, and directed it away from the crowd. Shoving off a policeman who was trying to catch him, this protester turned the water cannon onto nearby buildings, including the Cape Town headquarters of the National Party. To loud cheers and laughter from the crowd, he then jumped down from the truck. The police retaliated with batons and tear gas, hunting down purple-colored protesters trying to escape. (Within days, slogans went up Cape Town's walls, adapting the words of the Freedom Charter of 1955, which promised that "The People Shall Govern." Cape Town's graffitists wrote, "The Purple Shall Govern!")

Tutu was summoned to the cathedral, where he found hundreds of shocked protesters taking refuge. Many bore red welts across their bodies and faces. Having said at the beginning of the Standing for the Truth campaign that white people's involvement was essential if civil disobedience was to work, he was encouraged by the number of young whites there. He negotiated with the police to ensure safe passage for the protesters, then sought to lift their spirits. Moral right was on their side, he told them. They may have been beaten, but the prize for which they were striving was freedom for all, including the police. He shared with them his problem about being treated as a "protected species" but assured them that he would try to protect them as they left. He ended by saying:

> Say to yourselves, in your heart: "God loves me." In your heart: God loves me, God loves me. . . . I am of infinite value to God. God created me for freedom. . . . My freedom is inalienable. My freedom is God-given! I don't go around and say, Baas [boss], please give me my freedom. God loves me, I am of infinite value because God loves me and God created me for freedom, and my freedom is inalienable, God-given. Right! Now straighten up your shoulders, come, straighten up your shoulders like people who are born for freedom! Lovely, lovely, lovely!

So intent were the police on suppressing dissent that on Monday, September 4, two nights before the election, they stopped a visiting university choir from giving a concert in the cathedral. They also banned a service in the Buitenkant Street Methodist Church, a few blocks away, which was to have been addressed by Beyers Naude. Tutu, Naude, Colin Jones, and others arrived at the church to find an armored personnel carrier rammed up against the door. People were trapped inside the church, and a policeman was on top of the vehicle, trying to break in through a skylight. He scurried away as Tutu's group arrived, but then a senior officer arrived with a posse of men from Cape Town's main police station across the street. The police arrested Tutu's group and held them for some hours, keeping them off the streets while the riot squad roamed the city center, beating pedestrians indiscriminately. The wait in the cells was relieved by a moment of humor when Tutu plaintively called through the bars to the police, "I want my lawyer!" From the back of the cell, Essa Moosa, one of the city's human rights lawyers, responded: "I'm here!"

More than twenty people were killed in Cape Town's townships on election day, September 6. On the evening of Thursday, September 7, Matt Esau reported to Tutu that reports were circulating suggesting a far higher death toll. Tutu broke down weeping. He went to his chapel for evening prayers, spent the evening alone, and slept badly. Overnight he came to the conviction, with a clarity he had not experienced since writing his letter to John Vorster in 1976, that God was telling him to call for another march. On Friday morning, he told Esau that at a memorial service for the dead, to be held in the cathedral at lunchtime, he was going to call for a new protest on Monday. Taken aback, Esau appealed for more time. Tutu insisted on making his appeal that day, but agreed to postpone the march by two days, until Wednesday, September 13. Most of Cape Town's community and church leaders, among them Trevor Manuel and a fellow activist, Cheryl Carolus, heard about the march in the cathedral vestry a few minutes before its public announcement. They too were taken aback— the leaders of the Defiance Campaign had set aside the week after the elections as a time for regrouping. Tutu had a reputation for acting without consulting other leaders, and never was it more deserved than on this occasion. Reflecting on this years later, Tutu acknowledged:

> There was no political calculation involved, no careful assessment of the logistics. . . . In fact Cheryl Carolus was taking me to task a little bit, saying "But you haven't consulted the organizations." I said, "But God told me and I'm afraid we can't argue with God. . . ." It looks as if you are arrogant and presumptuous, yes, but the trouble is that I knew I was not my own master. At least *I* believed that.

Allan Boesak consented to Tutu's proposal, and the two duly issued an invitation to the people of Cape Town at the memorial service. Their announcement seized the public imagination, unleashing five furious days of consultation, lobbying, argument, and jockeying for position. The ferment reflected the success of the defiance campaign in achieving the main objective of nonviolent direct action—which is not to avoid violence at all costs but rather to put oneself at risk and thus draw out into the open the one-sided use of violence by an oppressor, exposing it for all to see. In Cape Town the strategy had worked with textbook precision. On election day, Gregory Rockman, a police lieutenant sickened by the behavior of his colleagues in Mitchell's Plain, played a crucial role in swaying public opinion when he broke ranks to tell a reporter from the South African Press Association that members of the riot squad were behaving like "wild dogs." In a subsequent breakthrough in the white establishment of Cape Town, the newly installed mayor, Gordon Oliver, attended Friday's memorial service. Asked by a journalist from Reuters a few minutes after the march was announced whether he would join it, he said yes.

By Monday, September 11, with minimal lobbying, a powerful domestic coalition was growing around the march. Tutu and Boesak saw their protest headlined as the mayor's march, attracting the support of the head of the Shell Oil Company and white opposition members of Parliament. They turned their attention to the international community. Despite—or perhaps because of—large-scale arrests of journalists and a ban on media coverage of police action, news of the protests had been broadcast and published around the world. From New York, Elie Wiesel telegraphed: "I am with you in spirit, but I wish I could be with you in person. . . . Be strong, stay well. We all need you. I am ready to help." A few days earlier, Margaret Thatcher and George Bush had responded to an appeal from Tutu, saying they were pressing the government to negotiate. Now Tutu wrote to thirteen heads of government. He and Boesak invited their ambassadors to a meeting at Bishopscourt and asked them to monitor the behavior of the police at the march. From Bishopscourt, the British ambassador, Robin Renwick, went to see the foreign minister, Pik Botha.

At Tuynhuys and in the adjoining ministerial offices in the H. F. Verwoerd Building in Cape Town, the government was split. On the one side were the security chiefs, who believed that if they lifted the lid on dissent the protests could ultimately bring down the government. The police drew up an application for a court order against Tutu and Boesak, in support of which a local police chief said that there had been 600 "unrest-related incidents" on election day and that the march could cause renewed unrest: "In view of prevailing emotions, it could give rise to the situation getting totally out of hand." On the other side, Robin Renwick found, Pik Botha needed no convincing that the march should be legalized. The person who had to make the final decision was F. W. de Klerk.

De Klerk was scheduled to be inaugurated as president on September 20. However, he had assumed power as acting president a month early after the cabinet chose his side in a showdown with P. W. Botha over a visit that de Klerk made to the Zambian president, Kenneth Kaunda. When de Klerk took office in August, Tutu had no hope that he would be an improvement on Botha: "I don't think we've got to even begin to pretend that there is any reason for thinking that we are entering a new phase," he said. "It's just musical chairs." Events on September 11 and 12 were to prove him wrong.

On the day Tutu and Boesak had discussions with the ambassadors, de Klerk asked his security chiefs at a meeting to outline their plans for handling the march. One of those present was Leon Wessels, the deputy police minister. He wrote later that, on hearing the plans, de Klerk "immediately expressed . . . his disappointment that there was no new approach." The president sent emissaries to talk to the march leaders. Wessels was sent to talk to Franklin Sonn. Johan Heyns, leader of the Dutch Reformed Church, flew from Pretoria to Cape Town, where he shuttled between Tuynhuys, the British Embassy and Bishopscourt. Heyns–who had previously helped lay the ground for state action against Tutu–now took a delegation of DRC leaders to ask Tutu and Boesak to accompany him to Tuynhuys to request permission to march. Tutu and Boesak rebuffed him. The Dutch Reformed leaders should rather join the march, they said. But Heyns was welcome, Tutu added, to approach the government on his own to get an assurance that the police would not use force. Late in the afternoon Vlok called to ask Tutu to cap the number of marchers and to apply to a magistrate for permission. Tutu was in a meeting with church leaders and leaders of the Defiance Campaign, and he put Vlok on a speakerphone. He refused both requests and, to the amusement of the gathering, told Vlok that he didn't mind if policemen lined the march route, as long as they kept their hands in their pockets. During the evening the justice minister, Kobie Coetsee, called to get details of the route. De Klerk announced that the government would allow the march: "The door to a new South Africa is open," he said, "it is not necessary to batter it down."

Tutu had no idea how many people to expect the next day. Perhaps there would be 1,000, he thought. Saint George's was full an hour before he arrived. The streets outside were teeming with people of all races. Black youngsters were doing the toyi-toyi or climbing up trees and traffic lights for a better view. White children from private schools wearing expensive blazers and straw boaters had come to join them, causing the eyes of Zubeida Jaffer, a victim of torture and harassment, to mist over with emotion. The police were nowhere to be seen; marshals from UDF, wearing red and yellow headbands, had taken over. Colin Jones led a brief service of "peace and mourning." To roars from the waiting crowd, Tutu, Boesak, Gordon Oliver, Jakes Gerwel, the UDF's copresident Zoli Malindi, the union leader Jay Naidoo, and Sheikh Nazeem Mohamed of the Muslim Judicial Council emerged from the cathedral. At first they tried to follow the traffic department's instructions to walk on the correct side of the road. It was hopeless—the citizenry had taken back the streets, blocking traffic in both directions.

In a spectacle not seen since the banning of the ANC and the PAC nearly thirty years earlier, an estimated 30,000 people moved in a triumphant wave down Cape Town's original shopping street, Adderley, to the railway station and around to the Grand Parade, the open square in front of the Victorian-style city hall. Behind the leaders, activists carried a banner reading "Peace in our city: Stop the killings." Ahead of them surged hundreds of chanting, stomping young people. Office workers cheered from their windows. At one time the march snaked for 1.6 kilometers (1 mile) around the city. Marchers carried a myriad of printed posters and handwritten notices; the UDF's banners; the ANC's flag of black, green, and gold; and a huge colorful banner reading "Women Unite for a Future South Africa." One poster read "Stop Vlokking us about." At the city hall, Tutu invited a crowd of all races to hold their hands in the air and addressed de Klerk:

> Mr. de Klerk, please come here! (Laughter.) We are inviting you, Mr. de Klerk, we invite you Mr. Vlok, we invite all the cabinet. We say, come, come here, can you see the people of this country? Come and see what this country is going to become. This country is a rainbow country! (Applause.) This country is technicolor! (Applause.) You can come and see the new South Africa! (Applause and whistles drown out his words.)

After Cape Town had cracked the government's ban on peaceful protest, an unstoppable flood of marches swept the country. Tutu took immense pride in the fact that his bishops were often in the front ranks: David Russell in Grahamstown on September 14; Duncan Buchanan—with Frank Chikane and Peter Storey—in Johannesburg on

September 15; Richard Kraft and John Ruston in Pretoria on the same day; Michael Nuttall with the renowned Catholic archbishop Denis Hurley in Durban on September 22.

Tutu's proclivity for unilateral, intuitive decisions often made him as unpopular with other church leaders as with politicians. His former pupil Buti Tlhagale defended his style, likening his instincts to those of an Old Testament prophet: "I don't know anywhere in the Bible where a prophet went to consult other prophets about an issue." Prophet or not, Tutu initiated a march—without proper consultation or a mandate—that proved a turning point in South Africa's shift from escalating confrontation to a path toward a negotiated settlement and democracy. The cabinet minister whom de Klerk put in charge of negotiations, Gerrit Viljoen, later told the *Financial Times*'s correspondent Patti Waldmeir that de Klerk's decision to allow the march was "a more fearful leap into the dark than any the president made later—including the release of Mandela." Robin Renwick described it as a crucial event in South African history. The veteran South African editor Allister Sparks in his authoritative study of the transition, considered September the culmination of de Klerk's conversion to negotiations.

De Klerk acknowledged in his autobiography that he could not have stopped the marchers from gathering: "The choice, therefore," he wrote, "was between breaking up an illegal march with all of the attendant risks of violence and negative publicity, or of allowing the march to continue, subject to conditions that could help to avoid violence and ensure good order." Responding rationally under pressure, he signaled, in the first major public decision of his presidency, that the Botha era was over. According to his autobiography, he had already decided to begin what he called a "democratic transformation process"; and he quickly moved to regain the initiative with a speed and sophistication unheard of among his predecessors. After his formal election to office, he learned that on the eve of the march his National Intelligence Service had coincidentally been holding secret talks in Geneva with two exiled leaders of the ANC: Thabo Mbeki and Jacob Zuma (later Mbeki's deputy as president of the country). He authorized the continuation of these talks. Early in October he agreed to meet Tutu, Boesak, and Chikane in Pretoria. Just before the meeting, he pre-empted one of their demands by announcing the release of Walter Sisulu and others jailed with Nelson Mandela in 1964. As the church leaders arrived for the talks, he startled them by first leading them into a photo call. Behind closed doors, de Klerk and Gerrit Viljoen discussed with them for more than two hours the steps needed to begin negotiations. Tutu was relieved to find no wagging finger—he came out impressed that "we were listened to."

A little over three months later, on February 2, 1990, de Klerk cleared the way for negotiations when he unbanned political parties. "I couldn't believe my ears," said Tutu, and promptly phoned de Klerk to congratulate him. On Saturday, February 10, de Klerk announced that Mandela would be released in Cape Town the next day. Tutu was in Johannesburg, where a young comrade came to the house in Orlando West early on Sunday to say there was a seat for him on a chartered plane leaving in a few hours. Tutu did not take it—he was going to baptize Trevor's first son that morning. Unable to get a seat on a scheduled flight back to Cape Town, he cadged a lift with a BBC television crew. The child was to be baptized Lizo Trevor Zukiso. At the baptismal font, Tutu added a fourth name: Inkululeko (Freedom). Directly after the service, he rushed to the airport.

From Cape Town's airport, Tutu's new personal assistant, Mazwi Tisani—who had just replaced Matt Esau—drove him directly to the city hall, where tens of thousands were gathered once again on the Grand Parade. On the way, Tisani told Tutu the ANC wanted Nelson and Winnie Mandela to stay at Bishopscourt that night. In the mayor's parlor, hours crept by as an array of dignitaries waited for Mandela. Outside, marshals began to lose control on the edges of a crowd that had waited in the sun all day in the hottest month of Cape Town's year. Looters broke into a liquor store. Police opened fire on them, forcing some of Tutu's staff at the back of the Parade to dive for cover. Reports came that people were being crushed. A group of young radicals and marijuana smoking Rastafarians broke into the city hall, demanding to see Mandela. Tutu remonstrated with them, to no avail. But then, like the Pied Piper, he led them through the building, out through a back door, and up to St. Mark's Anglican Church in the empty wastes of District Six. About 3,000 people from the Parade followed, but they drifted away when Mandela failed to show up.

Left with the hard-core remnant of the most angry militants, Tutu's staff began to wish they had not chosen a site strewn with so much rubble. Youngsters argued furiously with Tutu and with Muslim clerics. They accused Tutu of being "de Klerk's impimpi." One picked up a large rock. Tutu said he would take them back to the city hall. With the young people trampling on his heels, he returned to the Parade, where a line of the ANC's marshals was waiting. They let Tutu through but blocked the youngsters. "Go inside, Father," they said. "Let us deal with them." Back inside, Tutu found that the car carrying Mandela had been unable to get through the crowd and had turned back. As Allan Boesak repeatedly appeared on the balcony of the city hall to beg for patience, Tutu got on the telephone to Mandela. "You've got to come," he said, "or we will lose control." Mandela arrived early in the evening, and Tutu saw him face-to-face for the first time in thirty-five years. Then Mandela went out onto the balcony to deliver his first public address since 1964.

At Bishopscourt that night, the heads of government whose diplomats had the best contact lists began to call in on Tutu's private line to speak to Mandela: George Bush from Washington, Moshoeshoe II from Lesotho, and Kenneth Kaunda from Zambia. Tutu led the ANC leaders in singing one of the greatest Xhosa hymns, "Lizalis' idinga lako, Thixo nKosi yenyanyiso" ("Fulfill Your Promise, Lord God of Truth"). Nelson and Winnie Mandela spent their first night together in the guest flat upstairs. The next morning, Mandela gave his first news conference for 200 journalists at the only space big enough—the main lawn at Bishopscourt. He and Winnie also appeared for a photo op with Walter and Albertina Sisulu on the manicured terraces in front of the house. Tutu stayed away from the press conference and kept out of the formal shots. It was their day, not his. Some weeks later he told a journalist that he would not take part in negotiations for democracy. He had been an interim political leader, he explained, standing in for the real leaders. Now that role was over. He was a pastor, not a politician, and he had no intention of entering party politics. He wanted to have a lower public profile. He was more successful in fulfilling the first intention than the second.

CHAPTER 14

ROLLER-COASTER RIDE

Desmond Tutu was on the verge of euphoria as South Africa entered the new decade. After fifteen years of warning about a bloodbath, confronting the state, and keeping peace on the streets, he was exhilarated by the prospect of a negotiated transition to democracy. Quoting God's promises of liberation to Moses, he wrote to Anglicans in Cape Town after Mandela's release: "The road ahead may be long and hazardous but at long last it seems that what so many have prayed and fasted for, sacrificed and died for, were imprisoned, banned and went into exile for . . . seems more attainable than ever before." In his excitement, he allowed himself some hyperbole; in a reference to the events that followed the decisive confrontation at St. Nicholas Church in Leipzig the previous October, he wrote: "When Cape Town marched, not only South Africa followed but much of Europe as well. They marched in eastern Europe and the Berlin Wall fell. Autocratic communist regimes fell and Mr. Gorbachev carried out a more radical revolution than that of 1917 with little loss of life. . . . Praise be to God who has heard the prayers of his people when they cried to him." Exactly how hazardous the road ahead was to be became evident very quickly.

The influence on Tutu of his experiences elsewhere in Africa two decades earlier was discernible within weeks of Mandela's release. Determined that the church should not become "docile and quiescent," as he had described it in some liberated countries, he advocated what Latin American theologians called "critical solidarity" with pro-democracy forces—the churches would continue to campaign for justice, but as institutions with the gospel as their mandate they reserved the right to criticize their allies. The first steps in asserting the church's independence from the liberation movements were taken soon after Mandela's release, at a meeting of the Anglican synod of bishops in February 1990.

The synod happened to be meeting in Soweto, a short distance from the house in Orlando West to which Mandela and Winnie Mandela had returned a week earlier. At the suggestion of Michael Nuttall, Tutu invited Mandela to meet and address the bishops. Mandela spoke movingly of the ministry of prison chaplains, paid tribute to Anglicans such as Trevor Huddleston and Tutu—whom he called the "people's archbishop"—and told the bishops they had a crucial contribution to make in uniting the black community and in reassuring whites. Tutu and his bishops took up these suggestions later, but first they made three much more controversial decisions: to announce that they would call for an end to sanctions once the movement toward democracy was "irreversible," to urge the liberation movements to suspend the armed struggle, and to ban priests from belonging to political parties. The third decision was not announced for some time, but the first two caused immediate consternation among church activists.

The ANC was already worried that F. W. de Klerk's initiatives would seduce the churches. The previous September, Thabo Mbeki had warned that "the religious community is most vulnerable at this stage to being enticed by words which traditionally are ethically positive, i.e., words such as 'peace' and 'negotiation' which the Pretoria regime is currently using." In February, before the Anglican bishops met, the World Council of Churches' (WCC's) Program to Combat Racism, headed by Barney Pityana, had held a consultation in Harare, Zimbabwe, and called for sanctions to be intensified. The week after the bishops' meeting in Soweto, Pityana was in London, where he heard Tutu explain on BBC radio the synod's decisions. Back at his office at the WCC in Geneva, he wrote to Tutu about "how disappointing these positions were to us." Particularly regarding sanctions, the bishops had seen fit to depart from a definition of irreversible change carefully enunciated by the Organization of African Unity, the Non-Aligned Movement, the Commonwealth, and the United Nations. "It is important," Pityana said, "that we synchronize our strategies if we are to make an effective witness against apartheid."

As the march in Cape Town had shown, synchronizing strategies with others was not Tutu's highest priority. Believing that Pityana owed his job in Geneva at least in part to a glowing endorsement he had written, Tutu was wounded by the criticism. "I am disappointed that you are disappointed," he replied. On sanctions there was no difference in policy, only an insubstantial difference in wording. On armed struggle, the bishops' decision was in line with the negotiating concept developed by the Commonwealth in 1986. "I am saddened by your attack when it is clearly so uncalled for and totally unjustified," he added. "I hope you will see your way clear to apologizing for being so unfair." Pityana refused to backtrack. He acknowledged that the bishops had a right to promote their position on the armed struggle, but he pursued his concern on sanctions—their statement was likely to be misinterpreted, he said.

Within days of this interchange, it was overshadowed by the first major outbreak of violence in what became a low-level civil war in the province of Natal and the adjoining homeland of kwaZulu. On Sunday, March 25, Mangosuthu Buthelezi, chief minister of kwaZulu, addressed a rally of thanksgiving for the release of Mandela and other prisoners, organized in Durban by his Inkatha National Cultural Liberation Movement.* While Mandela was in prison, he and Buthelezi had maintained good relations by correspondence, but their followers had become bitter adversaries. Among those at Buthelezi's rally in Durban were members of Inkatha who had since 1987 been embroiled in conflict in the Vulindlela and Edendale valleys outside Natal's capital city, Pietermaritzburg. On their way home from the rally, young supporters of the ANC and UDF stoned Inkatha's buses, injuring some of the passengers. The stoning set off the "Seven-Day War," in which large groups of Inkatha's supporters invaded the Edendale valley, attacking people with assegais, pangas, and firearms and driving them from their homes. More than 100 people died; hundreds of homes were looted or destroyed; and as many as 20,000 people displaced.

Tutu was in Nairobi, en route to the United States, when the violence began. He canceled his visit, returned home, and joined a delegation of the SACC's leaders for talks with Buthelezi, Mandela, and de Klerk about the crisis. Their first trip was to the kwaZulu capital of Ulundi, to which they flew in an aircraft arranged by Bob Tucker, a sympathetic banker. It was the first time Tutu had been in Ulundi—previously, he would have regarded a visit there as conferring legitimacy on the homelands system, and it was a measure of how quickly his role had changed that now he did not think twice about going. Nevertheless, he approached the town with considerable trepidation, for he

---

* In Zulu, Inkatha yeNkululeko yeSizwe; an inkatha is a plaited coil of grass used to cushion loads carried by women on their heads.

had a rocky relationship with Buthelezi going back to the funeral of Robert Sobukwe, the PAC leader, twelve years earlier.

Tutu had been asked to preach at the funeral, in Sobukwe's hometown, Graaff-Reinet, in March 1978. Tutu; Buthelezi; Leo Rakale, the CR monk from Johannesburg; and others were already at the speakers' podium when Sobukwe's coffin was brought in, accompanied by hundreds of young people. Seeing Buthelezi, the young people swarmed around the podium, chanting slogans and insulting him as a "sellout," a "stooge," and—the most derogatory term of all in African culture—a "dog." Asked by a clergyman to leave, Buthelezi replied: "Let them kill me now. I am not going out. If it is my day to die, let me die here." When order could not be restored, Tutu asked Buthelezi to reconsider. Reluctantly, he agreed. Tutu asked the clergymen to form a protective wall around Buthelezi as he left, and himself led the way. Although Buthelezi was surrounded by aides and the clergy, youngsters surged toward him, kicking at the clergymen, shaking their fists, and shouting "Makabulawe!" ("Kill him!"). Tutu turned to remonstrate with them. Buthelezi reached a car only after his secretary had deflected a knife attack and his bodyguard had fired shots to clear the way. Sobukwe's friend and biographer, Benjamin Pogrund, who was prevented from speaking, turned to his wife and said, "That man with his enormous pride has been totally humiliated. God knows what price South Africa will be made to pay for it."

The week after the funeral, Tutu told a journalist that the youngsters were a "new breed of blacks who have iron in their souls." Reflecting on his comment nearly thirty years later, Tutu told the present writer: "He [Buthelezi] thought that was a condonation. . . . From that moment on, it was hell to pay, and our relationship has never really been restored to normalcy." Buthelezi said Tutu's real motive in asking him to leave the funeral had been "merely to give political credibility to a bunch of political thugs." The central committee of Inkatha passed a resolution describing Tutu as a "political opportunist." The correspondence and public exchanges in succeeding years were tetchy and disputatious at one moment, friendly and mutually supportive at another. Tutu disagreed with Buthelezi's participation in the homelands system and with his position on sanctions but recognized him as an important force and welcomed his insistence that kwaZulu remain part of South Africa. Buthelezi resented Tutu and the SACC for opposing him abroad but protested when the government withdrew Tutu's passport and, as South Africa's most prominent lay Anglican, respected Tutu's calling as a bishop. (He later regularly referred to Tutu as "my arch-bishop.")

On April 2, 1990, the delegation from the SACC arrived at the kwaZulu government buildings in Ulundi to find across the table not only Mangosuthu Buthelezi and the entire kwaZulu cabinet, but Inkatha's central committee and a delegation of Anglican clergy from the diocese of Zululand as well. After opening prayers, Buthelezi delivered a strident ten-page typed speech saying that the church leaders had come to the wrong place—the ANC was responsible for the violence. The leaders of the SACC replied by asking for the reactivation of a peace plan that local church leaders had been promoting the previous year. The key to what happened next is to be found in the opening lines of Buthelezi's text. "I have been," he said, "a very lonely Christian in my political leadership." In the discussion that followed, Inkatha's leaders gave vent to their own acute feelings of being alienated and under threat. They tore into the church leaders, charging them with siding with the ANC and caricaturing Inkatha as collaborationists with apartheid. The most chilling words were delivered by Prince Gideon Zulu, a member of the royal house. If Inkatha's opponents did not stop insulting the Zulu monarchy and subverting Zulu schoolchildren, he warned, what had happened in Pietermaritzburg would pale into insignificance compared with what would come.

From Ulundi, church leaders flew to Pietermaritzburg, where they pressed Mandela to hold a joint rally with Buthelezi and call for an end to the violence. The next day, Tutu returned to Ulundi on his own. As Buthelezi's archbishop, he decided, he wanted to pay him a pastoral visit. Buthelezi agreed, and they met for two hours over lunch, inaugurating a routine that, over the next four years, the staff at Bishopscourt named the "Ulundi shuttle." When Tutu perceived a particular crisis in negotiations or in violence, he would call Ulundi to ask for a meeting. Buthelezi would invariably agree. Within a day or two, Tutu and one or two staff members would catch a seven AM flight from Cape Town to Durban. Two hours later, they would transfer to a smaller aircraft—often sent by Buthelezi—for the short flight to Ulundi. There Tutu would meet Buthelezi in a conference room, often joined by other cabinet members and leaders of Inkatha (later relaunched as the Inkatha Freedom Party, IFP). They were very different men: Buthelezi a sensitive, proud traditional leader of royal blood in a society with strong rural roots; Tutu a self-deprecating, adaptable commoner, the product of a multicultural, multilingual, modern urban society. At the end of the meeting, the SABC television news crew assigned to Ulundi would arrive for interviews. Tutu and Buthelezi would both make friendly remarks. That night, the usual litany of television news reports about new killings would be briefly interrupted by Tutu and Buthelezi calling for tolerance and peace.

On Tutu's third day of ministry in Natal in April 1990, he toured the Edendale and Vulindlela valleys with Michael Nuttall; the Methodist leader Khoza Mgojo; and Matthew Makhaye, one of Nuttall's suffragan bishops involved in the peace efforts. Traveling from township to township, the bishops stopped at church after church stacked with bedding, clothes, and food, and filled with people driven from their homes, many of them still apparently in shock. The next week leaders in Natal and the national church went to Cape Town to see F. W. de Klerk, where Nuttall told him the police were taking sides and asked for a commission of inquiry to examine the causes of the conflict.

While Tutu's attention was on the violence, discontent was brewing over the bishops' prohibition against the clergy's joining political parties. The decision, imposed without prior consultation and announced without a supporting rationale, had come as a shock, particularly to young priests whose right to join a party of their choice had been snatched from them by the church within a month of its being recognized by the state. The clergy in Cape Town protested. Those who had secretly worked for the ANC while it was banned faced a clash of loyalties. Trevor Huddleston, who had been closely identified with the ANC for nearly forty years, thought it a "very dangerous decision." The Institute of Contextual Theology, which was instrumental in producing the Kairos Document, said that the bishops had denied priests freedom of association. But as it became ever clearer that partisan rivalry was an important ingredient in the growing violence of the transition, Tutu became ever more convinced that the bishops had been right. He noticed that at the enthronement of a new bishop on the East Rand, altar servers in their red robes used different salutes during the singing of the national anthem; one group raised the clenched fist of the ANC, another the open palm of the PAC. On a pastoral visit to Zeph Mothopeng, an Anglican who had become the leader of the PAC, he was given an "earful" about his bias in favor of the ANC. And Nelson Mandela raised no objection to the bishops' decision: he likened the clergy to traditional chiefs in rural areas, whom he discouraged from identifying with political parties because he believed it was divisive.

The unhappiness came to a head at a meeting of the Anglican Students' Federation in Pietermaritzburg in July 1990, when delegates called for a review of the policy. Tutu rejected their plea out of hand. The church would remain as involved as ever in the fight for justice, but not along party lines, he told them. Party membership had become a matter of life and death and was an obstacle to ministry in a parish: "Imagine when you have someone who says he is Inkatha and they want to come to confession, and they come for confession to a priest they know is ANC?" The vehemence of his arguments elicited nervous laughter from some students. It gave Tutu an opening for an intimidating counterattack. "It's serious; this is not a laughing matter," he said. "It's not a laughing matter when we have our priests killed. . . . It is not a laughing matter when you go into the house of a person and you find that they have got a fifteen-year-old killed. It isn't a laughing matter. . . . We are not playing marbles."

His views were reinforced when the violence spread from Natal to the Transvaal, first to the Vaal triangle and then to townships across the Reef. Tutu was in Canada in August 1990 when internecine conflict flared on the East Rand between Zulu-speaking migrant workers living in single-sex hostels and township residents in family units nearby. There had long been tension over issues that included migrant workers' reluctance to join political strikes and perceptions about these workers' treatment of township women. Rich Mkhondo, a correspondent for Reuters who grew up in an East Rand township, described in an account of a night attack how clashes typically unfolded:

The slaughter in my home township of Katlehong began to the sound of male residents whistling from house to house to warn of an impending attack by Zulu hostel dwellers. . . . The whistlers alerted township residents after they heard that Zulus, mostly supporters of the Inkatha Freedom Party, had just held a meeting in a hostel square at the west end of the township and decided to retaliate for the stoning and burning of a colleague's mini-bus by township residents, most of them supporters of the ANC. Within minutes, men, boys and some women from the township armed themselves with pick-handles, spears, knives, automatic rifles, stones and other weapons. The Zulus emerged from Kwesine hostel . . . and advanced towards the township. . . . Shots rang out from both sides and the battle began.

I saw a hostel-dweller chop at a youth with a panga and finish him off with a gun. An unlucky businessman was shot several times while trying to flee in his car, the back of his head torn open and his brains splattered on the car seat. . . . Several lifeless bodies lay strewn on open ground separating the hostel and the township. Residents led by aggressive youths repelled the Zulu attacks, barricading streets with rocks and sheet metal. The Zulus counter-attacked strongly and the battle intensified as houses and vehicles were stoned, damaged and looted. Police helicopters hovered overhead, aiming searchlights. . . . The police did not disarm Inkatha supporters who were brandishing weapons, and instead chased away armed residents. . . . Men wearing balaclavas burnt bodies, some of them beyond recognition. The next day police confirmed that 22 people were killed in the carnage and that more bodies were being found.

Tutu cut short his Canadian trip and flew home to Johannesburg, where he was thrown headlong into the crisis. With two local bishops, David Beetge and Duncan Buchanan; the SACC's president, Khoza Mgojo; and its general secretary, Frank Chikane, he toured townships across the Reef over successive days, making pastoral calls in homes, visiting refugees in halls, and addressing crowds of armed residents in impromptu meetings on the streets. Elias Maluleke of *City Press* described a visit to the townships of the West Rand, where residents were digging trenches in the streets in preparation for what they believed was an imminent attack:

Some residents welcomed the delegation warmly and sang praises to Tutu, while others turned the "peace mission" into a rowdy affair as they vented their anger and frustration. At one stage Tutu and Chikane were shouted down by a rowdy crowd in Kagiso which chanted: "No more peace, we want arms!" . . . In spite of being surrounded by crowds of angry people who brandished pangas, knives and other self-made weapons, Tutu did not flinch in his call for peace and urged residents to stop the . . . violence for the sake of their liberation. "By fighting and engaging in violent acts we give others the excuse to say we are not yet ready to govern ourselves," Tutu said. He said the church was not in a position to condone violence of any nature.

After the visit, Tutu's personal assistant, Mazwi Tisani, inadvertently captured the feelings of many in the delegation when he told Tutu of how he had felt standing in crowds of residents carrying pangas and axes. "Father," he quipped, "when you said, 'Let us pray,' I didn't want to close my eyes."

In Natal, the conflict pitched Zulu-speaking supporters of the ANC against Zulu-speaking supporters of the IFP. On the Reef, it could more easily be portrayed as tribal, at least on one side of the divide. In townships where men feared for the lives of their wives and children, the appearance on a street of a Zulu-speaking stranger could arouse deep suspicion. Rich Mkhondo has recorded how residents tested whether such a person might be a spy: "If he was suspected of being a Zulu from the remote rural villages, and thus a member of Inkatha, he would be shown a one rand coin and asked to identify it. Most rural Zulus pronounce 'r' like 'l,' so a Zulu would pronounce it 'land' rather than 'rand.' If he failed the test, he could easily be killed." Tutu worked vigorously to counter suspicion based on ethnicity. "In Soweto here," he told a funeral in Jabulani Stadium, "we have lived and continued to live harmoniously together. . . . If we quarrel, it is not because you are a Zulu, I quarrel maybe because your suit is . . . nicer than mine and so I am jealous. But we have never quarreled because of tribalism. It is a lie! It is a lie!"

Little more than a week after his tour of the Reef townships, Tutu was holding a regular synod meeting with his bishops at a conference center in Lesotho when two priests from the Vaal triangle brought news of twenty-three people killed in an attack on a hostel in Sebokeng township, and fifteen more killed when security forces opened fire on a crowd. He broke down and left the meeting, first for the chapel and then for his room, where Michael Nuttall found him weeping on his knees. Together they decided to propose that the bishops adjourn their meeting and make a collective pastoral visit to Sebokeng. Tutu later judged their action comparable with his letter to John Vorster and the march in Cape Town—an initiative inspired by God. At four AM the next day, a convoy of bishops headed for Sebokeng. After celebrating Eucharist in a local church, they toured the township in their red and purple cassocks, visiting the injured in the hospital and praying with the residents of burned-out migrant workers' hostels—many of whose companions had been shot by the police or troops two days earlier. They also stopped to speak to young people gathered on the streets of the most volatile part of the township, an area known as Beirut. Tutu got out of his car first. John Cleary of the Australian Broadcasting Corporation, a visiting religion correspondent, witnessed what happened next:

> I heard a noise and looked around and coming down the road was the
> one thing that you dread when you're in that situation, a convoy of

Casspirs, the big armoured vehicles with machine guns on top. You know they're loaded with police and teargas, and you think, "What is going to happen now?" By this time the other bishops had moved out of their cars and were pressing through this crowd of two or three thousand people. I could no longer see them but I heard the archbishop say, "Let us pray." Then the noise of the vehicles stopped. The crowd went quiet. There was no sound from the Casspirs, no sound of teargas canisters. So I looked around and there, behind me, were the Anglican bishops of Southern Africa–black, white, coloured, old, young–standing between the crowd and the Casspirs, with their arms outstretched. In that moment, I understood a little about what the Christian vision for a new South Africa cost people. I'd never witnessed that sort of courage before.

The violence of August and September 1990 was to reverberate years later in ways that affected the work of the postapartheid Truth and Reconciliation Commission and caused permanent damage to the relationship between Tutu and F. W. de Klerk. Tutu had been generous in his praise for de Klerk after February 1990, beginning a friendlier relationship than any he had enjoyed with a cabinet minister since Piet Koornhof. He was able to telephone de Klerk at will to relay concerns (and to hear de Klerk ask repeatedly when he was going to call off sanctions). At one point de Klerk even suggested that they should meet informally and relax over a beer or two. After the killings at Sebokeng, Tutu took an Anglican delegation to tell de Klerk how patients widely spread across different sections of the hospital had independently testified that men with blackened faces but white wrists and lower arms were among their assailants. Adriaan Vlok responded at a subsequent meeting ten days later with what Michael Nuttall called a "whitewash," and a police brigadier unwittingly disclosed that the earlier discussions with de Klerk had been secretly tape-recorded, raising questions about the president's integrity.

The two separate questions–the complicity of the security forces in the violence and de Klerk's knowledge of it–plagued the remainder of the transition. Some 14,000 South Africans died in political violence during the four years between Mandela's release and the first democratic election in 1994, more than double the number in the six years following the Vaal uprising of 1984. As the toll grew, Tutu and the church leaders held repeated talks with the president to make proposals for ending the killing, and grew increasingly frustrated with his failure to do so. Time and again Tutu–and other church and political leaders–blamed an evil "third force" for stoking the conflict. Slowly, evidence accumulated to substantiate the charge, and it pointed to the conclusion that certain generals of the police and army continued after 1990 to pursue the two-track strategy formulated in 1985: to couple negotiations with action to weaken the ANC's bargaining position. In November 1992, the judge Richard Goldstone, now the head of a standing commission of inquiry into violence, followed a lead provided by a hired killer's Diners Club card to order a raid on a secret military intelligence unit. The raid uncovered evidence which prompted de Klerk to order an air force general to investigate further. In December the general reported to de Klerk that members of the intelligence unit had held clandestine meetings in a private suite at Pretoria's main rugby stadium during which they had organized to supply weapons illegally to Inkatha and instigate public violence, with the aim of derailing negotiations and creating conditions conducive to an army coup. In addition, the investigation indicated that military operatives were fueling violence on the East Rand and were responsible for the indiscriminate massacres of commuters on suburban trains. The air force general pointed to the head of the South African Defence Force as one of the military leaders who was "caught up in the momentum of activities of the past." Two months before the election of 1994, Goldstone found evidence that police hit squads were continuing to operate, run by three police generals including the second in command of the police force–the man who had shown such discomfort at Vlok's negotiations with church leaders over the hunger strike five years earlier. After 1994, policemen and military agents applied to the Truth and Reconciliation Commission for amnesty for gunrunning and unlawfully supplying military training to Inkatha, for forewarning Inkatha members of police raids on hostels, and for conducting operations aimed at discrediting the ANC.

To suggest that the government followed a two-track negotiating strategy in the final years of apartheid is not to say that all participants were necessarily complicit in the overall vision, even before 1990. Among the Afrikaners who first put out feelers and then acted as conduits to the ANC in the late 1980s were enlightened academics who disagreed vehemently with P. W. Botha and whose integrity has never been impeached. Nor is it to say that de Klerk subscribed to the strategy when he came to power. Desmond Tutu warned ad nauseam in the 1990s that de Klerk's credibility was being eroded by the continuing violence, but he never went as far as some in the ANC, who accused the president of turning a blind eye to the violence so as to strengthen his bargaining position. Defending himself since, de Klerk has pointed out that before releasing Mandela, he summoned 800 police officers from across the country and told them they should keep out of politics. He repeated the exercise with the military later. He has also said that he acted every time he had firm evidence of crimes by the security force: he moved Vlok and defense minister Magnus Malan to lower-profile cabinet posts; he established a cabinet committee to control secret funds; he appointed Goldstone; he fired twenty-three army officers, including generals and brigadiers, when Goldstone revealed the activities of military intelligence; and he forced the suspension of the three police generals implicated in "third force" activities.

No evidence was ever forthcoming implicating de Klerk in violence. Thatcher's ambassador, Robin Renwick, who saw de Klerk regularly, told this writer that the president "did know that mayhem was going on" as a result of the activity of the security forces:

> His mistake . . . was, he has never been prepared to say as bluntly as he should have done that he was by no means properly in control of them. He used to say that to me at the time. . . . He has never been prepared to say this publicly, but he wasn't really in a position to fire 85 generals and that caused all his problems.

The CIA's contacts in South Africa led it to the same conclusion. A U.S. National Intelligence Estimate drawn up in 1992 suggested that although the prospects of a coup by the military or the police were remote, they would "increase dramatically" if de Klerk carried out a mass purge of conservative personnel. Asked by this writer in an interview if he had feared a coup, de Klerk would say only that the security forces were his last bulwark against chaos and he could not risk demotivating them: "It's an objective fact that if you fire the whole top echelon of the army and police, you are inviting tremendous conflict and a breakdown in authority. . . . If I overreact I can totally demotivate the security forces, because there was a real risk of anarchy breaking out."

For Tutu, the transition became, as he once described it, "a kind of roller-coaster ride," in which he alternately experienced euphoria and despair. Nine months into it, around his fifty-ninth birthday in October

1990, he was exhausted. His doctor, Ingrid le Roux—whose main work was running nutritional clinics in Cape Town's townships—advised him to take a rest for a full month. He canceled engagements for ten days. Five months later, he became ill with a urinary tract infection during a meeting of the synod of bishops in Namibia and had to be hospitalized for a week. Later tests gave an early warning of problems with his prostate gland. There were also indications that when under strain he was experiencing the effects of his childhood tuberculosis; the growth of his chest cavity had been abnormal, and his chest felt constricted.

Back at work in October 1990, he turned his attention to what became the heart of his contribution to a negotiated settlement: cajoling and lobbying black South Africans to unite for peace. Even if a hidden "third force" was instigating violence, he told them, it was unacceptable that they should become pawns in the hands of others. Black consciousness had clearly not accomplished its objective of instilling in blacks a sense of self-respect when they allowed themselves to be manipulated. His most eloquent and powerful public admonition was delivered at a lunchtime service at St. George's Cathedral during a week of prayer and fasting for peace the week before Easter 1991. There were many reasons for violence, he told the congregation. A period of transition was inherently unstable: "Yes, that is true." South Africa had no culture of tolerance of opposition: "Yes, that is true." There was economic deprivation: "Yes, that is true." The "ghastly single-sex hostels" of the migrant labor system were an explosion waiting to happen: "Yes, that is true." The security forces had on the whole behaved disgracefully: "Yes, that has added fuel to the fire." All this was true, he repeated.

But it is not all the truth. A lot of the violence is due to political rivalry. Political groups in the black community are fighting for turf and they do not seem to know, or certainly some of their followers don't seem to know, that a cardinal tenet of democracy is that people must be free to choose freely whom they want to support. . . .

Something has gone desperately wrong in the black community. . . . Ultimately we must turn the spotlight on ourselves. We can't go on forever blaming apartheid. Of course it is responsible for a great deal of evil. But ultimately, man, we are human beings and we have proved it in the resilience we have shown in the struggle for justice. We did not allow ourselves to be demoralized, dehumanized. We could laugh, we could forgive. We refused to be embittered at some of the worst moments in the struggle.

What has gone wrong, that we have seemed to have lost our reverence for life, when children can dance round someone dying the gruesome death of necklacing? Something has gone desperately wrong when our leaders are not listened to by their followers. There is much to admire in our political organizations, but there is much also which is not right. Some of those who belong to these organizations are totally undisciplined and you can't wage a struggle unless you are dedicated and disciplined.

Later he stopped just short of urging women to go on a sex strike, suggesting instead to members of the church's Mothers' Union that they should refuse to cook if their male relatives went out to fight: "You can't carry a baby for nine months in order for it to become cannon fodder for AK-47s."

He summoned black political leaders to Bishopscourt for a "summit" with church leaders in November 1990. It was attended by an unprecedented range of leaders from ANC, PAC, Azapo, and six homelands, who called on their followers to allow free political activity, without coercion or intimidation. But it was boycotted by Buthelezi; by Lucas Mangope, head of "independent" Bophuthatswana in the northwest of South Africa; and by Oupa Gqozo, the military leader of "independent" Ciskei in the Eastern Cape. Mandela and Buthelezi, whose discussions about a meeting had been bogged down in partisan wrangling, finally held their first face-to-face talks two months later, without facilitation by the church and to little noticeable effect. Tutu backed church and business leaders who brokered the signing of a National Peace Accord in September 1991, but his role was restricted by Inkatha's suspicion of church leaders. The accord had some success in communities where strong local leadership drove its implementation, such as Alexandra in Johannesburg—but the violence continued.

In December 1991, the national convention for which Tutu had been pleading since his letter to Vorster in 1976 began meeting, as the Convention for a Democratic South Africa. For the next two years, as the politicians argued over a basis for the new democratic state, the country lurched from crisis to crisis. It was as if the negotiators were traveling along the edge of a precipice, alternately walking and running, sometimes turning back, frequently brawling along the way, regularly driven off course by events that were sometimes out of, but at other times within, their control—coming to their senses only when it seemed they might all plunge over the edge together.

Tutu did not need to think through the question of taking on a new role of facilitator and conciliator; it came more easily to him than confrontation, and he moved into it instinctively. At the same time, he began in a more considered way to rethink the fundamental nature of his ministry. Halfway through his term as archbishop, after the signing of the peace accord, he spent a four-month sabbatical at the Candler School of Theology at Emory University, Atlanta. Even before going he had been hankering after a more contemplative lifestyle, and he returned intent on being less abrasive and on placing new emphasis on transformation.

Within weeks his intentions were subverted by a massacre. The Truth and Reconciliation Commission counted 112 massacres in the former Transvaal between 1990 and 1992. That which took place in the Vaal triangle on the night of June 17, 1992, was the worst. Soon after nine PM, between 300 and 500 men from the kwaMadala hostel near the township of Boipatong invaded the township and the neighboring shack settlement, Slovo Park. Wielding spears, axes, pangas, knobkieries, AK-47s, shotguns, and handguns, they put the township's informally organized Self-Defense Unit to flight. In little more than an hour they killed forty-six people, among them a nine-month-old boy, a pregnant woman, and an eighty-year-old woman. Sixteen of the men later explained to an amnesty panel of the Truth Commission that they were members of Inkatha who had taken over an abandoned hostel after being forced out of the townships by political strife. Constantly subject to attacks and unable to move around freely, the hostel residents had pressed leaders to avenge earlier killings. The amnesty panel contradicted a finding of the full commission that the police colluded with the attackers, but agreed that the police had dismantled barricades and dispersed Self-Defense Units shortly before the attack. The fact that hundreds of men had carried out an extended attack and returned to the hostel undetected strongly suggested their leaders had prior knowledge of the movements of police patrols, the panel found.

The day after the massacre Nuttall proposed to a distraught Tutu that they should visit Boipatong. With Peter Lee and an ecumenical delegation led by Frank Chikane, they toured the community, visiting the homes of the dead and injured, inspecting the wounds of toddlers, and praying with traumatized survivors. Chikane was in despair.

He told Tutu he was sick and tired of delegations visiting such sites again and again, arriving only after the killings had happened, unable to do anything to stop them. Tutu replied as a father to a son, but perhaps also addressing himself. Yes, he said, they should do all in their power to prevent evil. But they were clergymen, and their vocation was above all to be pastors. This required no more of them than that they should simply be with people in their pain, listen to them, and pray with them. To the people of Boipatong, he said: "We try to bring a little oil to pour on your wounds. We are bringing small little handkerchiefs; let us wipe your tears. We are also crying."

De Klerk visited Boipatong the following day in an attempt to show his sympathy. He was chased out by hostile crowds shouting "Kill the Boers!" His private secretary heard one police general mutter to another: "Now he can see what his fucking new South Africa looks like." Mandela was met by placards reading, "Mandela Give Us Guns." The latest round of constitutional talks had just deadlocked; Mandela suspended the bilateral discussions being held to overcome the deadlock. Tutu reentered the political process by calling from St. George's Cathedral for South Africa's expulsion from the forthcoming Olympics if the government did not meet a range of demands aimed at ending the violence. He and a group of congregants marched to Tuynhuys after the service to deliver his demands. The ANC was not prepared to go this far and instead called for athletes to wear black armbands. This idea was "frankly bizarre," Tutu said—whites could not have "both a Boipatong and Barcelona." His image among whites had been steadily improving since 1990, but now the spectacle of Tutu marching and taking a more radical position than the ANC sent it plummeting again. A slightly-built woman athlete who ran past him on his walk through Bishopscourt's streets early one morning turned back to scream at him: "You fucking communist wog!" The staff again began to hear abuse when they picked up overnight telephone messages from the office answering machine.

Ten days after the pastoral visit to Boipatong, Tutu returned to preach at the funeral on the township's soccer field. As rows and rows of coffins were laid out side by side in front of a crowd of thousands, the anger was palpable—unusually so, even for a mass funeral. A black youth kicked out at Mike Terry, executive secretary of the Anti-Apartheid Movement in Britain, as he arrived with Trevor Huddleston, who had been invited by the local council of churches. The politicians delivered a series of speeches described by Nuttall as "very strong" and by Peter Lee as "political invective." Huddleston delivered a homily commending the virtues of hatred: it was justified, he said, to hate evil. Tutu made no comment, but his discomfort was visible. Away from the stadium, while the funeral was still proceeding, youths caught a young man with dreadlocks whom they accused of belonging to Inkatha. In front of horrified photographers, a man came out of the mob, lifted a large rock high in the air, and smashed it down on the victim's head, setting off a frenzy of beating and stoning. The photographers saw the man being set alight: "A huge flame suddenly rose above the mob," one wrote, "[and] a collective scream of what sounded like joy rose with the flames."

Back on the field, Tutu began his sermon. He told the mourners that each one of them was made in the image of God, that God was neither blind nor deaf, but that as the Old Testament said, God was "in the fiery furnace with us." He spelled out his demands to de Klerk, appealed for discipline and dignity, and had the crowd chanting with him, "I am black and I am proud." The funeral ended peacefully. Peter Lee thought Tutu's sermon one of his great peacemaking moments.

Tutu's anxiety that the church should address its strictures to all parties was voiced a few weeks before the Boipatong massacre in a private repudiation of a call by the SACC for prayers for the downfall of the government. Tutu wrote to Frank Chikane that he would have approved of an appeal for the installation of a widely acceptable interim government. But the SACC's wording caused gratuitous controversy:

> I have no compunction in being harshly critical of the government. But I must be honest and say I would in camera dissociate myself and the [Anglican Church] from that statement. I would not do so in public because of my loyalty to the SACC. . . . If you meant to name sins . . . why were no words addressed for example to the black community, especially young people who were resorting again to necklacing, why no criticisms of Inkatha, and indeed of the ANC in the light of . . . our own knowledge of so many things that are not right in those organisations?"

The Boipatong massacre added impetus to a campaign of strikes and demonstrations that the ANC had begun after the deadlock in negotiations. When the confrontation escalated, Tutu resumed the role of mediator. In September 1992 he tried to avert a march on Bisho, capital of the Ciskei Bantustan, in telephone negotiations with the ANC and de Klerk. The march was part of a campaign to demand free political activity in homelands. His efforts failed, and during the march a group of ANC protesters tried to storm a gap in a fence to get into the town of Bisho. Bantustan soldiers opened fire, killing twenty-eight. The Truth Commission was later to allot a measure of responsibility for the deaths to the ANC's "lack of prudence." The bishop of Grahamstown, David Russell, on a pastoral visit to the site with Tutu, pointedly prayed to God that leaders would "not play games with your people, Lord."

The massacre at Bisho became one of the points in the transition when negotiators realized that they had to step back from the precipice. Mandela publicly signaled to de Klerk that he was willing to talk again; the two men met; and their parties worked out a basis on which to resume multiparty negotiations in 1993. They did so, however, at the cost of alienating Inkatha. Mangosuthu Buthelezi, whose behavior de Klerk was finding unpredictable and frustrating, entered an extraordinary alliance with the strongest defenders and beneficiaries of apartheid: right-wing Afrikaners who accused de Klerk of selling out the white man, and the leaders of the "independent" Bantustans of Bophuthatswana and Ciskei. Wearily, Tutu resumed the Ulundi shuttle.

In a round of visits not only to Buthelezi but also to leaders of homelands who had not attended the summit at Bishopscourt, Tutu tried to persuade them that their shared experience as blacks made them natural allies, not of whites who hankered after apartheid, but of the liberation movements. He was received politely, but there was no sign that he made any progress. His attempts to pursue a nonpartisan line had cut little ice with Buthelezi, who charged him with not expressing sympathy for Inkatha victims of violence. (Buthelezi withdrew his accusation only after being reminded of statements that Tutu had issued when members of Inkatha had been massacred.) He visited Bophuthatswana's president, Lucas Mangope—who was also educated by the Community of the Resurrection—for the first time. Mangope caused Tutu some soul-searching when he challenged him on why the churches had not extended even pastoral care to leaders of the homelands. In November 1992, Tutu confessed to Buthelezi that the churches had not given enough acknowledgement that kwaZulu and its king were not a creation of apartheid: "It's a self-indictment. . . . It was a very simplistic, naive form of political analysis."

In 1993, even as the ANC and the government made progress toward an agreement, thus beginning to establish a political center, forces unleashed by the violence threatened to tear the country apart. Supporters of the ANC stopped a light van carrying children to school up a winding dirt road in the hills near Pietermaritzburg and opened fire, killing six children and seriously injuring fifteen. They thought the van was driven by an Inkatha "warlord."* Some of the victims were the children of Inkatha officials. Tutu, Nuttall, and the SACC's leaders prayed at the site and visited the bereaved parents. The next day supporters of Inkatha took revenge, but they ambushed the wrong vehicle; five of the ten people they killed were members of the IFP. Later in the year, gunmen proclaiming allegiance to the PAC burst into a church in a suburb of Cape Town one Sunday night, lobbed hand grenades among the pews, and sprayed the 1,000 congregants with automatic rifle fire, killing twelve. Tutu's visit to the scene united, briefly, two rival denominations—the congregation that had been attacked was part of the Church of England in South Africa, a conservative grouping of Anglican origin which attracted members of the Anglican Church disenchanted with Tutu's leadership.

The event that came closest to moving South Africa into open civil war came on Holy Saturday, the day before Easter, in 1993, when a Polish immigrant and anticommunist zealot assassinated Chris Hani, the hugely popular general secretary of the South African Communist Party. Despite Tutu's rejection of the materialist aspects of the party's ideology, he was fond of Joe Slovo, its chairman, and was particularly attracted to Hani. Unlike the Christian church, the party was unequivocally identified with the struggle against apartheid. Moreover, Hani had amused Tutu at a meeting the previous year by singing, from memory, all the words of the hymn, "Lizalis' idinga lako, Thixo nKosi yenyanyiso". To the militant young comrades of the townships, Hani was a legend, and for ten days after his murder the country hung on the brink of anarchy. De Klerk had military power but no authority in the situation, so he stepped back and allowed Mandela to make a presidential-style appeal for calm. A memorial service at St. George's Cathedral had to be cut short when crowds grew too large, and angry young people clashed with the police on the Grand Parade. In the central business districts of Cape Town and three other cities, rioters set cars on fire, smashed windows, and looted shops.

* A member of the ANC applied for amnesty for the attack. It was refused.

Four million people stayed at home on the day of Hani's funeral. More than 120,000 gathered at the country's largest soccer stadium, outside Soweto, for a service that was broadcast live throughout the country. The service began with prayers by Christian, Hindu, Jewish, and Muslim leaders, followed by a series of speakers including Slovo and Mandela. The stadium was dangerously overcrowded. Banks of seating swayed from side to side as young people danced the toyi-toyi. Outside, peace monitors watched helplessly as gangs of youths burned houses nearby. Unidentified gunmen fired automatic weapons at police helicopters. Inside, monitors were concerned that ANC marshalls had lost control of the crowd. Tutu was the preacher, assigned the task of giving direction at the end of the service. It was the most important test he had ever faced of his skills in igniting and then channeling the feelings of a volatile crowd. He adopted as his text a familiar passage from Paul's letter to the Romans: "If God be for us, who can be against us?"* He greeted the mourners in five languages, conveying condolences to Hani's family in their home languages of IsiXhosa and Sesotho. The rabble-rousing started quickly: "Is there anyone here who doubts that Chris was a great son of the soil?" ("No!") "I don't hear you." ("No!") He paid tribute to Hani, mocked white South Africans' obsession with communism—"those who oppressed us were not communists"—and said that just as the resurrection followed the crucifixion, Hani's death could become a victory. Then:

> The death of Chris Hani gives . . . the government and all the key players another chance. We want to make a demand today. . . . We demand democracy and freedom. When? ("Now!") They don't hear you in Pretoria. They don't hear you in Cape Town. We demand democracy and freedom. When? ("Now!") We demand a date for the first democratic elections in this country. When? ("Now!")

South Africa was marching to victory, he repeated again and again, "the victory of light over the darkness of apartheid . . . the victory of life over the death of apartheid . . . the victory of goodness over the evil of apartheid." He invoked a phrase first used at the Cape Town city hall four years earlier:

> We are the rainbow people of God! We are unstoppable! Nobody can stop us on our march to victory! No one, no guns, nothing! Nothing will

---

* Romans 8:31.

stop us, for we are moving to freedom! (Whistles.) We are moving to freedom and nobody can stop us. (Whistles and cheers.) For God is on our side!

Finally, Tutu asked the tens of thousands spread out in front of him to lift their hands in the air. Mandela, Sisulu, and Slovo—who had been in jail or exiled when Tutu developed his techniques—sat enthralled, their eyes fixed on him, as he led the crowd in swaying their arms back and forth:

We will be free! ("We will be free!") All of us! ("All of us!") Black and white together! ("Black and white together!") We will be free! ("We will be free!") All of us! ("All of us!") Black and white together! ("Black and white together!") For we are marching to freedom! (Cheers, whistles.)

Hani's murder brought South Africa's leaders closer to the precipice than ever before. Having contemplated the drop below, they stepped back and resumed negotiations with a new sense of urgency. Tutu's confidence grew—if the transition had survived this crisis, it could survive just about anything. But Inkatha was resisting the setting of an election date, and Buthelezi and Mandela had not had bilateral talks in more than two years.

Early in June 1993, Tutu visited Pietermaritzburg for the consecration of a new bishop of Zululand and the unveiling of a statue of Mahatma Gandhi outside the local railway station. (A century earlier, Gandhi had been ejected from a train onto this station, because of his race. He went on to develop Satyagraha in South Africa to defend the rights of South Africans of Indian origin.) As the congregation at the consecration service exchanged greetings of peace, Tutu asked Buthelezi if he would meet Mandela. He agreed. The next day, Tutu and Nuttall pulled Mandela aside at a lunch after the unveiling and put the same question to him. He too agreed. Nuttall and Stanley Mogoba brokered the details in Tutu's absence abroad; and the two leaders, with delegations from their parties, met for nine hours in a Lutheran conference center outside Johannesburg on June 23. Reporting on the outcome was overshadowed by their failure to agree on a date for an election, but they agreed to a joint undertaking committing their parties to working for political tolerance. Mogoba—who cochaired the meeting with Tutu—and Nuttall believed that the most important achievement of the day was to have separated the two leaders from their delegations and arranged for them to have tea and lunch alone together. Tutu thought the joint undertaking "a quantum leap from where we have been" but was disappointed at the deadlock over the election date. Mandela had bent over backward to accommodate Buthelezi, Tutu said—even offering him the post of foreign minister in the first postliberation cabinet—but Buthelezi was a person who seemed incapable of making concessions.

Two years of negotiations produced agreement on an interim consti- tution, paving the way for the first democratic election in April 1994— without Buthelezi's agreement. So the Ulundi shuttle continued, apparently having some success weeks before the election. The govern- ments of Bophuthatswana and Ciskei had collapsed under pressure from the ANC's supporters, and Buthelezi and King Goodwill Zwelethini of the Zulus were holding out for a form of self- determination, when John Hall, a businessman who chaired the com- mittee that oversaw the National Peace Accord, convened a meeting of church leaders in Johannesburg. Hall was worried at the prospect of vio- lence in kwaZulu and Natal during the election. The meeting decided to seek an audience with Zwelethini. Through Buthelezi, the king agreed, and Hall and the church leaders dropped everything they were doing to travel to his palace at Nongoma in rural kwaZulu on April 15. After hearing their appeal, the king called in a television crew and recorded an emotional message saying that the killing was senseless: "Each and every Zulu who knows that I am his king—it must now stop."

On the day Hall and the church leaders met the king, Buthelezi was prevailed on by Washington Okumu—a Kenyan academic who worked with Africa Enterprise, an evangelical organization in Pietermar- itzburg—to make a final attempt at a settlement. Tutu was, by chance, at Union Buildings, the seat of government in Pretoria, four days later to hear the result. He was at a meeting of the committee planning the inauguration of a new president when news came in of a breakthrough in negotiations. Mandela, Buthelezi, and de Klerk appeared at a news conference next door to announce that Buthelezi would join the elec- tion. Tutu was ecstatic: "I'm over the moon. . . . It's just like a dream; we are not going to cease giving thanks to God that we have a God of surprises, a God who performs miracles all the time."

Tension among those who had been victims of apartheid was not limited to kwaZulu, Natal, and the homelands. In Cape Town, a split in the Coloured community was to lead to a confrontation between Tutu and some of his clergy who supported the ANC, a few days before the election. The community—descended from groups including white settlers, the indigenous Khoisan people of the Western Cape, and slaves from Malaya and Indonesia—was going through an identity crisis. Charles Albertyn, one of the regional bishops on whom Tutu relied for advice, described to the present writer the problem of the Coloured community as a struggle to come to terms with the fact that they had a foot in both the black camp and the white camp:

> You will never understand how difficult it is to describe [to an outsider]. On the one hand politically we're black and oppressed. . . . But socially and biologically and culturally, whites are our brothers and sisters. . . . There's a very strong bond between us. People used to say Afrikaners are particularly nasty against Coloured people because it's family quarrels and there's a lot of truth in that. . . . [We] were rebuffed on both sides. The whites were clear that [we] were not whites and the Africans make it quite clear that [we] are not black Africans.

Under apartheid, Coloured workers in the Western Cape were given preference in the allocation of jobs, housing, and amenities. With the approach of the election, their clergy listened to many of them discussing voting for de Klerk's National Party. Alarmed, eighty ministers from sixteen churches signed an advertisement taken out by the ANC declaring that "the Gospel values of an inclusive society" were best represented in the ANC's manifesto.

Seventeen of the signers were members of the Anglican clergy licensed to serve the diocese of Cape Town. Tutu summoned the full-time clergy to Bishopscourt, told them they had contravened the bishops' ban on identifying with a political party, and instructed them to apologize or lose their licenses. Sixteen—including the former staff members Chris Ahrends, Matt Esau, and Wilma Jakobsen—did so. Barney Pityana, who drew a salary from the University of Cape Town, was not at the meeting and refused to apologize. He wrote to Tutu that he had accepted the ban on membership in parties, albeit with reservations. Now it appeared to have been extended "to say that we are not to declare how we intend to exercise our democratic rights. I find that even more unacceptable. . . . The moral judgement of clergy should be respected and their autonomy in pastoral matters acknowledged." Tutu and Pityana had a stormy meeting at Bishopscourt. Tutu told Pityana he would have to withdraw his license. Pityana said in that case he did not want it. The discussion became heated, and Tutu ordered Pityana out of his office. Tutu was noticeably subdued for days afterward. Later he restored Pityana's license and patched up their relationship.

Millions of black South Africans voted for the first time in their lives on April 27, but few were more publicly exuberant than Desmond Tutu. Images of him dancing and throwing his clasped hands into the air in celebration were flashed around the world. So were his sound bites: "We are on cloud nine" and "It's like falling in love." He voted in Cape Town's Gugulethu township before touring polling stations, around which long lines stretched. Far from being frustrated at the delays, many voters afterward tried to outdo one another with stories about how long they had waited. Tutu was greeted with cheers and jubilation at most polling stations.

Tutu was an enthusiastic proponent of reassuring gestures to Afrikaners during the transition, taking time to give interviews to Afrikaans newspapers assuring them that their language would survive and supporting South Africa's return to international rugby under its traditional springbok emblem. He continued the effort in meetings of the committee planning the presidential inauguration. During negotiations, two national anthems had been adopted: "Die Stem" ("The Call"), which was dear to Afrikaner nationalism; and "Nkosi Sikelel' iAfrika." A proposal was brought to the inauguration committee that an English translation of "Die Stem" should be used. Tutu opposed the idea–the symbolism of using "Die Stem" would be diluted if it was translated, he said. His view prevailed. In one respect, however, he was unbending, even in the face of personal pressure from de Klerk.

As convenor of the religious subcommittee of the inauguration committee, Tutu planned the religious component of the ceremony as a multifaith event. On the day Buthelezi announced that he would join the election, de Klerk appealed to Tutu during a brief encounter to follow a previous inaugural tradition: that the head of the president's religious denomination should say the prayers. By then no one doubted that Mandela would be president, so the effect of de Klerk's plea would have been to have a Christian–Stanley Mogoba–as the only religious leader participating. De Klerk was a member of the Gereformeerde Kerk (Reformed Church), the smallest of the Afrikaans Reformed churches, and was clearly anxious about the feelings of his community. Tutu, mindful that South Africa had just replaced an explicitly Christian constitution with a secular constitution, would not give way.

On the Friday before the inauguration, May 6, Mandela visited a historic mosque in Cape Town. On Saturday, he went to a synagogue in the city. On Sunday he visited a Hindu temple near Johannesburg. That visit was followed by a huge Christian service of thanksgiving in the Soweto stadium from which Chris Hani had been buried. On Monday, May 9, Mandela returned to Cape Town, where the new Parliament formally elected him president. The mayor of Cape Town asked Tutu to introduce Mandela to the crowds awaiting him on the Grand Parade afterward. Tutu spoke from the balcony he had used after the march of September 1989:

> Friends, this is the day that the Lord has made and we will rejoice and be glad in it. This is the day for which we have waited for over 300 years. (Cheers.) This is the day of liberation (cheers) for all of us, black and white together. (Cheers.) . . . Fellow South Africans, I ask you: welcome our brand-new state president, out-of-the-box, Nelson Mandela!

The inauguration in Pretoria the next day was said to be the largest gathering of heads of state since John F. Kennedy's funeral. Nearly all of Africa's leaders were there. Others included Fidel Castro, Yasir Arafat, the duke of Edinburgh, and Al Gore—whose cavalcade, which also carried the first lady, Hillary Clinton, caused so much congestion that it was blamed for the delay in getting the inauguration under way. An early breakfast was held at the presidential mansion to gather the leaders in a single staging area. Tutu, the most recognizable South African present, bounced from group to group, greeting such old friends and acquaintances as Gore (with whom he had served on Harvard University's board of overseers), King Letsie III of Lesotho, Joaquim Chissano of Mozambique, and Malcolm Fraser and Bob Hawke of Australia.

The religious part of the ceremony comprised readings and prayers by Christian, Jewish, Hindu, and Muslim leaders. De Klerk made it clear to whose god he was praying when he took the oath as deputy president in a government of national unity. Instead of repeating after the chief justice, "So help me God," as Mandela had done, de Klerk said in Afrikaans: "So help me the triune God, Father, Son, and Holy Spirit." Tutu's closing prayer invoked the name of "Jesus Christ our Lord and Saviour" and continued in English, Afrikaans, Sesotho, and IsiXhosa:

Thank you O God for having brought us to this point in the history of our beautiful motherland, South Africa. Before our very eyes we see a miracle unfolding and our dreams becoming reality as the sun shines on a new dawn for us all, black and white together.

Thank you O God for freeing our country from racism and oppression and for liberating all our people. Thank you for the courage of those who initiated change. Thank you O God for those who sacrificed their freedom and even their lives in the struggle for justice. Thank you for bringing those who were previously enemies around the same table to achieve a negotiated settlement. Thank you for the miraculous way in which you transformed the election into a corporate act of nation-building. Thank you O God for all those, here and overseas, who have supported us with their prayers and love.

CHAPTER 15

A PROPER CONFRONTATION

In 1987, in a series of presentations to an Anglican church consultation, Desmond Tutu spelled out his vision for reconciliation in South Africa. In words similar to those addressed to the Eloff Commission five years previously, he likened the country under apartheid to the depiction of the world in the book of Genesis after the fall of Adam and Eve: a place in which harmony had been shattered by the effects of sin—alienation, disharmony, and separation. The church's calling was to work for the fulfillment of God's vision of "a new heaven and a new earth," in which "the wolf shall dwell with the lamb, and the leopard shall lie down with the kid."* But this would not be achieved without offending the powerful:

> Often there have been those who have wanted to provide a spurious kind of reconciliation . . . a crying of "Peace, peace," where there is no peace, a daubing of the wall with whitewash,† a papering over of the cracks instead of dealing with the situation as it demands, seriously facing up to the unpleasantness of it all. In South Africa, we have often heard people speaking disapprovingly of what they have called "confrontation," which they then opposed to "reconciliation." In this way . . . glorious gospel words have fallen into disrepute and have been horribly devalued so that many have come to think that "reconciliation" meant making peace with evil, immorality, injustice, oppression and viciousness of which they are the victims and, quite rightly, they have rejected such a travesty of the genuine article. How could anyone really think that true reconciliation could avoid a proper confrontation?

* Quotations from the Revelation of John 21:1 and Isaiah 11:6, respectively.
† A reference to Ezekiel 13:10.

Although Tutu developed this statement as a theological rationale for the struggle against apartheid, it also neatly summarized the thinking that underpinned his main preoccupation for the better part of the next two decades. As apartheid was dismantled, he insisted–initially in the churches, then to F. W. de Klerk, and eventually through the Truth and Reconciliation Commission–that if South Africans were to overcome the damage it had caused they had to face up to and work through its consequences. He advocated an explicitly Christian model of achieving reconciliation, involving three separate, successive transactions. Two of them required action from the perpetrators or beneficiaries of apartheid; the third involved a generous response from its victims. His best-known elucidation of the model was delivered at a national conference of South African church leaders near the town of Rustenburg, northwest of Johannesburg, nine months after Mandela's release.

The conference brought together an unprecedented range of South African churches. In an opening sermon, Tutu made the point that church leaders could not credibly preach reconciliation to the country if they were not reconciled among themselves. For this reconciliation to happen, he said, those responsible for apartheid first had to confess their sin: "Those who have wronged must be ready to say, 'We have hurt you by this injustice, by uprooting you from your homes, by dumping you in poverty-stricken homeland resettlement camps, by giving your children inferior education, by denying your humanity and trampling down on your human dignity and denying you fundamental rights. We are sorry; forgive us.' " In the second transaction, said Tutu, the victims were under a "gospel imperative" to forgive. In the third, those who had committed wrongs had to make restitution: "If I have stolen your pen, I can't really be contrite when I say, 'Please forgive me,' if at the same time I still keep your pen. If I am truly repentant, I will demonstrate this genuine repentance by returning your pen."

His sermon was followed by a moving apology for apartheid from another speaker, Willie Jonker, a theologian from Stellenbosch University, the intellectual heart of Afrikaner nationalism. The apology, endorsed the next day by the main white Dutch Reformed church, sent ripples through the Reformed church family and the Afrikaner community. From one side, black and Coloured Dutch Reformed churches questioned the sincerity of the white church and Tutu's right to accept the confession; from the other side, a furious P. W. Botha telephoned the church's moderator to protest. Tutu denied that he had spoken for the conference but said he refused to impose limits on God's grace. He supported his position by quoting an associate of Steve Biko, Malusi Mpumlwana, who had once told him that while being tortured by police he had looked up at his torturers and thought to himself, "By the way, these are God's children too, and . . . they need you to help them recover the humanity they are losing." Tutu said that the Dutch Reformed confession marked a "quite shattering" moment in the life of the country: "God has brought us to this moment. . . . I speak only for myself. I cannot, when someone says, 'Forgive me,' say 'I do not.' "

The conference approved a long declaration, including an eloquent collective confession of the churches' complicity in apartheid. Some months later Tutu asked F. W. de Klerk for a private meeting, at which he urged the president to make a formal apology for the suffering that apartheid had caused. De Klerk replied that his father, a member of one of the first apartheid-era cabinets, had helped to implement apartheid and that his father had not been a vicious man. Tutu responded that he was saying the policy was vicious, not its perpetrators; but he failed to persuade de Klerk. He was again disappointed by de Klerk when he took a delegation of Mfengu leaders in 1991 to plead for the return of land from which they had been forcibly ejected. One leader told de Klerk: "I used to have land, I used to have cattle, I used to have sheep, I used to have my own house. I'm seventy years of age. Now I have nothing." This cri de coeur, as Tutu described it, elicited not even a token gesture of regret from de Klerk or his colleagues.

Two years later, de Klerk did apologize: "It was not our intention to deprive people of their rights and to cause misery," he said, "but eventually apartheid led to just that. Insofar as that occurred we deeply regret it. . . . Yes, we say we are sorry." Tutu thought the apology was qualified and that de Klerk was not yet prepared to admit apartheid was intrinsically evil, but he urged that it be accepted. "Saying sorry is not an easy thing to do," he said. "We all often hedge our apologies. . . . We should be magnanimous and accept it as a magnanimous act." The issue would return to haunt their relationship during the proceedings of the Truth and Reconciliation Commission.

As the prospect of democracy drew closer, a gulf opened up over how to deal with past violations of human rights. The National Party, wanting pardons for those who had served it, proposed a comprehensive amnesty package covering all who had committed crimes with a political motive, whether they had fought for or against apartheid. The instincts of most ANC leaders were the opposite—in the vivid words of Thabo Mbeki, they thought that the way to deal with their former opponents was to "catch the bastards and hang them." From the beginning of the debate, Tutu advocated his three-stage model. There should be no Nuremberg-type trials, he said in November 1992; but there had to be confession, "a full disclosure" of crimes and then forgiveness, "a properly administered amnesty"; and finally, where possible, there had to be restitution: "Let us go . . . the Christian way, the way that says, yes there is a risk in offering people forgiveness; you don't know how they are going to turn out. But that's not . . . our business, that God's business, with that particular individual."

The way that was ultimately adopted was, in effect, Tutu's. The form it took—the establishment of the Truth and Reconciliation Commission—had, however, very little to do with him or with noble Christian ideals. It was rather the providential outcome of realpolitik, which reflected a convergence of pressures from three directions: idealistic human-rights advocates within the ANC, frightened generals of the old order, and a nongovernmental lobby coordinated by the man who was to become Tutu's deputy in the commission.

The pressure from within the ANC was a response to three inquiries, commissioned by the movement itself, into torture, ill-treatment, and executions in ANC detention camps in exile. In August 1993, the ANC's national executive reacted to a report from the final inquiry by calling for a "Commission of Truth" that would conduct a wide-ranging investigation of human-rights violations from all quarters in the apartheid era. Amnesty became a factor a few months later, as negotiators strove to overcome the last obstacles to a constitutional settlement. Generals in the security forces told Mbeki that if their men had to face trials at the hands of the new government, there would be no peaceful election. Mbeki relayed the warning to Nelson Mandela. In December 1993, negotiators tacked onto the end of the interim constitution what they clumsily named a "postamble"—a section promising amnesty for offenses committed in the course of past conflicts. "Without that," said the ANC's constitutional expert, Albie Sachs, "we could have ended up without an election, without a constitution, and without a country."

The postamble left the task of drawing up legislation to the first democratically elected parliament. At this stage the role of Alex Boraine, a former parliamentarian, became instrumental. Boraine had left Parliament three years before P. W. Botha's downfall, disgusted at Botha's failure to offer any path out of the country's impasse, to help establish a nongovernmental organization (NGO) to explore democratic alternatives to apartheid. In the early 1990s he began to examine the truth commissions through which other nations emerging from authoritarian government—principally in eastern Europe and Latin America—had dealt with their past. During the ANC's assumption of power Boraine became important in crafting the Promotion of National Unity and Reconciliation Act of 1995, which established the Truth and Reconciliation Commission (TRC). Parliament repudiated a blanket amnesty such as that granted in Chile after the regime of Augusto Pinochet. Instead, uniquely, it made amnesty conditional on individual application and on full disclosure of crimes. It grafted the amnesty apparatus onto the commission. In a second crucial decision unique to truth commissions, Parliament—lobbied by Boraine and nongovernmental groups concerned with victims' rights—changed the legislation during debate to mandate public hearings.

The first suggestion that Tutu should be one of the seventeen commissioners of the TRC was made by Michael Nuttall a few days after Parliament finalized the act in July 1995. In September the synod of bishops formally nominated him. His appointment wasn't inevitable, even as an ordinary member of the commission; three months after Mandela became president the previous year, he and Tutu had exchanged harsh words in public. Tutu attacked the government for failing to close down the apartheid arms industry and endorsed a criticism—first voiced by the activist Cheryl Carolus—that new members of Parliament who accepted large raises in pay had stopped the apartheid-era "gravy train" only long enough to climb aboard themselves. Mandela hit back by labeling Tutu a "populist" and saying that the archbishop should have discussed matters privately with him first. Tutu lashed back in the language he had used against apartheid cabinet ministers: Mandela was either lying or forgetful, he said, because he (Tutu) had raised the issues with the president at a private breakfast. (Tutu also famously criticized Mandela's colorful open-necked shirts. He said he did not mind the president wearing African-print shirts, which he wore himself, but Mandela's Italian-style shirts looked like pajamas. Even worse, the president wore them on occasions at which the black community judged them inappropriate, such as funerals. Mandela, equally famously, replied tongue in cheek that the criticism was amusing, coming from a man who wore dresses.)

Nonetheless, Mandela named Tutu chairman of the TRC. Alex

Boraine, who like Michael Nuttall before him could have expected the top job in an earlier era, was appointed Tutu's deputy. Tutu set out to model his relationship with Boraine on the relationship he had enjoyed with Nuttall, and together they planned the commission's first meeting at Bishopscourt. It was held on December 16, 1995, a national holiday which had originally commemorated an Afrikaner military victory over the Zulu nation but had been renamed the Day of Reconciliation.

The TRC was far bigger than Desmond Tutu. According to Priscilla Hayner, an expert on truth commissions, the TRC "dwarfed previous ... commissions in its size and reach." At the peak of its activities, it employed a staff of more than 300, directed by the commissioners and more than twenty additional committee members in four regional offices.* It operated three committees—one to investigate violations of human rights, the second to decide on amnesty, and the third to formulate recommendations for reparations and the rehabilitation of victims. At any one time, as many as three or four public hearings might be going on simultaneously, taking evidence from victims or considering applications for amnesty. The commission generated from within its ranks at least eight books—including indispensable accounts from Tutu and Boraine—and a number of other works have dissected its failures and its strengths. What follows, therefore, does not purport to be more than a short account of how Tutu, leading in customary style from the front, tried to create from an act of Parliament an instrument of healing and redemption.

The TRC's task was to investigate and report on gross violations of human rights—defined as killing, abduction, torture, and severe ill-treatment—in the period between the Sharpeville massacre of 1960 and Mandela's inauguration in 1994; to consider applications for amnesty; and to make recommendations to the government on reparations. At the core of Tutu's vision for its work was a sentence in the postamble of the constitution: "There is a need for understanding but not for vengeance, a need for reparation but not for retaliation, a need for *ubuntu* but not for victimisation." The Nguni word ubuntu—or botho in the Sotho group of languages—can be simply translated as "humaneness," but this English word fails to convey the African worldview. Explaining it for the predominantly white readers of Johannesburg's daily, *The Star,* as early as 1981, Tutu wrote of ubuntu-botho as observed in traditional African society:

---

* The present writer was appointed director of media liaison at the commission.

It referred to what ultimately distinguished us from the animals—the quality of being human and also humane. The definition is almost a tautology. The person who had ubuntu was known to be compassionate and gentle, who used his strength on behalf of the weak, who did not take advantage of others—in short he cared, treating others as what they were, human beings. . . .

Without this quality a prosperous man even though he might be a chief was regarded as someone deserving of pity and sometimes even contempt. . . . If you lacked ubuntu . . . you lacked an indispensable ingredient to being human. You might have much of the world's goods, and you might have position and authority, but if you did not have ubuntu, you did not amount to much. Even today, ubuntu is greatly admired and to be sought after or cultivated. Only someone to whom something drastic has happened could ever say that the death of a fellow human being left him cold.* Blacks would recoil from anyone in their community who ever displayed such callousness. He had lost his humanity; or was well on the way to doing so.

Tutu contrasted the western with the African notion of being human by setting the popular rendition of Descartes—"I think, therefore I am"—against Sotho and Nguni phrases that can be roughly translated as, "I am because you are; you are because we are," or "A person is a person through other people."† To the western ear, the standard formulation that Tutu developed later brings to mind Donne's "No man is an island": "None of us comes into the world fully formed. We would not know how to think, or walk, or speak, or behave as human beings unless we learned it from other human beings. . . . The solitary, isolated human being is a contradiction in terms."

In the TRC, Tutu advocated "restorative justice," which he described as characteristic of traditional African jurisprudence: "Here the central concern is not retribution or punishment but, in the spirit of *ubuntu,* the healing of breaches, the redressing of imbalances, the restoration of broken relationships. This kind of justice seeks to rehabilitate both the victim and the perpetrator, who should be given the opportunity to be reintegrated into the community he or she has injured by his or her offence."

* An allusion to a police minister during apartheid who said Steve Biko's death in detention "leaves me cold."

† In Tutu's home languages of IsiXhosa and Setswana respectively, "Umuntu ngumuntu ngabantu" and "Motho ke motho ka motho yo mongwe."

With this in mind, even before his formal appointment Tutu attempted to draw the deeply suspicious Afrikaner community into the process. Unaware of the extent of Boraine's involvement in setting up the TRC, he tried to persuade the government to appoint an Afrikaner as his deputy. His choice was Willie Esterhuyse, an academic at Stellenbosch University who had opened up the first contact between apartheid intelligence agents and the ANC in the 1980s. Tutu had more success in lobbying his fellow commissioners on the appointment of additional committee members. Distressed that the Afrikaner churches had no representation, he sought out Piet Meiring, a respected theologian from the University of Pretoria, and had him appointed a committee member. (Tutu also had high regard for the skills as a community activist of his former SACC fieldworker, Thom Manthata—a Catholic layman—and brought him in as another committee member.)

In the early days of the commission, Tutu took full advantage of his status to avoid prolonged wrangling over internal appointments. Alex Boraine felt that the full commission ought to make and debate nominations; Tutu insisted on naming a slate of candidates for its approval. He assumed for himself the chairmanship of the Human Rights Violations Committee, which was to hear from victims. He had little say about the makeup of the Amnesty Committee—its members were appointed by Mandela; and its decisions were final, not subject to review by the full commission—but he lobbied successfully to have Andrew Wilson, an independent-minded judge in Natal of whom Michael Nuttall thought a great deal, appointed as deputy chair. A key appointment initiated by other commissioners was that of Dumisa Ntsebeza, an activist and lawyer from the Eastern Cape, as head of the investigative unit. Ntsebeza's blunt honesty and independence of spirit were reminiscent of the younger Tutu, and he became the perceived "number three" of the commission—and, like the younger Tutu, a lightning rod for controversy.

Tutu delegated the detailed management of the TRC. Describing Boraine as a gifted organizer, he handed Boraine the kind of administrative tasks he had given Nuttall in the church. As with Nuttall, he also shared much of his decision making with Boraine, once likening Boraine to the TRC's "prime minister." Tutu kept his own schedule relatively clear and tried to keep an open door for commissioners and committee members. Very soon, though, he ran into difficulties.

The synod of bishops was a relatively homogeneous group. All the bishops were men. They had served the same cause and the same institution, the Anglican Church for most of their lives. All were opposed to apartheid, although some accepted only with reluctance the measures—such as sanctions—that most were prepared to support to end it. They operated according to long established conventions, which ensured that disagreements, with very few exceptions, were stated openly and resolved transparently. The TRC threw together a far more disparate group of people from far more diverse backgrounds. There were ten men and seven women. Most of them knew Tutu only by reputation and knew nothing about one another. The commission was dominated by antiapartheid lawyers, the clergy, and medical professionals, but it also included supporters or former supporters of apartheid. At the beginning, it was riven by political, racial, and personal suspicion.

Some commissioners were taken aback when the first three staff appointments went to whites.* Ntsebeza considered this a political mistake. Alex Boraine was suspect as a white liberal who had served in an apartheid Parliament; at early meetings Ntsebeza challenged him for using the personal pronoun "we" in relaying decisions to which not all commissioners had been party. Some whites failed to speak their minds on touchy issues, for fear of being seen as racist; others appeared upset when their antiapartheid credentials were questioned. When they went to Boraine for solace or advice, they took on the appearance of a white lobby.

The speed with which the commission had to be set up caused logistical nightmares. The law initially allowed it eighteen months to do its work, and the clock began ticking from its first meeting—when it had no offices, no staff, no furniture, and no equipment. Boraine, with the support of Tutu and the commission, broke state procurement rules, incurring censure from the auditor-general, in order to get off to a quick start. The role Tutu had allocated to Boraine was sometimes at cross-purposes with that of the commission's chief executive officer.

On occasion, divisions threatened to tear the commission apart. The most serious crisis was brought about by a witness in an amnesty hearing who claimed that Dumisa Ntsebeza's car had been used by operatives of the Pan Africanist Congress in an attack on a bar in Cape Town in 1993. The allegation had been relayed to Tutu and

* The author; Tutu's assistant, Lavinia Browne; and Boraine's assistant, Paddy Clark.

Boraine some months before the hearing. Skeptical about its veracity, they directed that it be investigated internally—by the very unit Ntsebeza headed. Both acknowledged later that this was a mistake; the probe failed to get to the bottom of the claim; and as the hearing loomed, they and the staff advising them became paralyzed. The public airing of the allegation rocked the commission, creating a split between black and white staff members. Tutu described the situation as "the commission's own O. J. Simpson case." Most black staff members assumed that Ntsebeza was innocent; most whites suspected that he was guilty. Tutu, applying the niceties of a well-developed western democracy, asked Ntsebeza to withdraw from the TRC's activities while the matter was being resolved. Ntsebeza refused; in South African racial politics, withdrawal would be seen as an admission of guilt. However, the crisis evaporated when the witness contacted Tutu to recant and Mandela, at the TRC's request, appointed Richard Goldstone to investigate. Goldstone subsequently cleared Ntsebeza's name.

Ultimately, the TRC's internal squabbles paled into insignificance against the overwhelming impact of its hearings on South African society. Previous truth commissions abroad had sat in secret and issued printed reports at the end of their work. South Africa, because civil society had lobbied Parliament, held hearings in public. Not only that; Tutu and Boraine decided that television cameras should be allowed into the hearings. The Human Rights Violations Committee consented with little difficulty; only a representative sample of victims would be giving evidence, and those who did not want publicity could simply give written statements. But the Amnesty Committee, run by judges horrified at the prospect of American-style televised trials, balked. The commission turned to the British experience in the hope that the judges would be more comfortable with it. A producer responsible for a series of BBC programs on trials in Scottish courts drew up a set of guidelines to ensure that the cameras would not be obtrusive. Still the judges refused. Tutu invited them to join him and Boraine for supper in the imposing surroundings of Bishopscourt, where he was still living shortly before his retirement as archbishop. They would not budge. In the end Tutu told them that their autonomy was limited to decisions about amnesty; overruled their objections; and, Boraine reported later, "padded off in his tracksuit" to go upstairs and watch a soccer match.

The result was that for more than two years, the country was awash with the hitherto concealed stories of abuses under apartheid. On days when several hearings were going on in different parts of the country, up to a third of evening news bulletins were devoted not to current affairs but to new revelations from the past. A team of television journalists produced a weekly documentary about the TRC. Facilitated by pioneering interpreters who rendered the proceedings in all the country's official languages, radio journalists provided news that penetrated even rural areas without electricity. English translations of the hearings were broadcast live. Underlying the good relationship between the commission and the media was Tutu's and Boraine's exceptional understanding of the role of independent journalists, gained during their years of campaigning against apartheid.

The commission deliberately put victims and survivors first, beginning in April 1996 with a four-week cycle of hearings in the four cities that were home to its regional offices. An early issue was the religious tone of the hearings. Boraine suggested that Tutu should refrain from wearing his full-length purple cassock; and commissioners in Johannesburg asked him to open their hearings with a period of silence rather than a prayer. Tutu, sure of his ground in a country in which four of every five people proclaimed adherence to a faith—and three in four the Christian faith—dismissed Boraine's suggestion. He told Boraine that Mandela, who had appointed him, knew he was an archbishop. He was supported by a Hindu commissioner. He tried to accommodate the request from Johannesburg but prayer was so integral to his life—he prayed, for example, at the beginning of every meeting and before his first car journey every day—that he abandoned the attempt. After fidgeting uncomfortably for a few moments at the opening of the region's first hearing, he overruled his colleagues and insisted on saying a prayer. Commission meetings stopped for prayers at midday, and commissioners twice went on retreat together.

From the first hearing in East London, Tutu seized the tool that Mandela had entrusted to him and sought to apply it for his ends. He singled out witnesses who embraced forgiveness and made their stories his leitmotif. Babalwa Mhlauli was the daughter of a man who had been abducted and killed by the police; his hand was cut off and was preserved in a jar on a senior officer's desk. Tutu lauded her when she told the commission, "I would love to know who killed my father. . . . We do want to forgive but I mean we don't know whom to forgive." He described as "extraordinary" the evidence of Beth Savage, the victim of an attack by the PAC on a golf club where a wine tasting was being held; she still had so much shrapnel in her body that she set off metal detectors at airports, but was nevertheless able to say, "I would like to meet that man who threw that grenade in an attitude of forgiveness and hope that he could forgive me too for whatever reason." Tutu highlighted the modest claims of relatives of the "disappeared" whose preoccupation–like that of many New Yorkers after September 11–was finding some remains, even just a single bone, to bury. Summing up the hearings, he praised the capacity of victims "to be magnanimous, refusing to be consumed by bitterness and hatred."

At the same time, Tutu reached out to encourage those who had enforced or benefited from apartheid to join the process. He reassured whites that the TRC was evenhanded, noting that it included the stories of victims of the liberation movements' armed struggle. During a hearing in the capital of the Free State, Bloemfontein, he made a pilgrimage to the nearby memorial to Afrikaner women and children who had died in British concentration camps in the Anglo-Boer War of 1899–1902. The next day, Afrikaans newspapers featured a photograph of him in his cassock, bending his head in prayer in front of a statue of two women and a dying child. He used the visit to argue for support of the TRC. The legacy of bitterness between Afrikaans- and English-speaking South Africans left by the camps, he said, could have been avoided if there had been a similar process a century earlier.

Tutu invested considerable emotional energy in the hearings. On one occasion in the opening round, an elderly victim of torture, Singqokwane Malgas, was overcome by emotion while describing the "helicopter"–a procedure in which he was hung upside down, his hands and feet manacled together, and spun around. Tutu put his own face down on the table in front of him and wept uncontrollably, disrupting the proceedings. Thereafter he could be seen biting his lip or his finger when his emotions threatened to get the better of him.

Halfway into the original eighteen-month life of the TRC stipulated by the law, the commissioners began to worry that the process was not working. Victims and survivors had been putting their pain on public display for six months, to no apparent effect. Whites were calling the TRC the "Kleenex commission," referring to the tears being shed. Racists mumbled in their clubs, bars, and homes that of course blacks were prone to exaggeration. The TRC had high hopes for the investigative unit, but it was becoming clear that a staff the size of five or six teams of detectives could hardly solve, in the space of two years, every major crime of the thirty-four-year period of the commission's mandate. The commission desperately needed applications for amnesty.

The theory behind amnesty was that a carrot-and-stick approach would generate applications: the carrot being the offer of a pardon in exchange for the truth, and the stick being fear of prosecution. But the deadline for applications was approaching, and there were only hints of policemen gingerly probing the possibilities. Then a lawyer in Pretoria representing five members of the security branch phoned Max du Preez, a crusading newspaper editor who had exposed the police death squads run from the farm Vlakplaas, and who now led the television team covering the commission. How, the lawyer asked du Preez, could he and a colleague get in touch with Tutu? Du Preez gave him a number for Tutu's staff in Cape Town, and an appointment was set up with a small TRC delegation. At the meeting Tutu put the lawyers at ease by praying and welcoming them in Afrikaans. They went on to explain that their clients were considering applying for amnesty but were nervous and first wanted an exploratory discussion. As proof of their bona fides, the policemen would supply a list of incidents in which they had been involved. The list arrived, and the commission quickly agreed to a further meeting.

About two weeks later, the lawyers and four of their five clients met Tutu and a delegation in the TRC's offices in Johannesburg. The most senior officer was a brigadier named Jan Hattingh Cronje, a former commander of Vlakplaas and later of the Northern Transvaal security police. He and his men had murdered so many people that they could not recall the number, but from their list it was already clear that they had a lot of blood on their hands. Yasmin Sooka, deputy chair of the Human Rights Violations Committee, was squeamish about meeting them. "We can't deal with these buggers," she told Tutu. He replied that if she wanted to be on the TRC she had no choice. She recalled in an interview how she greeted the policemen: "It was the most horrible experience, because we went around the room and we shook hands. . . . I remember going to the toilet and looking at my hand and washing it over and over again." The lawyers asked that their clients be placed in a witness protection program and discussed the question of legal aid. Tutu was more interested in fundamentals. "He actually explained what the amnesty process was about," recalled Sooka, "and how the big motivation was not revenge but rather to get this nation healed. I think on healing he kind of struck a note with them, because obviously that's the reassurance they were craving. . . . You got a sense of broken men."

The meeting was a turning point for the commission. It showed that the carrot-and-stick approach was beginning to work; the commission quickly learned that the Transvaal's attorney general had been about to order the arrest of Cronje and his men. Tutu again put pressure on the judges of the Amnesty Committee, this time to rush the applications into a hearing. In a blaze of publicity, Johannes van der Merwe, former head of the security police and national commissioner of police, stepped up to accept moral responsibility for the acts committed by his men—and to own up to his role in the bombing of Khotso House and the booby-trapping of hand grenades given to activists in the East Rand. In the series of hearings that followed over the next five years, thirty members of the Northern Transvaal security branch applied for amnesty for dozens of crimes committed between 1981 and 1990, including forty-five killings, twenty-two abductions, sixteen bombings or arson attacks on people's homes, twelve incidents of torture or serious assault, and the attempted murder of Smangaliso Mkhatshwa of the Catholic Bishops' Conference. As other policemen learned that the attorney general of the Transvaal was preparing criminal cases, the trickle of amnesty applications turned into a stream. Of the total of 293 applications from members of the former government's security forces, 229 came from the security police.

To illustrate the nature of the revelations, Tutu selected examples—as he had during victims' testimony—to which he turned repeatedly. He most frequently quoted the evidence of Dirk Coetzee, another former head of Vlakplaas, regarding how the police typically took detainees into the bush, murdered them, and disposed of their bodies. Coetzee told an amnesty hearing in Durban in November 1996:

> Knock-out drops . . . were administered to Sizwe Kondile [a student activist] in a drink whilst we were sitting around drinking ourselves, opening beer and whatever other drinks. . . . He eventually fell over backwards and lay on his back, and at a stage either Colonel Nic van Rensburg or Major Flemington said, "Well, chaps, let's get on with the job." In the meantime two junior officers . . . brought dense bushveld wood, big logs of it, with tyres, and one . . . took a Makarov pistol with a silencer on, and whilst . . . Mr. Kondile was lying on his back, shot him on top of the head. There was a short jerk and that was it. The four junior non-commissioned officers . . . each grabbed a hand and a foot, put it onto the pyre of tyres and wood, poured petrol on it, and set it alight. . . . Whilst that happened we were drinking and even having a braai [barbecue] next to the fire. Now, that I don't say to show our braveness, I just tell it to the Commission to show the callousness of it

and to what extremes we have gone in those days. And a body takes about seven hours to burn to ashes completely, and the chunks of meat, especially the buttocks and the upper part of the legs, had to be turned frequently during the night to make sure that everything burned to ashes.

Tutu resolutely resisted declaring that those responsible for atrocities were beyond redemption: "Yes indeed these people were guilty of monstrous, even diabolical, deeds [but] that did not turn them into monsters or demons. To have done so would mean that they could not be held morally responsible for their dastardly deeds. Monsters have no moral responsibility."

As the evidence of atrocities mounted, the commission turned its attention to the leaders under whom they had occurred. Desmond Tutu was instrumental in calling to account three leaders in particular: two former heads of state from the apartheid government, and—from the liberation movement—the woman people called the "mother of the nation." He did so not as a dispassionate adjudicator of the law, dispensing justice from Olympian heights to people he had never encountered. He was, rather, an emotional, committed advocate, dealing with people he already knew well and willing to bend over backward to persuade them to make the confessions by which they could appropriate the forgiveness they were being offered.

Tutu approached P. W. Botha for the first time since their confrontation in 1988 at Tuynhuys after the former police commissioner van der Merwe told the Amnesty Committee in October 1996 that Khotso House had been bombed on Botha's instructions. The commission could simply have issued a subpoena requiring Botha to appear before it in Cape Town. Anxious to avoid enraging Botha's supporters and conscious of his age—eighty—and ill health, Tutu readily accepted a suggestion from Boraine that he should visit the former president at his retirement home near the town of George on the southern Cape coast. Botha agreed to see Tutu in his daughter's home in George. In contrast to their last meeting, they had a rational two-hour discussion over tea and melktert ("milk tart," an Afrikaner delicacy). Botha denied doing anything that would have required him to apply for amnesty. He said that the allegations regarding Khotso House were incorrect, and also that its bombing did not fall within the definition of a gross violation of human rights (on the basis, it emerged later, of the contention that no one was injured). He nevertheless agreed to provide written answers to questions from the TRC and advised Tutu to talk to his police and defense ministers, Adriaan Vlok and Magnus Malan, respectively. Some months later, while the commission was awaiting Botha's answers, his wife died. Tutu returned to George for the funeral, prompting a black radio journalist to ask him to explain what he was doing there.

As the commission waited through much of 1997 for Botha's reply, more questions were emerging from a study of the minutes of his State Security Council. The Human Rights Violations Committee decided to subpoena him. Botha pleaded illness and was excused. The commission scheduled a new date and said it was prepared to hold the hearing in George. Botha still refused to attend. "I don't appear in circuses," he said. Nelson Mandela offered to accompany Botha to the commission, but to no avail. Eight years after relinquishing the presidency, Botha was summoned before a black magistrate in a small, sparsely furnished lower court in his hometown to face charges of defying the subpoena. Before the trial, Botha's lawyers tried to negotiate a compromise. Tutu and Boraine agreed to hold a closed, private hearing of the TRC, from which Boraine—an old parliamentary opponent of Botha—would withdraw. Negotiations continued until the morning Botha was due to appear, when Tutu met him privately in a final attempt at a settlement. Botha said he would speak only to Tutu and Mandela, not to the commission, which was trying to humiliate him and the Afrikaner.

In the trial that followed, Botha was forced to listen to Eugene de Kock, another former Vlakplaas commander whom the press called "Prime Evil." De Kock was brought from the jail cell where he was serving two life sentences and another 212 years' imprisonment to tell how he had bombed Khotso House. He accused Botha and other National Party leaders of deserting their men: "They want to eat lamb but they do not want to see the blood and the guts," he said. "They are cowards." The TRC's executive secretary, Paul van Zyl, gave evidence that minutes of State Security Council's meetings used words such as "eliminate" and "neutralise" when referring to its opponents. "It is quite clear . . . the word 'eliminate' means 'kill,' " van Zyl said. To substantiate the fact that people living across the street from Khotso House had been injured, Peter Storey—now teaching in Ohio after completing a term as a Methodist bishop—was flown home to describe the aftermath of the attack. He had found "utter devastation" at his church's apartment house, he said, with retirees and mentally disabled people in a state of confusion, their arms and faces lacerated and shrapnel embedded in the walls above their beds.

Tutu prefaced his evidence by expressing his reluctance to testify: "I tried to reach out to Mr. Botha," he told the court. "God did not call me to be a pastor of black people, God called me to be a pastor of his children. . . . Mr. Botha . . . is my brother because that is the interpretation of my faith and my baptism. . . . He is a member of my family, and God will ask me, 'What did you do to help redeem my child?' " After a long cross-examination by Botha's lawyers, Tutu asked the magistrate for permission to make a final appeal:

> Your worship, I believe that we still have an opportunity—although this is a court of law, and without suggesting that the accused is guilty of any violations, I speak on behalf of people who have suffered grievously as a result of policies that were carried out by governments, including the government that he headed. I want to appeal to him. I want to appeal to him to take this chance . . . to say that he may not himself even [have] intended the suffering. . . . He may not have given orders or authorised anything. . . . I am just saying that the government that he headed caused many of our people deep, deep anguish and pain and suffering. Our people want to be part of this country and to be part of reconciliation.
>
> If Mr. Botha was able to say: I am sorry that the policies of my government caused you pain. Just that. Can he bring himself to say I am sorry that the policies of my government caused you so much pain? That would be a tremendous thing and I appeal to him.

Botha did not respond. He was convicted of refusing to obey the subpoena, fined, and given a twelve-month prison sentence, suspended on condition that he did not repeat his offense. He was later acquitted on appeal, on a technicality: the law, which was being amended to extend the life of the commission, did not authorize the issue of a subpoena on the day it was signed. In its main report, issued in 1998, the commission identified Botha as "the man who took the State into the realms of criminality." It held him accountable for the deliberate unlawful killing and attempted killing of people opposed to the government, the widespread use of torture and other forms of severe ill-treatment, the forcible abduction of people resident in neighboring countries, and acts of arson and sabotage.

The TRC's confrontation in 1997 with Winnie Madikizela Mandela, by now the former wife of Nelson Mandela, had its origins in events that took place after she returned to Soweto in 1986 from a period of banishment in the Free State town of Brandfort. Madikizela Mandela, defiantly outspoken despite police harassment, restriction orders, arrest, torture, and imprisonment almost continuously since her marriage in 1958, became a magnet for young people who needed refuge and help. A number moved into rooms in the backyard of her house, around the corner from the Tutus' home in Orlando West. When they formed the Mandela United Football Club, she helped them buy uniforms in the colors of the ANC. In the middle of 1988, a dispute developed between members of the club and pupils at a school in Soweto over the use of a soccer field and assaults on teenage girls. Stories began to spread that the football club was terrorizing the neighborhood. The extent of Madikizela Mandela's alienation from her community was exposed in July 1988, when the pupils burned down her home, destroying possessions that included family records and photographs. Desmond and Leah Tutu, in England for the ten-yearly Lambeth Conference of Anglican bishops, were stunned—it was unthinkable that Sowetans would set alight the house of Nelson Mandela. Worse news followed. Soweto's firefighting service was so inadequate that when a fire broke out, neighbors would normally rush to help. Trevor Tutu, who also lived near the Mandelas, reported to his parents that when the Mandela home was burning, no one lifted a finger.

Madikizela Mandela and her "boys" moved to another house in the Diepkloof Extension area of Soweto. Back in South Africa, Tutu used the opportunity of a visit to Orlando West to try to talk to her about the football club. She refused to see him, saying that she was studying for exams. It later transpired that between August 1988 and February 1989 she and her associates were implicated, directly and indirectly, in assaults, kidnapping, attempted murders, and murders involving at least a dozen people, culminating in the abduction of four youths from a Methodist manse in Orlando West and the murder of fourteen-year-old Moeketsi "Stompie" ("Short One") Seipei in January 1989. From his prison cell, Nelson Mandela ordered the disbanding of the football club. Community and religious leaders formed a crisis committee to bring the reign of terror to an end. When Madikizela Mandela spurned their intervention, the Mass Democratic Movement and the ANC's exiled leadership issued statements branding her a maverick who refused to account to structures of the liberation movement and dissociating themselves from her. Two years later, after Mandela had been released, he stood by his wife when she went on trial and was convicted of kidnapping. In 1992 their marriage ran into trouble, with newspapers reporting on her infidelity and erratic behavior. Tutu, following his customary pastoral practice, did not wait for invitations. He called both Nelson and Winnie and arranged sessions with them on his next visit to Johannesburg. He never revealed the content of the pastoral discussions; the Mandelas divorced in 1996.

The TRC hearing to which Madikizela Mandela was summoned at the end of 1997 was traumatic for black South Africans. Three years after liberation, she was the Eva Perón of South Africa's poor and marginalized, adored in the shack settlements where people still lived in squalor. As her former husband prepared to retire and hand power to Thabo Mbeki, her supporters aspired to have her elected deputy president of the ANC, and thus Mbeki's logical successor. The truth about the football club was denied in much of the country. The farther one went from Orlando West or Diepkloof Extension, the more one heard that the stories were a concoction of lies, a "trick of the Boers" (and indeed there were indications that the club was riddled with informers and that the police had deliberately turned a blind eye to what was happening). In this view, Madikizela Mandela's conviction by a white judge in a white court was to be expected.

It would have been rank hypocrisy for Tutu to pretend at the hearing that he was a disinterested observer of what had happened in his community, and he made no attempt to do so. As well as making his customary round at the beginning, welcoming and greeting victims and prominent visitors, he hugged Madikizela Mandela. Then for nine tumultuous days—eight days longer than any apartheid leader had appeared before the commission—he presided over what became her public humiliation and disgrace. He kept an iron hand on the proceedings. He made cutting comments to white liberal lawyers who could not pronounce the African names of their clients. As perhaps only he could have done, he brought to order unruly spectators whose behavior threatened witnesses. One by one, frightened youngsters; criminal thugs; unstable accomplices; pleading, angry parents; temporizing, conscience-stricken community leaders; morally courageous political leaders; and brave Methodist ministers appeared to flesh out the sordid story of what had gone on in Madikizela Mandela's backyard. They told of beatings; of torture; of pouring battery acid into open wounds;

of kicking Stompie Seipei like a ball and slaughtering him like a goat, stabbing him through the neck with garden shears.

Peter Storey, one of those who had tried to negotiate the release of the abductees, was summoned back from America to give evidence in this case too. Drawing partly on his sermon at Stompie's funeral, he found the words to describe the implications of the child's death for which many had been grasping:

> It has exposed the deeper hidden wounds these years have carved into the people's souls . . . the erosion of conscience, the devaluing of human life, the evasion of truth, and the reckless resort to violence. And I think that part of the painful discovery that has come to these hearings . . . [is that] the primary cancer may be, and was, will always be, the apartheid oppression, but the secondary infection has touched many of apartheid's opponents and eroded their knowledge of good and evil. One of the tragedies of life, Sir, is [that] it is possible to become like that which we hate most, and I have a feeling that this drama is an example of that.

On the ninth day of the hearing, Madikizela Mandela had her chance to reply. Her evidence was broadcast live on television. In angry exchanges with a phalanx of lawyers appearing for witnesses and the commission, she issued what the *Washington Post*'s reporter Lynne Duke later described as an extraordinary string of denials: "Winnie saw no evil, heard no evil, did no evil, suspected no evil, even when people were beaten half to death on her property. . . . The spectacle was chilling." There was no hint of remorse, even less of repentance. Late in the day, Tutu decided to take a gamble before adjourning. He told the hearing—and the country, since the broadcast had displaced early-evening soap operas—of the Tutu-Mandela family relationship, of Madikizela Mandela's outstanding contribution to the struggle, and of how she had refused to see him in 1988. Anticipating the TRC's findings by a year, he said that "something went wrong, horribly, badly wrong. What, I don't know." Finally he threw the dice:

> There are people out there who want to embrace you. I still embrace you because I love you and I love you very deeply. There are many out there who would have wanted to do so if you were able to bring yourself to say something went wrong. . . . Say I am sorry; I am sorry for my part in what went wrong. . . . I beg you, I beg you, I beg you please—I

have not made any particular finding from what has happened here. I speak as someone who has lived in this community. You are a great person and you don't know how your greatness would be enhanced if you were to say sorry, things went wrong, forgive me. I beg you.

For a moment, the audience in the hall held its collective breath. Madikizela Mandela responded first by thanking the panel. Then she apologised to Stompie Seipei's mother and to the family of a doctor who had been killed, allegedly after treating the boy. Finally she turned to Tutu:

Thank you very much for your wonderful, wise words. . . . That is the father I have always known in you. . . . I am saying it is true, things went horribly wrong. I fully agree with that and for that part of those painful years when things went horribly wrong and we were aware of the fact that there were factors that led to that, for that I am deeply sorry.

On this note, the hearing ended. A storm broke over Tutu's head, in a way that had never happened when he pleaded with apartheid leaders to apologize. He had his defenders. Yasmin Sooka thought it a poignant moment, one of the "great cameos" of the commission. The poet Antjie Krog, in her book on the TRC, *Country of My Skull,* wrote of her exultation: Tutu had forced a perpetrator to bend the knee to his moral code. But such voices were few. According to his critics, Tutu had groveled, giving Madikizela Mandela an opportunity to make a cheap, insincere gesture. "He should have been more circumspect and more judicial," wrote Alex Boraine. "His hugging . . . and his declaration of love and admiration left the Commission wide open to the charge of bias." The country's leading judicial commentator, Carmel Rickard, reflected the legal establishment's unease with Tutu's dual role of pastor and quasi-judicial officer. His "legendary skills" had foundered, she said. "Why was the chairman of the commission abasing himself before her [Madikizela Mandela] to obtain some formula of repentance, when she had made it quite clear that she admitted no wrong?"

Tutu, as usual under fire, was unrepentant. Echoing his reaction to de Klerk's apology for apartheid four years earlier, he said, "I am not sure that we are right to scoff at even what might appear a halfhearted request for forgiveness. It is never easy to say, 'I am sorry.' . . . The prophet Isaiah speaks of the servant of God who is gentle and does not blow out a flickering flame." This did not mean he shied away from the truth. The following year he signed the commission's findings on Madikizela Mandela. It found that those who opposed her and the football club were branded as informers and killed. She knew of or took part in the activities of club members, or they were authorized or sanctioned by her, or both: "Further . . . she is accountable, politically and morally, for the gross violations of human rights committed by the Mandela United Football Club. The Commission finds further that Ms. Madikizela-Mandela herself was responsible for committing such gross violations of human rights."

Tutu never admired F. W. de Klerk in the way he had admired Winnie Madikizela Mandela, but he had far higher expectations for him than he ever had for P. W. Botha—probably too high. While working at Bishopscourt in the early 1990s, the present writer had the sense that Tutu longed for de Klerk to be a Beyers Naude—one of those Afrikaners who were not "clever and subtle" like nominally antiapartheid English-speakers, but for whom there were no half measures when they converted to the antiapartheid cause. De Klerk was no Beyers Naude—if he had become one, he would surely have been dumped by his party. Despite Tutu's disappointment with de Klerk, in 1992 he used his right as a Nobel laureate to nominate the then president jointly with Nelson Mandela for the Peace Prize. "These two," he wrote to the Norwegian Nobel Committee, "will have played and are playing a crucial role in the business of dismantling apartheid." The committee chose another candidate that year but returned to serious consideration of South Africans in 1993. The odds were against de Klerk; to Norway's antiapartheid forces, awarding the prize to him seemed a little like rewarding a man for stopping the beating of his wife. The committee was a week late in making its announcement. Before doing so, its secretary, Geir Lundestad, put in a rare call to Tutu. It had been more than eighteen months since Tutu's joint nomination. What, Lundestad asked, did Tutu think of the idea now? Tutu gave it his unreserved support. De Klerk and Mandela received the prize together in a tense joint visit to Oslo in December.

De Klerk was unhappy with the Truth and Reconciliation Commission from the outset. He considered his party's failure to win a comprehensive amnesty for all as probably its greatest defeat. After liberation, the party fought the ANC to get a law to which it would consent, but de Klerk was dismayed when Mandela presented him with a list of the commissioners. He would have preferred a body such as Chile had established, with the old and new governments represented equally. Mandela's vision was different; the TRC would be broadly representative of South African society, except that it would include only two members who had explicitly supported apartheid—one a right-wing opponent of the National Party. De Klerk decided that he could live with Tutu—although biased, he had proved his independence. He had much more serious reservations about Boraine, whose vehement opposition to apartheid in the white parliament had earned him a reputation among Afrikaner Nationalists as a "Boerehater" (an Afrikaner-hater). Writing of Boraine later in his autobiography, de Klerk said: "Beneath an urbane and deceptively affable exterior beat the heart of a zealot and an inquisitor."

De Klerk made his first presentation to the TRC before the amnesty hearings of the Vlakplaas commanders Cronje and Coetzee and their men. He acknowledged that security forces, frustrated by their incapacity to deal with revolutionary strategies, had developed "unconventional counterstrategies" which were planned on a "need-to-know" basis. But "within my knowledge and experience, they never included the authorisation of assassination, murder, torture, rape, assault or the like." Neither did he or his colleagues "directly or indirectly ever suggest, order or authorise any such action." When he gave evidence a second time, the confessions of the Security Branch's commanders and underlings had changed the landscape. He said in written evidence that the overwhelming majority of party members had been horrified at the revelations but they were not prepared to accept responsibility for the "criminal actions of a handful of operatives." In an oral submission, he reiterated his apology of 1993 for apartheid but added: "Many things happened which were not authorised, not intended and of which we were not aware. The recent information of atrocities I find as shocking and as abhorrent as anybody else."

At that point, de Klerk dug in. Under extensive cross-examination, he rejected "with every fibre of energy which I have" the contention that his government had presided over systematic, state-sanctioned violence: "It is unthinkable, [in] my whole physical, spiritual experience . . . unthinkable that anyone would callously say, because of this [threats to security] we relieve everybody of all moral and religious responsibility to act as Christians within the framework of the . . . law." Replying to a statement by Tutu that the abuses hardly constituted aberrations when they continued for so long and involved such senior figures, he questioned the veracity of applicants for amnesty who said their actions had been authorized from above. After the hearing adjourned, Antjie Krog saw Tutu slumped in his chair, "his shoulders covered in defeat." He had been desperate for a white South African leader to stand up, acknowledge the past fully, and find a way of taking responsibility for it so that the country could move on.

The next day, Tutu's face crumpled up in distress when a journalist asked him about the hearing at a news conference. Composing himself, he said he had hoped for statesmanship. He could not comprehend how de Klerk could insist he had been unaware of atrocities; he himself had reported allegations that the security forces were involved in the Boipatong massacre. (He may have meant Sebokeng.)

> There was an avalanche of information. To say I did not know . . . I find that hard to understand. I have to got to say that I sat there and I was close to tears. I feel sorry for him. I am devastated. [For him] to make an impassioned apology . . . and then to negate it. All that is required is to say that "we believed in this policy but it is a policy that brought about all of his suffering. It is a policy that killed people. Not by accident, deliberately. It was planned."

Later, Tutu would write that had he known in 1993 what he knew five years later, he would have vehemently opposed the award of the Nobel Prize to de Klerk, who had become "a small man, lacking magnanimity and generosity of spirit."

The commission's frustration at failing either to pin responsibility for violations of human rights on de Klerk, or to engage him in Tutu's effort to find a white leader to accept accountability for atrocities, was displayed in the embarrassing weakness of its finding against him. On the ground that he failed to disclose to the TRC that he had been told during his presidency that P. W. Botha authorized the bombing of Khotso House, the commission found him an accessory to gross violations of human rights. De Klerk challenged the finding, the commission backed down, and its main report in 1998 was issued with the relevant page blacked out. Four years later, the final report—issued after the Amnesty Committee had completed its work—recorded a watered-down finding saying merely that de Klerk had failed to make full disclosure and that in view of his knowledge, his statement that none of his colleagues had authorized gross violations was "indefensible."

The commission had more success, in varying degrees, with some of de Klerk's colleagues. Adriaan Vlok denied authorizing killings and

torture but conceded that words used in the State Security Council–
"eliminate," "neutralize," "take out," "destroy"–could have been "mis-
understood" by policemen. Roelf Meyer, a former deputy police
minister, said with the benefit of hindsight that more stringent steps
should have been taken to curb transgressions. The clearest acceptance
of responsibility came from Leon Wessels, also once a deputy police
minister but better known to Tutu as a member of Parliament for
Krugersdorp who had spoken out against the forced removal of Munsieville, and also the first Nationalist to apologize in Parliament for
apartheid. "I . . . do not believe," Wessels told the commission, "that
the political defence of 'I did not know' is available to me, because in
many respects I believe I did not want to know. . . . I had my suspicions
. . . but because I did not have the facts to substantiate my suspicions or
I lacked the courage to shout from the rooftops, I have to confess that
I only whispered in the corridors." There was no outcry when Tutu
hugged Meyer and Wessels after their testimony.

F. W. de Klerk acknowledged in his autobiography that the TRC
badly damaged his image. After its main report was published, a
newspaper headlined his presence at a meeting of the State Security
Council in 1984 at which an education minister wanted two teachers in
the Eastern Cape town of Cradock "removed." Fifteen months later the
teachers were among four people–one of them Babalwa Mhlauli's
father–murdered by the police. De Klerk told the newspaper the
intention had been that the teachers should be transferred to another
town. The writer, exploring the damage that the clash between Tutu
and de Klerk did to their relationship, asked de Klerk what had gone
through his mind when he heard of the deaths of the teachers. Did he
ever think, there's something wrong here? De Klerk's answer, given
Tutu's willingness to encourage "flickering flames," might have
enhanced the commission's potential to promote reconciliation had it
come eight years earlier.

De Klerk: I never knew about this and I was never part of any policies
authorizing it. But where maybe I failed was not asking more questions,
not going on a crusade about things . . . following up on a slight uncom-
fortableness you feel here and there. . . . In my case, I'm not saying I
didn't want to know. But I do think, with the advantage of hindsight,
that I was at times maybe not strong enough on following up on my
instincts. But that doesn't take away from the fact that at no time was
any decision taken of which I was part, where I felt, "This is actually

authorising assassination or cold-blooded murder." And I remember distinctly one incident, which I didn't write about [in the autobiography] and therefore will not identify, where I, at a function, got extremely upset, because what I heard was meaning that there had been what in my [judgement] would mean unacceptable behaviour. And I exploded in front of three of the top security people in South Africa.

The writer: Is this in the eighties?

De Klerk: Yes. And they took me aside and on their words of honour they assured me that my suspicions on that particular occasion were unfounded.

Writer: Do you recall generally what the nature of the issue was? That people had been killed?

De Klerk: Ja [yes], there were deaths involved. And on their word of honour [they] assured me . . . and it was people I had respect for.

Contrary to the commission's expectations, the presentation of its five-volume, 2,700-page main report in October 1998 focused local and international attention neither on its key declaration that apartheid, as a system of enforced racial discrimination and separation had been a crime against humanity, nor on its primary finding that most gross violations of human rights in South Africa had been committed by the former state through its security and law-enforcement agencies. Instead, the world was presented with news dominated by the ANC's violations. This was a consequence of the ANC's spectacularly shooting itself in the foot.

The commission, and Desmond Tutu in particular, had a number of run-ins with the party during its life, particularly over the suggestion of some of its officeholders that since it had fought in a just cause its members had no need to apply for amnesty. Tutu insisted that with regard to amnesty the law drew no distinction between fighters for and against apartheid; if they had broken the law, they needed amnesty if they wanted immunity from prosecution. He threatened to resign if the ANC refused to join the amnesty process. The party complied, but some of its leaders—and some commissioners—continued to have difficulty accepting the concept that it could be held responsible for violations. Some weeks before the main report was finalized, the commission sent out notices giving people and parties against whom it intended making findings the opportunity to make written representations. The draft findings sent to the ANC said that attacks on civilian targets (which were contrary to ANC policy), a land mine campaign on border farms, the killing of informers, and the torture and execution of suspected enemy agents or mutineers in its military camps in exile were all gross violations of human rights. They also held the ANC morally and politically accountable for violations committed by its supporters in the course of the "people's war" of the 1980s in the townships and by members of the self-defense units it had created and armed in the early 1990s.

The ANC reacted to its notice by asking to meet the commission. Dumisa Ntsebeza, acting in place of Tutu and Boraine, who had taken lecturing positions in the United States as the commission wrapped up its work, refused; it would have fatally damaged the TRC's credibility to grant a meeting to one party and not others. The ANC produced its representations late, after the report had gone to the printers, and then apparently lobbied sympathetic commissioners. Two days before the report was due, simultaneously, to be handed to Mandela and published, a group of commissioners argued that the question of a meeting be reopened. Tutu was staggered: "I really could not believe what I was hearing. . . . I had a hollow sensation in the pit of my stomach as I saw the whole enterprise sinking without trace." Their resolution was narrowly defeated, whereupon the group proposed that the ANC's late representations be considered. The vote was split evenly, seven for and seven against. Tutu settled the matter by voting against the proposal.

The next day, the eve of publication, the ANC announced it would apply for a High Court interdict to stop the commission from publishing any part of the report implicating the party until it had considered their submissions. Now Tutu was incensed; a delegation representing the 21,000 victims who had given statements to the commission—for him, the most important people in the process—had traveled to Pretoria, ready to meet Mandela the following morning. The prospect of victims' being slapped in the face was unbearable, and Tutu's anger spilled over into hyperbole. In a remark that still rankled the ANC's leaders years later, he told journalists: "Let me say I have struggled against a tyranny. I didn't do that in order to substitute another. If there is tyranny and an abuse of power, let them know I will fight it."

On publication day, beginning at six AM, teams of reporters from international news agencies and major domestic news outlets began to arrive at the venue of the handover. The report was scheduled to be handed to journalists when they arrived, on condition nothing was published before the report was handed to Mandela at noon. If the TRC's operation had gone according to plan, the reporters would have had up to six hours in which to read the report, increasing the chances that their stories would cover the full spectrum of findings. They would have seen twenty-four pages of findings against the former government and its allies. They would have seen six pages against the ANC and UDF, based on the party's own evidence, already published and canvassed fully at a high-profile hearing eighteen months earlier. But the report had to be withheld from journalists pending the outcome of the court case. With nothing to do, they waited around for four hours speculating on what the ANC had found so objectionable. When the court dismissed the application, they had little more than an hour in which to read the report and file copy. Their lead stories dealt with the controversy over the findings against the ANC.

The ANC's were not the only criticisms of the commission's report and operations. The most vocal academic critic of the TRC said it had let the beneficiaries of apartheid off lightly by making villains of a small number of perpetrators and by not including in its definition of gross violations of human rights the millions forcibly relocated from their homes. Other commentators accused it of bias in favor of the ANC and of failing to test evidence properly and to substantiate its findings fully. The Inkatha Freedom Party (IFP) and Mangosuthu Buthelezi challenged in court the finding that the party was responsible for gross violations and that Buthelezi was accountable in his representative capacity. (The case was settled by amending some findings and by including in the final report a statement by the IFP contesting others.) The commission also failed to flush out members of the military death squads. Only thirty-three members of the old South African Defence Force—mostly soldiers implicated by policemen in joint operations—applied for amnesty. And the commission lamented its inability to make breakthroughs of more substance than those of the Goldstone commission in its investigation of the violence of the transition.

Perhaps the principal achievement of the TRC was that the spectacle of policemen confessing to heinous crimes in front of television cameras, their words and images reverberating in news bulletins night after night, left white South Africans with no place to hide. They knew all about necklacings and "terrorist attacks"—the former government had seen to that, and had jailed or hanged many of those responsible. Now they saw the lengths to which some of their fathers, brothers, and sons had gone to preserve white privilege. They could turn off

their televisions or change channels during the news but, as Antjie
Krog warned them, "If you cut yourself off from the process, you will
wake up in a foreign country—a country that you don't know and that
you will never understand."

The drama notwithstanding—or perhaps because of it—the TRC
became a prophet without honor in its own country. Foreign leaders,
such as Shimon Peres of Israel and President Roman Herzog of Germany praised or awarded honors to Mandela, Tutu, and Boraine.
Amnesty in exchange for the truth, healing in place of retribution, was
hailed as something extraordinary in the life of nations, and ubuntu-
botho as an exciting new concept for humankind. At home, the commission was a victim of its own success: the gruesome revelations led
to popular calls for criminal trials and an end to amnesty; but that was
impossible, not least because it was only amnesty which produced
most of the revelations. Members and supporters of the liberation
movements applied for amnesty—998 from the ANC and 138 from the
PAC—and reactions to decisions became highly partisan. When your
side received amnesty, you rejoiced; when the other side received it,
you denounced the TRC. Because the commission's mandate was
gross violations of human rights, by its very nature it highlighted the
grubbiest, not the most glorious, episodes in the struggle of the past
three decades. It was as if South Africa, presented with a mirror reflecting the depths of moral depravity to which it had sunk under
apartheid, wanted to smash the mirror.

South Africa's most experienced investigator of political violence
and war crimes was Richard Goldstone, who after presiding over the
standing commission of inquiry into violence during the transition
went to The Hague as the first chief prosecutor of the International
Criminal Tribunals for the former Yugoslavia and Rwanda. After
preparing cases for those tribunals, he had no doubt that amnesty in
South Africa achieved more than the country could have expected
from prosecutions. Recording the history of human-rights abuses
would have taken "scores of long and costly trials," and the difficulty of
proving cases beyond a reasonable doubt would have resulted in
many acquittals. "In the great majority of cases," he told the present
writer, "I don't think the choice was amnesty or trial; it was amnesty or
nothing. . . . It would have been a very messy, unhappy situation."
Goldstone characterized the success of the TRC as analogous to that of
the tribunal on Yugoslavia. In the latter, people on each of the three
sides believed that they were victims and denied that they were perpe-

trators, "when in truth they were all victims and all perpetrators to a greater or lesser extent." The war crimes tribunal ended the denials. Similarly in South Africa:

> The greatest gift that the TRC has given to our people is a single history of what happened during the apartheid years in the area of serious human rights violations. Without the TRC there would undoubtedly have been roughly speaking two major histories . . . a black history which would have been approximately the truth, because the victims know what happened to them, and . . . a white history which would have been based on fabricated denials. . . . The TRC has put an end to those denials.

Could the TRC have worked without Desmond Tutu? Its members had to ask this question a year into their work, in January 1997, when Tutu was diagnosed with prostate cancer. Pumla Gobodo-Madikizela, a member of the Human Rights Violations Committee, had already seen evidence that the symbolism of his presence was vital among victims—it "validated the pain they had suffered." To Antjie Krog, working as a journalist looking on, the TRC without Tutu was unthinkable: "Whatever role others might play, it is Tutu who is the compass. . . . It is he who finds language for what is happening." He was soon back at work—the bulk of the prostate was removed and the cancer proved not to have spread. Later in the year, Alex Boraine felt it acutely when Tutu, at Leah's insistence, left the country for two months for hormone and radiation therapy.* And it was Boraine—the man who might have run the TRC himself—who at the end of its work judged that of all the commissioners, Tutu came closest to being indispensable: "I don't think the Commission could have survived without the presence and person and leadership of Desmond Tutu."

---

* Tutu was treated again for prostate cancer in 1999 and in 2006.

CHAPTER 16

INTERNATIONAL ICON

The contemplative lifestyle to which Desmond Tutu aspired after Nelson Mandela's release eluded him. After the wild fluctuations of the transition from euphoria to despair, and then to euphoria again, came the Truth and Reconciliation Commission. Once the TRC had completed its main report, he took a two-year visiting professorship in the United States to get out from under the feet of his successor as archbishop, Njongonkulu Ndungane. From Emory University in Atlanta, he traveled widely on speaking engagements, thanking old friends for past support, and, by lending them his celebrity status, returning the help they had given his cause when he was unknown. He also signed up with an American speakers' agency to supplement his small pension as a clergyman. This was an unexpectedly lucrative decision, which gave him financial independence to an extent he and Leah could never have imagined when they were living in a garage in the East Rand forty years earlier. Returning to South Africa in 2000 he set up an office in Cape Town, run by Lavinia Browne, the personal assistant who had served him for 15 years. He and Leah divided their time between Soweto, where they remodeled their home in Orlando West; and Cape Town, where he retained the house in the former white suburb of Milnerton that he had bought when he was at the TRC.

Tutu continued to crave more time for meditation and prayer. But this longing conflicted with many other impulses: his inability to say no to friends; the attractions of the money to be earned on the speaking circuit; the energy he drew from crowds; his enjoyment of the limelight; the satisfaction that expounding the gospel continued to bring him; his anxiety over the teething pains of democratic South Africa; and, most controversially, the compulsion he felt to speak out when he believed people to be suffering as a result of injustice, no matter how unpopular it made him.

• • • •

On issues concerning the Anglican Church, nothing kept Tutu's name in the public eye after his retirement as archbishop more than his attitude toward homosexuality. In the 1970s he had been tolerant of gays but had mentioned them in sermons alongside drug addicts and the poor; by the turn of the century, however, he had become perhaps the world's most prominent religious leader advocating gay and lesbian rights. His reevaluation of the status of gays and lesbians was occasioned by his acceptance that sexual orientation was probably not a matter of choice. "In fact," he said in one of his earliest public comments on the issue, in 1990, "given the kind of treatment homosexuals get in society . . . it would be one of the most stupid things to say, 'That is what I want to be.' " Once he had accepted that sexual orientation, like race or gender, was a given, the conclusion was inevitable: discrimination against gays and lesbians was as wrong as that against blacks or women: "We struggled against apartheid because we were being blamed and made to suffer for something we could do nothing about. It is the same with homosexuality."

Despite elevating the struggle for gay and lesbian rights, in principle, to that against racism, Tutu did not succeed in changing the policy of the Anglican Church in South Africa. This policy was that homosexual orientation was acceptable, but homosexual lovemaking was not. Logically, this required gay or lesbian Anglicans to be celibate–a policy that was applied to the clergy, at least nominally. Tutu felt bound as the leader of his church to accept the policy, but he dissented from it: "Why should we want all homosexual persons not to give expression to their sexuality in loving acts? Why don't we use the same criteria to judge same-sex relationships that we use to judge whether heterosexual relationships are whole or not?"

Anglican policy in southern Africa reflected policy in much of the worldwide communion. As the Lambeth Conference of bishops for 1998 approached, lobbies began pressing for change. As a retired bishop, Tutu did not attend the conference, which proved to be a disaster for those who wanted the church to reform its attitudes. Early discussions deteriorated into sometimes ugly confrontations, during one of which a bishop tried to drive the "demon" of homosexuality out of a gay priest. Proposals from bishops in east and west African churches sought to call on gays and lesbians to repent of their sin. The proposals failed, but the final conference resolution explicitly rejected "homosexual practice" as "incompatible with Scripture."

Privately, Tutu wrote to George Carey, who had succeeded Robert

Runcie as archbishop of Canterbury, that "I am ashamed to be an Anglican." In public, Tutu initially withheld comment, feeling that as a retired archbishop without a constituency to hold him accountable, he should refrain from complicating the lives of his former colleagues. He was unable to keep quiet for long. Although he turned down invitations to single-issue conferences on the subject, he began to include, in speeches and sermons, careful remarks which made his position clear. He approved in principle of church blessings for lesbian and gay relationships but stopped short of using the word "marriage" for the ceremony: "It just causes a lot of hassles. If you say you are blessing a union, I would prefer that." Exposure to specific instances of discrimination prompted more vigorous language, as when Jeffrey John, a canon of Southwark Cathedral in London, was forced to withdraw his acceptance of a nomination as a bishop because of his sexual orientation. From the cathedral in 2004, Tutu denounced such discrimination as being as unjust as apartheid ever was: "The Jesus I worship is not likely to collaborate with those who vilify and persecute an already oppressed minority."

While England's Crown Appointments Commission was considering a replacement for Runcie in 1990, a nonvoting member of the commission asked a member of Tutu's staff for details of his place and date of birth. The purpose was, he explained, to explore Tutu's eligibility to succeed Runcie. Tutu was not eligible—he was not in a position to swear allegiance to the queen of England—and in any event Robin Eames of Ireland was a more likely candidate if the church had looked outside England. Had Tutu been offered the appointment, there is no doubt he would have been strongly tempted to accept, for he loved the Anglican Communion. He saw it as a family—one, like his own, that was at times untidy, squabbling, and rambunctious but all the more lovable in consequence. He was attracted by the tolerance and inclusiveness of Anglicanism, by its appeal to reason as well as to tradition and scripture, and by the freedom of its constituent churches from the dictates of centralized authority.

It was, therefore, with sadness that from retirement he observed the conflict besetting the communion after the election of Gene Robinson, a gay man, as bishop of New Hampshire in 2003. He found it little short of outrageous that church leaders should be obsessed with issues of sexuality in the face of the challenges of AIDS and global poverty. And he also thought that Carey's successor, Rowan Williams, was too accommodating of conservatives who demanded that the churches of the United States and Canada should recant their tolerance for gays and lesbians under threat of expulsion from the communion. He told the present writer in an interview that if the conservatives did not like the inclusiveness of the Anglican Communion, "then [they] have the freedom to leave."

In his international ministry, Tutu responded to invitations, usually from churches or human rights lobbies, to make one-off visits designed by his hosts to help them achieve wider, long-term objectives. While he was archbishop, they were squeezed between his domestic commitments: for example, between the Cape Town march of September 1989 and the release of Nelson Mandela, he traveled on three separate trips to Egypt, Ethiopia and the Sudan; Israel/Palestine; and the United States. As a result, his interventions in any one country were sporadic and episodic by their very nature. Nevertheless, a common theme ran through his international campaigning, considered as a whole: democracy, human rights and tolerance, to be achieved by dialogue and accommodation between enemies. For some of Tutu's audiences, this message was not as welcome when preached in their countries as it was when they observed it being practiced in South Africa, demonstrating that it is sometimes easier to admire a prophet from afar.

Tutu's ministry outside South Africa began in earnest well before his retirement, when he was invited to give the keynote address to the fifth general assembly of the All Africa Conference of Churches (AACC) in Lomé, Togo, in 1987. The AACC was a council of Protestant churches, the continent-wide equivalent of the SACC in South Africa or of the World Council of Churches globally. Speaking on what it meant to witness for Christ in Africa, Tutu told the assembly, "We are true witnesses if we are on the side of the weak, the powerless, the exploited." Drawing on his experiences during the previous decade, when he traveled across the continent for the Theological Education Fund, he said that Africa's churches were the only institutions in a position to champion the interests of the voiceless and oppressed:

> It pains us to have to admit that there is less freedom and personal liberty in most of independent Africa than there was during the much-maligned colonial days. The gospel of Jesus Christ cannot allow us to keep silent in the face of this. . . . We must be committed to the total liberation of God's children, politically, socially, economically. . . . This is most obviously so for your sisters and brothers in South Africa, but it

would be true too for many in independent Africa for whom all that seems to have changed is the complexion of the oppressor.

Part of the reason Tutu was invited to Lomé was that the AACC had a leadership crisis. By the end of the assembly, he had been elected its president. At the same meeting, an Angolan church official, José Belo Chipenda, was chosen as the body's new full-time general secretary. Chipenda was a skilled and sophisticated church diplomat, fluent in Africa's three main lingua francas of government–English, French, and Portuguese. Together, the two men formed a decade-long partnership in which they worked for an "African renaissance," a phrase Tutu first adopted when he received an honorary degree from the National University of Benin in 1991.

Tutu's and Chipenda's terms of office coincided with what scholars have called Africa's "new struggle for democracy"–its "second wave" of liberation, which saw the number of multiparty democracies in the continent grow from just five in 1989 to thirty-six in 1995.* The AACC made it its business to support member churches–sometimes by prodding them, at others by backing efforts they initiated themselves–campaigning for human rights. Tutu's most important contribution to this struggle was the support he brought to member churches in visits to their countries. He exploited his international fame to arrange meetings with heads of state, often securing for his local hosts access that they were normally denied. Protected by his antiapartheid credentials, he was subject to fewer constraints than local church leaders when he spoke in public. Typically, his sermons dealt ostensibly with the oppression of apartheid; in reality the specific abuses with which he illustrated them would be common to South Africa and to his host country.

Tutu and Chipenda traveled to Zaire in 1989 to help the churches step back from the close relationship with Mobutu Sese Seko, which Tutu had seen developing in the early 1970s. Addressing theology students in Kinshasa, he might as well have been in South Africa when they spontaneously applauded him for saying that the Bible was "the most revolutionary book in a situation of oppression." God was on the side of the oppressed, he continued: "You are [here] to remind the church that whenever it is obedient to this Lord and Master, the

---

* The five in 1989, were Botswana, The Gambia, Mauritius, Senegal, and Zimbabwe.

church will end up, as its Lord and Master, on the Cross. Because when the church speaks up on behalf of the weak and the poor, the powerful and the rich don't like it. (Laughter.) . . . A church that does not suffer is not the Church of Jesus Christ. (Cheers.)" Amid tension between Mobutu and students, the authorities changed the venue of a service at short notice from a stadium to the grounds of Parliament. Officials told Tutu that they wanted to honor him by having him speak from where Pope John Paul II had addressed the nation. The real reason became clear when Tutu arrived on Sunday morning–the parliamentary complex was surrounded by iron fences and the congregation by troops. Nevertheless, a congregation of 15,000 came to hear him condemn Africa's violations of human rights, and its military dictatorships.

In the Marxist-Leninist dictatorship of Mengistu Haile Mariam in Ethiopia, Tutu preached at an outdoor service, surrounded by bishops of the Ethiopian Orthodox Church in richly ornamented robes, sheltering from the sun beneath colorful, lace-trimmed umbrellas. He used a passage from his South African sermons, which he had also used in Zaire: "God is a God who sides with the hungry and the poor and the marginalised, and so we are able to tell the powerful everywhere, we tell the oppressor everywhere . . . 'Watch it! Watch it! Watch it! Because God comes to deliver!' " In both Ethiopia and Angola, Tutu questioned officials of the ruling parties on how many of their people were Marxists. They gave numbers that were tiny in proportion to the total population; in Angola they estimated that 10,000 of 60,000 party members were truly Marxist-Leninist, in a country of 9 million. Tutu thereupon challenged the head of state, José Eduardo dos Santos, asking how dos Santos could develop the country while excluding Christians from power.

Three years later, in the early months of the Clinton administration, Bill Clinton and his vice president, Al Gore, used the opportunity of a visit by Tutu to the Oval Office to announce the United States' recognition of the Angolan government. According to Anthony Lake, Clinton's national security adviser, they chose Tutu's visit as the occasion for the announcement because the decision to recognize Angola was controversial, after the hostility of previous administrations to its government, and Tutu was probably the least controversial of any foreign figure in Washington.

Tutu and Chipenda also sought to minister in civil wars. In Liberia, hundreds of people rushed the aircraft on which Tutu arrived in 1994 for a joint mission with the Carter Center of Atlanta, founded by the former U.S. president Jimmy Carter. Troops from the United Nations, and West African troops, eventually gave up trying to keep the crowd away. Subsequently, in more than twenty meetings and public addresses, Tutu said that if South Africa could settle its problems, so could Liberia. However, the meeting he, Chipenda, and the Carter Center held with the warlord Charles Taylor was chaotic. The party was flown in a UN Chinook helicopter to see Taylor at Gbarnga, capital of the fiefdom he called Greater Liberia. They met in an old tea plantation house, where Taylor did most of the talking, in a loud and agitated voice. He promised a cease-fire, but a member of the AACC delegation, Hugh McCullum, vividly recalled Tutu's appraisal of Taylor as a highly unstable person whose word was not to be trusted. (Taylor became president in 1997 and was ousted in 2003, to face indictment on charges of war crimes and crimes against humanity.)

After South Africa's democratic government came to power in 1994, Nelson Mandela took advantage of Tutu's status, bypassing normal diplomacy in 1995 by sending him to ask the Nigerian military dictator Sani Abacha to release the winner of the country's annulled 1993 election, M. K. O. Abiola; and the former head of state, Olesegun Obasanjo.* The mission was unsuccessful, although Tutu had a private meeting with Abiola in which Abiola rejected, point by point, most of the claims Abacha made about the conditions of his detention. Later, when democracy began to falter in Zimbabwe, Tutu described Robert Mugabe, formerly "a splendid leader . . . one of the bright stars in the African constellation," as a "caricature of an African dictator" who had "gone bonkers in a big way." Mugabe replied in kind: "He is an angry, evil and embittered little bishop . . . a frightened man during the apartheid era."

Tutu also campaigned widely on other African issues. In Sweden in 1993, he called for the African continent's foreign debt to be scrapped, on the biblical principle of forgiving debts in a "year of jubilee." A strong proponent of interfaith dialogue, he was nevertheless sensitive to the concerns of AACC members in East and West Africa who felt threatened by Islamic fundamentalism, and appealed to Muslim nations to respect the freedom of worship of Christian minorities.

The most difficult and emotionally taxing mission that Tutu and Chipenda undertook for the AACC was to Rwanda in July 1995. Tutu went there the year after hundreds of thousands of Rwandans,

---

* Later the democratically elected president of Nigeria.

armed with pangas and nail-studded clubs called masus, and incited by
extremists from the majority Hutu group, hacked and beat to death
somewhere between 800,000 and 1 million of their neighbors–mostly
members of the Tutsi group but also Hutu moderates–in a period of
100 days. Chipenda and Tutu flew into Rwanda from neighboring
Burundi, where they had been mediating between rival politicians in
an attempt to help prevent a conflict between similar groups from
erupting into large-scale violence. In Bujumbura, the capital of
Burundi, nights in their hotel had been punctuated by the sound of
gunfire in the suburbs. As they checked into the Hôtel del Mille
Collines ("Hotel of a Thousand Hills," the "Hotel Rwanda" in the
film of that name), in Rwanda's capital, Kigali, it was much quieter; the
genocide was over and the country was ruled by a coalition installed
by the Rwandan Patriotic Front (RPF), which was led by the Tutsi and
had driven the *génocidaires* from power.

In Kigali Tutu and Chipenda joined a group of evangelical Christians from the organization African Enterprise, in an effort to show a
combined front of the evangelical and ecumenical strains in world
Christianity. From the day he arrived, Tutu counseled Rwandans
against pressing for "total justice" in response to the genocide. There
should be no blanket amnesty, and the truth had to be revealed, he
told a news conference, but justice needed to be tempered with mercy.
Preaching to 10,000 people at a Sunday service in Kigali's main stadium, he reached–perhaps unconsciously–for the words he had used
twenty-two years earlier in his report on the region for the Theological
Education Fund.

The history of Rwanda, he averred, was a story of "top dog" and
"underdog," in which two groups had striven for generations to dis-
lodge each other from power, imposing retribution when they succeeded and suffering it when they failed. He referred to the fact that the
Tutsi aristocracy favored by the Belgian colonial authorities had been
deposed from power on independence in 1962 and had waited thirty
years to return. The Hutu majority, he suggested, would be capable of
doing the same. The cycle of reprisal and counter-reprisal had to be
broken. The only way to do that was to move beyond retributive justice to restorative justice and forgiveness. Rwanda's coalition leaders
were in the stadium. Pasteur Bizimungu, the country's president–a
Hutu moderate–used his opportunity to speak to question–politely–
Tutu's case. They were ready to forgive, he said, but even Jesus had
said the devil could not be forgiven. Tutu wondered privately what Biz-

imungu's source was; nevertheless, he was grateful to receive a friendly hearing.

During the service at the stadium, José Chipenda told Tutu that the planners of the mission wanted him to visit the main prison in Kigali, where thousands of people suspected of genocide were being held. However, the government was not responding. Could Tutu ask Bizimungu directly to set up the visit? Tutu did so, and a group from the AACC and African Enterprise was given access that afternoon. The group members entered to find a sea of faces, singing, shouting, and cheering. The prisoners, dressed in pale pink overalls, were packed so tightly together from wall to wall that they had to squeeze against one another to clear a path for the visitors. They reported that there were more than 9,000 prisoners in a space built to hold 1,500, and that 500 had died; they had to sit and sleep in shifts because there was insufficient space for all to lie down at the same time. Tutu was appalled at the conditions. The prison, he told journalists on his way out, was a disaster waiting to happen.

The following morning, the program was changed on short notice. The reason was not made clear, but it appeared as if the government, disturbed by Tutu's apparent ambivalence over the rights and wrongs of Rwanda, wanted to bring home to him the full horror of the genocide. He was taken to see a small, worn redbrick church with an iron roof, situated in rolling hills at the end of a red dirt road about thirty kilometers (19 miles) south of Kigali. Part of the story of what had happened there was already known; the rest was told early in 2006, when a former governor of the local préfecture went on trial, charged with genocide and crimes against humanity, at the International Criminal Tribunal for Rwanda in Arusha, Tanzania. On April 14, 1994, a week into the killing, the governor, François Karera, told frightened Tutsi refugees at the Ntarama school that he would bring soldiers to protect them and that they should shelter in the church. The next day he allegedly led a convoy of six buses carrying about 200 soldiers and interahamwe (Hutu youth militia) to the church. "I don't want to see one Tutsi person alive in Ntarama sector by tonight," he is alleged to have told them. The attackers broke open the windows and lobbed in grenades—perhaps some of the 20,000 fragmentation grenades sold to Rwanda by South Africa. Then they slaughtered the survivors with guns and pangas.

Just outside the church, Tutu and the others found neat rows of bleached skulls, piled up high on a shaded platform roughly fashioned from tree branches. Led into the dimly lighted church, they made out in the gloom what at first glance seemed to be rubbish strewn on and between the low wooden benches. It took only seconds to discern the sickly-sweet smell of death, which pierces the mind so deeply that somehow it returns to the nostrils for days afterward. They were walking on and among the fifteen-month-old remains of human beings, lying where they had been cut down, their decayed flesh covered in rotting clothes. Coming out of the church, Tutu turned to gaze at the pile of skulls. Overwhelmed, he broke down, sobbing inconsolably. It was some time before he regained his composure enough to continue the journey to the nearby "Nelson Mandela Peace Village," where he gave a short speech likening its work to resurrection after crucifixion.

Back in Kigali for meetings with political leaders and the transitional national assembly, Tutu amended his approach slightly without allowing himself to be deflected from his core message. He told Bizimungu and his vice president, the RPF leader Paul Kagame, that they had to do something about the overcrowding in the prisons. This led to a creative discussion, during which Kagame, widely said to be the military strongman behind the government, acknowledged that it would be impossible to place every perpetrator on trial. Tutu prefaced his speech to the national assembly by spelling out explicitly what he believed to be self-evident: that the genocide was evil and inexcusable. But, he continued to maintain, it was not unforgivable.

Perhaps the moment at which Tutu touched Rwandans—or at least their church leaders—most directly was in an after-dinner speech. The churches were as torn by the genocide as any institution. Some of the clergy had bravely saved congregants; others had been accomplices or even killers, either wholeheartedly or to save their families' lives; and many who supported the deposed regime had fled the country. Tutu related a story he usually told in South Africa, which poked fun at prejudice by asking listeners to imagine nose size instead of skin color as the physical attribute determining access to privilege and opportunity. As elsewhere in the world, the story was greeted with hilarity. However, in this country it resonated at a particularly deep level. For although social anthropologists suggested that Hutus and Tutsis were politically rather than ethnically defined groups, the reality was that facial features were popularly thought to be an indicator of identity—the typical Tutsi was held to have a small, slim nose and the Hutu a broad, flat nose. Ending his speech Tutu revealed that he knew this. The laughter was more hesitant—rather nervous and scattered—as he dragged the issue into the open and drove his point home by paraphrasing Christ's words in Matthew's gospel: "Inasmuch as you did to the least of these, to this kind of nose, or that kind of nose, you did it to me. You killed this one because the nose is like this, you killed this one because the nose is like that, you killed God. You killed Jesus Christ."*

Desmond Tutu's most contested work outside South Africa was in countries where he urged governments to negotiate with those they regarded as terrorists. His first high level experience of the tension in Northern Ireland was at the Lambeth Conference of 1988. Backed by South Africa's bishops, the conference passed a resolution on "war, violence, and justice" expressing understanding for those who, after exhausting other means, resorted to "armed struggle." There was an uproar in the British media; the Irish Republican Army (IRA) described its campaign to force Britain out of Ireland as an armed struggle. Some newspapers accused the bishops of "blessing terror." Unhappy Irish bishops brought a new resolution of their own. Tutu called Robin Eames, head of the Church of Ireland, out of the conference hall; and they quickly agreed on a compromise—a condemnation of all violence "in the circumstances of Northern Ireland." Tutu's agreement was based on his acceptance that since all had the vote in Northern Ireland, Republicans could not be said to have exhausted peaceful means of pursuing their cause.

Three years later, preaching in a televised service from Christ Church Cathedral, Dublin, Tutu caused renewed offense to some Unionists. The British government had begun all-party talks but was refusing to deal with Sinn Fein and the Provisional IRA. Another two years were to pass before Margaret Thatcher's successor, John Major, acknowledged secret contacts with Sinn Fein. Tutu began by carefully condemning all violence, from whatever quarter. He continued with an appeal for negotiations to be inclusive: "Don't let any feel they have been left out. Any group, however small, which has grievances, real or imaginary, must not feel excluded; otherwise you can kiss good-bye to peace. Let them be represented by those they regard as their authentic spokespersons." As Tutu went out of the cathedral at the end of the service, journalists flocked around him wanting to know whether he was calling for talks with Sinn Fein. Tutu's answer was as guarded as his

* The reference is to Matthew 25:40.

sermon—the Irish had to decide for themselves. He returned to the cathedral for a meeting with Mary Robinson, the Irish president, who had been at the service. As he was on the way inside, the British ambassador intercepted him in a corridor and begged him to keep quiet. There were delicate developments afoot, the diplomat said, and he could ruin everything.

By Tutu's next visit, the delicate developments had borne fruit. Five months after the Good Friday agreement of 1998, and two weeks after Unionist leader David Trimble had met Gerry Adams of Sinn Fein for the first time, Tutu traveled to Belfast to address peace activists. With the peace process bogged down in a dispute over decommissioning, he reassured anxious questioners that South Africa had survived similar crises. Robin Eames, whose Unionist constituency appeared not to allow him the freedom of action which Tutu asserted in South Africa, had not yet met Adams. Tutu, however, decided to accept an invitation to Connolly House, the Sinn Fein headquarters in west Belfast. There, and in meetings with Trimble and John Hume of the Social Democratic and Labour Party, he explored ideas on how to resolve the deadlock. Three years later, he was again exposed to Northern Ireland's sectarian divisions when he visited a Catholic primary school in north Belfast that was the object of demonstrations by Unionists.

In the Middle East, Tutu's first appeals for negotiations and the recognition of a Palestinian state, controversial enough in any case, were complicated by other factors.

A harbinger of the heat that was to surround his participation in discussions over Israel and Palestine was a spirited argument in New York in 1987 with Ed Koch, the city's mayor. Tutu was invited to meet Koch in an arrangement made by his friend Hays Rockwell. The mayor's relations with black New Yorkers were such that Rockwell devised a stratagem for getting the two together; he went through the charade of inviting Tutu to his apartment, only to take him upstairs to a dinner party with neighbors at which Koch was also a guest. Rockwell recalled what ensued:

> We had a glass of wine and then Desmond and Ed started to argue and they fought for two and a half hours. . . . You know what the topic was? Same topic all the way through—should the nation-state of Israel have special status in the eyes of the nations? . . . Desmond's pain arose

from . . . [Israel's] having sold arms to the apartheid government. Koch said, "You can't hold Israel to higher standards than anyone else." Desmond argued, no, they became a nation-state because of their promise to be a light to the nations, and they're not a light to the nations when they sell arms to apartheid governments. . . . The hostess was in tears. She said the party was ruined. . . . But those guys . . . just went at it.

The topic of military cooperation between Israel and South Africa had been in the public arena in the United States since at least 1971, when C. L. Sulzberger reported in the *New York Times* on the close, if little-known, relationship between the two countries. There was, he wrote, "considerable military understanding," but specifics were "unconfirmable and wholly blanketed by security." Heavily edited documents from the late 1970s and 1980s, declassified through the work of the National Security Archive at George Washington University, show that the U.S. intelligence community kept a close watch on reports of military and nuclear cooperation. The former White House expert on counterterrorism, Richard A. Clarke, has recorded how he was sent to Israel in 1987, after passage of the Comprehensive Anti-Apartheid Act, to convey the message that defense relations with South Africa had to end. The Israeli cabinet apparently agreed, but the Defense Intelligence Agency and the State Department were still reporting on possible cooperation through 1989.

Tutu took up the issue publicly on a visit to New York early in 1989. In a pivotal address at the Stephen Wise Free Synagogue, he also widened his criticisms with comments that became a flash point for an ongoing, sometimes heated debate. He began by describing how the scriptures known to Christians as the Old Testament—and especially the teachings of Israel's prophets—had underpinned his own preaching against apartheid. "You have been a tremendous light to the world," he said. "We are proud to acknowledge the riches of our Jewish heritage." He paid tribute to Jewish antiapartheid stalwarts such as Helen Suzman. He thanked God that Israel had come into being as a nation. He asserted Israel's right to "territorial integrity and fundamental security against attacks from those who deny her right to exist." He condemned all terrorism, from whatever source. He praised the Israelis' protests against massacres in Lebanese refugee camps: "Those protestors did Israel proud, and have shown that as a country it is fundamentally democratic. It is not afraid of self-criticism."

Turning eventually to South Africa, he said—to repeated applause—that he did not understand "how people with your kind of history could allow the government of Israel, as distinct from the people, to have the kind of relationship with the government of South Africa that it has. . . . We cannot understand how Jews can cooperate with a government many of whose members were sympathetic to Hitler and the Nazis." To criticize such cooperation was not anti-Semitic, he added: "Whether Jews so accuse me or not, I will continue to be highly critical of Israel in this regard." Entering more uncertain territory with his audience, he went on to say there was another obstacle in the way of better relations between blacks and Jews—the question of the Palestinians:

> I have not spoken on this issue in public before tonight because of apprehension that I would be called anti-Semitic. I have to say I find it very, very difficult to understand Israel's policy in this regard. I do not know all the factors that are involved. My position is made more difficult because of two factors. I am Christian, many of the Palestinians are Christians, in fact many are Anglicans, and their anguish tears my heart apart. Secondly, it is because I am a black South African, and if you changed the names, the description of what is happening in the Gaza Strip and the West Bank could be a description of what is happening in South Africa.
>
> It is uncanny and it is deeply, deeply distressing. Israel cannot do that. It is out of line with her biblical and historical traditions. Israel, or shall we say, the Jews, having suffered so much, cannot allow their government to cause other people to suffer so much. Jews, having been dispossessed for so long, cannot allow their government to dispossess others. Jews, having been victims of gross injustice, cannot allow their government to make others victims of injustice. It is such a horrific contradiction.

Some months after Tutu's address, a delegation of Anglican archbishops visited Jerusalem following one of their regular meetings. Tutu missed the trip but accepted an invitation from the bishop of Jerusalem, Samir Kafity, to make a pilgrimage over Christmas. Israeli officials viewed the prospect of his visit to Palestinian Anglicans with considerable apprehension. It was to be two years before the government headed by Yitzhak Shamir tentatively talked to Palestinians in Madrid, and four years before another government negotiated with the

Palestine Liberation Organization in Oslo. Tutu had met Yasir Arafat in October in Cairo (where, as well as discussing the situation of Palestinians in territories occupied by Israel, he had urged Arafat to recognize Israel's right to exist). The Israelis were sensitive in particular to the possibility that Tutu would draw parallels between Israel and South Africa. As the trip neared, officials raised fears that he would fuel the intifada, the Palestinian uprising which had begun in 1987. Kafity began to receive death threats. Tutu heightened Israelis' anxiety when he repeated to the newspaper *Ha'aretz* the sentiments of his address at the Stephen Wise synagogue.

It did not help that from the early 1980s, Tutu had made comments which were not as carefully worded as those of 1989. In South Africa, blacks looked with suspicion upon whites who said "some of my best friends are black." Tutu, in the eyes of many Jews, was guilty of similar behavior when he countered charges of anti-Semitism by saying, "My dentist is a Dr. Cohen." He caused distress even to liberal Jewish friends when he discussed the influence of pro-Israel forces in the United States. He would have been on safe ground with them if, for example, he had said—as a writer in the *New Yorker* was to say much later—that the American Israel Public Affairs Committee was "a leviathan among lobbies." Instead, speaking at the Jewish Theological Seminary in New York after winning the Nobel Prize, he appealed for support for the antiapartheid cause, saying, "Jews are a powerful lobby in this land." A sympathizer from the seminary, Burton L. Visotzky, spelled out in a private letter how Tutu's words had been received:

Like oppressed blacks, we have developed an acute ear for the rhetoric of oppression. It is for this reason that some in our community were surprised to hear such phrases from you as "powerful Jewish lobby," or "the Jews must be different," or "there isn't an anti-Semitic bone in my body." This language is normally associated with the discourse of the less than philo-Semitic elements of our acquaintance. It raises the hackles of even the most sympathetic Jewish audiences. Part of the problem lies in our hypersensitivity but part . . . lies in a lack of awareness of our concerns and agenda. Unfortunately, these faux pas may become the focus of your listeners' attentions and the central message of your address can be lost in the shuffle.

To the degree that Tutu followed Visotzky's advice later, he reduced the scope for attacks on himself. However, in December 1989 a vocal pro-Israel group opened its files, found the remark made at the seminary, and used it and other statements to prepare to counter what it predicted would be a "spectacular anti-Israel blitz in the world media."

Tutu arrived in Jerusalem with Michael Nuttall and Njongonkulu Ndungane, his executive officer, to find an atmosphere similar to what had been called a "black Christmas" at home after the Soweto uprising. In protest against Israel's occupation of the West Bank and the suppression of the intifada, Palestinian Christians were celebrating only religious rites. Decorations and gifts were discouraged. The pilgrimage began quietly with a round of calls on religious leaders and at Christian, Jewish, and Muslim holy places.

On Christmas Eve, Tutu went to preach at Shepherd's Field near Bethlehem, which lay outside Beit Sahour, a mostly Christian town under siege by the Israeli army. Disembarking from their cars, Tutu, Nuttall, and Kafity were mobbed by thousands of Palestinians. Defying the Israelis, members of the crowd waved olive branches and chanted, "ANC, PLO," "PLO, Israel No." Women held up signs reading, "No to racism and occupation; yes to democracy and independence." Carols and readings from the New Testament were interspersed with the exuberant responses of an impromptu political rally. To applause, shouts, and whistling, Tutu stated his support for Palestinian nationhood. "But," he added, "we say also, dear brothers and sisters, the Jews have a right to their independent state as well." As in some African countries, his descriptions of the plight of black South Africans resonated strongly with the Palestinians, who laughed as he repeatedly paused during his recitation and reminded them: "I'm talking about South Africa." Tutu said that something earth-shattering had happened in Bethlehem on the first Christmas night, and God had chosen to relay the news to shepherds: "God has a special caring for those whom the world thinks are not important. . . . God sides with those whom the world despises. . . . God sides with those whom the world brutalises. . . . God is with those whom it oppresses." This was translated by one reporter into a statement that God was on the side of the Palestinians, angering South Africa's chief rabbi.

Later that evening the Israeli authorities called St. George's Cathedral during midnight Mass to say there was a bomb threat. A suspicious Bishop Kafity did not want to evacuate, but Tutu said it was better to be safe. The congregation completed the service in an open-air courtyard. In a sermon to an Arabic-speaking congregation on Christmas morning, Tutu urged Israel to talk to the authentic representatives of Palestinians. The following morning, on his way to Yad Vashem, the

Holocaust memorial, Tutu saw a slogan daubed outside the Cathedral compound reading, "Tutu is a black Nazi pig."

Most of his program was planned by the local church. Yad Vashem was placed on the schedule at Tutu's request, at the suggestion of a Jewish friend in South Africa. Samir Kafity obliged, but some lay Anglicans privately tried to talk the party out of going. "The Holocaust is not the other side of the story," one argued. "We [the Palestinians] were not responsible for the Holocaust." Tutu nevertheless went, spending an hour touring the memorial. He laid a wreath, said a prayer, and wrote in a guest book, "It is a shattering experience and the world must never forget our inhumanity to one another." Outside, he told journalists it was important to remind the world that human beings could sink to such levels. It was also important to remember forgiveness: "As our Lord would say . . . and also what comes from the prophets . . . [is that] the positive thing that could come is the spirit of forgiving, not forgetting, but the spirit of saying, 'God . . . this happened to us, we pray for those who made it happen. Forgive them. Help us to forgive and help us so that we in our turn will not make others suffer.' "

His remarks, added to those on the Palestinians, received an avalanche of criticism. Ed Koch, in a new column for the *New York Post,* called Tutu a "standard third-world radical" acting with malice. The American Jewish Congress said that if he could not bring himself to say anything about the culpability of Christians for the Holocaust, "he might at least have observed a respectful silence." The Anti-Defamation League of B'nai Brith said he had shown a profound naïveté about Judaism. Israel's minister of religious affairs challenged the comparisons with South Africa, denying that Israel's political system was based on a doctrine of superiority. A demonstrator at the inauguration of David Dinkins as the first black mayor of New York City threw a water-filled balloon at the podium as Tutu began to speak. The balloon hit a city councilor. In May 1990, seven members of the militant Jewish Defense League appeared at a church in Pasadena, California, where Tutu was preaching to shout at him, "Why do you hate the Jews?" and "Death to the PLO!"

The Christmas pilgrimage also led to the toughest discussions Tutu had experienced with Jewish leaders. They were arranged by the Episcopal Church in Cincinnati, Ohio, where a delegation headed by Alfred Gottschalk, president of the Hebrew Union College–Jewish Institute of Religion, challenged Tutu for failing to understand the precarious position of Jews in much of the world. An impassioned Tutu deplored the refusal of Arab countries to recognize Israel's existence for so long but defended his criticism of government policies. In some respects the treatment of Palestinians was worse than that of black South Africans, he said: "I have not said so in public but I have seen things that shocked me. I have not in the experience of apartheid . . . [seen that] when a child in a home . . . has been found to have thrown stones, that the home of that child is bulldozed or . . . sealed." But he drew a firm distinction between Jews and Israel: "I am not accusing Jews. I am accusing the Israeli government." The meeting issued a joint statement saying that the Jewish leaders believed Tutu's criticism of Israel was "asymmetric" but shared his concerns about being unfairly targeted as being anti-Semitic.

Ten years later, after the Oslo Accords and the TRC hearings, Tutu traveled to Tel Aviv at the invitation of Shimon Peres–now also a Nobel Peace laureate–for a meeting of the Peres Center for Peace. He was worried about how he would be received, but after the meeting he was grateful to be welcomed by both Palestinians on the West Bank and Jews in Jerusalem, and especially pleased to be questioned in Jerusalem about South Africa's truth and reconciliation process. But his sense of well-being did not survive the collapse of the peace process at Camp David in 2000 and the election of a new Israeli government. In 2002 he denounced Israeli policies again in a widely publicized speech in Boston, followed up with a declaration of support for divestment from Israel. He was roundly condemned by the Simon Wiesenthal Center in Los Angeles. With no end to the nearly sixty-year struggle in sight, he again sought to compare South Africa and the Middle East. On this occasion, he highlighted the differences, in remarks critical of both Israelis and Palestinians: "One reason we succeeded in South Africa that is missing in the Middle East today is quality of leadership– leaders willing to make unpopular compromises, to go against their own constituencies, because they have the wisdom to see that would ultimately make peace possible."

Tutu's style of campaigning was more restrained when he was abroad than when he was at home. In the same way as he tried to avoid embroiling himself too deeply in the decision-making processes of other Anglican churches, he declined invitations to join street demonstrations in countries other than his own. He made an exception early in 2003, when he was in the United States as a scholar in residence at the University of North Florida in Jacksonville.

During American and British preparations for war against Iraq, he told a British current affairs television program that it was "mind-boggling" to conceive of Prime Minister Tony Blair as aiding and abetting George W. Bush. Some weeks later he spoke by telephone with Condoleezza Rice, Bush's national security adviser at the time, to urge that the United States not go to war without a resolution by the United Nations Security Council. Military action in the absence of such a mandate would be immoral, he told Rice, and he would publicly condemn it as evil. So strongly did he feel that also he broke with his normal practice to accept an invitation to support one of the antiwar rallies held across the United States—and the world—on the weekend of February 15 and 16.

In freezing temperatures, he joined a crowd on the streets of New York estimated by the police at 100,000. Protestors stretched from a temporary stage near the United Nations and up First Avenue as far as he could see—twenty city blocks. Others spilled over into Second and Third avenues. It was neither the time nor the place for long-winded speeches, and Tutu confined his remarks to six minutes. He cracked a joke about the weather and said God was pleased to see them: "God says, 'Hey, aren't they neat?' " He said the just war theory provided that only a legitimate authority could declare war. In this case only the United Nations was such an authority. The theory also laid down that war had to be a last resort. In this case peaceful means had not been exhausted. He ended with a South African–style display of street oratory:

Now I ask you what do we say to war? ("No!") I can't hear you! (Laughter.) What do you say to war? ("NO!") What do you say to death and destruction? ("NO!") What do you say to peace? ("Yes!") I can't hear you. What do you say to peace? ("YES!") What do you say to life? ("YES!") What do you say to freedom? ("Yes!") What do you say to compassion? ("Yes!") Well, we want to say: President Bush, listen to the voice of the people. For many times the voice of the people is the voice of God. (Cheers.) . . . Listen to the voice of the people saying, give peace a chance. (Cheers.) Give peace a chance. And let's say once more so they can hear at the Pentagon, they can hear in the White House. What do we say to war? ("NO!") What do we say to peace? ("YES!")

EPILOGUE

For those who struggle for fundamental change in societies built on long-standing and deeply-embedded structural injustice, it is rare to achieve that change in their own generation, and even rarer to live long enough to see its first fruits. Gandhi saw India become independent but did not survive the violence surrounding partition. Martin Luther King, Jr., famously told the people of Memphis the night before his assassination that he had been to the mountaintop and seen the "promised land," but he never entered it. As Desmond Tutu approached his seventy-fifth birthday in 2006, he felt both vindicated and blessed: vindicated because, as he put it, he loved to be loved, and the demise of apartheid brought to an end the calumny he had endured as public enemy number one; and blessed to be part of a generation that saw the release of prisoners, the return of exiles, and the inauguration of democracy.

This is not to say that Tutu believed the transition to democracy fulfilled his or God's vision for South Africa. Tutu's own vision was built on the metaphor of a rainbow, which he first used during the Defiance Campaign of 1989. Inspired by thousands of demonstrators–including an unprecedented number of whites–waving their hands from side to side at his bidding, he described them as the "rainbow people of God." Mandela later appropriated this metaphor, incorporating it in his inaugural address. After liberation, what critics called "rainbowism" fell on hard times. Some people, though probably quite a small minority, rejected the nonracial vision. Opposition of more substance came from those who associated it with a naive, sentimental belief in a nonexistent multiracial harmony–or, even worse, with acceptance of a status quo in which blacks still lived in poverty and whites in comfort. Despite the criticism, Tutu doggedly continued to work for a nation in which each of South Africa's cultural and language groups exhibited its

own distinct beauty, but one also in which the beauty of the whole
exceeded the sum of its parts:

> You keep trying to remind people that it's a rainbow because the
> colours . . . remain distinct but related. They hold together in their dif-
> ference. And their differences are important . . . you ought to be glory-
> ing in them. It speaks of something that has to be evolving, it's not
> static. It is idealistic in a way. You're saying we want to reach a point
> where we celebrate who we are, and yet know that we can't be who we
> are unless you can be who you are.

Sixty years after first arriving in Sophiatown, Tutu returned to the
Church of Christ the King in 2004 to deliver the inaugural lecture:
"Naught for Your Comfort," named after Trevor Huddleston's book.
Ten years after Nelson Mandela's inauguration and a few months into
Thabo Mbeki's second term as president, Tutu measured reality against
the hopes expressed at liberation. He commended the government for
its achievements but issued a series of warnings, beginning with the
widening disparities in material wealth:

> We have all left the house of apartheid's bondage. Some, an elite few,
> have actually crossed the Jordan into the promised land. Others, too
> many, still wallow in the wilderness of degrading, dehumanizing
> poverty. . . . Much has been done. People have clean water and electric-
> ity who never had these before but we are sitting on a powder keg
> because the gap between the rich and the poor is widening and some of
> the very rich are now black.

He went on to question spending on armaments, the government's
policies on Zimbabwe, and—most controversially—the dominance of
Nguni-speaking leaders in government, which he said might stoke
ethnic resentments "that could explode one day." He added that a
vibrant democracy depended on "vigorous debate, dissent, disagreements and discussion. . . . No one is infallible. . . . No government can
be God." The speech was hardly reported and passed almost unnoticed. Three months later, he made many of the same points when he
delivered the annual Nelson Mandela Lecture in Johannesburg. He
omitted the warning about ethnic tension, but he also focused more
clearly on Mbeki. He lauded the president's contributions to the pro-

motion of unity, peace, and development in Africa. Then, in comments that led to a searing, months-long controversy, Tutu charged that the ANC under Mbeki's leadership demanded a "sycophantic, obsequious conformity," which required of members of Parliament that they should be no more than the party's "voting cattle."

Tutu's relations with Mbeki had been rocky since before the president took office in 1999, mainly over the Truth Commission. Mbeki contended that the TRC had criminalized the military struggle against apartheid; Tutu that felt the government was halfhearted and slow to deliver reparations. Mbeki's reluctance to lead an all-out campaign against South Africa's HIV/AIDS pandemic added to the issues on which they disagreed. Tutu was an early campaigner against AIDS—he made public service announcements on television promoting the use of condoms and safe sex. The Nelson Mandela Lecture was given wide publicity, and Mbeki used his weekly letter on the ANC's website to write a scathing rebuttal. He assailed Tutu as a populist—this contention was reminiscent of Mandela's response to Tutu's "gravy train" speech—who had no respect for the truth, was ignorant of the inner workings of the party, and had gratuitously insulted its members. The party followed up with a series of ten papers, "The Sociology of the Public Discourse in Democratic South Africa," which defended Tutu's right to his opinions but said that they coincided with the positions of a right-wing elite, which had made him an icon and then had hijacked his criticisms for their own ends.

A suggestion of why the ANC was so sensitive had been given earlier in 2004 by Moeletsi Mbeki, a political commentator and businessman who was the president's brother. Addressing the African audience of the news website AllAfrica.com, he said the government's power relative to that of the private sector and civil society was much weaker in South Africa than elsewhere on the continent. The ANC depended "to a huge extent" on its allies in the unions, nongovernmental organizations, and churches, he added: "That is why there is so much alarm when . . . Tutu disagrees with the ANC, because the churches bring huge constituencies to vote for the ANC."

A year after the spat, Mbeki used the tenth anniversary of the TRC's first meeting—the Day of Reconciliation in 2005—to give a reconciliatory speech praising the commission's work. Tutu for his part acknowledged in 2006 that the internal convulsions the party was experiencing over the choice of Mbeki's successor might be evidence of healthy dissent. But, he complained, the ANC still appeared to believe that "wisdom resides in the party"–it gave insufficient weight to the views and ideas of South Africans outside its ranks.

The ANC's sensitivity might also be read as an implicit acknowledgement that Tutu had authority over and above his influence on voters. Writing after the TRC's hearings, the South African writer and academic Njabulo Ndebele attributed to Tutu "considerable moral authority," which had left "an indelible mark on the national character of South Africa." Ndebele's assessment was shared, from another perspective, by the former vice president of the United States, Al Gore, who in an interview likened Tutu's authority to Gandhi's "truth-force." Gore–who, among Tutu's friends, has probably worked in closest proximity to the wielding of great national power–argued that moral authority was not irrelevant in national and international affairs: "His [Tutu's] power is the power to persuade. . . . The leveraging of moral authority to persuade people of the rightness of a particular course of action is a very tangible power. . . . Throughout history some of the most important changes of all have come because of the exercise of moral leadership on the part of individuals who may not have any formal political power at all." Secretary-General Kofi Annan of the United Nations valued Tutu's input in international affairs precisely because it came from outside the arena controlled by diplomatic convention. "Somebody with the voice of Desmond Tutu and his experience and stature brings a lot to the table," Annan told this writer. "They are often freer than organizations like the UN. . . . Often he can say things that we cannot say, and sometimes take a lead on issues where we perhaps do it more diplomatically. He has been a voice for the voiceless and he has really stood for human rights and human dignity around the world. . . . It's good to have that sort of independent voice around."

The foundations of Tutu's stature and his moral authority are to be found in his spirituality and his faith. It is in these also that his legacy can most clearly be discerned.

In a corner of the Tutu's small backyard in Orlando West is a tiny concrete chapel of vertical proportions, stark angles, and rich colors. Quiet and cool in summer amid the noise and heat of Soweto, it is a symbol of the constant pull Tutu has felt toward a life of silence and prayer. In 1993, as South Africa stood on the verge of civil war, an Anglican solitary, a nun living such a life, told him in the course of an extended correspondence to withdraw from the world for a while. "You have been a celebrity too long, and it is taking its toll, not only on you but also on those around you," she wrote. "You need once more to realise your nothingness before God, so that he can fill you with his love." Tutu was strongly attracted to her insights. Yet it was impossible for him to accede to them. He replied to her in an agonized letter, written in unusually self-justifying tones: "When the violence escalated and especially with the assassination of Chris Hani, I could not sit by quietly. . . . How could I say no when they asked me to be part of a delegation to pressure the Burmese government to release Aung San Suu Kyi?" The heart of his dilemma was that the craving for silence contradicted the forces driving his life: the compassion he inherited from his mother; the anger at injustice he developed, perhaps first at home and certainly later when he saw the suffering caused by apartheid; and the example set by the Community of the Resurrection, which taught him that the choice was not either prayer or social action: rather, prayer inevitably drove you off your knees into action. Most important, for Tutu to have withdrawn from the world of secular politics and principalities would have been to deny his African heritage.

Tutu's understanding of an omnipresent spiritual world, in which the ancestors and saints are as much part of one's experience as people now living, helped him to break down the barriers in modern Christianity, imported from western intellectual tradition, between the sacred and the profane, the spiritual and the secular. In Tutu's theology, elderly women in his congregation at Orlando West, even if they were treated as nonentities by their white employers, were people created in God's image, to be held in awe and reverence as if they were God. To allow such people to suffer was not simply wrong; it was blasphemous, "for it is to spit in the face of God." In a society that tolerated such blasphemy, the demands of the Bible—of the prophets of the Old Testament, of Christ's teachings in the New Testament—were revolutionary: "Why should you need Marxist ideology or whatever? The Bible is dynamite. . . . Nothing could be more radical."

With such language, Tutu stirred not only South Africans but people in other countries who were trying to relate faith to justice. While he expressed his faith through the sacraments and liturgies of the Anglican Church, that is not what distinguished him in the eyes of people ranging from teenagers in South African townships to international rock stars. "You get a sense with him that love is the higher law," said U2's Bono in an interview. "He represents a God who will go the longest way round to meet us, through the more obscure highways and byways. . . . [He stands] away from the platitudes, away from the niceties of usual religion." Bono was not even sure which church Tutu belonged to, and made of a joke of it: "I think he's Anglican, is that right? You know, let's be honest—death by cupcakes!" And Tutu's claims for justice transcended Christianity. Addressing students of the University of Khartoum in Sudan, he once outlined how all the major faiths—Buddhism, Christianity, Hinduism, Judaism, and Islam— compelled their adherents to strive for justice and peace.

If Tutu's lifelong advocacy of justice was difficult, demanding, and contentious, then his vision for how to bring about reconciliation was surely more so. In his formulation, ubuntu-botho equips you to look at your torturers, to realize that they need your help and to stand ready to enable them to regain their humanity. Such a philosophy scandalizes the world. Yet, extraordinarily, it empowers the survivors of torture, for it enables them to take control of their lives, to take initiatives instead of remaining trapped in victimhood, waiting helplessly for the perpe- trators to act. Thus ubuntu-botho gives contemporary, practical mean- ing to God's forgiveness of the people of Israel recorded by the prophet Hosea, and to Christ's words from the Cross: "Father, forgive them, for they know not what they do."* But ubuntu-botho does not allow perpetrators to escape the necessity of confessing and making restitution to survivors, since it places the needs of society—the restora- tion of relationship—at the heart of reconciliation. As Tutu once told a priest who challenged his views on the subject: "God's gift of forgive- ness is gracious and unmerited but you must be willing to . . . appropri- ate the gift."

By promoting a vision of reconciliation in which the principles of ubuntu or botho are applied to repair the fractures in society, Desmond Tutu held out to the world as it entered the twenty-first century an African model for expressing the nature of human community. It is perhaps in this contribution that future generations will find his great- est legacy.

* Hosea 11:1–9; Luke 23:34.

GLOSSARY

This glossary includes words from some of South Africa's eleven official languages, and also examples of the contorted, often perverse vocabulary spawned by racism and apartheid.

African: For most of the period covered in this book, this term was used to describe people of purely African descent. However, all who unreservedly identify themselves with the democratic South Africa now regard themselves as Africans.

Afrikaner: Descendant of the Dutch settlers, augmented later by Huguenots and Germans, who were the first whites to establish themselves in southern Africa.

apartheid: "Separateness." The Afrikaans name given to the policy of more rigid and comprehensively organized segregation introduced by the National Party after its accession to power in 1948. Pronounced "apart-hate."

Ausi: Big sister.

Bantu: Word derived from the Nguni word for "people," adopted by the apartheid government in place of "Native" to describe people indigenous African descent. See also *Native*.

Bantu Affairs and Development (BAD): The government department that controlled the lives of black South Africans under apartheid.

Basotho: The people of Lesotho, South Africa's neighbor. The prefix ba- denotes the plural; an individual member of the group is a

Mosotho. The language, Sesotho, is also spoken by millions of South Africans from the Sotho-Tswana linguistic group.

Batswana: The original inhabitants of the northwest of South Africa and Botswana. An individual member of the group is a Motswana. The language is Setswana.

black: Depending on the context, a term used to describe either the indigenous people of South Africa or all dark-skinned South Africans, including those of mixed race and Indian descent. The latter definition was promoted by adherents of the black consciousness movement who rejected the apartheid government's term "nonwhite" as a collective description.

Boer: Afrikaans for "farmer." See also *Afrikaner.*

boet, broer: Brother.

boy: In old white South African parlance, a male child if used in reference to a white person; a man of any age if applied to a black person.

Coloureds: Under apartheid law, people of mixed race. The term was also applied to people of Khoi heritage or descendants of Malay slaves.

dorp: Small town.

Eucharist, Holy Eucharist: The name formally used in the current South African Anglican Prayer Book for the celebration in which Christ's crucifixion is recalled by consuming bread, representing his body; and wine, representing his blood. Also referred to as Holy Communion, or as Mass by Anglicans who stress their Catholic heritage.

Europeans: Until the mid-twentieth century, a term used by white South Africans to describe themselves even if their families had been established in Africa for generations. Black South Africans were often called "non-Europeans."

Indians: South Africans of Indian descent.

IsiXhosa: The official name of the mother tongue of Desmond Tutu and his father's family, spoken originally by the people of the Eastern

Cape. In this book, the form "Xhosa" is usually used as an adjective, except in direct quotations. A major language of the Nguni linguistic group.

IsiZulu: The official name of the language spoken by members of the Zulu nation, also a major Nguni language.

girl: See *Boy.*

Holy Communion: See *Eucharist.*

kaffir: The most derogatory word that can be applied to black South Africans; the equivalent of "nigger" in the United States.

klevah: Streetwise. (As used in Arthur Maimane's *Hate No More*, Kwela Books, 2000.) See also *Tsotsitaal.*

koppie: Small hill.

Lifaqane: Sesotho term describing the upheavals of the early nineteenth century in the interior of South Africa; the word suggests a forced removal. See also *Mfecane.*

Mass: See *Eucharist.*

Mattins: Service of Morning Prayer. A variation of the usual spelling, matins, used by the Community of the Resurrection.

Mfecane: The upheavals of the early nineteenth century in the interior of South Africa. The word, more commonly used than its Sesotho equivalent (see Lifaqane), is probably based on the IsiXhosa verb, *ukufaca,* meaning to be weak and emaciated from hunger. (Davenport and Saunders, *South Africa, A History,* 13.)

moegoes: Ignorant country folk.

Motswana: See *Batswana.*

Native: Term used by whites to describe indigenous African people; in the earliest days, also used by African writers. It was replaced with the word "Bantu" by apartheid officials.

Nguni: See IsiXhosa and IsiZulu.

Rand, rand: When capitalized, abbreviation of Witwatersrand. When lowercase, South African currency.

Reef: Also used to describe the Rand, or the Witwatersrand.

Roman Catholic: Anglicans who value their Catholic heritage regard themselves as Catholic, and therefore insist on prefacing the word with "Roman" when referring to the church headed by the bishop of Rome.

Sesotho: See Basotho.

Setswana: See *Batswana*.

Sisi: Big sister.

situation: An uptight person, not streetwise. (As used in Arthur Maimane's *Hate No More.*) See *Tsotitaal.*

sjambok: Long rawhide whip.

township: Term used in South Africa to describe a segregated black suburb, usually in an urban area (formerly called a location).

tsotsi: A township thug.

tsotsitaal: Argot of the township streets.

Witwatersrand: The "ridge of white waters" that runs through Johannesburg, containing gold-bearing reefs. The word, sometimes abbreviated as the Rand, also describes the string of gold-mining towns over an eighty-kilometer (50-mile) east-west axis that it spawned. It is Africa's wealthiest industrial complex.

Xhosa: See *IsiXhosa*.

Zulu: See *IsiZulu*.

NOTES

KEY TO ARCHIVES

AAM	Anti-Apartheid Movement Archives, Bodleian Library of Commonwealth and African Studies, Rhodes House, Oxford.
ANC Records	Records of the African National Congress, Liberation Archives, University of Fort Hare, Alice.
Brenthurst	The Brenthurst Library, Johannesburg.
Bush Library	George H. W. Bush Presidential Library, College Station, Texas.
CPSA	Church of the Province of Southern Africa Archives, Historical Papers, William Cullen Library, University of the Witwatersrand, Johannesburg.
CR Archives	Archives of the Community of the Resurrection, Mirfield.
FedSem	Federal Theological Seminary Records, Liberation Archives, University of Fort Hare, Alice.
Huddleston Papers	Huddleston Papers, Bodleian Library of Commonwealth and African Studies, Rhodes House, Oxford.
Karis-Gerhart Collection	Karis-Gerhart Collection, Historical Papers, William Cullen Library, University of the Witwatersrand, Johannesburg.
King's	Tutu, Rev. DMB Student File, King's College London Archives, London.
Kistner Collection	Kistner Collection, Lutheran Theological Institute, University of KwaZulu-Natal, Pietermaritzburg.
Klerksdorp Archives	Archive of the Town Clerk of Klerksdorp, Transvaal. Archives Depot, Tshwane.
Methodist Archives	Methodist Archives, Cory Library for Historical Research, Rhodes University, Grahamstown.
Nahecs	National Heritage and Cultural Studies Archive, Liberation Archives, University of Fort Hare, Alice.
NSA	National Security Archives, George Washington University, Washington, D. C.
Paton Centre	Alan Paton Centre and Archives, University of KwaZulu-Natal, Pietermaritzburg.
Reagan Library	Ronald Reagan Presidential Library, Simi Valley, California.
SACC	South African Council of Churches Archives, Historical Papers, William Cullen Library, University of the Witwatersrand, Johannesburg.
SAHA	South African History Archive, University of the Witwatersrand, Johannesburg.
SAIRR Archive	SA Institute of Race Relations Archives, Historical Papers, William Cullen Library, University of the Witwatersrand, Johannesburg.
SANA	South African National Archives, Tshwane.

Suzman Papers	Helen Suzman Papers, Historical Papers, William Cullen Library, University of the Witwatersrand, Johannesburg.
Tambo Papers	O. R. Tambo Papers, Liberation Archives, University of Fort Hare, Alice.
UCT Archives	Desmond Tutu Papers, Manuscripts and Archives, University of Cape Town Libraries, Cape Town.
UL Archives	Archives of the University of Lesotho, Roma.
UNISA	University of South Africa Archives, Tshwane.
UWC	Desmond Tutu Collection, Mayibuye Centre, University of the Western Cape, Cape Town.
WCC	Theological Education Fund Archives, World Council of Churches Library and Archives, Geneva.

PROLOGUE

PAGE

1 *Bishopscourt was part:* Anne R. Kotzé, *Bishopscourt and Its Residents,* 5–9.

1 *Beyond the estate, to the south:* National Botanical Gardens, Kirstenbosch, historical plaque.

1 *In 1988, Tutu's second year: Drum* magazine (Johannesburg), July 1986.

1 *The route into the city:* Gavin W. Maneveldt, "Fynbos," at: www.botany.uwc.ac.za/envfacts/fynbos.

2 *This was District Six: South African Outlook,* January 1980, 2–11.

2 *Just a few weeks previously:* Republic of South Africa, *Government Gazette,* Vol. 272, No. 11157, February 24, 1988.

2 *In response, the South African:* Statement by church leaders, February 25, 1988; author's collection.

2 *On Monday, February 29:* Author's experience; BBC TV *Nine O'Clock News,* February 29, 1988; author's recording.

3 *A few of the clergy:* Author's experience.

3 *"The church has unmistakably":* James Robbins, BBC TV *Nine O'Clock News,* February 29, 1988.

3 *On Monday, March 14, the sheriff:* Evidence of Duma Khumalo, Theresa Ramashamola, Paula McBride, and J. S. Steinberg at hearings of the Truth and Reconciliation Commission (TRC), July 21 and 22, 1997; Mokhesi-Parker and Parker, *In the Shadow of Sharpeville,* 111–143, 172–195, 239–244; Diar, *The Sharpeville Six,* 3–4, 162–181, 249–253, 273–285, 290; Noonan, *They're Burning the Churches,* 44–47.

4 *When news came of the impending:* Transcripts of press conferences by Desmond Tutu, Cape Town and Johannesburg, March 16, 1988; author's collection. Answers to parliamentary questions by Margaret Thatcher, Hansard, House of Commons, 129/988–992, March 16, at: www.margaretthatcher.org/speeches; Thatcher to Trevor Huddleston, March 15, 1988, AAM Archives; J. Edward Fox to Chairman of the Committee on Foreign Affairs, House of Representatives, Washington D.C., July 26, 1988, Ronald Reagan Library.

4 *Tutu and his personal assistant, Matt Esau:* Renwick, *Unconventional Diplomacy,* 114. Matt Esau, observation to the author, March 16, 1988.

4 *Tutu told Botha:* Account of meeting from tape recording of Tutu and Esau's report, given to colleagues in Tutu's car as they returned to Bishopscourt, March 16, 1988, CPSA.

4 *He was opposed:* Martin Dolinchek, letter to *Daily News* (Durban), December 3, 1984; *Times* (London), July 10, 1982.

5 *"Our people have suffered":* Account by DMT, quoted in Wallis and Hollyday, 66.

6 *The following morning:* Diar, *The Sharpeville Six,* 267, 290.

6 *In the weeks following March 16: Journal of Theology for Southern Africa,* No. 63, June 1988, 68–87; statements in author's collection.

6 *Chikane laid the groundwork:* Convocation of Churches, May 30–31, 1988, press release, AB2701 P, CPSA.

6 *Early in June, Botha asked:* Adriaan Vlok, evidence to TRC Amnesty Committee, July 20, 1988.

7 *Two months afterward, a police team:* Eugene de Kock, evidence to TRC Amnesty Committee, July 20, 1988.

7 *"We were met by a scene out of hell":* Quoted by Vlok, evidence to Amnesty Committee.

7 *"You are leading people to confrontation":* Recording of Tutu and Esau's report on meeting with Botha, CPSA.

CHAPTER 1: CHILD OF MODERN SOUTH AFRICA

PAGE

9 *Here, until Desmond was four:* Sylvia Morrison, interview by author, July 2004.

9 *Klerksdorp's "location":* Sam Thusi Marawa, interview by author, December 7, 2004; Brown, *Golden Heritage,* 88–89; *Rapport* (Johannesburg), October 15, 2000.

10 *The very name of Makoeteng:* Reverend Itumeleng Tlhakanye, explanation to author, June 28, 2005.

10 *The chiefdoms of this group:* Mason, *Origins of Black People of Johannesburg,* 1–6, 14, 46–49, 703–705.

10 *She was letlomela:* DMT, interview by author, February 4, 2005.

11 *Zachariah was born:* Sylvia Morrison, explanation to author, December 29, 2005.

11 *He was proud:* DMT, interview by Hennie Serfontein, 1996.

11 *"She didn't say a word":* Morrison, interview by author, July 2004.

11 *The major groups:* Peires, *The House of Phalo,* 3, 18, 98.

11 *By this account:* Omer-Cooper, *The Zulu Aftermath,* 3–8, 24–48; Davenport and Saunders, *South Africa,* 13, 65.

12 *A number of historians:* Julian Cobbing, "The Mfecane as Alibi: Thoughts on Dithakong and Mbolompo," *Journal of African History* 29 (1988): 487–519; Mbongeni Zikhethele Malaba, " 'In a Mirror Dimly': An Analysis of Peter Becker's Biographies of Mzlikazi, Moshesh, and Dingane," in Lehmann and Reckwitz. See also Thompson, *A History of South Africa,* 83–84, 315–316. Davenport and Saunders, *South Africa,* give a useful summary of the evidence, 13–20.

12 *In this new narrative:* Alan Webster, "Unmasking the Fingo: The War of 1835 Revisited," in Hamilton, 256–276; Peires, *The House of Phalo,* 168–169.

12 *Whatever their origins:* Richard A. Moyer, "The Mfengu, Self-Defence, and the Cape Frontier Wars," in Saunders and Derricourt, 101, 107.

12 *"thus showing":* Ntantala, *A Life's Mosaic,* 96.

12 *Certainly, at and beyond:* Davenport and Saunders, *South Africa,* 65, 111–112, 189, 190; Janet Hodgson, "Christian Beginnings among the Xhosa," in Elphick and Davenport, 78–86.

13 *He declared that it would:* John Tengo Jabavu, "The Launch," in Mutloatse, 101–103.

13 *In his autobiography Mandela:* Nelson Mandela, *Long Walk to Freedom,* 12.

13 *Mandela, in an interview:* Nelson Rolihlahla Mandela, interview by author, March 20, 2003.

14 *There is no direct analogy:* Peires, *The House of Phalo,* 9.

14 *Before whites arrived:* This account is based on local histories, including Roelf Marx, *Klerksdorp;* Brown, *Golden Heritage;* Guest, *Voortrekkerdorp;* W. Grönum, *Die difaqane: Oorsprong, ontplooiing, en invloed op die Tswana* (MA-Verhandeling, University of the North-West, Potchefstroom); *Klerksdorp: City of People* (Klerksdorp: Klerksdorp City Council pamphlet).

14 *By some accounts:* Mason, *Origins of Black People of Johannesburg,* 627.

16 *In the 1930s, Klerksdorp's black residents:* Sam Thusi Marawa, interview by author, December 7, 2004.

16 *Only whites were enrolled:* Minutes of the Klerksdorp Town Council, September 25 and October 27, 1931; minutes of the Public Health Committee, April 28, 1933, Klerksdorp Archives.

16 *The community was diverse:* Elizabeth Mkhabela, interview by *The Citizen* (Johannesburg),

November 20, 1999; DMT, interview by author, February 4, 2005; Marawa, interview by author.

17 *In the weeks before and after Tutu's birth: Klerksdorp Record and Western Transvaal News*, Vol. 40, No. 2837, Friday, October 2, 1931; Vol. 40, No. 2838, Friday, October 9, 1931.

18 *By the time the delegates:* Davenport and Saunders, *South Africa*, 263–264; Hepple, *A Political and Economic History;* Beinart, *Twentieth Century*, 353.

18 *"Awaking on Friday morning":* Sol T. Plaatje, *Native Life in South Africa* (London, 1916), quoted in Mutloatse, *Reconstruction*, 115.

19 *However, unknown to the Tutus:* Paul Erasmus, interview by author, December 6, 2005.

19 *Its incidence rose: Acute Poliomyelitis (Infantile Paralysis),* Union of South Africa: Department of Health pamphlet, 1948.

20 *The house had three rooms:* Gloria Radebe, interview by author, November 27, 2004.

21 *"I enjoyed [as a child]":* DMT to Miss Clare Amner, April 1, 1986, AB1979 Da. 3.4, CPSA.

21 *Losing two:* Wilson and Ramphele, *Uprooting Poverty*, 108–112.

22 *"He drank often":* DMT, interview by Hennie Serfontein, 1996.

23 *"We had to speak English":* Elizabeth Kgosiemang, interview by author, December 7, 2004.

23 *"Once I saw black children":* DMT, interview by Hennie Serfontein, 1996; DMT, interview by Hanlie Retief, *Sarie*, October 2, 1991.

24 *In 1936, the white Parliament:* Wilson and Perrot, 574.

24 *Parliament was much less certain:* D'Oliveira, *Vorster, The Man*, 47–58.

24 *Among those who fought:* Gleeson, *The Unknown Force*.

24 *"It was actually a great honor":* DMT, interview by Carina le Grange, June 8, 1995.

25 *"Everybody believed":* DMT, interview by author, February 4, 2005.

25 *"We found it distinctly odd": New York Review of Books*, Vol. 32, No. 14, September 26, 1985.

25 *While living in Roodepoort West:* Accounts in *Christianity and Crisis*, November 27, 1984; DMT, address to the Charles Stuart Mott Foundation, Flint, Michigan, June 9, 2004.

26 *This white man in a big black hat:* Honoré, 1–2; DMT, interview by Trevor McDonald, *Paths of Inspiration*, BBC Radio 2, 1996.

CHAPTER 2: PRAISE POEM TO GOD

PAGE

27 *"The summit of our worship":* Community of the Resurrection, Mirfield, West Yorkshire, undated pamphlet made available to visitors in 2004.

27 *When the Community of the Resurrection:* Wilkinson, *The Community of the Resurrection*, 58–59, 71.

28 *An aristocrat, Gore:* Ibid., 6, 20, 65–67.

28 *There were limits:* Ibid., 76–77.

28 *Christianity was established:* Sundkler and Steed, *A History of the Church*, 7–9, 18, 30, 35.

29 *When officials:* Author's experience; Fetahi and Terrefe; Acts 8:25–40.

29 *This long heritage:* Church of the Province of Southern Africa, *Saints and Seasons*, 68, 96; Matthew 27:32.

29 *It was an all-pervasive reality:* Sundkler and Steed, *A History of the Church*, 91.

30 *So enthusiastic was she:* Jonathan N. Gerstner, "A Christian Monopoly: The Reformed Church and Colonial Society under Dutch Rule" in Elphick and Davenport, 24, 28; Sundkler and Steed, *A History of the Church*, 64; Van der Ross, *Up From Slavery*, 25.

30 *Their work began haltingly:* Elphick and Davenport, *Christianity in South Africa*, 3.

30 *This is partly because:* Hastings, *The Church in Africa*, 203. This account is based on Hastings, 199–206; on Peires, *The House of Phalo*, 87; and on two contributions to Elphick and Davenport: Elizabeth Elbourne and Robert Ross, "Combating Spiritual and Social Bondage: Early Missions in the Cape Colony," 34–38; and Janet Hodgson, "A Battle for Sacred Power: Christian Beginnings among the Xhosa," 70–71.

30 *"by the slow but certain progress":* Hastings, *The Church in Africa*, 205.

31 *They were seen often:* DMT, sermon preached in Moffat Church, Kuruman, October 9, 1988.

31 *Nxele took Christian concepts:* Hodgson, "A Battle for Sacred Power," in Elphick and Daven-
    port, 71–73. Descriptions of Nxele and Ntsikana are also based on Hastings, *The Church in
    Africa,* 218–221; Sundkler and Steed, *A History of the Church,* 146–149; Peires, *The House of
    Phalo,* 77–88; and David Dargie, "Christian Music among Africans," in Elphick and Dav-
    enport, *Christianity in South Africa,* 322–323.

32 *the role of the missionaries:* Elphick and Davenport, *Christianity in South Africa,* 4; Sundkler
    and Steed, *A History of the Church,* 402.

32 *The Anglican Church:* Hinchliff, *The Anglican Church,* 10–26, 45–48, 80, 153; Peter Lee,
    "Change and Challenge on the Reef," in Suggit and Goedhals, 130.

32 *Black evangelists took charge:* Davenport and Saunders, *South Africa,* 206–209; Sundkler and
    Steed, *A History of the Church,* 413.

32 *"From the outset":* Alban Winter, CR, "Till Darkness Fell," unpublished manuscript,
    AB178, CPSA, 6, 9, 14.

33 *In 1950, when the Archdeaconry: Watchman,* newsletter of the Diocese of Johannesburg,
    Vol. 20, No. 328, June 1950; Wilkinson, *The Community of the Resurrection,* 211.

33 *Black Methodists were organized:* Methodist Church of SA: Transvaal and Swaziland District
    Synod, *Synod Handbook, 1933–1934,* periodicals, Methodist Archives.

34 *Whenever we small boys:* Mothobi Mutloatse, "Mutloatse on Tutu," *Ecunews* (Johannesburg),
    December 1984, 16; DMT, interview by author, February 4, 2005.

34 *He was a shoe repairer:* DMT, interview by author, February 4, 2005.

35 *"If he says a mikado is a hippo":* Drum, August 1956, 63–65.

35 *Perhaps because we shared: Drum,* December 1984, 8–10.

36 *"He made learning so much fun":* DMT, "My Teacher–Mr. Nimrod Ndebele," undated copy
    of handwritten document, author's collection).

36 *"When we went to write":* DMT, interview by Hennie Serfontein, 1996.

37 *As in primary school:* DMT, interview by author, December 21, 2005; confirmed by Gloria
    Radebe.

37 *For lunch we used to get: Drum,* December 1984, 8–10.

37 *"My first foray":* DMT, *Tribute to Stanley Motjuwadi,* August 11, 1989, AB2701 S2 (1), CPSA.

37 *Forty years later: Drum,* November 1984, 6.

38 *In 1947 a 2.5-million-year-old skull:* John Noble Wilford, "Near-Intact Skeleton Offers
    Clues to Human Tree's Root," *New York Times,* December 10, 1998; Francis Thackeray,
    Mrs. Ples and Our Distant Relatives, Transvaal Museum: www.scienceinafrica.co.za/2001/
    may/ples.htm.

38 *In its more recent history:* Lucille Davie, *An Area Steeped in History,* Johannesburg News
    Agency: www.mogalecity.gov.za/visitors/history/

39 *My mother went where:* DMT, interview by Hennie Serfontein, 1996.

CHAPTER 3: A SENSE OF WORTH

PAGE

41 *"spawned onto the Reef":* "The 'Americans,' " *Drum,* September 1954, 19–22.

41 *The literary style:* Mphahlele, *Es'kia,* 309.

42 *Ultimately, it was the cacophonous:* Nkosi, *Home and Exile,* 13.

42 *The educated middle class:* "The 'Americans' "; interview by Es'kia Mphahlele in Stein and
    Jacobson, 56–58.

42 *The biographer of Raymond Raynes:* Mosley, *Raymond Raynes,* 72, 75.

43 *"an enormous benevolent empire":* Richard Elphick, "Mission Christianity and Interwar Lib-
    eralism" in Butler, Elphick, and Welsh, 68–69.

43 *In the 1930s, the empire employed:* Ibid.

43 *"colonialist in their attitude":* Nelson Mandela, *Long Walk to Freedom,* 42.

43 *Many, many, many of us:* DMT, sermon preached in Moffat Church, Kuruman, October 9,
    1988.

44 *He was so un-English:* DMT, "An Appreciation of the Right Rev. Trevor Huddleston, CR"
    in Honoré, 2; "Tribute: Archbishop Trevor Huddleston, CR", August 23, 1994, author's
    collection.

44 *"The children everywhere":* Home Letters, Chronicle of the Community of the Resurrection, No. 165, 1944.

44 *"I have seldom felt more devastated":* McGrandle, *Trevor Huddleston,* 159.

45 *"They showed us":* Khotso Makhulu, interview by author, April 17, 2004.

45 *The "stinking backyards":* Chronicle of the Community of the Resurrection, No. 176, 1946, 15–22; biblical reference is to the parable of the rich man and Lazarus, Luke 16:19–31.

45 *Between 1938 and 1945:* Packard, *White Plague, Black Labor,* 211–248.

46 *Once somebody started coughing:* DMT, interview by Hennie Serfontein, 1996.

46 *On his next visit:* Dominic Whitnall, interview by author, April 15, 2004; Dominic Whitnall to Trevor Huddleston, May 15, 1976, CR Correspondence, Huddleston Archives.

46 *"Even illness could not":* Drum, December 1984, 8–10.

47 *"In my tradition":* Mandela, *Long Walk to Freedom,* 24.

47 *From the nineteenth century on:* Luke Lungile Pato, "Reclaiming the African Heritage: The Indigenisation of Christianity within the CPSA" in Suggit and Goedhals, 149.

47 *"He would playfully close":* Drum, December 1984, 8–10.

47 *At the time he wrote his Senior Certificate:* Hartshorne, *Crisis and Challenge,* 62.

48 *"the three R's":* Ibid., 33.

48 *"They said we had to develop":* DMT, interview by Carina le Grange, June 8, 1995.

48 *Coming from a mission school:* Mmutlanyane Stanley Mogoba, interview by author, November 30, 2004.

48 *The Afrikaners were not:* DMT, interview by author, July 21, 2005.

49 *"When we were in the common room":* Ibid.

49 *Mogoba recalled students:* Mogoba, *Stone, Steel, Sjambok,* 5.

49 *When they went to the house:* DMT, interview by Trevor McDonald, BBC Radio 2, 1996.

49 *Opportunities for a full-time:* N. Barney Pityana, interview by author, February 23, 2005.

50 *In his best subjects:* Desmond M. Tutu's student record, UNISA; King's student file; UNISA calendars, 1951–1952; UNISA Examination Papers, Vol. 1, 1951; UNISA Examination Papers for External Students, November–December 1952, Vol. 1.

50 *"He was a 'situation' ":* Dr. Jiyana Mgojo Mbere, interview by author, June 30, 2005.

51 *"The very first time":* Nomalizo Leah Tutu, interviews by Hennie Serfontein, 1996.

52 *Like circumcision, lobola:* Southern African Anglican Theological Commission, *The Church and Human Sexuality,* 19–20; Luke Lungile Pato, "Reclaiming the African Heritage: The Indigenisation of Christianity within the CPSA" in Suggit and Goedhals, 149; Luke Lungile Pato, "Being Fully Human," *Journal of Theology for Southern Africa,* No. 97, March 1997, 59; DMT, interview by author, December 21, 2005.

52 *We were quite comfortable:* Nomalizo Leah Tutu, interviews by Hennie Serfontein, 1996.

53 *"If you only knew":* Moñala, letter dated November 17, 1953, AB2013 JK 7.1, CPSA.

CHAPTER 4: OBVIOUS GIFTS OF LEADERSHIP

PAGE

55 *For the new generation:* Sisulu, *In Our Lifetime,* 83; Sampson, *The Treason Cage,* 78.

55 *"We barely discussed the question":* Mandela, *Long Walk to Freedom,* 105.

55 *William Beinart, professor:* Beinart, *Twentieth Century South Africa,* 144.

56 *"The often haphazard":* Mandela, *Long Walk to Freedom,* 104.

56 *"conceived and gave birth":* David Botha, *Church and Kingdom in South Africa: Dutch Reformed Perspective,* address by moderator, Nederduitse Gereformeerde Sendingkerk, to the national conference of the South African Council of Churches, 1980.

56 *A study by the Methodist Church:* W. J. Gordon Mears, *An Outline of Methodism in the Transvaal,* 1972, Methodist Pamphlet Box 12, Methodist Archives.

56 *In the Eastern Cape:* Monica Wilson, in Wilson and Perrot, 11.

56 *Tiger Kloof—which also educated:* Steve de Gruchy, *Changing Frontiers,* 78.

57 *"Excitement ran high":* Mattera, *Memory Is the Weapon,* 139–140.

57 *The forced removal of natives:* New York Times, February 10, 1955.

58 *Sisi [big sister], you should have:* Jabavu, *The Ochre People,* 195.

58 *"the greatest display of police strength":* Daily Telegraph, February 10, 1955.

58 *"as if to rub salt":* DMT, Naught for Your Comfort Lecture, August 7, 2004, Christ the King, Sophiatown.

58 *"Sophiatown WAS a slum":* Huddleston, *Naught for Your Comfort,* 193.

59 *Again and again, I have heard:* Alban Winter, CR, *Till Darkness Fell,* AB178, CPSA, 47–48.

59 *In 1950 there were places:* Huddleston, *Naught for Your Comfort,* 161; Paton, *Apartheid and the Archbishop,* 69.

59 *A tiny minority of black pupils:* Hartshorne, *Crisis and Challenge,* 24–31.

59 *The church school system:* Jonathan Hyslop, "A Destruction Coming In" in Bonner, Delius, and Posel, 394.

59 *The Bantu must be guided:* Verwoerd, speech to the Senate, June 7, 1954, quoted in Rose and Tunmer, 261–266.

60 *Although Eiselen planned:* Hartshorne, *Crisis and Challenge,* 35, 67.

60 *"This is the most evil act":* Callinicos, *Beyond the Engeli Mountains,* 210.

60 *"That is the recognized pattern":* Cape Times, May 26, 1954.

60 *"Even a rotten system":* Paton, *Apartheid and the Archbishop,* 233–235.

60 *"It is my conviction":* Peart-Binns, *Ambrose Reeves,* 123.

60 *"the same hideous dilemma":* Huddleston, *Naught for Your Comfort,* 171–174.

61 *"The Bantu teacher":* Verwoerd, speech to the Senate, June 7, 1954.

61 *Trevor Huddleston wrote:* Correspondence and documents from AB2013 92 (x), CPSA, unless otherwise identified.

62 *His wealth was built:* Thompson, *A History of South Africa,* 206; Luthuli, *Let My People Go,* 154; Sampson, *Mandela,* 90, 109.

62 *"I wish you all success":* Oppenheimer, letter to DMT, Brenthurst Library.

63 *"I am sorry to hear":* Ibid.

63 *The Greek lessons had to be given:* Dale and Tish White, interview by author, July 6, 2005.

63 *I was somewhat disturbed:* Ambrose Reeves to principal, St. Peter's College, December 31, 1957, AB2414 student file, CPSA.

64 *When Tutu's class:* Alban Winter, CR, *Till Darkness Fell,* AB178, CPSA, 67–68.

65 *The previous principal:* Timothy Stanton, interview by author, September 18, 2004; Winter, *Till Darkness Fell,* 67–79; Minutes of the College Council, February 3, 1958, AB2414 A2.1, CPSA; *Theological Education and St. Peter's Rosettenville, April 1958,* report by Godfrey Pawson, AB2414 A5.1, CPSA.

65 *"I was amazed that he":* Mutloatse, "Mutloatse on Tutu," *Ecunews* (Johannesburg), December 1984, 17.

66 *Timothy Stanton arrived:* David Nkwe, interview by author, December 7, 2004.

66 *"almost a physical sensation":* DMT, interview by Bob Scott, Trinity Television, Trinity Church, Wall Street, New York, April 24, 2002.

67 *"I myself have been hopelessly":* DMT to Godfrey Pawson, December 9, 1958, AB2414 student file, CPSA.

68 *"her babes from whom":* Pawson, letter to "My dear Augustine," May 30, 1959, AB2414 student file, AB2013 92(x), CPSA.

68 *In a letter to Reeves, Pawson:* Pawson to Reeves and matron at Jane Furse Hospital, November 9, 1959, AB2414 student file, CPSA.

69 *The Anglican hierarchy:* Worsnip, *Between the Two Fires,* 139–153; Paton, *Apartheid and the Archbishop,* 279–281.

69 *The Johannesburg diocese:* Fee and allowance schedules, Ordination candidates, European, Correspondence (2) 1956–1959; and African, Correspondence 1953–1962, AB628 Diocese of Johannesburg, CPSA.

69 *"One policeman was standing":* Tyler, *Life in the Time of Sharpeville,* 18.

70 *His political instincts:* Peart-Binns, *Ambrose Reeves,* 189, 198–202, 211–218; Paton, *Apartheid and the Archbishop,* 237.

70 *It showed that the death toll:* Frankel, *An Ordinary Atrocity,* 115–116, 148–153, 229–241.

71 *"It was certainly one of those":* Sampson, *Mandela,* 132.

71 *"the wind of change is blowing":* Reason, *Africa,* 663; Sampson, *Black and Gold,* 66.

71 *Albert Luthuli was arrested in Pretoria:* Luthuli, *Let My People Go,* 199–200.

71 *Tambo left the country:* Callinicos, *Beyond the Engeli Mountains,* 254.

71 *Economically, international confidence:* Sampson, *Black and Gold,* 86.

71 *"the most impressive assertion"*: Lelyveld, *Move Your Shadow*, 315.

71 *Local and foreign investors*: Sampson, *Black and Gold*, 86.

72 *"I can't say that I was madly"*: DMT, interview by Carina le Grange, June 8, 1995.

72 *"He had the vision"*: Aelred Stubbs, interview by author, September 18, 2004.

73 *He continues to be a diligent*: AB2414 student file, CPSA.

73 *His white senior advisers*: Peart-Binns, *Ambrose Reeves*, 234–242; see also Peart-Binns, *Scourge of Apartheid*, 175–177.

74 *"I cannot get to Orlando"*: DMT to Stubbs, July 13, 1961, AB2414, St. Peter's student file, CPSA.

75 *Although marriage allowances*: Report of the Stipends Commission of 1963, AB1745, CPSA.

75 *"I dislike apartheid very much"*: Charge to the Thirty-Eighth Synod of the Diocese of Johannesburg, October 27, 1962, AB2668 PEO Johannesburg Diocese, CPSA.

75 *"Too much is being done"*: Entries in Stradling's diary for December 16 and 17, 1961, AB853, CPSA.

76 *You visit people who are sick*: DMT, interview by Academy of Achievement, www.achievement.org, June 12, 2004.

77 *"Whether or not the policy"*: Notes for a tape recording, February 1958, AB2414 A1.2, CPSA.

77 *"Please go ahead with it"*: Reeves to Stubbs, AB2414 student file, CPSA.

77 *"but the need of an African"*: Stubbs to Evans, June 11, 1961, and ensuing correspondence from Tutu's St. Peter's student file (AB2414, CPSA) and King's College student file.

CHAPTER 5: A BREATH OF FRESH AIR

PAGE

79 *"public enemy number one"*: Nelson Mandela, Foreword, in Tutu, *The Rainbow People*.

79 *The outgoing government*: Truth and Reconciliation Commission, *Report*, 1998, Vol. 1, 219, para 60.

79 *One of the few surviving government files*: Department of Bantu Administration and Development, File No. 100/6/460, Part I, Passport: Desmond Mpilo Tutu, SANA.

79 *"not a right but a privilege"*: "Statement by the Minister of the Interior in Parliament," September 8, 1953, in SAIRR, *Race Relations Survey 1952–1953*, 39.

80 *He has been described*: Peart-Binns, *Scourge of Apartheid*, 85–191; King, *A Good Place to Be*, 3.

81 *By the time the Tutus applied*: Peart-Binns, *Scourge of Apartheid*, 209–212; Lückhoff, *Cottesloe*, 116.

81 *While the Tutus*: Leslie Stradling to Stubbs, July 2, 1962, AB2414 student file, CPSA; correspondence between Stubbs and James F. Hopewell, TEF, July 11, 1962, DMT Scholarship Aid, FEDSEM, Area 11, TEF Projects 1965–1970, Box 106, WCC.

81 *"no mention of the TEF"*: DMT to Sydney Evans, February 1, 1962, King's student file.

82 *"stuck together with chewing gum"*: DMT, interview by author, April 5, 2005.

82 *The first leg up to Salisbury*: DMT to Stubbs, September 18, 1962, AB2414 student file, CPSA.

83 *"the familiar chorus"*: Sampson, *Anatomy of Britain Today*, 668.

83 *It was the era*: Transcript of a reply by Janet Dyson to DMT at reunion dinner, October 24, 1995, DMT office records.

83 *It was also a time*: Robinson, *Honest to God*, 12–24.

83 *King's College London*: Christine Kenyon Jones, *King's College London: In the Service of Society* (King's College, 2004), 6, 34–36, 102–104.

83 *Most foreign theology students*: DMT Scholarship Aid file, WCC; King's student file.

83 *"I really would not"*: Leah Tutu to Aelred Stubbs, September 30, 1962, AB2414 student file, CPSA.

84 *"But perhaps it will be more prudent"*: DMT to Stubbs, October 13, 1962, and all subsequent Tutu-Stubbs correspondence in this chapter from AB2414 student file, CPSA.

84 *Two-year old Naomi*: "Claude CR" to Aelred Stubbs, June 2, 1963, AB2414 student file, CPSA; Val Leslie to Aelred Stubbs, June 1962, AB2414 student file, CPSA.

84 *For Leah, however*: Malcolm Alexander, interview by author, October 4, 2004; Leah Tutu, interview by Hennie Serfontein, 1996.

85 *At thirty, he was older:* "Memories of Desmond," recollections of Tutu's classmates, July 2004 (Tutu office records).

85 *Oosthuysen was:* Oosthuysen, interview by author, September 12, 2004.

86 *"Brian and I":* DMT, King's Commemoration Oration, Celebrating the 175th Anniversary of the College, January 23, 2004.

86 *Tutu described Christopher Evans:* Ibid. See also Tutu, Foreword, in Ursula King, *Turning Points.*

87 *"I don't know what":* Mutloatse, "Mutloatse on Tutu," *Ecunews* (Johannesburg), December 1984, 17.

87 *"My grandfather, who was quite crusty":* Malcolm Alexander interview.

88 *"The Midlands Bank":* DMT, interview by Trevor McDonald, BBC Radio 2, 1996.

88 *Kenyon was a gregarious:* Martin Kenyon, interview by author, October 2, 2004; DMT, Lecture at the Centre for the Study of Global Governance, London School of Economics, February 1, 1995.

89 *Kenyon took him: The Guardian* (London), *Daily Telegraph and Morning Post* (London), and *Times* (London), June 25, 1963; Alexander interview; *Times* (London), July 27, 1966.

89 *Martin Kenyon came:* Kenyon to Trevor Huddleston, September 5, 1963 (Martin Kenyon files).

89 *"His results ... are really excellent":* Evans to Stubbs, July 1, 1963; Evans to TEF, July 24, 1963, AB2414 student file, CPSA.

90 *I am quite ready to accept:* Stubbs to Evans, July 12, 1962, AB2414 student file, CPSA.

90 *Forty years later:* DMT, interview by author, February 4, 2005.

90 *At St. Peter's, the CR fathers:* Geoffrey Pawson to Ambrose Reeves, December 11, 1958, AB2414 student file, CPSA.

90 *"It appears that of his impositions":* H. C. Juta to Stubbs, December 3, 1962, AB2414 student file, CPSA.

91 *"Of course I feel quite awful":* DMT to Leslie Stradling, February 1, 1963, AB2013 92 (x), CPSA.

91 *"Desmond was so ashamed":* Leah Tutu, interview by Hennie Serfontein.

91 *"a considerable test":* Christopher Evans to the University of Botswana, Lesotho, and Swaziland, September 2, 1969, DMT personal file, UL Archives.

91 *He was awarded:* Tutor's Terminal Report, D.M.B. Tutu, 1963–1964, King's student file.

92 *Stubbs believed:* Stubbs to Dr. Walter P. Cason, TEF, February 26, 1965; Stubbs to Dr. Charles W. Forman, TEF, December 13, 1965, AB2414 student file, CPSA.

92 *During the summer:* Correspondence from July to September, 1965, AB2013 92 (x), CPSA; AB2414 student file, CPSA; and King's student file.

93 *St. Alban's had been:* DMT to Evans, May 6, 1965, King's student file.

93 *"a later addition, introduced":* "History of St. Mary the Virgin, Bletchingley," pamphlet.

93 *Lambert had served:* Townend, *Burke's Genealogical History,* 383–385; Bell-Scott, *Uvedale and Mel: A Memoir.*

93 *Apart from the landed gentry:* John Ewington, interview by author, October 6, 2004; Sarah and Tim Goad, interview by author, September 26, 2004.

93 *By lunchtime, parishioners:* Ronald Brownrigg, "A Rector Remembers–1960–1974," handwritten manuscript.

94 *After three years:* St. Mary's parishioners' comments to the author, and Betty Bristow, interview by author, September 26, 2004; Ronald Brownrigg, interview by author, September 13, 2004; Ewington, Tim Goad interviews.

95 *Along with his academic qualifications:* Christopher Evans to the University of Botswana, Lesotho, and Swaziland, September 2, 1969, UL Archives.

95 *At the end of his year:* Geoffrey Parrinder to the University of Botswana, Lesotho, and Swaziland, August 23, 1969, UL Archives.

95 *"Islam is a potent force":* DMT Scholarship Aid file, WCC.

96 *A year after:* References from DMT Scholarship Aid file, WCC.

96 *He was very modest:* Christopher Evans to the University of Botswana, Lesotho, and Swaziland, September 2, 1969, UL Archives.

96 *He actively promoted:* Khotso Makhulu, interview by author, April 17, 2004.

97 *"I have just come away":* DMT to Sydney Evans, July 14, 1964, King's student file.

97 *In a nine-column: Sunday Times,* Johannesburg, October 28, 1962.
97 *Two days later: Rand Daily Mail,* Johannesburg, October 30, 1962.
99 *At the end of their visit:* DMT to Martin Kenyon, December 19, 1966; and January 6, 1967 (Kenyon files).

CHAPTER 6: CAMPUS PARENTS

PAGE
101 *Leah Tutu had told:* Uvedale Lambert to Aelred Stubbs, October 9, 1965, AB2414 student file, CPSA.
101 *"I don't want to sound":* DMT to Martin Kenyon, December 19, 1966 (Martin Kenyon files).
102 *"To get there we passed":* DMT, interview by author, April 26, 2005.
102 *The Federal Seminary:* Mostert, *Frontiers,* 982.
102 *"As far as the eye could see":* Jabavu, *Drawn in Colour,* 23–24.
102 *Lovedale not only trained:* Monica Wilson, in Wilson and Perrot, 4–12.
102 *"spent formative years":* Prospectus 2003, University of Fort Hare; Sampson, *The Treason Cage,* 117.
103 *In what the journalist Nat Nakasa: Drum,* June 1959; Alexander Kerr, "Never Accept Defeat," in Wilson and Perrot, 521.
103 *Charles Ranson:* "Notes on a Journey to Southern Africa, January 10 to March 8, 1959," C. W. Ranson, Reports 1957–1960, Box 18, Publications, WCC.
103 *"apartheid forced the church":* Simon Gqubule, interview by author, June 12, 2005.
104 *"He talked from handwritten notes":* Bishop Merwyn Castle, interview by author, June 10, 2005.
104 *Very few of the prescribed textbooks:* Academic Board minutes, AB1017 A1, CPSA; Stephen Gray, writing in *Mail and Guardian* (Johannesburg), August 19, 1998.
104 *A German expatriate:* Dr. K. Blaser, letter to Academic Board, 1967, Box 3, FedSem.
104 *Seminary archives show:* Minutes and reports, Boxes 4, 5, 7, FedSem; DMT, interview by author, June 22, 2005.
104 *"You had to eat in a particular way":* Thami and Ezra Tisani, interview by author, July 17, 2005.
105 *The college council:* Stubbs, letters to Tutu, March 26, 1966; May 6, 1966; and March 11, 1967, AB2414 student file, CPSA. Minutes of St. Peter's College Council, March 1, 1966; and November 3, 1966, AB1363 S22 (File 4), CPSA.
105 *Aelred Stubbs discussed:* Martin Kenyon, interview by author, October 2, 2004.
105 *"a rather dismal letter":* Pauline +OHP (Order of the Holy Paraclete) to Stubbs, December 23, 1967, AB2414 student file, CPSA.
105 *"an oasis of sanity and love":* DMT to Walter Cason, TEF, New York, February 17, 1967, Area 11, TEF Projects 1965–1970, Box 106, WCC.
105 *Simon Gqubule's daughters:* Gqubule interview.
105 *"I really don't know where":* DMT to Kenyon, June 5, 1968 (Kenyon files).
106 *In Cape Town, life was:* Castle interview.
106 *"Although the Homes":* DMT to Kenyon, March 5, 1968 (Kenyon files).
106 *The Community of the Resurrection:* Wilkinson, *The Community of the Resurrection,* 316.
106 *"we must teach our own people":* Timothy Stanton, interview by author, September 18, 2004.
107 *After the Lambeth Conference:* Reports and correspondence, AB1363 S22 (File 4), CPSA.
107 *The Methodists:* William R. Booth, in Stubbs, *The Planting of the Federal Theological Seminary of Southern Africa,* 1–5; Minutes of St. Peter's College Council, March 1, 1965; Stubbs to Bishop of Grahamstown, January 14, 1964, AB1363 S22 (File 3), CPSA.
107 *When the Methodists persisted:* Gqubule interview; memorandum on cooperation with Fort Hare, AB2414 A5.1, CPSA.
107 *Shortly before Tutu joined:* David Bandey, confidential letter to Robert Selby Taylor, July 28, 1966; Secretary of Bantu Education, letter to Fedsem (copy), May 23, 1967; Registrar, Fedsem, to the Secretary for Bantu Education, September 1967, Communications with University of Fort Hare, Box 32, FedSem.

108 *"I must state that in my view":* Aelred Stubbs to David Bandey, October 23, 1968 AB1363 S22 (File 4), CPSA.

108 *Students new to Fort Hare:* Thami and Ezra Tisani interview.

109 *"They really opened their home":* N. Barney Pityana, interview by author, February 23, 2005.

110 *"His support was important":* Ibid. Biko's account of the caucus is given in Arnold, *Steve Biko,* 10–11, 150.

110 *At the end of the mission week:* Pityana interview.

111 *We had been surrounded:* Ibid.

111 *"I can actually see police coming":* DMT, interview by author, June 22, 2005.

112 *"It has always been our belief":* J. M. de Wet to David Bandey, FedSem president, March 3, 1969; reply, March 4, 1969; J. M. de Wet to President, FedSem, August 15, 1969, Communications with the University of Fort Hare 1962–1969, Box 32, FedSem.

112 *The South African authorities:* Bernard Levin, *Times* (London), August 1972; republished in *South African Outlook,* Vol. 104, No. 1242.

113 *"I don't think Desmond":* Timothy Stanton interview.

113 *In a letter written:* Simpson, letter to the Principals of FedSem colleges, undated, AB2414 B2.2.2, CPSA.

113 *"I miss the children very much":* Leah Tutu to Martin Kenyon, April 16, 1969 (Kenyon files).

114 *"They were insisting":* Aelred Stubbs, interview by author, September 18, 2004.

114 *You started all this racket:* DMT to Stubbs, October 20, 1969, AB2414 student file, CPSA.

114 *It admitted students:* Mpho and Njabulo Ndebele, interview by author, June 25, 2005.

115 *"Bantu travel documents":* Department of Bantu Administration and Development, File No. 100/6/460, Part I, Passport: Desmond Mpilo Tutu, SANA.

115 *"There was no way":* Mpho and Njabulo Ndebele interview.

115 *"the rollicking story":* UBLS campus newsletter, January 10 and January 23, 1971.

116 *Tutu stood out:* Buti Tlhagale, interview by author July 4, 2005.

116 *"I hope you will not have thought":* Correspondence between DMT and Robert Selby Taylor, November 1969–July 1971, AB1363 T1, CPSA.

117 *"Mercifully the local authorities":* DMT, letter to friends, Christmas 1971, King's student file.

117 *When, in 1970, the WCC:* John de Gruchy, *The Church Struggle,* 123–134.

117 *Many black Anglicans:* Lee, *Compromise and Courage,* 300.

118 *The message declared that:* Karis and Gerhart, *From Protest to Challenge,* 417–420.

118 *"There are clergy in South Africa":* B. J. Vorster, letter to Bill Burnett and others, October 24, 1968, AC623 15.1.1, SACC.

118 *The prime minister:* Gill, *A Short History of Lesotho,* 216–222; Khaketla, *Lesotho 1970,* 207–225.

118 *He also imposed:* UBLS campus newsletters, January 22, 1971; February 11, 1972.

119 *"With the uncertainty":* DMT to Selby Taylor, July 19, 1971, AB1363 T1, CPSA.

119 *"I find myself wondering":* Sydney Evans to Shoki Coe, Theological Education Fund, August 25, 1971, King's student file.

119 *"He is a highly educated man":* Department of Bantu Administration and Development, File No. 100/6/460, Part I, Passport: Desmond Mpilo Tutu, SANA.

120 *On August 6, BOSS:* Letter from Prime Minister's Intelligence Adviser to Secretary for the Interior, December 22, 1971, Department of Home Affairs Archives, SANA.

120 *Without much hope:* DMT to Robert Selby Taylor, August 22, 1971; and September 22, 1971. Selby Taylor to Minister of the Interior, August 26, 1971. Selby Taylor to DMT, September 14, 1971, AB1363 T1 (File 1), CPSA.

120 *As months passed:* DMT, Christmas letter, December 1971, King's student file.

120 *"vigorous powers of argument":* Denis Fahy to UBLS, November 17, 1971, DMT staff file, UL Archives.

120 *His appeal was referred:* Letter from Prime Minister's Intelligence Adviser to Secretary for the Interior, December 22, 1971, SANA.

121 *"We won't breathe freely":* DMT to Vice Chancellor, UBLS, January 6, 1971, DMT staff file, UL Archives.

CHAPTER 7: TRANSFORMATION

PAGE

123 *The magistrate at Ladybrand:* Department of Bantu Administration and Development, File No. 100/6/460, Part I, Passport: Desmond Mpilo Tutu, SANA.

124 *The notebooks and the corresponding typed reports:* All reports of travel notes in this chapter from Boxes 123 and 124, TEF Archives, WCC.

124 *His first visit:* Reader, *Africa,* 649–662; Davidson, *Africa in History,* 339; Oliver and Fage, *A Short History of Africa,* 222–224; De Witte, *The Assassination of Lumumba,* especially 1–26, 119–124, and 140–143; Stephen R. Weissman, "U.S. Role in Lumumba Murder Revealed," *All Africa Global News* (allafrica.com), July 22, 2002.

125 *"Politically [the] country":* DMT travel notes, April–May 1972, WCC.

125 *He conferred official recognition:* Sundkler and Steed, *A History of the Church,* 762–783, 965–968.

126 *Tutu's reports:* DMT travel notes, February 1974, WCC.

126 *"Zaire is passing through":* DMT travel notes, April 1975, WCC.

127 *During the war Biafra:* Sundkler and Steed, 947–955.

127 *"Everybody trusts him":* DMT travel notes, March 1–21, 1973, WCC.

128 *He saw the Islam in Africa project:* DMT travel notes, April–May 1972 and February 1974, WCC.

129 *"The city looks prosperous":* DMT travel notes, August–September 1972, WCC.

129 *"The flags are out":* DMT travel notes, November–December 1973, WCC.

129 *"How do you speak about":* DMT travel notes, August–September 1972, WCC.

131 *Within days, Uganda's way":* Ibid.

131 *This is a sad country:* DMT travel notes, November–December 1973, WCC.

131 *"I don't know what":* DMT, email to author, June 6, 2005.

131 *Touring the white-ruled:* Betty Ward, interview by author, September 10, 2004; DMT, email to author, May 27, 2005; DMT travel notes, September 1973, WCC.

131 *Mozambique was "extremely depressing":* DMT travel notes, September 1973, WCC.

132 *"It is a wonder":* Ibid.

132 *Zambia had derived:* DMT travel notes, November–December 1973, WCC.

132 *"too many people are whisked":* DMT travel notes, November 11–30, 1974, WCC.

132 *He arrived in Ghana:* DMT travel notes, November 6–27, 1972, WCC.

132 *"did their job only too well":* DMT travel notes, March 1–21, 1973, WCC; Reader, *Africa,* 575.

132 *"I was reflecting on how little":* DMT travel notes, November 6–27, 1972, WCC.

133 *In Sierra Leone, a theologian:* Ibid.

133 *There is a mood:* Ibid.

133 *In Liberia:* Ibid.

133 *a mosaic of poverty:* DMT travel notes, November–December 1973, WCC.

133 *In Sudan:* DMT travel notes, ibid. and April 1975, WCC.

134 *Rwanda was now:* DMT travel notes, April 1973, WCC.

134 *Eighty-five percent:* Ibid.

135 *"Why do the expatriates live":* DMT travel notes, November–December 1973, WCC.

135 *"He [Parrinder] replied":* Tutu, Foreword, in Ackermann, *After the Locusts,* ix. Tutu does not identify Parrinder by name, but he confirmed the identification in an interview with the author, April 19, 2005.

136 *"Our people did not doubt":* DMT, Shoki Coe Memorial Lecture, Tainan Theological College, Taiwan, June 12, 1995, author's collection.

136 *To answer these questions:* DMT travel notes, April 1975, WCC; DMT, Shoki Coe Lecture.

136 *"They had to deny":* Tutu, Foreword in Oosthuizen, Kitshoff, and Dube, vii–viii; Tutu, "Some African Insights and the Old Testament," in Becken.

137 *"African theology has given":* Tutu, "Black Theology/African Theology–Soul Mates or Antagonists?" *Journal of Religious Thought,* Vol. 32, Issue 2, Fall–Winter 75, 25.

137 *"full of sorrow, bitterness":* John Mbiti, "An African Views American Black Theology (1974)," in Cone and Wilmore, 379–384.

137 *His most powerful defense:* Tutu, "Black Theology," September 1973 in ASATI Staff Institute, January 1975, Drawer 2, WCC.

CHAPTER 8: BLOODY CONFRONTATION

PAGE

141 *"The English-speaking churches":* Robert S. Bilheimer, quoted in Lückhoff, *Cottesloe,* 27.

142 *In a country as divided:* Lee, *Compromise and Courage,* 322.

142 *Tutu was nominated:* AB2013 B4, CPSA.

142 *"I was sure he would make":* Aelred Stubbs, interview by author, September 18, 2004.

142 *"whether [Tutu] commands much":* Star, July 4, 1974.

143 *Thirty years later:* Sipho Masemola, interview by author, December 1, 2004.

143 *"Johannesburg rejected me":* DMT to Stanley Mogoba, September 24, 1974, TEF Africa correspondence, FS5-73-1, WCC.

143 *"Had I been elected":* Tutu, foreword in Lee, *Compromise and Courage,* viii.

143 *He did not know Tutu:* Timothy Bavin, letter to author, October 2, 2004.

144 *The family was popular:* Interviews by author with members of St. Augustine's Church, Grove Park, October 3, 2004, including Alison Burtt, Daniel and Martin Cartwright, Bill Hartley, Christopher Towne, and Jane Upcott; Richardson, *A History.*

144 *Leah was later to describe:* Leah Tutu, interviews by Hennie Serfontein, 1996.

144 *"I had soaking wet shoulders":* Betty Ward, interview by author, September 10, 2004.

144 *One evening, Leah: Daily News* (Durban), June 7, 1976.

144 *"I think your coming would":* DMT to Bill Burnett, February 3, 1975; and reply, February 17, 1975, TEF Africa correspondence, WCC.

144 *"Leah was very, very upset":* DMT, interviews with author, August 16, 2005; and with Hennie Serfontein, 1996.

145 *"I do not want to apologise":* Star, March 13, 1975.

146 *Nobody knew exactly:* Kane-Berman, *Black Revolt, White Reaction,* 52–5.

147 *The congregation, numbering 1,500:* "Parish Questionnaire," AB1979 D6, CPSA.

147 *The only concern should be: Parishioner,* April, May, and September 1975.

147 *Ffrench-Beytagh had been:* Ffrench-Beytagh, *Encountering Darkness,* 89–132, 172–232; 277–282.

148 *Whitman wrote: Parishioner,* December 1975.

149 *He was also the priest:* Alan Paton, interview by author, June 6, 1980; published in *Star,* June 6, 1980.

149 *"Please let's not bicker": Parishioner,* November 1975.

150 *In the recollection of:* Philip Mokuku, interview by author, June 17, 2005.

150 *"playing, praying, and learning":* DMT in *Hope and Suffering,* 33–35.

150 *"in many ways it was whites":* Mutloatse, "Mutloatse on Tutu," *Ecunews* (Johannesburg), December 1984, 17.

150 *Passionate about reconciliation: Times* (London), October 6, 1975; *Star* and *Natal Witness,* October 30, 1975.

151 *Tutu turned down: Rand Daily Mail,* March 10, 1975.

151 *Khaketla told him:* DMT, interview by author, August 16, 2005.

151 *In the elective assembly:* AB1363 L17, CPSA.

151 *"There have been very few":* To Shirley Moulder, *South African Outlook,* Vol. 112, No. 1328, February 1982, 20.

152 *"deeply desolated. . . . It has been":* AB1979 D6, CPSA.

152 *"One man has—by God's grace":* Watchman, June 1976.

152 *His fear was based:* Lodge, *Black Politics,* 321–335; Anthony Marx, *Lessons of Struggle,* 60–72; Brooks and Brickhill, *Whirlwind before the Storm,* 67–85; Kane-Berman, *Black Revolt, White Reaction,* 48–52; Karis and Gerhart, *From Protest to Challenge,* 163–166, 202–204; Hirson, *Year of Fire, Year of Ash,* 142–143.

152 *"there wasn't a shot fired":* Joe Slovo, interview by Thomas G. Karis and Gail M. Gerhart, October 15, 1990, folder 35, A2675, Karis-Gerhart Collection; Barrell, *Conscripts to Their Age,* chap. 2.

153 *"a near irrelevance inside":* Barrell, *Conscripts to Their Age,* chap. 1.

153 *State repression:* Barrell, chap. 2.

153 *"I speak with words I hope": Rand Daily Mail,* May 1, 1976.

154 *"What do you say to justify":* DMT, interview by John Freeth, July 11, 2003.

154 *"I felt this pressure":* DMT, interview by author, August 16, 2005.

154 *"I am writing to you, Sir"*: Tutu, *The Rainbow People*, 3.

155 *"Most of our people"*: *Star*, June 25, 1976.

155 *"You hear people"*: *Star*, May 24, 1976.

155 *The resolution condemned:* AB2013 D1, CPSA.

155 *Tutu naively gave it to him:* DMT, interview by Carina le Grange, June 8, 1995.

155 *Pringle splashed it in full: Sunday Tribune*, May 23, 1976.

155 *"Does the Prime Minister"*: PC1/9/10/2/11, Paton Centre; published, with slight amendments, as an unsigned editorial in *Sunday Tribune*, June 13, 1976.

155 *"You can't appeal"*: Barney Pityana, interview by author, February 23, 2005.

156 *In a memoir of events:* Ndlovu, *The Soweto Uprisings*, 3–18, 45–48.

156 *On May 17: World* (Johannesburg), May 19, May 24, and June 1, 1976.

156 *On Sunday, June 13:* Murphy Morobe, evidence to TRC, July 23, 1996; Karis and Gerhart, *From Protest to Challenge*, 167–168.

156 *On June 16:* Brooks and Brickhill, *Whirlwind before the Storm*, 8; Kane-Berman, *Black Revolt, White Reaction*, 1.

157 *According to Bongani Mnguni:* Brink et al., *It All Started with a Dog . . .* , 58–59.

157 *It was not mythology:* Murphy Morobe, evidence to TRC.

157 *As Sophie Tema saw it: World*, June 17, 1976.

157 *"What do I say to black people"*: Peter J. Storey, notes of an emergency meeting at the South African Council of Churches, June 16, 1976 (Peter Storey files).

158 *"If they had meant to quell"*: Peter J. Storey, notes of a meeting of church leaders of the SACC, June 18, 1975 (Storey files); minutes of SACC executive committee and church leaders' meetings, June 16 and June 18, 1976, AC623 1.4.1, SACC.

158 *He left the meeting:* Brooks and Brickhill, *Whirlwind before the Storm*, 1–29; Kane-Berman, *Black Revolt, White Reaction*, 1–36.

158 *In the ten months:* Kane-Berman, 27.

158 *He was shocked:* David Bruno, interview by author, September 20, 2004.

158 *"Tell them that peace and order"*: *Parishioner*, July 1976.

159 *He wrote to Trevor Huddleston:* DMT to Trevor Huddleston, June 28, 1976, Stepney miscellaneous correspondence, Huddleston Archive.

159 *"What a magnificent occasion"*: *Parishioner*, August 1976.

160 *But preaching at:* Enthronement address, August 1, 1976 (Martin Kenyon files); Philip Mokuku interview.

160 *Leah sought work: Daily News*, Durban, November 3, 1977; DMT to Bill Burnett, December 2, 1976, AB1363 L16, CPSA.

161 *"We leave Bishop's House"*: Diary entry related by David Bruno, September 20, 2004.

161 *"grave and respectful politeness"*: Hastings, *The Church in Africa*, 303.

162 *"I have seldom felt"*: DMT, letter to bishops, June 18, 1977, AB1363 L16, CPSA.

162 *Tutu also admired:* Gill, *A Short History of Lesotho*, 63–114, 152–154; Sundkler and Steed, *A History of the Church in Africa*, 374–383.

162 *The son, now King Letsie III:* King Letsie III, interview by author, June 18, 2004.

163 *It is because blacks: Southern Cross*, Cape Town, April 3, 1977; *Rand Daily Mail*, March 24, 1977; *Star*, September 8, 1977.

163 *In a circular:* DMT letter postmarked November 24, 1977 (bishops: various), Huddleston Archive.

163 *Within half an hour:* Harold Snyman, evidence to TRC, September 10, 1997.

164 *"they did not take kindly"*: Amnesty Committee, TRC, decision on amnesty applications 3918/96, 3915/96, 6367/97 and 3521/96.

164 *"we give thanks for Steve"*: Tutu, *The Rainbow People*, 15.

164 *The first attempt:* SACC minutes, October 5, 1976, AC623 1.4.1; SACC statement, October 1976; letter to church leaders, January 21, 1977, AC623 1.8, SACC.

165 *In Cape Town:* Meeting notes, November 3, 1976, AB1363 L16, CPSA.

165 *He and Leah:* DMT to John Rees, December 1, 1975, AC623 1.4.1, SACC.

165 *Within a year:* Michael Carmichael, letter to Bill Burnett, September 30, 1977, AB2668, CPSA; Peter Storey, circular to heads of churches, November 23, 1977, AC623 1.8, SACC.

165 *Tutu wrote to Burnett:* DMT to Burnett, October 21, 1977, AB1363 L16, CPSA.

165 *He consulted:* DMT to Roy Snyman, February 27, 1978, AB1363 L16, CPSA.

165 *Burnett followed up:* Pastoral letter, November 23, 1977, AB1363 L16, CPSA.

166 *"I only hope":* Huddleston to DMT, December 29, 1977 (bishops: various), Huddleston Archive.

166 *But the South African Church Union:* Letter to *Seek* (Johannesburg), unpublished, March 14, 1978, A2 Correspondence, UCT Archives.

166 *"One wonders why the Bishop":* Axeman, newsletter of St. Boniface Anglican Church, Germiston, February 1978.

CHAPTER 9: THE JAZZ CONDUCTOR

PAGE

167 *Most of the 3,000:* Barrell, *Conscripts to Their Age,* chap. 3.

167 *In the weeks following:* Murphy Morobe, evidence to TRC, July 23, 1996.

167 *In October 1976:* Barrell, *Conscripts to Their Age,* chap. 3.

167 *"This action by us":* Secretary Cyrus Vance, Cable to African diplomatic posts, in Mokoena, 77–79.

168 *Tutu's former student:* Tlhagale, interview by author, July 4, 2005.

168 *"In the SACC":* Peter Storey, *South African Outlook,* Vol. 112, No. 1328, February 1982, 23.

168 *Its immediate predecessor:* Spong, *Come Celebrate!* 7–23.

169 *a "kind of whiz kid":* Michael Carmichael to Bill Burnett, September 30, October 28, December 13, 1977, AB2668, CPSA. Minutes of SACC executive, 1977, AC623 1.4.1.11; 1978, AC623 1.4.1.12–13, SACC.

169 *Handing over to Tutu:* Rees to DMT, May 8, 1979, AC623 7.3.14, SACC.

169 *He also gave:* Documents in AC623 7.23.4, SACC.

169 *"I tried on his shoes":* General secretary's report to 1978 national conference, AC623 1.3.18, SACC.

169 *"The church exists first":* DMT, "The Role of the SACC," June 8, 1978, AB1363 1.4.1.12–13, CPSA.

170 *The staff at the SACC quickly concluded:* Spong, *Come Celebrate!* 69.

170 *The council was the largest:* Ibid., 69–70; Sophie Mazibuko, in Tlhagale and Mosala, 13–18; author's observations and staff accounts to author, 1978–1982.

171 *"He wasn't the grand planner":* Dan Vaughan, remarks to author.

171 *He would say:* Joe Seremane, interview by author, February 8, 2005.

171 *Once he ordered:* DMT, Report of general secretary to SACC executive, March 12, 1980, AC623 5.6, SACC.

171 *He once wrote:* Correspondence with Anne Hughes, January 1980, AC623 5.2.1, SACC.

172 *The trial was important:* Cable from Ambassador William G. Bowdler to Secretary of State, Document 829, April 6, 1978, NSA.

172 *The accused decided:* Tokyo Sexwale, interview by author, November 7, 2005.

172 *"But as attempts to bring":* DMT, evidence in *State versus Mosima Sexwale and 11 Others,* Vol. 49, 2392–2405, AD1901, SAIRR Archive.

172 *Tutu's attitude toward violence:* Hofmeyr, Millard, and Froneman, 264.

173 *He said it should formally:* WCC document, December 1977, Document 614A, Kistner Collection.

173 *"How can you put that paper out":* Michael Carmichael to Bill Burnett, March 17, 1978, AB2668, CPSA.

173 *Sjollema's paper was merely:* Minutes of SACC executive, March 15, 1978, AC623 1.4.1.12–13, SACC.

173 *Radical in the original sense:* Eloff Commission, *Report,* 429.

173 *Johannesburg's largest daily:* Star, July 6, 1978; author's experience.

173 *In his paper, Kistner:* Background paper for the discussion of the problem of a "just revolution," Document 625A, appendix 2, Kistner Collection.

174 *The document was referred:* Report and assessment on SACC national conference 1978, AC623 1.3.18, SACC.

174 *"Our cry is":* Daily News (Durban), August 10, 1979; 1978 Lambeth Conference, Resolution 3.

174 *After some debate:* Author's notes; *Star* and *Pretoria News,* November 14, 1979; *Star,* December 6 and 10, 1979.

175 *In 1978, 26.3 billion:* Thompson, *A History of South Africa,* 217.

175 *Debate over using:* Luthuli, *Let My People Go,* 186.

175 *In 1976, the SACC:* "Investment in South Africa: Report Submitted by the Division of Justice and Reconciliation," SACC, 1977, 3604A, Kistner Collection.

175 *The participants were mostly:* Michael Carmichael to Bill Burnett, May 5, 1978, AB2668, CPSA.

175 *The SACC's lawyer:* Oliver Barrett to DMT, June 22, 1978, AC623 1.3.18, SACC.

176 *The conference excluded:* Author's report, *Daily News* (Durban), July 17, 1978.

176 *This resolution was:* DMT, "Is There Still Hope?" address to the Royal African Society, London, in *African Affairs,* Vol. 77, No. 309, October 1978, 567–570; *Star,* July 21, 1978; Associated Press, July 3, 1979.

176 *Speaking to Quakers: Bulletin* (Philadelphia), May 18, 1979.

176 *In a three-year project:* Barbara Waite, compiler, *"A Land Divided Against Itself: A Map of South Africa,"* Johannesburg: Black Sash, 1978; author's report, *Star,* March 13, 1978.

177 *In Zweledinga:* DMT, General secretary's report to SACC annual national conference 1979, AC623 1.3.19, SACC.

177 *I believe that you are unaware:* DMT to P. W. Botha, July 5, 1979, AC623 15.1.11, SACC.

178 *Botha's mother had been:* Dirk en Johanna de Villiers, *"PW,"* 1984, 9.

178 *"Although it is conceded":* P. W. Botha to DMT, August 29, 1979, AC623 15.1.11, SACC.

178 *Visiting European donor agencies:* Transcript of Danish interview, *Ecunews,* September 14, 1979.

178 *Botha's interior minister: Citizen* (Johannesburg), September 7, 1979.

178 *The president of the Methodist Church: Natal Mercury,* September 8, 1979.

178 *Right-wing Anglicans: Citizen,* September 7, 1979.

179 *Bill Burnett privately:* DMT, Internal SACC report, October 1979, AC623 5.6, SACC.

179 *"He is a man":* Bavin's open letter, September 11, 1979, author's copy.

179 *American diplomats:* U.S. consul general, Johannesburg, cable to secretary of state, September 6, 1979, Document 958, NSA.

179 *Koornhof had in preceding months:* DMT-Koornhof correspondence, AC623 13.2, SACC; DMT, general secretary's report to SACC executive, September 1979, AC623 1.3.18, SACC.

179 *During an eighty-minute meeting:* Anglican report on SACC church leaders' meeting, October 15, 1979, AB2668, CPSA.

179 *The police minister: Star,* October 10, 1979.

179 *They were at one:* Anglican report on SACC church leaders' meeting, October 15, 1979; SACC minutes of meeting, October 15, 1979, AC623 1.4.1, SACC.

180 *"I would much rather":* DMT, interview by Hennie Serfontein, 1996.

180 *Trevor, now working:* DMT, Christmas 1979, letter to friends, A2 Correspondence, UCT Archives.

180 *"I have also prayed":* DMT to minister of the interior, October 16, 1979, AC623 1.8, SACC.

180 *Tutu continued:* DMT-Koornhof correspondence.

180 *"I have written this letter":* DMT to prime minister, November 15, 1979, AC623 15.1.11, SACC.

181 *He called again for a national convention:* DMT, general secretary's report to SACC executive, March 12, 1980, AC623 5.6, SACC.

181 *One of the policemen:* Paul Erasmus, interview by author, December 6, 2005.

181 *One of the only:* Directorate of Security Legislation, Department of Justice, File 2/3/2/5862, SANA.

181 *"He did not hesitate":* Brigadier Willie Wentzel, interview by Hennie Serfontein, 1996.

181 *The government's response:* SACC telex, March 5, 1980, AC623 5.2.6, SACC.

181 *Church leaders:* AC623 5.2.6, SACC; AC623 1.5, SACC.

181 *"What a blunder":* Winnie Mandela to DMT, March 5, 1980, AC623 5.2.6, SACC.

182 *"I have no wish":* Robert Runcie to P. W. Botha, March 13, 1980, AC623 5.2.6, SACC.

182 *He described Tutu:* U.S. Senate, *Congressional Record,* March 6, 1980, S2290–91.

182 *Now the university's president:* Protests over passport withdrawal, AC623 5.2.6, SACC.

182 *The next weekend: Sunday Post,* March 9, 1980; Zwelakhe Sisulu, interview by author, 2005.

182 *To the young:* Buti Tlhagale interview.

182 *The newspaper described: Rand Daily Mail,* March 10, 1980.

182 *Soon Tutu: Daily News* (Durban), June 9, 1980.

183 *From Robben Island:* Nelson Mandela to DMT, undated, File C3.11.1–C3.11.2 Tambo Papers. (For reasons that are not clear, Tutu never received the letter.)

183 *Influenced by a visit:* Barrell, *Conscripts to Their Age,* chap. 4.

183 *Tambo's record:* Notes, January 19, 1980, and notebooks c. 1979–1980, A11.3.5, Tambo Papers. (My attention was drawn to this entry by Luli Callinicos's biography of Tambo.)

184 *The conference, inspired partly: Star,* July 26 and 27, 1979; *Ecunews,* August 3, 1979.

184 *Tutu was personally:* Author's report, *Star,* July 25, 1979.

184 *They were aimed:* Ibid.

184 *At the national conference in 1980:* Conference documents, AC623 1.3.20, SACC; *Star,* May 7 and 9, 1980.

185 *Joe Wing:* Message to the Churches, AC623 15.1.11, SACC.

185 *Bavin lived:* Bavin to Burnett, May 30, 1980, AB1363 J5, CPSA.

185 *The fifty-member group:* Author's observations.

186 *Swanepoel stopped:* Author's observations; *Star,* May 26, 1980.

186 *In the black women's:* Spong, *Come Celebrate!* 64.

186 *In their cells:* John F. Burns, *New York Times,* May 28, 1980.

186 *Tutu complained:* DMT, interview by Thomas Karis, February 28, 1984, Folder 39, A2675, Karis-Gerhart Collection.

186 *During a prayer service:* DMT to Bernard Spong, March 10, 1993, AB2546 T17, CPSA.

186 *P. W. Botha was furious: Star,* May 30, 1980.

186 *That weekend, Tutu:* DMT, statement, May 31, 1980, AC623 15.1.11, SACC; minutes of SACC executive with church leaders, June 4, 1980, AC623 1.4.14–16, SACC; DMT, letters to P. W. Botha, June 5, and P. G. J. Koornhof, June 10, 1980, AC623 15.1.11, SACC.

187 *In the interests:* General Secretary's Report, 1981 National Conference, AC623 5.6, SACC.

187 *Twenty church leaders:* Transcript of meeting between cabinet and church leaders, author's collection; Peter Storey, report to Central Methodist Church, Johannesburg, September 1980, AC623 5.1.11, SACC.

187 *The church leaders: Saturday Post,* August 9, 1980.

188 *"I can't say":* Draft of DMT's column, Kairos newspaper, AC623 5.7, SACC.

188 *Buti Tlhagale said:* Minutes of a meeting of theologians to evaluate talks, November 12, 1980, AC623 1.8, SACC.

188 *They saw those who led:* Broederkring members to author; Boesak, *Black and Reformed,* 80.

188 *"Moses went to Pharoah":* DMT, column for *Seek,* August 12, 1980, AC623 5.7, SACC.

188 *It took four months:* Correspondence at AC623 5.1.11, SACC; DMT to Botha, September 18, 1980.

188 *After South Africa's summer holidays:* DMT to P. W. Botha, February 11, 1981, AC623 13.2, SACC.

189 *It is not gas chambers:* General Secretary's Report to Executive Committee, February 23, 1981, AC623 1.4.1, SACC.

189 *"our sons, our fathers":* DMT, address at memorial service, Regina Mundi, AC623 5.7, SACC.

189 *"You appear to have opted":* Botha to DMT, March 12, 1981, AC623 13.2, SACC.

189 *In March 1981:* DMT, Report of General Secretary to Executive, April 10, 1981, AC623 5.6, SACC.

189 *Addressing the UN:* "Bishop Desmond Tutu Addresses UN Special Committee against Apartheid, March 23, 1981," pamphlet, UN Centre against Apartheid and UN Department of Public Information.

190 *He saw Jeane Kirkpatrick:* DMT, "Report on trip 4.3.81 to 9.4.81," AC623 5.6, SACC; *Associated Press,* March 25, 1981; minister of police to House of Assembly, Cape Town, September 10, 1981, Hansard col., 615.

190 *Ten days earlier:* Rowland Evans and Robert Novak, *Boston Globe,* March 22, 1981; Depart-

ment of State memorandum on Ambassador Kirkpatrick's conversations with SADF Lieutenant General Van der Westhuizen and Anglican Bishop Desmond Tutu, Documents 1150, March 20, 1981, and 1156, March 25, 1981, NSA; Associated Press, March 25, 1981.

190 *An angry Botha: Washington Post,* March 29, 1981.
190 *Tutu had intended:* Associated Press, April 1, 1981.
190 *Two senior staff members: Times* (London), April 3, 1981.
190 *In the first:* DMT, report on trip 4.3.81 to 9.4.81, AC623 5.6, SACC.
190 *As Tutu traveled home: Rand Daily Mail,* April 8 and 9, 1981.
190 *"It was a pretty good":* Erasmus interview.
191 *He responded: New York Times,* April 17, 1981.
191 *A few days later:* Directorate of Security Legislation, Department of Justice, File No. 81/90179, D. Tutu, SANA.
191 *That evening:* Presidium meeting minutes, April 10, 1981, AC623 7.13.4, SACC.
191 *Money, in particular:* Eloff Commission, *Report,* 297–299.
191 *A year before:* Executive Committee minutes, January 19, 1977, AB1363 1.4.1. 12–13, CPSA.
191 *The executive committee approved:* Michael Carmichael to Bill Burnett, September 30, 1977, AB2668, CPSA.
191 *However, it took:* Peter Storey, memorandum, June 1, 1979, AC623 1.4.1, SACC.
192 *Then auditors found:* DMT, General Secretary's Annual Report to Church Leaders, September 1980, AC623 1.8, SACC.
192 *This auditor found:* Minutes of Presidium meeting, December 2 and 3, 1980, AC623 1.5, SACC.
192 *Storey also criticized:* Storey to DMT, June 1, 1979, AC623 1.5, SACC.
192 *Both men were acquitted: Rand Daily Mail,* October 17, 1979; Eloff Commission, *Report,* 128.
192 *He claimed to represent:* Acknowledgment of check fraud, signed April 19, 1979 (Storey files); Christian League of Southern Africa and Reformed Independent Churches Association, letter to the secretary, President's Council, Cape Town, December 1981, author's collection; Leonard, *Apartheid Whitewash,* 22.
192 *Successive police ministers: Star,* November 20, 1978; October 10, 1979; May 30, 1980.
193 *The Dependants' Conference:* Annual reports, AC623 1.3.20, SACC.
193 *Its name, meaning: Ecunews,* No. 19, 1976.
193 *Most of its money:* Asingeni Fund report, undated, AC623 7.3.14, SACC.
193 *He also operated:* DMT to Dr. Warner Conring, Evangelical Church in Germany, October 22, 1980, AC623 7.3.14, SACC; Eloff Commission, *Report,* 381–382.
193 *Over time, the fund:* Eloff Commission, *Report,* 330–335; *Star,* July 17, 1978.
193 *The small, confidential:* Presidium Meeting minutes, April 10, 1981, AC623 7.13.4, SACC; *State versus John Charles Rees,* Supreme Court of South Africa (Witwatersrand Local Division), unreported judgment of Mr. Justice Goldstone, June 1983; *Cape Times, Star,* April 15, 1983; *Sunday Express* (Johannesburg), April 17, 1983.
194 *The meeting sent:* Presidium meeting minutes, April 13, 1981, AC623 1.5; Barrett, letter to SACC Presidium, April 13, 1981; AC623 7.13.4, SACC.
194 *After some months:* Minutes, reports, and correspondence at AC623 1.5 and AC623 5.4, SACC.
194 *First, during one of the fraud trials:* Eloff Commission, *Report,* 128.
194 *Newspapers that usually: Rand Daily Mail,* October 28, 1981; *Cape Times,* October 15 and 27, 1981.
194 *Worse for Tutu:* DMT, General Secretary's Report to 1983 National Conference, 18; AC623 5.6, SACC.
195 *He asked Rees:* DMT to Rees, November 9, 1981; Rees to DMT, November 20, 1981, Memorandum from Matthew I. Stevenson, 1982; AC623 7.13.4, SACC.
195 *A few days after:* Executive Committee Resolution, October 28, 1981, AC623 1.8, SACC.
195 *Its terms of reference: Government Gazette,* Pretoria, Vol. 197, No. 7942, November 20, 1981.
195 *The judge: State versus John Charles Rees,* judgment and sentence, June 1983.
195 *Wolfram Kistner:* Evaluation of 1983 National Conference, Document 1770, Kistner Collection.

195 *I resent such treatment:* DMT, General Secretary's Report to 1983 National Conference, AC623 5.6, SACC, 18–21.

196 *It ended with:* Minutes of 1983 National Conference, AC623 1.3, SACC.

196 *Trying to visit:* Peter Storey, e-mail to author, December 28, 2005; Tutu, in Storey, *With God in the Crucible,* 10; *Times* (London), February 1, 1981.

196 *After Rees's conviction:* Storey to DMT, May 21, 1998 (Storey files).

196 *They quickly restored:* Storey to SACC executive, May 27, 1983, AC623 1.3.23, SACC.

197 *The government commission:* New York Times Magazine, March 14, 1982.

197 *The commission contracted:* Eloff Commission, *Report,* 13–21.

197 *They argued that: Sunday Express* (Johannesburg), February 13, 1983.

197 *The police asked:* Police submission to Eloff Commission, AC623 13.2, SACC.

197 *Heyns opened the way:* Johan Heyns, "Evaluering van die Teologie van Biskop Desmond Tutu," submission to Eloff Commission, AB1363 S44.6 (File 4), CPSA.

197 *However, another:* David J. Bosch, submission to Eloff Commission, February 1983, AB1363 S44.6 (File 4), CPSA.

197 *Allister Sparks: Observer* (London), September 12, 1982.

197 *In the face of this, God:* Tutu, *The Rainbow People,* 55–56.

198 *Storey delivered: Rand Daily Mail,* June 1, 1983.

199 *In the view of Dan Vaughan:* E-mail from Dan Vaughan, January 16, 2006.

199 *Eloff's 450-page report:* Eloff Commission, *Report,* 304–307, 322, 427–443.

199 *"In no way":* C. F. Eloff, interview by author, December 11, 2004.

199 *He wrote a letter:* Eloff interview; *Ecunews,* Vol. 2, 1984, 11; Capital Radio, Mthata, BBC summary of world broadcasts, February 17, 1984.

CHAPTER 10: A FIRE BURNING IN MY BREAST

PAGE

201 *Black journalists:* For example, Jon Qwelane, *Star* (Johannesburg), April 14, 1981.

201 *His outspokenness:* Mandela, interview by author, March 20, 2003.

201 *Buti Tlhagale's:* Tlhagale interview, July 4, 2005.

201 *But whites' anger:* DMT, Christmas letter 1978, A2 Correspondence, UCT Archives.

201 *In 1978, incited:* Paul Erasmus, interview by author, December 6, 2005. SACC Executive Minutes, September 19 and 20, 1978, AB1363 1.4.1.12–13, CPSA; *Star,* September 11, 1978.

201 *A group calling: Star,* September 23, 1980; *Sowetan,* May 21, 1981.

201 *Tutu first drew up:* DMT, remark to author, June 26, 1997.

201 *He was enchanted:* Lenki Khanyile, interview by Hennie Serfontein, 1996.

201 *After his visit: Southern Cross,* May 3, 1981; *Ecunews* (Johannesburg), No. 10, 1981, June 19, 1981; SAIRR, *Race Relations Survey 1981,* 34.

202 *A security agency's:* Directorate of Security Legislation, Department of Justice, File No. 81/90179, D. Tutu, SANA.

202 *In a wide-ranging speech:* House of Assembly, September 10, 1981, Hansard cols. 613–616.

202 *Most members of the SACC's:* SABC, *Editorial Comment,* May 7, 1981, and May 20, 1983; *Citizen,* June 13 and November 27, 1984.

202 *One minute he seems:* Lin Menge, *Rand Daily Mail,* May 9, 1981.

203 *Helen Suzman:* Correspondence, 1981–1983, A2084 M61, Suzman Papers; Suzman to DMT, December 21, 1983, AB1979, Da 3.1, CPSA.

203 *He is a great character:* Paton to Huddleston, September 21, 1982, PC1/5/3/1–62, Paton Centre.

204 *You [the government]:* DMT, General Secretary's Report to SACC National Conference, June 21, 1982, AC623 1.3.22, SACC.

204 *"I am increasingly disturbed":* Burnett to DMT, May 28, 1981, AC623 1.8, SACC.

204 *"Desmond is Desmond":* Burnett to Michael Nuttall, bishop of Pretoria, July 10, 1981, AB1363 P26, CPSA.

204 *As confrontation with:* Letters, July and August 1981, AC623 1.8 and 13.2; Executive Committee Minutes, July 28–29, 1981, and October 27–28, 1981, AC623 1.4.1, SACC.

204 *Church leaders still:* Report to church leaders, October 1982; Russell to DMT, March 8, 1984, AC623 1.8, SACC.

204 *"The whole body":* Bishops of the Church of the Province of Southern Africa, statement, November 25, 1981, AC623 13.2, SACC.

205 *In a resolution:* Resolution, 1984 SACC National Conference, AC623 1.3.24, SACC.

205 *Tutu described:* Tutu, *The Rainbow People,* chap. 7.

205 *He had narrowly missed:* John de Gruchy, *The Church Struggle,* 193.

205 *He was a powerful:* Frederick Williams, New York, interview by author, August 8, 2003.

206 *In January 1983:* Van Kessel, *Beyond Our Wildest Dreams,* 15–18.

206 *"I'm not a thinker":* DMT, comment to author, June 26, 1997.

206 *In the 1970s:* Tlhagale interview.

206 *The three best examples: Sunday Times* (London), August 25, 1985.

206 *When an activist of the Pan Africanist Congress:* DMT to W. Z. Mafanya, April 3, 1980, A2 Correspondence, BC869, UCT Archives.

206 *He countersigned:* DMT and Naomi Tutu-Seavers letter, PAC/UN file, Nahecs.

207 *"Why are we so often":* DMT, Speech to National Forum, June 11, 1983, Reel 34, Folder 726, A2675, Karis-Gerhart Collection.

207 *Petrus Mokoena hurriedly:* Noonan, *They're Burning the Churches,* 58–60.

208 *Tutu, who had sent:* DMT, telegram to le Grange, AC623 15.1.11, SACC.

208 *On September 6:* TRC, *Report,* Vol. 3, chap. 6, para 260–279; Noonan, 61, 63.

208 *"It was a time":* Noonan, 62–63; *Ecunews,* Vol. 7, 1984, 10.

209 *Questions of peace and violence:* Unless otherwise indicated, information on the Nobel Prize processes is from interviews with the researcher Anne Ragnhild Breiby and the director of the Norwegian Nobel Institute and secretary of the Norwegian Nobel Committee, Dr. Geir Lundestad. Conclusions drawn are the responsibility of the author.

209 *"Their patience is remarkable":* Presentation speech by Gunnar Jahn, chairman of the Nobel Committee, at: www.nobelprize.org/peace/laureates/1960/press.html.

209 *The award to Luthuli:* Geir Lundestad, "The Nobel Peace Prize," in Levinovitz and Ringertz, 176.

210 *"You've got to give the prize":* Lunde, *Paradisveien,* 201–205.

210 *Lislerud was one:* Reported by Lunde.

211 *It selected him:* www.nobelprize.org/peace/laureates/1984/presentation-speech.html.

211 *On the afternoon:* James C. and Eulalie Fenhagen, interview by author, December 4, 2003.

211 *That night Leah: Star,* October 18, 1984.

211 *"It was a giveaway":* Esther B. Fein, *New York Times,* October 17, 1984.

211 *O Lord you have searched me out:* Psalm 139:1–4.

212 *The congregation prayed:* Associated Press, October 16, 1984; *MacNeil/Lehrer NewsHour; New York Times,* October 16, 1984.

212 *"Well, it means":* World News Tonight, ABC News, October 16, 1984.

212 *Tutu also compared: MacNeil/Lehrer NewsHour,* October 16, 1984.

212 *They flew first:* Hastings, *Robert Runcie,* 83.

213 *On Thursday:* Associated Press, United Press International, October 18; *Times* (London), October 19, 1984.

213 *This award is for mothers:* DMT, speech notes, AC623 5.2.1, SACC; Associated Press, October 18, 1984.

213 *Congratulatory messages:* AC623 5.2.1, SACC.

213 *Nelson Mandela:* Mandela, interview by author.

213 *Both P. W. Botha:* Associated Press, October 16–17, 1984; *Ecunews,* December 1984; SABC Comment, October 17; *Star,* October 20.

214 *Alan Paton wrote:* Open letter, October 18, 1984, PC 1/5/14/3/18-1, Paton Centre; PC 1/9/8/1/9, Paton Centre; published in *Sunday Times* (Johannesburg), October 21, 1984.

214 *The SACP throughout: African Communist,* No. 101, Second Quarter, 1985, 26–29.

214 *On Sunday, he spent:* Associated Press, October 21, 1984.

215 *He shared some:* DMT, e-mail to author, May 8, 2006.

215 *He had first asked: Star,* April 7, 1981.

215 *His desire to be:* DMT to Betty Ward, July 17, 1979, A2 Correspondence, BC869, UCT Archive.

215 *Yet Tutu's nomination:* Author's private source, May 1, 1981; Michael Nuttall, *Number Two,* 16.

215 *On the third day: Argus,* May 1, 1981.

215 *Bavin had proved:* DMT, interview with author, August 16, 2005.

215 *In the early 1980s:* Dale and Tish White, interview by author, July 6, 2005.

216 *"We wanted to get":* Terry Waite, interview by author, September 8, 2004.

216 *Runcie, who had once:* Bavin, letter to Anglican bishops, June 18, 1984, AB2668 PEO, Diocese of Johannesburg; Philip Russell to Runcie, June 4, 1982, AB1363 J5, CPSA.

216 *Runcie asked one:* Carpenter, *The Reluctant Archbishop,* 228–229.

216 *Separately, Runcie:* DMT, e-mail to author, October 29, 2005.

216 *Eight months later:* Bavin to Russell, June 18, 1984, AB2668, CPSA.

216 *"It would have made":* Bavin, letter to author, October 2, 2004.

217 *"I note that you":* DMT to Terry Waite, August 15, 1984, AC623 24.24.10, SACC.

217 *Trevor Huddleston:* Huddleston to Father Superior, CR, October 17, 1984, CR Correspondence, Huddleston Archive.

217 *The elective assembly:* Assembly record, AB2013 B5, CPSA.

217 *From the first round:* DMT, foreword in Lee, *Poor Man, Rich Man,* 9–10.

217 *One participant believed:* Private informant (elective assemblies are confidential).

218 *"Blocking was the order":* Norman Luyt to Russell, October 26, 1984, AB2013 B5, CPSA.

218 *the white laity:* Eric Richardson to Russell, received November 2, 1984, AB2013 B5, CPSA.

218 *"A revolt by moderate bishops": Sunday Times,* November 11, 1984.

218 *The bishops:* Press release, November 13, 1984, AC1966; private informants.

218 *"If the Russians":* DMT, Drawbridge Lecture, St. Paul's Cathedral, London, November 19, 1984, author's collection; *Star, Argus,* December 19, 1984.

219 *Philip Russell became:* Letters to Russell, December 10, 12, and 18, 1984, AB2546 J4, CPSA.

219 *Trevor Huddleston was hurt:* Huddleston to DMT, December 5, 1984, AC623 5.2.6, SACC.

219 *As Egil Aarvik:* Waite interview; Associated Press, December 10, 1984; Waite, *Taken on Trust,* 325.

219 *The threat, later found: Star,* August 23, 1985.

220 *At a news conference:* Press statement, January 2, 1985, AC623 10.8, SACC; presentation by DMT, Wesleyan University, Connecticut, March 2, 1984, BC869, UCT Archives.

220 *"I am surprised": New York Times,* January 3, 1985.

220 *The three-hour service:* Order of Service, AB2546 J4, CPSA.

220 *Tutu preached:* Philip Russell to Timothy Bavin, February 6, 1985, AB2546 J4, CPSA.

220 *There were few whites:* Stradling diary No. 37, entry for February 4, 1985, AB853, CPSA.

221 *To the conditions:* DMT, charge, AB2546 J4, CPSA.

221 *"I said to Desmond":* Philip Russell, interview by author, April 23, 2004.

221 *Just a short:* DMT to Russell, February 11, 1985, AB2546 J4, CPSA.

222 *Much of his first:* Pastoral letter, February 9, 1985, AB2546 J4, CPSA; *Star,* March 1, 1985; Nicholas Stubbing, letter to Mirfield, March 2, 1985, CR Archives.

222 *When three senior:* DMT interview.

222 *He appointed Peter Lee:* Diocesan Council minutes, June 15, 1985, AB1979 A62, CPSA; Norman Luyt to Christopher Ahrends, July 21, 1987, AB2546 J4, CPSA.

222 *Tutu had to counter:* Diocesan Council minutes, February 9, 1985 to June 7, 1986, AB1979 A62, CPSA.

222 *Peter Lee later wrote:* Lee, *Compromise and Courage,* 399–401.

222 *Merwyn Castle: Guardian* (London), November 26, 1985; DMT, e-mail to author, January 19, 2001; Castle to Philip Russell, November 21, 1985, AB2546 P8, CPSA; Diocesan Council minutes, December 7, 1985, AB1979 A62, CPSA.

223 *Recalling the outcome:* Sid Colam, remark to author; *Sowetan, Guardian,* April 4, 1985.

223 *The police gasoline-bombed:* Lee, *Compromise and Courage,* 408–412.

223 *On the East Rand: Star,* June 22, 1985.

224 *Two reporters: Star,* June 27, 1985.

224 *Many hundreds:* Kingston Erson, letter to Community of the Resurrection, Mirfield, July 10, 1985, CR Archives.

224 *Leaving the graveside: Star, Business Day* (Johannesburg), *New York Times, Washington Post, Times* (London), *Guardian* (London), *Financial Times,* July 11, 1985; DMT, interview by Hennie Serfontein, 1996.

225 *One of those:* TRC, *Report,* Vol. 2, chap. 3, para 398.

225 *Skhosana's sister:* SABC Television, *TRC Special Report,* February 9, 1985; Evelina Puleng Moloko, evidence to TRC, February 4, 1997.

226 *Television footage:* TRC, *Report,* Vol. 3, chap. 6, para 250.

226 *Thirty thousand people: New York Times, Washington Post, Guardian, Star,* July 24, 1975.

226 *We have a cause that is just:* Tutu, *The Rainbow People,* 98.

226 *A local priest:* DMT, interview by Hennie Serfontein, 1996.

226 *The ANC, in one:* Barrell, *Conscripts to Their Age,* chaps. 6 and 9.

227 *When two men:* Joseph Titus Mazibuko, evidence to TRC, February 4, 1997.

227 *Maki Skhosana:* TRC, *Report,* Vol. 3, chap. 6, para 519.

227 *Van der Merwe:* Judgment of TRC Amnesty Committee, Application of Eugene de Kock and twelve others, February 9, 2001.

227 *Tutu warned:* DMT statement to SA Press Association, AB1979, CPSA.

227 *He asked Botha: Sowetan,* August 2, 1985; *Star,* July 26–31, 1985; *Times* (London), *Guardian* (London), *New York Times, Christian Science Monitor,* July 29 and 30, 1985; *Sunday Star* (Johannesburg), August 4, 1985.

228 *"I will not listen": Sowetan, Guardian* (London), *New York Times,* August 2, 1985.

228 *Five days later:* Rich Mkhondo, *Star,* August 7, 1985; *Washington Post, New York Times,* August 7, 1985.

228 *In February 1986: Sowetan, New York Times, Guardian* (London), February 19, 1986; Associated Press, *Guardian,* February 22; Jon Qwelane, *Sunday Star,* and Alan Cowell, *New York Times,* February 23, 1986; *Christian Science Monitor,* February 24, 1986.

229 *Responding to events:* Barrell, *Conscripts to Their Age,* chaps. 8 and 9.

229 *Later Oliver Tambo:* Ibid., chaps. 7 and 9.

229 *On July 31:* Sampson, *Black and Gold,* 29–32; Waldmeir, *Anatomy of a Miracle,* 55.

230 *As the crisis developed:* Alan Hirsch, Sanctions and the South African Economy, Document 108A, Kistner Collection.

230 *"Things that . . . would": Washington Post,* September 14, 1985.

230 *When creditor banks:* DMT and Beyers Naude, statement, October 28, 1985, AC623 1.4.1, SACC.

231 *In October 1985:* Tutu, *The Rainbow People,* 101.

231 *On April 2: MacNeil/Lehrer NewsHour,* April 2, 1986.

231 *I have no hope:* Tutu, *The Rainbow People,* 111.

232 *Black political organizations: Sowetan,* April 4, 1986.

232 *Helen Suzman said: Star,* April 3, 1986.

232 *Some newspapers: Sunday Times* (Johannesburg), April 13, 1986.

232 *The security file:* Directorate of Security Legislation, Department of Justice, File 2/3/2/5862, SANA.

232 *Legal steps: Beeld* (Johannesburg), April 5, 1986.

CHAPTER 11: OUR BROTHERS AND SISTERS

PAGE

233 *Links between South Africa:* Massie, *Loosing the Bonds,* xv–xxiii, xxiv–vi, 17.

233 *During the nineteenth century:* Sundkler and Steed, *The History of Christianity in Africa,* 363.

234 *The mission it established:* Luthuli, *Let My People Go,* 19; Massie, *Loosing the Bonds,* xxiv–vi, 17.

234 *He had originally hoped:* DMT to Aelred Stubbs, April 25, 1965, AB2414 student file, CPSA.

234 *Powell and Tutu:* Bernice Powell Jackson, interview by author, July 3, 2003.

235 *Williams saw in Tutu:* Frederick Boyd Williams, interview by author, August 8, 2003.

235 *He had met the church's rector:* Hays Rockwell, interview by author, April 21, 2004.

236 *Complementing his work:* Frank Ferrari, interview by author, August 3, 2004.
236 *In 1980: New York Times,* May 4, 1980.
236 *The next year: New York Times,* February 15, 1981; *Washington Post,* September 23, 1981.
236 *After the government: New York Times,* March 14, 1982.
237 *How does one start:* DMT to Hays and Linda Rockwell, May 14, 1980 (Hays Rockwell files).
237 *At the request: Star,* June 1, 1982.
237 *South Africa rejected:* Documents in Senator Jacob K. Javits Collection, State University of New York, Box 33, Series 13, Subseries 2, Tutu, Bishop Desmond.
238 *Tutu's passport: Friend,* June 8, 1982; *Star,* August 19, 1982; *Rand Daily Mail,* September 2, 1982; *Friend,* September 3, 1982.
238 *Since the government:* DMT, General Secretary's Report to the SACC Executive, November 9, 1982, AC623 5.6, SACC.
238 *In the United States:* Daniel P. Matthews, interview by author, December 18, 2003.
238 *In the recollection of:* Edmond Browning, interview by author, May 21, 2004.
239 *We are not a fly-by-night:* DMT, tape recording of speech at Episcopal Church General Convention, New Orleans, September 1982, General Theological Seminary Library, New York.
239 *"sprouting horns or tails": Reuters/Diamond Fields Advertiser,* September 7, 1982; *Argus,* September 8, 1982.
240 *Just when you think:* Rockwell interview.
240 *He's a cross-over artist:* Williams interview.
241 *"These heads of banks":* Rockwell interview.
241 *F. W. de Klerk: Rand Daily Mail,* September 2, 1982.
241 *Tutu interpreted:* Itinerary, September 13–16, 1982, BC869, UCT Archives; notes of foreign policy press conference, September 15, 1982, Tutu file, General Theological Seminary, New York; *Sowetan,* September 17, 1982.
242 *"He taught me":* Powell Jackson interview.
242 *Hays Rockwell recalled:* Rockwell interview.
242 *Once, Fred Williams:* Williams interview.
242 *For his part:* Author's experience.
243 *Botha's . . . diplomacy:* DMT press statement, April 4, 1984, AC623 10.8, SACC.
243 *Trevor Huddleston tried:* Thatcher, *The Downing Street Years,* 514.
243 *Tutu wrote to Thatcher:* Asingeni Report No. 31, July 1984, AC623 1.3.24, SACC; *Star,* March 13, 1984.
243 *Officials of the Reagan administration:* Crocker, *High Noon in Southern Africa,* 199.
244 *Before his appointment:* Chester A. Crocker, "South Africa: Strategy for Change," in *Foreign Affairs,* Winter 1980–1981, 323–351.
244 *Tutu met Crocker: Rand Daily Mail,* February 7, 1984; hearing before Subcommittee on Africa of the Committee on Foreign Affairs of the House of Representatives, December 4, 1984, U.S. Government Printing Office.
244 *"What we did to P. W.":* Chester Crocker, interview by author, December 5, 2003.
244 *The CIA accurately predicted:* Jeffrey Herbst, "Analysing Apartheid: How Accurate Were U.S. Intelligence Estimates of South Africa, 1984–1994?" in *African Affairs,* January 2003, 101.
245 *"I wouldn't claim":* Crocker interview.
245 *"One day no one": Guardian,* November 20, 1999.
245 *In December 1984:* United Press International, December 20; *Star/*Reuters, December 21, 1984.
245 *"After their meeting":* Edward Lee, Q.C., letter to *Embassy,* Canadian foreign policy weekly, September 28, 2005.
245 *In May 1985: Times* (London), June 1, 1985; *Star/*Reuters, September 5, 1985; *Washington Post,* September 6, 1985.
245 *The announcement:* Reagan to DMT, October 19, 1984, Reagan Library.
245 *"Tutu's criticism":* Bruce Chapman, memorandum to Edwin Meese III, October 23, 1984, opened by Reagan Library in response to author's request under Freedom of Information Act #F2002-107.

246 *At the Security Council:* Associated Press, United Press International, October 23, 1984.

246 *In the closing weeks:* Associated Press, October 27 and 28, November 2; *New York Times,* October 28, 1984.

246 *"Perhaps he (Tutu)":* Associated Press, October 31, 1984.

246 *Randall Robinson:* Robinson, remarks to Juan Williams, *Washington Post,* December 12, 1984.

246 *With the help:* Financial Times, December 4, 1984; Sampson, *Black and Gold,* 166; Massie, *Loosing the Bonds,* 559.

246 *In the ensuing weeks:* Mary McGrory, *Washington Post,* December 13, 1984.

247 *Among the hundreds:* Financial Times, December 6; *Washington Post,* December 7 and 11, 1984.

247 *On Sunday December 2:* Washington Post, December 3, 1984.

247 *President Reagan returned:* President's schedule, Public Papers of the Presidents, December 7, 1984, 20 Weekly Comp. Pres. Doc. 1985, Reagan Library.

247 *Constructive engagement:* Associated Press, December 3, 1984.

247 *The following morning:* Washington Post, December 4, 1984.

247 *By Congressional standards:* "The Current Crisis in South Africa," hearing before the Subcommittee on Africa of Committee on Foreign Affairs of the House of Representatives, December 4, 1984, U.S. Government Printing Office.

248 *Tutu's presentation:* Associated Press, December 4, 1984; *Washington Post,* December 5, 1984.

248 *Across town:* Associated Press, December 4, 1984; *New York Times,* December 5, 1984.

249 *Cracks began:* Letter from thirty-five Congressmen to Bernardus Fourie, December 4, 1985, appendix B in Baker, *The United States and South Africa.*

249 *A letter to Reagan:* Washington Post, December 7, 1984.

249 *On the other side:* Ibid.

249 *the White House announced:* United Press International, December 7, 1984.

249 *In Johannesburg:* Star, December 6, 1984.

249 *In the event:* Associated Press, December 7, 1984; *Washington Post,* December 8, 1984.

249 *When Reagan ran out of time:* Leadership magazine, South Africa, June 1985.

249 *Tutu and Reagan:* United Press International, Associated Press, December 7; DMT notes for meeting (Dan Vaughan files); Reagan, remarks to reporters: www.reagan.utexas.edu/archives/speeches/1984/120784a.htm.

250 *After the meeting:* Reagan's remarks: www.reagan.utexas.edu/archives/speeches/1984/120784a.htm.

250 *but to people whose rulers:* The remark was reported by Reuters.

250 *Later in the day:* Reagan's remarks: www.reagan.utexas.edu/archives/speeches/1984/120784b.htm.

250 *Tutu emerged:* United Press International, December 7, 1984.

250 *Crocker felt that Tutu:* Crocker interview.

251 *In Pollsmoor:* Mandela, interview by author, March 20, 2003.

251 *After the meeting in the Oval Office:* Associated Press, December 7, 1984.

251 *There were times:* Reagan's remarks: www.reagan.utexas.edu/archives/speeches/1984/121084b.htm.

251 *In 1966, Robert F. Kennedy:* Rand Daily Mail, "Robert Kennedy in South Africa", souvenir booklet, 1966.

251 *In October 1984:* Gregory Craig (former aide to Edward Kennedy), interview by author, January 20, 2004.

252 *The contrasts:* Star, New York Times, January 6, 1985.

252 *On his last day:* New York Times, Star, January 14, 1985.

252 *Ted Koppel:* ABC News *Nightline,* March 18, 1985, transcript of show #996.

252 *"The last 25 years":* John Corry, *New York Times,* March 21, 1985.

253 *Twenty years later:* R.F. Botha, interview by author, November 2, 2005.

253 *Back in Washington:* See *Congressional Record:* 131 Cong. Rec. S 2794, Vol. 131, No. 27; 131 Cong. Rec. S 3991, Vol. 131, No. 41; 131 Cong. Rec. H 3388 Vol. 131, No. 67; 131 Cong. Rec. H 3816 Vol. 131, No. 73; 131 Cong. Rec. S 9335 Vol. 131, No. 92; 131 Cong. Rec. H 7087 Vol. 131, No. 106; 131 Cong. Rec. S 10715, Vol. 131, No. 106–part 2; 131 Cong. Rec. S 11047, Vol. 131, No. 110.

253 *None had spoken:* U.S. Senate, *Congressional Record,* 131 Cong. Rec. S 9335 Vol. 131, No. 92, July 11, 1995.

253 *Paul Simon:* U.S. Senate, *Congressional Record,* 131 Cong. Rec. S 3991, Vol. 131, No. 41.

253 *In the House: Congressional Record,* 131 Cong. Rec. H 3388 Vol. 131, No. 67, May 21, 1985.

253 *Walter Fauntroy: Congressional Record,* 131 Cong. Rec. H 3388 Vol. 131, No. 67.

253 *In the early debates:* See U.S. Senate, Steven D. Symms, August 1, 1985: 131 Cong. Rec. S 10715, Vol. 131, No. 106–Part 2; U.S. Senate, Helms, September 9, 1985, Cong. Rec. S 11047, Vol. 131, No. 110.

253 *This was particularly: New York Times,* March 14, 1982; Crocker interview; Craig interview.

253 *The moderate Republican:* Nancy Kassebaum Baker, interview by author, August 20, 2004.

253 *"He didn't look like":* Mark Helmke, interview by author, June 22, 2004.

254 *In Crocker's cast:* Crocker, *High Noon,* 253–259.

254 *Backing them up:* Crocker interview.

254 *By mid-1985:* Crocker, *High Noon,* 253–254, 271, 279–289.

254 *The flamboyant Pik Botha:* Lugar, *Letters to the Next President,* 219–223; Massie, *Loosing the Bonds,* 585–591; Crocker, *High Noon,* 275–278.

255 *Two weeks earlier:* August 24, 1985, transcript at: www.reagan.utexas.edu/resource/speeches/1985/82485c.htm.

255 *Trevor Tutu: MacNeil/Lehrer NewsHour,* August 26, 1985; *New York Times, Guardian,* August 27, 1985.

255 *"He has really been saying": Washington Post,* September 10, 1985.

255 *Huddleston pursued:* British Government, Correspondence with Government Departments, Prime Minister 1967–1995, MSS AAM 779, AAM.

255 *Van der Post:* Jones, *Teller of Many Tales,* 343–347, 365, 417–419, 431; Thatcher, *The Downing Street Years,* 533.

256 *"I know you will":* Huddleston to DMT, September 27, 1985 (Martin Kenyon files); Kenyon interview.

256 *He told her:* Patrick Keatley, *Guardian,* October 8, 1985; *Star,* October 4 and 8, 1985; Waite, interview by author, September 8, 2004.

256 *Thatcher had banned:* Lord Powell, interview by author, October 5, 2005.

257 *Thatcher tore into:* Thatcher, *The Downing Street Years,* 516–519; press conference, October 20, 1985: www.margaretthatcher.org/archive.

257 *In doing so:* Quoted in Sampson, *Mandela,* 342.

257 *"Support of this racist policy": New York Times,* October 29, 1985.

257 *In 1986 he refused: Business Day,* July 8, 1986; Lord Renwick, interview by author, September 27, 2005.

257 *According to Charles Powell:* Powell interview.

257 *But Lynda Chalker:* Baroness Chalker, interview by author, September 8, 2004.

257 *Anthony Sampson:* Sampson, conversation with author, October 2003.

258 *On May 19:* Commonwealth Group of Eminent Persons, *Mission to South Africa.*

258 *The following afternoon:* Crocker, *High Noon,* 304–306.

258 *"The Anti-Apartheid Act":* U.S. Senate, *Congressional Record,* 132 Cong. Rec. S 6383, Vol. 132, No. 69.

258 *In the House:* Massie, *Loosing the Bonds,* 608.

258 *In a handwritten letter:* Mary Rockefeller Morgan, letter to Reagan, Pocantico Hill Estate, Tarrytown, N.Y., delivered by courtesy of Laurance Rockefeller, July 4, 1986; Reagan to Morgan, July 7, 1986, 436530 CO 1411, Reagan Library.

260 *In the ten days:* Crocker, *High Noon,* 319–324.

260 *The final version:* Reagan, "Ending Apartheid in South Africa," address, Appendix C, Baker, 128–137.

260 *Tutu spent ninety minutes: MacNeil/Lehrer NewsHour,* June 13, *New York Times, Star,* June 14; *Star, New York Times, Financial Times,* July 22, 1986.

260 *Tutu decided: MacNeil/Lehrer NewsHour,* July 22, 1986; *Business Day, Star,* AP/*New York Times,* July 23, 1986.

261 *"Bishop Tutu is entitled":* Thatcher, press conference, September 12, 1986: www.margaretthatcher.org/archive.

261 *"He didn't know":* Crocker interview.

261 *On August 15:* Massie, *Loosing the Bonds,* 620.

261   *Edward Kennedy lobbied:* Craig interview; Lugar, *Letters to the Next President,* 234.
261   *White House records:* Phil Nicolaides, memo to Pat Buchanan, July 29, 1986, 437995 CO141; Carl Anderson, memo to Pat Buchanan, Mari Maseng, July 30, 1986, 437885 CO141; Pat Buchanan, memo to chief of staff, August 4, 1986; John M. Poindexter op-ed article for *Wall Street Journal,* September 24, 1986, 47554 CO141, Reagan Library.
261   *After the Senate's vote:* Pat Buchanan, memo to chief of staff, September 13, 1986, 464340 CO141; Phil Nicolaides, memo to Pat Buchanan, August 18, 1986, 436340, CO141; 435552 CO141, Reagan Library.
261   *"Blacks are suffering":* U.S. Senate, *Congressional Record,* 132 Cong. Rec. S 14460, Vol. 132, No. 133.
262   *Jesse Helms:* U.S. Senate, *Congressional Record,* 132 Cong. Rec. S 14460, Vol. 132, No. 133.
262   *On the day:* New York Times, October 3, 1986; Lugar, *Letters to the Next President,* 240.
262   *Tutu's singular:* Helmke, interview by author, June 27, 2004; Craig interview.

CHAPTER 12: THE HEADMASTER

PAGE
263   *Two months hence: Natal Mercury,* January 23 and 27; *Business Day,* January 24; *New York Times,* January 28; *Star, Citizen,* January 22; *Star,* January 25; *Guardian,* January 27, 1986.
263   *On his return home:* AB1979 Da 3.3, CPSA.
263   *a record of its meeting:* Minutes of BSG meeting, February 5, 1986, AB2546 B28, CPSA.
263   *Five years earlier:* Charles Albertyn, interview by author, December 15, 2005.
264   *Khotso Makhulu:* Makhulu, interview by author, April 17, 2004.
264   *Michael Nuttall:* Nuttall, *Number Two,* 15.
264   *More important, Leah:* DMT, comment to staff, 1987.
264   *When Makhulu's opposition:* Nuttall, *Number Two,* 14–17; King, *A Good Place to Be,* 63; recollection of Chris Ahrends.
264   *Tutu emerged: New York Times,* April 15, 1986; Michael Nuttall, *Leadership* (South Africa), No. 4, 1986, quoted in Nuttall, *Number Two.*
265   *In Soweto, Leah wept:* DMT to staff, 1987.
265   *Leslie Stradling:* Stradling diaries, book 38, AB2599, CPSA.
265   *Alan Paton told:* Paton to Buthelezi, August 14, 1986, PC1/5/1/10-9; Buthelezi to Paton, August 25, 1986, PC1/5/1/10-8, Paton Centre.
265   *Quoting the Letter of Jude: Ixthus,* Newsletter of Support Ministries, South Africa, November 1986.
265   *A counterpoint:* Order of Service for Enthronement, AB1966, CPSA; *Drum,* October 1986; *Cape Times, Business Day, Observer News Service,* September 8; *New Nation* (Johannesburg), September 11; DMT, letter of thanks to foreign guests, September 24, 1986, AB2546 E13 (File 2), CPSA; Stradling Diaries, September 7, AB2599, CPSA.
266   *Tutu structured:* Enthronment Charge, September 7, 1986, AB1966, CPSA.
266   *Building on his belief:* See also Tutu, *"An African Prayer Book,"* xvi; Tutu, Foreword, in John de Gruchy, *Cry Justice!* 11.
267   *The new archbishop: Cape Times, Business Day,* September 8, 1986; *Citizen,* September 4, 1986.
267   *When a few hundred:* Stradling Diaries, September 7, 1986; John Ruston to DMT, September 11, 1986, AB2546 P14(2), CPSA.
267   *The event was:* Pomerantz, *Where Peachtree Meets Sweet Auburn,* 334–340; Michael Peers, *Anglican Journal* (Canada), March 2000.
269   *"Bishopscourt is a charming":* DMT to Stephen Oliver, June 26, 1986, AB1979 Da 3.1, CPSA.
269   *The purpose of his letter: Citizen,* August 28, 1986.
271   *She prided herself:* Leah Tutu, interview by Hennie Serfontein, 1996.
272   *Trevor returned: Transvaler,* November 23, 1982; Associated Press, October 19, 1984; *Rand Daily Mail,* October 25, 1984.
273   *A year later: Star,* June 7, 1983.

273 *Desmond and Leah:* DMT to Trevor Tutu, March 7, 1978, A2, Correspondence, BC869, UCT Archives.
273 *"Your godson":* DMT to Trevor Huddleston, July 12, 1984, AB1979 Da 3.1, CPSA.
273 *In a publicity stunt:* United Press International, August 18, 1989.
273 *He was charged:* SA Press Association, August 4, 1997.
273 *"I write to you":* DMT, letter to R. F. Botha, October 2, 1992, AB2546 T17, CPSA.
273 *Botha did not reply:* Botha interview.
273 *For more than three years:* East Cape News Service, August 5, 1977; All Africa Press Service, December 8, 1997.
274 *In August 1997:* SA Press Association, August 7, 1997.
274 *His parents:* DMT statement, August 7, 1997; author's experience.
274 *Whatever Tutu felt:* Argus, February 11, 1989; *Fair Lady,* December 19, 1990.
274 *Some of the Tutus' British friends:* Malcolm Alexander, Ronald and Frankie Brownrigg interviews.
274 *In 1994 Tutu agreed:* Sunday Times Magazine (London), October 16, 1994.
274 *He later said:* Gyles Brandreth, *Daily Telegraph,* April 27, 2001.
276 *As part of his focus:* Cull, in Hulley; Cull to author.
276 *(In a demonstration . . .):* New York Times, March 24, 1986; Debbie Budlender, *"Assessing U.S. Corporate Disinvestment,"* Community Agency for Social Enquiry (CASE), 1989, 11–14.
277 *Since the 1960s:* Louis Bank, "All in God's Good Time," program for inauguration of the Diocese of False Bay, 2005.
278 *"The government has balkanised":* Albertyn interview.
278 *When Paton's newspaper commentary:* Nuttall to Paton, October 23, 1984, PC1/5/4/25, Paton Centre.
278 *By 1989 Nuttall's views:* Nuttall, *Number Two,* 129–132.
279 *Tutu responded:* Bishopscourt Update, No. 208, February 5, 1990, CPSA/UWC.
279 *This eased Tutu's load:* Michael Nuttall, interview by author, September 5, 2005.
279 *We bishops:* Nuttall, *Number Two,* 20–21.
280 *He gained that nickname:* Ibid., 20, 23.
280 *It was a cause:* Associated Press, July 31, 1978.
280 *In southern Africa:* Synod News Service, No. 13, June 4, 1989; and No. 26, June 6, 1989; *Bishopscourt Update,* No. 467, August 28, 1982, CPSA/UWC; Nuttall, *Number Two,* 109–111.
281 *Shortly before:* Fair Lady, December 19, 1990; DMT, comment to author, 1995.
281 *"liberation from sin":* Seek, August 1987.

CHAPTER 13: INTERIM LEADER

PAGE
283 *In October 1985:* TRC, *Report,* Vol. 2, chap. 1, para 154.
283 *He became aware:* Matt Esau to minister of justice, March 29, 1989; reply, May 23, 1989, AB2546 S40, CPSA; Mandela Prison Files, Vol. 24, Box 8, SANA.
284 *Tutu held consultations:* The story of the secret contacts is told by Allister Sparks, in *Tomorrow Is Another Country.*
284 *The police arrested:* TRC, *Report,* Vol. 2, chap. 1, para 160; Vol. 2, chap. 5, para 242, 254–268.
284 *In one of their early:* Chronology of intervention, July 17 and 18, 1987, AB2701 C3 (2), CPSA; Jaffer, *Our Generation,* 43–51.
286 *"Oh, absolutely":* Seek (Johannesburg), July 1987.
286 *In Johannesburg:* Citizen, June 16, 1987; *Star,* June 25, 1987; author's first bound collection of Tutu material for "Rainbow People of God," 1991 (Rainbow 1991 draft), 58–59.
286 *We expect them to reflect:* Rainbow 1991 draft, 59–61.
288 *In 1985, following:* Kairos Theologians, "Challenge to the Church: The Kairos Document," November 1985, 3rd impression.
288 *Tutu did not sign:* Africa Report, Vol. 31, No. 2, March–April 1986, 53.

288 *In May 1987, a consultation:* Lusaka Statement, AB2701 C3 (1), CPSA.

288 *Without opposition:* Statement, November 24, 1987, AB2701 C3 (1), CPSA.

289 *The committee's decision: ACTS,* Newsletter No. 17, January 1988, AB2701 C3 (1); G.G.S. Pegram to DMT, November 25, 1987, AB2546 N6 (2); Radio South Africa news bulletin, November 25, 1986, AB2701 C3 (1), CPSA; *Financial Mail,* December 4, 1987.

289 *Paul Erasmus:* Erasmus, interview by author, December 6, 2005.

289 *Pro- and anti-sanctions lobbies:* For example, Schlemmer, *Black Worker Attitudes;* Mark Orkin, *Disinvestment, the Struggle and the Future,* Ravan Press, 1986; Community Agency for Social Enquiry, statement, October 15, 1987, AC623 12.12, SACC.

289 *The diocese of Zululand:* Letter to Tutu, August 4, 1988, AB2546 Z3, CPSA.

289 *Michael Nuttall:* Newsletter, Diocese of Natal, February 1985, AB2546 S38, CPSA.

289 *On taking office:* Bishopscourt News Service, December 3, 1988, CPSA/UWC.

290 *Almost without exception: Bishopscourt Update,* No. 63, April 12, 1989, CPSA/UWC.

290 *It went first: Provincial Synod News,* No. 18, June 5, 1989, CPSA/UWC.

290 *Nuttall credited:* Nuttall, *Number Two,* 30–32.

290 *On February 24: Government Gazette,* Vol. 272, Nos. 11156 and 11157, Pretoria: Government Printers, February 24, 1988.

290 *Police roadblocks:* Wallis and Hollyday, *Crucible of Fire,* 1.

291 *Boesak likened:* Ibid., 28, 34, 39.

291 *Two days later:* Chikane, *The Church's Prophetic Witness,* 46.

291 *A delegation:* Statements and correspondence, *Journal of Theology for Southern Africa,* No. 63, June 1988, 74–77.

291 *In the meantime:* Ibid., 72–74.

292 *Tutu's eight-page rejoinder:* Ibid., 82–87.

292 *The willingness of a wide: Non-Violence News,* Justice and Reconciliation Division, SACC, Third Quarter, 1987.

293 *Frank Chikane:* Convocation resolutions, AB2701 P, CPSA.

293 *He told the SACC's:* DMT to Rob Robertson, June 3, 1988, AB2546 S38, CPSA.

293 *Church leaders followed up:* Rainbow 1991 draft, 111–113; Bishopscourt News Service, No. 6, September 6, 1988, CPSA/UWC.

293 *Within weeks:* Rainbow 1991 draft, 102; *Sunday Star,* June 19, 1988.

293 *In Cape Town:* Bishopscourt News Service, No. 22, November 2, 1988, CPSA/UWC.

294 *In the midst:* Rainbow 1991 draft, 102.

294 *One night:* Bishopscourt News Service, No. 6, September 24, 1988, CPSA/UWC.

294 *During the night:* Author's experience; *Seek,* November 1988.

294 *Early in 1989:* Author's experience.

294 *Stratkom's operatives:* TRC, *Report,* Vol. 6, section 3, chap. 1, para 122, 209–217; Erasmus interview.

294 *Stratkom's personnel:* TRC, *Report,* Vol. 6, section 3, chap. 1, para 124, 215.

295 *Security policemen interviewed:* Erasmus interview; Craig Williamson, interview by author, November 1, 2005.

295 *Tutu's status:* Amnesty Committee, TRC, decisions AC/99/0030, Jacques Hechter, and AC/2000/156, P. J. C. Loots.

295 *Chikane suffered:* TRC, *Report,* Vol. 2, chap. 2, para 325–326; statements, June 8, 1989, AB2546 S38, CPSA; evidence at trial of Wouter Basson, October 20–November 3, 2000.

295 *An affidavit: Bishopscourt Update,* No. 286, October 12, 1990, CPSA/UWC; TRC, *Report,* Vol. 2, chap. 2, para 325–326.

295 *Its operatives also hatched:* TRC, *Report,* Vol. 2, chap. 2, para 377–418; Amnesty Committee decision AC/2001/232, Carl Casteling Botha and seven others; Amnesty Committee evidence, March 13–16, June 13–23, September 28, 2001; Stiff, *Warfare by Other Means,* 344.

295 *One was placed outside:* Duncan Buchanan, bishop of Johannesburg, remarks to author.

296 *The head gardener:* Livingstone Nakani, contemporaneous account to author.

296 *Sam Nunn:* Edward J. Perkins, interview by author, June 23, 2005.

297 *"Before we could":* David Boren, interview by author, May 10, 2005.

297 *"I couldn't believe":* Perkins interview.

297 *Nunn announced: New York Times,* December 11, 1988.

297 *Back in Washington:* Boren interview.

298 *Three months after:* Memorandum for the president from James A. Baker III, May 2, 1989, Case No. 035266, ME001, NLGB Control No. 3117, WHORM, Subject File–General, Bush Library.

298 *A secret intelligence memo:* "South Africa: The ANC and the Superpowers," March 31, 1989, OA/ID CF01300, South Africa–ANC, John M. Ordway File, National Security Council, Bush Library.

299 *"Tutu is—without question":* Memorandum from David Passage for Brent Scowcroft, May 9, 1989, Case No. 035266, NLGB Control No. 3117, WHORM, Subject File–General, Bush Library.

299 *Tutu came away:* Bishopscourt Update, No. 70, May 20, 1989, CPSA/UWC.

299 *"Mrs. Sisulu has lived":* Bush's statement, June 30, 1989, at: www.bushlibrary.tamu.edu/re search/papers/1989/89063001.html.

299 *From Washington:* Sisulu, *In Our Lifetime*, 517–519.

300 *Baker told Bush:* Memorandum for the president from James A. Baker III, May 2, 1989.

300 *She said to de Klerk:* Powell interview.

300 *They went through:* Goldstone, *For Humanity*, 12.

300 *He sent appeals:* DMT correspondence, February 13, 1989, AB2546 M11, CPSA; *Bishopscourt Update,* Nos. 43 and 45, February 13–14, 1989, CPSA/UWC.

301 *Vlok said he was:* Bishopscourt Update, No. 46, February 16, 1989, CPSA/UWC; author's experience.

301 *Vlok's cooperative attitude:* Marcus White, account to author, 2005.

301 *Neither was the crisis:* Bishopscourt Update, No. 55, March 10, 1989, CPSA/UWC.

301 *Operating informally:* Bishopscourt Update, No. 126, August 2; No. 127, August 3; No. 128, August 7, 1989, CPSA/UWC.

302 *I told Mr. Vlok:* Bishopscourt Update, No. 134, August 10, CPSA/UWC.

302 *They were thrown:* Author's experience; jump street squads are described in a statement by the police informant Gregory Flat, AB2701 C3 (5), CPSA.

303 *On Saturday, August 19:* Bishopscourt Update, No. 138, August 21, 1989, CPSA/UWC; author's experience.

303 *Leaving the Strand:* Bishopscourt Update, Nos. 138 and 139, August 22, 1989, CPSA/UWC; *Weekend Argus,* August 19; Reuters, August 19; *Rapport* (Johannesburg), August 20, 1989; author's experience.

304 *The next day:* Bishopscourt Update, No. 138, August 21, 1989, CPSA/UWC; author's experience.

305 *He approached the microphones:* New Yorker, December 25, 1989, 66.

305 *Under Colin Jones:* See: www.nikolaikirche-leipzig.de/e/the_events_in_fall_1989/the_ events_in_fall_1989.html.

305 *We are involved:* Bishopscourt Update, No. 140, August 23, 1989, CPSA/UWC.

305 *The students listened:* Reuters, Associated Press, August 29, 1989; Chris Ahrends, interview by author, February 21, 2006.

306 *A week later:* Bishopscourt Update, No. 146, August 31, 1989, CPSA/UWC.

306 *The next day:* Bishopscourt Update, No. 149, September 1, 1989, CPSA/UWC.

306 *Watched by shoppers:* Weekend Argus, September 2 and 3; Bishopscourt Update, No. 150, September 2, 1989, CPSA/UWC.

307 *Say to yourselves:* Rainbow 1991 draft, 1991, 180–182; *Bishopscourt Update,* No. 157, September 9, 1989, CPSA/UWC; *New Yorker,* December 25, 1989, 68.

307 *So intent were:* Bishopscourt Update, No. 153, September 5, 1989, CPSA/UWC; Rainbow 1991 draft, 183; author's experience.

308 *Most of Cape Town's:* Matt Esau, interview by author, February 2, 2006.

308 *"There was no political":* DMT, interview by John Freeth, July 11, 2003, DMT office records.

309 *On election day:* Ben Maclennan, interview by author, February 1, 2006; *Sunday Star,* September 10, 1989.

309 *Asked by a journalist from Reuters:* Brendan Boyle, e-mail to author, February 1, 2006.

309 *Tutu and Boesak saw:* Sunday Star, September 10, 1989.

309 *From New York:* Elie Wiesel, telegram to DMT, September 9, 1989, AB2701 C5 (2), CPSA.

309   *A few days earlier:* George Bush to DMT, August 28, 1989; Robin Renwick to DMT, August 30, 1989, AB2701 C5 (2), CPSA.

309   *Now Tutu wrote:* DMT to prime minister of Greece, September 11, 1989, and annexation, AB2546 T17, CPSA; *Bishopscourt Update,* No. 162, September 20.

309   *On the one side:* De Klerk, *The Last Trek,* 159; Renwick, *Unconventional Diplomacy,* 138–139.

309   *The police drew up:* Notice of motion and affidavits, September 12, 1989, Directorate of Security Legislation, Department of Justice, File 2/3/2/5862, SANA.

309   *On the other side:* Renwick, *Unconventional Diplomacy,* 138.

310   *De Klerk was scheduled:* De Klerk, *The Last Trek,* 136–147; Prinsloo, *Stem uit die Wilderness,* 383–420.

310   *When de Klerk: Bishopscourt Update,* No. 135, August 17, 1989, CPSA/UWC.

310   *He wrote later:* Wessels, 62.

310   *Tutu and Boesak rebuffed: Bishopscourt Update,* No. 159, September 12, 1989, CPSA/UWC; Renwick, *Unconventional Diplomacy,* 138–139; Waldmeir, *Anatomy of a Miracle,* 138–139.

310   *Late in the afternoon: Bishopscourt Update,* No. 160, September 12, 1989, CPSA/UWC; author's experience.

310   *During the evening: Bishopscourt Update,* No. 164, September 22, 1989, CPSA/UWC.

310   *De Klerk announced:* Statement by acting state president, AB2701, C3 (5), CPSA.

310   *Tutu had no idea: Weekly Mail* (Johannesburg), September 15, 1989; *Argus,* September 13 and 14; Reuters, United Press International, September 13, 1989; *Cape Times,* September 14, 1989; Jaffer, *Our Generation,* 67; author's experience.

311   *"Mr. de Klerk, please":* Rainbow 1991 draft, 188.

311   *Tutu took immense pride: Bishopscourt Update,* No. 164, September 22, CPSA/UWC; Nuttall, *Number Two,* 39.

312   *"I don't know anywhere":* Tlhagale interview.

312   *The cabinet minister:* Waldmeir, *Anatomy of a Miracle,* 138; Renwick, *Unconventional Diplomacy,* 139; Sparks, *Tomorrow Is Another Country,* 101.

312   *De Klerk acknowledged:* De Klerk, *The Last Trek,* 159.

312   *After his formal:* Sparks, *Tomorrow is Another Country,* 113.

312   *Early in October: Bishopscourt Update,* No. 176–179, October 6–16; author's experience.

313   *"I couldn't believe": Bishopscourt Update,* No. 211, February 5, CPSA/UWC.

313   *From Cape Town's airport:* Account of Mandela's release and stay at Bishopscourt, author's experience.

314   *Some weeks later: Bishopscourt Update,* No. 219, February 26, 1990, CPSA/UWC.

CHAPTER 14: ROLLER-COASTER RIDE

PAGE

315   *Quoting God's promises: Good Hope,* newsletter of the Diocese of Cape Town, March 1990.

316   *Mandela spoke movingly: Bishopscourt Update,* No. 214, February 21, 1990, CPSA/UWC.

316   *Tutu and his bishops:* Statement, February 25, 1990, AB2546 A3, CPSA.

316   *The ANC was already:* Minutes, DRA September 1989 Consultation, Folder 26, Box 22, ANC Records.

316   *In February:* WCC Consultation on South Africa, statement, Harare, Zimbabwe, February 16–17, Folder 85, Box 18, ANC Records.

316   *Back at his office at the WCC:* Barney Pityana to DMT, March 6, 1990, AC623 2.2.4, SACC.

316   *Believing that Pityana owed:* DMT, telex to Emilio Castro, general secretary, WCC, September 3, 1987, AB2701 C5 (1); DMT to Pityana, March 7, 1990, AB2701 C5 (1), CPSA; Pityana to DMT, March 22, 1990, AC623 2.2.4, SACC.

317   *On Sunday, March 25:* Sampson, *Mandela,* 436; Nuttall, *Number Two,* 68–69, 74; Callinicos, *Beyond the Engeli Mountains,* 394; TRC, *Report,* Vol. 2, chap. 7, para 190–192; Vol. 3, chap. 3, para 263–292.

318   *Tutu had been asked:* Buthelezi, *Power Is Ours,* 121–124; *Sunday Times* (Johannesburg), March 12, 1978; *Rand Daily Mail* and *Star,* March 13, 1978; David Nkwe, interview by author, February 9, 2006; DMT, interview by author, August 30, 2005.

318   *Sobukwe's friend:* Pogrund, *How Can Man Die Better,* 376.

318 *The week after the funeral: Sunday Express* (Johannesburg), March 19, quoted by Buthelezi, *Power Is Ours,* 123; Tutu, interview by author, August 30, 2005.

318 *Buthelezi said Tutu's real motive:* Buthelezi, *Power Is Ours,* 123–4; *Daily News,* April 5, 1978.

318 *The correspondence and public exchanges:* Buthelezi, interview by Karis and Gerhart, Interviews, Folder 5, A2675, Karis-Gerhart Collection; Reel 35, Folder 469, A2675, Karis-Gerhart Collection; C4.22.2, Tambo Papers; AB1363 B1 (File 2), CPSA; AC623 5.2.6, SACC; May 1981 correspondence (Peter Storey files); AB2414 K5, CPSA; author's experience.

319 *On April 2, 1990: Bishopscourt Update,* No. 231, April 3, 1990, CPSA/UWC; memorandum by Mangosuthu Buthelezi, April 1, 1990, AB2668, CPSA; author's experience.

319 *From Ulundi: Bishopscourt Update,* No. 231, April 3, 1990, CPSA/UWC; author's experience.

320 *On Tutu's third day: Bishopscourt Update,* No. 232, April 10, 1990, CPSA/UWC.

320 *The next week leaders in Natal: Bishopscourt Update,* No. 235, April 12, 1990, CPSA/UWC.

320 *While Tutu's attention: Good Hope,* May and August 1990; *Bishopscourt Update,* No. 255, July 11, 1990, CPSA/UWC; letters between DMT and Sid Luckett, AB2546 N5, CPSA; Worsnip, *Priest and Partisan,* 126; ICT conference resolutions, AB2668, CPSA.

320 *But as it became: Bishopscourt Update,* No. 248, June 4, CPSA/UWC, and No. 255, July 11, 1990, CPSA/UWC; DMT, comment to author; Mandela, interview by author, March 20, 2003.

321 *The unhappiness came: Bishopscourt Update,* No. 255, July 11, 1990, CPSA/UWC.

321 *His views were reinforced:* TRC, *Report,* Vol. 3, chap. 6, para 528–529.

321 *The slaughter in my:* Mkhondo, *Reporting South Africa,* 48–49.

322 *Some residents welcomed: City Press,* August 26, 1990, quoted in *Bishopscourt Update,* No. 287, October 15, 1990, CPSA/UWC.

322 *After the visit:* Author's experience.

323 *Rich Mkhondo:* Mkhondo, *Reporting South Africa,* 52.

323 *"In Soweto here":* Tutu, *The Rainbow People,* 211; *Bishopscourt Update,* No. 294, November 2, 1990, CPSA/UWC.

323 *Little more than:* TRC, *Report,* Vol. 3, chap. 6, para 552; Nuttall, *Number Two,* 98–99; DMT, interview by John Freeth, July 11, 2003, DMT office records; *Bishopscourt Update,* No. 279, October 10, 1990, CPSA/UWC.

323 I heard a noise: Trenoweth, *The Future of God,* 7.

324 *After the killings: Bishopscourt Update,* No. 273, August 30, and No. 276, September 10, 1990, CPSA/UWC; author's experience; Nuttall to Vlok, October 17, 1990, AB2546 N5, CPSA; Nuttall, *Number Two,* 99–101.

324 *The two separate:* TRC, *Report,* Vol. 2, chap. 7, para 7; extrapolation from Kane-Berman, *Political Violence in South Africa,* 13.

324 *As the toll grew: Bishopscourt Update,* No. 282, October 10, 1990; No. 403, September 13, 1991; No. 407, October 7, 1991; No. 435, May 23, 1992; No. 454, July 10, 1992, CPSA/UWC.

325 *In November 1992:* Goldstone, *For Humanity,* 42–46.

325 *In December the general:* Staff Paper Prepared for the Steyn Commission on Alleged Dangerous Activities of SADF Components, December 1992, SAHA.

325 *Two months before:* Goldstone, *For Humanity,* 50–57; De Klerk, *The Last Trek,* 316–319.

325 *After 1994, policemen:* Amnesty Committee, TRC, decisions AC/2001/268; AC/2001/005; AC/2001/131; AC/2001/172; AC/2001/177. TRC, *Report,* Vol. 6, section 3, chap. 1, para 129, 132, 133, 174, 300; Vol. 2, chap. 7, para 100–123.

326 *Defending himself since:* De Klerk's statement, July 30, 1991, AB2701 C3(9), CPSA; De Klerk, *The Last Trek,* 210, 212, 266, 319.

326 *His mistake . . . was:* Renwick, interview by author, September 27, 2005.

326 *The CIA's contacts:* Director of National Intelligence, *National Intelligence Estimate 92–15,* 1982, NSA.

326 *"It's an objective fact":* F. W. de Klerk, interview by author, December 3, 2005.

326 *For Tutu, the transition:* Rainbow 1991 draft, 252.

327 *Back at work: Bishopscourt Update,* No. 488, March 5, 1993, CPSA/UWC.

327 *But it is not all the truth: Bishopscourt Update,* No. 349, March 27, 1991, CPSA/UWC.

328 *Later he stopped: Bishopscourt Update,* No. 388, July 27, 1991, CPSA/UWC.

328 *He summoned black:* Bishopscourt Update, No. 303, December 3, 1990, and No. 306, December 4, 1990, CPSA/UWC; Summit guest list, summit documents, AB2546, CPSA.

328 *Mandela and Buthelezi:* Mkhondo, *Reporting South Africa,* 31–32; Sampson, *Mandela,* 441.

328 *Tutu backed church and business leaders:* Minutes of National Peace Initiative preparatory committee, AB2546 N9, CPSA; *Bishopscourt Update,* No. 410, October 11, 1991, CPSA/UWC.

328 *The accord had:* Liz Carmichael, interview by author, September 22, 2004.

329 *Within weeks:* TRC, *Report,* Vol. 3, chap. 6, para 547.

329 *Soon after nine PM:* Mkhondo, *Reporting South Africa,* 143; Nuttall, *Number Two,* 101; Amnesty Committee, TRC, decision AC/2000/209.

329 *With Peter Lee:* Author's experience; *Bishopscourt Update,* No. 447, June 25, 1992, CPSA/UWC.

330 *De Klerk visited:* De Klerk, *The Last Trek,* 241–242; Mandela, *Long Walk to Freedom,* 596.

330 *Tutu reentered: Bishopscourt Update,* No. 446, June 22, 1992, CPSA/UWC; DMT, speech of February 23, 1993, AB2701 S2(3), CPSA.

330 *the spectacle of Tutu:* Author's experience.

330 *Ten days after:* Denniston, *Trevor Huddleston,* 190; Nuttall, *Number Two,* 103; Lee, *Compromise and Courage,* 422; author's experiences.

331 *"A huge flame":* Marinovich and Silva, *The Bang Bang Club,* 82–83.

331 *He told the mourners: Bishopscourt Update,* No. 449, July 5, 1992, CPSA/UWC.

331 *Peter Lee thought:* Lee, *Compromise and Courage,* 422.

331 *I have no compunction:* DMT to Frank Chikane, June 4, 1992, AB2546 S38, CPSA.

331 *The Boipatong massacre:* TRC, *Report,* Vol. 3, chap. 2, 399; *Bishopscourt Update,* No. 470, September 10, 1992, CPSA/UWC.

332 *The massacre at Bisho:* Sparks, *Tomorrow Is Another Country,* 151–152; 179–187; De Klerk, *The Last Trek,* 269–270; Mkhondo, *Reporting South Africa,* 154–159.

332 *His attempts to pursue:* Mangosuthu Buthelezi, memorandum, September 30, 1992; author's notes of meeting, AB2668; transcript of remarks to SABC, AB2701 S2(3), CPSA.

332 *Mangope caused Tutu:* DMT, contemporaneous remark to author; *Bishopscourt Update,* Nos. 473 and 474, October 6, 1992, CPSA/UWC.

332 *In November 1992:* Author's notes of meeting, November 11, 1992, AB2668, CPSA.

333 *Supporters of the ANC stopped:* TRC, *Report,* Vol. 6, section 3, chap. 2, para 243; *Bishopscourt Update,* No. 488, March 5, 1993, CPSA/UWC; TRC, *Report,* Vol. 3, chap. 3, para 401.

333 *Later in the year: Bishopscourt Update,* No. 511, July 26, 1993, CPSA/UWC.

333 *A memorial service: Bishopscourt Update,* No. 495, April 16, 1993, CPSA/UWC.

334 *More than 120,000:* Video recording of live funeral broadcast by SABC television, author's collection; Emails from Liz Carmichael, May 9 and 10, 2006.

335 *Early in June 1993:* Nuttall, *Number Two,* 83–87.

335 *Reporting on the outcome:* Joint Undertaking between Nelson Mandela and Inkosi Mangosuthu Buthelezi, AB2668, CPSA; Mogoba, *Stone, Steel, Sjambok,* 81; DMT, contemporaneous remarks, interview by author, August 30, 2005.

336 *After hearing their appeal:* Transcript of remarks of His Majesty the King of the Zulus to SABC and BBC crews, April 15, 1994, author's collection.

336 *On the day Hall:* Cassidy, *A Witness for Ever,* 172–190.

336 *"I'm over the moon":* DMT, remarks at Union Buildings, April 19, 1994; author's collection.

337 *You will never understand:* Charles Albertyn, interview by author, December 15, 2005.

337 *Alarmed, eighty ministers:* Advertisement and correspondence, AB2546 C31(2), CPSA.

337 *Barney Pityana:* Pityana to DMT, April 18, 1994, AB2546 C31(2), CPSA; Pityana, interview by author, February 23, 2005. DMT letter to bishops, May 25, 1994, AB2668, CPSA.

338 *Millions of black South Africans:* Author's experience.

338 *Tutu was an enthusiastic: Bishopscourt Update,* No. 413, October 11, 1991, CPSA/UWC; minutes of National Inauguration Committee, AB2546 I2, CPSA; author's experience.

338 *On the day Buthelezi:* Author's experience.

339 *Friends, this is the day:* DMT, Speech at the Grand Parade, Cape Town, AB2701 M1, CPSA.

339 *The inauguration:* Author's experience.

340 *"Thank you O God":* DMT, inauguration prayer, May 10, 1994, AB2546 I2, CPSA.

CHAPTER 15: A PROPER CONFRONTATION

PAGE
341 *Often there have been:* Papers delivered to Partners in Mission Consultation, November 9–14, 1987, author's collection.

342 *The conference brought: Bishopscourt Update,* No. 297, November 13, 1990, CPSA/UWC.

342 *The apology, endorsed:* Prinsloo, *Stem uit die Wilderness,* 442.

343 *Some months later: Bishopscourt Update,* Nos. 358 and 389, April 6, 1991, and July 27, 1991, CPSA/UWC.

343 *This cri de coeur:* Author's bound collection of Tutu material for "Rainbow People of God," 1991 (Rainbow 1991 draft), 308.

343 *"It was not our intention":* Reuters, May 11, 1993.

343 *"Saying sorry": Bishopscourt Update,* No. 500, May 10, 1993, CPSA/UWC.

343 *The National Party:* De Klerk, *The Last Trek,* 288–289.

343 *The instincts of most: Cape Times,* February 24, 1997, quoted by Alex Boraine in Rotberg and Thompson, 143.

344 *There should be no: Bishopscourt Update,* No. 483, November 11, 1992, CPSA/UWC.

344 *The pressure from:* Hayner, *Unspeakable Truths,* 60–64.

344 *Generals in the security forces:* Boraine in Rotberg and Thompson, 143–144.

344 *"Without that":* Boraine, Levy, and Scheffer, *Dealing with the Past,* 145.

344 *Boraine had left:* Boraine, *A Country Unmasked,* 14–46.

345 *In a second crucial:* Ibid., 49–52, 62–67.

345 *The first suggestion:* Nuttall, *Number Two,* 140–142.

345 *Tutu attacked:* DMT's statement, August 20, 1994, author's collection; *Cape Times,* September 27, 1984; SABC Radio interview, September 27, 1984.

346 *According to Priscilla Hayner:* Hayner, *Unspeakable Truths,* 41.

346 *The TRC's task:* "Promotion of National Unity and Reconciliation Act, No. 34 of 1995," Cape Town: Government Printer, 1995.

346 *At the core:* Postamble to "Interim Constitution, 1993," Cape Town: Government Printer, 1993.

347 *It referred to what: Star,* August 12, 1981, AC623 5.7, SACC.

347 *"I think, therefore I am":* Tutu, *No Future,* 35; Allen, *The Essential Desmond Tutu,* 5–6.

347 *In the TRC:* Tutu, *No Future,* 51–52.

348 *With this in mind:* Author's experience.

348 *Alex Boraine felt:* Boraine, *A Country Unmasked,* 85; author's experience.

348 *A key appointment:* Bell and Ntsebeza, *Unfinished Business,* 244.

348 *Describing Boraine:* DMT, opening address to TRC, December 16, 1995, author's collection.

349 *Some commissioners were:* Bell and Ntsebeza, *Unfinished Business,* 245; Boraine, *A Country Unmasked,* 86; Orr, *From Biko to Basson,* 84–87; *Weekly Mail,* Johannesburg, April 12, 1996; author's observations.

349 *On occasion:* Tutu, *No Future,* 161–164; Boraine, *A Country Unmasked,* 95–97; Bell and Ntsebeza, *Unfinished Business,* 264–286.

350 *Not only that:* TRC, *Report,* Vol. 1, chap. 11, para 19, 357; Boraine, *A Country Unmasked,* 271.

351 *Boraine suggested that Tutu:* Boraine, *A Country Unmasked,* 101; Meiring, *Chronicle of the Truth Commission,* 30.

351 *Tutu lauded her:* DMT, TRC evidence transcripts, April 16 and 18, 1996; Beth Savage, evidence, April 17, 1996; DMT, evidence transcript, May 10, 1996.

352 *He reassured whites:* DMT, evidence transcript, May 10, 1996.

352 *During a hearing:* Meiring, *Chronicle of the Truth Commission,* 51; Tutu, *No Future,* 31.

352 *On one occasion:* Singqokwane Malgas, evidence to TRC, April 17, 1996; Tutu, *No Future,* 109–110.

353 *At the meeting:* Roelof du Plessis, interview by author, November 3, 2005.

353 *They went on to explain:* Yasmin Sooka, interview by author, March 7, 2006.

353 *Yasmin Sooka:* Ibid.

354 *Tutu again put pressure:* Ibid.; Boraine, *A Country Unmasked,* 126.

354 *In a blaze of publicity:* Johannes van der Merwe, evidence to TRC, October 21, 1996.

354 *In the series of hearings:* TRC, *Report,* Vol. 6, section 3, chap. 1, para 253–255.
354 *Of the total:* Ibid., para 9.
354 *"Knock-out drops":* Dirk Coetzee, evidence to TRC, November 7, 1996.
355 *"Yes indeed":* DMT, Longford Lecture, February 16, 2004, author's collection.
355 *Anxious to avoid:* Tutu, *No Future,* 198; Boraine, *A Country Unmasked,* 198.
355 *Botha denied:* Reuters, Associated Press, SA Press Association, November 21, 1996; Tutu, *No Future,* 199.
356 *As the commission waited:* Reuters, November 18, 1997; Tutu, *No Future,* 199; Boraine, *A Country Unmasked,* 199–202, 205; Meiring, *Chronicle of the Truth Commission,* 337–338.
356 *In the trial:* Eugene de Kock, evidence in *State versus P. W. Botha,* June 1998, Collection AL3060, SAHA; TRC, *Report,* Vol. 6, section 3, chap. 1, para 16.
356 *The TRC's executive secretary:* Associated Press in *International Herald Tribune,* June 2, 1989.
356 *To substantiate:* Peter Storey, evidence in *State versus P. W. Botha,* AL3030, SAHA.
357 *Your worship, I believe:* DMT, evidence in *State versus P. W. Botha,* AL3060, SAHA.
357 *In its main report:* TRC, *Report,* Vol. 5, chap. 1, para 12, 102.
358 *The TRC's confrontation:* Winnie Mandela, *Part of My Soul Went with Him,* 106–108.
358 *A number moved:* Winnie Madikizela Mandela, evidence to TRC, December 4, 1997.
358 *Desmond and Leah Tutu:* Author's experience.
358 *Back in South Africa:* DMT, contemporaneous account to author.
358 *It later transpired:* TRC, *Report,* Vol. 2, chap. 6f, para 4–7, 95–97.
359 *Two years later:* Gilbey, *The Lady,* 252–269; Sampson, *Mandela,* 446–455.
359 *Then for nine:* Evidence at: http://www.doj.gov.za/trc/special/index.htm#mufch.
360 *It has exposed:* Peter Storey, evidence to TRC, November 26, 1997.
360 *In angry exchanges:* Duke, *Mandela, Mobutu, and Me,* 204–206.
360 *He told the hearing:* DMT, hearing transcript, December 4, 1997.
361 *Thank you very much:* Madikizela Mandela, evidence to TRC, December 4, 1997.
361 *A storm broke:* Tutu, *No Future,* 136; Duke, *Mandela, Mobutu, and Me,* 208; Krog, *Country of My Skull,* 259–260; Boraine, *A Country Unmasked,* 252–253; *Tablet* (UK), December 13, 1997.
361 *"I am not sure that we":* Tutu, *No Future,* 135–136.
362 *It found that those:* TRC, *Report,* Vol. 5, chap. 6, para 138.
362 *While working at Bishopscourt:* *Bishopscourt Update,* No. 169, October 4, 1989, CPSA/UWC.
362 *"These two":* DMT to Dr. Geir Lundestad, January 30, 1992, Box 29, MCH258, UWC.
362 *The odds were against:* Author's experience; DMT, contemporaneous account to author.
362 *De Klerk and Mandela:* De Klerk, *The Last Trek,* 297–299; Sampson, *Mandela,* 474.
362 *He considered his party's:* De Klerk, *The Last Trek,* 288–289, 370–371.
363 *De Klerk made his first:* Submission to TRC, August 1996.
363 *When he gave evidence:* Second submission to TRC, March 23, 1997; F. W. de Klerk, oral evidence, May 14, 1997.
364 *After the hearing:* Krog, *Country of My Skull,* 126, 128.
364 *There was an avalanche:* SA Press Association, Reuters, May 15, 1997.
364 *"a small man":* Tutu, *No Future,* 202–203.
364 *On the ground:* Boraine, *A Country Unmasked,* 303–304.
364 *Four years later:* TRC, *Report,* Vol. 6, section 1, chap. 4, para 29.
364 *Adriaan Vlok denied:* Vlok, evidence to TRC, October 14, 1997.
365 *Roelf Meyer:* Evidence of Roelf Meyer and Leon Wessels to the TRC, October 15, 1987.
365 *After its main report:* *Guardian* (London), *Mail and Guardian* (Johannesburg), May 28, 1999.
365 *De Klerk: I never knew:* De Klerk, interview by author, December 3, 2005.
366 *Contrary to the commission's expectations:* TRC, *Report,* Vol. 1, chap. 4; Vol. 5, chap. 6, para 77.
366 *The commission, and Desmond Tutu:* DMT, remarks to TRC news conference, November 4, 1996, author's collection; author's experience.
367 *The draft findings:* Boraine, *A Country Unmasked,* 306–314.
367 *Dumisa Ntsebeza:* DMT, letter to Ntsebeza, September 29, 1998, author's collection.
367 *"I really could not believe":* Tutu, *No Future,* 165–169.
367 *"Let me say":* *Independent* (London), October 30, 1998.
368 *The most vocal:* Mahmood Mamdani, in James and Van der Vijver, 58–61.

368 *Other commentators:* John Kane-Berman and Anthea Jeffery in Jeffery, *The Truth about the Truth Commission.*

368 *The Inkatha Freedom Party:* TRC, *Report,* Vol. 5, chap. 6, para 121; Vol. 6, section 5, chap. 4.

368 *Only thirty-three members:* TRC, *Report,* Vol. 6, section 3, chap. 1, para 9; Vol. 2, chap. 7, para 1; Vol. 5, chapter 6, para 53.

368 *Perhaps the principal:* John Allen, "Media Relations and the South African TRC–Riding a Tiger," paper prepared for International Center for Transitional Justice (ICTJ), New York, 2002; author's collection.

369 *Foreign leaders:* Author's experience.

369 *At home:* TRC, *Report,* Vol. 6, section 3, chap. 2, para 5; chap. 4, para 3; Allen, ICTJ paper.

369 *South Africa's most experienced:* Richard Goldstone, interview by author, March 3, 2006; Goldstone, *For Humanity,* 21.

370 *Could the TRC:* Gobodo-Madikizela, *A Human Being Died That Night,* 81; Krog, *Country of My Skull,* 152; Boraine, *A Country Unmasked,* 90, 268.

CHAPTER 16: INTERNATIONAL ICON

PAGE

372 *"In fact":* Fair Lady, December 19, 1990, 73.

372 *"We struggled":* Ecumenical News International (Geneva), March 3, 1998.

372 *"Why should we":* Tutu, Foreword, in Alexander and Preston, *We Were Baptized Too.*

372 *the conference, which proved to be a disaster:* Resolutions 1.10, V.1 and V35, 1998 Lambeth Conference, www.anglicancommunion.org; 1998 Lambeth Conference, www.religioustolerance.org; *Anglican Church News Service,* Item LC076, August 3, 1998.

373 *"I am ashamed":* DMT to George Carey, August 14, 1998; Carey to DMT, September 4, 1998; DMT to Carey, October 14, 1998, DMT office records.

373 *"It just causes a lot":* Canadian Press, April 20, 2004.

373 *"The Jesus I worship":* Anglican Church News Service (London), February 1, 2004.

373 *While England's Crown Appointments Commission:* Author's experience.

373 *He saw it as a family:* DMT, transcript of interview by Andrew Brown, July 25, 1988.

374 *He told the present writer:* DMT, interview by author, April 4, 2006.

374 *"It pains us":* Rainbow 1991 draft, 69.

375 *Part of the reason:* James R. Kangwana, AACC to DMT, June 17, 1987, AB2546 A9 (File 1), CPSA.

375 *Together, the two:* Bishopscourt Update, No. 324, February 28, 1991, CPSA/UWC.

375 *Tutu's and Chipenda's:* Wiseman, *The New Struggle for Democracy,* 1–3.

375 *He exploited:* Bishopscourt Update, No. 479, October 28, 1992, CPSA/UWC.

375 *Tutu and Chipenda:* José Belo Chipenda, interview by author, December 2, 2004; *Bishopscourt Update,* No. 53, February 27, 1989, and No. 54, February 27, 1989, CPSA/UWC.

376 *In the Marxist-Leninist:* Bishopscourt Update, No. 194, November 10, 1989, CPSA/UWC.

376 *They gave numbers:* Author's experience and notes; Chipenda interview.

376 *Three years later:* U.S. Newswire, Clinton's remarks, May 20, 1993.

376 *According to Anthony Lake:* Anthony Lake, interview by author, January 2004.

376 *In Liberia:* Anglican Update, August 25, 1994, CPSA/UWC; Hugh McCullum, e-mail to author, March 29, 2006; Liberian visit, documents, AB2701 T2, CPSA.

377 *After South Africa's:* DMT, "Report on Visit to Nigeria," author's copy.

377 *Later, when democracy:* BBC News, January 10, 2002; Reuters, January 12, 2002; *Ecumenical News International,* May 24, 2004; Robert Mugabe, *Sky News,* May 24, 2004.

377 *Tutu also campaigned:* DMT, "Kairos and the Jubilee Year," Address delivered in *Uppsala,* August 20, 1993, author's copy; *Bishopscourt Update,* No. 478, October 28, 1992, CPSA/ UWC.

378 *From the day:* Cassidy, *Ruination and Resurrection,* 52.

378 *The history of Rwanda:* Tutu, *No Future,* 207–209.

379 *The prisoners:* Author's experience; petitions in AB2701 T2, CPSA.

379 *Part of the story:* Indictment, Case No. ICTR-2004-74-1, International Criminal Tribunal

for Rwanda, June 8, 2001; Hirondelle News Agency, January 26, 2006, and June 2, 2003; McCullum, *The Angels Have Left Us*, 15; *East African,* April 21, 2003.

379 *Just outside:* Author's experience; *Times* (London)/Reuters, August 2, 1995; Cassidy, *Ruination and Resurrection,* 69–70.

380 *Back in Kigali:* Cassidy, *Ruination and Resurrection,* 71; Tutu, *No Future,* 209; author's experience.

380 *Perhaps the moment:* McCullum, *The Angels Have Left Us,* 63–94; author's experience.

380 *For although social anthropologists:* Discussed by Mamdani in *When Victims Become Killers.*

381 *"Inasmuch as you":* DMT, address, Kigali, Sunday July 30, 1994, author's collection.

381 *His first high-level experience:* Resolutions 27 and 73, 1988 Lambeth Conference, at: www.anglicancommunion.org; Rainbow 1991 draft, 108.

381 *Tutu's agreement:* Alf McCreary, *Nobody's Fool: The Life of Archbishop Robin Eames,* 253–255; author's experience.

381 *Tutu began by: Bishopscourt Update,* No. 361, April 30, 1991, CPSA/UWC; author's experience.

382 *With the peace process: Belfast Telegraph,* October 2, 1998.

382 *Tutu, however:* Author's experience.

382 *Three years later:* Press Association, November 6; *CNN.com,* November 7, 2001.

382 *A harbinger:* Hays Rockwell, interview by author, April 21, 2004.

383 *The topic of military cooperation: New York Times,* April 30, 1971.

383 *Heavily edited documents:* Director of Central Intelligence, interagency intelligence memorandum, "The September 1979 Event," Document 26, December 1979, in Mokoena, *The Declassified History,* 140–149; "Israel: Military and Nuclear Cooperation with South Africa, February 3," undated document, agency source excised with comment "Not responsive to request," unpublished collection of declassified documents on South Africa, NSA.

383 *The former White House expert:* Clarke, *Against All Enemies,* 43–45.

383 *The Israeli cabinet:* Documents 31 and 32, Mokoena, *The Declassified History,* 167–169.

383 *Tutu took up the issue publicly: Bishopscourt Update,* No. 44, February 14, 1989, CPSA/UWC.

384 *Israeli officials: Jerusalem Post,* November 3, 1989.

385 *Tutu had met: Bishopscourt Update,* No. 186, October 23, 1989, CPSA/UWC.

385 *As the trip:* Reuters, reported in *Daily Dispatch,* December 22, 1989.

385 *Kafity began:* Samir Kafity, interview by author, April 3, 2004.

385 *Tutu heightened: Jerusalem Post,* Associated Press, Reuters, December 22, 1989.

385 *It did not help:* Extracts from newspaper interview, December 26, 1989, author's collection.

385 *He would have been on safe ground: New Yorker,* July 4, 2005.

385 *Instead, speaking at:* Advertisement of Committee for Accuracy in Middle East Reporting in America, *Jerusalem Post,* December 22, 1989.

385 *Like oppressed blacks:* Burton L. Visotzky, letter to DMT, November 27, 1984, AC623 5.2.6, SACC.

385 *However, in December:* Committee for Accuracy in Middle East Reporting in America to *Jerusalem Post,* December 18, 1989.

386 *In protest against: Washington Post,* December 25, 1989.

386 *The pilgrimage began: Bishopscourt Update,* Nos. 206 and 207, February 5, 1990, CPSA/UWC.

386 *Disembarking from: Jerusalem Post, New York Times, Washington Post,* December 25, 1989.

386 *Tutu said that something: Bishopscourt Update,* No. 210, February 5, 1990, CPSA/UWC; *Times* (London), December 26, 1989; *Jerusalem Post,* December 29, 1989.

386 *A suspicious Bishop Kafity:* Kafity interview.

386 *In a sermon:* United Press International, December 25, 1989; *Jerusalem Post, Toronto Star,* December 26, 1989; *Bishopscourt Update,* No. 206, February 5, 1990, CPSA/UWC.

387 *Most of his program: Bishopscourt Update,* No. 210, February 5, 1990, CPSA/UWC; author's experience.

387 *His remarks, added:* Associated Press, January 5, 1990; Reuters, reported in *Citizen* (Johannesburg), December 30, 1989; *Jerusalem Post,* December 28, 1989; *New York Times,* January 2, 1990; *Bishopscourt Update,* No. 243, May 25, 1990, CPSA/UWC.

387 *The Christmas pilgrimage:* Transcript of meeting between Cincinnati and national Jewish

delegation and DMT, May 28, 1990; transcript of remarks to press, May 28; joint press statement, May 28, 1990, AB2701 S2(2), CPSA.

388 *Ten years later:* Tutu, *No Future,* 216.
388 *In 2002, he denounced:* Associated Press, April 13, 2002; *Boston Globe,* April 14, 2002; *Guardian,* April 29, 2002; *International Herald Tribune,* June 14, 2002; Reuters, June 21, 2002.
388 *"One reason we succeeded":* New Perspectives Quarterly, March 15, 2002.
388 *During American and British preparations:* Observer, BBC News, January 5, 2003.
389 *Some weeks later:* DMT, account to author, April 8, 2003.
389 *He cracked a joke:* Transcript of address, February 15, 2003, author's collection.

EPILOGUE

PAGE
391 *Martin Luther King, Jr.:* Martin Luther King, Jr., *I Have a Dream,* 203.
391 *Inspired by thousands:* Tutu, *The Rainbow People,* v.
392 *You keep trying:* DMT, interview by author, April 7, 2006.
392 *We have all left:* DMT, lecture, August 7, 2004, author's collection.
392 *Three months later:* DMT, lecture, November 2004, author's collection.
393 *He assailed Tutu:* Thabo Mbeki, *ANC Today, Online Voice of the African National Congress,* Vol. 4, No. 47, November 26–December 2, 2004: www.anc.org.za.
393 *The party followed up with: ANC Today,* Vol. 5, Nos. 2, 3, and 10.
393 *Addressing the African:* AllAfrica.com, February 6, 2004.
393 *A year after the spat:* Address by Thabo Mbeki, December 16, 2005, author's collection.
393 *Tutu for his part:* DMT interview.
394 *Writing after the TRC's hearings:* Njabulo Ndebele, in *Siyaya* (Cape Town), Issue 3, Spring 1998, 16.
394 *"His [Tutu's] power":* Al Gore, interview by author, November 29, 2004.
394 *"Somebody with the voice":* Kofi Annan, interview by author, November 29, 2004.
394 *"You have been a celebrity":* Martha Reeves to DMT, November 6, 1993; DMT to Reeves, November 19, Box 329, MCH258, UWC.
395 *In Tutu's theology:* Allen, *The Essential Desmond Tutu,* 8–9.
395 *"You get a sense":* Paul Hewson (Bono), interview by author, May 31, 2005.
396 *Addressing students: Bishopscourt Update,* No. 193, November 10, 1989, CPSA/UWC.
396 *In his formulation:* Tutu, *No Future,* 216–221.
396 *Thus ubuntu-botho gives:* I am indebted to L. Gregory Jones, *Embodying Forgiveness: A Theological Analysis,* 106–107, for the insight on Hosea. On these and succeeding pages, he discusses in some depth the expression of God's forgiveness in the Old Testament.

BIBLIOGRAPHY

Ackermann, Denise M. *After the Locusts: Letters from a Landscape of Faith*. Grand Rapids, Mich.: Eerdmans/Cape Town: David Philip, 2003.

Alexander, Marilyn Bennett, and James Preston. *We Were Baptized Too*. Louisville, Ky.: Westminster John Knox, 1996.

Allen, John. *The Essential Desmond Tutu*. Cape Town: David Philip, 1997.

Arnold, Millard, ed. *Steve Biko: Black Consciousness in South Africa*. New York: Vintage, 1979.

Baker, Pauline H. *United States and South Africa: The Reagan Years*. New York: Ford Foundation/Foreign Policy Association, 1989.

Becken, Hans-Jurgen, ed. *A Relevant Theology for Africa*. Durban: Lutheran Publishing House, 1973.

Beinart, William. *Twentieth Century South Africa*. Oxford: Oxford University Press, 2001.

Bell, Terry, and Dumisa Buhle Ntsebeza. *Unfinished Business: South Africa, Apartheid, and Truth*. Cape Town: Redworks, 2001.

Bell-Scott, Jill. *Uvedale and Mel: A Memoir*. Privately published, 1988.

Boesak, Allan. *Black and Reformed: Apartheid, Liberation, and the Calvinist Tradition*. New York: Orbis, 1984.

Bonner, Philip, Peter Delius, and Deborah Posel, eds. *Apartheid's Genesis*. Braamfontein: Ravan, 1993.

Boraine, Alex. *A Country Unmasked: Inside South Africa's Truth and Reconciliation Commission*. Cape Town: Oxford University Press, 2000.

Boraine, Alex, Janet Levy, and Ronel Scheffer. *Dealing with the Past: Truth and Reconciliation in South Africa*. Cape Town: IDASA, 1997.

Brink, Elsabé, Gandhi Malungane, Steve Lebelo, Dumisani Ntshangase, and Sue Krige. *Soweto, 16 June 1976: It All Started with A Dog. . . .* Cape Town: Kwela, 2001.

Brooks, Alan, and Jeremy Brickhill. *Whirlwind before the Storm: The Origins and Development of the Uprising in Soweto and the Rest of South Africa from June to December 1976*. London: International Defence and Aid Fund for Southern Africa, 1980.

Brown, Andrew. *Golden Heritage*. Privately published by Klerksdorp Public Library, 1983.

Budlender, Debbie. *Assessing U.S. Corporate Disinvestment*. Braamfontein: Community Agency for Social Enquiry (CASE), 1989.

Buthelezi, Mangosuthu Gatsha. *Power Is Ours*. New York: Books in Focus, 1979.

Butler, Jeffrey, Richard Elphick, and David Welsh, eds. *Democratic Liberalism in South Africa: Its History and Prospect*. Middletown, Conn.: Wesleyan University Press/Cape Town: David Philip, 1987.

Callinicos, Luli. *Oliver Tambo: Beyond the Engeli Mountains*. Claremont: David Philip, 2004.

Carpenter, Humphrey. *Robert Runcie: The Reluctant Archbishop*. London: Hodder and Stoughton, 1996.

Cassidy, Michael. *A Witness for Ever: The Dawning of Democracy in South Africa–Stories behind the Story*. London: Hodder and Stoughton, 1995.

Cassidy, Michael. *Ruination and Resurrection in Rwanda*. Pietermaritzburg: African Enterprise, 1995.

Chikane, Frank. *The Church's Prophetic Witness against the Apartheid System in South Africa*. Johannesburg: South African Council of Churches, 1988.

Church of the Province of Southern Africa. *Saints and Seasons*. London: HarperCollinsReligious, 1993.

Clarke, Richard A. *Against All Enemies: Inside America's War on Terror*. New York: Free Press, 2004.

Commission of Inquiry into South African Council of Churches. *Report of the Commission of Inquiry into South African Council of Churches*. Pretoria: Government Printer, 1983.

Commonwealth Group of Eminent Persons. *Mission to South Africa: The Commonwealth Report*. Harmondsworth: Penguin/New York: Viking Penguin, 1986.

Cone, James, and Gayraud S. Wilmore, eds. *Black Theology: A Documentary History*, Vol. 1. Maryknoll, N.Y.: Orbis Books, 1993.

Crocker, Chester. *High Noon in Southern Africa: Making Peace in a Rough Neighbourhood*. New York: Norton, 1992.

Davenport, Rodney, and Christopher Saunders. *South Africa: A Modern History*. Basingstoke: Macmillan, 2000.

Davidson, Basil. *Africa in History*. New York: Touchstone, 1995.

De Gruchy, John, ed. *Cry Justice: Prayers, Meditations, and Readings from South Africa*. London: Collins, 1986.

———. *The Church Struggle in South Africa*. London: SCM, 2004.

De Gruchy, Steve, ed. *Changing Frontiers: The Mission Story of the United Congregational Church of Southern Africa*. Gaberone: Pula, 1999.

De Klerk, F.W. *The Last Trek: A New Beginning*. London: Pan, 2000.

De Villiers, Dirk, and Johanna De Villiers. *PW.* Kaapstad: Tafelberg Uitgewers, 1984.

De Witte, Ludo. *The Assassination of Lumumba*. London: Verso, 2001.

Denniston, Robin. *Trevor Huddleston: A Life*. New York: St. Martin's, 1999.

Diar, Prakash. *The Sharpeville Six*. Toronto: McClelland and Stewart, 1990.

D'Oliveira, John. *Vorster: The Man*. Johannesburg: Stanton, 1977.

Duke, Lynne. *Mandela, Mobutu, and Me: A Newswoman's African Journey*. New York, Doubleday, 2003.

Elphick, Richard, and Rodney Davenport, eds. *Christianity in South Africa: A Political, Social, and Cultural History*. Los Angeles: University of California Press, 1997.

Fetahi, M. M. W. Rufael, and Haddis Terrefe, eds. *Refugee Service of the Ethiopian Orthodox Church*. Addis Ababa, Ethiopian Orthodox Church Refugee Counseling Service, 1988.

Ffrench-Beytagh, G. A. *Encountering Darkness*. London: Collins, 1973.

Frankel, Philip. *An Ordinary Atrocity: Sharpeville and Its Massacre*. New Haven, Conn.: Yale University Press, 2001.

French, Howard W. *A Continent for the Taking*. New York: Knopf, 2004.

Gilbey, Emma. *The Lady: The Life and Times of Winnie Mandela*. London: Vintage, 1994.

Gill, Stephen J. *A Short History of Lesotho*. Morija: Morija Museum and Archives, 1993.

Gleeson, Ian. *The Unknown Force: Black, Coloured, and Indian Soldiers through Two World Wars*. Rivonia: Ashanti, 1994.

Gobodo-Madikizela, Pumla. *A Human Being Died That Night*. Boston, Mass.: Houghton Mifflin, 2003.

Goldstone, Richard. *For Humanity: Reflections of a War Crimes Investigator*. New Haven, Conn.: Yale University Press, 2000.

Goodall, Eric, CR. *Forty Years On: Being a Record of the Birth and Growth of the Theological College of the Resurrection and St. Peter at Johannesburg*. Johannesburg: CR Press, 1941.

Gourevitch, Philip. *We Wish to Inform You That Tomorrow We Will Be Killed with Our Families*. New York: Picador, 1999.

Guest, Herman. *Voortrekkerdorp*. Klerksdorp: Klerksdorp Record, 1939.

Hamilton, Carolyn, ed. *The Mfecane Aftermath: Reconstructive Debates in Southern African History*. Johannesburg: Witwaterstrand University Press/Pietermaritzburg: University of Natal Press, 1995.

Hartshorne, Ken. *Crisis and Challenge: Black Education 1910–1990*. Cape Town: Oxford University Press, 1992.

Hastings, Adrian. *Robert Runcie*. London: Mowbray, 1991.

———. *The Church in Africa, 1450–1950*. Oxford: Clarendon, 1994.

Hayner, Priscilla B. *Unspeakable Truths: Facing the Challenge of Truth Commissions*. New York: Routledge, 2002.

Hepple, Alex. *South Africa: A Political and Economic History.* London: Pall Mall, 1966.

Hinchliff, Peter. *The Anglican Church in South Africa.* London: Darton, Longman, and Todd, 1963.

Hirson, Baruch. *Year of Fire, Year of Ash.* London: Zed, 1979.

Hofmeyr, J. W., J. A. Millard, and C. J. J. Froneman, eds. *History of the Church in South Africa: A Document and Source Book.* Pretoria: University of South Africa, 1994.

Honoré, Deborah Duncan, ed. *Trevor Huddleston: Essays on His Life and Work.* Oxford: Oxford University Press, 1988.

Huddleston, Trevor, CR. *Naught for Your Comfort.* London: Collins, 1956.

Hulley, Leonard, Louise Kretzschmar, and Luke Lungile Pato, eds. *Archbishop Tutu: Prophetic Witness in South Africa.* Cape Town: Human and Rousseau, 1996.

Jabavu, Noni. *Drawn in Colour: African Contrasts.* London: John Murray, 1960.

——. *The Ochre People.* Randburg: Ravan, 1982.

Jaffer, Zubeida. *Our Generation.* Cape Town: Kwela, 2003.

James, Wilmot, and Linda van der Vijver, eds. *After the TRC: Reflections on Truth and Reconciliation in South Africa.* Cape Town: David Philip, 2000.

Jeffery, Anthea. *The Truth about the Truth Commission.* Johannesburg: South Africa Institute of Race Relations, 1999.

Jones, J. D. F. *Teller of Many Tales: The Lives of Laurens van der Post.* New York: Carroll and Graf, 2001.

Jones, L. Gregory. *Embodying Forgiveness: A Theological Analysis.* Grand Rapids, Mich.: Eerdmans, 1995.

Kane-Berman, John. *Soweto: Black Revolt, White Reaction.* Johannesburg: Ravan, 1978.

——. *Political Violence in South Africa.* Johannesburg: South Africa Institute of Race Relations, 1993.

Karis, Thomas G., and Gail M. Gerhart. *From Protest to Challenge: A Documentary History of African Politics in South Africa,* Vol. 5, *1964–1979.* Pretoria: Unisa Press, 1997.

Khaketla, B. M. *Lesotho 1970: An African Coup under the Microscope.* Maseru: N. M. Khaketla, 2000.

King, E. L. *A Good Place to Be.* Cape Town: PreText, 1997.

King, Martin Luther, Jr. *I Have a Dream: Writings and Speeches That Changed the World.* San Francisco, Calif.: HarperSanFrancisco, 1992.

King, Ursula, ed. *Turning Points in Religious Studies: Essays in Honour of Geoffrey Parrinder.* Edinburgh: T. and T. Clark, 1990.

Kotzé, Anne R. *Bishopscourt and Its Residents.* Cape Town: Creda, 1992.

Krog, Antjie. *Country of My Skull.* Johannesburg: Random House, 1998.

Lee, Peter. *Poor Man, Rich Man: The Priorities of Jesus and the Agenda of the Church.* London: Hodder and Stoughton, 1986.

——. *Compromise and Courage: Anglicans in Johannesburg 1864–1999.* Pietermaritzburg: Cluster, 2005.

Lehmann, Elmar, and Erhard Reckwitz, eds. *Mfecane to Boer War: Versions of South African History.* Essen: Blaue Eule, 1992.

Lelyveld, Joseph. *Move Your Shadow.* London: Abacus, 1987.

Leonard, Richard. *Apartheid Whitewash: South African Propaganda in the United States.* New York: Africa Fund, 1989.

Levinovitz, Agneta Wallin, and Nils Ringertz. *The Nobel Prize: The First 100 Years.* Singapore: World Scientific, 2001.

Lodge, Tom. *Black Politics in South Africa since 1945.* Johannesburg: Ravan, 1983.

Lückhoff, A. H. *Cottesloe,* Kaapstad: Tafelberg Uitgewers, 1978.

Lugar, Richard G. *Letters to the Next President.* New York: Simon and Schuster, 1988.

Lunde, Einar. *Paradisveien: Dramatiske år i Afrika.* Oslo: Chr. Schibsted, 1995.

Luthuli, Albert. *Let My People Go.* London: Fontana, 1963.

Mamdani, Mahmood. *When Victims Become Killers.* Princeton, N.J.: Princeton University Press, 2001.

Mandela, Nelson. *Long Walk to Freedom: The Autobiography of Nelson Mandela.* Randburg: Macdonald Purnell, 1994.

Mandela, Winnie. *Part of My Soul Went with Him.* New York: Norton, 1985.

Marinovich, Greg, and Joao Silva. *The Bang Bang Club: Snapshots from a Hidden War.* New York: Basic Books, 2000.

Martin, David, and Phyllis Johnson. *The Struggle for Zimbabwe.* London and Boston: Faber and Faber, 1981.

Marx, Anthony W. *Lessons of Struggle: South African Internal Opposition.* Cape Town: Oxford University Press, 1992.

Marx, Roelf, ed. *Klerksdorp: Groeiende Reus 1837–1987.* Klerksdorp: Stadsraad van Klerksdorp, 1987.

Mason, Revil. *Origins of Black People of Johannesburg and the Southern Western Central Transvaal, AD 350–1880.* Occasional Paper No. 16 of the Archeological Research Unit, University of the Witwatersrand. Johannesburg: R. J. Mason, 1986.

Massie, Robert Kinloch. *Loosing the Bonds: The United States and South Africa in the Apartheid Years.* New York: Nan A. Talese/Doubleday, 1987.

Mattera, Don. *Memory Is the Weapon.* Johannesburg: Ravan, 1987.

McCullum, Hugh. *The Angels Have Left Us: The Rwanda Tragedy and the Churches.* Geneva: WCC, 1995.

McGrandle, Piers. *Trevor Huddleston: Turbulent Priest.* London: Continuum, 2004.

McCreary, Alf. *Nobody's Fool: The Life of Archbishop Robin Eames.* London: Hodder and Stoughton, 2004.

Meiring, Piet. *Chronicle of the Truth Commission.* Vanderbijlpark: Carpe Diem, 1999.

Meli, Francis. *South Africa Belongs to Us: A History of the ANC.* Harare: Zimbabwe Publishing House, 1988.

Mkhondo, Rich. *Reporting South Africa.* London: James Currey/Heinemann, 1993.

Modisane, Bloke. *Blame Me on History.* New York: Touchstone, 1986.

Mogoba, Mmutlanyane Stanley. *Stone, Steel, Sjambok.* Johannesburg: Ziningweni Communications, 2003.

Mokhesi-Parker, Joyce, and Peter Parker. *In the Shadow of Sharpeville: Apartheid and the Criminal Justice System.* London: Macmillan, 1998.

Mokoena, Kenneth, ed. *South Africa and the United States: The Declassified History.* New York: New Press, 1993.

Mosley, Nicholas. *The Life of Raymond Raynes.* London: Faith, 1961.

Mostert, Noël. *Frontiers.* New York: Knopf, 1992.

Mphahlele, Es'kia. *Down Second Avenue.* London: Faber and Faber, 1959.

———. *Es'kia.* Cape Town: Kwela, 2002.

Mutloatse, Mothobi, ed. *Reconstruction: Ninety Years of Black Historical Literature.* Johannesburg: Ravan, 1981.

Ndlovu, Sifiso Mxolisi. *The Soweto Uprisings: Counter-Memories of June 1976.* Randburg: Ravan, 1998.

Nkosi, Lewis. *Home and Exile: And Other Selections.* London: Longman, 1965.

Noonan, Patrick. *They're Burning the Churches.* Johannesburg: Jacana, 2003.

Ntantala, Phyllis. *Life's Mosaic.* Berkeley: University of California Press, 1993.

Nuttall, Michael. *Number Two to Tutu.* Pietermaritzburg: Cluster, 2003.

Oliver, Roland, and J. D. Fage. *A Short History of Africa.* London: Penguin, 1988.

Omer-Cooper, J. D. *The Zulu Aftermath: A Nineteenth-Century Revolution in Bantu Africa.* London: Longmans, 1966.

Oosthuizen, G. C., M. C. Kitshoff, and S. W. D. Dube, eds. *Afro-Christianity at the Grassroots: Its Dynamics and Strategies.* Leiden, Brill, 1994.

Orkin, Mark, *Disinvestment, the Struggle, and the Future.* Johannesburg: Ravan, 1986.

Orr, Wendy. *From Biko to Basson.* Saxonwold: Contra, 2000.

Packard, Randall M. *White Plague, Black Labor: Tuberculosis and the Political Economy of Health and Disease in South Africa.* Pietermaritzburg: University of Natal Press, 1990.

Paton, Alan. *Apartheid and the Archbishop: The Life and Times of Geoffrey Clayton.* London: Jonathan Cape, 1973.

Peart-Binns, John S. *Ambrose Reeves.* London: Victor Gollancz, 1973.

———. *Archbishop Joost de Blank: Scourge of Apartheid.* London: Muller, Blond, and White, 1987.

Peires, Jeff. *The House of Phalo: A History of the Xhosa People in the Days of Their Independence.* Cape Town: Jonathan Ball, 1981.

Pogrund, Benjamin. *How Can Man Die Better: The Life of Robert Sobukwe.* Johannesburg: Jonathan Ball, 1990.

Pomerantz, Gary M. *Where Peachtree Meets Sweet Auburn.* New York: Penguin, 1997.

Prinsloo, Daan. *Stem uit die Wilderness.* Mosselbaai: Vaandel-Uitgewers, 1997.

Randall, Peter, ed. *Apartheid and the Church: Report of the Church Commission of the Study Project on Christianity in Apartheid Society.* Johannesburg: Spro-Cas, 1972.

Reader, John. *Africa: A Biography of the Continent.* New York: Vintage, 1999.

Renwick, Robin. *Unconventional Diplomacy in Southern Africa.* Basingstoke: Macmillan, 1997.

Richardson, Kenneth V. *A History of St. Augustine's Church.* Grove Park: privately published, 1989.

Robinson, John A. T. *Honest to God.* London: SCM, 1963.

Rose, Brian, and Raymond Tunmer, eds. *Documents in South African Education.* Johannesburg: Ad. Donker, 1975.

Rotberg, Robert I., and Dennis Thompson. *Truth v. Justice.* Princeton, N.J.: Princeton University Press, 2000.

Sampson, Anthony. *The Treason Cage.* London: Heinemann, 1958.

——. *Anatomy of Britain Today.* London: Hodder and Stoughton, 1965.

——. *Black and Gold: Tycoons, Revolutionaries, and Apartheid.* London: Hodder and Stoughton, 1987.

——. *Mandela.* London: HarperCollins, 1999.

Saunders, Christopher, and Robin Derricourt, eds. *Beyond the Cape Frontier: Studies in the History of the Transkei and Ciskei.* London: Longman, 1974.

Schlemmer, Lawrence. *Black Worker Attitudes: Political Options, Capitalism, and Investment in South Africa.* Durban: University of Natal, 1984.

Sisulu, Elinor Batezat. *Walter and Albertina Sisulu: In Our Lifetime.* London, Abacus, 2003.

South Africa Institute of Race Relations. *Race Relations Survey.* Johannesburg: South Africa Institute of Race Relations. (Annual.)

South African Democracy Education Trust. *The Road to Democracy in South Africa,* Vol. 1, *1960–1970.* Cape Town: Zebra, 2004.

Southern African Anglican Theological Commission. *The Church and Human Sexuality.* Johannesburg: CPSA Publishing Committee, 1995.

Sparks, Allister. *Tomorrow Is Another Country.* Sandton: Struik, 1994.

Spong, Bernard, with Cedric Mayson. *Come Celebrate! Twenty-Five Years of the South African Council of Churches.* Johannesburg: SACC, 1983.

Stein, Pippa, and Ruth Jacobson, eds. *Sophiatown Speaks.* Johannesburg: Junction Avenue, 1986.

Stiff, Peter. *Warfare by Other Means.* Alberton: Galago, 2001.

Storey, Peter. *With God in the Crucible: Preaching Costly Discipleship.* Nashville, Tenn.: Abingdon, 2002.

Stubbs, Aelred. *The Planting of the Federal Theological Seminary of Southern Africa.* Lovedale: Lovedale Press, 1973.

Suggit, John, and Mandy Goedhals, eds. *Change and Challenge.* Marshalltown: Church of the Province of Southern Africa, 1998.

Sundkler, Bengt, and Christopher Steed. *A History of the Church in Africa.* Cambridge: Cambridge University Press, 2000.

Thatcher, Margaret. *The Downing Street Years.* London: HarperCollins, 1993.

Themba, Can. *The Will to Die.* Cape Town: AfricaSouth, 1972.

Tlhagale, Buti, and Itumeleng Mosala, eds. *Hammering Swords into Ploughshares: Essays in Honour of Archbishop Mpilo Tutu.* Johannesburg: Skotaville, 1986.

Thompson, Leonard. *A History of South Africa.* New Haven, Conn.: Yale University Press, 2001.

Townend, Peter, ed. *Burke's Genealogical and Heraldic History of the Landed Gentry,* Vol. 2. London: Burke's Peerage, 1969.

Trenoweth, Samantha. *The Future of God.* Alexandria, N.S.W., Australia: Millennium, 1995.

Truth and Reconciliation Commission of South Africa. *Report of the Truth and Reconciliation Commission.* Cape Town: Truth and Reconciliation Commission: Vols. 1–5, 1998; Vol. 6, 2003.

Tutu, Desmond Mpilo. *Hope and Suffering: Sermons and Speeches,* ed. Mothobi Mutloatse. Johannesburg: Skotaville, 1983.

——. *An African Prayer Book.* New York: Doubleday, 1995.

——. *No Future without Forgiveness*. New York: Doubleday/London: Rider, 1999.

——. *The Rainbow People of God*, ed. John Allen. New York: Doubleday, 1994.

Tyler, Humphrey. *Life in the Time of Sharpeville*. Cape Town: Kwela, 1995.

Van der Ross, R. E. *Up from Slavery: Slaves at the Cape*. Cape Town: Ampersand, 2005.

Van Kessel, Ineke. *Beyond Our Wildest Dreams: The United Democratic Front and the Transformation of South Africa*. Charlottesville: University Press of Virginia, 2000.

Waite, Terry. *Taken on Trust*. London: Hodder and Stoughton, 1993.

Waldmeir, Patti. *Anatomy of a Miracle: The End of Apartheid and the Birth of a New South Africa*. New York: Norton, 1997.

Wessels, Leon. *Die Einde van 'n Era: Bevryding van 'n Afrikaner*. Cape Town: Tafelberg, 1994.

Wallis, Jim, and Joyce Hollyday, eds. *Crucible of Fire: The Church Confronts Apartheid*. New York: Orbis/Sojourners, 1989.

Wilkinson, Alan. *The Community of the Resurrection: A Centenary History*. London: SCM, 1992.

Wilson, Francis, and Dominique Perrot, eds. *Outlook on a Century*. Lovedale: Lovedale Press, 1970.

Wilson, Francis and Mamphela Ramphele. *Uprooting Poverty: The South African Challenge*. New York: Norton, 1989.

Wiseman, John A. *The New Struggle for Democracy in Africa*. Aldershot: Avebury, 1996.

Woods, Donald. *Rainbow Nation Revisited*. London: André Deutsch, 2000.

Worsnip, Michael. *Between the Two Fires: The Anglican Church and Apartheid 1948 to 1957*. Pietermaritzburg: University of Natal Press, 1991.

OTHER RESOURCES

Barrell, Howard. "Conscripts to Their Age: African National Congress Operational Strategy, 1976–1986." D.Phil. thesis in Politics, Faculty of Social Studies, University of Oxford. The thesis is online at www.sahistory.org.za/pages/sources/barrel_thesis/index.htm.

Truth and Reconciliation Commission of South Africa, Web site: www.doj.gov.za/trc /trc_frameset.htm.

ACKNOWLEDGMENTS

My principal thanks are to my family: to Liz, love of my life, for far more than I can record here but including her role as researcher, editor, travel companion, transcriber of tapes, and proofreader; to Timothy, researcher, mapmaker, sounding-board, and editor, who unerringly pinpointed clumsy logic and language (he is forgiven for his more scathing remarks on the prose of early drafts); to John-Murray for research assistance and navigation in the UK and Geneva (forgiven for quite wrongly dismissing me in military lexicon as an "admin vortex"); to Kendra, for helping me to accommodate American language usage without sacrificing the South African voice; and to my parents, Cel and Mick Allen.

One of the reasons for Desmond Tutu's preeminence as a public figure has been his openness and his respect for journalists, their independence, and the truth. I knew this before I joined the Anglican Church as his media secretary; it was what attracted me to the job. What I did not know was how thoroughly not only Leah but his entire family had embraced and adopted as their own his vocation of hospitality. Together with hundreds, probably thousands, around the world, my family and I are deeply grateful for the warmth and good humor with which Desmond, Leah, Trevor, Thandi, Nontombi, and Mpho welcomed us into their lives. Thanks too to Mthunzi Gxashe and Joe Burris; it's not easy to be a Tutu son-in-law, and you guys have been no less welcoming.

Although mostly unnamed in this book, those who shared our lives at Bishopscourt, Braehead House, Church House, and the Truth and Reconciliation Commission in Cape Town, Khotso House in Johannesburg, Emory University in Atlanta, Trinity Church, Wall Street, in New York, and the wider church and religious community are no less a part of the story. Those who worked with us the longest at the time of greatest pressure were colleagues at Bishopscourt: Estelle Marinus,

Nonzame Sodlala, and Stewart Ting Chong in the media office, as well as Chris Ahrends, Gail Allen, Michael Battle, Merwyn Castle, Sid and Hazel Colam, Lavinia Crawford-Browne, Francis and Louise Cull, Carol Esau, Matt Esau, Wilma Jakobsen, Colin Jones, Ted MacKenzie, Patrick Matolengwe, Carola Meyer, Cynthia Michaels, Livingstone and Gladys Nakani, Njongonkulu Ndungane, Nosipho Lilian Ngoboza, Richmond Nkamande, Simone Noemdoe, Michael Owen, Geoff Quinlan, Wendy Sheen, Rowan Smith, Mazwi Tisani, Nolan Tobias, Margot Topham, and Marcus White.

Thank you to agents Lynn Franklin and Mary Clemmey, to Martin Beiser at Free Press and Judith Kendra at Rider for making the book possible. I am particularly indebted to Lynn for her friendship and caring and to Martin and Judith for wise and careful improvements to the text. Thanks to Wendy Sheen and Doreen Scott for long hours of transcribing tapes. The hospitality and support of Menna and Bruce McGregor in London and Liz Carmichael in Oxford were of enormous help. Thanks for help and support of various kinds to my sister and brother-in-law, Bev and Jon Edkins, in Durban and elsewhere in South Africa to Sally and Jonathan Cook, Jaco Engelbrecht, Pieter le Roux, Roy Murray, Michael and Dorrie Nuttall, Tom Scott, Alan and Esther Sherriff, Jonathan Young, and Beth Zinn. In the United Kingdom, thanks for hospitality and support to Jill Allen and Tessa George and in the United States to Laurie Callahan, Jamie Callaway, Charlie and Lynne D'Huyvetter, Karen Hayes, and Joshua White.

Invaluable advice and guidance were given by Einar Lunde and Geir Lundestad in Norway, John Carlin in Spain, Tom Bertrand, Tom Cahill, and Phillip van Niekerk in the United States and John de Gruchy, Jakes Gerwel, Antjie Krog, David and Maggie Nkwe, Christopher Saunders, Dan Vaughan, and Francis Wilson in South Africa. Thank you for help also to Thomas Mafora and Mosimanegape Tsabeng of Diocese of Matlosane, Martin Coetzee, Peter Fabricius, Simon Fabricius, Ahmed Kathrada, Ben Maclennan, Hennie and Hester Serfontein, Gerard Sharp, John Suggit, Sahm Venter, and Chris Vick in South Africa; to Sharon Gelman, Nadine Hack, Tami Hultman, and Reed Kramer in the U.S.; to Volker Faigle in Germany; and to Howard Barrell, Gavin Berriman, Suzannah Clarke, and Robin Denniston in the UK.

Much of this book is based on research undertaken with the assistance of archivists across South Africa, Europe, and the United States. No one has contributed to it as much as Carol Archibald, the superb archivist at the William Cullen Library of the University of the Witwa-tersrand, whose dedication and encyclopedic knowledge of the Angli-can Church's papers are unsurpassed. Thank you, Carol, and also to Kate Abbott and Michelle Pickover. I am grateful too for research as-sistance from Hugh McCullum in Canada and to the staff of the fol-lowing institutions:

Southern Africa: Brenthurst Library (Diana Madden); Jouberton Methodist Church (Itumeleng Tlhakanye); Klerksdorp Library (Magriet Benade, Doris Jiya); Lutheran Theological Institute, Pietermaritzburg (Georg and Inge Scriba); National Archives of South Africa; National Library of South Africa, Cape Town; Nelson Man-dela Foundation (Verne Harris, Anthea Josias); Cory Library, Rhodes University (Velile Victor Gacula, Shirley Stewart, Zweli Vena); South African History Archive (Kate Allan, Piers Pigou, Rolf Sorenson); St. Mary's Church, Munsieville (Gerald Lodi, Nelly Moropane); University of Cape Town Library, Manuscripts and Archives (Isaac Ntabankulu); University of Fort Hare Library (Sadie Forman, Mosoabuli Maamoe, Mark Snyders, Yolisa Soul); University of Fort Hare, National Heritage Centre (Babalwa Ramncwana, Cornelius Thomas); University of KwaZulu-Natal, Alan Paton Centre (Jewel Koopman); University of Lesotho Library (Matseliso Moshoeshoe, Celina Qobo); University of South Africa (Doreen Gough, Herma van Niekerk); University of the North-West (Theuns Eloff, Hester Spoelstra); University of the Western Cape Mayibuye/Robben Island Museum (Esther van Driel, Sim-phiwe Yako).

Switzerland: World Council of Churches Archives (Benigno Delgado, Stéphanie Knecht, Denyse Léger, Clare Medri).

United Kingdom: Bodleian Library of Commonwealth and African Studies, Ox-ford (Marion Lowman, Lucy McCann); Community of the Resurrection, Mirfield (George Guiver, Stephen Haws, Philip Nichols); King's College, London (Richard Burridge, Geoffrey Browell, Patricia Methven, Kate O'Brien).

United Nations: UN Archives (Marleen Buelinckx); UN Photo Library (Clara Gouy).

United States: General Theological Seminary (Emily Knox, Bruce Parker); George H. W. Bush Library, College Station, Texas; William J. Clinton Library, Little Rock, Arkansas; Library of Congress, Washington D.C.; National Security Archive, George Washington University, Washington D.C.; Princeton University Library; Ronald Reagan Library, Simi Valley, California; Schomburg Center, New York; Yale University Library (Martha Smalley).

Warm thanks for help with photographs to Cynthia Botha, Mau-reen Simons, Benny Gool, Louise Gubb, Peter Magubane, David Bruno, Paul Singleton, and Moegsien Williams, and, for interviews, to Michael Peers in Canada, Bono (Paul Hewson) in Ireland, Anne

Ragnhild Breiby and Geir Lundestad in Norway, Kofi Annan at the United Nations and the following in southern Africa, the United Kingdom, and the United States:

Southern Africa: Charles Albertyn, Pik Botha, José Chipenda, Michael Corke, Chris de Jager, F. W. de Klerk, Roelof du Plessis, C. F. Eloff, Paul Erasmus, Richard Goldstone, Simon Gqubule, Robin Harper, Wolfram Kistner, King Letsie III, Nelson Mandela, Sam Thusi Marawa, Sipho Masemola, G. G. Mbere, Mmutlanyane Stanley Mogoba, Philip Mokuku, Sylvia Morrison, Sally Motlana, Shirley Moulder, Mpho and Njabulo Ndebele, Joop Pinkaers, Barney Pityana, Gloria Radebe, Philip Russell, Joe Seremane, Tokyo Sexwale, Zwelakhe Sisulu, Yasmin Sooka, Timothy Stanton CR, Peter Storey, Buti Tlhagale, Thami and Ezra Tisani, Leon Wessels, Dale and Tish White, and Craig Williamson.

United Kingdom: Malcolm Alexander, Ronald and Frankie Brownrigg, David and Maggie Bruno, Richard Burridge, Lynda Chalker, John Ewington, Sarah and Timothy Goad, Anne Hughes, Gary Kemp, Martin Kenyon, Khotso Makhulu, Brian Oosthuysen, Charles Powell, Robin Renwick, Aelred Stubbs CR, Terry Waite, Betty Ward, Dominic Whitnall, and the congregations of St. Alban's, Golders Green, St. Mary's, Blechingley, and St. Augustine's, Grove Park.

United States: Michelle Bohana, David Boren, Ed Browning, Bill Cosby, Gregory Craig, Chester Crocker, Jim and Eulalie Fenhagen, Frank Ferrari, Wayne Fredericks, Al Gore, Priscilla Hayner, Mark Helmke, Samir Kafity, Nancy Kassebaum, Anthony Lake, Dan Matthews, James Ottley, Charles Perkins, Bernice Powell-Jackson, Hays Rockwell, Carlos and Deborah Santana, Wyatt Tee Walker, and Frederick Boyd Williams.

INDEX

ABOUT THE AUTHOR

JOHN ALLEN is a South African journalist who has reported on and worked with Desmond Tutu for thirty years. He has served as director of communications of South Africa's groundbreaking Truth and Reconciliation Commission, and of Trinity Church, Wall Street, in New York City. He is a former president of the South African Society of Journalists and has won awards in South Africa for defense of press freedom and in the United States for excellence in church journalism. He lives in Cape Town, South Africa.

PHOTO CREDITS